Israel Smith Clare

The World's History Illuminated - Vol. 05

Israel Smith Clare

The World's History Illuminated - Vol. 05

ISBN/EAN: 9783744651547

Printed in Europe, USA, Canada, Australia, Japan

Cover: Foto ©Thomas Meinert / pixelio.de

More available books at **www.hansebooks.com**

HEIDELBERG CASTLE, GERMANY.

THE WORLD'S HISTORY
ILLUMINATED

CONTAINING A RECORD OF THE HUMAN RACE FROM THE EARLIEST HISTORICAL PERIOD TO THE PRESENT TIME. EMBRACING A GENERAL SURVEY OF THE PROGRESS OF MANKIND IN NATIONAL AND SOCIAL LIFE, CIVIL GOVERNMENT, RELIGION, LITERATURE, SCIENCE AND ART ♣ ♣ ♣ ♣ ♣ ♣

COMPLETE IN EIGHT VOLUMES

Compiled, Arranged and Written by........ ISRAEL SMITH CLARE Author of "THE WORLD'S HISTORY ILLUMINATED," and "COMPLETE HISTORICAL COMPENDIUM."

REVIEWED, VERIFIED AND ENDORSED BY THE PROFESSORS OF HISTORY IN FIVE AMERICAN UNIVERSITIES, WITH AN INTRODUCTION ON THE EDUCATIONAL VALUE OF HISTORICAL STUDY

By MOSES COIT TYLER, A.M., L.H.D.

PROFESSOR OF AMERICAN HISTORY IN CORNELL UNIVERSITY.

"NOT TO KNOW WHAT HAPPENED BEFORE WE WERE BORN IS TO REMAIN ALWAYS A CHILD; FOR WHAT WERE THE LIFE OF MAN DID WE NOT COMBINE PRESENT EVENTS WITH THE RECOLLECTIONS OF PAST AGES?"—*CICERO.*

Volume V.—The Middle Ages and the Reformation

ILLUMINATED WITH MAPS, PORTRAITS AND VIEWS.

ST. LOUIS
WESTERN NEWSPAPER SYNDICATE .

COPYRIGHT, 1897,

BY

R. S. PEALE AND J. A. HILL.

TABLE OF CONTENTS.

Part II.—Mediaeval History—Vol. V.

CHAPTER IV.—RISE OF MODERN NATIONS.

SECTION I.

THE GERMAN EMPIRE AND THE CHURCH, 1603–1643
Conrad III., the First of the Hohenstaufen Kings of Germany.—His Quarrel with Henry the Proud of Saxony and Bavaria.—Margraviate of Brandenburg.—Berlin Founded.—Siege and Capture of Weinsberg by Conrad III.—Devotion of the Women.—Guelfs and Ghibellines.—Conrad III. Joins in the Second Crusade—His Death.—Frederick Barbarossa, King of Germany.—He Settles the Affairs of Germany.—Founding of the Duchy of Austria.—Revolt of the Lombard Cities.—Frederick Barbarossa's Expeditions to Italy.—He is Crowned King of Lombardy and Emperor.—Milanese Revolt.—Siege and Destruction of Milan.—Second Milanese Revolt.—Battle of Legnano.—Peace of Constance.—Frederick Barbarossa's Great Reign.—Rise of Henry the Lion, Duke of Saxony and Bavaria, and Head of the House of Guelf.—His Rebellion Against the Emperor Frederick Barbarossa.—He is Conquered by the Emperor and deprived of His Dominions.—He Asks the Emperor's Pardon and is Forgiven.—Frederick Barbarossa Joins in the Third Crusade.—His Accidental Death.—The Legend Concerning Him.—Reign of Henry VI.—His Acquisition of Naples and Sicily.—The Rival Kings of Germany, Otho IV. and Philip of Suabia.—Civil War.—Assassination of Philip.—Quarrel of Otho IV. with Pope Innocent III.—Otho IV. Excommunicated.—Frederick II. Becomes King of Germany.—Crowned Emperor.—His Fifteen Years' Absence from Germany.—His Character.—His Long Struggle with the Popes.—His Good Reign in Sicily.—His Quarrels with Popes Honorius III. and Gregory IX.—Excommunication of Frederick II.—He goes on the Fifth Crusade.—Crowned King of Jerusalem.—The Pope's Animosity.—Revival of the Lombard League Against Frederick II.—His Subjugation of the Lombards.—Frederick II. again Excommunicated by Pope Gregory IX.—Peace of San Germano.—Renewal of the Struggle.—Evils Caused by the Emperor's Long Absence from Germany.—His Son's Rebellion.—Frederick II.. Abolishes Private Wars.—An Imperial Tribunal.—Mongol Invasion of Germany.—Defeat and Death of Duke Henry of Lower Silesia at Liegnitz.—Revolt of the Lombards.—Frederick II. again Excommunicated by Pope Gregory IX.—His Quarrel with Pope Innocent IV.—The Pope's Arrogance Disgusts All European Sovereigns.—The Council of Lyons Excommunicates Frederick II.—Renewal of the Civil War Between the Guelfs and the Ghibellines.—The Emperor's Rivals, Henry Raspe of Thuringia and Count William of Holland.—The Struggle in Italy.—Cruelties of the Emperor's Partisans.—Peter de Vinea, the Emperor's Chancellor.—His Cruel Fate.—Death of Frederick II.—His Lofty Character.—Conrad IV. and Fall of the House of Hohenstaufen.—Naples and Sicily Seized by Popes Innocent IV. and Alexander IV., and Conferred on Charles of Anjou.—Manfred's Struggle with Charles of Anjou.—Battle of Benevento and Death of Manfred.—Execution of Conradine.—Richard of Cornwall and Alfonso the Wise of Castile.—Deplorable Condition of Germany During the Interregnum.—Rudolf of Hapsburg Elected King of Germany.—Overthrow and Death of Ottocar, King of Bohemia.—Founding of the Royal Austrian House of Hapsburg.—Restoration of Order in Germany.—Rudolf's Character.—His Death.—Adolf of Nassau, King of Germany.—His Disgraceful Proceedings.—His Dethronement and Death.—Albert I., of Austria, King of Germany.—Germany During the Thirteenth Century.—Christianization of Prussia.—Conquests of the Teutonic Knights and the Knights of the Sword.—Königsberg and other Cities Founded.—Marienburg.—Decay of the Royal Power in Germany.—The Seven Electors Entrusted with the Right to Choose the German Kings.—Growth of the German Towns.—The Free Imperial Cities.—League of the Rhine.—The Hanseatic League.—Its Extensive Commerce.—The Fehmgerichte.—German Architecture.—Cathedral of Cologne.—The Minnesänger.—Pope Boniface VIII. and Philip the Fair of France.—Avignon Becomes the Papal Residence.—Character of Albert I.—His Assassination.—Henry VII., of Luxemburg, King of Germany.—His Expedition to Italy.—Crowned King of Lombardy and Emperor.—His Death.—Disputed Succession and Civil War in Germany.—The Rival Emperors, Louis of Bavaria and Frederick the Fair of Austria.—Frederick's Defeat and Capture in the Battle of Mühldorf.—His Honorable Conduct.—Quarrel of Louis with

Pope John XXII.—Louis Excommunicated.—Pope John XXII. Deposed.—Louis Crowned Emperor by the Antipope Nicholas V.—Germany Made Independent of the Pope —Louis Excommunicated by Pope Benedict XII.—Errors of the Emperor Louis.—Revolt of His Subjects.—His Deposition and Death.—Charles IV., of Bohemia, King of Germany.—End of the Struggle Between the Guelfs and the Ghibellines.—Rise of the Swiss Cantons. —Austrian Tyranny over the Swiss.—League of Rutli.—Legend of William Tell and Gesler.—Battle of Morgarten.—The Eidgenossen.—Reign of Charles IV.—Plague.—Persecution of the Jews.— Bohemia Under Charles IV.—Founding of the University of Prague.—The Golden Bull.—Lawlessness and Confusion.—The Faust-recht.—Wenceslas, King of Bohemia and Germany.—His Bad Character.—Continued Lawlessness and Violence. —Rise of the Suabian League.—The Schlegler, the Löwen and the Hornerbund.—Wars Between the Knights and the Cities.—Growth of Austria.—Her Attempt to Conquer the Swiss.—Battle of Sempach and Patriotic Devotion of Arnold von Winkelried. — Independence of Switzerland. — Deposition of Wenceslas.—Rupert of the Palatinate, King of Germany.—Sigismund, King of Germany, Bohemia and Hungary.—The Great Schism in the Church.— Wickliffe and Huss.—Council of Constance.— Martyrdom of John Huss and Jerome of Prague.— Hussite War.— John Ziska's Victories.— The Elector of Brandenburg.— Sigismund Crowned Emperor.—His Death.—Albert II. of Austria, King of Germany, Bohemia and Hungary.—The Hapsburg-Austrian Dynasty.—Frederick III., King of Germany.— Council of Basle.— Concordat of Vienna.— Frederick III. Crowned Emperor.— Rapid Decline of the Royal Power in Germany.— Imbecility of Frederick III.—Feuds of the German Princes, Nobles and Cities.—Swiss Victories Over Duke Charles the Bold of Burgundy.—Maximilian I. of Austria, King of Grmany.—His Wife, Mary of Burgundy.—His Children.—His Great Power.— The Diet of Worms and the Land-friede.—The Imperial Chamber.—Maximilian's Defeat by the Swiss.—Peace of Basle—Maximilian I. Assumes the title of Emperor Elect.—The League of Cambray against Venice.—Maximilian's Penury.—The German Empire Divided into Circles.—The Aulic Council.—Importance of the Reign of Maximilian I.—Practical Independence of the German Princes. —Increase of Free Cities.—Patricians and Guilds.

SECTION II.

FEUDAL FRANCE. 1643-1717
Real Beginning of the French Monarchy Under Hugh Capet.—The Eight Principalities in France. —Reign of Robert the Pious.— He is Separated from His Wife by the Church.—Latin Civilization in France.—Supposed Approach of the End of the World.—Religious Awakening.—Erection of Churches.—Persecution of the Jews.—Reign of Henry I.—Famine in France.—The Truce of God. —Duke William II. of Normandy Establishes His Authority Over His Duchy.—Reign of Philip I.— Conquest of England by Duke William II. of Normandy.—His War with King Philip I.—Philip's Quarrel with the Church —The First Crusade.— Reign of Louis VI.—Extent of the French King's Dominions.—Enfranchisement of the Communes. —Different Constitutions of the Boroughs in the North and South of France.—Growth of the Royal Power.—Wars of Louis VI. with Henry I. of England.—Invasion of France by Henry V. of Germany.—The Oriflamme.—Marriage of Prince Louis with Eleanor of Aquitaine.—Death of Louis VI.— Extent of the French Kingdom.—Intellectual Activity.— Abelard and Heloise.— St. Bernard.— Reign of Louis VII.—He Goes on the Second Crusade.—Its Failure.—His Divorce from Eleanor of Aquitaine.—Her Marriage with Henry Plantagenet. —Henry Plantagenet Becomes King Henry II. of England.—Origin of the Enmity Between France and England.—Reign of Philip Augustus.—His Marriage with Isabella of Hainault.—His Policy. —War with England.—Philip Augustus Aids the Rebellious Sons of Henry II. of England Against Their Father.—Philip Augustus Joins in the Third Crusade.—His Jealousy of King Richard the Lionhearted of England.—His Return to France.—He Unites with Richard's Brother John.—Agnes de Méran.—War Between Philip Augustus and King John of England.—Philip Augustus Acquires John's French Possessions.—The Crusade Against the Albigenses.—War with Otho IV. of Germany, John of England and the Count of Flanders.— Battle of Bouvines.—Expedition of Prince Louis of France to England.—The War with the Albigenses.— Death of Philip Augustus.— Reign of Louis VIII.—His Conquest of the Albigenses.— Reign of Louis IX., or St. Louis.—Regency of His Mother, Blanche of Castile.—Acquisition of Languedoc by the Conquest of the Albigenses.— Good Reign of St. Louis.—War with England.— Sixth Crusade.—Captivity of St. Louis in Egypt. —His Ransom and Release.—Seventh Crusade.— Death of St. Louis at Tunis.—His Character.—His Canonization.—The Troubadours in the South of France.—The Trouvères in the North of France. —Courts of Love.—Reign of Philip the Bold.— The French Crown Acquires Toulouse and Navarre. —War Between the Houses of Anjou and Aragon in Sicily.—The Sicilian Vespers.—Philip the Bold's Invasion of Aragon.—His Death.—Reign of Philip the Fair.—Results of His Reign.— Decay of Feudalism. — The States-General.— End of the War with Aragon.—War with Edward I. of England.— Acquisition of Flanders by the French Crown.— Revolt of the Flemings.—Battle of Courtrai.— Peace with Flanders.—Philip the Fair's Quarrel with Pope Boniface VIII.—Seizure of Boniface VIII.—His Death.—Philip the Fair Procures the Election of Pope Clement V.—The Infamous Compact.—The Popes at Avignon.—Destruction of the Knights-Templars.—Martyrdom of Jacques du Molay.—Death of Pope Clement V. and King Philip the Fair.—Character of Philip the Fair.—Louis X. —Philip the Tall.—The Salic Law.—Charles the Fair.—Troubles in England.—Queen Isabella.— Philip VI., the First French King of the House of Valois.—Separation of France and Navarre.— Expedition of Philip VI. to Flanders.—His Quarrel with Edward III. of England.—Count Robert of Artois.—War between France and England.—The Flemings Espouse the English Cause.—English Naval Victory over the French off Helvoetsluys.— Truce between France and England.—Disputed Succession in Brittany.—The Countess de Montfort.—Murder of the Barons of Brittany.—Invasion of France by Edward III. of England.—Battle of Crecy.—Siege and Capture of Calais.—Heroic Conduct of the Six Burghers of Calais.—Truce between France and England.—The Black Plague.—Annexation of Dauphiny to France.—The First Dauphin.—Death of Philip VI.—Reign of John the Good.—He Arrests Charles the Bad of Navarre.— Invasion of Aquitaine by the English Black Prince. —Battle of Poitiers.—Surrender of King John the Good.—His Captivity in England.—Regency of the Dauphin Charles.—Etienne Marcel's Insurrection in Paris.—Meeting of the States-General.— Insurrection of the Jacquerie.—Peace of Bretigny.

TABLE OF CONTENTS.

—Ransom and Release of King John the Good.—Founding of the New Duchy of Burgundy.—John the Good's Voluntary Return to Captivity, and Death in London.—Reign of Charles the Wise.—War with Pedro the Cruel of Castile.—Battle of Navarrete.—Renewal of the War with England.—French Successes.—Death of the Black Prince.—Annexation of Brittany to the French Crown.—Revolt of the Bretons.—Death of the Constable du Guesclin and of King Charles the Wise.—Froissart.—Reign of Charles VI.—The Regency.—Popular Commotions.—Insurrection in Paris.—Revolt of the Flemings.—Battle of Rosbecque.—Increase of the Royal Power.—Execution of Popular Leaders.—Threatened Invasion of England.—Charles VI. Assumes the Government.—His Illness and Insanity.—Duke Philip the Good of Burgundy the Real Ruler of France.—Peace with England.—Quarrels between the Dukes of Burgundy and Orleans about the Regency.—Assassination of the Duke of Orleans.—The Armagnacs.—Civil War.—Invasion of France by Henry V. of England.—Battle of Agincourt.—The Queen's Alliance with Duke John the Fearless of Burgundy.—Massacre of the Armagnacs.—Assassination of Duke John the Fearless of Burgundy.—His Son and Successor, Duke Philip the Good of Burgundy, Joins the English.—Treaty of Troyes.—Marriage of Henry V. of England with the Princess Catharine.—Death of Kings Henry V. of England and Charles VI. of France.—The Duke of Bedford, the English Regent in France for the Infant King Henry VI. of England.—The Dauphin Assumes the Title of Charles VII., King of France.—Countess Jacqueline of Holland.—Coolness between the Dukes of Bedford and Burgundy.—English Successes in France.—Siege of Orleans.—Jeanne d'Arc.—She Raises the Siege of Orleans.—Her Successive Victories over the English.—Coronation of Charles VII. at Rheims.—Capture of Jeanne d'Arc, the Maid of Orleans.—Her Trial and Martyrdom.—Continued English Reverses in France.—Reconciliation of Duke Philip the Good of Burgundy with King Charles VII.—Expulsion of the English from France.—The States-General at Orleans.—Formation of a Standing Army for France.—The Dauphin's Wicked Conduct Toward his Father.—Death of Charles VII., the Victorious.—Reign of Louis XI.—His Character.—He Revokes the Pragmatic Sanction.—He Increases the Royal Domains.—League of the Public Good.—Treaty of Conflans.—Recovery of Normandy by Louis XI.—Duke Charles the Bold of Burgundy.—Enmity between Louis XI. and Charles the Bold.—Louis XI. Visits Charles the Bold at Peronne.—Louis XI. Held a Prisoner.—Obtains his Release by Signing the Hard Conditions Imposed by Charles the Bold.—Evades these Terms.—Intervenes in the Wars of the Roses in England.—Death of the Duke of Guienne.—War between Louis XI. and Charles the Bold.—Defeats of Charles the Bold by the Swiss at Granson and Morat.—He is Defeated and Slain by the Lorrainers at Nancy.—Marriage of Mary of Burgundy with Maximilian I. of Austria.—Her Death.—Seizure of Burgundy and Picardy by Louis XI.—His War with Maximilian I.—Last Days and Death of Louis XI.—Reign of Charles VIII.—The Regency of Anne of Beaujeu.—Rebellion of the Dukes of Bourbon and Orleans.—Anne of Brittany.—Her Marriage with Charles VIII.—Peace of Senlis.—Expedition of Charles VIII. to Italy.—His Death.—Reign of Louis XII.— His Good Character.—His Minister, George d'Amboise.—His Marriage with Anne of Brittany, the Widow of Charles VIII.—His Wars in Italy.—His Death.—Comines.

SECTION III.

FEUDAL ENGLAND, ... 1718–1813

Coronation of William the Conqueror at Westminster.—His Clemency at First.—Revolts in his Absence.— Devastation of Yorkshire.— Confiscation of English Estates.—Offices and Lands Conferred on Normans.— Lanfranc's Primacy.— The Norman-French Language.— Introduction of the Feudal System into England.—Waltheof's Fall.—Robert's Rebellion.— Bishop Odo.—Queen Matilda.—Threats of the Danish King Canute IV.—Domesday-Book.—Curfew Bell.—New Forest.—Wager of Battle.—Abolition of the Slave Trade and Capital Punishment.—Subjection of the English Church.—Death and Burial of William the Conqueror in Normandy.— His Character.— William Rufus.—His Tyranny.—His Character.—Lanfranc's Death.—William Rufus Robs the Church.—His Quarrel with Anselm.— Scottish Invasion of England.—William Rufus Obtains Normandy by Mortgage.—King's Forests.—Death of William Rufus.—Henry I.—His Charter of Liberties.—His Popularity and Learning.—His Character.—He Seizes Normandy and Imprisons his Brother Robert for Life.—Quarrels with Anselm.—Flemish Colony in Wales.—Robert's Son William.— War with France.—Battle of Brenneville.— Prince William's Sad Death.—Henry I. Bequeaths his Dominions to his Daughter.— Usurpation of Stephen of Blois.—Civil War.— Scottish Invasion of England.—Battle of the Standard.—Stephen's Defeat and Captivity.— Matilda's Haughtiness.—Her Defeat and Exile.— Her Son Henry Plantagenet Marries Eleanor of Aquitaine.—Becomes Stephen's Heir.—The Robber Barons.—Outlaws of the Forest.—Henry II., the First of the Plantagenets.— His French Possessions.— His Character.— Condition of England.— Restoration of Order.— Struggle Between Church and State.—Thomas à Becket.—His Primacy.—Constitutions of Clarendon.—Archbishop Becket's Quarrel with King Henry II.—Assassination of Becket.—His Canonization.—The King's Ultimate Triumph.— English Conquest of Ireland.—The Judiciary System.—Trial by Jury.—Rebellions of the Sons of Henry II.—His Penance at Becket's Shrine.—Defeat and Capture of King William the Lion of Scotland.—His Vassalage to Henry II.—Continued Rebellions of the Sons of Henry II.—His Death.—Richard the Lion-hearted.—His Character.—Massacre of Jews.—Richard the Lion-hearted as a Crusader.—His Captivity in Germany.—His Ransom and Release.—His War with France and Death.—John's Coronation at Westminster.— His Character.— His Murder of his Nephew, Arthur of Brittany.—His Loss of the Possessions of the Plantagenets in France.—His Quarrel with Pope Innocent III.— The Papal Interdict.—John's Humiliation.—Rebellion of the English Barons.— Magna Charta.— Patriotism of the Bishops of England.— Civil War.— Prince Louis of France Offered the English Crown.—King John's Death.— Henry III.— The Regency.—Marriage of Henry III. with Eleanor of Provence.—Influence of Foreigners.— Papal Revenues.—Redress the Condition of a Vote of Supplies.—Effort of Henry III. to Overthrow the Great Charter.— Rebellion of the Barons.— Simon de Montfort and the Origin of the House of Commons.— Battles of Lewes and Evesham.— Prince Edward as a Crusader.— Death of Henry III.—Roger Bacon at Oxford.—Rise of the Mendicant Orders.—Edward I.—His Character.—Conquest of Wales.—Restoration of Order.—Banishment of the Jews.—Death of the Maid of Norway.—John Baliol Made Vassal King of Scotland.—Baliol's Revolt.

—Capture and Massacre of Berwick.—Battle of Dunbar.—Baliol Dethroned.—First Conquest of Scotland.—Stone of Destiny.—Character of the Anglo-Scottish Wars.—War with France.—Arbitrary Taxation Forbidden.—Wise Laws of Edward I.—Peace and Alliance Between England and France Confirmed by two Marriages.—Scots Revolt under William Wallace.—Battles of Stirling and Falkirk.—Capture and Execution of Wallace.—Second Conquest of Scotland.—Robert Bruce Crowned King of Scotland.—Death of Edward I. —Edward II.—His Weak Character.—Piers Gaveston.—Marriage of Edward II.—The Barons Usurp the Royal Power.—Rebellion of the Barons.—Capture and Execution of Gaveston.—The War with Scotland.—Battle of Bannockburn.—Independence of Scotland.—Edward Bruce in Ireland.—Battles of Athenree and Dundalk.—Hugh Spenser and his Father.—Rebellions of the Barons and Queen Isabella.—Dethronement and Murder of Edward II.—Edward III.—His Character.—The Regency. —Queen Isabella and Roger Mortimer.—Peace of Northampton.—Mortimer's Tyranny.—His Execution.—Edward III. Seizes the Government.—Flemish Weavers in England.—Restoration of Order.—War with Scotland.—Battle of Halidon Hill.—Alliance of France and Scotland.—Quarrel with France.—Claim of Edward to the French Crown.—Beginning of the Hundred Years' War.—Naval Battle off Helvoetsluys.—Truce with France. —Renewal of the War.—Invasion of France by Edward III.—Battle of Crecy.—Scottish Invasion of England.—Battle of Neville's Cross.—Captivity of King David Bruce.—Siege and Capture of Calais. —The Black Plague.—Invasion of France by the Black Prince.—Battle of Poitiers.—King John the Good of France a Prisoner.—His Captivity in England.—Ransom and Release of King David Bruce. —Peace of Bretigny.—Ransom and Release of King John the Good.—His Voluntary Return to Captivity and Death in London.—The Black Prince's Court at Bordeaux.—He Restores Pedro the Cruel of Castile to his Throne.—Change in the Methods of Warfare.—Glories of the Reign of Edward III.—The English People.—The English Language.—Sir John Mandeville.—The Two Houses of Parliament.—Statute of Treasons.—Knights of the Garter.—Church Revenues in England.—Emancipation of the Serfs.—Statute of Laborers.—Labor Troubles.—Illness of the Black Prince.—English Disasters.—Internal Disorder and Misrule.—The Good Parliament.—John of Gaunt and John Wickliffe.—Death of the Black Prince.—Death of Edward III.—Richard II.—The Regency. —The Boy King's Popularity.—Wat Tyler's Rebellion.—Wickliffe and the First Reformation.—Chaucer, Langland and Gower.—War with France and Scotland.—Battle of Otterburn.—Prodigality and Profligacy of Richard II.—Council of Regency. —Tyranny of the Duke of Gloucester.—Sudden Vigor of Richard II.—Statute of Præmunire.—Death of Queen Anne.—Second Marriage of Richard II.—Arrest and Murder of the Duke of Gloucester.—Tyranny of Richard II.—Banishment of the Dukes of Hereford and Norfolk.—Confiscation of the Estates of Henry of Lancaster, Duke of Hereford.—His Return and Usurpation of the Crown.—Henry IV., the First King of the House of Lancaster.—Murder of Richard II. in Prison.—Edmund Mortimer, Earl of March.—Conspiracies and Rebellions.—Owen Glendower.—Rebellion of the Percies.—Battle of Shrewsbury and Death of Hotspur.—Archbishop Scrope's Rebellion and Execution.—Death of the Earl of Northumberland.—Seizure and Captivity of Prince James of Scotland. —Persecution of the Lollards.—Statute of Heretics.

—The First Martyrs in England.—Profligacy of Prince Henry.—Illness and Death of Henry IV.—Henry V.—His Individual Reform.—His Popularity.—Martyrdom of Lord Cobham.—Suppression of the First Reformation.—Renewal of the Hundred Years' War.—Invasion of France by Henry V.—Capture of Harfleur.—Battle of Agincourt.—Second Invasion of France by Henry V.—Siege and Capture of Rouen.—Conquest of Normandy.—Treaty of Troyes.—Henry V. Regent of France.—His Death.—Henry VI.—Duke of Bedford.—Jeanne d'Arc.—The English Driven from France.—The Regency in England.—Marriage of Henry VI.—Murder of the Duke of Suffolk.—Jack Cade's Rebellion.—Wars of the Roses Begun by the First Battle of St. Albans.—The Duke of York Claims the Crown.—Nevil, Earl of Warwick.—Battles of Bloreheath, Northampton, Wakefield, St. Albans and Mortimer's Cross.—Dethronement of Henry VI.—Edward IV., the First King of the House of York.—Battle of Towton.—Marriage of Edward IV.—The Woodvilles.—The Earl of Warwick Deserts Edward IV.—His Defeat and Death at Barnet. —Margaret's Defeat at Tewkesbury.—Murder of Prince Edward and Henry VI.—Margaret's Exile in France.—Invasion of France.—Edward IV. Outwitted by Louis XI.—Death of the Duke of Clarence.—Tyranny of Edward IV.—Printing Introduced by Caxton.—Death of Edward IV.—Edward V.—Plot of Richard, Duke of Gloucester.—Murder of Lords Rivers, Grey and Hastings, and of Edward V. and his Brother.—Richard III.—Plots Against Him.—Henry Tudor, Earl of Richmond, Claims the Crown.—Defeat and Death of Richard III. at Bosworth.—Henry VII., the First of the Tudor Kings.—Results of the Wars of the Roses.—Destruction of the Ancient Nobility.—Loss of Constitutional Liberty.—Decline of Civilization.—Coronation and Marriage of Henry VII.—His Character.—His Hatred of the House of York.—His Avarice.—The Impostors, Lambert Simnel and Perkin Warbeck.—Statute of Allegiance.—End of Feudalism.—Revival of Learning.—The King's Extortions.—Statute of Liveries.—Star Chamber. —Marriage Alliances.—Chapel of Henry VII.—His Bequests.—His Death.

SECTION IV.

ITALIAN STATES, ... 1813-1823

Italy under the German Emperors.—Guelfs and Ghibellines.—Mediæval Italian Civilization.—Republic of Venice.—Republics of Genoa and Pisa.—Republic of Florence.—The Medici.—Duchy of Milan.—Duchy of Savoy.—Papal Rome.—Cola di Rienzi.—Kingdom of Naples and Sicily.

SECTION V.

SPAIN AND PORTUGAL, ... 1823-1839

Wars between the Moors and the Christian Spaniards.—Kingdoms of Asturias, Leon, Castile, Aragon and Navarre.—Moorish Kingdom of Granada.—Kingdom of Portugal.—Kingdom of Spain under Ferdinand and Isabella.—Conquest of Granada.—The Inquisition.—Banishment of the Jews from Spain.

SECTION VI.

KINGDOM OF SCOTLAND, ... 1839-1854

Ancient Caledonia.—Scots and Picts.—The Angles.—Introduction of Christianity by St. Columba. Kenneth Mac Alpin, First King of all Scotland.—His Successors.—Macbeth.—Malcolm Canmore.—

TABLE OF CONTENTS.

Alexander I.—David I.—William the Lion.—Alexander II.—Alexander III.—The Maid of Norway.—John Baliol.—English Conquest of Scotland.—William Wallace and Robert Bruce.—Battle of Bannockburn.—Independence of Scotland.—David Bruce.—Edward Baliol.—House of Stuart.—Robert II.—Robert III.—James I.—James II.—James III.—James IV.—Battle of Flodden Field.

SECTION VII.

THE SCANDINAVIAN KINGDOMS, . . . 1854-1861
Origin of the Scandinavian Kingdoms. — Denmark. — Norway. — Sweden. — Margaret and the Union of Calmar.—House of Oldenburg.—Independence of Sweden.

SECTION VIII.

RUSSIA, OR MUSCOVY, ... 1862-1871
The Slavs, or Slavonians.—Novgorod and Kiev.—Rurik, the Founder of the Russian Empire.—Oleg.— Igor.— Sviatoslav.— Vladimir the Great.—Christianization of Russia.—Sviatopolk.—Varoslav.—Petty Russian Principalities.—Andrew of Susdal.—Moscow Founded.—Mongol Conquest of Russia.—The Tartar Supremacy.—Alexander Nevski.—Ivan I.—Dimitri II.—Vassili III.—Ivan the Great.

SECTION IX.

KINGDOM OF POLAND, ... 1871
The Poles.—Piast. — Boleslas I., First King of Poland.—Ladislas IV.—Casimir the Great.—Louis the Great of Hungary. — The Jagellos. — Great Power and Extent of the Polish Kingdom.

SECTION X.

KINGDOM OF HUNGARY, ... 1872-1874
The Magyars, or Hungarians.—Arpad.—Geisa.—Stephen the Pious, First King of Hungary.—Geisa II.—Saxons and Flemings in Transylvania.—Andrew II. and the Golden Privilege.—Louis the Great.— Sigismund.— Matthias Corvinus.— Hungary's Decline.

SECTION XI.

BULGARIA, SERVIA, AND BOSNIA, . . . 1874-1875
Kingdom of Bulgaria.—Servian Kingdom and Empire.—Kingdom of Bosnia.

SECTION XII.

END OF THE EASTERN EMPIRE, . . . 1875-1880
Capture of Constantinople by the Latin Crusaders.—The Latin Empire.—The Greek Emperors of Nice.—Of Trebizond.—Restoration of the Greek Dynasty at Constantinople.—The Palæologi.—The Turks in Europe.—They Take Constantinople.—End of the Eastern Empire.

SECTION XIII.

ZINGIS KHAN'S TARTAR EMPIRE, . . 1881-1890
The Mongols.—Zingis Khan's Conquests.—His Sons.—Octai, His Successor.—Batou's Conquests and Kipzak Empire.—Further Conquests in China.—Yelu. — Kayuk. — Mangoo. — Kublai Khan. — Mongol Chinese Emperors. — Kipzak Empire. — Zagatai Empire.—Mongol Persian Empire.

SECTION XIV.

TAMERLANE'S TARTAR EMPIRE, . . . 1890-1898
Tamerlane's Birth, Childhood, Education and Early Exploits.—His Conquests, Government and Death.

SECTION XV.

RISE OF THE OTTOMAN TURKISH EMPIRE, 1899-1907
Origin of the Ottoman Turks.—Solyman.—Orthogrul.—Othman I, Founds the Ottoman Empire.—Orkhan.—The Turks in Europe.—Amurath I.—Adrianople the Turkish Capital.—The Janizaries.—Bajazet I.—His Conquests.—His Defeat and Capture by Tamerlane at Angora.—Mohammed I.—Amurath II.—Mohammed II.—Capture of Constantinople.—It Becomes the Turkish Capital.—Conquest of Greece.—Bajazet II.

PART III.—MODERN HISTORY.

CHAPTER I.—DAWN OF THE MODERN ERA.

SECTION I.

PROGRESS OF CIVILIZATION AND INVENTION, 1915
Invention of the Art of Printing.—Invention of Gunpowder and the Mariner's Compass.—Revival of Learning.—Decay of Feudalism and Chivalry.

SECTION II.

THE SEA-PASSAGE TO INDIA, ... 1916
Prince Henry of Portugal and Portuguese Maritime Discoveries.—Discovery of the Cape of Good Hope by Bartholomew Diaz.—Vasco da Gama's Voyage to India and Founding of Calicut.

SECTION III.

THE DISCOVERY OF AMERICA, ... 1916-1920
Christopher Columbus.—His Great Discovery.—His other Voyages.—His Death.—Amerigo Vespucci.—The New Continent Named in His Honor.—Sabastian Cabot's Voyages, Discoveries and Explorations.—The Aborigines of America.

CHAPTER II.—SIXTEENTH CENTURY.

SECTION I.

DISCOVERIES AND EXPLORATIONS, ... 1921-1923

Gaspar Cortereal.—Diego Columbus.—Discovery of Florida by John Ponce de Leon.—Discovery of the Pacific Ocean by Balboa.—Discovery of Mexico by Cordova.—Ferdinand Magellan's Circumnavigation of the Globe.—Vasquez de Ayllon.—Stephen Gomez.—Pamphilo de Narvaez.—Explorations of John Verrazzani and Jacques Cartier.—Discovery of the Mississippi River by Ferdinand De Soto.—Discovery of the Amazon River by Orellana.—Alarçon, De Cabrillo and Coronado on the Pacific Coast.

SECTION II.

THE SPANISH EMPIRE IN AMERICA, . . 1923-1936

Mexico and Peru.—Early Mexican History.—The Toltecs.—The Chichimecs and Other Nations.—The Aztecs, or Mexicans.—Rise of the Aztec Empire.—Aztec Civilization, Government, Religion and Customs.—Reign of Montezuma II.—Conquest of Mexico by the Spaniards under Fernando Cortez.—Mexico, or New Spain, under the Spanish Dominion.—Empire of the Incas in Peru.—Conquest of Peru by the Spaniards under Francisco Pizarro.—Peru under the Spaniards.—Discovery and Conquest of Chili by the Spaniards.—Wars with the Araucanian Indians.—South America under the Spaniards.

SECTION III.

PORTUGUESE IN ASIA AND AMERICA, . . 1936-1938

Rise of the Portuguese Colonial Empire in Asia.—Cabral and Almeida.—Albuquerque.—He Obtains Cochin.—Conquers Goa, Malacca and Ormuz.—Portuguese Colonies in Ceylon and on the Coromandel Coast.—Conquest of the Molucca and Sunda Islands.—Macao, in China.—Portuguese Influence in Arabia and Eastern Africa.—Splendor of Ormuz.—Extent of the Portuguese Dominion.—Its Decline and Fall.—Cabral's Discovery of Brazil.—Its Colonization by the Portuguese.

SECTION IV.

RISE OF THE EUROPEAN STATES-SYSTEM, 1938-1952

The European States-System.—The Balance of Power.—Europe at the Beginning of the Sixteenth Century.—Spain.—France.—England.—The Germano-Roman Empire.—Other European States.—Wars of Charles VIII. and Louis XII. of France in Italy.—League of Cambray against Venice.—Holy League against Louis XII.—English Victories over the French and the Scots.

SECTION V.

FRANCIS I., CHARLES V., HENRY VIII., 1952-1958

Francis I. of France.—Battle of Marignano.—Death of Ferdinand of Spain.—Charles I. of Spain.—Peace of Brussels.—Cardinal Ximenes.—Charles I. of Spain Becomes Charles V. of Germany.—His Vast Dominions.—Henry VIII. of England.—Field of the Cloth of Gold.

SECTION VI.

CHARLES V. AND THE REFORMATION, 1958-1970

Corruption of the Church and Previous Efforts at Reform.—Dr. Martin Luther.—Pope Leo X. and the Sale of Indulgencies.—Beginning of the Reformation by Luther.—Luther Excommunicated.—He Burns the Pope's Bull.—Luther Before the Diet of Worms.—Under the Ban of the Empire.—Confinement in Wartburg Castle.—His German Bible.—Dr. Carlstadt and the Anabaptists.—Philip Melanchthon.—Extension of the Reformation.—The Peasant Revolt in Germany.—Franz von Sickingen.—Thomas Münzer.—Subjection of the Revolted Peasants.—Progress of the Reformation.—Activity of Luther and Melanchthon.—The Protestation.—The Augsburg Confession.—Ulrich Zwingli and the Reformation in Switzerland.—Religious War in Switzerland.—Battle of Kappel and Death of Zwingli.

SECTION VII.

CHARLES V., FRANCIS I. AND THE TURKS, 1970-1985

First War Between Charles V. and Francis I.—French Invasion of Navarre.—The French Driven from Milan.—French Invasion of Italy.—Defection of the Constable de Bourbon.—French Retreat from Italy.—Death of the Chevalier Bayard.—Bourbon's Invasion of France.—Invasion of Italy by Francis I.—Battle of Pavia.—Captivity of Francis I.—Peace of Madrid.—Release of Francis I.—Holy League against Charles V.—Second War Between Charles V. and Francis I.—Capture of Rome by Cardinal Colonna.—By the German and Spanish Armies.—Captivity of Pope Clement VII.—Successful Career of Francis I. in Italy.—Andrea Doria.—Ladies' Peace of Cambray.—Alarming Progress of the Turks.—Conquest of Egypt and Syria by Selim I.—Solyman the Magnificent.—His Conquests.—Invasions of Hungary.—Battle of Mohacz.—Siege of Vienna.—Hungary Divided Between Austria and Turkey.—Expedition of Charles V. against Tunis.—Third War Between Charles V. and Francis I.—Truce of Nice.—Expedition of Charles V. Against Algiers.—Fourth War Between Charles V. and Francis I.—Peace of Crespy.—Persecutions of the Netherlanders.—Of the Vaudois.—Death of Francis I.

SECTION VIII.

WAR OF RELIGION IN GERMANY, . . 1986-1998

The League of Schmalkald.—Lutheranism in Würtemberg.—The Anabaptists in Münster.—Lutheranism in Saxony, Brandenburg and the Palatinate.—The War Between Charles V. and His Protestant German Subjects.—Perfidy of Maurice of Saxony.—Battle of Mühlberg.—Captivity of John Frederick of Saxony and Philip of Hesse.—The Augsburg Interim.—Maurice of Saxony Makes War on Charles V.—Peace of Passau.—Seizure of Lorraine by Henry II. of France.—Siege of Metz by Charles V.—Religious Peace of Augsburg.—Abdication, Retirement and Death of Charles V.

SECTION IX

LUTHERANISM AND CALVINISM, . . . 2003-2005

The Lutheran and German Reformed Churches.—John Calvin at Geneva.—Calvinism in France, Scotland and the Netherlands.

SECTION X.

CATHOLIC CHURCH AND THE JESUITS, 2005-2010
  The Catholic Church.—The Inquisition.—The Papacy.—Council of Trent—Ignatius Loyola and the Society of Jesus.

SECTION XI.

THE REFORMATION IN SCANDINAVIA, . 2010-2012
  Sweden's Liberation from Denmark by Gustavus Vasa.—Establishment of Lutheranism in the Three Scandinavian Kingdoms.

MAPS IN VOLUME V.

Europe, A. D. 1200 .... 1600, 1601
Feudal France in the Time of the Early Plantagenets 1640, 1641
Feudal France during the Hundred Years' War.. 1714, 1715

Europe, A. D. 1400 .... 1810, 1811
Discoveries in America 1910, 1911
Europe in the Time of the Reformation 2000, 2001

cle that he spared both the town and its inhabitants.

It was during the siege of Weinsberg that the war cries which resounded throughout Germany and Italy for three centuries were first heard. The king's troops took their name from their battle shout "Waiblingen," the name of a village which had been the home of the Hohenstaufen family. The rebel count's soldiers shouted their leader's name "Welf." These designations were subsequently assigned to the two great parties in the Germano-Roman Empire, which are most familiar to us in their Italian form of *Guelfs* and *Ghibellines*.

In the meantime the Papacy was divided between Innocent II. and Anacletus, the Antipope; but Innocent II. had triumphed over his rival, who died about A. D. 1139. Upon the accession of Conrad III. to the German throne, Pope Innocent II. sought to strengthen himself by a close alliance with King Roger of Sicily, who was so formidable a foe that both the Eastern Roman and the Germano-Roman monarchs, Manuel I. and Conrad III., formed a coalition against him. The Pope's authority was for a time set at defiance in Rome itself by the people, who were instigated by the stern denunciations of priestly ambition by the famous monk, Arnold of Brescia, who threw off the authority of the Pope and established a Senate and a Patrician named Giordano.

There was now a lull in German affairs, and the German people could devote their attention to the great subject which was occupying the minds of the people of all Christendom—the Crusades. Conrad III. engaged in the Second Crusade with King Louis VII. of France, the German king furnishing an army of seventy thousand men for the great expedition, A. D. 1147. Conrad III. was accompanied by his nephew Duke Frederick of Suabia, his old enemy Count Welf, and the flower of the German chivalry. He acquired a reputation for valor and intrepidity in the East, but accomplished no definite results. He returned to Germany two years later, broken down in health. Soon after his return Count Welf again rebelled, but was defeated. Conrad III. died in A. D. 1152, while making preparations to go to Rome to be crowned Emperor.

In pursuance of Conrad's advice, the German nobles elected his young nephew, the Duke of Suabia, to the dignity of King of Germany. The new sovereign is generally known as FREDERICK BARBAROSSA, the surname signifying "Red Beard." He was thirty-one years of age at his accession, and was considered a model of chivalry. He was a man of generous and noble impulses, and of strong and imperious will, so that he was devotedly loved by his friends and as implacably hated by his foes, as he could be harsh and stern in asserting his rights.

Frederick Barbarossa sincerely desired to end the struggle between the Guelfs and the Ghibellines, and was happily in a position to do so. His mother was a sister to Henry the Proud, whose son, Henry the Lion, of Brunswick, was the chivalrous monarch's cousin, as well as his personal friend. Henry the Lion was already Duke of Saxony, and the king bestowed upon him the duchy of Bavaria, thus making him the most powerful prince in Germany, as well as head of the house of Guelf. Frederick Barbarossa compensated Henry, Margrave of Austria, for relinquishing Bavaria by erecting the Austrian territory into a separate and independent duchy, to be held as a fief of the German crown, and made it hereditary in both the male and female line.

Frederick Barbarossa led six military expeditions to Italy, for the purpose of subduing the rebellious Italians, who were founding independent republics, and openly setting the German monarch's authority at defiance. Animated by patriotism and by a love of freedom, the Lombard cities, headed by the haughty Milan, formed an effective burgher militia, and endeavored to cast off the imperial authority. This refractory spirit manifested itself in this king's first campaign, when, in accordance with a long-established usage, he reviewed his troops in the plains near Piacenza and required the princes and cities of Northern Italy to do him homage.

Frederick Barbarossa proceeded to Italy in A. D. 1154, and at a great Diet held at Roncaglia he received the submission of all the Italian states. The young German king came with the intention and the power to restore the imperial authority in Italy, and he instantly set about doing so. Complaints were made to him by the enemies of Milan, and that city had deeply offended him by refusing to acknowledge his authority and to furnish him the supplies to which he was entitled. Frederick Barbarossa therefore decided against Milan. Tortona, an ally of Milan, was likewise accused, and also condemned. The German king destroyed Asti and Chieri, and took and burned Tortona, the allies of Milan. He spared the lives of the inhabitants, who found refuge in Milan.

Frederick Barbarossa received the Lombard crown at Pavia; after which he proceeded to Rome, and was there crowned Emperor by Pope Adrian IV., who was Nicholas Breakspear, the only Englishman who ever became Pope. Frederick Barbarossa only obtained the imperial crown by giving up Arnold of Brescia, the remarkable Italian monk who had sought to bring back Rome to its ancient republican simplicity. Imbued with the ideas of the renowned French philosopher Abelard, Arnold of Brescia traversed Italy, denouncing the Pope's temporal power and the unworthiness of the clergy. While he was at Rome, busy with his project for a new Roman Republic, Pope Adrian IV. laid the city under an interdict; and the Roman Senators, unable to withstand the entreaties of the Roman people, submitted to the Pope and expelled Arnold. The monkish reformer fled, but was overtaken by Frederick Barbarossa's troops and made prisoner; and the Emperor handed him over to the Prefect of Rome, by whom he was tried, convicted and beheaded in the Castle of St. Angelo, in A. D. 1155.

Thus the Pope's authority was reëstablished in Rome. The Emperor also reduced Milan to submission, and placed the imperial eagle on the spire of its great cathedral; in token of his supremacy. But before very long the Pope and the Emperor commenced quarreling over the territories of the Countess Matilda, and this dispute soon developed into an effort on the Pope's part to deprive the Emperor of all his rights over Rome and his Italian possessions. Upon the death of Pope Adrian IV., in A. D. 1159, two Popes were elected—Alexander III. by the papal party, and Victor IV. by the imperial party. Each Pope excommunicated his rival and his followers, and the whole of Christendom was divided into two parties. Alexander III. was the more generally acknowledged pontiff; and a war which broke out between the Emperor and the cities of Lombardy enabled this Pope to offer a determined resistance to his powerful enemy, the Emperor Frederick Barbarossa.

After Frederick Barbarossa's return to Germany, the Milanese renewed their defiance of the Emperor, and destroyed Lodi and several other Lombard cities that adhered to the Emperor. Thereupon Frederick Barbarossa led a second expedition against the revolted city, A. D. 1159. The Emperor had his regalian rights determined by jurists according to the Code of Justinian, and when Milan refused to submit to the decision he uttered the ban of the Empire against the refractory city.

A fierce war ensued between the Emperor and the Milanese. Frederick Barbarossa took and destroyed Crema, a city in alliance with Milan, and also forced Milan to surrender, after a siege of three and a half years. After the carroccio, or carriage, that supported the chief banner of the city had been broken to pieces, and after the citizens had humbled themselves before the victorious Emperor, the walls and houses of Milan were leveled with the ground, and the inhabitants were forced to settle in four widely-separated points of their territory. The other Lombard towns were so terrified by the destruction of Milan that they received the imperial legate, or Podesta, within their walls.

The fall of Milan put an end to the resistance against the imperial authority in Lombardy, and made the situation of Pope

Alexander III. dangerous in Rome. Sicily was so torn with violence and civil war that it no longer afforded the Pope his usual refuge, and he fled into France, where he remained three years. During this period the Antipope died, and was succeeded by Guido of Crema, who assumed the name of Paschal III. As the Emperor Frederick Barbarossa was detained in Germany by the events which occurred in that country, Pope Alexander III. seized the opportunity to return to Rome, A. D. 1165.

Frederick Barbarossa's first successes in Italy made him the most powerful sovereign in Europe. The Kings of Poland and Hungary did homage to him for their crowns, and the Emperor rewarded the Duke of Bohemia for his faithful services by erecting his duchy into a kingdom. Frederick Barbarossa married Beatrice, the heiress of Franche-Comte, or the Free County of Burgundy; thus annexing that portion of Burgundy to the German kingdom.

Frederick Barbarossa personally disliked Pope Alexander III., and he therefore refused to acknowledge his election and resisted his authority. For this course, the Pope excommunicated him, and united himself with the Lombard cities, which were exasperated by the tyranny of the imperial legate; and the entire Guelfic party in Italy rallied to the Pope's support, and a furious war ensued. Even Cremona and other cities which had formerly opposed Milan joined the coalition against the Emperor, which was definitely organized in A. D. 1167 under the name of the *Lombard League*. The Milanese, who headed the revolt against the imperial authority, had rebuilt their city, and had founded the city of Alexandria, which was named in honor of Pope Alexander III.

The Emperor's power was seriously menaced by the Lombard League, and about the same time the Eastern Emperor Manuel I. obtained a footing in Italy and gained over Ancona. Frederick Barbarossa, who had left Italy, soon returned with a powerful army, and vainly attempted to take Ancona, after which he marched against Rome.

The Pope instantly fled, but Frederick Barbarossa's advantage was neutralized by the breaking out of a pestilence in his army, which forced him to a hasty retreat from Italy.

Frederick Barbarossa returned to Italy in A. D. 1174 with a powerful army, and laid siege to Alexandria, but was compelled to retire by the army of the Lombard League. As Henry the Lion of Brunswick, Duke of Saxony and Bavaria, and head of the house of Guelf, refused to aid the Emperor, the German army was disastrously defeated by the gallant Milanese in the decisive battle of Legnano, about fifteen miles from Pavia, A. D. 1176. Frederick Barbarossa himself was missing for several days. The heroism displayed by the chivalrous Emperor won the respect of the Lombard confederates and of the Pope; and in 1177 a truce of six years was agreed upon at Venice, by which the Pope and the Emperor were reconciled. Frederick Barbarossa recognized Alexander III. as Pope, and was allowed to hold the Countess Matilda's territories until his death, when they were to revert to the Pope. Frederick Barbarossa returned to Germany at the conclusion of this Lombard war.

At the expiration of the six years' truce, in A. D. 1183, a permanent treaty of peace was concluded at Constance, in Suabia. By the Peace of Constance the Emperor ceded to the towns all rights inside their walls. He allowed them to administer their own laws and to make peace on their own account. He retained the old regalian rights—the right to quarters, food and clothing for his army when he was in the territory of these cities; but these regalian rights were defined, and precautions were taken against future disputes. He allowed the Consuls to be retained, but they were nominally invested by him, and each Lombard city was to admit an imperial judge of appeal.

The Peace of Constance made the Lombard cities virtually independent, while they continued to constitute a part of the Germano-Roman Empire. Thus left to themselves, these cities became the chosen resorts of great men and the nurseries of science and art; but their liberation from imperial rule left them divided among themselves and arrayed against each other, with no power capable of harmonizing their disputes.

Frederick Barbarossa afterwards gained another advantage over the Pope. William II., the Norman King of Sicily, had been the Pope's most faithful ally. The Emperor married his son Henry to Constance, the daughter of Roger, the first Norman King of Naples and Sicily. On the death of William II., the reigning Norman king, who was childless, Henry would be the direct heir to the crown of Sicily.

As King of Germany, Frederick Barbarossa was a great and wise monarch. He was not wholly successful in abolishing private warfare, the great curse of his kingdom, but he imposed a check upon it by requiring those who indulged in it to give three days' notice to their enemies. All who refused to do so were to be treated as outlaws. Frederick Barbarossa likewise encouraged the growth of the cities by granting them important privileges and making some of them free. His acts were so judicious and popular that he won the support and affection of the whole German nation, even the German prelates being loyal to him.

Thus strong in the support and attachment of his German subjects, the great Emperor was able to bid defiance to the Pope's power in Germany, there being no opposition for the Pope to intrigue with. A papal legate once ventured to assert in the German Diet that the Empire was dependent upon His Holiness, thus raising such a storm of fury that his life was saved only by the Emperor's personal interposition. Had Henry IV. been a sovereign of the same stamp and vim, he might have reigned as a great and successful monarch, and escaped the humiliation to which he was subjected by Pope Gregory VII.

Henry the Lion had for a long time enjoyed the favor and friendship of the Emperor Frederick Barbarossa, and advanced in power and prosperity. He had conquered the Slavonic provinces of Pomerania and Mecklenburg; had made war on the Frislanders on the Baltic, and the peasant republic of the Ditmarsens, in Holstein; and had obtained possession of an extensive dominion. He had established mines in the Hartz mountains. He had founded cities and bishoprics—Lübeck, Munich and Ratzburg—and attracted settlers from the Netherlands. But his ambition and acts of violence against princes and clergy were as well known as his great feats in war; so that the brazon lion that he erected before the citadel of his principal city, Brunswick, might be considered an emblem of his rapacity, no less than of his strength. His success made him haughty and arrogant, and his overbearing manner at length aroused the jealousy of the other German princes.

In A. D. 1176, having become angry with Frederick Barbarossa because he refused to bestow the city of Goslar upon him, Henry the Lion took a mean advantage of the Emperor, deserting him in the most critical period of his war with the Lombard cities, and returning to Germany with his troops. This defection caused the Emperor's defeat in the battle of Legnano, from which field Frederick Barbarossa escaped with difficulty. The Emperor is said to have begged Henry the Lion on his knees not to desert him, but in vain.

When Frederick Barbarossa returned to Germany, in A. D. 1178, he determined to punish Henry the Lion for his defection. The complaints that arose on every side against Henry the Lion gave the Emperor the opportunity that he desired, and Frederick Barbarossa therefore summoned Henry to appear before the Diet at Worms. Henry refused to appear; and, with the sanction of the Diet, the Emperor put the refractory prince under the ban of the Empire, and declared his two duchies, Saxony and Bavaria, to be forfeited. A part of East Saxony was given to Bernhard of Anhalt, son of Albert the Bear; a portion of West Saxony was bestowed on Philip, Archbishop of Cologne, who was also granted ducal rights in these territories; and the duchy of Bavaria, greatly weakened by the separation of Styria, was conferred on Otho of Wittelsbach. The Wittelsbachs were devoted to the Hohenstaufen family, and afterwards received the Palatinate of the Rhine.

1181 Henry came to Erfurt, where the Emperor was holding a Diet, prostrated himself at the Emperor's feet, and humbly asked pardon of his sovereign. Greatly af-

FREDERICK BARBAROSSA ASKING AID OF HENRY THE LION.

But Henry the Lion was only subdued after a bloody war, and withstood his foes for two years. Only when Frederick Barbarossa himself took the field against him was he thoroughly subdued. In A. D. fected by the sight of his old friend so humbled, Frederick Barbarossa frankly forgave the head of the house of Guelf. The Emperor could not restore Henry's duchies of Saxony and Bavaria, but permitted him to retain for himself and his family his hereditary possessions of Brunswick and Luneburg. Henry agreed to live for three years at the court of his father-in-law, King Henry II. of England. During Henry's sojourn in England his wife gave birth to a son, from whom the present royal family of England is descended.

Frederick Barbarossa had become venerable for his years, but his military ardor had not abated. Having subdued all his foes, he participated in the Third Crusade, A. D. 1189, along with Kings Richard the Lion-hearted of England and Philip Augustus of France, in order that he might end his heroic career in the same manner that he had commenced it. From this expedition the chivalrous Emperor never returned, and he never lived to reach Palestine, being drowned in crossing a small stream in Cilicia, in June, A. D. 1190.

The affection which the German people bore Frederick Barbarossa was so strong that the tidings of his accidental death were at first received with incredulity, and then with an outburst of the most profound sorrow. In after years the German people looked back to this chivalrous Emperor as their greatest champion, and he still lives in the legends of the German nation. There arose a tradition that Frederick Barbarossa was not dead, but was only plunged with his knights into an enchanted sleep in a cavern of the Kyffhauser Berg (or hill), in Thuringia, where, armed *cap-a-pie*, they would remain until the ravens should cease flying around the mountain, when they would make their appearance and restore Germany to her former greatness.

Frederick Barbarossa's son and successor, HENRY VI., crushed a new revolt of Henry the Lion, after which he went to Italy, where he was crowned Emperor. After the death of William II., the last Norman King of Naples and Sicily, Henry VI. desired to take possession of that kingdom, the inheritance of his Norman wife Constance; but the Neapolitan nobles, who dreaded Henry's ambition and avarice, opposed this project, and endeavored to place one of their own number, the brave Tancred, on the throne of Naples and Sicily. A war followed, in which Henry VI. subdued the Neapolitans, by the equipment of fresh armaments with ransom money which he obtained for the release of King Richard the Lion-hearted of England, and by the aid of the German Crusaders. After obtaining possession of Naples and Sicily he took a frightful revenge, filling the prisons with Neapolitan nobles and bishops, some of whom were blinded and impaled, while others were burned or buried alive. The plunder was conveyed to the Hohenstaufen castles by heavily-laden pack horses. Henry died suddenly in A. D. 1197 at the early age of thirty-two, leaving behind him a two-year-old son, who was intrusted to the guardianship of Pope Innocent III.

The claims of the infant son of Henry VI. were disregarded by the German nobles, and the result was a disputed succession and a civil war of ten years in Germany. The Ghibellines elected a Hohenstaufen prince, PHILIP of Suabia, brother of Henry VI.; while the Guelfs chose OTHO IV., of Brunswick, son of Henry the Lion. Philip was acknowledged in the South of Germany, while Otho IV. was recognized in the North. During the ten years' civil war which followed, the greatest lawlessness and violence prevailed, and frightful ravages were committed, sixteen cathedrals and three hundred and fifty parishes with churches perishing in the flames. The assassination of Philip at Bamberg by the hasty Palsgrave, Otho of Wittelsbach, in A. D. 1208, restored peace for a short time. Otho IV. was now generally recognized as king throughout Germany, and the next year he proceeded to Rome, where he was crowned Emperor by Pope Innocent III.

Pope Innocent III. was a politic prince, and ranked next to Gregory VII. (Hildebrand) among the Popes. He acted on the principle that the Pope is superior to temporal princes—a principle almost universally acknowledged during the Middle Ages. He endeavored to persuade the Emperor Otho IV. to confirm all previous donations and renounce all claims to feudal rights in Rome and Central Italy. But the Emperor sought a quarrel with the Pope, invaded the estates of the Church in Tuscany, and marched into the dominions of the youthful Frederick II. of Sicily. Thereupon Pope Innocent III. excommunicated Otho IV. and pronounced his deposition, at the same time sending the young Frederick II. into Germany as a rival for the German and imperial crowns. The German princes obeyed the Pope's order by electing Frederick II. to the German throne; and after another civil war, and the defeat of Otho IV. by King Philip Augustus of France in the battle of Bouvines, in A. D. 1214, Otho IV. retired to private life, and thus remained until his death at Brunswick in 1218.

FREDERICK II.—the son of Henry VI. and the grandson of Frederick Barbarossa—was crowned King of Germany at Aix la Chappelle in 1215, and in 1220 he was crowned Emperor at Rome by Pope Honorius III.

Frederick II. soon became a powerful enemy of the Pope. He was absent from Germany for the first fifteen years of his reign. Upon leaving Germany he induced the German princes to elect his young son Henry King of Germany, and made him regent of the kingdom under the guardianship of Engelbert, Archbishop of Cologne.

A large part of the reign of Frederick II. concerns itself with Italian affairs. Though Frederick II. was of German blood, he was a Sicilian by birth, and was thus endowed by nature with certain qualities and habits of mind which did not belong to his Teutonic blood. He had been carefully educated in the wisdom of the Arabians, and entertained a friendly feeling towards the Mohammedans and the Oriental mode of life. His reign was a constant struggle between the papal and imperial powers. His position as King of Lombardy and King of Naples and Sicily threatened the existence of the Pope's temporal power, while his skeptical turn of mind and his liberal religious views menaced the authority of the Church. His bitter hatred of the Pope caused him much trouble in the end.

The first years of the reign of Frederick II. were the happiest. He was free to carry out his own policy in his own kingdom of Sicily, which enjoyed a security and prosperity during his reign which it had not enjoyed under his predecessors. He established law and order, compelling the nobles to cease their lawlessness, and thus protecting the weak and helpless. He encouraged learning and the arts by founding the university of Naples, and by aiding those of Bologna and Salerno. The Italian language began to assume its modern form during his beneficent reign.

The Emperor's good understanding with Pope Honorius III. was soon disturbed by Frederick's delay to lead the Fifth Crusade to the Holy Land, which he had promised to do as the price of his coronation as Emperor. Honorius III. censured the Emperor for his tardiness. The next Pope, Gregory IX., pursued the same course, and excommunicated Frederick II. in 1227 for venturing to fall sick at the time that the Pope expected him to embark for the Holy Land. The Emperor treated the sentence of excommunication with utter contempt, and this so angered Gregory IX. that he threatened Frederick II. with still greater penalties in A. D. 1228. There was in Rome a powerful party devoted to the Emperor through gratitude for his generous assistance to them in a time of famine; and this party, indignant at the Pope's course toward the Emperor, drove Gregory IX. from Rome.

The Pope, who had excommunicated Frederick II. for his delay in leading the Fifth Crusade when he was ordered, now endeavored to prevent him from sailing when he was ready; but the Emperor disregarded the Pope's mandate, and proceeded on his expedition to Palestine, where he arrived in September, A. D. 1228. The animosity of Pope Gregory IX. pursued Frederick II. to the Holy Land, and arrayed the Knights Templars and the Knights of St. John, as well as the ecclesiastics, against the refractory Emperor. The two orders

BATTLE OF BOUVINES.

THE GERMAN EMPIRE AND THE CHURCH.

of knighthood absolutely refused to fight under the banner of Frederick II. and grossly insulted him. Nevertheless, the Emperor proceeded in his work, seized Jaffa, and entered into a treaty with Sultan Malek Kamel of Egypt, with whom he had long been on terms of friendship; thus obtaining Jerusalem, Nazareth and Bethlehem for the Christians.

Frederick II. then proceeded to Jerusalem to complete his pilgrimage to the Holy Sepulcher. He had not arrived at the Holy City before the Archbishop of Cæsarea appeared with instructions from the Patriarch of Jerusalem to declare the Emperor under excommunication and to place Jerusalem under an interdict. Even the Holy Sepulcher was under the ban of the Church. The pilgrims were forbidden to pray in that holiest of places, and prayers there delivered were pronounced unholy. No Christian rite could be celebrated before the Christian Emperor—a disgrace which was inflicted in the face of all Mohammedans.

As soon as Frederick II. arrived at Jerusalem he visited the Church of the Holy Sepulcher. The church was silent, and not a priest made his appearance. During the Emperor's stay in Jerusalem no mass was celebrated in the city or its suburbs. An English Dominican monk, named Walter, performed but one service on Sunday morning. Frederick II. again proceeded in great pomp, and in all his imperial apparel, to the Church of the Holy Sepulcher. No prelate or priest of the Church of Jerusalem was there who ventured to utter a blessing. The Archbishops of Palermo and Capua were present, but do not appear to have participated in the ceremony. The imperial crown was placed on the high altar. The Emperor took it up with his own hands, and put it on his head, thus crowning himself King of Jerusalem without being consecrated by the Church.

Frederick II. returned to Europe in A. D. 1229, finding that the Pope had revived the Lombard League against him, and was even seeking to instigate all Europe in a crusade for his overthrow. As soon as the Emperor arrived in Italy he recovered all the towns which the Lombard League had conquered. Pope Gregory IX., not intimidated by these reverses, renewed the excommunication against Frederick II., and declared his subjects absolved from their allegiance. The Emperor then marched toward Rome; whereupon negotiations were opened, which ended in the Peace of San Germano, concluded between Frederick II., Pope Gregory IX. and the Lombard League, August, A. D. 1230, the Pope freeing the Emperor from the excommunication.

Frederick II. then aided the Pope in persecuting the religious sect of the *Paterini*, which had ventured to dispute the extraordinary power claimed by the priests of the Romish Church. Jealous of the Emperor's great influence in Italy, Pope Gregory IX. soon brought about another war with him by instigating the Milanese to encourage the Emperor's son Henry, King of the Romans, to rebel against his father.

The Emperor's absence from Germany during the first fifteen years of his reign encouraged the German nobles to make the authority of the regent, his son Henry, King of the Romans, only nominal, and also to increase their own power to such an extent that they became almost independent of their sovereign. Private wars distracted every part of Germany, and robbery and violence again prevailed all over the country. As Henry grew to manhood he gave constant evidence that he did not inherit his father's noble qualities. He was mean, rash and violent; and it was his father's long absence from Germany that encouraged him to rebel, and to declare, to the German princes assembled at Boppart in A. D. 1234, his intention to seize the German throne. The Emperor Frederick II. returned to Germany the next year, and easily crushed his son's rebellion. Henry attempted to poison his father, but was imprisoned in Apulia for the remainder of his life.

During this visit to Germany, the Emperor Frederick II. married the princess Isabella, the sister of King Henry III. of

England. He held a great Diet at Mayence, where he endeavored to abolish private wars by declaring all such strifes unlawful, except in cases where justice could not be otherwise obtained. He also established an *imperial tribunal*, to try all causes not affecting princes of the Empire. This was a good beginning, but Frederick II. left Germany again too soon to complete his work. In A. D. 1236 he returned to Italy, where his struggle with the Pope required his presence; leaving his son Conrad in charge of the German kingdom.

A few years afterward the very existence of the German nation was imperiled by a destructive inundation of Asiatic hordes into Europe. Vast hosts of Mongols, or Moguls—of whom we shall speak hereafter—had overrun the vast plains of Russia and Poland. They burst into Germany in A. D. 1241, and defeated and killed Duke Henry of Lower Silesia in a terrible battle at Liegnitz, the Silesian force being entirely cut to pieces; but so terrible was the slaughter of the victorious Mongols on this occasion that they retired from Germany in utter dismay, turning southward into Hungary.

Frederick II. gave his kingdom of Naples and Sicily a new code of laws, and encouraged trade, industry and poetry. But when he endeavored to force the Lombard cities to fulfill the stipulations of the Peace of Constance and to discharge the regalian rights pertaining to him as Emperor, a furious war broke out in Northern Italy. Aided by the Ghibellines, under the cruel tyrant, Ezzelino da Romano, in Padua, Vicenza and Verona, and supported by his faithful Saracens whom he had settled in Southern Italy, Frederick II. defeated the allied army of the Lombards in the battle of Corte Nuova, A. D. 1237. He captured the Podesta of Milan, who was a son of the Doge of Venice, and put him to death in punishment for his rebellion. This execution so enraged the Venetians that they joined the Lombard League against the Emperor, while the Genoese likewise espoused the Guelfic cause.

When Frederick II. pursued his conquest with severity and threatened Milan with a fate similar to that which it had experienced from Frederick Barbarossa; and when he presented his illegitimate son, the brave and handsome Enzio, with the island kingdom of Sardinia, Pope Gregory IX. again excommunicated the Emperor, espoused the cause of the Lombard cities, and sought to raise up enemies on all sides against Frederick II., accusing the free-thinking Emperor of being an enemy to the Christian religion and a secret Mohammedan. The Emperor retorted these accusations in some violent written replies, repaying invective with invective; but, as public opinion was on the Pope's side, the Church triumphed in the quarrel.

Pope Gregory IX. summoned a general council of the Church at Rome to ratify the excommunication; but the Pisans captured the Genoese fleet which conveyed the English and French bishops, some of whom were drowned and others taken prisoners during the battle—a circumstance which prevented the council from accomplishing anything.

After the death of Pope Gregory IX., in A. D. 1241, at the age of almost a century, the position of the Emperor Frederick II. appeared to become more favorable; but Innocent IV., who became Pope in A. D. 1243, was the Emperor's bitter personal enemy. Frederick II. at once acknowledged Innocent IV. as Pope and made offers for a reconciliation; but Innocent IV., who was resolved to crush the Emperor, refused to accept any settlement of the quarrel except the unconditional submission of Frederick II. In order to place himself beyond the Emperor's reach, Innocent IV. fled from Rome and took refuge in the free city of Lyons, which was not yet a part of the Kingdom of France.

The Pope's arrogance, and the bitter and cruel hostility which he manifested towards the Emperor Frederick II., disgusted the great sovereigns of Europe. Even St. Louis, King of France, refused to permit Innocent IV. to take up his residence in the French dominions. James I., King of Aragon, courteously declined to receive the Pope in his kingdom. When King Henry III. of

England was appealed to for this purpose, he bluntly replied: "We have already suffered too much from the usuries and simonies of Rome; we do not want the Pope to pillage us." Henry III. had only a short time before dismissed the papal legate at the demand of the English barons, with the hearty exclamation: "The devil take thee away to hell!"

The crowned heads of Europe were alarmed by the growing power and the insatiable ambition of the Pope, who claimed authority over all the kingdoms of the world, the right to set up and pull down whom he pleased, and whose claims were well expressed by the following remark of Innocent IV.: "We are no mere man; we have the place of God upon earth!" Innocent IV. was not content with merely asserting his pretensions. He promptly proceeded to enforce them by the power of the sword.

Thus being obliged by the coldness of the great powers of Europe to remain at Lyons, Pope Innocent IV. summoned a council of the Church at that city. This council convened in June, A. D. 1245, but was very far from representing the entire Church. The Pope accused the Emperor Frederick II. of many crimes, and charged him with being false to the Church, a believer in Mohammedanism, and a blasphemer of God. The learned jurisconsult, Thaddeus of Suessa, ably and fearlessly defended Frederick II.; but the animosity of Innocent IV. prevailed over every form of law and justice recognized by the Church. The council excommunicated the Emperor, declared him to have forfeited his dominions, absolved his subjects from their allegiance to him, threatened his adherents with the ban of the Church, urged the Pope to appoint a new king for Sicily, and ordered the German princes to elect a new king for Germany.

When the Emperor was informed of the council's decision he exclaimed haughtily: "I hold my crown of God alone; neither the Pope, the council nor the devil shall rend it from me!"

The civil war between the Guelfs and the Ghibellines was now renewed with the most desperate fury in Italy and Germany. The Emperor's enemies conspired against his life, and he was in constant peril everywhere. The Pope seemed desperate and unscrupulous enough to use any means, and base enough to sanction any plot. The better nature of Frederick II. was overcome by this disreputable method of warfare, and he became suspicious and cruel. The Emperor's partisans injured his cause with the Northern Italians by their severities, and he speedily lost ground among them.

The Pope's efforts to find a new King of Germany and Emperor did not succeed as he had hoped they would. None of the crowned heads of Europe would assist him in his war against Frederick II. by accepting the imperial crown and thus acknowledging his assumed right to deprive Frederick II. of that crown.

In Germany the prelates and clergy espoused the Pope's cause and won over many of the princes and nobles who desired to increase their own power at the expense of the imperial authority. But the Emperor had still a large following of patriotic nobles, who loved their country better than their party; and the German cities, now growing more wealthy and powerful, sustained Frederick II. almost unanimously.

The papal party finally elected HENRY RASPE, Landgrave of Thuringia, to the German throne, A. D. 1246; but he was never acknowledged sovereign, and was defeated at Ulm, in Suabia, by Conrad, son of Frederick II., soon after which he died powerless and forsaken in Wartburg castle, A. D. 1247. After some trouble in finding a candidate who would accept the German throne, the Pope caused COUNT WILLIAM OF HOLLAND, a youth of twenty, to be proclaimed Emperor. William was strongest in the North of Germany, where he allied himself with the Welfs; but CONRAD IV., the son of Frederick II., prevailed in Southern Germany. The imperial towns and most of the German nobles sided with Conrad IV.

In the meantime hostilities between the

Guelfs and the Ghibellines raged with terrible fury in Italy. The fiery temperament of the vindictive Italians caused deeds of frightful atrocity. Family was arrayed against family, city against city, and neither age nor rank refrained from the conflict. Frederick II. was at first successful, crushing the revolt in Naples and Sicily, and throwing his enemies wholly on the defensive. But monstrous cruelties were perpetrated by Ezzelino, the leader of the Ghibelline nobility, in his attacks upon the Guelfic cities in Northern Italy, until he met with his merited punishment in the prison of Milan. These excesses neutralized Frederick's success in Southern Italy, and in A. D. 1247 Parma revolted from Frederick II., who failed in his attempts to take the city, though he besieged it for many months. His illegitimate son Frederick captured Florence; but his son Enzio was taken prisoner by the Bolognese, who kept the fair-haired king in captivity for the remaining twenty years of his life.

Peter de Vinea, born in A. D. 1190, raised himself by his eloquence and legal knowledge from a low condition to the office of Chancellor to the Emperor Frederick II., who reposed such confidence in him that his influence was unbounded. The Emperor's courtiers, envious of Peter's exalted station, managed by means of forged letters to make Frederick II. believe that his Chancellor held a secret and treasonable intercourse with the Pope. Because of this supposed crime, Peter de Vinea was sentenced to be paraded through all the cities of the Kingdom of Naples, and to be tormented to death.

The fallen Chancellor was taken to San Miniato, in Tuscany, where his eyes were put out. He was led through the villages, mounted on an ass; while a crier shouted: "Behold Master Peter de Vinea, the chief councilor of the Emperor, who betrayed his master to the Pope! See what he has gained by his dealings. Well may he say, 'How high was I once, and how low am I brought!'" But Peter was determined that the Emperor should not have the pleasure of parading him through the towns of Apulia. On the way to Pisa, the unfortunate Chancellor dashed out his brains against a pillar to which he had been chained (A. D. 1249). The great Florentine poet, Dante, who was born soon after this tragedy, and who lived near its scene, has vindicated the good name of the great statesman who had been so falsely and unjustly accused:

"I swear
That never faith I broke to my liege-lord,
Who merited such honor; and of you,
If any to the world indeed return,
Clear he from wrong my memory, that lies
Yet prostrate under envy's cruel blow."

Frederick II. for a long time maintained his lofty attitude, and the number of his enemies only increased his courage. But worn out by the constant struggle which the animosity of Popes Gregory IX. and Innocent IV. had forced upon him in both Italy and Germany, the great Emperor's heart finally broke; and he died in the arms of his beloved son Manfred, in Southern Italy, in the fifty-sixth year of his age, A. D. 1250. Having confessed, he received absolution from the faithful Archbishop of Palermo. His body was carried in state to Palermo, where it was interred in a magnificent tomb. This was perfectly proper, as he had always been one of the wisest and best rulers that Sicily ever had.

Frederick II. had a cultivated mind, and possessed great aptitude for science and poetry; while he was likewise distinguished for his courage, heroism and personal beauty. Surrounded by pomp, luxury, and all sorts of pleasures, he would have had all pretensions to happiness had not his free-thinking spirit resisted the Church, and had he only learned to moderate his desires and control his passions. The malice of his enemies pursued him to the grave, describing him as dying unreconciled to the Church, miserable, deserted, and conscious of the desertion of all; while his son Manfred was maliciously accused of smothering him with a pillow.

The great power of the German Emperors in Italy ended with the death of Frederick II. The towns of Northern Italy soon became strong enough to resist the occasional

DEATH OF EMPEROR FREDERICK II.

efforts of the Emperors to control them, and in Southern Italy the power of the Emperors was soon obtained by other claimants. The successors of Frederick II. were so occupied with German affairs that they were unable to devote much attention to Italy.

Upon hearing of the death of Frederick II., Pope Innocent IV. returned to Rome in triumph. He declared Naples and Sicily to be lapsed papal fiefs, and excommunicated Conrad IV. and Manfred, the sons of Frederick II., who desired to take possession of their paternal inheritance. Conrad IV. soon died; but his chivalrous half-brother, Manfred, defended Southern Italy with his German and Saracen troops so gallantly and successfully that most of the towns tendered their allegiance, and the Guelfic troops were obliged to retreat into the papal territories. Distress at this circumstance hastened the death of Pope Innocent IV.

The next Pope, Alexander IV., pursued his predecessor's policy toward the Hohenstaufen dynasty, whom he resolved to deprive of Naples and Sicily at any price. He accordingly conferred that beautiful kingdom as a papal fief on the energetic and tyrannical Duke Charles of Anjou, brother of St. Louis, King of France, on condition that he should conquer it by Guelfic aid and with French troops, and should pay an annual tribute to the papal court. Manfred valiantly defended his paternal inheritance, but was defeated and slain by the army of Charles of Anjou in the bloody battle of Benevento, A. D. 1266. His remains were interred in a simple grave, to which every one of his soldiers contributed a stone.

The battle of Benevento broke the power of the Ghibellines, and Naples and Sicily fell into the possession of the stern and victorious Charles of Anjou, who made the unfortunate kingdom feel all the miseries of conquest. The Ghibellines were punished with death, imprisonment and exile, and their possessions were divided among the French and Guelfic soldiers.

THE LAST OF THE HOHENSTAUFEN.

The oppressed Ghibellines now called Conradine, the youngest son of Conrad IV., from Germany into Italy. This prince possessed the lofty spirit and heroic courage of his illustrious ancestors. He went to Italy for the purpose of recovering the Hohenstaufen inheritance, with the aid of his youthful friend, Frederick of Baden, and a few faithful adherents. He was joyfully welcomed by the Ghibellines, and marched triumphantly through Northern and Central Italy, putting the Pope to flight, and entering the Kingdom of Naples. He won the battle of Scurcola, but his over-hasty advance caused his defeat by the troops of

DEATH OF MANFRED IN THE BATTLE OF BENEVENTO.

Charles of Anjou, who were watching in ambuscade. His troops were killed or dispersed; and Conradine himself was betrayed into the power of Charles of Anjou, who beheaded him and his faithful friend, Frederick of Baden, at Naples.

The few remaining Hohenstaufen princes likewise experienced a cruel fate. King Enzio died in prison at Bologna, as already noticed. The cruel Charles of Anjou permitted Manfred's sons to end their lives in prison; and Margaret, the daughter of Frederick II., was ill-treated and threatened with death by her husband, Albert the Uncourteous, of Thuringia, so that she fled by night from the Wartburg castle. In her agony at her separation from her two sons, she bit one of them in the cheek while embracing him, so that he retained the mark and was called Frederick the Bitten.

Pope Alexander IV. died A. D. 1261, and was succeeded by Urban IV., a Frenchman. Upon the death of Frederick II., in A. D. 1250, his son Conrad IV. succeeded him as King of Germany. In consequence of the unscrupulous efforts of Popes Innocent IV. and Alexander IV., Germany was in such a condition of anarchy that Conrad IV. found it a hard task to accomplish anything for his kingdom. After the death of Frederick II. the imperial authority had become only nominal, and private wars and the violence of the nobles imperiled life and property throughout Germany. Conrad IV. had to maintain a hard fight for his crown. His death in A. D. 1254, in the midst of the struggle, ended the Hohenstaufen dynasty in Germany.

The death of Conrad IV. left William of Holland the sole King of Germany. He was considered of little importance by either party; and his death in A. D. 1256, in a war with the Frislanders, left the German princes free to choose a new king. The chief candidates for the German throne on this occasion were two foreign princes— RICHARD OF CORNWALL, brother of King Henry III. of England, and ALFONSO THE WISE, King of Castile—both of whom bribed the electors. The party headed by the Archbishop of Cologne chose Richard of Cornwall, while the party led by the Archbishop of Treves elected Alfonso the Wise. Richard came to Germany and was crowned at Aix la Chapelle, but he only visited the country three times thereafter, and took no interest in its affairs; while Alfonso never set foot in the kingdom.

This period, when Germany was virtually without a sovereign, is called the *Interregnum*, and constitutes the darkest period of German history. There being no central government in the land, violence and lawlessness prevailed throughout the country, and the strong alone could obtain justice. The nobles and the knights degenerated into marauders and robbers. No traveler was safe without the protection of an armed escort, and only within the strong walls of the towns did industry venture to engage in its accustomed pursuits. The princes and bishops occupied the Interregnum in enlarging their territories and possessing themselves of privileges, while the knights and vassals waylaid and plundered the weak and defenseless. They led a wild and predatory life in their castles, which were built upon the banks of navigable streams or near frequented highways, as is shown by the ruins. They dragged travelers into their dungeons for the purpose of extorting a heavy ransom. They plundered the wagons of the mercantile towns, and behind their strong walls they bade defiance to the powerless laws and tribunals.

This deplorable condition of affairs in Germany was ended by the death of Richard of Cornwall in A. D. 1271. Until this event the Pope had intentionally held aloof from German affairs, as the vacancy of the imperial throne increased his own importance and prevented the rise of a rival. It now became evident to His Holiness that the condition of anarchy which prevailed in Germany was detrimental to the Church as well as to the Empire, because the papal revenues could not be collected without the aid of the imperial power. Finally Pope Gregory X. notified the Electors, the German princes who chose the king, that if they did not elect a proper person for King of Germany he would himself appoint one. The Pope's threat had its effect, and the Interregnum ended in A. D. 1273.

During the Interregnum many of the German princes and bishops had assumed the rights of sovereignty. To retain what they had gained, the Electors sought to prevent the choice of any prince to the German throne whose lands and vassals rendered him formidable; while they also required an energetic man, who should be able to restrain the prevailing lawlessness and to break the threatening power of Ottocar, King of Bohemia, and Duke of Moravia and Austria. All these qualities were possessed by COUNT RUDOLF OF HAPSBURG, who was accordingly elected King of Germany through the influence of the Archbishop of Mayence, with whom he had been on friendly terms (A. D. 1273).

The choice of Rudolf of Hapsburg was a wise one, as that prince was a brave and resolute man, fully alive to the evils from which Germany was suffering, and anxious to put an end to them. His moderate hereditary estates in Alsace did not alarm the German princes; his courage, strength and skill had long been proved and acknowledged; but his piety and the inclination he had always manifested to the Church was what especially contributed to his election. Therefore, when Rudolf of Hapsburg pledged his word that he would respect the property and rights of the Church and the interests of the German princes, his election was generally recognized, and Alfonso the Wise of Castile was induced to abdicate.

Rudolf had likewise won the Pope's support by a solemn pledge not to interfere with Charles of Anjou in Sicily or in Tuscany, and somewhat later he recognized the Pope's territorial sovereignty by relinquishing to Pope Nicholas III. the imperial claims over Rome and the bequest of the Countess Matilda. Thus strengthened, Rudolf of Hapsburg devoted himself with vigor to the task of restoring order throughout Germany.

Ottocar, King of Bohemia, who had added Austria, Styria, Carinthia and Carniola to his native kingdom, alone refused to acknowledge or do homage to Rudolf, hoping to be himself elected King of Germany. But Rudolf declared war against him in 1276, marched into his territories with the aid of his Swiss and Alsatians, and with the assistance of the German princes whom he had connected with his dynasty by marriages with his numerous daughters, and forced Ottocar to relinquish Austria and the neighboring territories and to do homage for his Bohemian crown. As Ottocar renewed the war upon Rudolf's retirement, Rudolf again took the field against him; and in the great and decisive battle of Marchfeld, in 1278, Ottocar was defeated and slain.

Only Bohemia and Moravia were left to Ottocar's son Wenceslas. With the consent of the German princes, Rudolf conferred Austria, Styria, Carniola and Carinthia on his sons Albert and Rudolf. Soon afterward he bestowed Carinthia on his father-in-law, Count Meinhard of Tyrol; leaving Albert in possession of Austria, Styria and Carniola. In this way Rudolf became the founder of the illustrious royal Austrian House of Hapsburg, which has ever since possessed and ruled the Austrian territories.

As before said, Rudolf of Hapsburg was elevated to the German throne when the royal and imperial authority had been almost totally wiped out. His task was to restore it and to reëstablish the supremacy of the civil law. As he avoided all interference in the affairs of Italy, he was able to devote his entire energies to Germany. After a series of campaigns and battles, mainly in Suabia, against the rapacious Eberhard of Wurtemberg, and in Burgundy, he finally succeeded in recovering many of the fiefs, lands, privileges and revenues that had been alienated from the German crown.

But Rudolf's greatest service was in securing the peace of Germany and in restoring law and order to the distracted country. He traversed the whole kingdom with his army, and called the lawless nobles and robber knights to a severe account. In

Thuringia alone he caused twenty-nine knights to be executed, and destroyed sixty castles. In Franconia and on the Rhine he destroyed more than seventy fortresses in a single year.

Rudolf won the affection of the German people by his simplicity, virtue and honesty, as well as by his intelligence, his impartial justice and his military achievements. He was only deficient in the poetical magnanimity of the Hohenstaufen. He died at Gomersheim, in September, A. D. 1291, at the age of seventy-four, during one of his military expeditions for the suppression of lawlessness, and was buried at Spire.

Just before his death, Rudolf of Hapsburg had endeavored to have his son Albert elected to the German throne, but had failed because the German nobles regarded the revenues of the kingdom as insufficient for the maintenance of two sovereigns. After Rudolf's death, the Electors chose the insignificant COUNT ADOLF OF NASSAU to the throne of Germany, at the instigation of Gerhard, Archbishop of Mayence, Adolf's cousin, from fear of the power of the Hapsburgs, and from dislike for Rudolf's cruel and avaricious son Albert.

Like Rudolf of Hapsburg, Adolf of Nassau endeavored to enlarge his own small territories, but was unable to do much against the nobles, who opposed him and sought to limit his powers. He formed an alliance with King Edward I. of England, who supplied him with a large sum of money on condition that he should make war on France. Adolf used this money in purchasing Thuringia and Misnia from the worthless Landgrave, Albert the Uncourteous; but this disgraceful transaction involved Adolf in a war with Albert's sons, Frederick the Bitten and Diezman, whom their degenerate father had sought to deprive of their inheritance, and who were sustained in their refusal by their vassals and by many of the German princes.

The public disgust at Adolf's dishonest proceeding, and the discontent of the Electors of the Palatinate, Mayence, Treves and Cologne, whom Adolf had deprived of their unjustly acquired tolls of the Rhine, had aided in forming a party favorable to Adolf's rival, Albert of Austria, the son of Rudolf of Hapsburg, who was accordingly chosen to the German throne. Adolf resisted this action, but Albert marched to the Rhine and defeated his dethroned rival in the battle of Göllheim, near Worms, A. D. 1298; Adolf himself being hurled from his horse by Albert's lance and slain in the tumult. His remains were interred in the cathedral of Spire; and ALBERT I., of Austria, became undisputed King of Germany, A. D. 1298.

Before proceeding with the events of Albert's reign, we will take a general review of the condition of Germany during the thirteenth century. For some time the Germans had been making steady progress eastward. They had acquired Brandenburg in the preceding century, and since then they had come in possession of Holstein, Mecklenburg, Pomerania and Lower Silesia; all of which had been Slavonic countries, except Holstein, which was Scandinavian. All these had now became Germanized by the slow progress of colonization. A monk named Christian began preaching Christianity in Prussia about the beginning of the thirteenth century. He was resisted by the heathen Prussians, who were also a Slavonic people, and who held fast to their pagan belief, in consequence of which a Crusade was preached against them.

About A. D. 1230 during the reign of Frederick II., the *Teutonic Knights* came to Prussia and commenced its conquest. In 1237 the *Knights of the Sword*, another German order, which had already conquered Livonia, became united with the Teutonic Knights. Many warriors from every portion of Europe joined the order of the Teutonic Knights, to aid in the conquest of Prussia. In 1245 the Teutonic Knights founded the city of Königsberg, which was named in honor of King Ottocar of Bohemia, who had taken part in the Crusade; and by 1260 most of Prussia was conquered. A great revolt of the native Prussians broke out in that year, but it was suppressed after a severe struggle. German colonies were settled in Prussia, and founded the cities of Culm, Elbing, Thorn and others. In 1309 the Teutonic Knights made Marienburg their headquarters, and held Prussia in subjection, while it gradually became Christianized and Germanized, the Teutonic order conducting the government of the conquered country, while the native peasantry sank into the condition of serfs.

The absence of the Emperors from Germany, and the long struggle with the Popes, resulted in the serious loss of their power as Kings of Germany. By neglecting their duties as German kings, and exerting their main efforts for the Empire, the Emperors allowed the German princes to seize gradually all the privileges of the German crown and to render themselves practically independent. The Hohenstaufen sovereigns deliberately relinquished many of their most valuable rights as Kings of Germany, for the purpose of acquiring some immediate advantage as Roman Emperors. Denmark, Poland and Hungary became independent kingdoms, and Burgundy was slowly absorbed by France.

The German princes had always refused to permit the German crown to be made hereditary, and in the thirteenth century a change was made in the mode of electing the sovereign. This privilege was vested in seven *Electors*—three spiritual princes and four secular princes. The three spiritual Electors were the Archbishops of Mayence, Cologne and Treves—all in the West of Germany. The four secular princes were the Duke of Saxony, the Margrave of Brandenburg, the Palsgrave of the Rhine, and the King of Bohemia. These seven Electors ranked above all the other German princes, and constituted a separate college in the German Diet. The Pope claimed the right to revise the action of the Electors and to reject any candidate whom he considered unsuitable, and this right was usually acknowledged. The King of Germany had the right to the imperial crown, which could be conferred on him by the Pope only; and thus was derived the Pope's claim.

Another important feature of this period was the growth of the German towns. As the great duchies fell into decay the towns that had been dependent upon them became independent, managing their affairs in their own way, but acknowledging the Emperor's supremacy, and therefore called *free imperial cities*. The deputies of these cities at length constituted a third college in the imperial Diet, and voted on an equality with the Electors and the princes. The free cities usually supported the king's authority, but were almost always at war with the German nobles and bishops. For their mutual protection against these enemies, the free cities organized leagues or confederations among themselves; the most celebrated of which were the *League of the Rhine* in Western Germany, and the *Hanseatic League* in Northern Germany.

The League of the Rhine embraced the cities of Worms, Spire, Mayence, Strasburg, Basle and seventy others. The Hanseatic League comprised Hamburg, Bremen, Lübeck, Stralsund, Riga and about eighty other commercial cities, and maintained fleets and armies. It was formed in 1241 for the protection of the commerce of the Northern seas against piracy. It possessed the entire trade of the Baltic and a large part of that of the North Sea. Its principal foreign depots were London, in England; Bruges, in Flanders; Bergen, in Norway; and Novgorod, in Russia. The Hanseatic military and naval forces frequently defeated the armies and fleets of the Northern kings; and the Kings of England and France accorded the league a marked degree of respect. For a long time the Hanse towns carried on an active commerce with England, the export trade of which country was wholly conducted by the Hanseatic merchants. The English called these merchants *Easterlings;* whence the word *Sterling*, as still applied to English money. Hanseatic commerce extended even to Northern Asia and to China, by way of Novgorod.

Germany had no uniform code of laws. In the thirteenth century the laws of Saxony were codified by Eike of Repgord, and those of Suabia were codified by a Suabian priest. In Westphalia the violence of the times gave rise to a singular class of courts of justice, called *Fehmgerichte*. These were tribunals which convened in open day, usually under some tree; but the proceedings were kept secret. Only such crimes as were punishable with death were tried in these courts. If an accused person was condemned he was instantly hanged. Any one who did not appear after having been summoned three times was assumed to be guilty, and was certain to be put to death sooner or later.

In those lawless times the weak and oppressed were glad to find any court which gave them some opportunity of obtaining justice. Accordingly appeals began to be made to the Fehmgerichte from every portion of Germany. Finally men of free birth, from any part of the kingdom, were permitted to become free judges; and many thousands of all classes availed themselves of the privilege. For some time the Fehmgerichte did real good; as the German nobles who did not care for their Emperor-king trembled when they received the summons of some free judge to appear before a secret tribunal at a certain date. But as the Fehmgerichte grew in power they were frequently reckless and unjust; and many, particularly the clergy, denounced them in the strongest terms. These courts lost almost all their power in the sixteenth century, but traces of them remained long afterwards among the peasantry of Westphalia.

The Hohenstaufen era was noted for a marked revival of architecture in Germany, of which the still-unfinished cathedral of Cologne is a noble specimen. This was also the epoch when those love singers, the *Minnesingers*, or *Minnesänger*, flourished. Several of the Hohenstaufen Emperors, particularly Frederick II., were poets. The most noted of the Minnesingers were Heinrich von Waldeck, Wolfram von Eschenbach, Gottfried von Strassburg and Walther von der Vogelweide.

Pope Boniface VIII. strenuously endeavored to uphold the papal power; and, in endeavoring to prevent the taxation of the French clergy, he became involved in a violent quarrel with King Philip the Fair of France, who treated the Pope's bulls of excommunication with contempt and imprisoned the papal legate in France, and whose officers in Rome made the Pope a prisoner. Boniface died of vexation at his humiliation, shortly after his forcible release by the Romans. His second successor, Clement V.— who had been Archbishop of Bordeaux, and who had been elected Pope through the influence of King Philip the Fair—removed to Avignon, in the South of France, where the Popes resided seventy-two years (1305-1377), entirely under French influence.

Albert I. was the first of the Austrian Kings of Germany. He lacked all the qualities which had made his father, Rudolf of Hapsburg, so beloved by the German people, and sought to maintain his authority by extreme harshness and tyranny. He was an energetic but a severe sovereign, and his inflexible disposition could be read in his gloomy and one-eyed visage. He was also more selfish and ambitious than his father, and desirous of extending his estates and advancing the fortunes of his family. He therefore sought to gain possession of Bohemia and the county of Holland. His son Rudolf was King of Bohemia for a few months, but that kingdom at length passed from his family. He also tried to dispossess the Landgrave Frederick of Thuringia of his territory, but failed in that undertaking.

Albert's aggressions aroused the hostility of those whom he attempted to rob for his own aggrandizement. Feared and hated, he was finally assassinated by his nephew John of Suabia, at Windisch on the Reuss, near Hapsburg castle, May, 1308, after a reign of ten years, just as he was preparing to subdue the free Swiss. John expiated his deed in a cloister; but Albert's wife and daughter took a terrible revenge upon the three nobles who aided John of Suabia in the assassination—Wart, Balm and Eschenbach—and upon all their friends and relatives.

Albert's unpopularity prevented the Electors from choosing his successor from the Austrian House of Hapsburg; and Count Henry of Luxemburg was elected King of Germany with the title of HENRY VII. With the consent of the Bohemian states, the new king married his son John to Elizabeth, the granddaughter of King Ottocar; and in this way John became King of Bohemia, the crown of which long remained under the Luxemburg dynasty.

In 1310 Henry VII. led an expedition to Italy, where he was joyfully welcomed by the oppressed Ghibellines; and the great poet Dante, of Florence, celebrated his appearance by a Latin essay called *Monarchy* and by songs that were soon sung by everybody. Henry VII. was crowned King of Lombardy at Milan in 1311. He collected with rigor the taxes that were due in the towns of Northern Italy, and met with an honorable reception in the Ghibelline city of Pisa.

But notwithstanding all his efforts to assume the character of a prince desirous of reconciliation, the Guelfs and the haughty Florence under the leadership of King Robert the Wise of Naples rose against Henry VII. for cause. The Pope himself opposed him, and the King of Naples threw a garrison into Rome. Henry VII. forced this garrison to retire into the Leonine City, where they held the Church of St. Peter against him. Thus cut off from the great cathedral, Henry VII. was crowned Emperor in the Church of St. John Lateran, June 29, A. D. 1312.

Henry VII. now endeavored to crush the Guelfic revolt, and raised an army, which he led into Tuscany with the intention of chastising Florence; but the fatal air of Rome had so undermined his constitution that he died on his march, August 24, A. D. 1313. His body was taken to Pisa, and was buried in the Campo Santo, or churchyard of that city. This event changed the situation. The Germans, deprived of their sovereign, disbanded and recrossed the Alps; and the Guelfs were again in the ascendency.

Henry VII. died in the flower of his age, and was the last of the German Emperors who exercised any real authority in Italy. He was a man of great abilities and of noble character. The Guelf Villani wrote of him as follows: "He was a man never depressed by adversity; never in prosperity elated with pride or intoxicated with joy." The successors of Henry VII. were not Emperors in the sense in which that title can be employed to describe him and his predecessors. They were mainly the leaders of a faction of the Italian people, and some of them were never crowned Emperor.

The death of Henry VII. was followed by another civil war in Germany, occasioned by a disputed succession. Some of the Electors chose DUKE LOUIS OF BAVARIA for King of Germany; while others adhered to DUKE FREDERICK THE FAIR OF AUSTRIA, the eldest son of King Albert I. Louis was crowned at Aix la Chapelle, and Frederick the Fair went through the same ceremony at Bonn. Thus Germany had two rival kings, both of whom appealed to the sword, and thus inaugurated a sanguinary civil war, which lasted eight years (A. D. 1314–1322).

As a general rule, the towns supported Louis, while the nobles sustained Frederick the Fair. Frederick's cause found an energetic and vigorous leader in his brother Leopold. Notwithstanding the superior strength of the Austrian party, Louis, who was an excellent general, maintained his own cause successfully, particularly after Leopold's force had been weakened by the war with the Swiss. The civil war was decided in favor of Louis by the decisive battle of Mühldorf in A. D. 1322, where Frederick the Fair was defeated and taken prisoner by his rival's skillful general, Seyfried Schwepperman. Frederick was confined in captivity in the castle of Trausnitz, in the Upper Palatinate.

Notwithstanding Frederick's defeat and capture, his brother Leopold and other princes continued the war and attempted a new election. They were sustained by Pope John XXII., who had quarreled with Louis for aiding the Ghibellines of Milan and as-

CAPTURE OF FREDERICK THE HANDSOME AT THE BATTLE OF MÜHLDORF.

suming the title of King of the Romans without the Pope's sanction. Louis haughtily asserted that he owed his dignity to the German electors and not to the Pope, whereupon the Pope excommunicated him and laid all those parts of Germany that supported him under an interdict. Anxious to restore peace to Germany, Louis liberated his rival in A. D. 1325, upon the condition that he should renounce all claims to the German crown and persuade his party to consent to peace.

As neither the Pope nor Frederick's brother Leopold would be bound by Frederick's promise or listen to the proposal for peace, Frederick, true to his word, returned to captivity, as he had promised to do before his liberation provided he failed to persuade his partisans to make peace. Frederick's honorable conduct so affected his chivalrous competitor that the two rivals thereafter lived in the closest friendship, and Louis would have consented even to share the German crown with Frederick the Fair, but the Electors would not consent to such an arrangement.

The death of Leopold of Austria in 1326 did not put an end to the struggle, as the contest continued with increased animosity between Louis and Pope John XXII. In 1327 Louis led an expedition to Italy to obtain the Lombard and imperial crowns. He remained in that country three years. He was at first quite successful, as he was supported by the Ghibellines. He proceeded to Rome, declared Pope John XXII. deposed, and caused an Antipope to be elected with the title of Nicholas V., who crowned him Emperor. As the former adherents of Louis refused to aid him by sending subsidies to pay his mercenary troops, he exacted heavy levies of money from the Italian towns; whereupon the Romans revolted, and Louis fled, taking the Antipope Nicholas V. with him.

After Louis had returned to Germany he took measures to make that country entirely independent of the papal dominion. The Germans were ready to support their king in spite of the Pope, whose interference in Germany they had learned to dread. The German cities especially were hostile to the Pope, who was thus deprived of the popular sympathy and support which had made his predecessors strong in Germany against Henry IV. and Frederick II.

At the Diet convened at Frankfort in 1338 the German princes sustained the cause of Louis against the Pope. The Electors assembled at Rense, on the Rhine, and all of them, but the blind King John of Bohemia, who was jealous of the Bavarian dynasty, and who was also a bitter personal enemy of Louis, united in a solemn declaration that the King of Germany, or Emperor of the Romans, derived his power and his title solely from the choice of the Electors of Germany, and not from the Pope in any sense. This declaration of the Electors was accepted by the Diet and proclaimed by the Emperor, and became a part of the law of the land; Louis declaring that the election of Emperor was directly derived from God, that the Pope's confirmation only lowered the dignity of the Empire, and that all who thought otherwise were guilty of high treason. This law established the independence of the German Empire.

Pope Benedict XII., the successor of John XXII., renewed the excommunication of the Emperor Louis the Bavarian, and resolved on pronouncing his deposition and seeking to find a successor for him. The German princes and people were ready to sustain their king against the Pope, but Louis soon lost the esteem of the German princes by his avarice and his desire to enlarge his territories, which led him into many unjust and violent measures.

The Emperor Louis had elevated his son Louis to the dignity of Margrave of Brandenburg in 1323; and he also desired to confer the Tyrol upon the same son, but he was unable to do so, because the Tyrol belonged to Margaret Maultasch, who was already married to a son of King John of Bohemia. Louis, however, did not scruple to dissolve this marriage and to grant to Margaret a dispensation to marry his son Louis. In all Roman Catholic countries marriage is considered a sacrament, the Pope alone being able to dissolve it or to grant a dispensation for a second marriage during the life of a first partner. In attacking a right which all regarded as vested in the Pope, Louis shocked the consciences of his subjects and alienated many of his best adherents, while his open efforts to enrich and aggrandize his own family aroused the jealousy of the German nobles.

This feeling was increased when, upon the death of Count William IV. of Holland, Louis granted the counties of Holland, Zealand and Hennegan in fief to his own son William. When the Electors were convened in 1344 they gave significant expression of their discontent. In 1346 Pope Clement VI. pronounced the deposition of the Emperor. Louis had so thoroughly alienated his subjects that the Electors readily took advantage of the Pope's action as a pretext to get rid of their obnoxious sovereign. They therefore elected the Margrave Charles of Moravia, son of King John of Bohemia, to the German throne, with the title of CHARLES IV. (A. D. 1346).

Louis exerted all his energies to preserve his crown. At the head of his army he visited the imperial free cities, and satisfied himself of their loyalty. As Charles IV. was unable to obtain admittance into Aix la Chapelle or Cologne, he was crowned King of Germany at Bonn, in the presence of a few faithful knights. After the death of Louis from apoplexy in the midst of a great boar hunt, October 11, A. D. 1347, Charles IV. became sovereign; and, though the Bavarians at first made some opposition, he was acknowledged undisputed sovereign in 1349. Thus ended the long contest between Guelfs and Ghibellines—between the Popes and the German Emperors.

Until the reign of Louis the Bavarian, the German kings had generally relinquished their hereditary lands upon receiving the crown. Louis retained his lands; and this course was adopted by his successors, because the revenues of the German kingdom were inadequate to maintain the royal dignity, the kings being obliged to depend upon their private resources. This change had a bad effect, because it made the German king more careful of his own individual possessions than of the kingdom in general.

In the meantime a series of events occurred which led to the founding of the Swiss Republic. This series of events began during the reign of Albert I., of Austria, whose severity led to the rise of the Helvetic Confederation. Helvetia, or Switzerland, was a component part of the German Empire, and was under the protection of Prefects, who there exercised the highest offices of jurisdiction. These offices were at first filled by the rich and powerful Dukes of Zähringen, who founded Berne and other Swiss cantons. After the extinction of the ducal house of Zähringen, the Counts of Savoy in the South and the Counts of Hapsburg in the North raised themselves to a position above the other feudal lords by their power and possessions. The Counts of Hapsburg were in possession of the Landgravate of Aargau, and, in the name of the German Empire, exercised the functions of protectors over the three forest cantons of Uri, Schwyz and Unterwalden, situated in the Alpine mountain region on the borders of Lake Lucerne.

The people of Uri, Schwyz and Unterwalden spoke the German language, and acknowledged allegiance only to the German king, but always maintained their freedom. Like many districts of the German Empire, these three forest cantons formed a league for their mutual protection. This league may have existed from a very early date, but the earliest written compact between them bears the date of August 1, A. D. 1291.

The Counts of Hapsburg held large estates within the limits of the three forest cantons, and when they became Dukes of Austria and Kings of Germany they endeavored to reduce Uri, Schwyz and Unterwalden under the ducal sovereignity of Austria. To further this purpose, Albert I., King of Germany and Duke of Austria, gave permission to the Vögte, or governors, who ruled the

Hapsburg lands, to enforce the laws of the German Empire over the free forest cantons, and to oppress the simple, warlike and freedom-loving mountaineers. This oppression caused the three forest cantons to form the *League of Rutli*, under the leadership of Walther Furst, Werner Stauffacher and Arnold Melchtal, who met at Rutli and swore under the open canopy of heaven to live and die in defense of freedom and country. Each of these three leaders chose ten associates from his own canton, and the thirty-three repeated the oath of freedom and then proceeded to incite their countrymen to revolt.

The tyrannical measures of Albert I. drove the Swiss mountaineers to desperation. In connection with this oppression is a famous legend, now generally discredited, though it had been for a long time accepted as a historical fact. This is the story of William Tell and Gesler—one of the best-known legends of the Middle Ages. According to this legend, Gesler was one of the tyrannical Austrian governors expelled by the Swiss. He placed the ducal cap of Austria in the market place of Altorf, and ordered all who passed to bow to the cap, in token of submission. William Tell refused to bow to the cap, and was thereupon imprisoned. Being a good archer, Tell was promised his freedom if he would shoot an apple from his son's head. Tell hit the apple and received his freedom, saying to Gesler: "Had I killed my son, I would have killed you." Tell is said to have been at once seized by order of the enraged tyrant, and conveyed across the lake of Lucerne in a boat in which were Gesler and his attendants; but a violent storm having arisen during the passage, Tell, who was a skillful boatman, was released in order that he might conduct the boat in safety to the shore; and no sooner had the shore been reached, than Tell leaped from the boat, and soon afterward dispatched an arrow into the tyrant's heart, killing him instantly.

The revolted Swiss mountaineers seized the Austrian bailiffs and officers and expelled them from the country. Albert I. instantly marched against the Swiss confederates, but was assassinated on his march by his nephew John of Suabia, as already noticed. His son Leopold, the next Duke of Austria, took the field against the Swiss; but his army was overwhelmingly defeated by a few hundred Swiss mountaineers in the narrow pass of Morgarten, November, A. D. 1315. The flower of the Austrian nobility perished in this battle, beneath the clubs of the sturdy peasants of Uri, Schwyz and Unterwalden.

Thenceforth the power of the Hapsburgs declined in Switzerland; and Uri, Schwyz and Unterwalden maintained their position as distinct members of the German Empire. By the accession of the town of Lucerne, in 1332, the entire shore of Lake Lucerne came into the power of the Helvetic Confederation, which was soon joined by the towns of Berne, Zurich, Zug, Glarus and many others. Thus strengthened, the Helvetic Confederation increased its power by seizing or buying the lands of the neighboring nobles whenever occasion required. The confederacy assumed the title of the *Old League of High Germany*; and its members were called *Eidgenossen*, "Confederates." Gradually the name which properly belonged to the canton of Schwyz spread over the whole of Helvetia, which thus came to be called *Switzerland*, and the people *Swiss*.

Charles IV. was crowned King of Germany a second time at Aix la Chapelle in A. D. 1349, and in 1355 he proceeded to Rome and was crowned Emperor by Pope Innocent VI. Ten years later—A. D. 1365—he was crowned King of Burgundy at Arles. He was a sagacious monarch, intent on his own interests and the aggrandizement of his family, the Luxemburg dynasty; and he regarded money and property as of more value than honor or fame.

Through Charles IV. the imperial power lost all respect in Italy, where he allowed the imperial privileges to be purchased by the towns and the princes. Though the contests between Guelfs and Ghibellines ceased in Italy, they only gave place to contentions between the princes and the free towns concerning the extension of their respective territories. Mercenary troops, called Condottieri, were now employed instead of the earlier militia; and the enterprising leaders of these bands often controlled the fate of states and obtained possession of their governments. The efforts of Charles IV. in Germany were likewise mainly directed to the gratification of his avarice and lust of territory. He sold the privileges and liberties of the imperial free towns; he granted letters of nobility for money; and he annexed some of the other German territories to his hereditary possessions.

In the beginning of the reign of Charles IV., Germany was ravaged by a dreadful plague, which spread its desolations throughout Europe. It broke out in 1349 and carried hundreds of thousands to their graves in a short time. The Jews were generally suspected of causing the pestilence by poisoning the springs and rivers, and multitudes of them were massacred by the ignorant and fanatical mob. King Charles IV. and the Church were obliged to resort to severe measures to protect the unoffending Jews from persecution by the bigoted people.

As King of Bohemia, Charles IV. was a good sovereign, and under his beneficent rule that kingdom attained its highest prosperity. He summoned artists and artisans from other parts of Germany and from Italy into Bohemia; and in that country under his benign reign Carlsbad and other towns and a number of villages were founded, agriculture and trade were encouraged, roads and bridges were planned, and heaths and forests were brought under cultivation. With the Pope's consent and with the coöperation of the Italian poet Petrarch, Charles IV. founded the university of Prague, the first German university, which soon had from five thousand to seven thousand students, and at once became celebrated throughout Europe. He made Prague, the capital of Bohemia, a most splendid city.

Charles IV. greatly enlarged the territories of the Bohemian crown. He obtained the Upper Palatinate through his wife as her dowry; and he annexed all Silesia and Lower Lusatia to Bohemia, and also the Mark of Brandenburg, which he obtained from the ducal house of Bavaria.

In A. D. 1356 Charles IV. granted the first imperial code of laws, known as the *Golden Bull*, which defined the manner of electing the King of Germany by the seven Electors. The King of Bohemia was made the first secular Elector, and the Archbishop of Mayence was assigned the duty of convening the electoral college, which was to meet at Frankfort. The king was to be chosen by a majority of the votes of the Electors, and was to be crowned at Aix la Chapelle. The Electors were made independent of the German crown by being declared absolute sovereigns within their own respective territories. There was to be no appeal from their courts unless they refused to dispense justice. Their persons were declared sacred. Thus the authority of the German crown was almost totally destroyed, and the German sovereign was thenceforth to be little more than a mere figure-head of the Empire, the German princes thus becoming more powerful than the sovereign himself.

The imperial authority had fallen into utter decay, and confusion and lawlessness prevailed throughout Germany. The laws concerning disturbance of the public peace were almost wholly disregarded; and the only law which prevailed was the *Faustrecht*, or club-law, which called upon every man to take care of himself, alliances being formed to do this more effectually.

The Emperor Charles IV. died in A. D. 1378, and was succeeded by his son WENCESLAS, who had been chosen King of the Romans by the Electors in 1376. He was a bad monarch to both Bohemia and Germany. He was a rude, hot-headed man, of cruel temper, and addicted to drink and to low pleasures. He led a dissolute life in Bohemia, devoting himself to hunting, quarreling with his nobles and with the clergy, and rendering himself hateful and contemptible by his cruelty and by his barbarous treatment of the Vicar Nepomuk, whom he ordered to be thrown from the bridge of Prague into the Moldau.

Wenceslas so thoroughly neglected the German Empire that the country fell into the same confusion and violence that prevailed during the Interregnum. The German nobles became wholly lawless. The towns in Suabia, in Franconia and on the Rhine were obliged to form the *Suabian League*, similar to the League of the Rhine, the Hanseatic League and the Helvetic Confederation, in order to preserve the peace of the country and to defend themselves against the rapacious nobles. The lawless knights, who gained their living by plunder and highway robbery, and who were menaced by the Suabian League, formed leagues in opposition to those of their enemies. These leagues of knights were the *Schlegler*, the *Löwen* and the *Hornerbund*.

The leagues of the knights and those of the towns were constantly engaged in war with each other, until finally the murder of the Bishop of Salzburg by a Bavarian duke gave rise to the *great cities' war*, which caused extreme distress in Southern Germany. The citizens were victorious in Bavaria; the courage of the Nuremburgers rendered the fortune of the war dubious in Franconia; but in Suabia, where the valiant enemy of the towns, Eberhard the Grumbler, of Wurtemberg, headed the nobility, the burghers suffered great loss near Döffingen, and yielded to the iron ranks of the knights of Hesse and the Palatinate at Worms and at Frankfort. The indolent Wenceslas cared nothing for Germany, and made no effort to restore order and peace throughout the Empire, nor to win back the lost privileges of the German crown.

In the meantime the duchy of Austria had been rapidly growing in power and importance. Carinthia was annexed to it in 1335, and the Tyrol in 1369, the latter coming into the possession of the Austrian duke by bequest from Margaret Maultasch. These provinces were ever afterward a portion of the Austrian territories. Duke Leopold of Austria—nephew of the Duke Leopold who was vanquished by the Swiss in the battle of Morgarten in 1315—now determined to profit by the confusion prevalent in Germany by attempting to conquer the freedom-loving Swiss, because some towns belonging to him had been admitted into the Helvetic Confederation. He was joined by many princes and nobles who were jealous of the growing power of the Swiss.

Duke Leopold led several thousand of the flower of the Austrian and German chivalry, with a host of armed nobles, into Switzerland, A. D. 1386. Fourteen hundred Swiss confederates were posted on the heights of Sempach. Finding it impossible for his cavalry to force the narrow mountain pass, the Austrian duke ordered his knights to dismount and storm it on foot. They were rapidly surrounding the Swiss confederates with a living wall of steel, when one of the Swiss leaders, Arnold von Winkelried, a gallant knight of Unterwalden, resolved to sacrifice his life for his country, crying to his countrymen: "Dear brothers, I will open a way for you; take care of my wife and children!" Then rushing upon the bristling lances of the Austrian and German chivalry, he cried: "Make way for liberty!" Throwing himself on the iron-clad ranks of the Austrian knights, and seizing as many of their lances as he could grasp and plunging the points of them into his body, he fell dead; but his gallant plunge "made a path" for his countrymen into the ranks of the foe, and they rushed upon the Austrians and killed or routed their whole force, Duke Leopold and six hundred and fifty-six of his nobles being among the slain, A. D. 1386.

Two years after the glorious victory of the Swiss at Sempach, the people of Glarus achieved another victory over the Austrians at Näfels (A. D. 1388). These two brilliant Swiss triumphs forced Austria to respect the independence of the Swiss cantons, and the Helvetic Confederation was likewise permitted to retain the towns that had voluntarily joined that league; but the independence of Switzerland was not fully established until 1499, and was not formally acknowledged until 1648.

The inability of King Wenceslas to restore law and order in Germany induced the

HEROIC DEATH OF ARNOLD VON WINKELRIED AT THE BATTLE OF SEMPACH.

1628

Electors in a Diet at Lahnstein, in A. D. 1400, to declare him dethroned, "because he had not aided the peace of the Church, had sold the title of duke to the rich and crafty Visconti in Milan, had not maintained the public peace, and had governed tyrannically and with cruelty in Bohemia." The Electors had been instigated to this proceeding by Pope Boniface IX., one of the two rival pontiffs who at that time divided the dominion of the Church. Wenceslas desired to depose both Popes, and Boniface IX. struck this decisive blow at him in retaliation.

The Electors chose RUPERT OF THE PALATINATE to succeed Wenceslas as King of Germany, A. D. 1400. The new sovereign was the grandson of that Rupert who had founded the university of Heidelberg in the year of the battle of Sempach, A. D. 1386. The deposed Wenceslas was still supported by a strong party; and Rupert was not properly aided by his adherents, so that he was but little more than nominal king. In spite of many good qualities, Rupert was not equal to the difficulties of his station. He was obliged to grant to the German princes and estates the right to form confederations and to maintain the public peace in their own way. When he endeavored to restore Milan to the Germano-Roman Empire he was defeated by the Italian Condottieri, who had discovered a more scientific system of tactics. He likewise failed in his efforts to restore tranquillity to the Church. Rupert died A. D. 1410.

Germany was now divided by a disputed succession. Some of the Electors chose JOBST, Margrave of Moravia, to the German throne; while others elected SIGISMUND, Margrave of Brandenburg and King of Hungary, a brother of Wenceslas, and therefore belonging to the Luxemburg dynasty. Jobst died soon afterwards, and Sigismund was thereupon unanimously chosen king by the Electors. He had displayed some good qualities, and high hopes were entertained of him by the German people; but he disappointed their expectations, as we shall presently see.

When Sigismund ascended the German throne the Church had been divided for a quarter of a century. Pope Gregory XI., a Frenchman, had reëstablished the papal residence in Rome by moving there from Avignon in 1377, thus yielding to the general desire of Christendom outside of France. Gregory XI. died the following year (A. D. 1378), the very year of the death of the Emperor Charles IV. and the accession of Wenceslas. The conclave of cardinals convened at the Vatican immediately after his death to elect a new Pope. As there was no Roman acceptable for the papal office, the conclave chose a Neapolitan, who took the title of Urban VI. The French cardinals, indignant because the new Pope refused to return to Avignon, left him. Another election was held, at which Robert of Geneva was chosen Antipope, under the name of Clement VII. (A. D. 1378). The Antipope went with the French cardinals to Avignon. His election was sustained by France, and thus began the *Great Schism*, which divided the whole of the Western, or Romish Church.

A council of the Church was convened at Pisa in 1409 to heal the schism in the Papacy. This council pronounced the deposition of the two reigning Popes, Benedict XIII. at Avignon and Gregory XII. at Rome, and declared the Holy See vacant. The council then elected a new Pope, who took the name of Alexander V. Instead of putting an end to the schism, this election only complicated matters, as the two deposed Popes each had supporters, so that there were now three Popes ruling at the same time, each of whom excommunicated the other two. The damaging truths which the three rival Popes told of each other destroyed men's reverence for the Church; and several great Reformers —John Wickliffe in England and John Huss in Bohemia—preached against the abuses in the Church and the vices of the clergy.

John Wickliffe was one of the most celebrated men of this period. He was a native Englishman and a professor in Oxford university. He was a learned man, well versed in scholastic subtleties. He taught that the Pope was no longer Head of the Church, and that Church councils were unnecessary. He rejected many articles of faith, such as confession and transubstantiation, and also objected to the celibacy of the clergy. He died in 1384.

John Huss, who was a professor in the university of Prague, was the most famous of Wickliffe's many adherents. He was excommunicated by the Pope, but in spite of this he was daily gaining new followers, one of the most zealous of whom was Jerome Faulfisch, a Bohemian nobleman, better known as Jerome of Prague. The Germans in the university of Prague favored the doctrines of the new Reformers, and were therefore curtailed of their privileges by Wenceslas, who was still King of Bohemia though he had been deprived of the German crown, and who changed the constitution of the university in 1409, giving three votes to the Bohemians in the university, and only one each to the Saxons, the Bavarians and the Poles. Enraged at this arbitrary action, the German professors and students left the institution, and thus brought about the founding of several other German universties, one of which was that of Leipsic, in Saxony.

The Reformers were now in the ascendency at Prague, and Huss was made Rector of the university. He assumed a bolder tone, and commenced denouncing in the strongest terms the abuses in the Church and the doctrines which he considered false. His boldness aroused the hostility of the clergy, but nevertheless he persisted in teaching his doctrines and grew bolder in his denunciations of the errors of the Church. The Pope at length excommunicated Huss and laid the city of Prague under an interdict until it should consent to expel the bold Reformer. The Bohemians refused to expel Huss, as he taught them what they considered a purer faith than that of the Romish Church, and because his principles were fast arousing in them a national spirit, which all men perceived would sooner or later result in the separation of Church and State, if not checked.

At the earnest solicitation of Sigismund, Pope John XXIII. convened a great council of the Church at Constance, in Suabia, to heal the schism in the Papacy and to reform the Church of its corruption. The *Council of Constance* was in session four years (A. D. 1414–1418); and was attended by the Emperor Sigismund and Pope John XXIII., and also by eighteen thousand clergymen and by learned men from all the universities of Europe—in all about one hundred and fifty thousand persons.

The first act of the Council of Constance was to depose the three rival Popes or to persuade them to abdicate. John XXIII. promised to resign; but broke his promise by fleeing in disguise, during a tournament, to Schaffhausen, in Switzerland, and taking refuge in the castle of Duke Frederick of Austria, where he recalled his abdication. Thereupon the council declared itself independent of and superior to the Pope, and joined Sigismund in punishing the refractory. Sigismund outlawed Duke Frederick of Austria and ordered the Swiss confederates to make war on him. Berne therefore attacked the Austrian duke, and was joined in the struggle by the other Swiss cantons. Duke Frederick was obliged to make peace, and Sigismund restored to him most of his estates. The Swiss refused to relinquish what they had conquered. Among their conquests was Aargau, which contained Hapsburg castle, the hereditary seat of the Dukes of Austria.

In the Council of Constance the French and Germans desired first to reform the Church, and then elect a new Pope; but their plans were frustrated by the Italians, who insisted upon an election of Pope before all other things. The opinion of the Italians prevailed, and Martin V. was chosen to the papal chair. He was a man of moderation, and sought during his pontificate to remedy many of the abuses which had crept into the Church during the Great Schism.

After putting an end to the schism in the Papacy, the Council of Constance directed its efforts against heresy. The dead Wickliffe's doctrines were condemned and his writings were sentenced to the flames. His remains were cast into the Severn. John

Huss was summoned to appear before the council to answer the charge of heresy. Being provided with an imperial safe-conduct by Sigismund, Huss and his friend, Jerome of Prague, proceeded to Constance, against the advice of their friends, meeting with evidences of popular sympathy all along the route.

When Huss arrived at Constance the Pope received him graciously. Said the pontiff: "If John Huss had slain my brother, I would not permit, as far as is in my power, any harm to be done to him in Constance." A few days later the great Bohemian Reformer was seized and cast into prison. Several conferences were held, and Huss explained his doctrine, but the result was unsatisfactory. The council desired him to recant, but he persistently refused, as did Jerome likewise. Finally Huss was degraded from the priesthood, and both he and Jerome were handed over to the imperial power. Both were condemned to be burned to death.

Huss perished at the stake in 1415. When the fire was raging around him he was again asked to recant, but he refused, and suffered his horrible torture with the most heroic fortitude. The Council of Constance was of the opinion that promises made to heretics were not binding; and Sigismund made no effort to save the great Reformer, notwithstanding his solemn promise of safety to Huss. Roman Catholic writers urge in palliation of Sigismund's conduct on this occasion that Huss and Jerome were put to death by the civil power, not only for the crime of heresy, but likewise for preaching sedition and for high treason. Jerome was martyred the year after Huss (A. D. 1416).

The martyrdom of Huss and Jerome aroused a storm of indignation in Bohemia and led to a furious religious war of eighteen years (A. D. 1416-1434), during which the Hussites took a terrible revenge on the Empire and on the Church for the cruel death of the two great Reformers. The cup, which, according to the views of Huss, was not to be withheld from the laity, was carried before the Hussite armies as the symbol of their cause; for which reason they were called *Utraquists* and *Calixtines*. A heavy vengeance was inflicted upon the priests who refused to administer the cup. Vainly did the Pope fulminate an interdict against the Hussites, whose numbers increased daily. They stormed the town-house of Prague and murdered the counselors, which so enraged the old King Wenceslas, who was still sovereign of Bohemia, that he died of apoplexy (A. D. 1419).

Sigismund, as the brother of Wenceslas, was the heir to the Bohemian crown, and at once proceeded to take possession thereof Instead of seeking to conciliate the Hussites, Sigismund arrayed them in a determined body in opposition to him by ordering a general crusade against them. The whole Bohemian nation rose in arms to prevent the bigoted monarch from taking possession of the kingdom. Their armies were led by the valiant John Ziska, a great military genius. Vainly did Sigismund lead three imperial armies against the Hussites. His troops fled in dismay before the wild fury of the enraged people. The Hussites burned the Bohemian churches and convents, and carried their ravages into the neighboring countries. The name of Ziska, who became blind during the war, was a terror to the enemies of the Hussites, and he led his followers from victory to victory.

After Ziska's death, in A. D. 1424, the Hussite armies were led by Procopius, a blind priest, who also proved a great general and a formidable foe to the German Empire and the Romish Church. He drove back the imperial armies which endeavored to conquer Bohemia, after which the Hussites under Procopius the Great and Procopius the Little ravaged Saxony and extorted tribute from Brandenburg and Bavaria.

Finding that force was useless, Sigismund undertook to negotiate with the Hussites, and his action was sustained by the Council of Basle, which convened in A. D. 1431. The Hussites were then divided into two parties—the *Calixtines*, or *Utraquists*, who were willing to return to the Church on condition of being permitted to receive

JOHN HUSS BEFORE THE COUNCIL OF CONSTANCE.

the cup in the Lord's Supper and preaching in their own language; and the *Taborites*, who desired a complete separation from the Romish Church.

Being granted their demand, the Calixtines returned to the Church in 1433; whereupon they were attacked by the Taborites, who considered the Calixtines traitors to the Hussite cause; but the Taborites were decisively defeated near Prague in 1434, and the two Procopiuses were killed. Sigismund then ratified the treaty that had been made between the council and the Calixtines, and succeeded in bringing about a peace by the dexterity of his Chancellor, Schlick; whereupon he was acknowledged King of Bohemia (A. D. 1434), thus ending the famous *Hussite War*.

Sigismund did not remain faithful to the treaty. After being crowned he sought to put down the Calixtines and to restore the former Romish worship. The glory of Bohemia was humbled in the dust. Several decades later a small party of the former Hussites separated from the Church and formed a separate sect, since known as the *Bohemian and Moravian Brethren*, "poor, scripture-proof and peaceful."

In 1415 Frederick, Landgrave of Hohenzollern, bought the Mark of Brandenburg from King Sigismund, and received the dignity of an imperial Elector with his new dominions, which ever afterwards remained under the Hohenzollern dynasty, which now occupies the thrones of Prussia and the German Empire. Sigismund, who was now King of Germany, King of Hungary and King of Bohemia, was crowned Emperor in 1433, and died in 1437.

The male line of the Luxemburg dynasty expired with Sigismund, who was succeeded as King of Bohemia and King of Hungary by his son-in-law Albert II., Duke of Austria. In 1438—the year after Sigismund's death—ALBERT II. was chosen King of Germany, and thenceforth the German throne was occupied by the Hapsburg-Austrian dynasty until the end of the Germano-Roman Empire in 1806, with the brief intermission of a few years after the failure of the male line in 1740. Albert II. was a well disposed and energetic sovereign, but he was unable to effect anything of importance during his short reign of less than two years (A. D. 1438-1439). He died suddenly in a campaign against the Turks in 1439.

In 1440 Duke Frederick of Styria, the nephew of Albert II. was chosen King of

STATUE OF HUSS ON THE LUTHER MONUMENT AT WORMS.

Germany with the title of FREDERICK III. The new sovereign was endowed with domestic virtues, but lacked energy and possessed slender talents for government. The revenues of the German crown were inadequate to his acting with decision in anything, and the different states comprising the German Empire looked coldly upon any measure which did not directly affect themselves.

The Council of Basle, which had been summoned by Pope Martin V. just before his death in 1431, was still sitting, and remained in session eighteen years (A. D. 1431-1449). The council was convened to settle the disputes of the Hussites. It opened with but a small attendance of prelates, March 3, 1431. When this was known, Pope Eugenius IV. ordered the council to dissolve, and convoked another at Bologna, in Italy. The members of the Council of Basle refused to leave, and summoned the Pope to appear before them. When he refused they elected an Antipope. The Emperor Sigismund offered his services as mediator, and his services were accepted. Some time afterward the Pope recalled his order to dissolve the council, and permitted it to proceed. While the Hussite controversy was still unsettled, and until its settlement, the Pope and the prelates were in complete accord; and Catholic history represents this period of harmony as "The bright days of the Council of Basle."

As there was a prospect of union between the Greek and Roman Catholic Churches, and as the Greek deputation preferred going to some Italian city, the Pope desired to remove the council to Ferrara; and thenceforth Pope Eugenius IV. no longer recognized the Council of Basle, whereupon it elected Felix V. as Antipope. King Frederick III. of Germany sustained Pope Eugenius IV. in his quarrel with the Council of Basle, but the German states sided with the council, whereupon a quarrel broke out between the Pope and the German Electors. With the aid of his secretary, Æneas Sylvius, Frederick III. succeeded in effecting a reconciliation between the German princes and the Pope.

The General Council assembled at Ferrara, but the breaking out of the plague in that city caused its removal to Florence. The two Councils of Basle and Florence lasted during the entire pontificate of Eugenius IV. A kind of union was effected between the Greek and Roman Catholic Churches by the Council of Florence, but this union was not permanent. This council was visited by the Eastern Emperor, John Palæólogus, and the Patriarch of the Greek Church, with a train of courtiers and Greek clergy. The Eastern Emperor—in order to gain the aid of Western Christendom against the Ottoman Turks—offered to recognize the Pope's supremacy; but the authorities at Constantinople refused to ratify the treaty signed to that effect; and fifteen years later (A. D. 1453) the Eastern Empire fell before the conquering Turks.

Pope Eugenius IV. died just as Germany had sent Æneas Sylvius, who had been secretary to the Council of Basle, to Rome, to tender submission to the legitimate Pope.

The next Pope, Nicholas V., was recognized by the Germans; and the Concordat of Vienna was concluded between that Pope and King Frederick III., by which the Holy See recovered nearly all the powers of which it had been deprived by the Council of Basle. By this concordat all the claims against the exactions of collectors and the abuses of ecclesiastical administration were fully satisfied. Episcopal elections were restored to their primitive condition. Each church named its pastor, who was to be confirmed by the Holy See. This concordat served as the basis of ecclesiastical jurisprudence in Germany until 1803, and its ratification put an end to the schism in the Church.

King Frederick III. hoped to recover some of the lost authority of the German crown by the aid of the friendship of Pope Nicholas V.; but the time for this had passed. The German princes had advanced too far on the way to practical independence to be turned back, and the German king's alliance with the Pope was now powerless to effect anything important for either the King of Germany or the Pope.

In 1452 King Frederick III. was crowned Emperor at Rome by Pope Nicholas V. He was the last Emperor crowned at Rome, and the last, except one, who was crowned by the Pope. Upon ascending the imperial throne he confirmed the title of archduke to the Austrian House of Hapsburg, and granted many privileges to it, elevating the archdukes to a dignity next to that of the Electors.

The Emperor Frederick III. very much desired to join in the crusade which the Pope proclaimed against the Ottoman Turks, who had taken Constantinople in 1453, and who were menacing Germany. But the German states were unwilling to sustain the Emperor in this enterprise, as they did not fear any danger from the Turks, and dreaded the Emperor's alliance with the Pope, which they had no desire to strengthen. Thus the task of driving back the Turks devolved entirely upon the Poles and the Hungarians. The Turks laid siege to Belgrade, but were driven back in 1456 by the Hungarians under the command of the regent, the valiant John Hunníyades of Transylvania.

Ladislas, who had succeeded his father Albert II. as Duke of Austria, and as King of Hungary and King of Bohemia, died in 1457. The Emperor Frederick III. endeavored to seize the Austrian territories, but was obliged to relinquish Upper Austria to his brother Albert, and retained Lower Austria only. To atone for this disappointment, he then endeavored to obtain possession of the crowns of Bohemia and Hungary, but did not succeed in either effort. The Bohemians conferred their crown upon George Podiebrad, who had already ruled the kingdom as regent; while Matthias Corvínus, the worthy son of John Hunníyades, was elected King of Hungary by the Hungarian Diet. The Emperor Frederick III. vainly endeavored to oppose these elections, and he was finally obliged to recognize both these sovereigns.

Frederick III. had great trouble in preserving his crown even in Lower Austria. The people of Vienna rebelled against him in 1462, and were aided by the Emperor's brother Albert. Frederick III. was forced to yield Lower Austria, with Vienna, to his brother Albert for eight years. Albert soon became as unpopular as Frederick III. himself; and by his death, in 1463, Frederick III. obtained possession of all the Austrian territories except the Tyrol.

The power of the German crown had sunk into utter contempt. The Emperor was unable to enforce his authority, and his interference in German affairs only caused trouble without accomplishing anything. The German princes made themselves independent of the Emperor, and exercised the privilege of private warfare without hesitation. Accordingly the reign of Frederick III. was signalized by many internal wars which produced great suffering to the German people.

The Suabian League was engaged in a furious war with Albert, "the German Achilles," the valiant Margrave of the Brandenburg territories of Bayreuth, in Franconia—a war in which nine battles were fought and two hundred villages reduced to ashes. The vicinity of the Rhine and the Neckar was desolated by the War of the Palatinate, during which the Palsgrave Frederick the Victorious achieved a brilliant victory near Seckenheim in 1461, and made prisoners of his enemies, Ulrich of Wurtemberg, the Margrave of Baden and the Bishop of Metz; but he was unable to prevent the deposition of his ally, the exiled Archbishop Dieter of Mayence, in whose defense he had taken up arms.

In 1471 George Podiebrad, King of Bohemia, died, and the Emperor Frederick III. made another attempt to obtain the crown of that kingdom. The Bohemian states elected Ladislas, the son of King Casimir IV. of Poland, King of Bohemia. The Emperor and Pope Paul II. induced Matthias Corvínus, King of Hungary, to attack Bohemia; but Frederick III., soon becoming jealous of the great power of the Hungarian king, turned against him and transferred his aid to Ladislas. Thereupon King Matthias Corvínus overran Austria and compelled the Emperor to flee from Vienna. The valiant King of Hungary kept possession of Austria until his death in 1490, when the Emperor Frederick III. recovered his estate and made another effort to become King of Hungary. When he failed in this attempt he endeavored to obtain the Hungarian crown for his son Maximilian; but the Hungarian magnates, jealous of Austria, conferred the crown of Hungary upon King Ladislas of Bohemia.

During the reign of Frederick III. the Eidgenossen, or Swiss confederates, rapidly advanced in power and importance. Charles the Bold, Duke of Burgundy, was one of the wealthiest and most powerful princes of his time; being lord of the duchy of Burgundy, the free county of Burgundy and most of the Netherlands. Not satisfied with these extensive territories, he desired to found a dominion like the old kingdom of Lotharingia, or Lorraine, by securing the whole region between France and Germany, between the North Sea and the Mediterranean.

In 1476 Charles the Bold became involved in a war with the Swiss, the quarrel having been instigated by the crafty King Louis XI. of France. In this war the Swiss fought with more than their accustomed courage, and defeated the Burgundian duke most disastrously in two bloody battles, one at Granson in 1476 and the other at Morat in 1477. A few months afterward the Duke of Burgundy made war on the Duke of Lorraine, who, aided by the Swiss, defeated him in the battle of Nancy, in which Duke Charles the Bold himself was slain. These great victories over the powerful Duke of Burgundy raised the renown of the Swiss to a high degree, and did much toward arousing in them a national feeling, though they still continued to be a portion of the German Empire.

Milan and Lombardy became entirely independent of the German Empire during the reign of Frederick III., who relinquished the government of the archduchy of Austria and the German Empire to his son Maximilian, who had been elected King of Germany in 1486. The Emperor Frederick died in 1493, after a reign of fifty-three years (A. D. 1440-1493).

MAXIMILIAN I., the son and successor of Frederick III., was a man of greater courage and talents than his weak father, and was called "the last knight." During the lifetime of his father there had been negotiations for the marriage of Maximilian with Mary of Burgundy, the daughter of Duke Charles the Bold, but these negotiations had been broken off. Upon the death of Charles the Bold, Mary married Maximilian of her own free will, thus bringing to him the rich inheritance of Franche-Comte, or the free county of Burgundy, and the Netherlands. The duchy of Burgundy had been seized by the rapacious King Louis XI. of France, who, after the death of Duke Charles the Bold without male heirs, claimed the duchy as a lapsed fief of the French crown.

Mary died in 1482, leaving to Maximilian two children, Philip and Margaret. Philip was heir to his mother's territories, but during his minority these lands were ruled by his father, who was by inheritance Archduke of Austria, and Duke of Styria, Carinthia and Carniola, and Count of Tyrol. Thus Maximilian I. was one of the most powerful sovereigns that had reigned over Germany for a long time.

When King Charles VIII. of France invaded Italy in 1494 Maximilian I. was anxious to oppose him, as he feared that the French monarch was aiming at the imperial crown. For the purpose of securing the aid of the German states, Maximilian I. summoned a Diet, which convened at Worms in 1495. This famous Diet gave the German Empire a new constitution, by which the private wars that had so long been the curse of Germany were abolished. As the German princes refused to sacrifice any of their real or pretended rights, every proposal that appeared likely to increase the king's power, or to diminish the power of the princes, encountered a determined resistance. The constitution finally agreed upon at this imperial Diet at Worms by Maximilian I. with the Electors, the nobles, the bishops, and the representatives of the free imperial towns, while striking a death-blow to the right of private warfare, completely undermined the German sovereign's authority.

The imperial constitution framed by this Diet at Worms put an end to private war by establishing the *Landfriede*, "Land-peace," by which any one was forbidden to seek self-redress by appealing to arms on his own account, under penalty of being outlawed and put under the ban of the Empire. The German princes urged their sovereign to create an imperial tribunal by which all the quarrels that had formerly been settled by arms might be tried; and though Maximilian I. was greatly averse to surrendering any of his kingly rights, he consented to this scheme, in order to secure the assistance of the imperial Diet against King Charles VIII. of France. Accordingly an *Imperial Chamber* was constituted, which was to be composed of a judge and sixteen assessors, the judge to be appointed by the king, and the assessors to be selected by the German states and to be confirmed by the king. Persons who refused to submit to the jurisdiction of the court were to be outlawed and put under the ban of the Empire. Provision was made for the expenses of the Imperial Chamber by the assessment of a common tax.

Maximilian I. was always hostile to the Imperial Chamber and threw every obstacle in its way, but it continued to exist until the end of the Empire in 1806, without possessing much real power or doing much good. The Swiss, who offended Maximilian I. by entering into an alliance with the French and assisting them in their efforts to conquer Italy, refused to submit to the Imperial Chamber and denied their contingent of taxes. In 1499 Maximilian I. attempted to reduce them to submission by force of arms, but was defeated and compelled to make a disgraceful retreat, and was obliged to forego his demands in the Peace of Basle, A. D. 1499, by which he acknowledged the exemption of the Swiss from imperial taxation and from the jurisdiction of the Imperial Chamber. Switzerland remained nominally a portion of the Germano-Roman Empire for a century and a half longer, until 1648, but the concessions wrung from Maximilian I. in the Peace of Basle rendered the Swiss practically independent.

Being unable to accomplish much at home, Maximilian I. attempted to interfere in the affairs of other countries. As he was about to march to Rome in 1508 to be crowned Emperor, he was stopped by the Venetians, who refused to permit him a passage through their territory. With the sanction of Pope Julius II., Maximilian I. assumed the title of *Emperor-elect*, without being crowned at all—a title borne by all succeeding Kings of Germany.

The refusal of the Venetians to allow Maximilian I. to pass through their territory incurred for them the Emperor's bitter hostility; and in 1508 he very readily united with Pope Julius II., King Louis XII. of France and King Ferdinand the Catholic of Spain in the *League of Cambray* against Venice. He afterwards joined the *Holy League* against Louis XII. of France. The Emperor Maximilian I. was generally unsuccessful in his wars.

The German states perceived that peace was their great need, not war, and by refusing to supply the Emperor with troops and money they rendered him powerless to embroil them very deeply in wars with other nations. The revenues of Maximilian's hereditary estates, on which he was obliged to depend, did not enable him to carry on very expensive wars; and his luxurious habits subjected his finances to a very great strain. He was frequently so much in need of money that in order to replenish his purse he descended to acts unbecoming his august position, as when he served as a private in the army of King Henry VIII. of England at the siege of Terouenne in the latter's war with France, receiving as pay one hundred crowns a day. Maximilian I. professed a desire to lead a crusade against the Turks; but the German states distrusted both the Emperor and the Pope who supported him, and therefore refused to grant him any aid.

In 1501 the German Empire was divided into *Circles* for the better administration of justice. Six Circles were then formed—Bavaria, Suabia, Franconia, Upper Rhine, Westphalia, and Lower Saxony. In 1512 four new Circles were formed out of Maximilian's hereditary dominions and the territories of the Electors who had been excluded from the first division. These were Austria, Burgundy, Lower Rhine, and Upper Saxony. Thus Germany was divided into ten Circles, each of which had its own states, or legislative assembly, over which one or more directors presided. The government of a Circle was assigned the duty of enforcing the decisions of the Imperial Chamber, and was required to maintain order within its own dominions.

It required some years for this new system to get into operation, and even then its results fell far below the expectations of its founders, though it was a great improvement upon the lawlessness of the preceding three centuries. This arrangement raised the power of the German princes to a still greater height, so that they became absolute rulers in their own respective territories.

Maximilian I. ruled well in his hereditary dominions, and inaugurated many useful reforms, among which was the establishment of a tribunal afterwards called the *Aulic Council*, which was charged with the duty of hearing appeals from lower courts, and which finally became a court of appeal for all Germany.

At one time Maximilian I. cherished the hope of exchanging the imperial crown for the papal tiara. He even pawned the archducal mantle of Austria, to procure funds to bribe the cardinals. He wrote to his daughter Margaret: "To-morrow I shall send a bishop to the Pope, to conclude an agreement with him that I may be appointed his coadjutor, and on his death succeed to the Papacy, that you may be bound to worship me—at which I shall be very proud."

The Emperor Maximilian I. held a Diet at Augsburg in 1518, where he endeavored to induce the German states to assist him in a crusade against the Ottoman Turks. On his way home from this Diet, he died at Wels, in Upper Austria, A. D. 1519.

The reign of Maximilian I. forms the transition period between mediæval and modern times. This chivalrous Emperor himself, with his valiant deeds in battle and tournament, may well be considered the "last knight" on the imperial throne of Germany. His fondness for the decaying chivalric poetry, his marriage with Mary of Burgundy, his wars in the Netherlands and in Italy, are all stamped with the mediæval character. But at this time, also, began a more refined political science and a greater intercourse among nations, which, along with the new discoveries and inventions, brought about the modern epoch.

The power of the Emperors had undergone a considerable change in its character during the fourteenth and fifteenth centuries. They did not derive their power from their position as sovereign of Germany, but from their hereditary wealth and influence. The authority of Maximilian I. and his successors was uncertain in Germany, though they were supreme in their hereditary dominions.

The various princes of the German Empire had become practically independent by the time of the reign of Maximilian I.; and each German state had its states, or legislative body, which was modeled after the Diet of the Empire. These states, or legislatures, possessed the sole power of levying taxes and granting funds to their rulers, and sometimes they required them to give an account of the manner in which they disposed of the funds. These states usually resisted the efforts of the Austrian Emperors of Germany to drag them into foreign wars, because they perceived that these struggles were for the special benefit of Austria rather than of Germany.

Many of the imperial cities had become free, and had acquired such power that they were able to uphold their rights against the most powerful princes of the Empire. The representatives of these free cities constituted the third college in the imperial Diet.

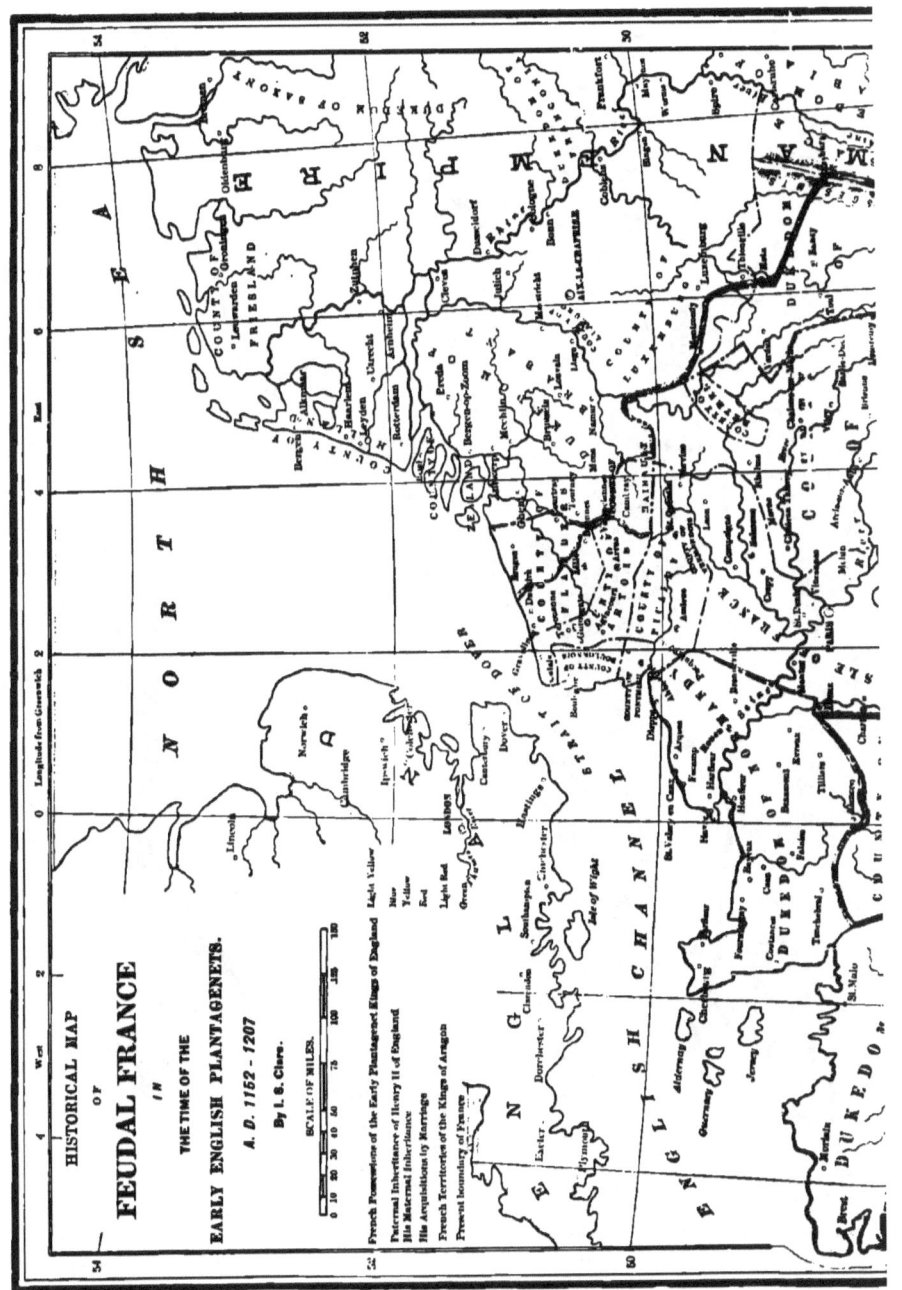

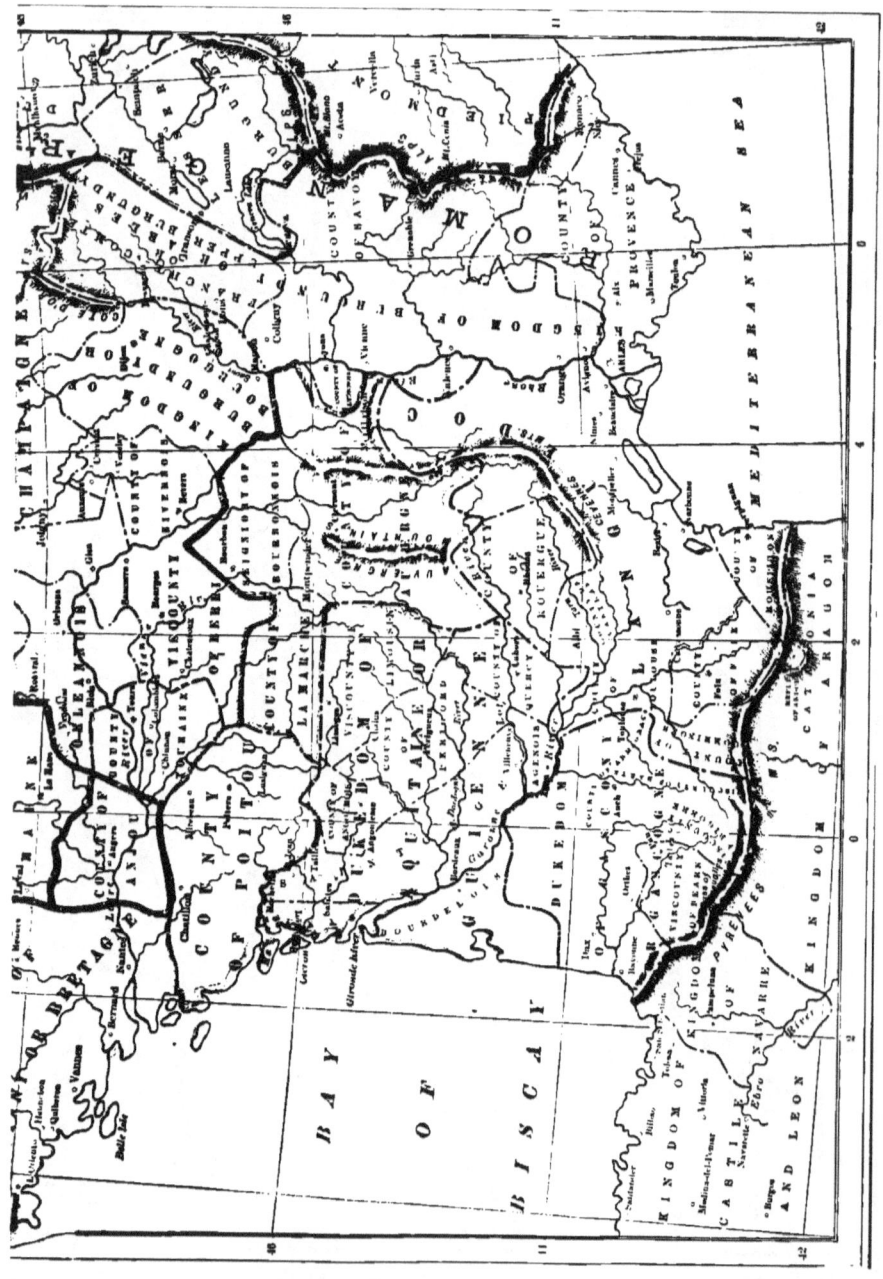

The Hanseatic League was at the zenith of its power and glory during the closing period of the Middle Ages. The government of the cities was contested by the *patricians*, or old families, who constituted a distinct class, and by the *guilds*, or unions of the various trades. The guilds held the ascendency in many of the German cities, and the government was democratic in such cities.

SECTION II.—FEUDAL FRANCE.

HE real history of the Kingdom of France commences with the accession of HUGH CAPET, the founder of the Capetian dynasty of French monarchs, A. D. 987. His elevation to the French throne was considered the triumph of the French nationality over what had been generally regarded as the foreign rule of the Carlovingian dynasty. The illustrious royal race founded by Hugh Capet ruled France in continuous succession for eight centuries, until overthrown by the great French Revolution of 1789.

The reign of Hugh Capet was disturbed by the restlessness and ambition of the French nobles. There were at this time eight powerful principalities in France, each independent of the French crown—namely, Burgundy, Aquitaine, Normany, Brittany, Gascony, Flanders, Champagne and Toulouse; and the royal authority was most insignificant.

Hugh Capet reigned nine years (A. D. 987-996), and proved himself an able and sagacious monarch. The first years of his reign were disturbed by the efforts of Duke Charles of Lorraine to seize the French throne, but these efforts failed, and Hugh Capet's power was firmly established. Charles of Lorraine was taken prisoner, and died in captivity a few months later, A. D. 992.

Hugh Capet sought to secure the support of the powerful nobles of the South of France, and was likewise careful to gain the favor of the Church by conferring rich possessions upon the clergy. He also restored to the monasteries throughout his kingdom the privilege of free election, which had been discontinued since the reign of Charles the Bald. After securing the succession by causing his son Robert to be crowned at Orleans, Hugh Capet died peacefully at Paris, October 24, A. D. 996, in the fifty-seventh year of his age.

ROBERT THE PIOUS succeeded his father as King of France without opposition, in the twenty-fourth year of his age. He had been a pupil of the celebrated Gerbert, afterwards Pope Sylvester II., under whom he acquired a fair education. He excelled in music, and passed his hours in composing hymns and in deeds of charity, to which his amiable and benevolent disposition inclined him.

Having married his fourth cousin Bertha, King Robert the Pious was excommunicated by Pope Gregory V., and his kingdom was laid under an interdict. After some years of spirited resistance to the ecclesiastical authorities, Robert was obliged to divorce his beloved Bertha, whom he never ceased to cherish. He submitted to the Church in order to regain for his subjects the enjoyment of their religious rites, of which the papal interdict had deprived them.

The general belief that the world would come to an end in the year A. D. 1000 overspread all Christendom just before that year's approach, and this belief manifested itself in a marked degree in France. It found expression in a movement joined in by all classes, for the restoration and improvement of the churches and monasteries, and for the erection of new edifices of a similar character. "It was the beginning of that wonderful architectural movement of the Middle Ages which has covered Europe with its glorious monuments of Christian art and Christian self-devotion." The Abbey of St. Martin at Tours, the magnificent Church of St. Aignan at Orleans, the cathedrals of Perigueux, Angoulême and Cahors, are some of the numerous remarkable structures erected during the reign of Robert the Pious. The splendid abbeys of Clugny and Vezelai, and that of St. Sernin at Toulouse were founded later in the eleventh century.

The general gloom which prevailed at the approach of the year 1000 caused people to neglect the preparation of the coming year's crops, and the consequence was a famine.

It was in the midst of the religious enthusiasm occasioned by this superstitious belief that the news reached Europe of the profanation and destruction of the Holy Sepulcher by Hakem, the Fatimite Khalif of Egypt. The Jews were suspected of having instigated this outrage, and they were everywhere cruelly put to death, especially in France. King Robert the Pious himself directed the attack upon them at Sens, A. D. 1016.

In 1006 Robert the Pious married Constance, daughter of the Count of Toulouse, a woman of imperious will and overbearing disposition, who had her royal husband completely under her control. The chronicles of the time give us numerous anecdotes as examples of the meek patience with which the king submitted to her tyranny, and the affectionate ingenuity with which he shielded others from the same tyranny. Constance brought a train of attendants, and attracted many of the gay and polished natives of Aquitaine to her court, thus introducing the superior civilization and refinement of the South of France into the Northern provinces.

The last years of Robert the Pious were troubled by the revolt of his sons, who were goaded into rebellion by the insolent and factious conduct of their mother Constance. The king took the field against his rebellious sons, and, after a bloody campaign in Burgundy, reduced them to submission. Robert never recovered from the shock caused him by the unnatural conduct of his sons. He was attacked with illness immediately after subduing the revolt, and died at the castle of Melun in A. D. 1031, after a reign of thirty-five years, leaving the crown to his son, HENRY I.

Constance sought to set aside the claims of her elder son, King Henry I., in favor of her youngest and favorite son Robert, and the French kingdom was again distracted by civil war. Eudes, the great Count of Blois, Chartres and Champagne, supported the queen-mother with such vigor that Henry was under the necessity of soliciting the aid of Robert the Devil, Duke of Normandy. With the Norman duke's assistance, Henry reduced his mother and her partisans to submission. In the settlement of the kingdom Henry generously provided for his mother, and assigned the duchy of Burgundy to his brother Robert, whose descendants held it for over three centuries. Overcome with mortification at her defeat, Constance died at Melun in July, A. D. 1032.

To reward Duke Robert the Devil of Normandy for his aid, King Henry I. was obliged to cede to that powerful vassal the territories of Gisors, Chaumont, Pontoise and the entire district of the Vexin, situated between the Oise and the Epte. This acquisition of territory extended the frontier of Normandy to within twenty miles of Paris.

About this time a terrible famine of three years ravaged France, inflicting the most dreadful suffering upon the country. The Church took advantage of the general consternation and despondency to impose a check upon the evil practice of private warfare, by proclaiming the "*Truce of God*," which provided that no act of violence should be committed from Wednesday evening to Monday morning The truce was never rigidly enforced, but it was never abolished, and it vastly mitigated the miseries of private war, and contributed much toward restoring social order and public confidence by aiding the progress of agriculture and commerce, which were placed under its special protection. So little was the authority of Henry I. respected that the leading French nobles, such as the Counts of Toulouse, Flanders and Champagne, eclipsed the king in power.

Duke Robert the Devil of Normandy was suspected of having obtained his ducal throne by murdering his elder brother Richard III. He furnished ground for this suspicion several years afterward, by going on a pilgrimage to the Holy Land, after having compelled the Duke of Brittany to become his vassal. Robert the Devil made his illegitimate son, William II., afterwards the Conqueror of England, his successor on the ducal throne of Normandy in case he should never return from his pilgrimage; and the Norman barons willingly accepted William II., and took an oath of allegiance to the young duke, who was then a lad of seven years. Robert the Devil set out on his pilgrimage and reached Jerusalem, but died at Nice, in Bithynia, on his return homeward, A. D. 1035.

Upon hearing of Robert's death, the Norman barons refused to acknowledge William II. on account of his illegitimacy. William was at first supported by King Henry I., but the French monarch at length turned his arms against the young Norman duke. William II. decisively defeated King Henry I. at Mortemer in 1058, and by a second great victory at Varaville he forced the king to abstain from interference with the affairs of Normandy and established his own authority firmly over his duchy.

King Henry I. died in August, A. D. 1060, and was succeeded on the throne of France by his eldest son, PHILIP I., the child of his third wife, a Russian princess. Philip I. was a boy of eight years when he became King of France, and during the first seven years of his reign the government of the French kingdom was wisely administered by his uncle and guardian, Count Baldwin V. of Flanders. Baldwin's death in 1067 left King Philip I. his own master, though he was still less than fifteen years of age. The youthful king was possessed of fair abilities and a good education, but from a very early age he manifested a strong tendency to voluptuousness and debauchery, and these soon became the most prominent traits of his character.

During Philip's minority Duke William II. of Normandy invaded and conquered England. Before starting on his expedition William visited his youthful suzerain at St. Germain-en-Laye, and solicited his aid; but the young king's counselors induced their sovereign to decline the Norman duke's request, because they feared that if William succeeded he would become too powerful a neighbor, while in case of failure France would expose herself to the just enmity of England. Duke William II. was not dispirited by his youthful king's refusal, and prosecuted his project to a crowning success. After conquering England he was crowned king of that country at Westminster Abbey on Christmas day, A. D. 1066.

The acquisition of the English crown by the Norman duke made that great vassal of the French monarch a more powerful sovereign than his royal suzerain himself, thus arousing Philip's jealousy. In 1075 the king took the field against William in support of Alan, Count of Brittany, who had rebelled against his Norman liege-lord. Philip I. united his forces with those of Alan, and compelled the Duke of Normandy to raise the siege of Dol and retire with considerable loss. Some time afterward Philip I. encouraged Robert Courthouse, Duke William's eldest son, to rebel against his father. For several years that prince maintained a desultory warfare in Normandy without accomplishing any decisive result.

For a long time the Duke of Normandy bore King Philip's aggressions with remarkable patience, but he finally resolved to put a stop to them. He demanded that Philip should restore the Vexin district, which the French crown had unlawfully recovered during William's minority. The king replied to this demand by an insulting refusal, whereupon the Norman duke marched into the disputed district, frightfully ravaged it, and took and burned the town of Mantes. William was thrown from his horse amid the ruins of the town and severely injured. He was removed by his attendants to Rouen, and afterward to the monastery of St. Gervais, near that city, where he died six weeks later, September 10, 1087.

King Philip's habitual immorality now involved him in a contest with the Church. As his private revenues were inadequate to defray the expenses of his infamous pleasures, he endeavored to increase them by selling bishoprics and other ecclesiastical dignities to the highest bidder. Pope Gregory VII. (Hildebrand) was aroused to intense indignation by this wholesale simony, and he threatened to excommunicate and depose the French king if the practice was not discontinued. Afraid to face the stern Pope, King Philip I. submitted and for a while obeyed the papal mandate; but when the Pope was in the midst of his famous struggle with King Henry IV. of Germany in the War of Investitures, the King of France relapsed into his old ways, and the Pope considered it best not to proceed to extremities against Philip.

In A. D. 1092 King Philip I. imprisoned his good wife Bertha in the castle of Montreuil, simply because he became tired of her after she had borne him several children. In the same year he seduced and carried off Bertrade de Montfort, the wife of the Count of Anjou, the most beautiful woman in the French kingdom. The countess exacted a promise from the king that he should marry her, and Philip I. readily found two bishops who pronounced the blessing of the Church upon the infamous union. The Count of Anjou, the lawful husband of Bertrade, and the Count of Flanders, the step-father of King Philip's lawful wife Bertha, took up arms against the king. Pope Urban II. excommunicated the guilty couple in 1094, and forbade Philip I. to use any of the ensigns of royalty until he should abandon Bertrade and perform penance for his sin. The king really cared very little for the papal anathema, but desired to save his crown, and thus made an outward submission to the Pope, who paid no further attention to his acts.

Philip I. continued to live with Bertrade, and caused her to be crowned as his queen at Troyes. She bore him four children, but their legitimacy was never admitted. In the meantime his first and lawful wife Bertha died of a broken heart in her prison at Montreuil. The excitement which led to the First Crusade now drew attention from the king's private life; and Pope Urban II., occupied with his zeal for the recovery of Jerusalem, permitted Philip I. and Bertrade to live together as husband and wife without any further molestation for the rest of their lives.

King Philip I. died in A. D. 1108, after a reign of more than forty-seven years—one of the longest reigns in French history. He was succeeded on the French throne by his son LOUIS VI., surnamed *le Gros*, "the Fat," because of his corpulence. Louis VI. was one of the best of French sovereigns. When he ascended the throne the immediate dominions of the King of France embraced only the five cities of Paris, Melun, Etampes, Orleans and Sens, with the territory surrounding each. These towns were separated from each other by the strong fortresses of nobles, who interrupted the communication between them and engaged in a regular system of brigandage, pillaging travelers and seizing and imprisoning them in their castles, from which the captives were only enabled to escape by the payment of a large ransom. These robber nobles trampled on all public law, and there was no order or security in any part of the French kingdom.

King Louis VI. devoted himself first to restore law and order in his kingdom, and he effected this result by encouraging the people to unite and resist the rapacious and lawless barons. Suger, Abbot of St. Denis, who was made the king's confidential friend and prime minister, induced the Church to give the king and the people a hearty and effective support in their struggle with the lawless nobles. This contest continued eight years, and resulted in what is called the *Enfranchisement of the Communes*. Encouraged by King Louis VI., the various communes combined for mutual defense against the lawlessness of their feudal lords, compelling them to grant security of personal freedom and those great privileges of internal organization and self-government which made the commons, or *tiers état*, "third estate," one of the great constituent orders of France and a check upon the power of the great feudal nobility.

Although King Louis VI. contributed so much to this movement, he does not deserve credit for originating it, as the communes were organized by the citizens themselves, and not by any sovereign, being the result of a simultaneous popular rising throughout France for defense against oppression, for the maintenance of the rights of property, and for the protection and development of commerce. King Louis VI. aided in making the movement successful by becoming the champion of public order, by devoting himself to redress wrongs and reform abuses, and by asserting the supremacy of the French crown over all its vassals, most of whom had renounced all thought of subordination.

The forms of municipal government were not the same in the North and in the South of France. The cities of the South had always retained the municipal privileges which the ancient Romans had conferred upon them. They now merely asserted them by choosing their own local magistrates and by arming for the common defense. The liberties of the towns of the North were usually wrung from their feudal lords. A third class of French towns consisted of those which were voluntarily enfranchised by their feudal lords and granted personal freedom, security of property and certain commercial privileges, but which were without the right of choosing their own magistrates or conducting their own governments.

The increase of the royal power was another result of the organization of communes. The king was often invoked to mediate between the nobles and the people; and, as both sides considered his decision final, he came to be recognized as the supreme power in the kingdom. Most of the boroughs were required to contribute annually to the royal treasury and to furnish a specified force of militia upon the king's requisition. With the supplies which they thus obtained, the Kings of France were enabled to extend the royal domains and to force their rebellious vassals to respect their authority. Aided by the wise counsels of the Abbé Suger, Louis VI. governed his kingdom with such firmness and intelligence that he restored the royal power in France, revived the national prosperity, and enlarged his dominions to something like their ancient and natural dimensions. His merits as a sovereign are abundantly attested by the affection which his subjects bore him.

The reign of Louis VI. was marked by several wars. Duke Robert II. of Normandy, while returning from the Holy Land, was captured by his brother, King Henry I. of England, and spent the remainder of his life in captivity in Cardiff castle, in Wales. His son, William Cliton, escaped from Henry's pursuit, and appealed to the King of France to place him in possession of his father's duchy of Normandy. Louis VI. responded to the young Norman prince's appeal, and engaged in a war of several years with Henry I. of England. Henry had lately erected the strong castle Gisors on the frontier of Normandy. The English defeated the French in the battle of Brenneville, the first conflict between the two nations (A. D. 1124). William Cliton was slain in 1128, thus removing the main cause of the war between France and England.

Henry I. of England was a shrewder politician than Louis VI., and he contrived to involve his rival in a war with Henry V. of Germany. Pope Calixtus V. had been driven out of Italy by the German king and compelled to seek refuge in France. The Pope convened a Council at Rheims and thundered an excommunication against the German Emperor, who resolved to destroy the town where so gross an insult was offered to him.

Thereupon the King of France unfurled the *Oriflamme*. The vassals of the crown flocked to the sacred standard, and Louis VI. soon had two hundred thousand men to oppose the German Emperor, who hastily retreated across the Rhine into his own dominions.

The *Oriflamme*, or sacred banner of France, was said by the monks to have been placed in the monastery of St. Denis, the patron saint of France, by an angel from heaven in the times of Clovis or Charlemagne. The staff was of gold, and the flag was of red silk covered with golden flames, whence its name. It was not the standard of the king, but of the kingdom, and it was only brought forward on the most important occasions. The unfurling of the Oriflamme was the signal for all the vassals of France to assemble around their king and to follow him to war. When displayed in battle it was a signal that no quarter would be given. Many fabled virtues were attributed to this banner, and it was believed that its presence would insure victory; but the falsehood of this was proved in the great defeat of the French by the English at Creçy in 1346. The Oriflamme entirely disappeared in the reign of Louis XI., near the close of the Middle Ages. The respect in which the Oriflamme was held is shown by the oath administered to its bearer:

"You swear and promise, on the precious body of Christ Jesus, here present, and on the bodies of Monseigneur St. Denis and his companions, here also, that you will loyally, in your own person, guard and govern the Oriflamme of our lord the king, also present, to the honor and profit of himself and his kingdom, and that you will not abandon it for the fear of death or any other cause, but that you will in all things do your duty, as becomes a good and loyal knight, towards your sovereign and liege-lord."

For the purpose of strengthening himself in France, King Henry I. of England procured the marriage of his only daughter, Matilda, the widow of the German Emperor Henry V., to Geoffrey Plantagenet, the eldest son of Foulques V., the reigning Count of Anjou. This was a shrewd proceeding; as Count Foulques V. resigned his county of Anjou in favor of his son Geoffrey in 1129, and started for the Holy Land, thus bringing one of the most important parts of France under the influence of the English crown.

On the death of King Henry I. of England, in 1135, his nephew, Count Stephen of Blois, usurped the crown of England, which rightfully belonged to Matilda, and also claimed the duchy of Normandy, which was contested by Geoffrey Plantagenet in right of his wife, thus giving rise to a bloody war for the possession of the duchy. Geoffrey Plantagenet was vanquished, and Stephen's son won Normandy with the aid of the French king.

Louis VI. made another gain at this time. William X., Duke of Aquitaine, for the purpose of atoning for his crimes, went on a pilgrimage to the shrine of St. James of Compostella, in Spain, where he died in April, A. D. 1137. Before starting on his pilgrimage, Duke William X. made his only daughter Eleanora the sole heiress of his dominions, and placed her under the guardianship of King Louis VI. on condition that she should be married to the king's son Louis le Jeune, the heir to the French crown. Louis VI. gladly accepted this offer, as it brought to his son and heir almost all of France south of the Loire; and the marriage was solemnized in the cathedral of Bordeaux, in August, A. D. 1137.

King Louis VI. himself died on the day before his son's marriage, and his son LOUIS VII. became King of France (A. D. 1137). The French kingdom now extended from the river Somme and the frontiers of Flanders to the Adour and the Pyrenees. On his death-bed Louis VI. addressed his son Louis thus: "Remember, my son, that a kingdom is a public trust, for the exercise of which you must render a strict account after your death."

The reign of Louis VI. was a period of great intellectual activity in France, and was made illustrious by a number of great lights, such as Roscelin, St. Anselm, Pierre Abelard, St. Bernard and William de Champeaux.

Pierre Abelard, the renowned French philosopher, the restorer of philosophy in the Middle Ages, was born A. D. 1079, and taught with extraordinary success in Paris.

He simplified and explained everything, presenting philosophy in a familiar form and impressing it on men's minds. In the height of his popularity he became violently enamored of his pupil Heloise, and forgot his duty to himself and mankind. After his cruel punishment he renounced the world and became a monk, but he found no peace, as he was charged with heresy and condemned by the Church, through the instrumentality of St. Bernard. He sought and found his brothers and more than twenty of his companions. He observed the strictest rules of the order, and so distinguished himself by his ability and acquirements that he was selected to lead the monkish colony to Clairvaux, and was made abbot of the new monastery, an office which he held for the rest of his life. His fame attracted many monks, a number of whom attained distinction, among them Pope Eugenius III., six cardinals and many bishops. In 1128 St. Ber-

ABELARD AND HELOISE.

a refuge in the famous monastery of Clugny, in Burgundy, where he died two years later, A. D. 1142.

St. Bernard, Abbot of Clairvaux, in Burgundy, was born of a noble Burgundian family. He was carefully trained by pious parents, and sent to study at the university of Paris. At the age of twenty-three he entered the monastery of Citeaux, in Burgundy, just then founded, accompanied by nard prepared the statutes for the order of Knights Templars. Popes and princes desired his support, and referred their disputes to his decision.

St. Bernard was the principal promoter of the Second Crusade. At the Council of Vezelai, in 1146, he spoke as by inspiration before the French king and nobles, and gave them their crosses with his own hand. He then preached the Crusade in Germany, where he persuaded King Conrad III. to join in the great expedition, but refused the command which was offered to him. His prediction of success was not verified, as the Crusade was without results.

St. Bernard was the violent foe of Arnold of Brescia and of Abelard. He steadily refused the offers of several achbishoprics and other ecclesiastical dignities, preferring to remain a mere abbot. His character and his writings have secured for him the title of "the Last of the Fathers." The power, tenderness and simplicity characterizing his sermons and other works have secured for him the admiration of both Catholics and Protestants. Dante introduces him in the last cantos of the *Paradise*, with profound reverence, admiration and love. Luther studied his writings with similar feelings.

Louis VII. did not inherit his father's talents or good sense. In 1141, four years after his accession, he quarreled with Pope Victor III. about the right to appoint an Archbishop of Bourges. The Pope was sustained by the Count of Champagne, and the next year war broke out between the king and this powerful vassal. Louis VII. was obliged by his superstitious fears to yield two years afterward, thus giving the Holy See another triumph.

Louis VII. participated in the struggle between the Counts of Blois and Anjou for the possession of Normandy, by espousing the cause of Geoffrey Plantagenet, and secured him in the possession of that great duchy. Finally a compromise was effected, by which Count Stephen of Blois retained the throne of England during his life, while Geoffrey Plantagenet's eldest son Henry was named as Stephen's heir.

Count Thibault of Champagne had rebelled against the king, but had been reduced to submission and pardoned. But Thibault took up arms a second time; and Louis VII., exasperated at his conduct, attacked his castle of Vitry, and set it on fire, but the flames spread to a village close by and destroyed a church and many of its inmates. Shocked at this accident, the king made peace with Count Thibault; and, as an atonement for the dreadful accident, Louis VII., in connection with Conrad III., King of Germany, engaged in the Second Crusade, A. D. 1147; but both monarchs were unfortunate in that undertaking, and after losing all but a few of their followers they returned to Europe.

The government of the French kingdom was well administered by the Abbé Suger during the king's absence in the Holy Land. The Abbé Suger was one of the wisest statesmen that France ever produced, and vainly sought to prevent the king from engaging in the Crusade. Under the beneficent administration of this able statesman, Louis VII. found his kingdom in excellant condition upon his return home. By the death of the Abbé Suger, in January, 1152, Louis VII. lost his ablest counselor. The death of this great statesman was followed by the greatest political blunder of Louis VII.

The king had reason to suspect the fidelity of his wife, Queen Eleanora, during his absence in Palestine; and when he returned to France he confided his trouble to the Abbé Suger, who implored him to conceal and overlook his queen's conduct, if possible, for the good of France. The high-spirited Eleanora regarded her weak husband with contempt, and the breach between them daily widened. Both demanded a divorce; and in March, 1152, the Council of Beaugency declared the marriage null and void.

Eleanora then resumed her rank as Duchess of Aquitaine, and assumed the government of her hereditary dominions, thus depriving the French crown of more than half of its possessions. Six weeks afterward she married Henry Plantagenet, Duke of Normandy and Brittany, and Count of Anjou, Poitou, Touraine and Maine. On the death of King Stephen of England, in October, 1154, Henry Plantagenet ascended the English throne as Henry II., thus becoming the most powerful sovereign in Europe. Thus was laid the foundation of the lifelong enmity between King Louis VII. of France and King Henry II. of England.

For twenty years Louis and Henry were engaged in almost continual war, as the French king claimed the right of feudal superiority over the English monarch. During his war with the Duke of Normandy, Louis besieged Rouen; and, after granting the citizens of the beleaguered town a truce, he perfidiously assaulted the city, but was justly punished by a vigorous repulse.

Louis VII. was no match for Henry Plantagenet, who contrived to obtain the advantage over his rival on every occasion, but Louis} gave Henry considerable trouble during his reign. He sheltered and protected the exiled Primate of England, Thomas à Becket, and aided and encouraged the rebellion of Henry's wife, Queen Eleanora, and her sons Henry, Geoffrey and Richard, against their father; but when Henry had crushed the rebellion of his wife and sons the French monarch was glad to make peace with the King of England.

Louis VII. died September 18, A. D. 1180, and was succeeded as King of France by PHILIP AUGUSTUS, his son by a third marriage with Alice, the sister of Count Thibault of Champagne. Philip Augustus was fifteen years old at his accession. His surname, according to some writers, was given him because he was born in August. Other writers consider his surname as synonymous with the word *Great*. Soon after his accession he married Isabella, daughter of Count Baldwin of Hainault and niece of Count Philip of Flanders, who received as her dowry the town of Amiens and the promise of a part of Flanders at her uncle's death.

The first act of Philip Augustus indicated his future policy to increase the royal power at the expense of the great feudatories of France. He forced the powerful Duke of Burgundy, who had robbed the Church and had refused to make restitution, to make adequate reparation for the injuries which he had inflicted, and to submit himself to his sovereign's clemency. When the Burgundian duke submitted, the king treated him with wise generosity.

In 1182 Philip Augustus gave another example of the decisive energy of his character by banishing the Jews from the French kingdom and confiscating their synagogues to the Church, and by imposing heavy penalties upon profane swearers, blasphemers, gamblers, and the heretical sect of the Paterini, many of the last suffering death.

War between France and England was renewed in A. D. 1187, and a large portion of the English king's possessions in the duchy of Berri was overrun by the French monarch before King Henry II. of England could arrive. A truce was concluded before a battle was fought, and Philip Augustus and Henry II. met near Gisors in 1188 to conclude a definite peace. At this meeting intelligence was received of the capture of Jerusalem by the valiant Sultan Saladin of Egypt, and the aged Archbishop of Tyre powerfully appealed for assistance against the Moslems. Losing sight of their own interests, the French and English kings concluded a treaty of peace with each other, and solemnly pledged themselves to assume the cross and rescue the Holy Land from the Mohammedans. The example of the two kings was followed by the chivalry of France, Normandy and England, and two years were devoted to preparing for the Third Crusade.

In spite of their treaty, the war between the Kings of France and England was renewed the next summer (A. D. 1189). Philip Augustus found an efficient ally in Richard the Lion-hearted, the son of King Henry II. of England, who openly rebelled against his father and did homage to the French king for his possessions in France. The English monarch was obliged to sue for peace and to sign a humiliating treaty, thus making an unqualified submission to his powerful rival, renouncing all pretension to the sovereignty of Berri, purchasing by a heavy ransom the restitution of the towns taken by the French, and consenting that all the barons who had taken up arms in behalf of his son Richard the Lion-hearted should remain vassals of that valiant prince. Henry II. of England died in 1189, from grief and mortification, and was succeeded in his dominions by his son Richard the Lion-hearted.

Kings Philip Augustus and Richard the Lion-hearted united with the German Emperor Frederick Barbarossa in the Third Crusade. The French and English monarchs led a joint expedition in 1190, reaching Palestine in the Spring of 1191. Their first operation in the Holy Land was the siege of Acre, of which Richard the Lion-hearted was the hero, as he was of the entire Third Crusade. Philip Augustus was more of a statesman than a warrior, and was very jealous of his ally's glory. The two kings quarreled, and Philip Augustus returned to France after the capture of Acre, after first solemnly swearing to respect Richard's rights and territories.

The French monarch at once proceeded to Rome, where he sought to persuade Pope Celestine III. to absolve him from his oath to the King of England; but the Pope, to his great credit, refused to grant Philip's request. Philip Augustus then returned to France, fully determined to strike a decisive blow at Richard the Lion-hearted at the first opportunity. The occasion soon presented itself. Richard's brother John was busily conspiring to deprive his brother of the crown of England and of the duchy of Normandy, and the French monarch at once aided the young prince in the plot. John did homage to the King of France for both Normandy and England, and Philip Augustus proceeded to overrun Richard's dominions in France. The valiant King of England, while returning from the Holy Land in 1192, had been made a captive by the Duke of Austria, in revenge for an insult to the German banner after the capture of Acre, and only obtained his release after a year's captivity by the payment of a heavy ransom by the English people, just as his brother John and the French king believed that their projects were about to be crowned with complete success.

Soon after his release Richard the Lion-hearted made his appearance in Normandy at the head of his barons, recovered the territory which Philip Augustus had wrested from him, and severely defeated the French king at Fretteval, near Vendome, July 15, A. D. 1194. Hostilities proceeded without any decisive result until January, A. D. 1199, when Pope Innocent III. compelled both parties to make peace, and a treaty was concluded by which each king retained his actual possessions. In April of the same year Richard the Lion-hearted was killed while besieging one of his vassals at Chalus, in Normandy, thus relieving Philip Augustus of his ablest adversary. Richard's brother John then became his successor as King of England, Duke of Normandy and lord of all the other vast possessions of the English crown in France.

Philip Augustus then espoused the cause of Duke Arthur of Brittany, King John's nephew, who disputed with his uncle the crown of England and the sovereignty of Normandy; but the French king did not proceed to an open rupture with John, as he was too deeply involved in a quarrel with the Church to hazard a foreign war.

After the death of his first wife, Isabella of Hainault, Philip Augustus married Ingelberga, daughter of the King of Denmark, a princess described as beautiful, amiable and virtuous; but when he first met her he conceived such an aversion to her that he compelled the French bishops to grant him a divorce. Ingelberga then appealed to Pope Celestine III., who refused to sanction the action of the French bishops in granting the divorce. In spite of the Pope's refusal, the French king married the beautiful Agnes de Méran, daughter of the Marquis of Istria. Pope Celestine III. vainly sought to turn Philip Augustus from his purpose.

The next Pope, Innocent III., who was a pontiff after the style of Hildebrand, commanded the disobedient King of France to put away Agnes and to live with his lawful wife. When the king refused to do so, Pope Innocent III. laid France under an interdict, and the French churches were closed for eight months, during which the people of France were deprived of all their religious rites, except the baptism of infants and the extreme unction for the dying. The growing discontent of the French people obliged their sovereign to yield to the Pope, and he accordingly put away Agnes, who died several months afterward. Philip Augustus reinstated Ingelberga in her outward position, but treated her with the most brutal severity in private. Upon the king's submission, the Pope released France from the interdict.

Philip Augustus was prevented by his quarrel with the Pope from taking active measures against King John of England in support of the claims of Prince Arthur of Brittany to the crown of England and the duchy of Normandy. A compromise was therefore agreed upon, by which the Infanta Blanche of Castile, the niece of King John of England, was married to Prince Louis, the eldest son of King Philip Augustus. John bestowed on his niece as a dowry the sum of thirty thousand marks of silver and the city and county of Evreux, and appointed her the sole heiress of his dominions in France in case he died without direct heirs. Philip Augustus induced Prince Arthur of Brittany to renounce all pretensions to John's dominions and to do homage to John for his duchy of Brittany. After these matters had all been arranged, Prince Louis of France and Blanche of Castile were married, May 23, A. D. 1200.

But peace was not yet restored. King John of England became violently enamored of the beautiful Isabella of Angoulême, the affianced bride of Hugh de Lusignan, Count de la Marche, and thereupon repudiated his own wife, Hawise of Gloucester, and carried off Isabella and married her. The Count de la Marche demanded justice; and, as this demand was sustained by the nobles of Poitou and Limousin, King Philip Augustus, as the feudal lord of King John and all these nobles, summoned John to appear at his court in Paris, in May, 1202, to answer the charges brought against him. The King of England disregarded the French king's summons, whereupon war ensued between the two kings.

Philip Augustus instantly invaded Normandy and reduced several important towns. John made an effort to defend his French territories and captured the Count de la Marche and Prince Arthur of Brittany, who had been selected by the French monarch to lead the revolt in Poitou against the King of England.

Arthur's fate is shrouded in mystery, but it was generally believed at that time that King John himself murdered his nephew in the castle of Rouen and cast his body into the Seine, April 3, 1203. This atrocious crime caused John to be bitterly hated by his subjects. Poitou rose in rebellion against him and supported the French monarch. Philip Augustus next invaded Normandy, and by the spring of 1204 he overran the entire duchy and annexed it to the French crown. In 1205 the French king conquered and annexed the counties of Saintonge and Angoulême.

In 1206 King John crossed the Channel from England and feebly attempted to recover his lost possessions; but after some insignificant successes he was obliged to make peace, renouncing all claim to the sovereignty of the duchies of Normandy and Brittany and the counties of Anjou, Poitou, Maine and Touraine. Thus only the duchy of Aquitaine and the Channel Islands remained as the sole possessions of the King of England in France. Philip Augustus also acquired the counties of Artois and Vermandois and the duchy of Auvergne, and thus in the course of three years he had almost doubled the size of the French kingdom. These acquisitions of territory made France second among the states of Europe in power and population, the Germano-Roman Empire being first.

The King of France was now a powerful territorial sovereign, and had steadily pushed the policy upon which he had conducted his reign—the increase of the royal power at the expense of the power of the French nobles. In the South of France the king's authority and possessions were very much augmented by the Crusade against the Albigenses. As the people of Southern France were an enlightened community in which the arts and sciences were liberally cultivated and a spirit of free inquiry encouraged, they had never rendered the same blind and unquestioned obedience to the Pope which had characterized their countrymen in the Northern provinces.

The sect of the Albigenses, which had arisen in the course of time in Languedoc, denounced the ambition and corruption of the court of Rome, and denied the Pope's supremacy and the doctrines of the sacrifice of the mass, purgatory and image worship. Pope Innocent III. determined to crush the bold heretics, and turned them over to the Inquisition, giving that horrible tribunal full power to search out and punish their heresy. The Pope's messengers sought to induce Count Raymond VI. of Toulouse, the protector of the Albigenses, to surrender his subjects to the terrible tortures of the Inquisition; and when he refused they threatened him with the Pope's vengeance. Indignant at this insult, one of the count's attendants killed one of the Pope's envoys, January, A. D. 1208. Pope Innocent III. thereupon excommunicated Count Raymond VI. and proclaimed a Crusade against him. In 1209 bands of fanatical warriors under Simon de Montfort overran the fertile district of Languedoc and spread death and desolation wherever they appeared, destroying cities, towns and villages, massacring the inhabitants and converting that beautiful region into a vast wilderness. After a war of six years the Crusaders conquered Languedoc, and Count Raymond VI. of Toulouse was deprived of his territories, which were bestowed upon Simon de Montfort, the leader of the Crusaders.

In 1213 Pope Innocent III., having laid England under an interdict, invited the French king to undertake the conquest of that country. Philip Augustus accordingly collected a large army at a heavy expense; but as he was about to set out on his expedition he was forbidden by the papal legate to invade England, as King John had in the meantime submitted to the Pope, who thereupon allowed John to rule as his vassal, making England a papal fief. The French king obeyed the Pope's mandate, although he was highly incensed at the Pope's treatment of him.

Philip Augustus then marched northward against the Count of Flanders, who had renounced his allegiance to the King of France and formed an alliance with King Otho IV. of Germany, the nephew of King John of England. This action of the Count of Flanders caused Philip Augustus to side with Frederick of Hohenstaufen, afterwards the Emperor Frederick II., which was a great gain for the young German prince.

Philip Augustus gained important advantages over the Count of Flanders, who endeavored to check him by allying himself with King Otho IV. of Germany, King John of England, and all the great nobles of the Netherlands. With an inferior force Philip Augustus won a great and decisive victory over the allied German, English and Flemish troops, one hundred and fifty thousand strong, under King Otho IV. and the Earl of Salisbury, King John's illegitimate brother, at Bouvines, between Lille and Tournay, August 27, A. D. 1214. This was one of the hardest fought battles of history, and the King of France, who made the attack, routed his foes with great loss, taking many of their leaders prisoners, among whom were the Count of Flanders and the Earl of Salisbury. The French king's victory put an end to the power of Otho IV. of Germany, and established his rival, Frederick II., on the German throne.

King John of England, who had completely failed to effect anything, and had retreated within the farthest limits of Poitou, was granted a truce for five years on payment of sixty thousand marks. The Counts of Flanders and Boulogne forfeited their fiefs to the French crown, and the Count of Flanders passed the remainder of his life in captivity. The chief result of the war was the moral prestige acquired by the French crown and kingdom.

After King John had returned to England the barons of that kingdom forced him to grant Magna Charta, the foundation and bulwark of English constitutional liberty. Pope Innocent III. bitterly denounced the

Great Charter and forbade the English king and his barons to observe it, on penalty of excommunication. The English barons defied and disobeyed the Pope, and the civil war between them and their king was renewed. Driven to despair by their unscrupulous sovereign, the barons invited Prince Louis, son of the King of France, to come to England and assume the crown of that kingdom. Philip Augustus consented very reluctantly to allow his son to assume the English crown, and Louis embarked at Calais for England in May, 1216. He landed at Sandwich, where he was welcomed with joy, and was conducted to London and proclaimed King of England in right of his wife, Blanche of Castile, granddaughter of Henry Plantagenet. John retreated to the North of England, and his cause grew so weak that Louis seemed on a fair way to be successful.

John's sudden death, October 19, 1216, instantly changed the entire situation, as England was freed from her tyrant, and his son, the legitimate heir to the English crown, was an innocent child. The English barons quickly deserted the French prince whom they had invited to become their sovereign, and espoused the cause of the young King Henry III. Thus abandoned by his partisans, the situation of Prince Louis became very critical. The Pope excommunicated him and his adherents, and his father refused to come to his aid. He was defeated in several battles on land and sea, and was shut up in London, where he was forced to capitulate and to renounce all claim to the crown of England, when he was allowed to return to France.

In 1216 Count Raymond VI. of Toulouse and his chivalric son Raymond seized the sword to recover their lost inheritance. They were joyfully received by their people, and in the fall of 1217 they triumphantly entered Toulouse, their capital. Simon de Montfort at once laid siege to Toulouse, but was slain in June, 1218. All Languedoc at once acknowledged the Count of Toulouse as its ruler and expelled the son and heir of Simon de Montfort. Pope Honorius III. proclaimed another Crusade, and invited the King of France to seize the dominions of Count Raymond VI. Philip Augustus sent an army under his son Louis into Languedoc, but after an inglorious failure the prince abandoned the Crusade. Count Raymond VI. died in 1222, and was succeeded in his estates by his son, Count Raymond VII.

Under Philip Augustus the political condition of France underwent an entire change. Before his reign the King of France had been merely the feudal chief of a confederacy of princes, but now he became an absolute monarch. Thus Philip Augustus was the first king of the national monarchy of France, because under him France first assumed the character of a united nation.

Philip Augustus was one of the ablest and best sovereigns that ever reigned over France. He was prudent, energetic, firm and persevering. He governed his subjects with wisdom and justice, however selfish his policy may have been toward others. He was surpassed in these qualities by few, if any, of his successors. He was a generous friend to the city of Paris, which he enlarged and refortified, and adorned with noble edifices. He liberally encouraged the rising schools of Paris, and endeavored to make that city the intellectual center of Europe. He did much to establish a regular administration of justice throughout France, and to introduce a proper fiscal system.

Upon the death of Philip Augustus, in 1223, his son LOUIS VIII. became King of France. The new reign began with a war with King Henry III. of England. After two campaigns a truce of five years was concluded, and Louis VIII. devoted his attention to the more important struggle with the Albigenses in Languedoc. The Council of Bourges, in 1225, had excommunicated Count Raymond VII. of Toulouse, and had transferred his territories to King Louis VIII. In the summer of 1226 Louis VIII. led a large army into Languedoc, and by the middle of autumn he was in possession of all the important towns except Toulouse, which was still held by Count Raymond VII. At the end of the campaign Louis VIII. died at Montpensier, in Auvergne, November 8, A. D. 1226; leaving the French crown to his young son LOUIS IX., generally known as ST. LOUIS.

During the minority of St. Louis the French kingdom was ruled by his mother, Blanche of Castile, as regent. Blanche was a woman of strong good sense and firmness, and governed wisely and well. Just after the death of her husband some of the leading nobles of France formed a coalition for her overthrow, but she succeeded in maintaining her authority, and after a contest of five years reduced the rebellious barons to submission, A. D. 1231.

The following anecdote fully illustrates the good character of Queen Blanche: Some villagers, who were serfs of the priests of Notre Dame, were unable to pay certain contributions which their lords had demanded of them. The angry priests thrust the poor serfs into prison. The prison was so small that the inmates were scarcely able to move, and were almost suffocated for want of air.

When Blanche heard of this she was very much shocked and sent to the priests, requesting them to release the imprisoned serfs, and offering to be security for the money demanded of the poor men. The priests were highly indignant, declaring that the queen-mother had no right to interfere between them and their serfs. The priests then seized the wives and children of the poor men, and crowded them into the same place, where many were suffocated to death. Thereupon Blanche repaired to the prison with her attendants and ordered them to force open the doors. Her attendants were so fearful of offending the churchmen that no one obeyed her. The queen-mother herself then took the ax and commenced breaking open the door. Her boldness so encouraged her attendants that they came to her aid, and the doors were soon forced open. The poor prisoners were brought out, and many of them fainted when they felt the fresh air. Those who were able to speak showered their blessings upon her. Blanche's kindness did not end here, as she made the released serfs forever free.

During the regency of Queen Blanche the war with the Albigenses was ended, to the advantage of the French crown. A treaty was signed at Paris in 1229 by young King St. Louis, who had been crowned in the meantime, and by the papal legate and Count Raymond VII. of Toulouse. The Count of Toulouse was granted a small part of his former possessions in fief during the remainder of his life. At his death this territory was to be conferred on Alfonso, Count of Poitiers, brother of King St. Louis, who was to marry Jeanne, the only daughter of Count Raymond VII. The rest of Languedoc was definitely annexed to the French crown. The marriage between Alfonso and Jeanne occurred in 1241. For the purpose of consolidating the conquered land, the Inquisition was established at Toulouse in 1229, and for a long period the people of Southern France were at the mercy of this horrible tribunal and groaned under its tortures.

In 1234, when St. Louis was nineteen years of age, he married Marguerite, daughter of Raymond Beranger IV., Count of Provence, a bride of thirteen years, selected for him by his mother. Queen Blanche had carefully educated her son; and, though she had too much inclined him toward superstition, she had succeeded in laying the foundation of the noble character which was in the future to render this good sovereign deservedly renowned.

In 1241, when his brother Alfonso had married Jeanne of Toulouse, St. Louis assigned this prince the county of Poitou and the duchy of Auvergne, in accordance with the provisions of their father's will. This action of the young king brought to a crisis a formidable conspiracy among the barons of Poitou against the sovereign claims of St. Louis and his family, based on the former connection of Poitou with the royal race of Plantagenet which occupied the throne of England. The conspiracy was headed by the Count de la Marche, whom Queen Isabella had married within a few months after the death of King John of England. Isabella desired to recover the former French possessions of the English crown for her son, King Henry III. of England.

St. Louis took the field to uphold his brother's claims, and King Henry III. of England crossed over to France to aid his supporters; but the English and their French allies were badly defeated in the desperate battle of Saintes, July 22, A. D. 1242. The rebel barons were reduced to submission, and Henry III. of England was obliged to accept a truce of five years, which was signed in March, 1243. In accordance with this treaty all of Aquitaine as far as the Gironde was annexed to the French crown.

An important result of this war was the loss of the independence of the feudal nobility of France, and the firm establishment of the supremacy of the French crown over its vassals. From this time feudalism declined in France, and the royal power gradually grew stronger. In 1246 the French crown was further strengthened by the marriage of the king's brother Charles, Count of Anjou and Maine, with Beatrix, the heiress of Provence.

In 1244 St. Louis was seized with a violent illness. As he lay in a state of lethargy he imagined that a voice from heaven told him to take up the cross against the Moslems, and scarcely had he recovered his speech than he made a vow to lead a Crusade. His mother and all his wisest counselors vehemently opposed the enterprise, but the king considered his vow a sacred bond, which men were not permitted to unloose. After devoting four years to putting his kingdom in order, he carried out his project.

In August, 1248, St. Louis led the Sixth Crusade; and, leaving the government to be administered by his mother as regent, he sailed for Palestine, taking his queen and his brothers with him. But, instead of leading the expedition to the Holy Land, he invaded Egypt; and, after taking Damietta, he was made a prisoner by the Sultan of Egypt, but was released on the payment of a heavy ransom, and a ten year's truce was concluded. St. Louis returned to France after the death of his mother in 1253, arriving in Paris in September, 1254.

For the next sixteen years France was blessed with peace, and greatly prospered under the wise government of her good king. Justice was scrupulously administered throughout the kingdom, and all classes reposed such confidence in the king that they accepted his decisions without question. St. Louis was accessible to all his subjects, even the humblest. He patiently investigated and redressed all complaints brought before him. He ruled with moderation, but also with firmness, and gradually strengthened the power of the French crown.

St. Louis, the best of the Capets, put an end to feudal violence; established the equality of nobles and serfs before the law, instituting royal courts of justice for the redress of individual wrongs; and gave France a new code of laws, and placed her in the front rank of the powers of Europe.

St. Louis had a truly upright and benevolent disposition. His temper was mild and forgiving, but also brave and firm. No man had more meekness in prosperity, nor more fortitude in adversity. His integrity was inflexible under all circumstances, and he was governed solely by religious principle. His piety did not deprive him of the qualities worthy of a king. His liberality was wholly consistent with a wise economy. The king's revenues at that time arose from his own estates, not from the purses of his subjects. His grandeur depended upon a judicious economy. Unlike his predecessors, St. Louis did not consider the founding of a monastery or the erection of a church an expiation for sin. When speaking of this subject, he was accustomed to saying: "Living men are the stones of God's temple, and the church is more beautified by good manners than by rich walls."

St. Louis maintained great state and regularity at his court, but in his own dress he preserved the plainness of a private individual. He earnestly applied himself to the reformation of abuses. Under the shade of an oak in the forest of Vincennes, near Paris, he heard the complaints of his subjects and redressed their wrongs. The code of laws which he framed still goes by his name.

St. Louis administered justice with the strictest impartiality. His brother Charles, Count of Anjou and Provence, had a dispute with one of his vassals. The cause was tried before the count's officers, and a decision was of course given in his favor. The vassal appealed to the king's court, and this so angered Charles that he cast him into prison. Upon hearing of this, the king instantly summoned his brother into his presence, and sternly addressed him thus: "Because you are my brother, do you suppose you are above the laws?" The king at once ordered Charles to release his vassal and to let the law take its course. The count obeyed, but his vassal could not find a lawyer with courage sufficient to undertake his cause. When the king heard of this he appointed an agent for that purpose. The cause was discussed with the strictest impartiality, and a decision was rendered in favor of the vassal, who was reinstated in his possessions.

Under all the Capets a council had existed, consisting of all the king's vassals and the officers of his household. The constitution of this council was now changed, and it became a superior court with the name of the *Parliament of Paris*, to which appeal might be made from all the other courts of France. This court was likewise employed to register the king's edicts. Sometimes the court remonstrated against the royal edicts, and sometimes they positively refused to sanction them by registering them. In this case the king was obliged to appear before the court and order it to register his edict. There was then no other alternative for the court than to obey, as it was a maxim of French law that the power of all officers and magistrates was suspended in the king's presence. When the king attended the Parliament of Paris his seat was on a couch under a canopy, and on such occasions he was said to hold a *Bed of Justice*.

Feeling that his illustrious grandfather, Philip Augustus, had unjustly acquired some of the French possessions of the English crown, St. Louis voluntarily restored to King Henry III. of England in 1259 the viscounty of Limousin and the counties of Perigord, Quercy and Saintonge. The King of England in return renounced his claims to the duchy of Normandy and the counties of Anjou, Poitou, Maine and Touraine. The English king and his barons, after years of civil war between them, agreed to submit their controversies to the arbitration of St. Louis, thus paying the good French monarch the highest tribute in their power.

In 1262 Pope Urban IV. offered St. Louis the crown of Sicily, but the good king refused it because it was not rightfully his, nor would he permit his son Robert to accept it. The king's brother Charles, Count of Anjou and Provence, was not so scrupulous, and readily accepted the Pope's offer. St. Louis did not discourage his brother, but neither did he give him any active assistance.

Charles went to Rome in 1265, where Pope Clement IV., the successor of Pope Urban IV., crowned him King of Sicily. Charles promised to hold Sicily as a papal fief, that the island kingdom should revert to the Pope in case Charles left no direct heirs, and that it should never be held by the German Emperor. But Charles was obliged to conquer his new kingdom, in which his only partisans were a few native traitors. The Pope provided him with an army by proclaiming a crusade against Manfred of Hohenstaufen, the valiant son of the German Emperor Frederick II., the legitimate King of Sicily, and by levying the tax usually assessed upon churchmen for the prosecution of a holy war.

Charles of Anjou assembled a large army of Frenchmen, with which he invaded Sicily and defeated and killed Manfred in the bloody battle of Benevento, A. D. 1266, thus becoming master of Sicily. Manfred's brother Conradine attempted to make himself King of Sicily, but was defeated by Charles of Anjou in 1268, taken prisoner and beheaded by order of Charles at Naples. Charles afterward aspired to the sovereignty of all

DEATH OF ST. LOUIS.

Italy and to the imperial crown, but his ambitious schemes were utterly thwarted by Pope Gregory X.; and the next Pope, Nicholas III., compelled Charles to resign his offices of Vicar of Tuscany and Senator of Rome.

In 1270 St. Louis undertook the Seventh Crusade, to rescue the Christians in Palestine from the cruelty of Sultan Bibars; but instead of proceeding to the Holy Land, he sailed to Africa to attack the Moors of Tunis. After landing at Tunis, the French monarch besieged that city; but a plague which broke out in the French camp carried St. Louis and many of his soldiers to their graves. This worthy king died August 25, A. D. 1270, at the age of fifty-six, and after a reign of forty-four years.

St. Louis was not a great king according to the ordinary standard, but he was an example of the inherent power of high moral and religious principle faithfully and consistently put in practice through a whole life-time. He was neither a great general nor a man of learning. He often forbore to seize advantages which rightly belonged to him, because of his extreme moderation and conscientiousness; but he exercised a greater influence upon Europe than any other sovereign of his time, and no monarch was ever more fortunate in promoting the advancement and happiness of his subjects. Voltaire thus briefly but justly summed up his character: "It is not given to man to carry virtue to a higher point." The Church rewarded the merits of St. Louis; as Pope Boniface VIII. canonized him as a saint in August 1297, twenty-seven years after his death; wherefore his title.

During the period of the Crusades—embracing the twelfth and thirteenth centuries—the *Troubadours* and *Trouvères* flourished in France. The Provençal language, formed from the Latin as learned and spoken by the Burgundian conquerors of the region between the Alps and the Rhone, possessed the first mediæval literature of Europe; and its improvement dates from the accession of a Count of Barcelona as King of Burgundy and Provence in A. D. 1092, and the subsequent introduction of a refined taste acquired from the Arabs of Spain. The Troubadours were the poets of the South of France, and the earliest of them were natives of Provence and wrote in their native dialect. Thenceforth the Provençal language became the language of poetry, and was universally studied and admired for several centuries; after which it suddenly ceased to be cultivated, and is now obsolete, though there are immense numbers of Provençal manuscripts in the Royal Library of Paris.

The Troubadours were usually persons of little education, who had the faculty of rhyming, which they derived from the Arabs of Spain. They possessed the happy art of fascinating their hearers by the harmony and simplicity of their verses. Their works were highly prized, and their visits were acceptable at court and castle. They roved about at will, being welcomed wherever they went. Their songs were mostly filled with complaints of the cruelty of the ladies whom they professed to admire, and with compliments to their beauty; and the flattery which these songs contained rendered them more delightful to those for whom they were intended. The songs of the Troubadours derived new inspiration from the Crusades; and the heroes of those holy wars—among whom was King Richard the Lion-hearted of England—were as proud of their fame as poets as they were of their renown as knights.

The Trouvères, or poets of the North of France, arose a century later than the Troubadours, or about the close of the twelfth century, when they originated those tales of chivalry which afforded nearly all the secular reading in the Middle Ages. Their language was formed from the Latin spoken by the Franks who conquered Northern Gaul, and differed as much from the Provençal, or language of Southern France, as the Burgundian dialect differed from the Frankish. Both dialects were called *Romance*—a name which in the course of time was applied to the class of compositions most characteristic of the first French writers. The *Romance Wallon*, spoken North of the Loire, was likewise called the *Langue d' Oui*; while the *Romance Provençal* was named the *Langue d' Oc*. The Romance Wallon, or Langue d' Oui, very much resembled the modern French language. The adventurous spirit of the Normans is clearly displayed in the Romances of the Trouvères.

An acquaintance with the poetry and romances of the Troubadours and Trouvères constituted an essential part of the education of French gentlemen and ladies during the Middle Ages. The taste for poetry was carried to such excess that every lady eminent for rank or beauty had her poet. While the gentlemen had their tournaments and trials at arms, the ladies had their *courts of love* and trials of wit. At these meetings all poets were challenged to appear and to recite their verses. Judges were appointed to decide on the merits of the competitors, and prizes were awarded to the successful poet with great parade and pomp. These courts of love were the resort of the idle of both sexes, and were presided over by a lady of the highest rank. In the progress of time they assumed more solemnity, and difficult cases of precedence and nice points of etiquette and lover's quarrels were submitted to their decision; and the most stubborn knight was not bold enough to disregard their injunctions.

St. Louis was succeeded as King of France by his eldest son PHILIP THE BOLD, who made a mournful entry into Paris, May 21, 1271, after his return from Africa, having brought with him the dead bodies of his illustrious father; his wife Isabella; his sister Isabella, Queen of Navarre; and his uncle Alfonso, Count of Poitou and Toulouse, and his wife Jeanne. The new king's character was quite a contrast to that of his father. His education had been neglected, and his character was feeble, suspicious, and destitute of any elements of greatness. The death of Alfonso and Jeanne without heirs gave all their vast possessions to the king. The Pope now received a portion of these territories—the city of Avignon and the surrounding county of Venaissin—in accordance with an agreement with Count Raymond VII. of Toulouse; and these territories remained in the possession of the Holy See until the great French Revolution of 1789.

The possessions of the French crown were likewise increased by the death of the king's brothers, Jean Tristan and Pierre, without heirs, which gave the crown the counties of Valois and Alençon. In 1274 King Henry Crassus of Navarre died; and his widow, a French princess, fled to the court of Philip the Bold for protection. The French king received her kindly, and when her daughter reached a marriageable age he married her to his son and heir, thus uniting the crowns of France and Navarre. The large county of Champagne likewise belonged to the crown of Navarre, and thus came into the possession of the son of King Philip the Bold.

In 1284 Philip the Bold made war against Aragon to sustain his uncle Count Charles of Anjou and Provence, King of Sicily. The French had incurred the bitter hostility of the Sicilians because of their cruel and tyrannical treatment of them, and the oppressed Sicilians formed a conspiracy to transfer the crown of their kingdom to King Pedro III. of Aragon, who claimed it in right of his wife Constance, the daughter of Manfred, the last of the Hohenstaufen Kings of Sicily. Pedro III. solicited the assistance of the Eastern, or Greek Emperor, Michael Palæólogus, who promised to aid him. John di Procida, a Sicilian noble, who had been grievously wronged by the French, was the leader of the conspiracy.

The secret of the plot was kept for two years by the conspirators, who comprised a great portion of the people of Sicily. Charles of Anjou was partially aware of his peril, and was making ready to meet it, when a chance occurrence precipitated hostilities. On Easter day, A. D. 1282, a French soldier in the suburbs of Palermo grossly insulted a bride in the presence of her friends. He was attacked with fury, and the cry of "Death to the French" resounded through the streets of the city, just as the church bells sounded for vespers, or evening prayers. The shout spread like lightning through Palermo's streets, and the inhabitants assailed and massacred the unsuspecting French. So great was the slaughter in Palermo that in the course of two hours but one Frenchman escaped with his life. In a few days eight thousand Frenchmen were massacred throughout Sicily, and that island became an independent kingdom under King Pedro III. of Aragon. This frightful massacre is called the *Sicilian Vespers.*

Pope Martin IV. excommunicated King Pedro III. and offered his kingdom of Aragon to Charles, the second son of the King of France. Philip the Bold invaded Aragon in the spring of 1285, to place his son on the throne of that kingeom. The Sicilian Vespers had aroused intense indignation in France, and the French king was heartily sustained by his subjects. After invading Aragon, Philip the Bold besieged and took Gerona, which had made a defense of almost three months; but the capture of the French fleet by De Lauria so disheartened Philip that he retreated back into his own kingdom. During his retreat he died at Perpignan, October 5, 1285, at the age of forty, after a reign of fifteen years. King Pedro III. of Aragon died shortly afterward, November 11, 1285, of the same malignant fever that had ended the life of Philip the Bold.

PHILIP THE FAIR succeeded his father, Philip the Bold, as King of France (A. D. 1285). His reign of twenty-nine years is one of the most important in French history. He so increased the royal power in France that it became a despotism ; the independence of the great vassals being totally destroyed, so that they were reduced to complete submission to the crown. The king persistently advanced the bourgeoisie, or middle classes, whom he protected against the nobility, but whom he also made subservient instruments in effecting his absolute rule.

In the reign of Philip the Fair feudalism in France began to give way to civil institutions. Thoughout the kingdom justice was administered in the king's name, and the Parliament of Paris became the recognized organ of the supreme central administration. The States-General, or the great legislative body of the French nation, seems to have been in this reign, in its modern constitutional form, composed of the three distinct and equal orders, the nobles, the clergy, and the *tiers état*, or third estate, consisting of the representatives of the French people. Philip the Fair likewise struck the first successful blow at the papal power which had held every state in Europe in subjection, and shattered it so thoroughly that it ceased to be formidable.

In the beginning of his reign Philip the Fair ended the war which his father had commenced with Aragon. His brother, Charles of Valois, on whom the Pope had conferred the crown of Aragon, relinquished his claims to it; and the rightful King of Aragon agreed that his brother James should restore Sicily to the house of Anjou reigning in Naples. This could not be accomplished, and Sicily remained independent of the French dynasty of Naples. This arrangement was effected by the mediation of Philip's kinsman, King Edward I. of England.

Philip the Fair took advantage of the English king's difficulties with Scotland to make an effort to seize the duchy of Guienne, or Aquitaine, under the pretext of a quarrel between some English and Norman barons at Bayonne, which led to a furious war between the merchant seamen of the two nations, unsanctioned by either government. The English obtained such advantages in 1293 that the French king interfered, summoning the King of England as Duke of Aquitaine to appear before him in January, 1294, to answer for the conduct of his subjects.

King Edward I. appeared before his French suzerain by his representative, who was his brother Edmund, Earl of Lancaster. Philip the Fair demanded that the duchy of Aquitaine, or Guienne, should be placed in his possession until the dispute could be settled; but when he had obtained possession of the chief towns of the duchy he threw off the mask, declared Edward I. contumacious because he did not appear in person, and pronounced all the English king's fiefs in France forfeited to the French crown.

King Edward instantly took the field to maintain his rights, and was aided by the Duke of Britanny, Count Guy of Flanders, and Adolf of Nassau, King of Germany. The war commenced in Gascony in 1294, and lasted two years, with the general advantage on the side of the French monarch. The English king was prevented by his war with Scotland from making a determined effort, and was likewise hampered by frequent revolts of the Welsh. Pope Boniface VIII. endeavored to bring about a peace, but failed, and aroused the enmity of the French king.

In 1297 Philip the Fair invaded Flanders with a large army and reduced that province to submission. Pope Boniface VIII. again offered his mediation, which was accepted by all parties, and a treaty of peace between England and France was signed in June, A. D. 1299. In accordance with the terms of this treaty, King Edward I. married Marguerite, the eldest sister of Philip the Fair; while Edward's son Edward, the first English Prince of Wales, was affianced to Philip's daughter Isabella, then only six years old. By this arrangement, the King of England abandoned the cause of his ally, Count Guy of Flanders; and the King of France left his allies, the Scots, to the vengeance of the English monarch.

By this peace with England, Flanders was left completely at the mercy of King Philip the Fair, and in A. D. 1300 a large French army under Charles of Valois invaded that province. Donai, Bethune and Damme surrendered without offering any resistance. Count Guy of Flanders threw himself into Ghent, where he prepared to resist the French; but when he perceived his hopeless situation he yielded to the representations of Charles of Valois, who assured him that the King of France was kindly disposed toward him. The Count of Flanders thus surrendered the city of Ghent, with himself, his two sons and his leading nobles.

The victorious Charles of Valois at once sent his prisoners to Paris, where they were treated with a harshness which might have been expected from the unscrupulous character of Philip the Fair. Count Guy and his two sons were imprisoned in the gloomy fortress of the Chatelet, and the Flemish barons were confined in the various fortresses near Paris. The French king declared the county of Flanders forfeited, and annexed it to the French crown.

A few months afterward King Philip the Fair visited Flanders with his queen, Jeanne of Navarre, and was joyfully received by the Flemings, who had never liked Count Guy. The county of Flanders was one of the richest prizes that had ever fallen to the lot of the French monarch, and Philip the Fair returned to Paris in high glee, leaving Jacques de Châtillon as his viceroy in Flanders. The new viceroy was well suited to represent the most unscrupulous of sovereigns.

The Flemings soon discovered that by accepting the King of France as their sovereign they had placed themselves in the power of a stern tyrant, who treated their political privileges with contempt. His exactions soon commenced crippling their commerce, and the insolent French viceroy trampled upon their liberties. At length a determined blow was struck for their freedom. One night in March, A. D. 1302, the tocsin sounded at midnight in Bruges, whereupon the citizens seized their arms and massacred all the French in the city, three thousand in number. The French viceroy, Jacques de Châtillon, fled to Paris.

King Philip the Fair instantly sent an army under Count Robert of Artois into Flanders to reduce the revolted burghers to submission. This splendid army was defeated by the revolted Flemings at Courtrai, July 11, 1302; so many of the French knights and higher officers being killed that their gilt spurs were collected by the bushel after the battle; while Count Robert of Artois, the French commander, and Jacques de Châtillon, the viceroy, were also among the slain.

The King of France met this disaster with characteristic resolution, and immediately went to work to repair it. He arranged a year's truce with the Flemings, and during this truce he made such preparations that at its expiration he was enabled to take the field with an army of seventy thousand well-equipped troops, while he attacked the northern coast of Flanders with a fleet of Genoese galleys, which he had taken into his pay. The Flemings were defeated by this Genoese fleet in a naval engagement, and the French king achieved a most important victory over the Flemish army eighteen days after the campaign had commenced, August 18, 1304.

The Flemings were a more resolute race than Philip the Fair had supposed. They rallied from their reverse in three weeks' time, and again confronted him with an army of sixty thousand men. Their determined patriotism won his admiration, and he offered them honorable terms of peace. By the treaty signed June 5, 1305, the French king assigned to the eldest son of the late Count Guy de Dampierre the county of Flanders in fief, and promised to respect the ancient liberties and privileges of the Flemings. The Flemings paid the French monarch a large indemnity for the expenses of the war, and placed four of their chief towns and all of French Flanders in his possession as a guaranty of the payment of the indemnity. Thus ended the first struggle of the valiant burghers of Flanders for the preservation of their liberties.

While engaged in his struggle with the Flemings, Philip the Fair was also occupied with a bitter quarrel with Pope Boniface VIII., one of the ablest of the Roman pontiffs. This fierce quarrel had commenced near the close of the thirteenth century, but it had not attained its full strength until the beginning of the fourteenth century.

Pope Boniface VIII. was a man of haughty, overbearing temper, and endeavored to recover for the Papacy the power which it had wielded under Gregory VII. and Innocent III. But King Philip the Fair had a better understanding of the spirit of the age, and knew that such an effort on the part of the reigning Pope was hopeless. The French king did not hesitate to advance the royal power at the expense of the Church. It appeared only right in the eyes of the King of France and his subjects that the clergy, who were in possession of a very considerable part of the wealth of the kingdom, should bear their proportion of the public burdens.

The war between Philip the Fair and King Edward I. of England had involved almost all the other nations of Europe, whose sovereigns sided with one or the other of the warring monarchs. The Pope endeavored to act as umpire between the French and English kings, but his proffered mediation was declined, and the war proceeded with increased violence.

This furnished Boniface VIII. the opportunity for which he had long been watching; and in 1296 he summoned both kings to appear before him to answer for their unjust exactions, and issued a bull forbidding the clergy to pay any tax or subsidy to any secular ruler without the consent of the Holy See, also forbidding any such ruler to demand or accept such payment on penalty of excommunication.

King Philip the Fair retaliated by issuing a decree closing his kingdom to all strangers, forbidding all appeals to another potentate, and prohibiting the exportation from the French kingdom, without the royal consent, of any coined or uncoined gold or silver, plate, jewels, arms, horses or military stores. The Pope was not named in the king's edict, but it was aimed at him, as the proceeding rendered it impossible for him to receive the large revenue paid him annually by the French clergy. Alarmed by the prospect of losing this revenue, the haughty pontiff receded in some degree from his position; and an apparent reconciliation was effected between Boniface VIII. and Philip the Fair, but this seeming peace was of short duration.

The Jubilee of A. D. 1300, in which Pope

Boniface VIII. saw Rome filled with pious pilgrims from every part of Christendom, caused him to form a false estimate of the moral strength of the Papacy in Europe, and so flattered his pride that he renewed all his pretensions and most indiscreetly undertook measures by which he hoped to force the King of France to submission. But the Pope had to deal with a monarch who scrupled at nothing to accomplish his ends, who did not fear the Pope's spiritual weapons, and who was very well aware that the time had passed when those instruments could be employed against the sovereign of a compact and powerful kingdom.

Philip the Fair had demanded homage from the Viscount of Narbonne and the Bishop of Mauguelonne, who held their fiefs of the Church. The Pope forbade them to obey the French king, and sent the Bishop of Pamiers to France as his legate to settle the dispute. This prelate was personally obnoxious to Philip the Fair, who suspected him of treasonable designs. The legate treated Philip with such insolence that the king arrested him and gave him into the custody of the Archbishop of Narbonne.

Thereupon the Pope issued a bull couched in language the most insulting to Philip the Fair, summoning the French bishops to meet in council at Rome and there arrange a plan for the settlement of the disorders which he professed afflicted France. The French king caused the Pope's bull to be publicly burned in Paris, and for the first time summoned the States-General, the grand council of the French nation; and that legislative body convened in April, A. D. 1302, and enthusiastically pledged the king the support of the nation in his controversy with the Pope.

Several months afterward Boniface VIII. issued the celebrated bull *Unam Sanctam*, wherein he asserted the papal claims with more than his former audacity, saying: "There are two swords, the spiritual and the temporal. * * * Both are in the power of the Church; the one, the spiritual, to be used *by* the Church, the other, the material, *for* the Church; the former that of the priests, the latter that of kings and soldiers, to be wielded at the command and by the sufferance of the priests. One sword must be under the other, the temporal under the spiritual. * * * The spiritual instituted the temporal power, and judges whether that power is well exercised. * * * If the temporal power errs it is judged by the spiritual. * * * We therefore assert, define and pronounce that it is necessary to salvation to believe that every human being is subject to the Pontiff of Rome."

The Pope excommunicated Philip the Fair, April 13, A. D. 1303. The French king retaliated by charging Boniface VIII. with a series of scandalous crimes and demanding that he should be tried by a general council of the Church.

Philip the Fair now determined to get Boniface VIII. into his power by seizing the Pope's person. It is uncertain whether the King of France intended to punish His Holiness or merely to prevent him from committing any additional acts of hostility, but it is quite clear that he meant to seize him. Boniface VIII. announced that on September 8 (A. D. 1303) he would publish a bull deposing Philip the Fair and forbidding his subjects to render him any further allegiance. Two of the French king's partisans—William de Nogaret, an eminent lawyer, whose ancestors had been persecuted by the Inquisition at Toulouse; and Sciarra Colonna, a younger son of the noble Roman family of Colonna—determined to carry out the king's wishes without delay, but it does not appear that they had any orders from the king to that effect.

The Pope was then residing in his native city, Anagni. De Nogaret and Colonna hastened to Italy, and at the head of several hundred armed men stormed the Pope's palace, compelled his defenders to surrender, and forced their way into the venerable pontiff's presence, finding His Holiness seated on his throne, crowned with the tiara, arrayed in the stole of St. Peter, and grasping the keys in his hand. The bold

COLONNA TAKES POPE BONIFACE VIII. PRISONER.

Pope did not flinch in the presence of his foes, though deserted by his friends. Nogaret overwhelmed his illustrious captive with the most furious reproaches; and Colonna is said to have struck him with his iron gauntlet, and to have been prevented from killing him only with the greatest difficulty. The captive Pope was then set on a vicious horse, with his face towards the animal's tail, and led through the town to prison.

Two days afterward the people of Anagni rose against Nogaret and Colonna and their soldiers, drove them from the town, and released the Pope, who hastened to Rome to take vengeance on his enemies. Mortification at his humiliation and his ungovernable temper, along with the infirmities of age, hastened the death of the venerable Boniface VIII., who died October 11, A. D. 1303. Some accounts tell us that he was seized with a fever which ended in frenzy and death. Other writers, perhaps more reliable, speak of him "as sadly but quietly breathing his last, surrounded by eight cardinals, having confessed the faith and received the consoling offices of the Church."

Though freed from the violence of Pope Boniface VIII., King Philip the Fair pursued the dead pontiff's memory with unrelenting hostility. He demanded that the new Pope, Benedict XI., should call a council to condemn Boniface VIII. for heresy and other crimes. Benedict XI. refused to pursue his predecessor's memory, and pronounced a sentence of excommunication against the individuals concerned in the arrest of Boniface VIII. and against all others who might have aided or encouraged their proceedings in any manner, among whom it was very clear that he included the King of France himself. Pope Benedict XI. died very suddenly a month afterward, and it was very generally believed that his death was hastened by poison administered by the French king's agents.

Philip the Fair now resolved that the next Pope should be a Frenchman, and one who would consent to be his dependent and instrument. By bribing the cardinals he obtained their promises to elect to the Papacy the person whom he nominated. He then summoned the unscrupulous Bertrand de Goth, Archbishop of Bordeaux, to his presence, and offered to make him Pope if he would swear to comply with six conditions, five of which were named to him then and there. These conditions were: To remove all the ecclesiastical censures pronounced against Philip the Fair and his supporters; to grant him a tenth of the revenues of the Church in France for five years; to condemn the memory of Boniface VIII; to restore the Colonna family to their honors; and to confirm several persons nominated by Philip the Fair as cardinals. The French king reserved the sixth and last condition to be named thereafter, but the archbishop solemnly swore to grant it when it should be demanded of him.

When the disgraceful bargain had been concluded, the King of France caused the archbishop to be elected Pope, and the new pontiff assumed the title of Clement V., June, A. D. 1305. He was crowned at Lyons, and established his residence at Avignon, on the Rhone, instead of at Rome, as we have before noticed. By this change Pope Clement V. placed himself entirely in the power of Philip the Fair, whom he soon found a most relentless master. The new Pope promptly fulfilled the five conditions which the King of France had named to him, and awaited the announcement of the sixth condition with considerable anxiety. For the next seventy-two years (A. D. 1305 –1377) the Popes continued to reside at Avignon; and, being thus within the French kingdom, they were wholly under French influence.

Since their expulsion from Palestine the Knights Templars had continued to exist as one of the wealthiest and most powerful institutions in Europe; comprising a body of fifteen thousand veteran knights, exempt from the royal jurisdiction and governed by their own peculiar laws and officers, and being established in every country of Europe. Their immense wealth, their pride and avarice, and their insolent treatment of the people made them unpopular wherever they were established. By their resistance to some of the tyrannical measures of Philip the Fair they had aroused that monarch's hostility, and he determined to destroy them as an order. He was made the more eager to proceed against them by the prospect of confiscating all their great wealth in France.

For the purpose of accomplishing the destruction of this order, which was largely ecclesiastical and under the Pope's immediate protection, it was essential to obtain the assistance of the Church. Accordingly, when Clement V. was fairly established in the Papacy, Philip the Fair named to him the sixth condition which the Pope had sworn to grant, and which was the destruction of the Knights Templars. At first the Pope shrank with horror from such a proceeding, but he was utterly helpless in the French king's hands, and was obliged to do his master's bidding.

Jacques du Molay, the Grand Master of the Knights Templars, and the other chief officers of the order, were invited into France on the pretext of taking measures with the Pope for a new crusade. Philip the Fair at first received them with distinction, but they were soon seized and imprisoned, October 13, A. D. 1307. The property of the order throughout France was seized by the officers of the crown, and all the Knights Templars in the kingdom were arrested and cast into prison. Philip the Fair accused them of idolatry, atheism, Mohammedanism and many infamous practices. They were doubtless innocent of the charges which the French king brought against them, whatever their faults were.

Many of the unfortunate Knights Templars were forced by torture to confess the crimes of which they were accused and of which they were innocent, and the confessions thus obtained were used to fix the guilt of the order. Others endured their sufferings with heroic fortitude and protested their innocence to the very last. Nevertheless, with the evidence which he had obtained, Philip the Fair procured the condemnation of the order by the States-General in May, 1308, and forced Pope Clement V. to consent to the sacrifice of the Knights Templars. Many of them were burned to death, dying with the unflinching bravery which had made their order invincible in battle. In the Council of Vienne, in March, 1312, Pope Clement V. solemnly abolished the order of Knights Templars throughout Europe, and bestowed their landed estates and all their privileges on the Knights of St. John.

Two-thirds of the movable property of the Knights Templars were conferred on the King of France as compensation for his expenses in the prosecution, and this amounted to a large sum. The last victims of the French king's tyranny and caprice were Jacques du Molay, the Grand Master of the unfortunate order, and the Preceptor of Normandy, who were kept in prison for seven years and finally burned at the stake, in Paris, in March, 1314, protesting their innocence to the very last, and dying with a courage and fortitude which caused the spectators to shed tears.

Pope Clement V. died a few weeks afterward, April 20, 1314; and King Philip the Fair himself passed to his grave November 29th of the same year. Philip the Fair was one of the most unscrupulous of the French kings, and was also one of the most successful. He succeeded in everything that he undertook. He humbled the Church by his treatment of Popes Boniface VIII. and Clement V. By crushing the Knights Templars he struck the severest blow that had yet been inflicted upon the feudal nobility. He restored the supremacy of the civil law in France, and protected the common people against the aggressions of the nobles, though he himself did not respect the rights of the masses. He may be deservedly ranked among the greatest of French kings, on account of his great abilities and the success of his measures. But, with all his talents, he was so unscrupulous, rapacious, vindictive and cruel that he won no lasting good for his kingdom, and left a character noted for its dishonesty.

Philip the Fair's three sons reigned in succession. The eldest of these, LOUIS X., became King of France upon his father's death in 1314. Louis X. was surnamed *le Hutin*, "disorder," or "tumult," from the tumultuous conduct of the French nobles. He reigned but two years, during which a violent reaction set in from all classes—the nobles, the clergy and the commons—against the despotism established by Philip the Fair. Each class recovered a part of its lost rights, and the nobles contrived to exalt their own power at the expense of the commons. Louis X. died in June, 1316, without an heir. About four months afterward his queen, Jeanne of Navarre, gave birth to a son, who died six days later, and is not generally classed among the Kings of France.

Philip, the brother of Louis X., had been appointed regent when that king died; and upon his infant nephew's death he caused himself to be crowned King of France at Rheims, January 9, A. D. 1317. Thus began the reign of PHILIP THE LONG, which lasted six years. The Duke of Burgundy claimed the French crown for his niece, the Princess Jeanne, the daughter of Louis X. by his first wife; but Philip the Long convened the States-General, which enacted a law declaring females incapable of inheriting the French crown. This measure is called the *Salic Law*, because it was based upon an obscure article in the barbarous code of the Salian Franks, which prohibited the transmission of the allodial property of the tribe to women. This measure silenced all opposition to Philip the Long and confirmed him in his usurpation. The Salic Law has ever since remained an essential part of French constitutional law. In after ages it proved of the greatest benefit to France by excluding foreign princes from the throne, and keeping the sovereignty in the possession of a dynasty of native French kings.

Philip the Long was a mild and generous sovereign, and was the author of many useful laws, one of which declared the royal domain inalienable. He died in 1322, without a son; whereupon his brother, CHARLES THE FAIR, the third and youngest son of Philip the Fair, became King of France. Taking advantage of the civil war between King Edward II. of England and his barons, Charles the Fair endeavored to seize the duchy of Guienne, or Aquitaine, and captured La Rochelle. The English king sent his wife Isabella, the sister of the French monarch, to Paris, in May, 1325, to negotiate a peace; but Isabella had no sooner arrived in France than she began plotting against her husband, and her brother aided her with men and money. She returned to England in September, 1326, and brought on the rebellion which ended in the dethronement and murder of her husband. Charles the Fair restored Guienne to Edward III., the next King of England, upon the payment of an indemnity of fifty thousand marks sterling. Charles the Fair died January 31, 1328, without a male heir. Two months afterward his queen gave birth to a princess.

The direct line of the House of Capet, which had occupied the throne of France in continuous succession for more than three centuries, was ended by the death of Charles the Fair in 1328. The popular belief was that this failure of heirs was a Divine punishment for the crimes of Philip the Fair. Upon the birth of the posthumous daughter of Charles the Fair, the French nobles conferred the crown upon Count Philip of Valois, grandson of Philip the Bold and nephew of Philip the Fair. The new king was the first cousin and the nearest male relative of Charles the Fair, and was regarded as having a lawful right to the French crown under the Salic Law. He was crowned at Rheims, May 29, 1328, and is called PHILIP VI. With him began the Valois branch of the House of Capet, which occupied the French throne for more than two and a half centuries (A. D. 1328–1589).

The new monarch was thirty-five years of age at his accession, and was endowed with many good qualities. He was brave, generous and affable, and was fond of pomp and display. He established a magnificent court, which became the habitual residence of the great French nobles and of the blind King John of Bohemia and the Kings of Navarre and Majorca, with their splendid retinues. In the midst of this magnificence, King Philip VI. was silently increasing the royal power in France until the sovereign became as strong and despotic as during the reign of Philip the Fair.

Philip VI. commenced his reign by establishing the Count and Countess of Evreux on the throne of Navarre. The countess was the daughter of King Louis X., and was only prevented by the Salic Law from inheriting the French crown upon her father's death. In return for the services of Philip VI. in placing them on the throne of Navarre, both she and her husband renounced their pretensions to the French crown.

At this time the Flemings revolted against their ruler, the Count of Flanders, and that prince solicited assistance from King Philip VI. The French monarch promptly marched to the aid of the Count of Flanders, defeated the Flemings in the battle of Cassel, and reëstablished their count's authority.

The French king now considered himself strong enough to summon King Edward III. of England to appear at his court and do feudal homage for his duchy of Guienne. The English king, being unprepared for war, considered it more prudent to obey, and accordingly did homage to Philip VI. at Amiens in 1329. But Edward III. made a secret reservation, in his council of state, not to surrender his rights as an independent sovereign, and to vindicate those rights at the proper time.

The King of England waited six years; during which the French monarch made an enemy of his brother-in-law, Count Robert of Artois, who had been one of his most devoted and useful friends. Count Robert had sought by a base imposture, and, as it was believed, by causing two of his relatives to be poisoned, to recover the county of Artois, which had been taken from him in a former reign. His fraud was detected, and he was sentenced to perpetual banishment, while his property was confiscated. He had fled from the kingdom before this sentence was pronounced, and immediately began plotting against the King of France, whom he hated for not shielding him from the consequences of his crimes. Fearing the exiled count's enmity, King Philip VI. pursued Robert from country to country, causing the various princes to refuse him the refuge which he sought. At length Robert fled to England, where he was heartily welcomed by King Edward III., the jealous and vigilant rival of the French king, A. D. 1333.

The ceaseless plotting of the exiled Count of Artois at the English court caused King Philip VI. to bring matters to a crisis. Early in A. D. 1336 he proclaimed Robert of Artois a traitor and an enemy of France, and forbade all his vassals of whatever rank, in or out of France, to receive or aid him on penalty of confiscation of their fiefs. The King of England accepted the insult as addressed to himself, regarded it as a declaration of war on the French king's part, and therefore commenced making energetic preparations for war.

The Flemings, under their celebrated leader, James Van Artevelde, the noted brewer of Ghent, now espoused the English monarch's cause; and, by Van Artevelde's advice, King Edward III. formally assumed the title of King of France in 1337, claiming the French crown because his mother was a daughter of Philip the Fair—a claim of course made invalid by the Salic Law. The Flemings instantly acknowledged the English king as their feudal lord, and in 1339 he crossed over to Flanders, from which he invaded France. The first campaign was indecisive, and the English retired into Hainault.

In the spring of 1340 King Edward III. returned to Flanders with a formidable fleet and a considerable army. In the meantime a French army had been sent into Hainault; and the French fleet, which consisted of four hundred well-manned and equipped ships, was sent into the Flemish waters to prevent the English king from landing. The French forces posted themselves near the mouth of the Scheldt at Helvoetsluys. The English fleet approached in the afternoon of June 23, 1340, and attacked the French fleet the next morning. The battle continued until late in the afternoon, and the French were overwhelmingly defeated with the loss of thirty thousand men and the capture of almost their whole fleet. The French navy was annihilated, and England's maritime supremacy was fully established. The English loss was slight in comparison with the French. King Edward III. himself was slightly wounded.

Several weeks afterwards the King of England invaded France with a large army, in which were sixty thousand Flemings under James Van Artevelde, and besieged Tournay, but he obtained no advantage. A truce was concluded, which both parties observed beyond the period named, until the middle of the summer of 1342; but a permanent peace was prevented by a new source of trouble which reopened the quarrel between the two kingdoms.

Count Charles of Blois and Count John de Montfort disputed the succession to the duchy of Brittany. The King of France sustained the claims of Charles of Blois, his nephew; while the King of England espoused the cause of John de Montfort, whom he created Earl of Richmond. In August, 1341, Charles captured the town of Nantes, which was held by John de Montfort, took his rival prisoner, and sent him to Paris. The Countess de Montfort now took up her husband's cause and defended it very ably and gallantly. She threw herself into the town of Hennebon, which she occupied, until the arrival of a large reinforcement, sent to her aid by King Edward III., forced the French to raise the siege, A. D. 1342.

King Edward III. himself came over, but nothing definite was accomplished, and a truce of three years was signed between the English and French kings, which included the allies and partisans on both sides, January 19, 1343. Neither party intended to observe the treaty, but Philip VI. first violated it. Before the end of the year he invited fifteen of the most powerful barons of Brittany to a tournament at Paris, and then treacherously arrested them on an unsustained charge of intriguing with the English. They were beheaded without trial by order of the French king, November 29, 1343; and early in 1344 three Norman barons were seized and executed in the same manner.

The royal murder of these nobles aroused a feeling of universal indignation against King Philip VI. Edward III. proclaimed that the King of France had violated the treaty, declared war against him in 1345, and invaded France in 1346 with thirty thousand infantry. He landed at Cape La Hogue, in Normandy, June 12, 1346, and marched almost to Paris, ravaging the country with fire and sword; after which he retreated into Flanders, pursued by Philip VI. with an army of one hundred thousand Frenchmen.

The King of France sought to force the English monarch to an engagement, in which he hoped that his great superiority of numbers would give him the victory. Edward III. skillfully eluded his antagonist until he had crossed the Somme and secured his retreat into Flanders; after which he took position on the edge of the forest of Creçy, about twelve miles from Abbeville, where he awaited the French king's approach. Having failed to prevent the English from passing the Somme, Philip VI. crossed that stream at Abbeville, and marched hastily toward the English king's position, before which he arrived August 26, 1346.

The French king intended to postpone the attack until the next day, but his advanced troops engaged without his orders, thus bringing on the great battle of Creçy, in which the French were decisively defeated with the loss of twelve hundred knights, eighty bannerets, thirty thousand men-at-arms, and many princes, counts and superior officers. The Counts of Alençon and Flanders, and the veteran knight-errant, the almost-blind old King John of Bohemia, were among the slain. The victorious English gave no quarter; and King Philip VI., who had fought with valor in the disastrous battle, fled from the sanguinary field and took refuge at Amiens. The English victory was owing to the bravery of King Edward's heroic son Edward, the Prince of Wales, called the *Black Prince*, from the color of his armor, who commanded the first division of his father's army; and also to the steadiness and skill of the English archers, before whose destructive showers of arrows the undisciplined French hosts were unable to stand.

After the battle of Creçy, King Edward III. laid siege to Calais, the gate to France, while his fleet blockaded the town by sea. The inhabitants had made an obstinate defense for nearly a year, when, threatened with all the horrors of famine, they were finally forced to surrender to the victorious invaders, August 4, 1347. It is said that the King of England, exasperated at the stubborn resistance of the citizens of Calais, agreed to spare the inhabitants, if six of the principal citizens were brought to him, with halters about their necks, ready for hanging; whereupon Eustace St. Pierre, a wealthy merchant of Calais, offered himself as the first victim, and five other leading citizens followed his noble example. When the six citizens appeared before Edward III., the stern monarch ordered them to execution; and their lives were only spared through the earnest entreaties of the English nobles, of King Edward's heroic son, the Black Prince, and of his noble-hearted queen, Philippa, who fell on her knees before her husband and exhorted him not to violate the laws of religion and honor by so inhuman an act. King Edward III. expelled the French inhabitants of Calais and peopled the city with English; and for two centuries that important town remained in the possession of the English.

A truce of ten months was concluded between the two kings, September 28, 1347, and Edward III. returned to England. At the end of the truce hostilities were not resumed. During the years 1348 and 1349 the Black Plague raged throughout France, carrying off hundreds of thousands; and in Paris alone fifty thousand persons fell victims to its ravages, among whom were the Queens of France and Navarre.

Philip VI. imposed a tax on salt, called the *Gabelle*, thus originating the government monopoly of salt, which afterwards became so profitable to the French treasury and so obnoxious to the French people. In 1350 Humbert II., the Dauphin of Vienne, so called from the *Dolphin*, or *Dauphin*, which he carried as his emblem, retired into a monastery. As he was childless he ceded his hereditary estates to Philip VI. for the king's grandson, Prince Charles, afterwards King Charles the Wise, for two hundred thousand florins to be paid him by Philip VI.

Philip VI. died August 22, 1350, after a reign of twenty-two years, and was succeeded as King of France by his son, JOHN THE GOOD, who was then thirty-one years old. John the Good resembled his father in character; being proud, obstinate, presumptuous, cruel, fond of pomp and luxury, display and pleasure. He was likewise brave, and could be generous when he desired to be so. He sincerely wished to be a model knight.

At the beginning of his reign King John the Good seized Raoul de Nesle, the Constable of France, and put him to death without trial; after which he conferred the office of Constable on Charles de la Cerda, to whom he also granted the county of Angoulême, which had been ceded to the French crown by Charles the Bad, then King of Navarre, on condition of obtaining other territories in exchange. John violated his agreement by refusing to give these territories, thus making the King of Navarre his bitter enemy. Charles the Bad brought many afflictions on France during the reign of John the Good. He vowed vengeance against the Constable Charles de la Cerda, and fulfilled his threats by causing the Constable to be assassinated in his bed in January, 1354.

QUEEN PHILIPPA AMONG THE POOR.

BATTLE OF POITIERS.

King John the Good instantly prepared to invade Charles the Bad's kingdom of Navarre and his county of Evreux; but, as the King of Navarre was a most formidable foe, the French monarch agreed to a reconciliation, which was arranged by their relatives. The reconciliation was a mere pretense; and the King of Navarre instigated the Dauphin Charles, the son of John the Good, to lead a party in opposition to his father. This proceeding aroused the French king to the utmost fury. Upon hearing of it he hastened to Rouen, where the Dauphin, as Duke of Normandy, held his court, and personally arrested Charles the Bad, whom he would have put to death had not the Dauphin persuaded him against so harsh an action. The King of Navarre was then sent to Paris, and imprisoned in the Chatelet, where he was treated harshly, April, 1356.

The cause of the King of Navarre was championed by his brother Philip in the summer of 1356; and with many discontented French nobles, Philip joined the English Duke of Lancaster and made war on the French king in Normandy. John the Good marched against his enemies and drove them back, after which he besieged the fortress of Breteuil, which belonged to the King of Navarre.

While engaged in the siege of Breteuil, King John the Good was informed that the English Black Prince with eight thousand troops had marched out of his duchy of Guienne and had advanced into the French monarch's territories as far as Bourges. The King of France instantly raised the siege of Breteuil, and hastened by forced marches into Poitou in order to cut off the Black Prince's communications and intercept his retreat into Guienne. John the Good threw his army of sixty thousand Frenchmen across the route of the Black Prince. The Black Prince hereupon offered to surrender the conquered territory and give up the war, if he were permitted to retreat unmolested; but this was prevented by the obstinacy of the French monarch, who insisted on terms of unconditional submission.

Seeing that he must either fight or surrender, Edward the Black Prince took up a strong position at Poitiers, where he awaited the French attack, undismayed by the vast numerical superiority of the army of King John the Good. On the morning of September 19, 1356, the French king made a gallant attack upon the English army, but was defeated most disastrously. The French were thrown into confusion by the deadly volleys of arrows from the English archers, and broke and fled before the decisive charge of the Black Prince's troops. Only one French division, that commanded by King John the Good in person, endeavored to check the English advance; but this division was beaten, and John himself was taken prisoner. The French lost twenty-five hundred nobles and knights, and from seven thousand to eight thousand common soldiers. The prisoners taken by the victorious English numbered more than three times the entire English force.

Edward the Black Prince treated the captive French king with the utmost respect and magnanimity, and generously sought to make him forget his captivity. John was taken to Bordeaux, and in the spring of 1357 he was conveyed a captive to London by the victorious Black Prince, who continued to treat the unfortunate French monarch with the utmost generosity; and during the four years of his captivity in the English capital John was treated by King Edward III. more like a guest than a prisoner, and was assigned the old palace of the Savoy for his residence. Unsuccessful efforts were made for the restoration of peace, but a truce was concluded for two years from Easter, 1357.

The Dauphin Charles, who made his escape from the battle of Poitiers, arrived at Paris ten days afterward, and assumed the government of the French kingdom as lieutenant-general. The king's capture had thrown all France into confusion, and the Dauphin summoned the States-General at once. It was manifest that the commons intended to profit by the opportunity to recover some of their lost rights. They were led by Etienne Marcel, the Mayor of Paris, and by Robert Lecoq, Bishop of Laon, both very able and patriotic men.

The Dauphin was obliged to concede the just and moderate demands of the commons, but he also obtained an order from his father to disregard all his promises as well as the acts of the States-General. This led to an insurrection of the Parisian populace, who released Charles the Bad of Navarre and urged him to assert his claim to the French crown, which would have been indisputable had he not been related to the royal family on his mother's side, thus being excluded by the Salic Law. The insurgents murdered two of the Dauphin's most trusted counselors in his presence and forced him to sanction their proceedings.

The Dauphin Charles was now a prisoner in the power of Marcel, who permitted him to retire from Paris to Compiègne, where the nobility speedily joined him. The States-General convened and sustained the Dauphin, and a powerful reaction set in in favor of the royal cause. A civil war of five months ended in the Dauphin's triumph and the defeat of the cause of popular liberty.

At this time a sanguinary insurrection of the French peasantry burst forth, in consequence of the miserable condition of serfdom in which the peasants had so long been kept by the despotic nobility. This great popular revolt is known as the *Insurrection of the Jacquerie*, from Jacques Bonhomme, the name given in derision to a French peasant. The insurgent peasants sacked the feudal castles, and put to death their inmates, without respect to age or sex. After the peasants had been repulsed in an attack upon one of the towns, they were hunted down like wild beasts, and thousands of them were brutally massacred. Many of the rural districts were almost depopulated, and presented a sad picture of ruin and desolation.

Charles the Bad of Navarre continued his war against the French kingdom for some time longer, and the Dauphin signed a treaty of peace favorable to the Navarrese king in August, 1359, for the purpose of obtaining peace. It became known at the same time that the captive King John the Good had concluded a treaty of peace with King Edward III. of England, ceding to that monarch the duchies of Aquitaine and Normandy, the viscounty of Limousin, and the counties of Poitou, Touraine and Saintonge—in all about one-half of the Kingdom of France—in absolute sovereignty.

This humiliating treaty aroused the indignation of the Dauphin, who summoned the States-General; and that body repudiated the treaty, with a patriotic declaration that the French people were willing to endure any hardships rather than agree to such a disgraceful dismemberment of the kingdom.

King Edward III. was so enraged at the rejection of the treaty by the States-General that he invaded France in October, 1359, and forced the Dauphin to consent to a treaty called the Peace of Bretigny, in May, 1360. The terms of this treaty were as humiliating to France as those of the one that had been rejected; as the duchy of Aquitaine, the viscounty of Limousin, and the counties of Poitou, Saintonge and Angoumois were ceded to the King of England in full sovereignty, or independently of all homage to the French crown. Edward III., however, renounced for himself and his son, the Prince of Wales, all claims to the crown of France and all pretensions to the duchy of Normandy and the other ancient possessions of the Plantagenets north of the Loire. King John the Good was to be set free on the payment of a ransom of three million crowns, in six annual installments. The captive king was to be released when the first half million crowns were paid, and was to place some of the chief lords of France in the English king's power as hostages for the payment of the other installments.

The Dauphin raised the requisite sum with extreme difficulty, and John the Good was restored to his freedom. He was joyfully received by his subjects, as peace at any price seemed sweet to them because of the exhausted condition of the kingdom.

The last of the ancient house of the

Dukes of Burgundy died in 1361; and, as there were no direct heirs, King John the Good claimed the duchy as the nearest male relative of the last duke, disregarding the claim of King Charles the Bad of Navarre, which was at least as good as his own, and seized the duchy of Burgundy and annexed it to the royal domain.

Count Louis of Anjou, the French king's second son, was one of the hostages delivered to Edward III. of England for the fulfillment of the Treaty of Bretigny; but the young prince broke his parole, made his escape from Calais, and hastened to Paris. John the Good was a faithful knight, and was intensely mortified by his son's breach of faith. He therefore resolved to atone for the bad faith of Louis by voluntarily returning to England and surrendering himself as a prisoner again.

Before leaving France for England, John the Good granted the duchy of Burgundy to his youngest and favorite son Philip in fief, as a reward for that prince's heroism in the battle of Poitiers, where he fought bravely at his father's side. This grant was a fatherly proceeding on the king's part, but it was also an act of short-sighted and mistaken policy. Philip the Bold, the new Duke of Burgundy, thus founded the later ducal house of Burgundy, which became a powerful rival to the royal family of France in the next century.

King John the Good returned to England in January, 1364, to voluntarily resume his captivity. King Edward III. received him with courtesy and distinction. Soon after his arrival in London, John fell a victim to a fatal illness, which ended his life April 8, 1364, at the age of forty-five.

John the Good was succeeded on the throne of France by his son CHARLES V., surnamed *le Sage*, "the Wise." Unlike his father, Charles the Wise was quiet and studious in his habits, was a well-educated man for the age in which he lived, and was cautious and prudent by nature. His physical weakness prevented him from engaging in a soldier's rough life; but he had the happy faculty of promptly recognizing and readily employing the men best adapted to execute his plans—a faculty so essential in the sovereign of a great and powerful kingdom. This quality caused him to select Bertrand du Guesclin as the chief commander of his armies, and to firmly sustain that great general, who had given evidence of his remarkable military genius at the beginning of this reign.

When Charles the Wise became King of France he annexed the province of Dauphiny to the French crown, and thereafter the French king's eldest son and heir was called the *Dauphin*, as the eldest son of the British monarch has been styled the *Prince of Wales*.

When Charles the Wise ascended the throne of France a civil war was raging in the Kingdom of Castile in Spain, between King Pedro the Cruel and his illegitimate brother, Henry of Trastamara. Henry was driven into France, where he implored the aid of the French king; and in 1365 Charles the Wise sent an army under Du Guesclin into Spain, whereupon the Castilians instantly rose in revolt against Pedro the Cruel, who was obliged to flee from Castile, and Henry of Trastamara obtained the Castilian throne without striking a blow.

Pedro the Cruel sought refuge at the court of Edward the Black Prince at Bordeaux, whom he induced to march into Spain with ten thousand troops to restore him to the throne of Castile. Pedro's army, commanded by the Black Prince, defeated Henry's force, under the command of Du Guesclin, in the battle of Navarette, April 3, 1367. Du Guesclin's force was routed with terrible slaughter, Du Guesclin himself being taken prisoner; but Henry escaped, and found refuge with Pope Urban V. at Avignon.

This Castilian war produced very important results for France. Pedro the Cruel failed to furnish the funds to pay the Black Prince's troops, who were mercenary soldiers called the *Free Companies;* and the Black Prince himself was unable to raise the money for this purpose when he returned to Bordeaux. The army dispersed in many bands, discontented and angry, and commenced perpetrating such outrages in the Black Prince's dominions that he was obliged to demand their retirement. They then entered France, and committed such excesses that the inhabitants of the suffering districts were aroused to fury against the Black Prince.

For the purpose of raising funds to pay these mercenary troops, the Black Prince imposed a heavy tax upon his subjects. The nobles remonstrated, and refused to pay the tax. In 1368 three of the most powerful of these nobles appealed to the King of France, as lord-paramount, to protect them against the exactions of the Black Prince. Charles the Wise had secretly encouraged this disaffection, and had chosen his time very well. The Black Prince was slowly dying of an incurable disease, and Edward III. was aged and feeble. The French people felt deeply humiliated by the sacrifices made by the Treaty of Bretigny, and the French provinces ceded to England desired a reunion with the Kingdom of France.

Charles the Wise first secured the services of the Free Companies, and sent them into Spain under Du Guesclin to restore Henry of Trastamara to the throne of Castile, in which he succeeded. Pedro the Cruel was defeated and taken prisoner, and slain soon afterward; whereupon Henry of Trastamara, with whom the French king had concluded an offensive and defensive alliance, was acknowledged King of Castile. The King of France now threw off the mask by repudiating the Treaty of Bretigny and summoning the Black Prince to appear before him to answer the complaints of his vassals.

War broke out at the same time in the North and South of France. The cautious policy of Charles the Wise succeeded, and the French obtained a great advantage through the failing health of the Black Prince, who became so ill that he was obliged to relinquish his command and to return to England in 1370. By the end of the year 1372 Du Guesclin, who had been made Constable of France, had recovered the entire region between the Gironde and the Loire. Brittany was overrun in 1373, and most of the fortresses in that duchy came into the French king's possession.

King Edward III. now sent a large army into France under John of Gaunt, Duke of Lancaster, who landed in that country in July, 1373. Charles the Wise adopted the Fabian policy, and his generals steadily retired before the English commander, refusing to engage in a decisive conflict. Said the French king to his commanders: "Let the storm rage; retire before it; it will soon exhaust itself."

The wisdom of the French monarch's policy was vindicated by the result. When the Duke of Lancaster arrived at Bordeaux he had lost about a third of his army by sickness, fatigue, capture or death, in the many petty attacks with which he was harassed by the French on his march; and twenty-four thousand out of his thirty thousand horses had died. The work of destruction was completed by the privations and sufferings of the winter, so that the English army was ruined without having an opportunity to fight one battle. The towns and castles of Gascony quickly deserted to the French side; and by the end of 1374 the only important places which the English held in France were Calais, Bordeaux and Bayonne. Pope Gregory XI.—who restored the papal residence to Rome in 1377—arranged a truce between France and England in June, 1375. The Black Prince died in 1376; and his father, King Edward III., passed to his grave in 1377; so that France was thus relieved of her two most inveterate foes.

Immediately after the death of King Edward III. the united fleets of France and Castile made a descent upon the coast of England, and ravaged the shores of the Isle of Wight and the neighboring counties. The English possessions in the duchy of Guienne and the duchy of Brittany were wholly conquered and annexed to the French crown; while the King of Navarre, who was detected in another effort against the King of France, was obliged to purchase peace by surrendering several of the strongest castles in his kingdom.

The annexation of Brittany to the crown of France, in 1379, greatly offended the Bretons, who were unwilling to surrender their independence. They promptly revolted against King Charles the Wise and recalled their exiled duke, who landed at St. Malo in August, 1379, and was welcomed with enthusiasm. All the Breton generals in the French service resigned their commands and joined their countrymen. Even the noble-hearted Du Guesclin, who was devotedly attached to King Charles the Wise, resigned his office and retired from court. The king implored the Constable to resume his post, and Du Guesclin consented, but firmly declined to fight his own countrymen. Charles the Wise obstinately persisted in his designs against Brittany, thus hopelessly alienating the Bretons from the French crown.

The misgovernment of the Duke of Anjou now produced troubles in Languedoc. The English took advantage of the circumstance to seize several towns and castles along the frontier of Languedoc, and the French king sent Du Guesclin to drive out the invaders. Du Guesclin fell a victim to illness, dying while engaged in the siege of Châteauneuf de Randau; and the governor of that fortress, who had sworn not to surrender to any but Du Guesclin himself, brought the keys of the fortress to the Constable's tent and quietly laid them on the dead hero's breast. All France mourned for Du Guesclin. King Charles the Wise deeply lamented his death, and caused his remains to be conveyed to Paris and buried with almost royal honors in the Abbey of St. Denis, among the Kings of France.

Charles the Wise died two months after his general, September 16, 1380. He was one of the best of French kings. Though he ruled despotically, he sincerely desired and constantly sought the welfare of his subjects; and his success in recovering the provinces held by the English in France was alone sufficient to rank him as one of the most renowned Kings of France. His kingdom was indebted to him for many wise and useful laws. As he was himself a learned man, he liberally patronized learning. He founded the Royal Library of Paris, and liberally encouraged the arts, particularly architecture. He built the vast and celebrated Hotel de St. Pol, at Paris, which became his favorite residence. He also began the famous fortress of the Bastile.

During this period flourished the eminent French historian Jean Froissart, who was born in 1337. He was patronized by Philippa of Hainault, the queen of Edward III. of England, who always welcomed the gay poet and narrator of chivalric deeds. In 1366 Froissart accompanied Edward the Black Prince to Bordeaux. On the death of his protectress, Froissart renounced his connection with England; and, after different adventures as a diplomat and a soldier, he became domestic chaplain to the Duke of Brabant, who was a poet like Froissart, and of whose verses, with some of his own, he formed a kind of romance called *Meliador*. He again visited England in 1395, and was introduced to King Richard II., but when that monarch was dethroned he returned to Flanders, where he died in 1401. Froissart's historical writings strikingly illustrate the character and manners of his age, and are greatly prized for their graphic simplicity and minute details. They comprise a period of almost eighty years, ending in A. D. 1400.

Charles the Wise was succeeded on the French throne by his son, CHARLES VI., surnamed *the Well Beloved*, who was not yet twelve years of age. The boy king's four uncles instantly commenced quarreling about the regency, and at length agreed to a compromise. The Duke of Anjou was proclaimed regent during the young king's minority; the custody of the king's person was assigned to the Dukes of Burgundy and Bourbon; and the Duke of Berry was made governor of Languedoc and Aquitaine. In accordance with the command of Charles the Wise on his death-bed, Oliver de Clisson, the trusted lieutenant of Du Guesclin, was made Constable of France.

The Duke of Anjou was a man of notorious avarice; and the unjust and oppressive taxes which he imposed upon the French people occasioned a formidable popular insurrection in Paris and violent commotions throughout the French kingdom, and order was restored with great difficulty. After quiet was restored, the young king returned to Paris, accompanied by his uncles, May, 1382. Immediately afterwards the Duke of Anjou, who had been adopted by his cousin Joanna, Queen of Naples, as her heir, started for that kingdom, where he died in 1384. The regency in France then devolved on Philip the Bold, Duke of Burgundy, the ablest of the young king's uncles.

The Flemings having revolted against their ruler, Count Louis of Flanders, a French army was sent to subdue them. In the battle of Rosebecque, in which the King of France himself was present, the Flemish leader, Philip Van Artevelde, and twenty-five thousand of his followers, were defeated and slain by the French commanded by Oliver de Clisson, the Constable of France, November, 1382.

The great victory at Rosebecque strengthened the royal power in France. All the French towns which had resisted the tyrannical exactions of the monarch were obliged to yield, and all their citizens who had taken a conspicuous part in the popular movement were mercilessly put to death, three thousand being led to the scaffold in Paris alone (A. D. 1382.)

All the unpopular taxes were reimposed, and the king levied a fine of nine hundred and sixty thousand francs upon the citizens of Paris, after which he graciously pardoned them for their share in the disturbances. Among the other cities of Northern France which were punished in the same manner as Paris were Rheims, Troyes, Châlons, Orleans and others. This subversion of the rights and liberties of the French people was the direct cause of the civil wars which distracted France in the latter part of this king's reign.

Count Louis of Flanders died in January, 1384, leaving no male heir. Duke Philip the Bold of Burgundy, who had married the only daughter of Count Louis, came into possesion of his dominions, consisting of the counties of Flanders, Artois, Rethel and Nevers, and other territories in Champagne. The Burgundian duke also soon obtained the duchy of Brabant, thus becoming one of the most powerful sovereigns in Europe. He soon settled the troubles which had for a long time existed between the Counts of Flanders and the people of Ghent, and peaceably extended his authority over the entire province. By marrying his eldest son to the daughter of Duke Albert of Bavaria, Philip the Bold had connected himself with one of the most powerful families of Germany; and in 1385 he brought about the marriage of his nephew, King Charles VI. of France, with Isabella, the daughter of Duke Stephen of Bavaria —a union destined to be the source of great trouble to France.

In 1386 the French collected a formidable army and a large fleet to invade England, but losses by tempests and the quarrels of the French commanders caused the failure of the expedition, and the remnant of the fleet that had escaped the storms was captured or destroyed by the English fleet in the harbor of Sluys. An effort to renew the expedition in 1387 likewise failed, on account of the enmity of the Duke of Brittany toward the Constable Oliver de Clisson.

In 1388, when Charles the Well Beloved was twenty-one years old, he was induced by the entreaties of his subjects and the advice of the Cardinal-Bishop of Laon to end the regency by assuming control of the government himself. The young king accordingly relieved his uncles, the Dukes of Burgundy and Berry, of their duties; and these powerful dukes left the court, not daring to resist the king's action. The Cardinal-Bishop of Laon, who had advised the king to dismiss them, was found dead on the day of their departure, with evidences of having been poisoned.

Charles the Well Beloved had no taste for the duties of royalty, and left the government to his ministers, of whom the most influential was the Constable, Oliver de Clisson. These ministers concluded a three years' truce with England, and introduced many useful reforms into the government, so that these three years were comparatively tranquil.

The king's uncles now sought to destroy De Clisson, whom they bitterly hated. One night in June, 1392, the Constable was attacked and left for dead in the street by a band of bravos led by a nobleman named De Craon, whom the king's uncles had instigated to the deed. De Craon fled to the Duke of Brittany. Enraged by this attack upon one of the highest officers of state, the young king took an oath to signally avenge it. He demanded the surrender of De Craon, but the Duke of Brittany replied that he knew nothing of De Craon or his offense. Thereupon the king took the field against the Breton duke to punish him for his falsehood and for his complicity in the attempted murder.

On his march against the Duke of Brittany, Charles the Well Beloved was seized with a dangerous illness, which produced insanity. He partially recovered his reason soon afterward, but from this time he was never capable of sustained effort or close application; and during the rest of his life he was a hopeless imbecile, with frequent fits of violent mania, and with rare lucid rational intervals. As the king was incapable of administering the government, the Duke of Burgundy was made regent, and one of his first acts was to deprive De Clisson of the office of Constable and to drive him into exile. During one of the king's lucid intervals a definite treaty of peace was concluded with England; and the Princess Isabella, a child six years of age, was married to King Richard II. of England, A. D. 1396.

From 1400 to 1407 the Dukes of Orleans and Burgundy quarreled about the regency. Duke Philip the Bold of Burgundy died in April, 1404; but his son and successor, John the Fearless, continued all his father's pretensions, and intensified the quarrel with the Duke of Orleans, whom he caused to be assassinated November 23, 1407, thus making himself the real master of the French kingdom.

In 1410 a league was organized by the murdered duke's sons, the young Duke Charles of Orleans and his brother, with the Dukes of Berry, Bourbon and Brittany, and Count Bernard d' Armagnac and the Constable d' Albret, for the overthrow of Duke John the Fearless of Burgundy. The leader of this league was the Count d' Armagnac, whose daughter was married to the young Duke of Orleans; and thenceforth the partisans of the house of Orleans were known as *Armagnacs*.

Bernard d' Armagnac collected a large army in the South and West of France, and ravaged the country as far as the very gates of Paris. In 1411 the Armagnacs obtained possession of Paris, but were driven out by Duke John the Fearless of Burgundy and compelled to retreat to Orleans. The Duke of Burgundy then caused many of the adherents of the Armagnacs in Paris to be put to death, and the streets of the capital were deluged with the blood of the defeated party.

The Armagnacs were now in a desperate situation, as they were outlawed by the king and pursued with brutal fury by the triumphant Duke of Burgundy. Their only alternative was to solicit the aid of England, and accordingly in 1412 they entered into a treaty with King Henry V. of England, agreeing to aid him to recover the former possessions of the Kings of England in the South of France. The young English king agreed to assist the Armagnacs with a force of four thousand select English troops. The discovery of these negotiations by the imbecile French king led to a civil war in France, which resulted in driving Duke John the Fearless of Burgundy from power, and he was forbidden to come to Paris without the king's permission, thus making the Armagnacs complete masters of the government. As the king was an imbecile, his son, the Dauphin Charles, was the real ruler of the French kingdom. The civil war ended in 1414 and reduced France to a very low condition.

Profiting by the weakness of France, King Henry V. of England claimed the French crown, and demanded the French king's daughter Catharine in marriage and the restitution of Normandy and of all the provinces ceded by England to France by the Treaty of Bretigny, threatening war in case of refusal. In consequence of the weak condition of France, the Dauphin did not resent the insult offered by the King of England; but offered him his sister Catharine in marriage, with a large dowry in money, and the duchy of Aquitaine and the viscounty of Limousin. The young English king instantly rejected the Dauphin's offer and invaded France, landing at the mouth of the Seine with an army of thirty thousand men, August 14, 1415, and laying siege to Harfleur, which surrendered to him a month afterward.

As the English army was greatly weakened by disease, King Henry V. determined to defer active operations until the next year, and marched northward toward Calais, where he intended to go into winter quarters. His army had now been reduced to eleven thousand men, and on his march to Calais he was attacked at Agincourt by an army of a hundred thousand Frenchmen under the Constable d'Albret, who endeavored to intercept his retreat, October 25, 1415. After a battle of three hours, the French were as signally defeated by the English at Agincourt as they had been at Crecy and Poitiers, through the heavy volleys of the English archers. Ten thousand Frenchmen were killed, of whom there were eight thousand knights, over a hundred noblemen and seven princes of the blood royal. Among the slain were the Constable d'Albret and the Dukes of Alençon and Brabant. Fourteen thousand were taken prisoners, among whom were the Dukes of Orleans and Bourbon. After the battle of Agincourt, the English king retired to Calais, as the weakened condition of his army prevented him from following up his victory.

The Count d'Armagnac was now made Constable of France. The Dauphin died in December, 1415, and was succeeded by his brother John, Duke of Touraine, who died a little more than a year afterward, believed to have been poisoned by the Constable. The French king's third son, Charles, a boy of fourteen, now became Dauphin. He was fully devoted to the Armagnacs, among whom he had been educated, and was wholly under the influence of the Constable d'Armagnac, who undertook to remove the queen from power by inducing the Dauphin to punish her for her scandalous life. Her paramour was seized, tortured, and drowned in the Seine; while the queen herself was sent into an honorable but strict captivity in the castle of Tours.

Thenceforth Queen Isabella entertained the most furious and vindictive hatred toward her son. Duke John the Fearless of Burgundy had maintained a sullen neutrality throughout the war with the English, and he and Queen Isabella had hitherto been declared enemies. Their hatred of the Armagnacs was now their bond of sympathy and union. Before the queen had been long in confinement she contrived to open negotiations with the Duke of Burgundy, who marched to Tours with a military force and released her.

Queen Isabella declared herself regent of France, and the civil war was renewed with increased fury. The English took advantage of the distracted state of the kingdom, and captured Caen, Bayeux and some other towns in Normandy. In May, 1418, the Burgundians entered Paris, being admitted by a citizen who had become angry with the Constable d'Armagnac. Thereupon a frightful massacre of the Orleanist faction followed; the Constable, several bishops and many nobles being cruelly put to death. The streets of Paris were a general scene of massacre for three days; a band of Parisian assassins called *Cabochiens*, under the leadership of a butcher named Capeluche, taking up the work of the triumphant Burgundian faction.

One of the Orleanist leaders secured the

Dauphin's escape to Mehm at the beginning of the massacre. Several weeks afterward the queen-regent and Duke John the Fearless of Burgundy entered Paris and were welcomed with joy. The Cabochiens resumed their bloody work, and were restrained with difficulty by the Duke of Burgundy, who was obliged to hang their leader, Capeluche.

Early in 1419 King Henry V. of England took Rouen and conquered all of Normandy. Both the Burgundian and Orleanist factions endeavored to open negotiations with the invader; but he haughtily refused to treat with either, and marched to Pontoise, whence he menaced Paris. The threatened English conquest of all France now caused the factions which distracted the kingdom with civil war to become reconciled for a short time.

Tauneguy Duchâtel, the Orleanist, or Armagnac leader who had effected the Dauphin's escape from Paris, resolved to put an end to the life of Duke John the Fearless of Burgundy, knowing that his professions could not be relied upon. Accordingly, while the Burgundian duke was engaged in a conference with the Dauphin on the bridge of Montereau he was attacked and assassinated by Tauneguy Duchâtel and other Armagnac leaders, September 10, 1419.

The assassination of John the Fearless produced the most serious results. Philip the Good, the murdered duke's son and successor, at once entered into an alliance with the English, sinking all patriotic considerations in his desire to avenge the murder of his father. The queen-regent, who desired to punish her son the Dauphin, supported the new Duke of Burgundy. The Parisians, who were devotedly attached to the Burgundian duke, also espoused the English cause.

The queen-regent's party at once opened negotiations with the English; and in April, 1420, the insane King Charles VI., at the dictation of his queen and Duke Philip the Good of Burgundy, signed the Treaty of Troyes—by far the most humiliating treaty ever subscribed by a French sovereign. It was agreed that Henry V. of England should marry the Princess Catharine, the French king's daughter; that he should be declared regent of the French kingdom and heir to the French crown at the death of the imbecile Charles VI.; that the crowns of France and England should thereafter be permanently united under one sovereign; and both the contracting parties bound themselves to enter into no engagement whatever with the French king's son Charles, "calling himself the Dauphin of Vienne," except by the mutual and unanimous consent of all parties to the treaty.

Thus the demented Charles VI. was forced to betray his country and repudiate his own son. The civil war in France between the Burgundian and Orleanist factions had reduced French courage and patriotism to so low a state that this treaty —the most humiliating transaction in French history—was joyfully received throughout Northern France. After the terms of the treaty had been settled, Henry V. and the Princess Catharine were married with great pomp at Troyes, June 2, 1420.

In the meantime the Dauphin Charles and his partisans had retired south of the Loire, where the people were favorable to the Dauphin, who was the last champion of French national independence against foreign dominion, notwithstanding his despicable character and his lack of military skill.

King Henry V. of England died August 31, 1422. His son and heir was but nine months old. The insane King Charles VI. died at Paris less than two months later, October 21, 1422. The infant son of Henry V. was crowned at Paris as Henry VI., King of England and France. At the same time the Dauphin, the son of Charles VI., was proclaimed King of France at Melun with the title of Charles VII. John, Duke of Bedford, the uncle of the infant King Henry VI., became the English regent of France. His main support was his alliance with Duke Philip the Good of Burgundy. The French national party repeatedly sought to detach the Burgundian duke from his alliance with the English, but without avail, and in 1423 that alliance was strengthened by the marriage of the Duke of Bedford with one of the sisters of the Duke of Burgundy.

When the Dauphin became the rightful King of France by the death of his father Charles VI., in 1422, he was so poor that a shoemaker refused to give him credit for a pair of shoes. When the infant Henry VI. was peaceably crowned at Paris most of the great cities of France sent deputies to swear allegiance to the English, and the wise administration of the Duke of Bedford appeared to have reconciled the French to an English government. Charles VII. himself seemed to have lost all hope, as he abandoned himself to indolence and dissipation, neglecting public affairs. His friends vainly sought to inspire him with better thoughts; and one of them, when asked his opinion of some festival which occupied the young king's attention, replied: "Sire, I do not believe it possible for any one to lose a kingdom with greater gayety."

Charles VII. caused himself to be crowned King of France at Poitiers, and established his government at Bourges, wherefore the English contemptuously styled him "King of Bourges." But his party was by no means contemptible; as he was sustained by almost all of France south of the Loire, by the Duke of Anjou and by the Counts of Alençon and Clermont. He also had the aid of a large body of troops furnished by the Duke of Milan and by the King of Scotland. The Scots in his service were commanded by the Earl of Douglas, whom Charles VII. created Duke of Touraine. The Scotch Earl of Buchan was made Constable of France, but soon became a prisoner to his enemies. In 1423 and 1424 Charles VII. was unable to obtain any advantage, and was beaten by the Duke of Bedford in two pitched battles.

A peculiar circumstance now prevented the English and the Burgundians from acting together in perfect accord and with the vigor essential to follow up their successes. This was the distasteful marriage contracted by Jacqueline, Countess of Hainault and Holland, with the Duke of Brabant, the cousin of Duke Philip the Good of Burgundy, who was his nearest relative and heir. Unable to endure her husband, the countess fled from Hainault in 1421, obtained from the deposed Pope Benedict XIII. (Pedro de Luna) a decree of divorce, and soon afterward married Humphrey, Duke of Gloucester, a younger brother of the Duke of Bedford. This marriage menaced the Burgundian duke's right of succession to Jacqueline's territories. Duke Philip the Good therefore interfered, encouraged the Duke of Brabant to resist, challenged the Duke of Gloucester to mortal combat, and captured Jacqueline and held her in captivity at Ghent until the case could be decided by the legitimate Pope, Martin V.

Thus a breach was opened between the English and the Burgundians, and the Duke of Bedford lost faith in the Duke of Burgundy, whose defection from the English cause he only considered a question of time. The breach was still further widened by the decision of Pope Martin V., who divorced Jacqueline and Humphrey. Jacqueline escaped from the custody of Duke Philip the Good of Burgundy, and a bitter struggle followed between her and the Burgundian duke, in which the countess was defeated. Humphrey submitted to the Pope's decision and returned to England, while Jacqueline was forced to recognize the Duke of Burgundy as the heir to her dominions and to promise not to marry again without his consent.

These transactions produced a suspension of hostilities for several years between the French and the English. But King Charles VII. did not take advantage of this respite; and the jealousies and plots of his adherents, along with the weakness of his own character, rendered his position more critical and embarrassing with the progress of time.

Finally the Duke of Bedford resolved to try a decisive campaign; and in October, 1428, he laid siege to Orleans, whose capture would open the entire region south of the Loire to the English. Orleans was defended by Dunois, one of the bravest of the French knights. Both sides were very well aware that if Orleans would be captured the fate of France would be decided. The English besieging force was commanded by the Earl of Salisbury.

Unable to relieve Orleans, Charles VII. was preparing to yield to his unhappy fate and to retire into Dauphiny; but was diverted from this disgraceful course by the exhortations of his mistress, the famous Agnes Sorel, whose many virtues somewhat atoned for her only crime.

The English met with a great loss in the death of their commander, the Earl of Salisbury, who was killed by a cannon-shot while directing the siege; but this loss was atoned for early in 1429 by the total defeat of the French army in a sally while trying to intercept a convoy of herrings that were being conveyed to the English camp, wherefore this action was called the *Battle of the Herrings.*

After this French repulse the Count of Clermont retired from Orleans with two thousand of the garrison, thus leaving the people of the beleaguered city alone to defend themselves against the English. Reduced to great extremities, and without any hope of succor, they offered to surrender the city to the Duke of Burgundy to be held in trust for their duke, who had been in captivity in England since the battle of Agincourt. The Duke of Burgundy agreed to the proposal; but the Duke of Bedford, whose distrust of the Duke of Burgundy had steadily increased, rejected the proposal; whereupon Duke Philip the Good retired to Flanders in anger, and ordered all his vassals to withdraw from the English army.

When Orleans, the last stronghold of the French, was thus on the point of surrender, the beleaguered city was relieved, and the deliverance of Charles VII. effected, by one of the most extraordinary circumstances recorded in history.

Joan of Arc, or Jeanne d' Arc, a poor peasant girl of Domremy, in Lorraine, about seventeen years of age, had been told by a prophecy that France could only be delivered from its English invaders by a virgin; and her mind became impressed with the belief that she herself was divinely commissioned to effect this great object.

Jeanne d' Arc was born January 6, 1412, in the village of Domremy, on the river Meuse, on the borders of Lorraine and Champagne. Her father was a poor peasant, having only a few sheep and cattle. He had three sons and two daughters. Jeanne never learned to read or write. She usually made two crosses at the top of the letters which she dictated. She was taught to sew and spin, to repeat the Pater Noster and the Credo. All accounts say that she was simple, chaste, modest, patient, charitable and pious. Said one: "I would that God had given me as good a daughter as she was." An English commissioner said that he could not learn anything about her that he would not have wished to find in his own sister.

Jeanne worked in the field with her father, plowing, weeding, harvesting, and she also watched the sheep. She spun and assisted in the household work, and when she had no work to do she was found kneeling in the village church. While in the fields, whenever the church-bell rang, she knelt and prayed. She reproached the bell-ringer for not being always prompt, and promised him money if he would be more exact. A girl named Hauviette, her companion from childhood, thus testified concerning Jeanne: "Many's the time I have been at her father's; she was a good girl, simple and gentle." A laborer testified that she used to tend the sick and give to the poor. Said he: "I know it well; I was a child then, and she tended me."

She nourished her soul by prayer and the contemplation of nature. From her father's door she could see the borders of the great oak forest of the Vosges. Her favorite resort was a beautiful beech-tree that was visited by the country people, who danced under its shade, celebrated as the haunt of fairies. At her trial she asserted that her godmother told her that she saw fairies under that tree, but that she herself never did.

Jeanne's visions came to her in midday in

her father's garden, or on the blossoming heath; and these visions appeared to her as angels and saints, surrounded by an aureole of light. We have nothing but her account of these supernatural appearances, which were seen only by herself. She never varied from her statements, from first to last. Her faith in these visions was her support amid her trials, and the strength by which she overcame obstacles. She first beheld these visions when she was twelve years of age. One summer day she saw an extraordinary light while she was working in her father's garden, and a voice told her to "be good and trust in God." At her trial she said that she was frightened, and that from that moment she consecrated herself as a virgin to God.

A vision again appeared to her while she was keeping sheep alone in the meadows, and then she saw the figure of an archangel with wings and a very noble air, with other angels. She saw these figures "with her bodily eyes." She said that St. Michael told her that she was to save France, and that she must go to the aid of King Charles VII. Jeanne wept, and told the archangel that she could not mount a horse or command an army. The archangel told her to go to Vaucouleurs and find the captain there, who would send her to the king.

This vision was in 1425, when she was only thirteen years old, and was the vision in which her mission was first revealed to her. She did not, however, at first believe that it was St. Michael. The vision was repeated three times, and the archangel spoke of "the pity that there was for the Kingdom of France." She afterwards saw two female saints—St. Marguerite and St. Catharine—who constantly talked to her. She called them her "Voices," and had the most profound respect for them. She kissed the earth where they had stood, and wept when they had gone because they had not taken her with them. Her Voices spoke to her twice or thrice a week, telling her that she must go and deliver France from the English invaders. Her soul struggled between her dread greatness of the task and its responsibility, and her conscientious sense of the duty to submit to this high call.

As Jeanne grew up, the beautiful female saints continued their visits to her more frequently, floating in an atmosphere of light, their heads adorned with crowns, their voices gentle and sweet. She declared that she had three counselors; one of whom remained near her, a second came and went, and the third advised with them. The conviction became gradually fixed in her mind that she was the person mentioned in an old prophecy of Merlin, current in the country, which declared "that a woman should one day destroy France, and a virgin from the Marches of Lorraine should restore it." With this conviction came this pure soul's resolution to consecrate her life to the work.

And now Jeanne had to encounter difficulties. Her father had suspected her condition of mind, and was troubled by it. He swore that he would rather see her drowned than go with the army. He was unable to understand her state of mind, and the prophetess was without honor in her father's house. Her hardest trial was to choose whether she would disobey her parents or the angels. Her parents endeavored to keep her at home by a trick. A young man cited her before the court of the Bishop of Toul, alleging that she had promised to marry him; but she went to Toul and easily convinced the officials that there was no truth in the assertion.

As she was resolved to go to Vaucouleurs, she obtained permission to visit an uncle and remain with him several days. This uncle's name was Durand Laxart, and he resided at the village of Petit Bury. He was her first convert, and at her request he proceeded to ask Captain Baudricourt to send her to King Charles VII.; but the captain considered it all nonsense, and told the old man that he had been deceived by his niece and that he had better go home and give her a good slapping. The old man's faith in his niece's mission was shaken by the captain's view of the matter, and he went back and informed Jeanne of it, but she induced him to take her to see Captain Baudricourt at

Vaucouleurs. Jeanne's only arguments were her own strong conviction and her evident piety; but these finally broke down the coarse-minded captain's resistance, and he ended by sending her with an escort of seven men to King Charles VII. at Chinon, with a pass from Duke Charles of Lorraine.

Thus Jeanne d' Arc departed on her mission in February, 1429, when she was only seventeen years of age. She had to cross France through a country overrun by bands of both French and English soldiers, where there was neither road nor bridge, without female attendants. This was a perilous journey of about two hundred and fifty miles; but this pure-minded girl, full of faith, feared no danger and encountered none. She adopted a soldier's attire for protection, and did not lay it aside until she was taken prisoner.

She probably felt justified in this by having heard in the Golden Legend that her patroness, St. Marguerite, had assumed a soldier's dress in an emergency. But her best protection was the purity of her soul. There was an atmosphere of awe and religion around her. She was given the soldier's garb by the inhabitants of Vaucouleurs. Captain Baudricourt gave her a sword. Her uncle Laxart and another villager bought her a horse for sixteen francs. The people of Vaucouleurs followed her out of the town with good wishes, so much had their hearts been touched by her piety and sweetness.

A knight and a squire took charge of her escort, and one of her brothers was in the party. They had many doubts and suspicions, and some of her guard were at one time half inclined to throw her into a quarry as a sorceress; but she was calm and serene, and constantly assured them that they should safely reach the Dauphin. She desired to stop at every village to hear mass, however great might be their peril, and gradually impressed them with the same serene confidence. Said she: "Fear nothing; God clears the way for me. For this was I born." It appeared almost a miracle when they found themselves at the end of their journey eleven days after it had begun.

She now considered how she would persuade King Charles VII. to trust himself, his cause and his armies to the guidance of a poor peasant girl. Her faith solved this question also. While the king was hesitating whether he would even admit her to an audience, she decided the question by the impression which she made on all who approached her, as she did at Vaucouleurs. Her confident words, her fervent and constant prayers, her frequent communions, her fastings, her holiness of life, her sweetness, her simplicity, her modesty, her good sense, created a movement in the public mind which few were able to resist.

After deliberating three days, King Charles VII. consented to see her. Perhaps he would have refused if his affairs had not been so desperate, but even this ray of hope appeared sufficient to cling to in his despairing condition. Besides, in overcoming the first and smaller difficulties, Jeanne constantly acquired additional force by which to overcome future and greater ones. The mere fact that she had been able to come to the king through such perils encouraged him to believe in her. Her hopeful and confident promises of relieving Orleans, which she uttered on her journey, had been reported to the besieged in that city; and Dunois, the commander of the garrison, sent to King Charles VII. to inquire as to the meaning of these rumors. An influence thus appeared to flow out from her own deep faith, to create a prestige, an enthusiasm in other minds.

For the purpose of proving the maiden's power, King Charles VII., upon admitting her to an audience, mingled with his courtiers; but Jeanne went to him directly, and was not embarrassed, though he denied that he was the king. Said she: "Gentle Dauphin, my name is Jeanne la Pucelle. I come from the King of Heaven to tell you that you are the lawful heir of France, son of the king, and that I am to deliver Orleans, and then take you to Rheims to be crowned King of France"

It is also said that she revealed to the king what was known only to himself, herself and God—that recently in his oratory he had silently prayed that if he were the true heir to the French crown he might recover his kingdom, but if he were not the true heir that he might at least escape to Spain or Scotland.

At this time, March, 1429, Jeanne was over seventeen years old. She was beautiful, of a fine figure, tall, and had a sweet and penetrating voice. Many were in favor of confiding in her at once. Among these were the Duke d' Alençon and the nobles from Lorraine. But old and more cautious statesmen desired more evidence. So it was decided to send her to Poitiers, where were the Parliament and a university, and to consult the doctors and the theologians, as well as the wisest of the civilians assembled there.

Here she encountered a new trial. The spirit was now to be examined and judged by the letter. Jeanne perceived that the struggle would be hard, but she knew that she should surmount it. Said she: "I know well that I shall have hard work to do at Poitiers, but my Master will aid me. Let us go, then, in God's name."

It is very interesting to see how she evaded the difficulties, overcame the objections, and quietly set aside the learned cavils of the doctors by the simplicity and directness of her replies. They first asked her what signs she could show them to prove her mission. She answered: "I have not come to Poitiers to show a sign. Give me some men-at-arms and lead me to Orleans, and I will show you signs. The sign I am to give is to raise the siege of Orleans." One of the doctors responded thus: "But if God wished to deliver the city he could do it without soldiers." Jeanne replied: "The soldiers will fight, and God will give them the victory." Brother Seguin of Limousin asked her, in his provincial dialect, in what idiom her angels spoke. She answered: "In a better idiom than yours." Said he, somewhat angrily: "Do you believe in God?" Jeanne replied: "I have more faith in God than you have." The sharp man was thus silenced.

Still the doctors proceeded with their examinations, asking repeated questions and suggesting many learned difficulties. Said Jeanne: "Why do you ask me all these things? I do not know even my A, B, C; but I have come, by God's command, to raise the siege of Orleans and crown the king."

Having nothing more to say, the doctors finally decided in the maiden's favor, to which they were somewhat influenced by the great reverence which she inspired among the people of Poitiers by her holiness and piety, as she had before done at Chinon and Vaucouleurs. Jacques Gelu, Archbishop of Embrun, also took the same view in a treatise which he composed in reply to questions asked him. The devil was not believed to have any power over a virgin. Therefore, as her power could not be from below, the logical inference was that it was from above.

King Charles VII. then assigned Jeanne a command. A brave and wise counselor of the king was to attend her as esquire. She had two pages, two heralds, a chaplain, valets and guards. In a letter to his mother, Guy de Laval thus referred to the maiden: "It was beautiful to see her, in white armor, sitting on a black horse, with a small ax in her hand."

The Voices told her to send for an old sword, marked with five crosses, which was behind the altar in the chapel of St. Catharine de Fierbois. The armorer went; and such a sword was found among a heap of old weapons which had formerly been given to the chapel, and which lay near the altar. But what Jeanne loved most was her standard; on one side of which was a likeness of the Savior, seated on the clouds of Heaven, with angels adoring Him; while on the other side was written *Jhesus Maria*. Jeanne always carried this standard in the midst of battle, seldom using her sword; as she said that she did not wish to kill any one, and that she loved her standard forty times more than her sword.

The soldiers of whom Jeanne now assumed command were almost as savage as wild beasts, but she soon tamed them. She sent all bad women out of the camp. She made the troops and their officers confess and cease swearing. La Hire, who had feared neither God nor man, no longer ventured to utter an oath. Observing his embarrassment for want of his accustomed expletives, Jeanne permitted him sometimes to swear by his staff. Says Michelet: "The devils had been changed into little saints."

As the troops marched along the banks of the Loire from Blois to Orleans, in beautiful spring weather, Jeanne had an altar erected in the open air, where they all communed. They had been made young again by a generous ardor, which had broken through the crust of evil habit and sin, and which allowed some ray of love to warm their hearts. At night she lay down in her armor. She had no fear. She desired to go up on the side of the river where the English had built their castles or forts around Orleans. Seized with a peculiar awe, the English allowed her to enter Orleans, April 29, 1429; and in eight days she drove the English from the city, which they had been besieging for eight months.

Few events in military history surpass the valor and skill with which Jeanne d' Arc planned and executed the attacks on the English forts, or the ardor which the French troops, inspired by her, manifested in their repeated assaults. The English, in-inflamed by rage, cursed her and insulted her, but always fled before her. She wept upon beholding the dead bodies of the enemy, slain without confession. When Talbot, the English commander, threatened to have her burned to death, she exclaimed: "Come out; and if you can take me in single combat you *may* burn me."

Dunois testified: "Before she came to Orleans eight hundred or one thousand of my soldiers could not resist two hundred English. After she came, four hundred or five hundred of mine could conquer any number of English soldiers. I think she was sent by God, and her skill in war was more divine than human. I saw it in many things—in this among the rest. May 27, early, we attacked the Boulevard of the Bridge. Jeanne was wounded by an arrow, which entered half a foot, between her neck and shoulder. She went on fighting as before. The battle lasted all day. At eight in the evening I thought we ought to retreat. La Pucelle came to me and asked me to wait a little longer. She then went into a trellis of vines, alone; remained in prayer half an hour; returned, and seizing her banner in her two hands, went to the ditch. As soon as they saw her the English trembled and were taken with a panic. Our soldiers, on the other hand, seemed inspired with new courage, and assailed the fort, meeting no resistance."

Jeanne had to meet the opposition of some of the French officers, who desired to act without her or against her advice, and left her out of their councils. She sprang up suddenly at night, while sleeping with Charlotte, a daughter of the treasurer of the Duke of Orleans, and exclaimed: "My God! The blood of our people is running on the ground. It was ill done. Why was I not wakened? Quick—my arms, my horse!" She galloped off at full speed, and met the French troops fleeing. When they saw her they turned back, attacked the English fort again and captured it. She then returned to the city; but only took a few slices of bread, dipped in wine and water, for refreshment, which was sometimes the only nourishment she took during the entire day.

Jeanne resolved to pass the whole of Ascension Day in prayer. The French captains took advantage of her absence to have a little consultation about their position. They apparently regarded her inspiration as better to animate than to direct, better to impel than to guide, better in the field than in the council. But their wisdom was folly in comparison with her inspiration. She chose the means with as much wisdom as she pursued the end with zeal. She observed that they were concealing something from her, and said: "Tell me what you have determined. I can keep this secret and greater ones also."

It appears that the French officers had resolved to wait for reinforcements before attacking the strongest forts of the English before Orleans; but Jeanne said: "You have been at your counsel, I at mine. The counsel of my Lord will stand; yours will come to naught. Let all be ready early tomorrow for the attack. Much blood will flow, and I also shall be wounded." Yet this proud and firm nature was melted to tears by the cruel insults of the English. Said she: "The King of Heaven knows that they speak falsely." Presently she said that she felt consoled, because she had news from her Master.

The French captains had resolved not to yield to her, and refused to open the gates; but the next morning after Ascension Day she forced them by her overpowering energy to do so, and hurled an impetuous assault upon the principal fort of the English. This fort was so strongly intrenched by the river and a deep fosse as to be well-nigh impregnable, and was garrisoned by the flower of the English chivalry. The Duke d' Alençon afterwards examined this fort, and said that he would have undertaken to defend it for seven days against any force that could have been brought against it. But all of Jeanne's predictions were verified that day. Having crossed the ditch and been the first to plant a ladder against the walls, she was wounded. They carried her from the walls and took off her armor. She was overcome by pain and fright, and began weeping; but presently her Saints appeared to her, and she recovered her heroism.

Pulling the arrow from her own wound with her own hands, she said that she would rather die than have the charms muttered over the wound which were usually used by the soldiers. She prayed earnestly to God, and was consoled. In the meantime the French, wearied with the long and useless struggle, were everywhere retreating. Long after noon had passed, the English appeared to have gained the day; but Jeanne implored the French officers to renew the attack, and, seeing her standard near the walls, she rode toward it, exclaiming: "If it touches the walls we shall enter!"

As soon as the French troops saw her they turned and rushed forward in an overflowing tide against the fort and commenced climbing its walls. The English, having believed that she had been killed, were terrified as at the sight of an apparition, and fled. A shot struck down the bridge over which the English commander was passing into the fort, and he was drowned in the ditch. At the same moment the people of Orleans opened their gates, and multitudes of them attacked the fort from the other side. Instantly the fort was occupied, and its defenders were driven out or slain. The bells of Orleans rang all night for joy, and the *Te Deum* was chanted in the churches.

The English were in full retreat the next morning, which was Sunday. Jeanne would not permit them to be pursued, but had an altar erected in the plain in full sight of the fleeing foe. Said she: "For the love of St. Dimanche (Sunday) do not kill them to-day. Do not attack them first. My Master does not wish us to fight to-day. Let them go—that is enough."

When the first part of her prediction was thus accomplished, Jeanne desired to fulfill the rest. Said she: "Now, noble Dauphin, let us march to Rheims. I shall last only a year, or a little longer; I must be well employed." The politicians smiled at what they considered a childish folly in the maiden, thus to insist on the ceremony of coronation; but her folly was wisdom, as the great mass of the people thought they ought to accept as their king him who was the rightful heir, and who should be regularly crowned. Jeanne's assertion was to the multitude like a voice from heaven, concerning the first point, in the king's behalf. If he were crowned at Rheims the French nation would accept him as its true and legitimate sovereign. Jeanne, who was one of the people, understood this better than the courtiers; and, fortunately for the king, she was able to overrule the selfish and timid counsels of the courtiers, and to induce the king to undertake this perilous march of about two hundred miles through the midst of his enemies.

JOAN OF ARC WOUNDED.

RHEIMS CATHEDRAL.

By Jeanne's wisdom and valor, the town of Jargeau, twelve miles from Orleans, was taken by storm. Presently the celebrated Falstaffe arrived with large reinforcements for Talbot; but Jeanne constantly encouraged and animated afresh the doubting Frenchmen. Said she: "If these English were hanging to the clouds we should get them." She asked the officers: "Have you good horses?" They inquired: "What! must we fly?" She replied: "Oh, no! But you will need them to-day in pursuing the English. The gentle king will have the greatest victory to-day he has ever won." Well did Jeanne fulfill the prophecy; as Crecy, Poitiers and Agincourt were avenged on that day. Falstaffe fled; Talbot and other English officers were taken prisoners, and two thousand English were slain, at Patay, where, four months before, Falstaffe, with two thousand English, had defeated Dunois at the head of four thousand French.

Jeanne wept at the sight of this bloodshed, and endeavored to prevent the French from ill-treating their prisoners. One of the prisoners was struck on the head near her; whereupon she sprang from her horse, held his head in her arms, had a priest brought to him, comforted him, and encouraged him to face death with courage.

The French people had faith in Jeanne, but the nobles doubted and distrusted her. She was always obliged to overcome their resistance. They did not believe that she could take Orleans, but she took it. They lacked courage to go to Rheims, and offered a campaign on the Loire instead. She accepted their offer, and ended the campaign in a week, taking Jargeau, June 12, 1429, and Baugency after a siege of two days, June 15–17, 1429, and routing the hitherto victorious Talbot and Falstaffe at Patay, June 18, 1429. On that day (June 18, 1429) the English prestige came to an end, and one fortified city after another had opened its gates to the French king. The French generals offered no more positive resistance to Jeanne's commands; but some jealous hearts were filled with envy of her influence, and these sought privately to weaken her power over King Charles VII. During the entire march to Rheims, the king's counselors were always advising one thing, while Jeanne was urging another. When they arrived at Troyes the officers declared that they could not take so large and well defended a town, and that it could not be left in their rear with safety, so that they had better return. The Archbishop of Rheims was of this way of thinking, but one old counselor argued more wisely, reconciling earthly and heavenly wisdom. Said he: "When the king undertook this march he did so not because of his great force or abundance of money, or because it seemed possible, but merely because Jeanne said, 'Go and be crowned at Rheims!' Let us now do as she says. Ask her if we shall attack the city."

Jeanne, being then called, asked: "Shall I be believed?" The king replied: "If you say what is reasonable I will believe you." Jeanne repeated: "Shall I be believed?" The king replied: "Yes!" Jeanne then said: "Then, noble Dauphin, tell your people to assault the town; for, by my God, you shall enter Troyes, by force or love, in two days." Said the Chancellor: "If we could be sure of entering in six we would wait; but I have my doubts of it." Jeanne replied: "Six? You shall be masters of Troyes to-morrow!" She then led them to the assault and took Troyes, July 9, 1429.

Jeanne next led the victorious French into Rheims, July 15, 1429; and King Charles VII. was crowned in that city with all the usual ceremonies, July 17, 1429. On this occasion Jeanne occupied the highest place, holding her standard in her hand. She then cast herself on her knees, weeping, and said: "O gentle king, now is accomplished the will of God, that I should raise the siege of Orleans and bring you to be crowned here, to show that you are the right king and that the kingdom belongs to you."

Touched by the sight of the people, who came singing hymns to welcome the king,

Jeanne said: "Oh, the good people! When I die I should like to be buried here." Dunois asked: "When will you die, Jeanne?" She replied: "I cannot tell—when God wills. I would that he would let me return to my father and mother, and keep sheep again. They would be so glad to see me. But I have done what the Lord commanded."

The old chronicle says that Jeanne turned her eyes toward heaven, and all the lords who were present never saw so clearly, as in her looks then, that she came from God.

Quoting the words of the French generals, Wallon says that the English had become thoroughly demoralized; and this remarkable maiden had in one week taken all the principal English fortresses on the Loire, defeated the best English officers and troops in the field, caused all the great cities to open their gates, and had marched to Rheims without opposition through a territory which had been wholly in the possession of the English a month before. Wallon says that Jeanne inspired a wonderful enthusiasm, and also displayed an extraordinary military ability. She rode her horse and wielded her lance like an old knight. She appeared to understand the details of war by intuition.

The French people had good reason to believe in the heroine. Her modesty had not been impaired by her great fame. She claimed no merit, but said: "My work is but a ministry." She exhibited the same constant piety as before, observed daily prayers and masses, and maintained the same purity of life. In her presence evil thoughts departed from the most impure minds. Every night she staid with the most virtuous women in the place where she might be.

The heroine made no pretensions to miraculous power, although she performed works almost miraculous. Said one: "Nothing like these acts of yours have been told of, even in any book." She replied: "My Master has a book which the wisest clerk has never read." When some women of Bourges asked her to touch crosses and chaplets, she laughed, and said: "Touch them yourselves; they will be quite as good."

Jeanne now felt that she had finished her mission, and she implored King Charles VII. to permit her to return to her home and her sheep. The old chronicle says that it was great pity to hear her ask to be allowed to go back to her peasant's home and tasks, as her reward in the midst of her great triumph. Two of her brothers, Pierre and Jean, had followed her to Rheims, where she was met by her father Arc and her uncle Laxart.

The letters-patent of King Charles VII. exempted the village of Domremy from all taxes, for the sake of this renowned heroine, Jeanne d' Arc, the *Maid of Orleans*. Charles VII. also gave letters of nobility to the young maiden and to all her family, including the female descendants.

Still more remarkable was the tribute paid to the virtues of the valiant Maid of Orleans in after-times. After the allied armies had defeated the Emperor Napolean I. in the memorable campaign of 1814, they came to the village of Domremy while on their march to Paris. At that hallowed spot the German troops refrained from plunder or from doing any injury to the inhabitants, out of respect to the memory of this renowned heroine, this savior of France in the fifteenth century.

Jeanne felt that her mission was ended when King Charles VII. was crowned at Rheims. Thenceforth he had a smooth way ahead of him, and cities and towns opened their gates before him wherever he went. The sagacity of the heroine's judgment was vindicated by the result, as all France now appeared ready to submit to its legitimate, native king.

Jeanne's mind now became clouded, though it was still full of energy. She lost ground on the whole, both before the foreign enemy and among her own countrymen, though she still manifested an heroic and almost superhuman courage, and though she still gained victories. Hitherto she had succeeded in everything that she had undertaken, but thenceforth she sometimes failed.

Jeanne's first reverse was under the walls of Paris. Eventually, the French officers, jealous of her fame, allowed Duke Philip the Good of Burgundy, the ally of the English, to make her a prisoner in a sally from the town of Compiègne, May 23, 1430. The valiant maiden had a premonition of her fate, and had foretold it, but she did not lose her wonderful force of character in full view of this sad prospect.

At the moment of her great danger under the walls of Compiègne the bells were rung to summon the soldiers to her rescue. This last homage was useless, as none came to the heroine's relief. The governor of the city treacherously ordered the gates to be closed against her in order to shut her out. Jeanne had rebuked this infamous man for his evil habits. He afterwards came to a tragic end, his wife having persuaded his barber to strangle him.

Thus the heroic Maid of Orleans was taken prisoner by her enemies when she was only eighteen years of age, after a military career of but a year. The English thirsted for the blood of the young heroine, whose only crime was that of bravely and patriotically defending the independence of her native land; and the Duke of Bedford, the English regent in France, endeavored to buy her from the Burgundians, in which he finally succeeded by the instrumentality of the Church. The Bishop of Beauvais and the Inquisitor-General demanded her of Jean de Ligny, who finally sold her to the English for ten thousand francs. Jean de Ligny's wife threw herself at her husband's feet and entreated him not to dishonor himself, but he had taken the money.

After passing six months in different prisons, the heroic Maid of Orleans was taken to Rouen and placed in an iron cage, with fetters on her limbs. Although she was to be tried by an ecclesiastical court for heresy and sorcery, she was kept in the English prison in the capital of Normandy, and was guarded by rude soldiers, who did not scruple to offer her coarse insults. The trial was conducted by Pierre Cauchon, Bishop of Beauvais—a name, like that of Caiaphas, doomed to eternal infamy as a cruel persecutor who sought, under the forms of law and justice, pretexts to satisfy the malice of vindictive foes by the judicial murder of an innocent captive.

Barante says that the entire judicial proceeding was a series of falsehoods, of traps set for the unsuspecting victim—repeated violation of justice and established rights, under a hypocritical appearance of following the customary rules. A priest who pretended to be her friend was sent into her prison, after which notaries were placed behind her walls to write down what she might say to the priest. The notaries were ashamed of such a task, and declined to perform it.

When brought before an assembly of doctors and divines this poor girl displayed a courage as great as she had ever exhibited in leading the hosts of France to battle and to victory. The doctors and divines who tried her allowed her no counsel, but her honesty and good sense were the best helps by which she escaped the snares in which they endeavored to entrap her. She gave way to neither anger nor fear in consequence of their threats and violence. The assembly was frequently astonished by the readiness and beauty of her answers. They asked her if she knew that she was "in the grace of God." She replied: "It is a great thing to answer such a question." Jean Talri, one of the assessors, remarked: "Yes, Jeanne, it *is* a great question, and you are not bound to answer it." The bishop cried out to the assessor: "You had better be silent." Jeanne replied: "If I am not, may God make me so; if I am, may God keep me so. But if I were not in the grace of God, I should not have known what to do." The manuscript says: "They were much astonished, and for that time finished the examination."

They asked her again about her standard. She replied: "I carried it instead of a lance, so as not to kill any one. I have never killed any one." For the purpose of accusing her of magic, they asked her what virtue she supposed there was in the standard. She answered: "I said to it, 'Go boldly among the English,' and then I followed it myself." They asked her why she brought it to the altar at Rheims. She replied: "It had been where there was danger; it was right that it should be where there was honor." They inquired: "What did the people mean in kissing your hands, feet and garments?" She responded: "The poor people came gladly to me because I did them no wrong. I supported and helped them, as I had the power." Thus simple, innocent truth was too much for craft.

Jeanne sometimes spoke very sublimely. Once she said: "My Voices, to-day, have told me to answer you very boldly." She strictly followed their advice. She rebuked the Bishop of Beauvais for his part in the trial, and warned him of the awful responsibility which he would encounter. She asserted: "Bethink you what you do, for truly I am sent of God. You put yourself in great danger. Yes, I am come from God. I have nothing to do here. Send me back to God from whom I came." They endeavored to make her say that the Voices had inspired her with un-Christian feelings. They asked her: "Were the inhabitants of Domremy Burgundians?" She replied: "There was only one Burgundian in the village; and I could have wished that his head were cut off, provided it was the will of God." They inquired: "Did the Voices tell you you ought to hate the Burgundians?" She answered: "I did not love them so well after I found that the Voices were for the King of France." They inquired: "Did you have a great desire to injure the Burgundians?" She replied: "I had a great desire and wish that the king should have his kingdom again." They asked: "Do you think you did well in leaving home without the consent of your father and mother?" She answered: "They have forgiven me." They asked: "Do you think, then, that you did not sin in acting so?" She responded: "If God commanded me, ought I not to have done it? Though I had a hundred fathers and mothers, I would have left them if God had ordered it."

The judges could not conceive that Jeanne should have seen the archangel Michael and the saints, and they thought it quite probable that she should have had intercourse with fairies and evil spirits. They endeavored to make her say that she had talked with fairies under the May-tree; but she answered that others had declared that they had seen fairies there, but that she herself had never seen any. She admitted that many people who had the fever visited the May-tree and drank of the neighboring fountain, but she did not know whether they were cured or not. She had heard some old people say that they saw fairies under the May-tree, but she did not know whether it was true or not.

They asked her: "Did you not tell the soldiers that you would turn aside the English arrows?" She answered: "I only told them not to be afraid; but many were wounded at my side, and I was wounded myself." They asked her if she had ever been where she saw the English killed. She replied: "Who of us has not seen war? But of such sad things let us speak softly and with a low voice." An English nobleman who was present was touched by this reply, and said: "I would she were an Englishwoman."

The judges asked: "Was it well done to attack Paris on our Lady's Day?" She replied: "It is well to keep the festivals of our Lady; it would be well to keep them every day." They inquired: "Do your saints hate the English?" She answered: "They love whatever God loves, and hate what He hates." They asked: "Does God hate the English?" She responded: "As for God's love or hate for the souls of the English, I know nothing; but I know that He will cause them all to be driven from France, except those who die here." They inquired: "Jeanne, do you know by revelation whether you will escape?" She replied: "This has nothing to do with your trial. Do you wish me to accuse myself?" They asked: "But have the Voices told you nothing about it?" She answered: "This does not concern the trial. I leave the matter in the Lord's hands."

After all their examinations, the judges failed to make out any case against her concerning sorcery, and they were obliged to abandon that charge. The only points against her were wearing a man's dress and declining to submit to the decisions of the Church. It was contrary to a text in Deuteronomy to wear a man's dress. But the real point against her consisted in the conflict between God's authority, speaking in her heart, and the authority of the visible Church.

They asked her if she would submit to the decision of the Church as to whether her Voices had told her the truth or not, and let the Church decide on all her words and actions. She answered: "I love the Church, and would support it with all my power; but as to my works, I must leave them to the judgment of God Who sent me." When the same question was repeated, she replied: "Our Lord and the Church are all one." They then contrived a distinction, for the purpose of inducing her to reject the authority of the visible Church. They told her that there was a distinction between the Church Triumphant above, consisting of God and the saints, and the Church Militant below, and asked her to which she submitted. She responded: "To the Church Triumphant." They then asked: "And do you refuse to submit to the Church Militant?" She said: "I will answer no more to-day."

But there were some honest men among the counselors who could not bear this. Three of them were bold enough to visit Jeanne in her prison and to tell her that the true Church Militant was not composed of her enemies, but of the Pope and the General Councils, and that she might appeal from her prejudiced judges to the Pope and to the Council of Basle, which was then about to be convened. One of the counselors had courage sufficient to advise the heroine publicly, before the tribunal, to submit to the Council of Basle. She asked: "What is a General Council?" Brother Isambert replied: "It is a congregation of the Universal Church, and is composed of your friends as well as of the other party." She answered: "Oh! in that case I submit." The bishop thus addressed Isambert: "Be silent!" He also forbade the notary from writing down Jeanne's answer. The poor girl said: "Alas! you write what is against me, but not what is for me."

The account of the trial from the record of March 31, 1431, contains the following question and answer. The question put to her was: "Will you refer yourself to the judgment of the Church on this earth, for all you have said and done, good or bad? Especially, will you submit to the decision of the Church concerning all the charges made against you for different offenses and crimes, and in regard to the whole of the present process?"

Her answer was: "As to all that is required, I refer myself to the judgment of the Church Militant, provided it commands nothing which I am unable to do; and I consider it impossible to declare that my Voices and Revelations have not come from God. Nothing in the world will make me declare this. Whatever God causes me to do, whatever he commands or shall command—that I must not fail to do, for any man alive. It is impossible for me to take back this. In case the Church wishes me to do anything contrary to the commands I have received from God, I never can consent for anything in the world."

Then she was asked: "If the Church Militant declares your Revelations to be illusions, or to be diabolical, will you submit to the Church in this matter?" She answered: "I will submit to God, Whose commandments I shall always obey. I know that the matters spoken of in this process have been done by the order of God. Whenever I affirm in this process that I have acted by God's order, I can never deny it. If the Church commands the contrary, I shall submit to no one in the world, but only to God, Whose commands I shall always obey."

They then asked her: "Ought you not to

submit to the Church of God on earth—that is, to the Pope (our Lord), to the cardinals, archbishops, bishops, and other prelates of the Church?" She replied: "Yes; I do submit—provided that God is obeyed first."

After the examinations were concluded, the Bishop of Beauvais selected twelve articles from what he chose to consider the heroine's answers, and sent them to the leading doctors and ecclesiastical tribunals for their opinions. These twelve articles were so drawn up as to make it only possible to give such a reply as would condemn her. The main point was her refusal to submit to the tribunal of the Church if it should contradict the Voice of God in her own soul. She was therefore practically condemned, as Luther and the other leaders of the Reformation a century later were condemned, for denying the authority of the Church Militant. Jeanne was also condemned for wearing men's clothes, and for believing in revelations which probably came from evil spirits.

The English now very much desired that the heroine who had so ruined their cause should be burned. She became ill about this time, and the great Earl of Warwick very much feared that she might die a natural death. Said he: "You must cure her. The king has bought her. She must be burned! You must not let her die!"

This Earl of Warwick—who manifested such rancor against a poor peasant girl who had so deeply wounded English pride—was the brave and gallant knight of that age, the model gentleman, full of chivalric ideas. He made a pilgrimage to the Holy Land, and did not miss a tournament by the way. He himself gave a tournament at the gates of Calais, challenging the entire chivalry of France.

It was intolerable to the English that a poor maiden had so frightened them, that she had driven them half the length of France, that she had taken them in their fortresses and had conquered them in the field. The vengeance of English pride thus severely mortified could only be satisfied by burning the young heroine to death.

This being Passion Week, they refused her the sacraments of the Church. The object of the Bishop of Beauvais was to make her submit to the Church and confess that her visions were deceptive. He did not care what became of her after that. He therefore tried every means to induce her to submit; threatening her with torture and fire if she refused, and promising her the mercy and protection of the Church if she submitted. But the heroine stood firm in her refusal day after day. Deprived of the outward consolations of religion, she relied on her faith.

Said she: "For my *faith*, I submit to the Church below; for my *acts*, I will submit only to the Church of Heaven. I would rather die than revoke what I have done by the Lord's commands." She was told: "But you cannot hear mass on Good Friday, except you submit." She replied: "Our Lord can let me hear it without you." She was then asked: "Will you submit to the Church Militant?" She answered: "Provided it does not command what is impossible." The next question to her was: "Do you not think you ought to obey the Pope and the bishops, and the Universal Church?" Her reply was: "Yes, our Lord being first obeyed." She was next asked: "Do your Voices forbid you to submit to the Church Militant?" She answered: "They do not, our Lord being obeyed first."

Finally, a public display was prepared, May 24, 1431. Two scaffolds were constructed. The cardinals, bishops and doctors were seated on one scaffold; Jeanne, with the executioner and priests, on the other. The English assembled in crowds, expecting that she would be burned; but the bishop's object was to obtain a public abjuration from the heroine. She for a long time refused to sign anything; but being threatened with instant death by burning if she refused, and being promised pardon and protection if she consented, while being also exhausted by the long discussions and arguments, she finally agreed to sign a short form of abjuration in which she submitted to the Church and confessed that her Voices might have deceived her, saying at last: "I submit to the Church." This abjuration occurred in the cemetery of St. Ouen, near the beautiful church of that name.

A much longer form of abjuration was than presented for her signature. This infuriated the English, who were impatient in their desire to have the poor girl burned to death, and they commenced throwing stones at the bishop, also shouting: "You have not earned the king's money; you are going to let her escape." The Earl of Warwick said: "Things go badly if she escapes." The holy man replied: "Never mind; we will soon have her again." They pronounced her pardon, which was a sentence of life-long imprisonment; and then they sent her back to the English prisons, instead of committing her to the guardianship of the Church.

After thus making a partial submission to the Church, Jeanne resumed her female dress in obedience to its commands. But it had been arranged that she should not escape. After being received by the Church to penitence and absolved from the excommunication, she had expected to be released. Erard, the preacher who had obtained her abjuration, had promised that she should be restored to liberty. As she had been sentenced to life-long imprisonment as a salutary penance "on the bread of grief and water of anguish," she was justified in demanding that her imprisonment should be in the prisons of the Church. This was suggested to the bishop by several; and Jeanne said: "Men of the Church, carry me to your prison, so that I shall not be any more in the hands of the English!" But this was not the bishop's intention, and he clearly showed himself to be an accomplice of the English by saying: "Take her back to the place where you found her."

Insults were thereafter offered to the heroine in her cell, and she was chained as before. Some witnesses said that her woman's dress was carried away while she was asleep. At any rate, they must have intentionally left the man's dress where she could get it, and the design of this was doubtless to tempt her to put it on again. She said: "Gentlemen, you know I am forbidden to wear that." Finally, however, she put on the soldier's garb, as she had no other, or because she felt more secure by so doing. They then cried out: "She is taken." The judges came, and would not listen to her complaints and excuses. Said she: "Put me among women, and I will wear a woman's dress."

The judges asked her: "Why have you again worn your man's dress?" She answered: "Because it is more proper to wear a man's dress than a woman's when I am among men." She also said that she had a right to wear it again, because they had violated their promises to let her go to mass and to take off the irons from her limbs. Continuing their examination, the judges said: "You abjured your errors, and promised not to wear the man's dress again." She replied: "I had rather die than be thus chained; but if you will take off the irons and let me go to mass, put me in a good prison and let me have a woman with me, I will be good and do what the Church commands."

The judges, desiring to find some foundation for the charge of "relapse," asked her if she had heard her Voices again since Thursday, the day of her abjuration. She made no attempt to escape the snare, but promptly replied: "Yes." They asked: "And what did they say to you?" She answered: "God has taught me, by St. Catharine and St. Marguerite, that I have committed a sad treachery in abjuring to save my life; that I damned myself to save my life." She also said that her Voices had told her what to do that day, to answer the preacher fearlessly from the scaffold, because he was a false preacher. She said: "If I should admit that God did not send me I should damn myself. It is true that God sent me. My Voices told me that I did very wrong in confessing that what I have done was not well done."

The clerk who wrote down her answers asserted that she said that she wore a man's dress to protect her modesty. The judges decided that she should be delivered over to the civil authorities to be put to death. When it was announced to her that she must die the cruel death by fire, her woman's nature gave way, and she commenced weeping bitterly and tearing her hair, crying out: "Alas! shall my body be burned, which I have preserved pure and uncorrupt? I had rather be beheaded, seven times over, than be burned."

On her way to execution, she cried out: "O Rouen, Rouen, must I die here!" She was taken to the scaffold at nine in the morning, May 30, 1431, after having taken the communion by the bishop's permission. Men's minds on one side were more and more giving way to remorse, pity and grief; while a corresponding rage was increasing on the other side. Those who manifested the least sympathy for her were in imminent peril from the English, but still they managed to show such sympathy.

Three friends who remained with the heroine to the last were Brother L' Advenu, Brother Isambert, and Massieu, one of the secretaries—all three of whom the English had threatened for having given her their advice and manifested pity for her during the trial. The people along the streets also wept as she passed on her way to the scaffold, her sweet face still wet with a woman's tears. The priest who had falsely pretended to be her friend in the prison, for the purpose of betraying her confidence, repented, burst through the guards, flung himself down before her, accused himself aloud of his treachery, and implored pardon from the poor girl and from God. The priest would have been instantly killed by the enraged English if the Earl of Warwick had not interfered.

A sermon was preached as the introduction to the dreadful ceremony. At the close of this sermon, the valiant Maid of Orleans wept and asked the forgiveness of all, while she forgave their wrongs against herself, and implored them to pray for her. Even the hard-hearted Bishop of Beauvais and the cruel English were touched and were unable to refrain from tears; but still the bishop pronounced to her the sentence: "We cut you off from the Church as a relapsed penitent, as a rotten member; we give you over to the secular power, entreating it to moderate its sentence and spare you the pain of death and mutilation of limb."

She kissed the cross given her by an English soldier, and then ascended the wooden pile raised on a foundation of plaster. Looking on the city and the silent multitude about the scaffold, she exclaimed: "O Rouen, Rouen! I fear me much thou wilt have to suffer for my death!" She shrieked aloud upon seeing the executioner apply the fire. The priest who stood by her paid no attention to the flames. She then forgot herself and entreated him to leave the scaffold.

When the flames commenced rolling up around her she first cried out for water. Then she called on God, and finally said: "My Voices have not deceived me." In the midst of the flames she saw that the safety and deliverance that her Voices had promised were not the deliverance from death, but the deliverance of her soul. She appeared to have an inward light which "quenched the violence of the fire." Her last words were "Jesus! Jesus!"

All this was testified by the priest who had just descended from the scaffold. Wallon says: "She finished her prayer in heaven." Even the rude English soldiers shed tears, and exclaimed: "We are lost! We have burned a saint! Would God my soul were where hers is now!" Some endeavored to laugh. One man had sworn that he would throw a fagot on the pile. As he approached he heard her cry to Jesus; whereupon he became ill and almost fainted, and was carried to a neighboring tavern. Said he: "I saw a dove escape from her mouth." The executioner went in utter dismay to Brother Isambert to confess, and could not believe that God would forgive him.

Thus perished the valiant Jeanne d' Arc. the Maid of Orleans—the most renowned heroine of all history—a martyr to the cause of her country's independence. This poor young maiden, taken prisoner in war, suffered for no other crime than for defending with matchless heroism her country and her king. She was a woman in the Age of Chivalry, when the greatest thing talked of was the duty of protecting afflicted dames and damsels—a virgin in an age when the worship of the Virgin had almost taken the place of the worship of God. Yet in that age they united savage cruelty with pharisaic hypocrisy, and tried this poor peasant girl for heresy and sorcery, endeavoring to lead her by falsehoods and deceptions into self-accusation; and, when all these arts of bishops and noblemen were thwarted by the transparent truth and holy innocence of the young heroine, they dragged her to the stake and burned her to death, under a shallow pretext which could not deceive any one.

We see in this how much has been gained to the world by the change from the Middle Ages. And yet there are those who talk of the "Ages of Faith"—who lament the degeneracy of our own times, and grieve that the Age of Chivalry has passed forever. In the beginning of our own century was a great leader, who, like Jeanne d' Arc, had led the French armies against the English. He was their most inveterate foe—the invader of every nation which his insatiate ambition could covet and his wonderful military genius could hope to overcome. Yet, after deluging Europe with a sea of blood, he was finally made a prisoner by this same English nation, which had spent millions of treasure and hundreds of thousands of lives to check his victorious course. And yet, many considered it too harsh a punishment when he was placed in a remote island, though surrounded with friends, books, comforts and luxuries. Thus, we see how much more magnanimous is the nineteenth century than was the fifteenth—how much the world has advanced in four centuries. How different the treatment of Napoleon Bonaparte, the despoiler of nations, was to that of the Maid of Orleans, the defender and restorer of her country's independence.

Though Jeanne d' Arc suffered death by the sentence of the Roman Catholic Church, at the demand of the English, in May, 1431, a tribunal of the same Church reëxamined and reversed this sentence twenty-five years later, A. D. 1456. King Charles VII., whose failing fortunes the valiant Maid of Orleans had restored, but who had ungratefully made no effort to save her in her peril, was now better advised, and in 1450 he ordered a new trial of her case. In consequence of this royal demand, and in compliance with the request of the martyred heroine's mother and brothers, Pope Calixtus III. directed the Archbishop of Rheims and the Bishops of Paris and Coutances to preside at the trial, which took place in 1456.

This investigation lasted from seven to eight months, and witnesses came from all parts to testify in the heroine's favor. The old people from Domremy, her native town; the younger companions of her childhood; Dunois and the Duke d' Alençon, her comrades in military leadership; Louis de Contes, her page; D' Aulon, her squire; Pasquerel, her confessor; those who saw her in her prison, and those who stood near her at the scaffold; even the officials and notaries employed by her enemies—all testified in this trial to different traits in her lovely character.

These witnesses all testified to Jeanne's pure and modest life in her father's home, her simplicity of character and her inspired firmness of soul during her famous career, her patience amid her sufferings after she had been sold to the English, her boldness before the tribunal of her enemies, and the sudden illuminations which showed her the crafty purposes of her judges. After hearing this evidence the Court of Revision declared that the charges under which the heroine was condemned were calumnious and false, and that the sentence under which she had suffered martyrdom was null and void; thus vindicating the memory of the valiant maid. The Court of Revision ordered that this decree be read publicly in the city of Rouen, where she had been so cruelly put to death, and likewise in the city of Orleans, which she had delivered from the English.

Thus there is no history which is substantiated by more authentic materials than that of Jeanne d' Arc, and it is a remarkable fact that we have almost as full and exact an account of her life as if we had known her ourselves. The records of her trial and of the Court of Revision have been preserved in the Royal Library of Paris for four and a half centuries. Ninety witnesses—thirty-four of them from her native town—had testified in her favor before the Court of Revision; and three of the greatest of French generals—Dunois, the Duke d' Alençon, and De Gaucourt—bore witness to her military prowess; while we also have her own words given in reply to thirty public and private examinations during her trial; so that her whole life is revealed to us.

Not satisfied with putting the Maid of Orleans to death with the utmost barbarity, the English sought to blast her reputation and destroy her character by the sentence of the ecclesiastical tribunals. They also cast her ashes into the Seine, so that no monument might ever be erected over her remains; but they had unconsciously erected a far nobler and more enduring monument to her memory in the trial itself. In the city of Rouen, the scene of her martyrdom at the hands of her cruel foes, is a beautiful monument, surmounted by a statue of the heroine, commemorating her ill-fated end.

The four and a half centuries which have passed since the death of the Maid of Orleans have purified her memory from the stains with which ignorance and prejudice had soiled it, and the nineteenth century has done full justice to the heroine of the fifteenth. Patient research has discovered, among the contemporary memoirs of her time, and in the records of her trial and the Court of Revision, the amplest means of vindicating her pure and noble virtues. The most brilliant French authors have embalmed her memory in prose and verse, and one of the most renowned of German poets has beautifully illustrated her character in one of his most charming dramas; but, beautiful as is Schiller's drama, any one who reads the simple memoirs of her life and the events of her brief career must feel that these constitute a far nobler poem, as nothing can surpass the touching beauty of the facts themselves. In the language of Maria Lowell, an American poetess, the young heroine can truly be called

"The whitest lily on the shield of France,
With heart of virgin gold."

Says the great French historian, Michelet: "It was fit that the savior of France should be a woman. France herself is a woman. She has the fickleness of the sex, but also its amiable gentleness, its facile and charming pity, and the excellence of its first impulses."

It has frequently occurred, after the death of any one who has deeply moved the popular mind, that a belief has prevailed that the person was still living and would reappear. This belief has often induced impostors to come forward who pretended to be that very person. It was so in the case of Jeanne d' Arc. A false Jeanne d' Arc made her appearance in 1452, twenty-one years after the execution of the Maid of Orleans, claiming to be that veritable personage. She wore a man's dress, went about amusing herself and feasting, and imposed on many.

An amiable young maiden, daughter of Claude de Lys and grandniece of Jeanne d' Arc, was the very picture of her illustrious grandaunt. Brought up in the same house and surrounded by memories of Jeanne, this maiden thought herself destined to continue the heroine's career. Dressed in men's clothes, she exercised herself in the use of arms and became a perfect equestrian. She was prepared to show, if occasion required, that the blood of the Maid of Orleans was not extinct; but the occasion never presented itself, and she married and lived a quiet life.

Having finished the account of the wonderful career of Jeanne d' Arc, we will proceed with the narrative of events which followed her martyrdom. The Duke of Bedford had expected that the execution of the heroine would turn the tide of war in his favor. He caused the young Henry VI. of England to be crowned King of France in the cathedral of Notre Dame in Paris, but the ceremony aroused no enthusiasm, and the hostile conduct of the Parisians soon caused Henry VI. to retire into Normandy. Although the Maid of Orleans no longer led the French armies, victory still perched upon the French banners, and reverses fell thick and fast upon the English. The French forces under Dunois took Chartres, and the English under the Duke of Bedford were defeated in a pitched battle at Lagny.

The Duchess of Bedford, the sister of Duke Philip the Good of Burgundy, died in November, 1432, thus severing the tie which bound the Dukes of Burgundy and Bedford, whereupon a coolness sprang up between them, which was soon increased by the remarriage of the Duke of Bedford without consulting or communicating with the Duke of Burgundy. Disgusted with the English alliance, Duke Philip the Good openly broke with the English regent, and entered into negotiations with Charles VII.

A reconciliation was arranged between the King of France and the Duke of Burgundy in 1435; and, as the Duke of Bedford had died in the meantime, Philip the Good openly espoused his king's cause against the English, but made Charles VII. pay liberally for this reconciliation. The French king rendered ample satisfaction to Duke Philip the Good for the murder of his father, pleading his extreme youth at the time of the murder in extenuation of his share in the crime. He ceded the counties of Macon and Auxerre, and some territories on the Somme and in Ponthieu, to the Burgundian duke. The King of France also released the Duke of Burgundy from all homage to the French crown, thus recognizing him as an independent sovereign.

Thus all France was again united, after twenty-nine years of civil war. Isabella of Bavaria, the mother of King Charles VII., who had been the cause of so many woes to France because of her reckless intrigues, died at Paris three days after the treaty between the King of France and the Duke of Burgundy was signed. As she had been universally despised, her funeral was performed hastily at St. Denis, without any of the honors due to her rank.

Duke Philip the Good of Burgundy now united his arms with those of King Charles VII., and their combined forces drove the English from Paris in the spring of 1436. The French king proclaimed a general amnesty, and was joyfully acknowledged by the Parisians as their sovereign. The long reign of violence caused brigandage to succeed the war upon so large a scale that great efforts were needed to suppress the evil. Many of the French king's soldiers formed themselves into marauding bands and terrorized the country, but they were exterminated with a stern hand by the Constable de Richemont.

As Charles VII. was now secure in the possession of the French crown, he manifested a degree of energy and vigor for which none had given him credit. In October, 1439, he summoned the States-General at Orleans, and in that body he published a highly important measure. By this he abolished the old feudal levies of the nobles, and made it high treason for the nobles to enroll troops without the king's permission. He established a regular military force for the defense of the French kingdom, to be paid out of the public treasury, and the officers to be appointed by the king. This was the origin of the standing army of France, and was the death-blow to feudalism in that kingdom. The Dukes of Bourbon and Alençon and some of the other French nobles rebelled against this measure, and the Dauphin Louis was persuaded to join in the rebellion; but it did not receive the popular support, and was sternly discountenanced by Duke Philip the Good of Burgundy, so that King Charles VII. was enabled to reduce the rebellious nobles to submission.

In the meantime the English had suffered some severe reverses in Normandy and Gascony. In 1444 a truce of twenty-two months was concluded between the French and the English, and a marriage was negotiated between King Henry VI. of England and Margaret of Anjou, niece of the French king's queen. This marriage occurred at Nancy in the spring of 1445. The war between the French and the English was renewed in 1449. The English steadily lost all their conquests in France, and by the close of 1453 only the towns of Calais and Guines with the narrow strip of adjacent territory remained in their possession.

The wars had so depopulated the North of France that wolves and other beasts of prey infested even the city of Paris. In 1437 the wolves entered the city by the Seine and devoured about fifteen persons. The next year they entered Paris a second time, killed four women and severely bit seventeen other individuals, eleven of whom died of their wounds. There was especially one formidable wolf, called *Courtland*, because he had no tail, that became an object of universal fear. When any person was leaving the city, it was said, "*gardez vous de Courtland*," which subsequently passed into a proverb.

No sooner had France been freed from the power of a foreign foe than Charles VII. found his peace disturbed by the artifices and cabals of his eldest son Louis, the Dauphin. This prince was a monster of depravity, and employed assassins to murder a nobleman who had incurred his dislike. When the attempt was discovered the king severely reproved his son's treachery; and Louis, impatient of control, retired into Dauphiny, firmly resolved never again to be subject to his father's power. He is accused of having poisoned Agnes Sorel, his father's beloved mistress; but his character is adequately tarnished by undeniable crimes, without those which have no other foundation than mere suspicion.

The people of Guienne, particularly the citizens of Bordeaux, had always been remarkable for their attachment to the English. After they had remained subject to Charles VII. for some time they grew weary of a government which disregarded their privileges and loaded them with oppressive taxes. Deputies were sent to England to entreat King Henry VI. to receive the people of Guienne again under his protection and to send troops to aid them in expelling the French. The English king sent Talbot, the most distinguished general of the time, to Guienne with a military force. At first Talbot won several victories and conquered most of the province, but the French king assembled his forces and overpowered the little English army near Castillon, where Talbot and his gallant son were slain and most of their troops were killed or taken prisoners. Bordeaux surrendered to the army of King Charles VII., after a short siege. Several of its citizens were exiled; two castles called the Chateau Trompette and the Chateau Ha were erected to keep the inhabitants in subjection; and the duchy of Guienne, or Aquitaine, was permanently annexed to the crown of France.

Thus Charles VII., surnamed *the Victorious*, was sovereign of the whole kingdom of France, except the town of Calais on the strait of Dover, which remained in England's possession two centuries longer. His last years should have been his happiest, as France was then freed from civil and foreign wars, but that was the most unhappy period of his life. He abandoned himself wholly to his favorites and mistresses, thus entirely neglecting the affairs of state.

After the Dauphin Louis had retired into Dauphiny he became the center of every intrigue against his father, and married a princess of the house of Savoy against his father's wishes. His cruelties and exactions in that province were so intolerable that his subjects were obliged to appeal to the king. Charles the Victorious sent Dammartin to arrest the disobedient Dauphin, in 1456; but Louis had been informed of Dammartin's approach, and fled to Burgundy, where Duke Philip the Good received him with all the respect due to the son of his king. The French king sent frequent embassies to the Burgundian duke, demanding that he should withhold his protection from the disobedient Dauphin, and warning him that "he nourished a serpent who would repay his hospitality by attempting his life." The Duke of Burgundy disregarded these remonstrances, although he knew that the Dauphin had excited his own son, the Count of Charolois, to rebellious acts. The Dauphin finally took refuge at the Flemish court at Brussels.

King Charles the Victorious was so exasperated against his son that it was with difficulty that he was prevented from disinheriting him and bequeathing the French crown to his second son. The king sank into a state of insanity, which he had inherited from his father. He was positively informed that his wicked son had bribed the royal domestics to poison him. The king's apprehensions became so great that he abstained wholly from eating for several days, not knowing from whom he could safely receive food; and he finally died for want of nourishment, in July, 1461, in the fifty-ninth year of his age and the thirty-ninth of his reign.

The wars of Charles the Victorious show that the spirit of chivalry was fast declining. We find no traces of that individual heroism which gives the history of the wars with Edward III. of England and the Black Prince such a romantic interest, and Agincourt was the last great battle in which the superiority of the English archers was made available. The bow and arrow were gradually superseded by the use of fire-arms; gunpowder having been invented a century before by the German monk Berthold Schwarz. Cavalry, hitherto the most important part of an army, was considerably diminished in value by the new system of tactics.

These changes in the art of war had great influence on the political condition of society; as the knights and the small landed proprietors, who had hitherto possessed much influence by the importance of their services, sunk suddenly when these services were performed by mercenary soldiers. Thus the power of the feudal aristocracy was destroyed, and the royal power in France became absolute.

Charles the Victorious was succeeded as King of France by his son, LOUIS XI., who was in Flanders at the time of his father's death, in 1461. He instantly returned to France, stopping at Rheims for his coronation, after which he hastened to Paris and assumed the government, being escorted to the capital by Duke Philip the Good of Burgundy and his son with about fourteen thousand cavalry.

Louis XI. was one of the most remarkable of French kings. He was thirty-nine years old at his accession, and was therefore in the prime of life and of matured experience. He had for some years ruled Dauphiny as an independent prince in defiance of his father's will, and had learned the difficult and delicate business of statecraft, thus becoming proficient in the art of judging men. He was by nature a man of cool, clear understanding, profound sagacity and strong will, and had learned to sacrifice every personal feeling and interest to the success of his plans.

Louis XI. ascended the French throne with the determination to destroy the last vestige of feudalism and to erect an absolute monarchy upon the ruins of the Feudal System. His constant policy during his entire reign was to reduce the great nobles of France to a position of insignificance and to concentrate all the powers of the state in the hands of the sovereign.

He was fully qualified for the success of his plans. Government was a science with him; as he had studied it profoundly, and had learned how to profit to the fullest extent by the weaknesses, the vices and the passions of mankind. He was a consummate master in the arts of dissimulation and duplicity, and made it his chief object to overreach and circumvent others, considering successful fraud the most conclusive evidence of talent. He made use of cajolery, corruption and perfidy where his predecessors would have used violence. He understood perfectly how to play off one class of interest against another, how to foment the seeds of discord and estrangement so as to profit thereby afterward. When he saw fit he treated the victims entrapped by his cunning with a tyrannical cruelty seldom surpassed, thus showing that his heart was callous to the most ordinary feelings of human nature.

Such a character as Louis XI. in the station he occupied necessarily produced important results in France and on the general policy and social condition of Europe. His history was full of strange contrasts and anomalies. He realized his objects as a sovereign by unscrupulously sacrificing all his obligations as a man. Few kings have done more to extend the power and exalt the dignity of France, and few have left a personal portrait of darker or more odious coloring upon the pages of history.

Louis XI. commenced his reign by treating his subjects as if they were a conquered people. He deprived all officers appointed by his father of their situations, took a malicious delight in undoing all that his father had done, limited the provision made for his brother, oppressed his subjects with heavy taxes, plundered the nobles and insulted the clergy. He revoked the *Pragmatic Sanction*, the celebrated measure of his father's reign by which the liberties of the Church in France were guarded against the papal encroachments. This proceeding was promptly resented by the nobility and the clergy, and was a cause of trouble throughout this reign. Though anxious to oblige the Pope, Louis XI. first sided with him and then with his own subjects, according to the requirements of his policy, and skillfully managed to avoid an open quarrel with either.

In 1462 King John II. of Aragon borrowed a considerable sum of money from Louis XI. for the prosecution of a war against the revolted Catalans, and placed the counties of Roussillon and Cerdagne in the French king's hands as security. Soon afterward Louis XI. increased his dominions by concluding a treaty with Duke Philip the Good of Burgundy by which he paid four hundred thousand crowns to redeem the towns of Abbeville, Amiens and St. Quentin, which his father had ceded to the Burgundian duke by the Treaty of Arras. Count Charles of Charolois—son of Philip the Good, and afterwards Duke Charles the Bold of Burgundy—who had hitherto been a devoted friend of Louis XI., now became that king's inveterate enemy, because he believed that Louis had committed an act of spoliation of his father in this transaction.

In the meantime the tyranny and wanton cruelty of Louis XI. had aroused a feeling of deep hostility toward him among all classes of his subjects. The Duke of Brittany and Count Charles of Charolois entered into an alliance against the king, who had sought to incite a war between them for his own purposes; and in 1464 this alliance was joined by the disaffected French nobles, the chief of whom were the Dukes of Lorraine, Nemours, Alençon, Bourbon and Berry. This coalition of French nobles assumed the name of the *League of the Public Good*. Civil war ensued.

Without waiting for his allies, Count Charles of Charolois advanced toward Paris; and Louis XI., eager to save his capital, hastened to reach it before his rival. The two armies encountered each other at Mont l'Hery, July 16, 1465. Both desired to avoid an engagement; but the Seneschal of Normandy, one of the leaguers, precipitated a battle, and was himself one of the first who was slain. The greater part of both armies fled from the field, and when night put an end to the conflict each army believed itself defeated. It was proposed in the Burgundian camp to take advantage of the night in order to make good their retreat, and they were very much suprised in the morning at finding themselves masters of the field. Says Philippe de Comines: "This unexpected victory was the source of all the calamities which the Count of Charolois afterwards experienced, for it inspired him with so much confidence in his own skill and prowess that he disregarded all advice."

Though he failed to obtain the victory, Louis XI. made himself master of Paris, and gained the Parisians to his side by his promises and flattery. The unscrupulous king now began to practise the advice given him by Francisco Sforza, Duke of Milan, who had counseled the French monarch to promise the leaguers all that they demanded, to foment dissensions among them after they had disbanded their troops, and then attack them in detail. This was just the plan that Louis XI. was calculated to execute.

The crafty king accordingly made a truce with the leaguers, went into the hostile camp, and pretended to feel a wonderful revival of affection for Count Charles of Charolois. He made similar demonstrations of esteem to all the principal leaguers, and expressed the greatest desire to regain their friendship on any terms short of resigning his crown. The treaty was accelerated by an unexpected circumstance, which caused Louis XI. to consent to the article which he had thus far most persistently refused.

The leaguers had insisted on the duchy of Normandy as an appanage for the king's brother; and Louis XI. had rejected the proposal, as he feared that the possession of so important a province might prove a step to the crown. But while this matter was still a subject of negotiation, the Normans, who were eager for provincial independence, everywhere opened the gates of their towns to the forces of the league. When tidings of this condition of affairs in Normandy reached King Louis XI., he determined to make a merit of granting what he was unable to withhold any longer, and immediately signed the Treaty of Conflans, A. D. 1465.

By this treaty Louis XI. relinquished the important line of the Somme to Duke Philip the Good of Burgundy; consented that the Duke of Berry should be made Duke of Normandy; ceded the counties of Etampes and Montfort to the Duke of Brittany; and raised the Count de St. Pol to the office of Constable of France. Each of the other members of the league reaped some advantage from the treaty. After the Treaty of Conflans had been signed, the League of the Public Good was dissolved.

Louis XI. resolved from the first not to execute these humiliating conditions. By the treaty he accomplished his purpose to gain time and divide the leaguers, after which he set to work to deprive them of their possessions and to humble them. The Parliament of Paris refused to ratify the grant of Normandy to the Duke of Berry, on the ground that the king had no right to alienate the possessions of the crown; and Louis XI. soon put an end to the duke's authority in that province.

Louis XI. then instigated a quarrel between the Dukes of Berry and Brittany, marched his forces toward Caen, and summoned the Duke of Brittany to appear before him. The Duke of Brittany, terrified and surprised, agreed at the conference to surrender to the king all the towns that his troops garrisoned in Lower Normandy. The rest of Normandy yielded to the king's threats and violence; and the Duke of Berry, destitute of friends, money, spirit or counsel, considered himself fortunate in escaping with his life to the court of the Duke of Brittany. Normandy enjoyed its qualified independence only two months; and Louis XI. put several of the Norman nobles to death without any of the formalities of justice, because of their desire to obtain that independence.

Count Charles of Charolois was very indignant when he was informed of the king's proceedings in Normandy, but Louis XI. had provided sufficient employment for Charles by instigating the factious citizens of Liege and Ghent to revolt. After capturing Rouen without encountering any resistance, Louis XI. formally resumed the government of the duchy of Normandy in January, 1466.

While Count Charles of Charolois was engaged in suppressing the insurrection in Liege and Ghent, his father, Duke Philip the Good of Burgundy, died, June, 1467; whereupon Charles came into possession of the rich inheritance of the duchy of Burgundy, and is known as Charles the Bold. The young Duke of Burgundy forced the citizens of Ghent and Liege to submit to very severe terms, and increased his treasury by exacting heavy pecuniary punishments from the insurgents; after which he prepared to turn his attenion to France, where Louis XI. was rapidly recovering all that he had relinquished by the Treaty of Conflans.

In 1468 Louis XI. invaded Lower Normandy and Brittany with two powerful armies, and took several frontier towns, when he was informed that Duke Charles the Bold of Burgundy was rapidly advancing toward the Somme with a gallant army. Before the arrival of the Burgundian duke the king had forced the Dukes of Berry and Brittany to sign a treaty of peace with him, by which they consented to renounce their alliance with the Duke of Burgundy and to pledge themselves to aid the king against him.

Charles the Bold was at Peronne when he received tidings of this treaty, and was so surprised and enraged that he was with the greatest difficulty prevented from hanging the herald who brought him the news. He instantly demanded of Louis XI. the faithful execution of the Treaty of Conflans, threatening war in case of refusal. Instead of answering the Burgundian duke's threat by instantly marching against him, the king took a most extraordinary step to get rid of his vigorous rival, whose presence at the head of an army encouraged all the disaffected spirits in the French kingdom. Relying on his own superior address, and in opposition to the earnest entreaties of his most trusted counselors, Louis XI. yielded to the advice of Cardinal de Balue, by adopting the extraordinary resolution of seeking a personal interview with Charles the Bold, hoping thus to divert the Burgundian duke's attention to other objects, or to excite jealousy between him and his allies. A few days before starting to meet Charles the Bold, Louis XI. sent emissaries to instigate another rebellion in Liege against the Duke of Burgundy.

After procuring a written safe-conduct from the Duke of Burgundy, the French king started for Peronne with a small escort in October, 1468. When he arrived at Peronne he was greatly alarmed at meeting in the camp of Charles the Bold several nobles who had fled from his dominions to escape his tyranny; and to escape their vengeance he requested the Duke of Burgundy to lodge him in the castle of Peronne. Charles the Bold granted the king's request and treated him with great courtesy.

Negotiations were then commenced between Louis XI. and Charles the Bold; but after these negotiations had continued several days news arrived that the people of Liege had broken out into another and fiercer rebellion and had murdered the Burgundian officers and several of the clergy, being instigated thereto by the emissaries whom the crafty French king had sent for that purpose before he started for Peronne. Upon hearing of this revolt the Duke of Burgundy burst into a furious rage, and ordered the gates of the castle of Peronne to be closed and guarded, thus making Louis XI. a close prisoner. In his rage Charles the Bold resolved to put his royal prisoner to death, and make the Duke of Berry, the captive king's younger brother, King of France in his stead.

Louis XI. was in dreadful suspense for three days; but, resorting to his accustomed arts, he bribed all those courtiers whom he supposed would likely have any influence over the Duke of Burgundy, among them Philippe de Comines, the historian, from whom is derived the account of this affair. At length, through the influence of Comines, Duke Charles the Bold was induced to release the captive king on the most humiliating conditions to Louis XI. The king bound himself by a solemn oath on a relic which he regarded with the most superstitious veneration to execute the Treaty of Conflans in good faith, and to grant the counties of Champagne and Brie to the Duke of Berry in place of the duchy of Normandy.

Louis XI. was also obliged to accompany

LOUIS XI. MEETING CHARLES THE BOLD AT PERONNE.

Charles the Bold to Liege to aid the Duke of Burgundy in reducing that rebellious city to submission. The king and the duke both vented their anger and disappointment upon the unfortunate city for the rebellion incited and assisted by the French king himself. Liege was taken by storm, and most of its inhabitants were massacred, while many of those who escaped perished from hunger and cold. Louis XI. was then released, whereupon he went to Tours to lay plans to avenge his humiliation.

The Parisians were much amused at the manner in which Louis XI. had been outwitted, and they taught their parrots to cry out "Peronne, Peronne." But the king revenged himself for their jest by ordering all the tame animals in the city kept for pets to be killed.

No sooner had Louis XI. been released than he resolved not to submit to the terms exacted from him by Charles the Bold at Peronne as the condition of his release. He therefore refused to bestow the counties of Champagne and Brie upon his brother, the Duke of Berry, as the possession of those provinces would make that prince the neighbor as well as the ally of the Duke of Burgundy; and he determined to substitute the more distant duchy of Guienne, or Aquitaine, instead. The king's plan was betrayed to Charles the Bold by Cardinal de Balué. The cardinal's letters fell into the king's possession, and the cardinal was arrested and confined in an iron cage in the castle of Loches—a punishment which he richly deserved, as he was the original inventor of such a barbarous torture.

Louis XI. then persuaded his brother, the Duke of Berry, to accept the duchy of Guienne, or Aquitaine; and that prince accordingly renounced his alliance with the Duke of Burgundy and offended him by refusing to marry his daughter and heiress Mary, A. D. 1469.

Both the King of France and the Duke of Burgundy now took part in the Wars of the Roses in England, Louis XI. siding with the House of Lancaster, and Charles the Bold with the House of York. The French king's failure to restore Henry VI. to the English throne greatly encouraged the Burgundians and depressed Louis XI. to a corresponding degree.

The people of Guienne and Gascony regretted the loss of their national independence, and intrigued with their new duke, the French king's brother, the Duke of Berry, to throw off the French yoke, A. D. 1472. The Duke of Guienne accordingly renewed his old alliance with Duke Charles the Bold of Burgundy, and the Duke of Brittany took up arms to aid them.

Louis XI. sought to avert the danger with which he was threatened by the league against him by offering the most humiliating concessions to the allies, and caused his brother's sudden death by poison; while a French army laid siege to Lectoure, which was defended by Count John d' Armagnac, who manifested the utmost activity in the old Gascon interest. The town was taken by storm and burned, and John d' Armagnac and the inhabitants of the town were massacred by the victorious French troops, while John's wife was forced to take a beverage which produced her death in two days, A. D. 1472.

Undismayed by the loss of his most important ally, Duke Charles the Bold of Burgundy took the field against King Louis XI. in June, 1472, and took and barbarously sacked the town of Nesle, in the county of Picardy. The Burgundian duke was repulsed in his attempts to take Beauvais, near the end of July, and was forced to consent to a truce of five months, which was afterwards extended for more than two years.

Louis XI., took advantage of this truce to avenge himself on the feudal nobles who had refused to submit to his will. The Duke d' Alençon was deprived of his estates and imprisoned for life. Count James d' Armagnac, Duke of Nemours, was decapitated in Paris; and his children were placed under the scaffold, so that they might be sprinkled with their father's blood, and thus be warned never to make war against their suzerain, the King of France. The Duke of Lorraine died very suddenly, and was believed to have been poisoned by the French king's emissaries.

The impetuous Duke Charles the Bold of Burgundy frequently renewed the war with King Louis XI., and was bribed as frequently to grant fresh truces. The Constable St. Pol, who had seized some of the towns on the confines of Burgundy, encouraged the animosities of both parties, as their agreement would have proved his ruin. Equally distrusted by the king and by the Duke of Burgundy, the Constable acted with impartial treachery toward both, thus insuring his ultimate destruction, though he deferred it by his artifices for some time.

In 1475 Duke Charles the Bold of Burgundy entered into an alliance with King Edward IV. of England and the Duke of Brittany, by which the English king agreed to revive the claims of his predecessors to the French crown. In the summer of that year Edward IV. landed at Calais with a splendid army of thirty thousand men; but the Duke of Burgundy, having lost half of his army in a foolish invasion of the territory of Cologne, was unable to furnish any aid to the King of England; and, as the other allies of Edward IV. proved lukewarm, that monarch's expedition failed. The Constable St. Pol had promised that he would surrender St. Quentin to the allies of the Duke of Burgundy, but when the English army appeared before the town it was fired upon and forced to retire.

These circumstances afforded Edward IV. an honorable excuse for putting an end to the war, of which he was already weary, and the liberal offers of Louis XI. contributed largely to the same result. The crafty King of France literally bribed the English monarch and the principal English nobility, who remained disgraceful pensioners of the French sovereign for several years. The two kings had an interview at Pequigny, in which they soon arranged the terms of a treaty for seven years, by which Louis XI. agreed to pay the expenses incurred by Edward IV. in the war, and betrothed his son, the Dauphin Charles, to the English king's eldest daughter, engaging to have the marriage performed as soon as the parties reached the proper age.

Charles the Bold of Burgundy was so incensed at the treaty between the two monarchs that he refused to be a party to it, but he afterwards concluded a truce with Louis XI. in order to enable him to continue his unjust war against the Swiss and the Duke of Lorraine. In accordance with the terms of the treaty between the Kings of France and England, the Constable St. Pol was to be surrendered to Louis XI. Seeing that his ruin was inevitable, the Constable fled to the court of the Duke of Burgundy, but Charles the Bold delivered him to the French king. The Constable's treason was so evident that he was promptly condemned by the Parliament of Paris, and was executed on the Place de Grève, December 10, 1475. This execution was the boldest blow which Louis XI. had thus far struck against the great feudal nobility of France. In addition to his vast possessions and his great personal influence, the Constable St. Pol was a member of the imperial family of Luxemburg, had married a sister of the queen of Louis XI., and was connected by marriage with several of the royal families of Europe.

Duke Charles the Bold of Burgundy had exacted a large price for his abandonment of the Constable St. Pol. This ambitious prince was already one of the wealthiest and most powerful sovereigns of Europe. His great grandfather, Philip the Bold, who had been granted the duchy of Burgundy in fief by his father, King John the Good of France, in 1363, had also acquired by inheritance and marriage Franche-Comté, or the Free County of Burgundy, and also the counties of Flanders and Artois, with Mechlin, Antwerp and other towns. His son John the Fearless (1404-1419) and his grandson Philip the Good (1419-1467) extended their possessions still farther over the Netherlands, and built up a dominion that vied with Italy in civilization, industry and prosperity. Philip the Good was one of the richest and most powerful princes of his time, and his Netherland chivalry were celebrated for their splendor, adroitness and polished manners. The wealthy manufacturing and commercial towns of Ghent, Bruges, Brussels, Antwerp, Louvain, Mechlin and others possessed great privileges and liberties, and a warlike militia. Charles the Bold—who, as we have seen, succeeded his father Philip the Good in 1467—enlarged his dominions and raised the splendor of his chivalrous court to the highest degree.

Charles the Bold was a man of vigor, courage and warlike spirit; but his ambition and his violent passions rendered him rash, obstinate and insolent. He sought to found a new Burgundian kingdom by making himself master of the entire region between the Rhine and the Alps on the east and the territories of the French crown on the west, from the Mediterranean on the south to the North Sea on the north; but his efforts were frustrated by the crafty Louis XI.

In pursuance of his ambitious designs, Charles the Bold proceeded to take possession of the duchy of Lorraine, driving out the young Duke Réné. As the price of the deliverance of the Constable St. Pol into his hands by the Duke of Burgundy, Louis XI. permitted Charles the Bold to seize Lorraine without himself opposing it, but he instigated the Swiss to treat the Duke of Burgundy with such insolence that, after making himself master of Lorraine, Charles the Bold turned his arms against the brave mountaineers. The King of France was well convinced that an encounter with the hardy Swiss would ruin his powerful rival, and events justified his calculation.

Charles the Bold led a stately and splendidly equipped army across the Jura against the Swiss; but he suffered so disastrous a defeat in the battle of Granson, March 2, 1476, that the survivors were dispersed in disorderly flight; and his admirable artillery and his magnificent camp filled with costly stuffs, with gold, silver and precious stones, came into the possession of the victorious Swiss, who did not know their value.

Maddened by the disgrace of this defeat, Charles the Bold led a new army against the Swiss a few months afterward; but the Swiss again defeated him in the battle of Morat, June, 1476, the flower of the Burgundian chivalry being left dead upon this fatal field, and the victors being again enriched with an immense booty. The Swiss canton of Berne wrested the Valais from the ducal house of Savoy, the ally of Burgundy; and the Duke of Lorraine recovered his lands from the vanquished Duke of Burgundy, reëntering his capital, Nancy, in triumph; while the subjects of Charles the Bold broke out into open disaffection and reproached him bitterly for his ambition and rashness.

With the recklessness of despair, and meditating nothing but vengeance, Charles the Bold rejected every proposal of peace, and took the field against the Duke of Lorraine by invading that prince's territories and laying siege to Nancy. Duke Réné, by means of funds furnished to him by Louis XI., collected an army of twenty thousand Swiss, Alsacians and Lorrainers, and marched to the relief of his capital; and in a decisive battle in the frozen fields before Nancy, in January, 1477, Charles the Bold suffered a third disastrous and decisive defeat, and was slain in a frozen morass during his flight from the fatal field.

The Duke of Burgundy owed his defeat and death largely to the treachery of the Italian condottieri in his service, commanded by the Count of Campobasso. This Italian officer had long been attached to the Duke of Lorraine, had sworn to compass the ruin of his master, Charles the Bold, and had almost openly bargained for the assassination of the Burgundian duke. With almost inconceivable credulity, Charles the Bold continued to trust him, though warned of his treachery; and when Louis XI. sent him word to beware of the treacherous Italian, the unfortunate Charles declared the letter to be the strongest evidence of Campobasso's fidelity, saying: "If evil were designed, Louis would be the last to send me warning."

Scarcely had the armies of the Dukes of Burgundy and Lorraine met on the fatal field of Nancy than Campobasso deserted with his condottieri, leaving fourteen desperadoes to assassinate Charles the Bold in the tumult. Dismayed by this unexpected defection, the Burgundians gave way at the first onset; and after the battle was over the dead body of Charles the Bold was found lying under a heap of slain, so disfigured with wounds as to be scarcely recognized. His generous foe, the young Duke of Lorraine, when shown the dead body, took hold of the right hand and uttered the simple words: "God rest thy soul! thou hast caused us much evil and sorrow." The Duke of Lorraine then ordered the body to be honorably interred.

The death of Charles the Bold put an end to the Burgundian dominion. Louis XI. instantly seized the Burgundian territories, and, claiming the duchy of Burgundy as a lapsed fief, annexed it to the French crown, to which it remained united thereafter. Louis XI. proclaimed himself the guardian of Mary of Burgundy, the daughter of Charles the Bold, who was his kinswoman, and pledged himself to watch faithfully over her interests.

Mary offered to unite her dominions to those of the King of France by a marriage with the Dauphin, but Louis XI. was base enough to betray Mary's letters to the factious citizens of Ghent, thus inciting a revolt of the Flemings against the princess. The revolted citizens condemned two of Mary's most faithful servants to death as traitors; and, in spite of her entreaties, the enraged mob caused the condemned servants to be executed in the market-place of Ghent, and the princess returned to her palace sad and disconsolate.

Mary, after vainly appealing to the French king to carry out his promises to her in good faith, and with the full approval of her subjects, married the Archduke Maximilian of Austria, afterwards the Emperor Maximilian I. The marriage was solemnized August 18, 1477, much to the chagrin of Louis XI., who had hoped to marry the Dauphin Charles to the Burgundian princess, or, at least, to defraud her of her inheritance.

The marriage of Mary of Burgundy with Maximilian of Austria laid the foundation of the future greatness of the Austrian House of Hapsburg, and was the source of the jealous enmity between that dynasty and France, which produced so many wars in Europe during the next two centuries. Louis XI. vented his rage on the Duke of Nemours, who had been a member of the League of the Public Good, and had been jealously watched by the French king ever after. The Duke of Nemours had been arrested in August, 1476; and after a cruel imprisonment of a year he was executed in August, 1477.

After the death of Mary of Burgundy, in 1482, by a fall from her horse while hawking, the people of Ghent chose her infant son and daughter, Philip and Margaret, for their sovereigns, and placed them under the guardianship of their father Maximilian. Louis XI. renewed his treacherous intrigues for the purpose of instigating a rebellion in the towns of the Netherlands against Maximilian. Ghent renounced Maximilian's authority; the guilds of Bruges kept him a prisoner for some time; the duchy of Brabant wavered; but, nevertheless, Maximilian, by his courage and conduct, induced the whole of the Netherlands to recognize his guardianship of his infant children.

Louis XI. kept the duchy of Burgundy and the county of Picardy. Margaret, the daughter of Mary and Maximilian, was affianced to the Dauphin Charles, and was sent to France to be educated. It was agreed that she should receive as a dowry Franche-Comté, or the Free County of Burgundy, and the counties of Artois, Macon and Auxerre, which, in the event of the failure of issue of the marriage, or the non-performance of the marriage, were to revert to her brother Philip, the son of Mary and Maximilian. Louis XI. renounced his claims to French Flanders, and agreed never again to encourage revolt among the Flemings. Such were the conditions of the Treaty of Arras.

We have already alluded to the Treaty of Pequigny, by which the Dauphin Charles was betrothed to the Princess Elizabeth, the daughter of King Edward IV. of England. The English king was enraged at the insult to him conveyed by the Treaty of Arras, and prepared to invade France; but his sudden death in April, 1483, relieved Louis XI. of all danger.

Louis XI. was now at the height of his power, and had vastly enlarged his dominions by means generally more or less dishonorable. In addition to the territories wrested from the house of Burgundy at the death of Charles the Bold, Louis XI. about this time came into possession of the duchy of Anjou by the bequest of Réné, the last duke of that province; and a year afterward he obtained the counties of Maine and Provence by the same bequest. The duchy of Guienne and the counties of Alençon and Perche were annexed to the possessions of the French crown by less honorable means. The counties of Roussillon and Cerdagne also became the property of the French crown, having been pawned by King Ferdinand the Catholic of Spain. The duchy of Brittany was the only great feudal fief of France that yet remained independent of the French crown. The boldness with which Louis XI. had struck at the French nobles had awed them into submission, and his acknowledged diplomatic skill and success had made him one of the most influential and powerful monarchs of Europe.

In the midst of his prosperity, Louis XI. was stricken with apoplexy while sitting at dinner one day in March, 1480, which at once deprived him of his sense and speech. Though he partially recovered from this attack, his health was never fully restored. He perceptibly declined day after day, and he dreaded death more and more as the fatal day came nearer. Everything appeared to inspire him with jealous fear. He removed his queen from the court, and kept his son a close prisoner in the castle of Amboise. He always retained in his suite Louis, Duke of Orleans, the first prince of the blood royal, whom he had barbarously deprived of the advantages of education. He compelled this prince to marry the princess Jane, who possessed an amiable disposition, but with whom he had no issue.

Conscious, as he had himself told his son, "that he had grievously oppressed his people," Louis XI. lived in constant dread of their revenge. He therefore shut himself up in the strong castle of Plessis les Tours, which he fortified by digging ditches and placing iron spikes in them. As he did not dare to trust his own subjects, he was guarded night and day by a band of Scottish archers, who had orders to shoot any person who approached the castle without first making himself known. The gates of the castle were never opened, but such persons as were allowed to enter were admitted through a small gate called the *wicket-gate*, through which only one person could pass at a time. The cruel tyrant's dread of the nobles was so great that the princes of his own family, even his own daughters, were forbidden to visit him without invitation. The avenues to this miserable abode were lined with gibbets instead of trees.

The three companions of his solitude were his barber Oliver Daim, his hangman Tristan l' Hermite, and his physician Jacques Coctiers. The cruel tyrant was a miserable slave to the last of these intimate associates, who was an artful quack and pretended that an astrologer had predicted that according to the decrees of fate the physician himself should die four days before the king. The wretched monarch therefore watched over the life of the unscrupulous physician with the utmost care, loaded him with presents, and submitted to all his insolence.

Fearing that his subjects might deprive him of his government because of his increasing imbecility, the tyrant made a great show of attention to business, and pretended to read all the documents committed to his secretaries, though he could not see a single word. In order that he might be promptly informed of what was transpiring in all parts of his kingdom, he established regular posts. Though these were employed in the king's service, citizens were permitted to ride post horses on payment of a certain sum. In order to persuade mankind that his health was perfectly restored, the unhappy king sent embassies to foreign princes, wore the most elegant robes instead of the plain and shabby dress that he had hitherto worn, and sacrificed additional victims to his suspicious cruelty and undying revenge.

The miserable king sought to divert his thoughts by amusements. As hunting had been his favorite diversion when he was in health, he caused many rats to be caught and turned loose in his chamber, where he hunted them with cats. But as he soon became tired of this pastime, his attendants devised a more innocent diversion; collecting the peasants, dividing them into bands and distributing them in the meadows about the castle, where some played on the pipes, while others danced and sung. To conceal the ravages of disease, the wretched king, now dressed with splendor, looked at the peasants from the windows of the castle; but when he perceived that any one observed him he instantly retired, and did not again appear that day.

The nearer death approached the more he dreaded it, and he sought to prolong his life by all the arts of superstition. He kept various relics about his person, and little leaden images were stuck around in his cap. He constantly addressed his prayers to these images, and caused holy oil to be brought from Rheims and kept it on his table. The Pope sent the unhappy king various articles of assistance from Rome, and even the Sultan of the Ottoman Turks sent a deputation of holy relics from Constantinople. The wretched monarch feared to accept these last, as they came from un-Christian hands. His chief hope was in the prayers of Francis de Paule, a pious hermit of Calabria, whom he had brought to his castle, and before whom he frequently fell on his knees, begging him to prolong his life; but the honest hermit announced to the despairing monarch that his case was hopeless, and recommended him to prepare for another world.

Thus deprived of his last hope, and finding himself to be growing weaker day by day, Louis XI. sent for his son, and exhorted him not to govern without the aid and advice of the princes and nobles, not to change the great officers of state at his accession, not to continue the oppressive taxes, and to make his administration as unlike his father's as possible. The chief anxiety of Louis XI. was to die on Saturday, which he considered the most fortunate day; and this wish was gratified, as he died Saturday, August 30, 1483, in the sixty-first year of his age and the twenty-second of his reign.

Few sovereigns have been more execrated than Louis XI. More than four thousand persons were executed for state offenses during his reign, and he took a fiendish delight in witnessing their torments. He, however, diligently attended to the administration of justice, and made several judicious regulations in the law courts; and although he oppressed his subjects very much he never permitted others to do so. He was the first to establish posts in France, to gratify the restless desire for news; and the first printing-press was made in Paris during his reign.

Upon the death of Louis XI., in 1483, his son, CHARLES VIII., surnamed *the Courteous*, a boy of thirteen years and in feeble health, became King of France. That age was the legal age of majority; but the weakness of his constitution, and the ignorance in which he had been reared, rendered him unfit to take the government in his own hands. Louis XI. had by his will appointed his daughter, Anne of Beaujeu, guardian to her brother, the young king. This princess was a woman of excellent understanding, high spirit and vigorous resolution, possessing much of her father's craft, without any of his cruelty and perfidy.

The princes of the blood royal, particularly the Dukes of Bourbon and Orleans, considered it beneath their dignity to submit to the control of a woman, declaring that as the Salic Law excluded females from the French crown it also rendered them incapable of exercising the regal functions; and the States-General was summoned to decide on this important question. Contrary to the expectation of the princes of the blood royal, the States-General confirmed the will of Louis XI. and acknowledged Anne of Beaujeu as regent, but appointed a council of twelve of the principal nobles to assist her in the administration. Thereupon the Dukes of Bourbon and Orleans appealed to arms, but the promptitude of the regent disconcerted their plans. The Duke of Bourbon was forced to submit to whatever terms Anne was pleased to dictate, while the Duke of Orleans was obliged to seek refuge in Brittany. By the death of the Duke of Bourbon soon afterward, the regent Anne of Beaujeu became Duchess of Bourbon; that prince having been her husband's elder brother.

Though the inhabitants of the duchy of Brittany had always manifested a strong love of independence and had shown themselves unwilling to become incorporated with either the duchy of Normandy or the Kingdom of France, the discontent of a large part of the Bretons induced them to solicit the assistance of the King of France against their duke, but they discovered when too late that a powerful ally soon becomes a master. King Charles VIII. sent them an army far exceeding the number of troops that had been stipulated for. He garrisoned the towns of Brittany with French troops, and claimed the duchy in right of the ruling family of Blois, the former rivals of the Montforts, the house of Blois having bequeathed their pretensions to the French king.

The Bretons discovered their error when too late, submitted to their duke and joined him with all their forces; but they were totally defeated by the French army at St. Aubin, July 28, 1488, their bravest leaders being either killed or taken prisoners, and the whole of Brittany being thus placed at the mercy of the victorious invaders. The Duke of Orleans and the Prince of Orange were among the prisoners taken by the triumphant French. The regent Anne of Beaujeu imprisoned the Duke of Orleans, but released the Prince of Orange.

The Duke of Brittany was thus obliged to make peace on very disadvantageous terms, and grief hastened his death, which occurred in September, 1488. He left two daughters, one of whom soon followed her father to the grave. The surviving daughter, Anne, the heiress of Brittany, was only a child of thirteen, but conducted herself with great wisdom under all the difficulties of her situation. Her subjects were divided into several parties concerning her marriage.

The regent Anne of Beaujeu resolved to seize the opportunity of annexing the duchy of Brittany to the territories of the French crown, and induced her brother, King Charles VIII., to demand that Anne of Brittany should not assume her title of duchess until the question of succession had been judicially decided between herself and the King of France, and that she should submit herself to his guardianship. As Anne of Brittany rejected these demands, a French army invaded the duchy and took Brest and other important towns.

The French invasion of Brittany alarmed England, Germany and Spain, as those nations were extremely jealous of the rapid growth of the French power; and they formed an alliance to preserve the independence of Brittany. In the spring of 1489 an English and Spanish army landed in Brittany, but no decisive action occurred. The English soon retired; and in the summer of 1490 the young Duchess of Brittany was persuaded to contract a marriage by proxy with the Archduke Maximilian of Austria, the widower of the Duchess Mary of Burgundy, and afterwards Emperor Maximilian I. Anne of Brittany then assumed the title of Queen of the Romans, but to her disappointment she obtained no aid from Maximilian, who was then engaged in a war with Hungary. In the meantime the duchy of Brittany was reduced to great suffering.

In 1490 King Charles VIII., then twenty years of age, assumed the government of France. He immediately released the Duke of Orleans, to whom he was tenderly attached, and effected a reconciliation between that prince and his sister, the regent, Anne of Beaujeu, Duchess of Bourbon. By this consummation the Count of Dunois, who had been the chief counselor of the

CHARLES VIII. MEETS ANNE OF BRITTANY.

Duchess Anne of Brittany, was won over to the king's side.

The Count of Dunois had advised the marriage of Anne of Brittany with the Archduke Maximilian of Austria; but, as that prince never assisted her against the power of France, the Count of Dunois induced her to end her trouble by marrying the King of France. Reduced to utter despair and deserted by Maximilian, she consented to this arrangement. The Duke of Orleans contrived an interview between King Charles VIII. and Anne of Brittany at Rennes. The king and the duchess were well pleased with each other; and their marriage was solemnized at the chateau of Langeais, in the province of Touraine, in December, 1491. Thus the duchy of Brittany became fully united with the crown of France; and, in order to make this union permanent, it was stipulated in the marriage contract that if Charles VIII. should die without issue the queen should marry his successor, or if he were married she should marry the next heir of the French crown.

The marriage of Charles VIII. with Anne of Brittany was a double insult to Maximilian of Austria, as it deprived him of his bride and his daughter Anne of a husband, that princess having been betrothed to Charles VIII. in her childhood. The counties of Artois, Charolois, and Franche-Comté or the Free County of Burgundy, which had been ceded by Maximilian as his daughter's dowry, were restored to him. The Archduke of Austria was unable to avenge the insult thus offered him, because of his war with Hungary and troubles in Flanders, which kept him thoroughly occupied. He submitted with as good grace as possible, and when the Burgundian territories just named were restored to him he made peace with France by the Treaty of Senlis in May, 1493.

Peace was soon afterward concluded between France and England by the payment of a large sum of money to King Henry VII. of England as indemnity for his expenses in the war in Brittany. Peace was also made between France and Spain; the French king ceding to King Ferdinand the Catholic of Spain the counties of Roussillon and Cerdagne, which King John II. of Aragon had pawned to Louis XI. of France; but the money for which they had been pawned was not returned to the King of France.

France was now at the highest pitch of power; and King Charles the Courteous resolved upon enforcing some claims which he had upon the Kingdom of Naples, and for this purpose he invaded Italy with eighteen thousand men; and, after receiving the submission of many Italian cities, he entered Rome and Naples in triumph. But when the King of France considered his Italian conquests secure, a powerful coalition was formed against him by the Italian princes, the Emperor Maximilian I. of Germany, and Ferdinand and Isabella of Spain. The allies attempted to cut off Charles's retreat to France, but he defeated their united forces in the battle of Fornovo, and reached his kingdom in safety; but all his conquests in Italy were lost to him. The whole kingdom of Naples was soon recovered from the French by the able Spanish general, Gonsalvo de Cordova, "the Great Captain." The events of these Italian wars of Charles the Courteous will be more fully narrated in another part of this volume.

In 1497 Charles the Courteous sent another expedition into Italy to retrieve his fallen fortunes, but soon concluded a truce with his enemies, and his troops returned. He had ruined his health by debauchery, but he now suddenly surprised and gratified his friends by dismissing the companions of his guilty pleasures and forsaking his evil habits. He then applied himself diligently to public affairs and introduced many salutary reforms in the government, thus seeming to live only for the good of his subjects. He dismissed all unjust judges and unworthy persons from their offices. He showed a determination to effect a reform in the manners of the clergy, whose extreme ignorance and vices had made them contemptible in the eyes of the people, when his life was suddenly cut short.

Charles the Courteous was suddenly attacked with apoplexy at his splendid new palace at Amboise, April 17, 1498, falling senseless to the ground as he said to one of his attendants that he hoped he should never commit another sinful act, and dying soon afterward on a wretched bed to which he had been carried, in the twenty-eighth year of his age and the fifteenth of his reign.

Charles VIII. was a sovereign with a good natural disposition. His kindness of manner and his amiable qualities endeared him to all who knew him, and it is said that he never uttered an expression which could wound the feelings of any human being. His courtesy and affability acquired for him the surname of *the Courteous*. Two of his servants are said to have died of sorrow for his death; and his widow, Anne of Brittany, was almost crazy with grief. But his father's barbarous policy in depriving him of the advantages of education and confining him in the company of menials produced the worst effects on his character, giving him a taste for sensual pleasures, because he knew no other, and causing that mixture of obstinacy and indecision in his character so commonly perceptible in persons of vigorous minds and little information.

On the death of Charles the Courteous, in 1498, without children, his third cousin, the Duke of Orleans, ascended the throne of France with the title of LOUIS XII., and was the only King of France belonging to the Orleans-Valois branch of the dynasty of the Capets. He was anointed at Rheims, May 27, 1498, and was crowned at St. Denis, July 1, 1498. He was the grandson of the Duke of Orleans who had been assassinated by Duke Philip the Good of Burgundy in 1407, and was the great-grandson of King Charles the Wise. He was in the prime of life at the time of his accession. The calamities which he had suffered in the early part of his life produced a beneficial effect upon his character. Louis XII. was one of the best kings that ever wore a crown. He was so solicitous for the welfare of his subjects, and was so beloved by them in return, that he was called "*the Father of his People.*"

Immediately on his accession, Louis XII. rewarded the zeal and fidelity of George d'Amboise, Archbishop of Rouen, by appointing him prime minister; and never did a favorite better deserve the confidence of his master. During his entire administration this minister caused the sciences and trade to flourish. He was a munificent patron of literature, and his general conduct caused him to be as much beloved as his sovereign. He labored zealously to effect a reformation among the clergy, and promoted this reformation by his own example; as he would hold but one benefice at a time, and devoted two-thirds of the revenue of that benefice to the relief of the poor and the repair of churches.

The first care of Louis XII. was to lessen the taxes and to improve the administration of justice. Being importuned to remove from the command of the army a brave old general, De la Trimouille, who had taken him prisoner at the battle of St. Aubin, Louis XII. magnanimously replied: "It does not become the King of France to revenge the injuries of the Duke of Orleans." His niece and former rival, Anne of Beaujeu, Duchess of Bourbon, was distinguished by special marks of favor and regard; and those who had taken part against him in his struggle with that princess during the minority of Charles VIII. were assured that they need have no fear of losing their positions.

Anne of Brittany, the widow of Charles VIII., had retired to Nantes soon after the death of her husband, and had resumed the government of the duchy of Brittany, living like an independent sovereign. Louis XII. was already married to a wife whom Louis XI. had forced him to espouse, and who was a princess of blameless reputation and great merit, though deformed in person. In order to carry out the treaty for the union of the duchy of Brittany with the French crown, it was necessary for Louis XII. to divorce his wife and marry Anne of Brittany, as he had no children. Pope Alexander VI. granted a dispensation for this purpose; re-

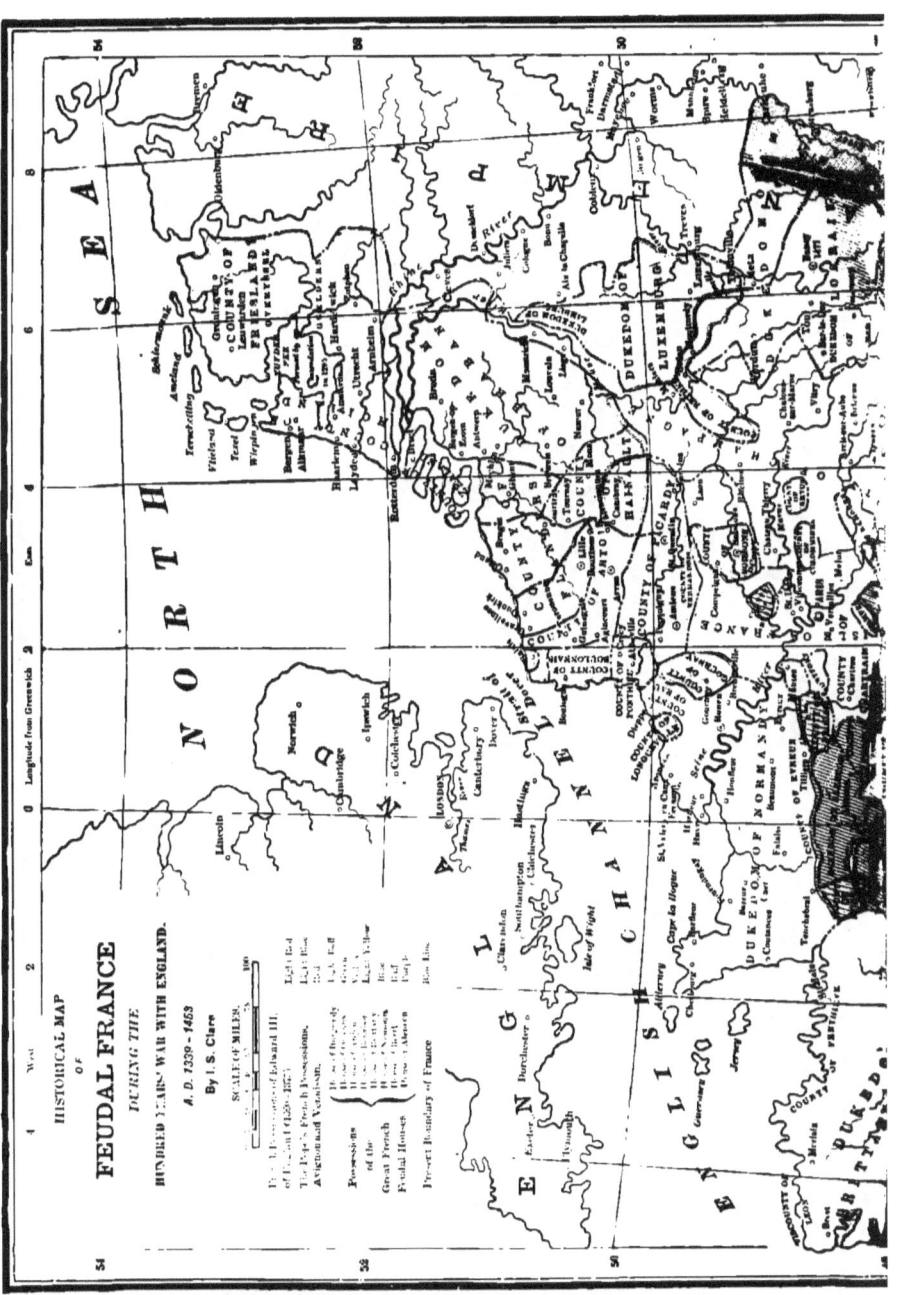

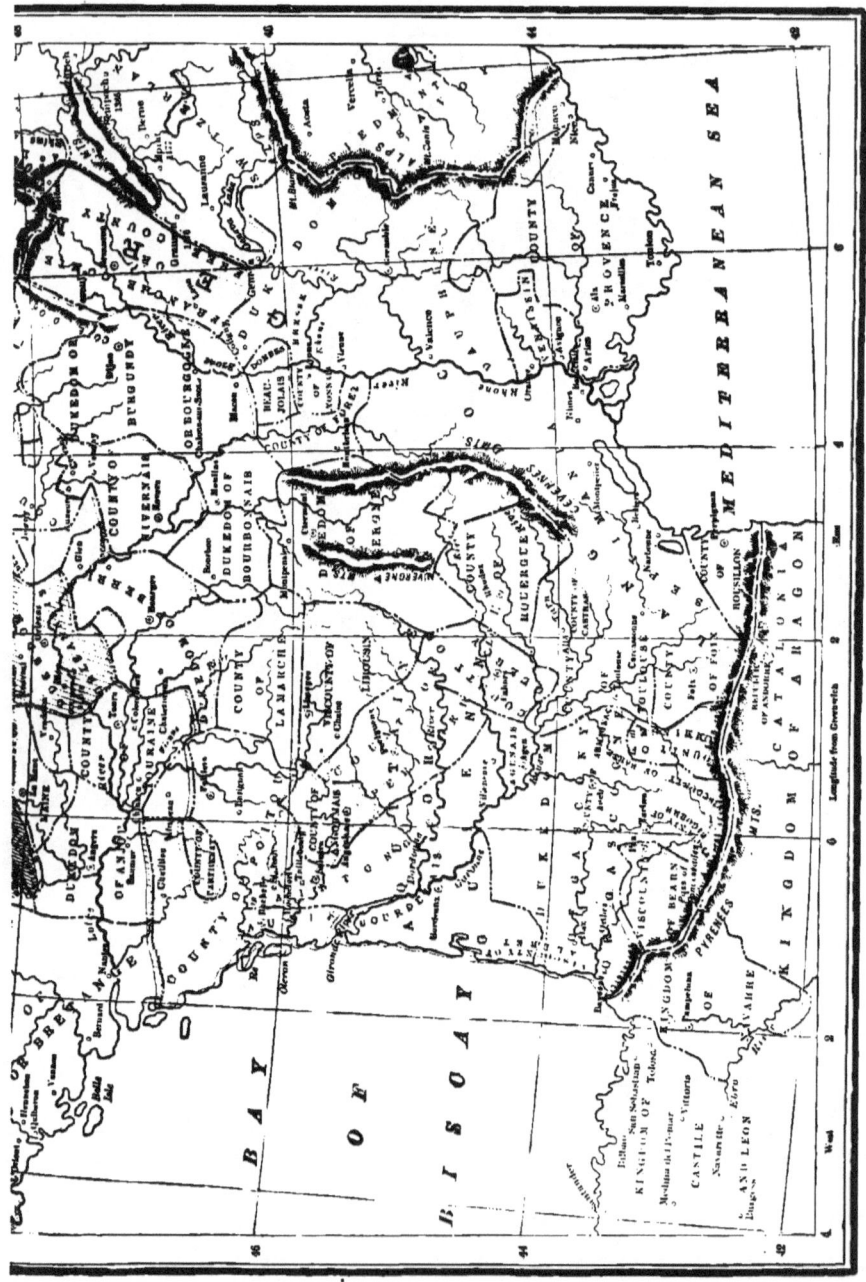

ceiving in return for his share in the transaction the title of Duke of Valentenois, in Dauphiny, and a handsome pension for his son, Cæsar Borgia. Louis XII. then married Anne of Brittany. The queen retained the administration of the duchy of Brittany; and it was stipulated that if there should be no children by this marriage Brittany should revert to the descendants of its ancient dukes, and that if two sons were born to Louis XII. and Anne the second son should be Duke of Brittany.

Anne was quite remarkable for the propriety of her conduct and for her simple manners. Her court was a model of decorum. She was always surrounded by a numerous train of young ladies, whom she employed in embroidering and other work suitable to their rank. She herself would sit at work in the midst of these ladies. She was a very excellent woman, and was one of the best of the Queens of France. Her heart is still preserved in the Royal Library of Paris, inclosed in a gold case.

In 1499 King Louis XII. sent an army into Italy to enforce his hereditary claims upon Milan. The French conquered Milan and Genoa, and Louis XII. and King Ferdinand the Catholic of Spain wrested Naples from its king, Frederick; but a quarrel arose between the robbers, and the Spanish king forced the French monarch to yield his claim upon Naples. In 1508 Pope Julius II., the Emperor Maximilian I. of Germany, King Ferdinand the Catholic of Spain, and King Louis XII. of France formed the powerful League of Cambray against the Republic of Venice; but the Pope and Louis soon quarreled and open war ensued, and the Venetians secured the alliance of the Pope and the King of Spain. The French defeated the combined forces of their enemies in the great battle of Ravenna, on the 11th of April, 1512. In the following year (1513) King Henry VIII. of England invaded France and won the *Battle of the Spurs*, near Tournay.

Anne of Brittany, the wife of Louis XII., died in 1514. The king was sincerely attached to her, and was deeply afflicted by her death. Louis XII. now concluded peace with all his enemies but the Swiss, who refused to treat with him. By the terms of the treaty Louis XII. paid a large indemnity to England and married the Princess Mary, the sister of King Henry VIII., August 7, 1514. Louis XII. died a few months after this marriage, January 1, 1515, and was deeply mourned by his subjects. As his only children were two daughters, his heir was his cousin Count Francis d'Angoulême. On his death-bed Louis XII. sent for this prince, and, embracing him, said: "I am dying; I commend my subjects to your care."

The French people justly venerated the memory of Louis XII., because he diminished the old taxes one-half and never imposed any new ones, notwithstanding his long wars and many reverses. He vindicated his economy by frequently saying: "I had rather see the courtiers laugh at my avarice than my people weep on account of my expenses."

During this period flourished the celebrated French historian Philippe de Comines, who was born in 1447, and whose *Memoirs* present a vivid and reliable account of the court of Louis XI. and of the chief events and general character of the age in which he lived. This great mediæval French historian died in 1511.

SECTION III.—FEUDAL ENGLAND.

AS WE have seen, the battle of Hastings made WILLIAM THE CONQUEROR King of England, and he was the first of the four Norman kings who ruled that kingdom. At his coronation in Westminster Abbey on Christmas Day, A. D. 1066, both English and Norman nobles were present, and good order prevailed inside the building. The question asked these nobles was: "Will you have William, Duke of Normandy, for your king?" Both parties answered "Yes," with loud acclamations. But the Norman soldiers outside, imagining that the noise signified violence against their duke, attacked the multitude who had assembled about the doors from innocent curiosity, and even set fire to houses in the vicinity. King William the Conqueror, after receiving his English crown from the Archbishop of Canterbury, succeeded in quieting the tumult; but only after a sense of personal wrong had been added to the national despair of the vanquished English.

William the Conqueror loved justice, and endeavored to reconcile his Anglo-Saxon subjects to his rule by enforcing the laws impartially on rich and poor, both English and Norman-French alike. He sought to learn English, for the purpose of better understanding and governing his new subjects. He placed his Norman countrymen in all civil and military commands, and divided among them the estates of those English soldiers who had fallen at Stamford Bridge and Hastings, but he first left all other proprietors in possession of their lands. He erected strong castles to overawe London, Winchester and other English cities; but he was careful to confirm all the commercial and other privileges which those cities had enjoyed. By thus covering the hand of steel with the glove of velvet, the Norman Conqueror of England so far silenced opposition that he considered it safe to revisit his duchy of Normandy, taking many English earls with him to swell his royal train and display the wealth of the conquered kingdom, while they served as hostages for the good behavior of their Anglo-Saxon countrymen.

King William's absence from England was a disaster to the kingdom, as his officers were neither so just nor so wise as their master; and their violence and avarice excited animosity between the Normans and Angle-Saxons, which was not appeased for several centuries. About half of England yet remained unconquered. The men of the Danelagh scorned submission to the Norman Conqueror, and offered their homage to Sweyn II., King of Denmark, who entered the Humber with a large fleet and army in A. D. 1069 and besieged and took York, massacring the Norman garrison of three thousand men.

Great numbers of the English, who had hitherto smothered their discontent, now felt encouraged to cast off the Norman yoke, and the kingdom was everywhere ready for revolt. But William the Conqueror now acted with exceeding and effectual severity. After bribing the Danish invaders to return to Denmark, he turned upon the armed rebels of the Danelagh with a tiger-like ferocity; ravaging the sea-board so that no Dane should find either foothold or plunder thereafter, and laying waste with fire and sword the old fertile region of Deira, between the Humber and the Tees, the heart of the rebellion. The devastation was so complete that for the space of sixty miles north of York the entire region remained for half a century without a human being, a barren waste, and marked only by blackened ruins. One hundred thousand people, who had fled from their homes to the woods when William appeared, died of starvation after returning to the ashes of their homes.

This cruel work was performed in midwinter, but the hard-hearted king at once started for the West of England, where the revolt was still formidable; the starving army toiling painfully on its way, with the tireless king at its head, through an unbroken wilderness, covered with snow drifts and crossed by swollen streams; and with the fall of Chester the rebellion was virtually ended.

Many of the vanquished Danes and Saxons

The vindictive Norman King of England then began a wholesale confiscation of the estates of the vanquished rebels. These confiscated lands were divided among the Norman knights and nobles who had fought under King William's standard, while the former Anglo-Saxon and Danish owners of the lands either found refuge in foreign

WESTMINSTER ABBEY.

CLOISTER.

countries or organized in hostile bands and waged a desultory warfare with their Norman conquerors. Hereward, a Saxon noble, retired to the isle of Ely, where, protected by almost impenetrable marshes, he bade defiance to the Norman power for a long time. But William built a causeway across the swamps and finally forced the valiant Saxon chief to surrender.

took to the woods as robbers and outlaws. Others proceeded to Constantinople and enlisted in the guards of the Eastern Emperor. Many of the fugitive Danish and Saxon nobles were hospitably received by Malcolm Canmore, King of Scotland—among them being Edgar the Atheling and his two sisters, one of whom married the Scottish king.

After the Saxon rebellion had been suppressed William the Conqueror put Normans into all high places in church and state; and Lanfranc, an Italian monk, whose piety and learning had already wrought a great reformation in the Norman monasteries, was now created Archbishop of Canterbury. Necessarily, all the business of the government and of the courts of justice, the services of the Church, except such as regularly employed Latin, and the exercises of the schools, were conducted in the Norman-French language. Thus Norman-French came largely into use, even among English people; but the English masses still continued to talk in their Anglo-Saxon tongue.

The Norman Conquest of England was now complete, and William the Conqueror turned his attention to the organization of the government, with a view to its future security. For this purpose he put Normans into all places of power and trust; and the military power of the government was based on the Feudal System, which had already prevailed in Continental Europe for several centuries, and which the Norman Conqueror introduced into England as a bulwark to his throne. Under this system the great Norman lords were granted well-nigh absolute power over the persons and property of their English tenants, on certain conditions, the most important of which was that they should come to the king's support with all their vassals whenever he should call them to arms. These nobles, or barons, usually living in strongly fortified castles, and constantly surrounded by devoted bodies of vassals, thus became petty sovereigns, passing their time in hunting, or in making war on each other, and sometimes on the king himself. Although the Feudal System was a bulwark to the Norman Conqueror's throne against the vanquished English, that system became the chief danger to the throne when the spirit of disaffection infected the Norman nobility, who had been made powerful and independent.

The completeness of William's confiscation of the English lands is seen in the fact that he was enabled to grant vast estates to his more powerful Norman followers; his half-brother Odo, Bishop of Bayeux, receiving two hundred manors in Kent, with as many in other parts of England; and grants almost as large being conferred on the king's ministers, Fitz-Osbern and Montgomery, and on such barons as the Mowbrays, the Warrens and the Clares; while the poorest Norman soldier of fortune had a part in the spoil, and the humblest Norman rose to wealth and power in his illustrious duke's new dominion.

The last Englishman who retained any power or importance was Waltheof, son of the famous Siward, Earl of Northumberland. After being received into the Norman Conqueror's favor, Waltheof married the Lady Judith, William's niece, and was presented with three rich earldoms. The high-spirited Norman barons, who always resented the imperious temper of their duke, had become still more restive after he had been elevated to a royal dignity; and at a wedding party, when the wine was flowing freely, an actual revolt was proposed. The Saxon Waltheof assented to the proposal of the Norman lords, but with his cooler judgment the next morning he revealed the plot to his wife. As Judith hated her husband she availed herself of this means to accomplish his ruin.

King William was then in his duchy of Normandy, where he received a letter from Lady Judith informing him of the conspiracy and exaggerating Waltheof's guilt. Waltheof himself hastened to Normandy to detail the entire affair to William. But the king's mind was influenced against the Saxon chief; and, contrary to his usual justice, he nursed his wrath until a day of retribution. Before William's return to England his officers quelled the revolt, with the assistance of the English themselves; but the punishment of the rebels was reserved for the king himself, and he executed it with unusual severity. Some of the offenders were blinded, and others were immured in dungeons; but Waltheof, the least guilty, suffered the heaviest penalty, being condemned and beheaded as a traitor. His faithless wife gained nothing by her treachery; as she soon fell under the king's displeasure, passing the rest of her life in shame and remorse, and being universally detested.

Thousands visited Waltheof's tomb as a martyr's shrine. The English believed that the Conqueror's good fortune deserted him on the day of Waltheof's execution. Peace departed from him; and "his bow was broken, his sword blunted." William's last years were visited by the heaviest sorrows. His eldest son, Robert, a turbulent and misgoverned youth, desired to become Duke of Normandy even during his father's life-time, and was joined by a party of turbulent young courtiers in a rebellion against his father. King Philip I. of France, who was always jealous of the Duke of Normandy, gave Robert a castle on the Norman frontier for his headquarters, whence he and his wild companions sallied forth to ravage Normandy.

William besieged the castle, and in a fight beneath its walls father and son met in deadly combat, both being concealed by their helmets. Wiliam was wounded, and his cry for help first made known to his rebellious son that the latter was about to slay his own father. Robert was instantly stricken with remorse and terror, and fell on his knees, imploring his father's pardon. Peace was restored for a time, through the intervention of the barons, and particularly of Matilda, William's worthy wife and Robert's mother. Robert then made his first visit to England, and was assigned the command of an expedition into Scotland.

The Scots and the Welsh were pacified; but King William had to encounter a nearer enemy in his half-brother Odo, Bishop of Bayeux, to whom he had intrusted the government of England during his absence in Normandy. Odo desired to be a king, but his ambition soon aspired to a higher dignity. He used his royal brother's treasures to buy votes in Rome, and bribed the same brother's soldiers to enter his service, for the purpose of transporting an army to Italy and making himself Pope by force in the place of Gregory VII., Hildebrand, whose arrogance and insolence had offended all princes of Christendom. The king returned from Normandy just in time to check his ambitious half-brother's bold enterprise. William arrested Odo with his own hands, and sent him to Normandy, where he was imprisoned in the castle of Rouen. William's good queen Matilda died soon afterward, worn out with cares and sorrows, and the Conqueror seldom smiled thereafter.

The Conqueror's wife Matilda was the daughter of the Earl of Flanders, through whom the present royal family of England traces it descent from Egbert, the first king of all England. The famous *Bayeux Tapestry*—so called from being kept at Bayeux, in Normandy—was the handiwork of Matilda; and was a piece of canvass sixty-eight yards long and nineteen inches wide, on which scenes and figures giving a complete pictorial history of the Norman Conquest of England were embroidered in wool.

William had many enemies. King Canute IV. of Denmark prepared an immense fleet, being secretly encouraged by people in the North-east of England, and hoping to recover his grandfather's island kingdom. This Danish fleet was "glued to the coast" by head-winds, which the superstitious believed to have been raised by the spells of wierd women; but the magic in the case was no other than that which was wrought by English gold, with which King William's emissaries bribed the Danish leaders.

For the better organization of his kingdom, and for the more certain collection of its revenues, William the Conqueror ordered a general survey of the estates of the English realm—the most celebrated act of his reign. Commissioners were appointed in all the cities and towns of England, except London and the four Northern counties —Northumberland, Cumberland, Westmoreland and Durham—to make an exact registration of all estates and capital. The reports of these commissioners were arranged and copied on vellum into the two great volumes of the *Domesday Book*, which is still preserved in the Tower of London, and in which Englishmen may yet see the landed possessions of their ancestors eight centuries ago accurately described. From this famous register the crown dues were carefully calculated and rigidly collected. Domesday Book and Windsor Castle are the most celebrated of the works of William the Conqueror yet remaining.

William the Conqueror established the curfew bell, which was rung from every church-tower and monastery in England, at sunset in summer, and at eight o'clock in the evening in winter, as a signal for the people to cover the fires on the hearth and to retire to rest. The law of the curfew was designed as a safeguard against conflagrations, and had prevailed for a long time in different parts of Europe, where fires were frequent and extensive in the wood-built towns.

Among the worst acts of William the Conqueror was his conversion of large tracts of land into hunting grounds. He formed the *New Forest*, in Hampshire, by laying waste an extensive tract reaching from Winchester to the English Channel, burning sixty villages and driving the inhabitants from their homes. "He loved the tall deer as if he were their father," according to an old rhyme; and the killing of the king's game called forth a severer punishment than the murder of a man.

William the Conqueror introduced a mode of trial called *Wager of Battle*, or *Single Combat*; by which an accused person was permitted to challenge his accuser to mortal combat, and if he came out of the struggle victorious he was pronounced innocent, otherwise he was declared guilty.

The Norman Conqueror abolished the slave trade, which had long been a source of wealth to the merchants of Bristol; and he formally abolished capital punishment, only one person suffering death for crime during his entire reign. He likewise became a friend and patron of the Jews, who were then a despised and persecuted people, and permitted them to erect dwellings and synagogues in all the principal towns of England.

William the Conqueror was a true Roman Catholic, and strengthened the Church by establishing ecclesiastical courts, which proved the source of so much trouble in the reign of Henry II.; but he bluntly refused obedience to the Pope's command to do homage for his realm. When Pope Gregory VII., Hildebrand, called on William to

WINDSOR CASTLE.

do fealty for his realm the Conqueror rejected the demand in this vigorous style: "Fealty I have never willed to do, nor do I will to do it now. I have never promised it, nor do I find that my predecessors did it to yours." No papal letters could be received in his kingdom without his permission. He required the Norman bishops and abbots, whom he had appointed to the places of their English predecessors, to lead the most exemplary lives, and he instantly dismissed those whom he found unworthy.

William the Conqueror met with a characteristic end, losing his life on an errand of vengeance in 1087, after reigning over England twenty-one years. He had become corpulent during the latter years of his life; and once, while suffering from illness, he had been made the subject of a silly jest by King Philip I. of France. William felt so deeply mortified by this treatment that after recovering he laid waste the French king's lands bordering on the duchy of Normandy, and burned the town of Mantes. While riding through the burning town his horse reared among the hot embers that filled the road and stumbled upon a burning brand, and the Conqueror of England received mortal injuries from the pommel of his saddle from which he died at Rouen several weeks afterward. Just before his death he divided his dominions among his three sons; bequeathing the duchy of Normandy to his eldest son Robert, the Kingdom of England to his second son William Rufus, and a large treasure to his youngest son Henry.

After receiving the announcement of their inheritance William Rufus and Henry hastened to secure it, leaving their dying father in the care of hirelings. As soon as the king had drawn his last breath his attendants rushed to horse, eager to secure their own interests under the new reign. The lowest servants stole every article which they could find, and fled, leaving their dead master on the floor unattended. The obsequies of the Conqueror were attended to by a poor knight named Herlouin, who as sole mourner attended the dead king's remains to Caen, to be interred in a magnificent abbey which William had erected in that important city of Normandy.

Peace was denied the unhappy Conqueror even in death. Caen was at that very moment a prey to a conflagration, which destroyed a large part of the city and dispersed the funeral procession, leaving only a few monks about the corpse. Just when the words "Ashes to ashes, dust to dust" were about to be chanted, a voice rang through the abbey forbidding the burial of the body, because the ground where the grave was dug had been unjustly taken from its rightful owner, the complainant's father. The funeral rites were suspended while witnesses were examined and money was counted out to pay for the ground; after which the mortal remains of William the Conqueror, Duke of Normandy and King of England, were laid at rest.

There was a grandeur about the Norman Conqueror that was not characteristic of any other King of England. This was alike manifest in his fearless humanity and in his dauntless ferocity. He was reserved, haughty, severe in his rule, ruthless in his revenge, "stark to baron or rebel," but "mild to them that loved God;" thus inspiring a mingled sense of respect and awe in all about him—a sense doubtless heightened by a consciousness of his great physical strength, as no ordinary man was able to swing his battle-ax or bend his bow. With a ferocity having few parallels in all history, he blotted out rebellious towns, and brought a death-like silence on offending districts; while, with a humanity in remarkable contrast with the spirit of the age in which he lived, he formally abolished capital punishment. He could brook no opposition, and was like a raging lion to all who withstood him, except to Anselm, the good Abbot of Bec, in whose presence he was always gentle and patient.

WILLIAM RUFUS—whose surname signified "the Red," because of his ruddy complexion—who became King of England upon his father's death, in 1087, seized the royal treasures and several fortresses, upon his arrival in England, before making known his father's death. Archbishop Lanfranc then hastened to crown him before any opposition could be offered; and that ceremony was performed September 26, 1087, seventeen days after his father's death. His uncle, Odo, Bishop of Bayeux, headed a party which attempted to crown the new king's elder brother, Duke Robert of Normandy, King of England; but William Rufus made such fine promises to the English that they heartily rallied to his cause, thus enabling him to crush the rebellion raised in Robert's interest.

The English soon had reason to regret their loyalty to the cause of William Rufus, as he forgot all his promises of good laws as soon as all danger to his throne was past; and, instead of the light taxes that they had been promised, they were required to bear the heaviest burdens to supply the king's extravagant wants. Wherever the king and court went they did as much damage as an invading army; as the king's followers lived at free quarters on the country people, and frequently plundered and sold the property of their hosts, also washing their horses' legs with the liquor that they did not drink. Thus William Rufus was a selfish tyrant, not deterred by law or religion from using his great talents entirely in the pursuit of pleasure and power.

William Rufus was his father's equal in personal courage, violence of temper and strength of will ; but he was the Conqueror's inferior in all the higher moral qualities. He was coarse and profane in speech, mean and covetous in disposition, and prodigal and licentious in his habits. He kept his ministers busy contriving means to extort new taxes from his subjects.

Archbishop Lanfranc's death, in A. D. 1089, was a cause of intense sorrow to the English. Though an Italian, and thus a foreigner to both Normandy and England, he was the friend, advocate and protector of the common people—a noble office which became inseparable from the duties of Primate of the Church in England.

William Rufus hated the Church for the same reason that a robber hates the judge— because it was the only power which could rebuke and measurably restrain his evil passions. A law of the realm bestowed on the crown the revenues of vacant bishoprics and abbeys. He refused to fill such vacancies as long as possible, so that he might appropriate their incomes to himself, or sold them to the most unworthy persons ; and when the vacant sees were filled he burdened them with enormous taxes. By these means he robbed the Church of its rights and the people of their religious privileges. The money which the king thus obtained was used for the gratification of his desire for debasing pleasures, and for the enrichment of his worthless courtiers.

For some years after Lanfranc's death William Rufus kept for his own use the great revenues of the archbishopric of Canterbury, but finally a severe illness awakened his conscience, whereupon he appointed the good Abbot Anselm to the office of Archbishop of Canterbury. When William Rufus recovered his health he resumed his old crimes, but he found Anselm to be a firm and able antagonist. After a long and angry contest between the king and the Primate, Anselm retired from England and took refuge with the Pope.

William Rufus and his brothers Robert and Henry spent several years in wars with each other for the possession of their father's entire dominions. Many of the Norman barons had estates in both England and Normandy, and found it impossible to serve two masters who were so at variance as were William Rufus and Robert. William Rufus failed in an attempt to wrest Normandy from Robert in 1090, after which these two brothers became reconciled and turned their arms against their younger brother Henry, whom they vanquished.

William Rufus was recalled from Normandy by an invasion of England by Malcolm Canmore, King of Scotland, who was induced to make peace and to do homage to the King of England for his crown. Malcolm Canmore again invaded England in 1093, but was defeated and slain in a battle at Alnwick Castle in the same year. As a precaution against such Scottish inroads, William Rufus rebuilt Carlisle, which had been in ruins for a long time, erected a strong castle at that frontier town, and peopled it with colonists from the South of England.

A few years later William Rufus obtained the duchy of Normandy from his brother Robert in an unexpected manner. It was at this time that Christendom sprang to arms and engaged in the First Crusade to wrest Palestine from the hands of the Seljuk Turks, who had conquered the Holy Land and ill-treated the Christian pilgrims to the Holy Sepulcher on Mount Calvary. Duke Robert of Normandy was one of the leaders of the First Crusade. To obtain the necessary funds, he mortgaged his entire duchy of Normandy to his brother, King William Rufus, for ten thousand marks. William Rufus raised this sum by extorting the money from all classes of his subjects, even forcing the churches to melt their gold and silver plate to furnish their share. With this sum Duke Robert joined the army of the Crusaders, and William Rufus took possession of the mortgaged duchy of Normandy.

Under William Rufus one-third of all the

pected of discharging the fatal arrow, but he always denied it, though he fled from the kingdom. The dead king's body was conveyed by a poor charcoal-burner in his cart to Winchester, where it was buried without religious rites. William Rufus was the third of his family who suffered violent deaths in the New Forest; and the poor people whose homes had been destroyed for this cruel pastime considered his fate a proof of the just retribution from Heaven for the Conqueror's heartless cruelty. William

THE TOWER OF LONDON.

lands in England were *King's Forests*, in which the king's will was the only law— an adequate reason why they were the favorite resorts of the godless king and his reckless followers. William Rufus met with a tragic death, in the year A. D. 1100, while hunting in the New Forest, which his father had made in Hampshire; being pierced to the brain by an arrow from one of the hunting party, whether by design or accident was uncertain. Walter Tyrrel, one of the hunting party, was sus-

Rufus was never married. He built two historical edifices in London—the Tower and Westminster Hall.

HENRY I., the brother and successor of William Rufus and the youngest son of William the Conqueror, was also hunting in the New Forest when he heard of his brother's death. He instantly put spurs to his horse and hastened to secure the royal treasury at Winchester; after which he galloped off to London, was saluted as King of England by the bishops and barons, and was crowned in Westminster Abbey three days after the death of William Rufus; thus usurping the English crown by forestalling his elder brother Robert, who was loitering on his way home from the Holy Land.

As Henry I. was at first opposed by the barons, who espoused his absent brother Robert's cause, he followed the example of his dead brother William Rufus by falling back on the support of the English. He soon conciliated all parties by granting a *Charter of Liberties*, in which he solemnly swore to observe the laws of Edward the Confessor; renounced the right to plunder the Church by allowing its sees and abbeys to remain vacant; promised not to sell or lease the vacant benefices of the Church; and bound himself to exempt his vassals, the Norman barons, from certain exactions and restrictions, on condition that the barons granted the same relief to their own vassals, the English people. He removed the evil companions of his brother William Rufus from the positions to which they had been appointed by that king, and recalled Anselm to the archbishopric of Canterbury.

Henry I. had been born and educated in England and spoke its language well, while also being a great favorite with the English people. His writs and charters were issued in English, instead of Latin. His learning, unusual in that age, acquired for him the surname of *Beauclerc*, the "Fine Scholar." He pleased the English people most and gained the support of the Scots by marrying Edith, the daughter of Malcolm Canmore, King of Scotland, and a great-granddaughter of Edmund Ironside; thus uniting the Saxon and Norman dynasties, and restoring in the descendants of this princess the ancient line of Cerdic and Odin. Upon her marriage with Henry I., Edith took the Norman name of Matilda, or Maud.

The character of Henry I. was a strange combination of virtues and vices. He was unscrupulous, false-hearted and revengeful; but he promoted the welfare and happiness of his subjects, encouraged manufactures, improved the coinage, established a system of weights and measures, repealed the odious law of the curfew, and reorganized the courts of justice. The system of justice established by Henry I. is the system now existing in England and the United States, with modifications and improvements. When he endowed the great towns of England with charters of freedom he struck a heavy blow at the Feudal System in his kingdom and gave a great impulse to liberty.

Upon returning from the Holy Land, Robert took undisputed possession of the duchy of Normandy, his old inheritance, which he had mortgaged to William Rufus; after which he proceeded with his army of Crusaders to enforce his claims to the English crown. But the unbounded enthusiasm of the English people at the marriage of King Henry I. with an English princess could not be overcome; and when Robert landed in England, and raised his standard as the rightful heir to the English crown, he found himself opposed by sixty thousand resolute English yeomanry. The two brothers pitched their camps in sight of each other, but both dreaded to begin the unbrotherly strife; and, after several days had thus passed, a treaty was made between them, through the exertions of Archbishop Anselm and others, Robert renouncing his claims to the English crown for a pension of three thousand marks a year for himself, while his followers were pardoned.

No sooner had Robert returned to his duchy of Normandy, and the Norman barons in England dispersed to their castles, than Henry I. began to confiscate the estates of all the barons implicated in the rebellion in Robert's interest. Indignant at his royal brother's treachery, the chivalrous Robert instantly summoned his vassals to renew the war. Claiming that Robert had thus broken the treaty, and finding that the barons of Normandy were dissatisfied with their duke, Henry I. crossed the Channel and invaded Normandy with a large army in 1106, defeated Robert's army and took Robert himself prisoner, received the homage of all Robert's vassals and thus took possession of Normandy, and then returned to England with his captive brother Robert, who was doomed to life-long captivity in Cardiff Castle, in Wales.

It is said that Robert having once attempted to escape, Henry I. caused his captive brother's eyes to be put out with a hot iron; so that this noblest of the sons of William the Conqueror lingered twenty-nine years in sightless captivity, finally dying in his dungeon a blind old man of eighty years, A. D. 1135, the very year of the death of Henry I.

In the meantime a quarrel ensued between King Henry I. and Archbishop Anselm, in consequence of the king's claim that the bishops and abbots should be nominated by the crown and be its vassals. Anselm defended the Pope's right to make such nominations without kingly interference. Henry I. was finally obliged to yield some of his pretensions, and the Pope's power in England was thus strengthened.

Henry I. settled a colony of Flemings in Wales, in the district of Ross in Pembrokeshire. These Flemish colonists engaged in the tilling of the soil and the manufacture of cloth. They increased rapidly in numbers and in prosperity, and held their own against the Welsh princes who sought to expel them.

Henry's cruel treatment of his brother preyed unceasingly on his mind, and thenceforth he did not have a moment's happiness. He vainly endeavored to stifle his remorse by founding monasteries and erecting churches. Though suffering under the burden of one crime, he was meditating the commission of another, that of murdering his nephew William, Robert's son, a boy of ten years, whose rightful claims to the duchy of Normandy kept his royal uncle in continual dread and prevented him from enjoying what he had acquired so unjustly; but Henry I. failed in his attempts to get possession of the young prince, who took refuge with King Louis VI. of France.

The French king's attacks on Normandy, in the name of the young refugee Norman prince, kept King Henry I. in continual disquiet. The armies of the Kings of England and France encountered each other at Brenneville, near Rouen, the capital of Normandy, in which the English were victorious, and which was the first battle between the English and the French. As each party desired to take prisoners for ransom rather than take life, only three knights were slain out of the many engaged in the battle.

King Henry I. reaped much sorrow and little joy from his ambitious and unjust schemes, and his last years were rendered sad and gloomy by the death of his good queen Matilda in 1118, and also by the melancholy death of his only son, Prince William, by shipwreck in 1120.

The king and his son had been on a visit to Normandy to secure the acknowledgment of the young prince as heir to all his father's dominions and to complete a marriage contract with the daughter of the Count of Anjou. After both matters had been arranged satisfactorily, they embarked in different ships to return to England. Some accident delayed the *White Ship*, in which Prince William had taken passage. The prince had ordered some wine to be given to the crew, and the sailors drank so freely that many of them became intoxicated. When the vessel got to sea the drunken pilot ran it upon a rock and all but one on board perished. When Henry I. was informed of the terrible catastrophe he fainted away, and is said to have never smiled again.

The only surviving child of King Henry I. was Matilda, wife of the German Emperor Henry V. For want of a son, Henry I. resolved to bequeath his dominions to his daughter, although neither Normans nor Saxons had ever tried the hazardous experiment of putting the crown on a woman's head. After the death of her imperial husband, Matilda was married to Geoffrey Plantagenet, Count of Anjou, on which occasion all the barons of both Normandy and England did homage to her as their liege-lady. The nobles repeated their oaths of fealty after the birth of Henry Plantagenet, Matilda's son with her second husband; and two years later, A. D. 1135,

King Henry I. died, bequeathing all his dominions to Matilda.

Before Matilda could return to England to take the crown that was her lawful right, it was usurped by Count Stephen of Blois, nephew of Henry I. and grandson of William the Conqueror by his daughter Adela, Countess of Blois. Stephen, who was affable in his manners and familiar in his address, had made himself a general favorite with the citizens of London, thus paving his way to the throne.

Stephen of Blois and his brother Henry had been invited to England by King Henry I., who had conferred honors and estates upon them. In return, Stephen and his brother professed great gratitude and affection for Henry I., and expressed their desire for the accession of his daughter to the English throne; but as soon as Henry I. had died Count Stephen hastened to London, and by misrepresentations induced the Archbishop of Canterbury to crown and anoint him King of England. The religious rite of kingly consecration was highly reverenced, and a bull which Stephen obtained from the Pope confirming his title increased the respect in which it was held. Normandy followed England's example by acknowledging STEPHEN, who thus became King of England and Duke of Normandy, A. D. 1135.

The usurper did not have quiet possession of his throne, as Matilda appealed to arms to enforce her rights, thus involving England in civil war. Her uncle, King David I. of Scotland, invaded the North of England to enforce his niece's right to the English crown. With an army of wild and lawless Highlanders, the Scottish king inflicted havoc on both the supporters and the enemies of Matilda. The Archbishop of York took the field against this army of marauding Scots, and utterly routed them in the great *Battle of the Standard*, at North Allerton, in Yorkshire, A. D. 1138, driving them across the border.

Matilda herself came to England the next year with a small body of troops to claim her kingdom, and was joined by many barons who had become restive under Stephen's iron rule. Matilda's chief supporter was her half-brother, Robert, Earl of Gloucester; while Stephen's brother, Henry, Bishop of Winchester, the papal legate in England, likewise espoused her cause for a time, being offended in a violent quarrel between his brother and the clergy. Stephen was defeated and taken prisoner in a battle at Lincoln in 1141, and was sent in chains to Gloucester Castle.

MATILDA then entered London, and was solemnly acknowledged Queen of England by an assembly of the clergy. Her authority seemed about to be established over the entire kingdom; but her haughty manners and her violent temper, so much in contrast with Stephen's generous and good-natured ways, soon changed her friends into foes and cost her the crown. She peremptorily rejected the three conditions proposed by her supporters—the restoration of the laws of Edward the Confessor; the confirmation of Stephen's son Eustace in his father's inherited estates; and Stephen's release from captivity, on his promise to renounce all pretensions to the English crown and to enter a monastery.

The Pope's legate in England, offended by Matilda's rejection of his advice, took up arms against the haughty queen; and her brother and chief defender, Earl Robert of Gloucester, was soon afterward made prisoner in battle. Matilda was obliged to exchange the captive king for her captive brother, and the flames of civil war raged more fiercely than ever for some years. The rapid approach of Stephen's heroic wife with an army, and the ringing of the alarm bells of London, caused a general uprising of the people, thus compelling Matilda to flee in haste from the city, and she found refuge inside the walls of Oxford Castle.

Stephen, again at liberty and at the head of his army, speedily surrounded Matilda's place of refuge, disposing his troops in such a manner as apparently to cut off every avenue of escape. The garrison in the castle ran short of provisions; and Matilda, with three devoted knights, clad herself in white to resemble the snow that then covered the ground, passed silently through the lines of Stephen's army in the night, crossed the frozen Thames, and took refuge among her loyal subjects in the West of England, whence she retired to Normandy four years afterward. About the same time her brother, Earl Robert of Gloucester, died.

The situation changed as Henry Plantagenet, Matilda's son, grew to manhood. That prince had spent some years in Scotland, whence he made raids into England; and by his military talents he revived the confidence of his party. When he was seventeen years old he was made Duke of Normandy, with the suzerainty of Brittany, by his mother's consent; and upon his father's death, soon afterward, he became Count of Anjou and Maine. By his marriage with the great heiress, Eleanor of Aquitaine, a few weeks after her divorce from her first husband, King Louis VII. of France, he came into possession of the large duchy of Aquitaine and the counties of Poitou and Touraine. Thus Henry Plantagenet was lord of the whole western half of the Kingdom of France, his territories in that country being far more extensive than those of the French king himself.

Henry Plantagenet's promotion in rank and wealth induced the barons of England to invite him thither, and in 1153 he crossed the Channel with an army collected from his French provinces, thus renewing the civil war with Stephen. But the bishops of England, under the lead of Theobald, Archbishop of Canterbury, weary of the strife that had been the cause of such calamity to the kingdom, brought about a treaty at Winchester, A. D. 1153. Stephen and Henry Plantagenet spoke with each other from opposite sides of the Thames, and agreed that Stephen should remain King of England during his life and that Henry should be his successor. It was also agreed that the grants of crown-lands which Stephen had made should be canceled, that the new castles should be demolished, and that the foreign troops should be dismissed. Henry Plantagenet then returned to France, and peacefully ascended the English throne upon Stephen's death the next year, A. D. 1154.

Stephen was influenced to this treaty by the death of his eldest son and by the defection of his leading nobles, some of whom had turned against him, while more of them had abandoned the struggle and retired to their estates. This showed the practical workings of the Feudal System.

To gain the support of the barons, Stephen had permitted them to erect new castles on their estates at the commencement of his reign, and had also granted new titles of nobility to his chosen adherents. Thus one hundred and twenty-six castles were erected, many of which were of great strength and built on inaccessible heights. Secure in these strongholds, the barons lived like petty princes, defying the king's authority and renewing old family quarrels. They plundered the country in the vicinity of their estates, and taxed their tenants to the point of starvation. Even the churches were despoiled of their wealth. The wealthy were waylaid as they journeyed, and were held or tortured for ransom. These nobles acquired the title of *Robber Barons.*

Following the example of the Robber Barons, criminals and outcasts, idle soldiers and starving peasants, in all parts of England, took to the woods and became outlaws, thus making it perilous to travel in some districts without the protection of an armed escort. Banded together, sometimes in large numbers, these outlaws of the forest set the laws and the authorities at defiance, or retreated to their hiding places in the dense recesses of the forest, where they were safe from pursuit. Many of these bandits were rude and ruthless men, and spared neither age nor sex; while others were generous and courteous, and robbed the rich for the purpose of relieving the wants of the poor.

It is almost impossible to describe the anarchy and misery which afflicted England during Stephen's reign. Towns were deserted; farms were neglected; the sanctuaries were filled with helpless, starving people; and thousands fled in terror from the country.

HENRY II., or Henry Plantagenet, Duke of Normandy, Brittany, Aquitaine and Gascony, and Count of Anjou, Maine, Poitou and Touraine, who became King of England upon Stephen's death in 1154, was the first of the renowned dynasty of the Plantagenets who occupied the English throne for three hundred aud thirty-one years (A. D. 1154-1485). As Duke of Aquitaine he was, besides being suzerain of Gascony, feudal lord of the counties of Saintonge, Angoumois, La Marche, Perigord, Quercy, Agenois, Bearn, Auvergne, the seigniory of Bourbonnois, and the viscounty of Limousin. Being feudal lord of all the Western provinces of France, from the English Channel on the north to the Pyrenees on the south, he possessed far more extensive territories in France than his suzerain, King Louis VII. of France; and when he became King of England he was a greater monarch than his lord-paramount, and was one of the most powerful sovereigns of Europe.

The reign of Henry II. was one of the most important in English history, and was contemporary throughout with that of Frederick Barbarossa in Germany. Henry II. was a man of hard, practical sense, of great firmness and energy, and had been carefully educated. He delighted in the society of learned men, and was a man of broad, liberal views in many respects.

No king ever ascended the English throne under more peculiar circumstances—circumstances in some respects more appalling—than greeted the first of the illustrious French family of the Plantagenets on his accession to the sovereignty of this island kingdom. During Stephen's wretched reign the whole structure of society had fallen to pieces, regard for law and respect for religion having been swept away in the general wreck. The spirit of lawlessness, which commenced with the nobility, had permeated the priesthood and the peasantry. When priest and noble turned robber, it is not surprising that the helpless peasant either became an outlaw, or deserted home and harvest-field, and fled in consternation beyond the sea. The best elements of society had become demoralized for the time being. Though only twenty-one years old when he became King of England, Henry II. undertook the task of reconstruction with a courage and an intelligence that challenge admiration. His efforts were principally directed to the restoration of order and the correction of the abuses of the Church.

One after another of the Robber Barons was subdued, and their castles were razed to the ground; while the outlaws of the forest were mercilessly hunted down. The crown-lands were also reclaimed, and the foreign soldiers were expelled. The king issued two sweeping edicts, in order to increase the royal power and to weaken the baronage still more. One of these edicts, issued in 1159, substituted the payment of money, called *shield money*, for the personal services of the barons in time of war; thus enabling the king to keep a paid standing military force. The other edict, issued in 1181, restored the militia; making every freeman a soldier, always to be properly armed, and subject to the king's call in time of national danger.

The struggle of Henry II. with the Church was more difficult and more dangerous than that with the barons. Under the Saxon and Danish Kings of England the judges and the bishops sat together on the civil benches; but William the Conqueror had established separate courts for ecclesiastical cases, over which the bishops alone presided. Criminals among the clergy were thus put beyond the jurisdiction of the civil authorities, and by a canon of the Church the priesthood could not impose the death penalty upon one of their own order, so that these priestly criminals were likewise exempt from extreme punishment. Under such a condition of things, it is no wonder that the Church had become arrogant and independent, or that during the first few years of the reign of Henry II. one hundred murders were committed by priests, some of whom were punished merely by some trifling penance or degradation in office, while the others suffered no punishment whatever.

The struggle between church and state which now convulsed England was far more violent than the contest between King Edwy and St. Dunstan or the controversies which William Rufus and Henry I. had with Archbishop Anselm. Thomas à Becket, the son of a London merchant, was the first Englishman since Waltheof who had risen to great power in England. He had improved many fine talents by studying law at Bologna, in Italy; and after his return to his native land King Henry II. lavished offices, revenues and honors upon him. He was created Lord Chancellor, and was followed by an army of knights. Great nobles, and even the king, often accepted his hospitality and sought his aid in the education of their sons. Henry II. finally appointed Becket to the dignity of Archbishop of Canterbury, thinking he was securing a useful instrument for his struggle with the Church, but in this expectation he was sadly disappointed.

Becket's character appeared to experience a sudden and complete change from the time that he became Primate of the Church in England. The man who had before been the king's bosom friend and companion— the man whom Henry II. had raised from poverty to affluence, from the position of tutor to his children to the highest ecclesiastical dignity in England—now withdrew from court, and immediately abandoned his former pomp and adopted habits of austerity and asceticism. Instead of the costly banquets in which he had formerly indulged, he now subsisted on a scanty fare of bread and water. He tore his flesh with the scourge, and daily washed the feet of thirteen beggars in imitation of his Master's humility. All this was practically to declare hostility to his king.

Becket at once made himself the uncompromising champion of the Pope's supremacy in England, and this action on his part was highly resented by King Henry II. The chief point of controversy was the claim of the Church to judge all crimes committed by persons in her employ, independently of the civil courts. Soon after Becket's consecration as Archbishop of Canterbury a clerk committed a disgraceful crime and sought to conceal it by murder. The king ordered that the offender be given up to justice. Archbishop Becket kept him in the bishop's prison, and insisted that he could only be punished by removal from his office.

At the summons of King Henry II., a great council of nobles and bishops convened at the castle of Clarendon in January, 1164. With the consent of this assembly, an important charter called the *Constitutions of Clarendon* was given to the English people. This charter provided that the civil courts should have a certain jurisdiction over the ecclesiastical tribunals, and that even priestly criminals, when convicted by the church courts, should be stripped of their orders and turned over to the civil authorities for punishment.

After violent resistance, Archbishop Becket swore to support the Constitutions of Clarendon; but when Pope Alexander III. published a bull annulling this charter the English Primate expressed great sorrow and contrition for his former submission, and sought to unite all the English bishops in a league against King Henry II. The king turned upon the archbishop with such fury that Becket fled from the kingdom. King Louis VII. of France, who had many causes of jealousy against the King of England, gladly received the refugee Primate with all the honors due to a saint and a martyr; and Becket remained an exile in France for six years (A. D. 1164-1170).

In 1170, while Becket was still absent from England, Henry II. caused his eldest son Henry to be crowned as associate monarch by the Archbishop of York. Becket obtained a sentence from Pope Alexander III. declaring that the Archbishop of Canterbury alone had the right to crown any English sovereign, deposing the Archbishop of York and excommunicating all the bishops of England who had taken any part in this ceremony of coronation. As King Henry

II. was then in Normandy, Becket returned to England and was received with shouts of welcome by the clergy and by the common people, both of whom regarded the Primate as their champion against royal tyranny. Becket came back as haughty and determined as ever, and immediately caused it to be published that he brought with him the sentence of excommunication pronounced by the Pope against the Archbishop of York and two other bishops who had taken part in the coronation of Prince Henry, "the Younger King."

When King Henry II. was informed of Becket's haughty conduct, and of his triumphal entry into Rochester and Southwark, he was overcome by a fit of anger, during which he exclaimed: "What cowards have I brought up in my court. Is there none of my servants who will rid me of this pestilent priest?" Four knights in attendance on the king in Normandy—Reginald Fitz-Urse, William de Traci, Hugh de Moreville and Richard Brito—took the angry king at his word, proceeded to England and assassinated Becket before the altar of Canterbury Cathedral, December 11, 1170. The murdered Primate was one of the most remarkable men that England ever produced; being "a prelate of the most lofty, intrepid and inflexible spirit, who was able to cover to the world, and probably to himself, the enterprises of pride and ambition under the disguise of sanctity, and of zeal for the interests of religion."

Henry II. had intended to arrest Becket, but the news of the assassination of the Primate filled the king with consternation. Henry II. solemnly protested his innocence of complicity in the murder, and the Pope accepted his oath and consented to be appeased. Becket's tomb was revered as a martyr's shrine. In one year a hundred thousand pilgrims flocked thither from all parts of Christendom, and miracles were said to have been wrought by the holy relics. The murdered Primate was canonized by the Pope under the title of St. Thomas of Canterbury. The assassins went on a pilgrimage to Jerusalem, where they died; and on their tomb was inscribed this epitaph: "Here lie the wretches who murdered St. Thomas of Canterbury."

The struggle between church and state ended in the king's ultimate triumph. The clergy and the laity were made equal before the law. The supremacy of the state over the Church was achieved. Although Henry II. assented to a modification of the Constitutions of Clarendon after the assassination of Becket, this modification was merely nominal; the practise of the courts and the submission of the bishops showing that the king still retained all the substantial fruits of victory.

One of the most important events of the reign of Henry II. was the conquest of Ireland and the annexation of that island to the realm of England. In the very year that Henry II. became King of England, A. D. 1154, Nicholas Breakspear, the only Englishman who ever became Pope, was elected to the Chair of St. Peter and assumed the title of Adrian IV. Pope Adrian IV. immediately granted authority to King Henry II. to conquer Ireland, which was then divided into five native kingdoms—Ulster, Munster, Leinster, Connaught and Meath.

Many of the Celtic tribes of Ireland, the ancient Hibernia, had early embraced Christianity; and the conversion of the inhabitants was completed by St. Patrick in the fifth century. After the Saxons had conquered Britain the Irish made peace with them, instructed them in religion and founded schools among them. St. Bridget flourished in the sixth century, when the principal monastery of Ireland contained over a thousand monks. The piratical Danes ravaged Ireland as well as England and the Continent, and subdued the Irish people, who were under different chiefs. The Danes oppressed the conquered Irish with heavy taxes, subjecting the master of every house to a *nose-tax*, so called because the master of the house was required to pay an ounce of gold annually or have his nose cut off.

The Danes were finally defeated by Brian

MURDER OF THOMAS Á BECKET.

Boru, King of Munster, who fought twenty-five battles with the Northern invaders. This famous Irish hero maintained a large army and a fleet of three hundred vessels. To test the order prevailing in his kingdom, Brian Boru directed that a beautiful virgin should traverse it unprotected, carrying a costly ring on a wand; which she did without molestation. In the year A. D. 1000 Brian Boru was elected king of all Ireland, and the Irish people enjoyed peace and prosperity under his wise and vigorous administration, while intercourse was opened by Irish ambassadors with the various courts of Europe. Brian Boru finally broke the power of the Danes in Ireland in the great battle of Clontarf, near Dublin, A. D. 1014, but purchased his victory with the cost of his life. After his death Ireland was again divided, and devastated by wars between the rival chiefs or kings.

Although Pope Adrian IV. had granted to King Henry II. the right to invade and conquer Ireland as early as 1154, nothing was attempted in that direction until 1169. As it was usual for one of the five kings of Ireland to take the lead in the wars among them, he was styled king of the whole island. At this time Roderic O'Connor, King of Connaught, was elevated to that dignity. Dermot MacMorrough, King of Leinster, had kidnapped the daughter of the King of Meath, who was strengthened by the alliance of the King of Connaught, and was thus enabled to invade Leinster and punish its king. Thereupon Dermot Mac Morrough appealed to the King of England for aid against the other Irish kings.

King Henry II. readily accepted Dermot MacMorrough's offer, but as he was then occupied in his French dominions he only gave letters-patent authorizing all his subjects to aid the King of Leinster to recover his dominions. Relying on this authority, Dermot MacMorrough returned to Bristol, in England, where, after some difficulty, he concluded a treaty with Richard de Clare, Earl of Pembroke, surnamed *Strongbow*, who agreed to aid the exiled King of Leinster in recovering his dominions on condition of receiving Dermot's daughter Eva in marriage and being declared heir of his kingdom. Being thus assured of aid from England, Dermot MacMorrough returned privately to Ireland, and concealed himself during the winter in the monastery of Ferns, which he had founded.

In the spring of 1169 Robert Fitz-Stephen, a Norman knight, landed in Ireland at Bannow, on the Bann, a creek near Wexford, with one hundred and thirty knights, sixty esquires and three hundred archers. They were soon joined by Maurice Pendergast, who brought over ten knights and sixty archers about the same time; and with this small band they besieged and took Wexford, A. D. 1169. The Norman adventurers were reinforced by one hundred and fifty men under Maurice Fitz-Gerald, and the entire band composed a small army which struck awe into the barbarous Irish. Roderic O'Connor, King of Connaught and chief monarch of Ireland, ventured to oppose the Norman invaders, but he was defeated; and the Prince of Ossory was obliged to submit soon afterward and to give hostages for his future good behavior.

Being thus reinstated in his hereditary Kingdom of Leinster, Dermot MacMorrough soon entertained hopes of extending his dominion over all Ireland. With these views he sought to expedite Strongbow, who had been thus far prohibited by King Henry II. from crossing over into Ireland. Demot MacMorrough endeavored to arouse his ambition by the glory of the conquest of Ireland, and to excite his avarice by the advantages which that conquest would procure. He expatiated on the cowardice of the Irish and on the certainty of success.

Strongbow first sent over Raymond, one of his retinue, with ten knights and seventy archers; and after receiving permission for himself from King Henry II., soon afterward, he landed in Ireland with two hundred cavalry and a hundred archers. All these English forces were now combined and became irresistible, although altogether they only numbered about eleven hundred men. The Irish were so barbarous that they were unable to withstand this Anglo-Norman chivalry, and were everywhere routed. Strongbow speedily took the city of Waterford soon after landing, A. D. 1170, and also took Dublin by assault. Soon afterward Strongbow married Eva, Dermot MacMorrough's daughter; and Dermot himself died about the same time, bequeathing his Kingdom of Leinster to Strongbow, according to the treaty between them.

Ireland was thus practically subdued, as nothing was capable of resisting the further progress of the English arms; and Henry II. was now willing to share personally in those honors which the Norman adventurers had already secured. He therefore landed in Ireland in 1171 with five hundred knights and some soldiers, simply to take possession of a kingdom already conquered and to receive the homage of his new subjects. He confirmed most of the Irish chiefs in possession of their estates, on condition of feudal homage; and after appointing Strongbow as his Seneschal, or Lord Lieutenant, of Ireland, he returned to England to receive the congratulations of his subjects and the Pope's confirmation of his new sovereignty.

Thus seven centuries ago the English conquered the Emerald Isle with trifling expense of blood and treasure, and that beautiful island has ever since been an appendage of the English crown. But the English authority was merely nominal; and for centuries Ireland remained in a condition of complete anarchy, torn by the contentions of the Anglo-Norman lords and the native Irish chiefs.

One of the most interesting works of the reign of Henry II. was his improvement of the judiciary system founded by Henry I. He divided England into six judicial districts, each with three traveling judges, who went regularly on their circuits, having jurisdiction over noble and peasant, and trying all cases brought before them. In this way the subject was spared the great expense of a journey to London, and justice was made easily accessible to all the people of England.

The most radical change during the reign of Henry II. was that made in the form of trial. We have alluded to the method of trial called the Ordeal, or the Judgment of God, and also to the form called Compurgation, when the accused was convicted or acquitted on the oaths of his kinsmen or neighbors—both of which modes were brought from Germany by the Anglo-Saxons. We have also referred to the method of Wager of Battle, or Single Combat, introduced by William the Conqueror.

The first mention of Trial by Jury handed down to us occurred during the reign of Henry II., when by the Assize of Clarendon, in 1166, twelve freemen chosen from the hundred, and four from each township, acting in the double capacity of judges and witnesses, presented alleged criminals for the Judgment of God or the Wager of Battle. The same Assize abolished Compurgation.

The Plantagenets inherited the tendency to family quarrels, along with their dominions, from the Norman dynasty. The four sons of Henry II. were aided and abetted by their mother, Queen Eleanor, and by her former husband, King Louis VII. of France, in rebellion against their father. War broke out in Henry's French dominions; and at the same time his English kingdom was invaded by the Scots from the north and by the Flemings from the east.

These calamities aroused the king's sluggish conscience, and he determined to make peace with the murdered Thomas à Becket. Accordingly in 1174 he returned to England from Normandy on a pilgrimage of penitence, and when he came within sight of Canterbury Cathedral he dismounted and walked bareheaded and barefooted to Becket's tomb, where he fasted and prayed all day and all night; after which he caused the whole brotherhood of monks to be assembled, presented each of them with a scourge, and begged them to apply the lashes severely to his bare back, "for the good of his soul." The next day he received absolution for all his crimes and errors; and soon afterward he was informed that on the same day his army in the North had defeated and captured King William the Lion of Scotland near Alnwick Castle. This happy omen was regarded as proof of St. Thomas's forgiveness and of the favor of Heaven. King Louis VII. of France also made peace; Henry's rebellious sons returned to obedience; and King William the Lion of Scotland, with all his nobles and bishops, did homage to Henry II., acknowledging himself and his posterity as vassals of the Plantagenets.

The domestic peace of Henry II. did not last very long. He had assigned Ireland to his youngest and favorite son, John; but that prince showed his wretched unfitness to govern, by driving the Irish chiefs into rebellion, and his father was obliged to recall him. Another son, Prince Henry, died in France, in the midst of the rebellion which he renewed against his father; and Richard, the eldest surviving son and therefore now the heir to his father's dominions, as soon as his brother Geoffrey with whom he had been at war had been killed in a tournament at Paris, also took up arms against his father. Soon after Geoffrey's death his widow gave birth to a son, who was named Arthur, and whom Henry II. invested with the duchy of Brittany, of which, as Duke of Normandy, he was the feudal lord.

Henry II. was so humiliated and enfeebled by the unnatural conduct of his sons that he finally agreed to all the demands of his enemies, one of which was a free pardon to the barons who had taken part in Richard's rebellion. After the treaty of peace had been signed, the king, who was then sick in bed, asked to see the list of the rebels that he had consented to pardon; and then the unhappy king saw with grief and amazement that his youngest and favorite son John's name was at the head of the list. His heart was broken by this last stroke of ingratitude, and he turned his face toward the wall, saying: "Now let the world go as it will, I care for nothing more." He died of fever after a few weeks' illness, at the castle of Chinon, on the Loire, in the county of Touraine, July 6, A. D. 1189, in the fifty-eighth year of his age and the thirty-fourth of his reign.

Henry II. was succeeded in all his dominions by his second son, RICHARD THE LION-HEARTED, whose rebellion had hastened his father's death. Richard's penitence for his undutiful conduct toward his father was lasting, and was productive of good for England, as he discarded the men who had supported him in his rebellion, and retained his father's faithful ministers in office, making them his counselors and friends.

Richard the Lion-hearted was in no sense an Englishman, and his reign had very little influence on English history. He was a Frenchman by birth, education and character; and during his ten years' reign he visited England but twice, and then only for a few months at a time. He was a valiant Crusader, a model knight, a brilliant poet, a gallant hero of romance. His most famous acts were connected with the Third Crusade, of which he was the principal hero. He was a skillful musician, and was familiar with the songs of the Troubadours.

Richard the Lion-hearted was of heroic stature, of noble and commanding appearance; and was possessed of the most indomitable courage, of unusual strength and of great endurance. He loved tilts and tournaments better than royal courts, daring deeds on hard-fought battle-fields more than cares and responsibilities of government. His very name, embalmed in song and story, has become a synonym for Chivalry. In him the king was subordinate to the knight. He was fearless of danger and mighty in battle, courteous to a gallant enemy and generous to a fallen foe.

Notwithstanding Richard's knightly virtues, beneath his iron armor there beat a hard, cold, selfish heart. Like his father he had an ungovernable temper. He was ambitious, haughty, domineering, revengeful, cruel, unscrupulous. He stained his knightly honor by many a dark and brutal deed. He cared little for the happiness or welfare of his subjects, his ambition being limited to the power to gratify an inordinate love of military glory and daring adventure. The

English have always been dazzled by his brilliant personal qualities and proud of his world-wide renown.

Richard's hatred of unbelievers—a highly Christian sentiment, according to the ideas of those times—produced deplorable consequences on the day of his coronation. The London Jews, who were numerous and wealthy, offered gifts of gold to celebrate the occasion, hoping thus to propitiate the royal favor. But the king had forbidden them to approach the banqueting-hall; their messengers were driven away; and suddenly a rumor was circulated that the king had ordered a general massacre of all the Jews. An ignorant, fanatical and blood-thirsty mob thereupon slaughtered these despised and defenseless people, burned their houses and seized their hidden treasures.

As the news of this horror in London spread to other cities of England the same frenzy seized the inhabitants, the same terrible scenes were enacted, the same horrible massacre of innocent and helpless Hebrews. At York five hundred Jews, with their families, fled for refuge to the castle, which was soon surrounded by an armed and furious mob. The Jews vainly offered their wealth as a ransom for their lives. Hoping for neither justice nor mercy, they plunged their daggers into the bodies of their own wives and children rather than see them fall victims to their infuriated enemies, and then set fire to the castle and perished in the flames. King Richard the Lion-hearted had accepted their gifts and issued a proclamation in their favor, but he took no adequate measures for their protection.

In the summer of 1190 Richard the Lion-hearted united with King Philip Augustus of France and the chivalrous German Emperor Frederick Barbarossa in the Third Crusade. The Kings of England and France had arranged to proceed together to the Holy Land. To raise money for this Crusade, Richard sold crown-lands, offices, titles and pardons, and even released King William the Lion of Scotland from his allegiance, also restoring to him the fortresses of Berwick and Roxburgh, the proudest acquisitions of King Henry II. When rebuked by one of his friends for his lavish disposal of crown property, Richard is said to have replied: "I would sell London, if I could find a purchaser."

Richard left the government of England in charge of his Chancellor, William Longchamp, Bishop of Ely, and started on his expedition to Palestine. The Kings of England and France met at Vezelay, where they discovered that their combined armies numbered one hundred thousand men. They sailed from different ports on the Mediterranean, but storms forced both to pass the winter in Sicily, where their warm friendship was changed into rivalry and hatred.

At Messina Richard was joined by the Princess Berengaria of Navarre, to whom he was already betrothed. As the marriage could not be performed in Lent, she sailed in company with her sister for the Holy Land. The vessel was once more overtaken by storms and driven into a port in the island of Cyprus, where the ladies suffered very rude treatment, and the crews of two attendant vessels were murdered in their presence. When Richard heard of this insult he landed in Cyprus, defeated its king, Isaac, in two battles, took him prisoner and loaded him with chains, assuming the sovereignty of the island for himself. The rejoicings for this victory over King Isaac were completed by Richard's marriage.

Upon arriving in Palestine the Kings of England and France found all the Christian forces occupied in the siege of the important seaport of Acre, which had withstood them two years. The arrival of the Crusaders inspired the Christian besieging army with such courage that Acre was soon forced to surrender, A. D. 1191. But Philip Augustus had now grown envious of the superior fame of Richard the Lion-hearted, and soon returned to France, after first taking a solemn oath not to meddle with England or Normandy. Richard's career in the Holy Land was full of stirring incidents of battle and adventure. He fought his way one hundred miles from Acre to Ascalon, where he defeated the renowned Sultan

PERSECUTION OF THE JEWS.

BATTLE BEFORE ACRE.

Saladin of Egypt in a great battle, A. D. 1192.

At this juncture Richard the Lion-hearted received important news from England. His brother John had usurped the regency, and, in alliance with the King of France, was attempting to deprive Richard of all his dominions. Richard, in great alarm for his English and French Dominions, embarked to return home; after first concluding a truce with Saladin by which the Christian pilgrims were permitted to visit the Holy Sepulcher unmolested, and relinquishing his purpose to attempt the recovery of Jerusalem, the goal of so many hopes, whose walls were in sight, but which he was never destined to enter.

Richard started by sea on his return home in 1192; but his vessel was wrecked in the Adriatic, and Richard landed at a port on that sea, whence he attempted to make his way to England by land through Germany, disguised as a merchant. He was recognized at Vienna by Duke Leopold of Austria, who seized him in revenge for his insult in causing the German flag to be torn down from the battlements of Acre and the English banner to be raised instead. The Duke of Austria sold his royal captive to his sovereign, Henry VI. of Germany, who loaded him with chains and imprisoned him in the little castle of Trifels, in the Tyrol.

Richard's enemies all hastened to take advantage of his misfortune. King Philip Augustus of France invaded the duchy of Normandy, and Richard's own brother John demanded the crown of England. Both sent messengers to the Emperor Henry VI., offering him a large sum of money to keep Richard in life-long captivity.

In the meantime Richard's mother Eleanor besought Pope Celestine III. to interfere for her captive son's release; setting forth the shame in permitting the champion of Christendom, the hero whose strong right arm had struck down so many enemies of the Cross, to languish in captivity. Finally, after a year's imprisonment, the captive king was summoned before the Diet of the Germano-Roman Empire to plead his own cause. His eloquence and the fame of his great exploits in the Holy-Land moved the hearts of the German princes and bishops; and the Emperor Henry VI. was forced, by the Pope's threat of excommunication and by the indignation of the German princes and prelates, to release Richard the Lion-hearted on the payment of a ransom of one hundred and fifty thousand marks by the English people. All classes in England were reduced to the greatest distress to raise this sum, the churches even melting down their plate. The English people, who remembered John's merciless extortions, joyfully welcomed Richard the Lion-hearted, who arrived in England in 1194, after an absence of four years.

His brother John was startled by the announcement from King Philip Augustus of France: "Take care of yourself, for the devil is unchained." John hastened to leave the country, but returned at Richard's command, and confessed on his knees his traitorous designs, at the same time humbly begging for pardon. Said Richard with characteristic generosity: "I hope I shall as easily forget his ingratitude as he will my forbearance."

After remaining in England but a few months, Richard the Lion-hearted crossed over into France to engage in hostilities with King Philip Augustus. When Richard was informed that the Viscount of Limousin, one of his French vassals, had found hidden treasure in one of his fields, he demanded its surrender, according to the common law that made treasure-trove the property of the feudal lord. The Viscount of Limousin refused compliance, and Richard at once besieged him in his castle of Chalus, but received a mortal wound during the siege, so that the hero of the Third Crusade perished in a private quarrel, April, 1199.

Richard's brother JOHN, surnamed *Lackland*, then became King of England, lord of Ireland, Duke of Normandy with the suzerainty of Brittany, Duke of Aquitaine with the suzerainty of Gascony, Count of

Anjou, Maine, Poitou and Touraine; and was crowned at Westminster the next month, May, A. D. 1199.

John was a weak, cowardly, incompetent, cruel, tyrannical and licentious sovereign; and his reign was one of continued misfortune for England. He was as base and cowardly as Richard the Lion-hearted was generous and chivalrous. His brazen boldness in the midst of safety speedily vanished in the presence of danger. He was grossly impious in his treatment of the sacred rites of the Church; but he was childishly superstitious, wearing charms and relics about his person as a safeguard against evil. Other Kings of England have been corrupt, but John was the most basely licentious of all of them.

John's nephew, Prince Arthur of Brittany, the son of his dead brother, Geoffrey Plantagenet, claimed John's territories in France; and King Philip Augustus of France espoused the cause of the young prince, who was a mere boy of fifteen. The King of France was unable to render Prince Arthur any active aid at first; but John's abduction of Isabella of Angoulême, the affianced bride of the Count de la Marche, afforded King Philip Augustus an opportunity of fulfilling his promise to the young prince. In the war which followed, King John took his youthful nephew prisoner, with many of his adherents, most of whom were starved to death. Prince Arthur himself was believed to have been stabbed to death by his wicked and cruel uncle in the castle of Rouen, A. D. 1203. The young prince's sister Eleanor was kept in close confinement by John until she wasted away and died.

King Philip Augustus, as John's feudal superior for his provinces in France, summoned him to answer for the murder of Prince Arthur; and, as John refused to appear, the French king declared all of his fiefs and lordships in France forfeited to the French crown, being sustained in that action by the "Peers of France." The universal horror produced by John's crime wrought powerfully against that despicable tyrant; and King Philip Augustus took castle after castle, and wrested from John by conquest the counties of Anjou, Maine, Poitou and Touraine, and finally the duchies of Normandy and Brittany; so that the duchy of Aquitaine, or Guienne, and the Channel Isles were the only French possessions remaining to the Plantagenets. The Channel Isles—Jersey, Guernsey and Alderney—still remain in England's possession.

John raised a large army and invaded the French territories to recover his lost possessions; but when the hostile armies were on the eve of battle he proposed peace, and fled ignominiously to England in the very midst of the negotiations. It was in consequence of the loss of his French territories that John received the surname of *Lackland*. This loss was a great gain for England in the end; because, when her kings had lost their feudal possessions in France, they were obliged to confine their attention to England, and thus became Englishmen, instead of being any longer French princes ruling England.

King John was next involved in a violent quarrel with Pope Innocent III. about the appointment of an Archbishop of Canterbury. John had secured the election of John de Gray to that dignity by the monks; but the Pope annulled the election and forced the monks of Christ's Church, Canterbury, to choose Stephen Langton. Langton was a good man, but the Pope's action was a violation of English rights in church and state. The angry king punished the monks for their compliance with the Pope's commands, by turning them out of doors, seizing their lands and treasures, and thus reducing them to beggary.

For the purpose of forcing John to compliance, Pope Innocent III. threatened to lay his kingdom under an interdict. The despicable king made light of the Pope's threat. In 1208 Innocent III. made good his threat, and the papal interdict fell upon England with all its horrors. The whole country was at once plunged into the deepest gloom. To the people the interdict was nothing less than the curse of God. The blessings and benedictions of religion were suddenly denied to every one except the innocent babe and the dying. During the four years that England thus remained under the Pope's curse it was as though a pestilence had spread its horrors over the land. The churches were closed, and their bells were not rung. "No knell was tolled for the dead; for the dead remained unburied. No merry peals welcomed the bridal procession; for no couple could be joined in wedlock."

John still remained obdurate; and after waiting two years for his submission, Pope Innocent III. finally excommunicated the obstinate king A. D. 1210. Even this did not have the desired effect upon the contumacious monarch; and two years later, A. D. 1212, Innocent III. pronounced a decree deposing John from his throne, absolving all his subjects from their allegiance to him, and declaring a crusade against him, so that it was made lawful and Christian for any man to kill the deposed monarch. Nothing could be more deplorable than John's situation at this time. Furious at his indignities, jealous of his subjects, not knowing whom to trust, and fearing a plot against his life, he shut himself up an entire night in the castle of Nottingham, and allowed no one to come near him.

The crusade preached against John by the Pope called upon all Christian princes and barons to make war upon the excommunicated and deposed king. Innocent III. especially commissioned the King of France to execute his decree of deposition, and Philip Augustus readily undertook to enforce the Pope's final decree. John continued defiant for a time, and if his English subjects hated him they had no love for Philip Augustus. Mustering a gigantic fleet, the Earl of Salisbury crossed the Channel and attacked the French at the mouth of the Seine, after which his victorious armies ravaged the coast of Normandy; thus ending the danger of a French invasion for the time.

John continued defiant for a while longer. Europe now impatiently watched the struggle between the Head of Christendom and the King of England—the struggle in which the Church was either to triumph or to be overthrown. But Pope Innocent III. was too refined a politician for either the King of England or the King of France. The astute pontiff only intended to intimidate and humble the refractory king, not to ruin him. The Pope therefore intimated to John, through his legate in England, that there was only one way by which the king could secure himself against impending danger, and that was to place himself under the protection of the Pope, who was a merciful father, ever willing to receive a repentant sinner to his bosom.

John was too much intimidated by the manifest danger of his situation not to embrace every means offered for his safety. Finding no encouragement in his resistance, and the elements of opposition in his own kingdom gathering about him like a thick cloud, his bravado forsook him, and he yielded to all the Pope's demands, assenting to the truth of the papal legate's remonstrances, and taking an oath to perform whatever stipulation the Pope should impose upon him; so that his submission to Innocent III. was as abject and humiliating as it was sudden and complete.

King John having thus sworn to perform any command which the Pope might impose, the crafty papal legate, Pandolf, managed the barons so well, and intimidated the despicable king so effectually, that he persuaded John to take the most extraordinary oath in all history. Every true Englishman felt a share of the national shame when this degenerate descendant of William the Conqueror, this cowardly son of Henry Plantagenet, this craven-hearted brother of the lion-hearted Richard, laid his crown at the feet of the papal legate, and on his knees before the legate took a solemn oath acknowledging himself a vassal of Pope Innocent III. and his Kingdoms of England and Ireland as papal fiefs, in the following words:

"I John, by the grace of God, King of

England and lord of Ireland, in order to expiate my sins, from my own free will and the advice of my barons, give to the Church of Rome, to Pope Innocent III. and his successors, the Kingdom of England and all other prerogatives of my crown. I will hereafter hold them as the Pope's vassal. I will be faithful to God, to the Church of Rome, to the Pope my master, and his successors legitimately elected. I promise to pay him a tribute of a thousand marks yearly; to wit, seven hundred for the Kingdom of England, and three hundred for the Kingdom of Ireland."

This was the only time in England's history of a thousand years that a King of England surrendered the independence of his country to a foreign potentate. After thus doing homage to the Pope for his crown, restoring the monks and nuns to their possessions, and recognizing Langton as Archbishop of Canterbury, John received back his crown as the Pope's vassal; while the papal legate trampled under his feet the tribute which the humiliated king had consented to pay. Upon his submission, Pope Innocent III. recalled his hostile decrees, and forbade King Philip Augustus of France to make war on the King of England, who was now the Pope's vassal, and whose kingdom was now one of the territories of the Church.

Thus, by the most humiliating and scandalous concessions, did King John avert the threatened blow. In this way, by repeated acts of cruelty, by expeditions without result and humiliations without reserve, did this despicable monarch become the detestation of all mankind.

The degradation of England enraged the barons, whose indignation had already been aroused by King John's disregard of their rights. Archbishop Langton was a true Englishman, and was faithful to his high office as an advocate and champion of the people's rights. He convened a council of barons and bishops at St. Edmundsbury, November 20, 1214, to whom he showed a recently found copy of the Charter of Liberties granted by King Henry I., and urged the assembled bishops and barons to insist upon the renewal and enforcement of the charter. Accordingly, the barons assembled their vassals and proceeded to rebellion against their king. John suddenly found himself face to face with all England in arms against him; and, being deserted by all his vassals except seven knights, he was obliged to grant all that his great vassals demanded.

The rebellious barons assembled a large army at Stamford, whence they marched to Brackley, about fifteen miles from Oxford, where the king then resided. Hearing of their approach, John sent Archbishop Langton, the Earl of Pembroke and other members of his council, to inquire what were the liberties which the revolted barons so much desired. The barons delivered a schedule containing the principal articles of their demands, of which the code of Edward the Confessor and the Charter of Liberties granted by Henry I. constituted the ground-work. As soon as these demands were shown to the king he burst into a furious rage and asked why the barons did not also demand his kingdom, swearing that he would never comply with such humiliating demands.

But the barons were now too strong for the weak king to cope with. They chose Robert Fitz-Walter for their general, dignifying him with the title of *Mareschal of the Army of God and of the Holy Church*, and proceeded to make war upon the king without further ceremony. They besieged Northampton, took Bedford, and were welcomed with joy in London. They wrote circular letters to all the nobility and gentry who had not yet declared in their favor, and threatened to ravage their estates in case of refusal or delay.

The terrified king, in utter consternation, first offered to refer all controversies to Pope Innocent III. alone, or to eight barons, four to be selected by himself, and four by the whole body of the revolted barons. The barons rejected John's proposition with scorn. He then assured them that he would submit at discretion, and that it was his supreme pleasure to grant all their demands.

A conference was therefore appointed, and all things were arranged for this most important settlement.

Accordingly, the king's commissioners met the revolted barons in the meadow called *Runnymede*, on the Thames, between Staines and Windsor—a place ever since held in reverence as the spot where the standard of constitutional freedom was first unfurled in England. There the barons appeared with a host of knights and warriors, June 15, 1215; while the king's representatives and forces came at the same time. Both sides encamped apart, like open enemies. The armed barons would admit of but few abatements; and, as the king's agents were mainly in the interest of his enemies, few debates ensued. On the same day King John signed and sealed the charter demanded of him—a charter which remains in force to the present day—the famous *Magna Charta*, "Great Charter"— the bulwark and foundation of English constitutional liberty; on which are based all the liberties enjoyed by the people of Great Britain and the United States—the most precious heritage of all the English races of the world.

Some of the most important principles of this great charter of English freedom can be traced to Anglo-Saxon origin, having been set aside by the Norman Conquest of England; while others were brought from the reigns of Henry I. and Henry II.; but all were made more broad and liberal, and were couched in the most explicit terms. The preamble of Magna Charta is as follows:

"John, by the grace of GOD, King of England, Lord of Ireland, Duke of Normandy and Aquitaine, and Count of Anjou; to his archbishops, bishops, abbots, earls, barons, justiciaries, foresters, sheriffs, governors, officers, and to all his bailiffs and liegemen, greeting:

"Know ye, that in presence of God, and for the health of our soul and the soul of our ancestors and heirs, and to the honor of God, and to the exaltation of His Holy Church, and for the amendment of our kingdom; by advice of our venerable fathers, Stephen, Archbishop of Canterbury, Primate of all England, and Cardinal of the Holy Roman Church; Henry, Archbishop of Dublin; William of London, Peter of Winchester, Jocelyn of Bath and Glastonbury, Hugh of Lincoln, Walter of Worcester, William of Coventry, and Benedict of Rochester, bishops; Master Pandolf, our lord the Pope's subdeacon and servant; Brother Aymeric, master of the Temple in England; and the noblemen William Marescall, Earl of Pembroke, William Earl of Salisbury, William Earl of Warren, William Earl of Arundel, Alan de Galloway, Constable of Scotland, Warin Fitzgerald, Peter Fitzherbert, Hubert de Burgh, Seneschal of Poitou, Hugh de Neville, Matthew Fitzherbert, Thomas Basset, Alan Basset, Philip de Albiney, Robert de Roppelaye, John Marescall, John Fitzhugh, and others our liegemen; we have granted to GOD, and by this our present charter confirmed, for us and our heirs forever."

The first clause is as follows: "That the English Church shall be free and enjoy her whole liberties inviolate. And that we will have them so to be observed, appears from this that of our mere good will we granted, and by our charter confirmed, the freedom of elections which was reckoned most necessary for the English Church, and obtained the confirmation thereof from our lord the Pope Innocent the Third, before the discord which has arisen between us and our barons; which charter we will ourselves observe, and will that it be observed in good faith by our heirs forever. We have also for us and our heirs forever granted to all the freemen of our kingdom, all the underwritten liberties to have and to hold to them and their heirs from us and our heirs"

The first clause just related secured the liberties of the Church in England. Other clauses remedied the grievances of the barons as tenants of the crown, and among these provisions was a specification that "no scutage or aid (assistance in money from a vassal to his lord) except in the three general feudal cases, the king's captivity, the knighting of his eldest son and the marrying of his eldest daughter, shall be imposed, but by the great council of the kingdom."

Measures were likewise inserted to prevent the arbitrary seizures of the lands of the nobles by the crown. After thus securing their own rights, the barons placed the liberties of the people on as sound a basis. It was ordained that all the privileges and immunities granted to the barons by the king should be extended by the barons to *their* vassals. The king bound himself not to grant any writ empowering a baron to levy any scutage or aid from his vassals, except in the three feudal cases already referred to.

It was also ordained that one weight and one measure should be established throughout the kingdom. Merchants should be allowed to transact all business, without being exposed to any arbitrary tolls and impositions. The merchants and all freemen should be permitted to go out of the kingdom and return at their pleasure.

The towns were secured in the enjoyment of their municipal privileges and their ancient liberties, immunities and free customs, their freedom from arbitrary taxation, their rights of justice, of common deliberation, of regulation of trade. This memorable article reads thus: "Let the city of London have all its old liberties and its free customs, as well by land as by water. Besides this, we will and grant that all other cities and boroughs and towns and ports have all their liberties and free customs." Aids were not to be required of these cities and burgs except by the consent of the great council of the kingdom.

No towns or individuals were to be obliged to make or support bridges, except by ancient custom. The goods of every freeman were to be disposed of according to his will. If he died intestate his heirs were to succeed to their possession. No officer of the crown had the right to take any horses, carts or wood without the owner's consent.

It was provided that the king's courts of justice should be stationary, that they should no longer follow the king's person, and that they should be open to every one. Circuits were to be regularly held every year. The inferior tribunals of justice—the county courts, sheriff's turn and courtleet— were to meet at their appointed times and places. The sheriff was incapacitated to hold pleas of the crown, and was not authorized to put any person on trial from mere rumor or suspicion, but upon the testimony of lawful witnesses. The following are the two most important provisions securing the liberties of Englishmen: *"No freeman shall be taken, or imprisoned, or dispossessed, or outlawed, or banished, or in any way destroyed; nor will we pass upon him, nor commit him, but by the lawful judgment of his peers, or by the law of the land.*

"To no man will we sell, to none will we delay, to none will we deny, right or justice."

Those who suffered otherwise in the reigns of John and his two immediate predecessors were to have their rights and possessions restored to them. It was also provided that every freeman should be fined in proportion to his fault, and that no fine should be levied on him to his utter ruin. Even a villain or rustic was not to be deprived of his carts, plows and farming implements. Even the worst was not to be deprived of the means of livelihood.

Many irregular exactions were abolished, or assessed at a regular rate. The undertenants or farmers were protected against all lawless exactions of their lords in precisely the same terms as the barons were protected against the lawless exactions of the crown. The abuses of wardship were reformed; and widows were protected against the compulsory marriages to which they had been subjected for the profit of the crown. It was provided that the bishops and the greater barons were to be summoned to the great council of the nation by special writ, and all tenants-in-chief through the sheriffs and bailiffs, at least forty days before.

The last clause is as follows: "Wherefore we do will and firmly do command that the Church of England be free; and that all men in our kingdom have and hold all the aforesaid liberties, and rights, and grants, well and in peace, freely and quietly, fully and wholly, as aforesaid, to them and their heirs, from us and our heirs forever. It is also sworn, as well on our part, as on that of the barons, that all the things aforesaid shall be observed in good faith and without evil intention. Witnessed by the above and many others. Given by our own hand, in the mead called Runnymede, between Windsor and Staines, this fifteenth day of June, in the seventeenth year of our reign."

One copy of this precious document still remains in the British Museum, injured by age and fire, but with the royal seal still hanging from the brown, shriveled parchment. Says the late John Richard Green, the eminent English historian: "It is impossible to gaze without reverence on the earliest monument of English freedom which we can see with our own eyes and touch with our own hands, the Great Charter to which from age to age patriots have looked back as the basis of English liberty." Hallam truly calls Magna Charta "the keystone of English liberty."

All the benefits conferred by the Great Charter were not realized by the English people for hundreds of years thereafter. Though its provisions were frequently ignored and openly trodden under foot by John and his successors, the great principles of liberty and justice which these provisions embodied were never forgotten by the English people. Amid the oppressions of aftertimes, these principles became the centers around which clustered the national hopes, the goal toward which the national efforts were directed. These principles were the beacon lights in an almost shoreless sea of misgovernment, guiding an oppressed people in their struggle for constitutional freedom. These principles are to-day the foundation and the bulwark of those liberties and privileges which render England and the United States the freest and happiest nations on the globe. Such was the foundation of the free constitution of England.

The unflinching patriotism of Archbishop Langton and most of the bishops of the Church of England in this momentous crisis should never be forgotten. Langton himself was the leader of the opposition to John's tyranny and the Pope's assumptions. The bishops and the barons stood side by side at Runnymede, indifferent alike to the king's execrations and the Pope's anathemas.

A council of twenty-four barons was appointed to force the king to comply with his solemn oath, with the right of declaring war against the king if he infringed its provisions; and the charter was published throughout the kingdom, and was sworn to at every hundred-mote and at every town-mote by the king's order.

King John, in an outburst of impotent rage, flung himself on the floor and gnawed like a wild beast at sticks and straw and anything that came within his reach, crying: "They have given me four and twenty over-kings!" But he promised the more readily, because he did not intend to perform. Before daybreak he had ridden from Windsor; and he lingered for months along the southern shores of England, the Cinque Ports and the Isle of Wight, while his agents were enlisting foreign troops in Continental Europe.

A special envoy from King John laid before Pope Innocent III. a copy of the Great Charter, which John declared had been wrenched from him by violence. The Pope, considering himself the real sovereign of England, declared that his rights had been encroached upon. He therefore annulled the Great Charter and excommunicated all who sustained it. Archbishop Langton courageously and patriotically refused to pronounce the papal bull of excommunication, and was suspended from the Primacy by Pope Innocent III. for his faithful exercise of the duties of his position as the champion of the liberties of England.

Strengthened by the Pope's bull, and still more by an army of foreign soldiers, King John broke all his promises, starved Rochester into submission, and marched from south to north, laying waste the kingdom with fire and sword, as far as the borders of Scotland. From Berwick the king turned back to oppose his enemies in London, where fresh papal anathemas fell upon the barons and the city. But the burghers of London defied Pope Innocent III. in the following words: "The ordering of secular matters appertaineth not to the Pope." Simon Langton, the Primate's brother, caused the bells to be rung and mass to be celebrated as before.

With the undisciplined militia of England, the barons were unable to cope with the king's trained foreign troops, and they sought the alliance of King Alexander II. of Scotland; but John compelled the Scottish monarch to stay in his own kingdom. In despair, the barons sought aid from France, offering the crown of England to Prince Louis, son of King Philip Augustus, who had married John's niece, Blanche of Castile, the granddaughter of Henry II. Prince Louis accepted the offer of the English barons, in spite of the Pope's excommunications, landed in England in May, 1216, with a large French army, took Rochester Castle, and made a triumphal entry into London amid the rejoicings of the citizens. The French prince seemed on the point of carrying everything before him, when King John, overcome by illness, shame and vexation, died suddenly at Newark, October 18, 1216, in the eighteenth year of his reign, leaving behind him the reputation of being the worst king that ever reigned over England.

John's wickedness was the source of two great benefits to the English people. The one was Magna Charta. The other was the loss of the French possessions of the Plantagenets, which was a piece of good fortune to England, because it forced her kings to confine their attention at home.

HENRY III., John's eldest son by his second wife, Isabella of Angoulême, succeeded his father as King of England and Duke of Aquitaine, being then a boy of ten years. He was crowned at Gloucester ten days after his father's death. William, Earl of Pembroke, a brave, able and upright man, who was made regent, or Protector of the Realm, during the youthful king's minority, exercised all the real power; and under his vigorous rule England was soon reduced to order. His first act was the renewal of Magna Charta, which John had violated.

Prince Louis of France, whom the barons had invited to wrest the crown of England from King John, alarmed his English supporters by granting English lands to his French followers; and accordingly the barons deserted him and joined the party of young Henry III. The Earl of Pembroke, with a few hundred knights, defeated the French troops under Prince Louis in a battle in the streets of Lincoln, in 1217; and an English squadron defeated a superior French naval force off Dover. Finding the hearts of the English turning to their legitimate king, Prince Louis left England never to return, renouncing all claim to the English crown.

Unfortunately for England the good Earl of Pembroke died in 1219, and was succeeded in the regency by Hubert de Burgh, a brave and faithful officer, whose gallant defense of Dover Strait and Castle had chiefly contributed to the defeat of the French invasion. He was succeeded by the Bishop of Winchester, a native of Poitou, whose extortions had occasioned many of the miseries of John's reign. By his advice, the young king invited a multitude of Frenchmen from Poitou into England, assigning them all the important positions in the court, and lavishing honors and riches upon them; thus disgusting his English subjects.

King Henry III. married Eleanor of Provence—a country at that time a part of Southern France, and celebrated for its wealth and luxury, as well as for the gay and brilliant genius of its inhabitants. The young queen brought with her to England a multitude of Provençal courtiers: and the marked indulgence shown them by the king increased the displeasure of the English.

The English people found a greater grievance in the exactions of the Italian clergy, who obtained a larger revenue from England than did the king himself. The Pope claimed the entire income of all vacant livings; one-twentieth from those which were occupied; one-third from all that exceeded one hundred marks a year; and one-half from those held by non-residents.

The Pope, as over-lord of England, had filled many vacant livings with foreign priests, and even demanded a share in the government of the kingdom. The king and his regent were frequently at variance with each other, and both were at times arrayed against the Pope. There was, however, one thing in which the King of England and the Pope were always agreed—the mutual effort to wring the last farthing from the poverty-stricken people.

The Pope worked upon the weakness of King Henry III. by bestowing the crown of Sicily upon his second son—a gift which only involved the king in an enormous debt, no less than in ridicule and disgrace. The Sicilian kingdom was one of the "fiefs of St. Peter," which the Pope claimed the right to grant to any one at his pleasure.

The king's brother, Richard, Earl of Cornwall, likewise desired to play a part in the affairs of Continental Europe. His great wealth, derived from the tin mines of his earldom, induced the German princes to elect him their sovereign, as we have seen in the history of the German Empire; but he was never crowned Emperor at Rome, and therefore he gained nothing but the empty title of King of the Romans, in exchange for his vast treasures.

The extortions of King Henry III., and his subserviency to foreign favorites, disgusted the brave barons of England. In 1225 a great council was summoned to deliberate on the question of supplies to the crown. A grant was made on condition of a new confirmation of Magna Charta. Thereafter the practice prevailed of making a confirmation of the Great Charter, or a redress of grievances, the condition of voting money to the crown. Some of the dearest rights now enjoyed by the people of England were retained or acquired in this way.

In 1227, when Henry III. was twenty-two years old, he assumed the government himself. He began his full assumption of power by endeavoring to make Magna Charta subordinate to the royal prerogative, in the following declaration:

"Whenever and wherever, and as often as it may be our pleasure, we may declare, interpret, enlarge or diminish the aforesaid statutes and their several parts by our own free will, and as to us shall seem expedient for the security of us and our land."

This declaration was the keynote of the policy of Henry III. for forty years; while the barons, distracted by feuds among themselves, stood idly by. The history of the entire period is only a dreary and monotonous record of royal recklessness and folly, of royal beggary and extortion. When in need of money, the king would swear on his honor as "a man, a Christian, a knight and a king," to preserve the provisions of the Great Charter inviolate; but the awful words had hardly died away among the arches of Westminster Hall, after his wants had been supplied, before he broke every solemn promise and trampled the provisions of the Great Charter under his feet in mere wantonness. Under the influence of the crown, even the courts of justice became but a legalized system of extortion and robbery, the judges on the circuits compounding felonies and selling justice to the highest bidder.

The chief of the king's French courtiers was Simon de Montfort, son of the Simon de Montfort who led the Crusaders who extinguished the unfortunate creed of the Albigenses, in the South of France, in blood a generation before. King Henry III. had elevated this Simon de Montfort to the dignity of Earl of Leicester, and had given him his own sister in marriage. But unlike the king's other French favorites, Simon de Montfort faithfully served the interests of the English people, who rewarded him with their enthusiastic devotion. He sustained Grosseteste of Lincoln—the best English bishop of that time—in his resistance to the Pope's unjust demands.

In 1257 England suffered from a dreadful famine, in consequence of a failure of crops. This calamity brought matters to a crisis in 1258. The king's brother, Earl Richard of Cornwall, King of Germany, sent a supply of corn from Germany to England for the relief of the starving English people; but King Henry III. seized the corn and sold it for his own profit. This enraged the barons, who met in arms at Oxford and insisted upon a Council of Regency to be chosen, half by the king and half by themselves.

King Henry III. being still in need of money, even after his outrageous transaction, he summoned the barons to a great council at Westminster. The barons obeyed the king's summons, but they came at the head of their men-at-arms. As Henry III. entered Westminster Hall and gazed upon the stern array of mail-clad barons, whose clanking swords alone broke the general silence, he inquired in sudden alarm: "Am I a prisoner?" The patriotic barons responded: "No, you are our sovereign; but your foreign favorites and your prodigality have brought misery upon the realm, and we demand that you confer authority upon those who are able and willing to redress the grievances of the public."

As the king was powerless to resist, he consented to the demands of the barons, as specified in the *Provisions of Oxford*, providing for a council of twenty-four barons, one half to be appointed by the barons and the other half by himself, empowered to act in behalf of the realm. Parliament was ordered to meet three times every year, whether summoned by the king or not; and "twelve honest men" were to represent the commonalty.

But the barons were soon divided, and many who sought honors and lands joined the royal party; but the more patriotic, with all the representatives of the English people, sustained Simon de Montfort, Earl of Leicester, who, with a reinforcement of fifteen thousand Londoners, achieved a brilliant victory over the king's army in the great battle of Lewes, in Sussex, in which King Henry III. and his gallant son, Prince Edward, were taken prisoners, May 14, 1264.

Earl Simon de Montfort, who was now the real head of the realm, summoned a Parliament in the king's name, inviting representatives of the people of England, to be composed of two knights from each shire, two citizens from each city, and two burgesses from each borough, to take their seats side by side with the bishops and the barons. This memorable Parliament convened at Westminster in January, 1265, and was the foundation of the future *House of Commons*, or popular branch of the English Parliament —the real beginning of true representative government. The House of Commons has ever since been the chief guardian of the rights and liberties of the people of England. John's tyranny gave rise to Magna Charta, the corner-stone of English constitutional liberty; while the oppressions of Henry III. led to the origin of the House of Commons, the bulwark and defense of that liberty. The two were wonderful landmarks in the progress of the Anglo-Saxon race.

But the English were soon called upon to mourn the death of their great leader—the founder of the House of Commons. Prince Edward, having escaped from captivity, speedily raised an army, with which he won a decisive victory in the great battle of Evesham, in Worcestershire, over the patriot forces under Earl Simon de Montfort and his son, both of whom were slain, August 4, 1265. This victory released the king from captivity; but no attempt was made to undo the great work of this illustrious patriot and statesman, whose name ranks with that of Archbishop Langton as an early champion of the English people's rights and liberties; and the right of the English people to representation in Parliament was permanently established.

As soon as the civil war between Henry III. and his barons was ended, Prince Edward, with a gallant array of barons, sailed for the Holy Land, to take part in the Seventh Crusade, A. D. 1270. The illustrious name of Plantagenet, and traditions of the chivalrous deeds of Richard the Lion-hearted, drew all the Christian forces

ROMAN PONTIFF AND GERMAN EMPEROR.

THE BLACK PRINCE (PRINCE EDWARD OF WALES).

GERMAN DUKE—GERMAN LADIES.

EBERHARD II. ("THE GREINER").

THE 12TH AND 13TH CENTURY.

of the East about the young prince, who won several victories over the Saracens, and struck such terror into their hearts that they sent an assassin to murder him. In trying to wrench a poisoned dagger from the assassin, Prince Edward was wounded in the hand during the scuffle; and this wound might have proven fatal had not his affectionate and devoted wife, Eleanor of Castile, who had accompanied her husband to Palestine, sucked the poison from his wound. After concluding a ten years' truce with the Saracens, Prince Edward sailed from Palestine on his return to England; and when he reached Sicily he heard of the death of his father, King Henry III., which occurred November 16, 1272.

During the dark and turbulent reign of Henry III. a steady light began to shine from the great University of Oxford, whose foundations were laid by Alfred the Great four centuries before; but the spirit of inquiry excited by the Crusades, with the new knowledge brought home from the East, had produced a great revival of zeal for the study of philosophy, law and ancient literature. In the great universities of the Middle Ages, thirty thousand scholars, traveling far over land and sea, were frequently assembled at one time about some celebrated teacher.

One of the most famous of these Schoolmen was Roger Bacon, whose wonderful mind was stored with all the learning of his time concerning the world of matter, no less than the mind and works of man. His lectures at Oxford were listened to by throngs of eager students, many of whom begged their daily bread, while others had followed their teacher's example in lavishing ample fortunes upon books and costly experiments, renouncing all ambition of honor or wealth, in search of the more precious treasures of wisdom. Roger Bacon was the father of English science. His physical researches anticipated many modern discoveries, the use of gunpowder in war among the rest.

Bacon, who was a Franciscan monk, furnished an example of the peril of great learning in an ignorant age, as did St. Dunstan three centuries before him. Although he was admired and reverenced by his pupils, his superiors in the Church saw nothing in his geometrical lines and circles but charms to force the attendance of evil spirits, and could comprehend the Greek, Hebrew or Arabic sentences which he repeated in his studies as nothing else than the language of these evil spirits. He was condemned by the council of his own Franciscan order; and passed the last ten years of his life in a dreary dungeon, deprived of his cherished books, and even of pens and parchment.

The *Mendicant Orders*, or *Begging Friars*—as the two monkish orders of the Franciscans and the Dominicans were called—bound themselves to absolute poverty and the service of the poor, owning nothing, living by daily alms, relieving distress, and acting as physicians and nurses as well as priests. During the civil war between Henry III. and his barons these mendicant monks were the steady friends of the people. They at first renounced learning, but soon had control of the University of Oxford, which became the firm foe of papal exactions and the stronghold of English freedom.

The chivalrous EDWARD I., who became King of England upon the death of his father, Henry III., in November, 1272, did not arrive in England on his return from the Holy Land until May, 1274. Edward I. was a true Englishman, and is ranked as the greatest of the Plantagenets. He was tall and of majestic appearance, and was noted for his skill in archery and in the exercises of knighthood. He was a wise legislator, an able statesman, a vigorous ruler, a great warrior and a gallant knight. His efforts to reform the laws acquired for him the title of the *English Justinian*. Because of the unusual length of his legs, his enemies in Berwick nicknamed him *Longshanks*.

Edward I. was as much distinguished for his mental power as for his kingly generosity. Under his fostering care the administration of justice became more regular and secure in England. He was by nature a despot and doggedly tenacious of the royal prerogative, but he was just and even generous to his law-abiding subjects. To others he was severe and even cruel. His natural sternness was tempered by gentleness and affection in his domestic relations; but he would not shield any one from the consequences of his crime, not even his own son, who was once sent to prison like a common felon.

As Edward I. had no dominions in Continental Europe except Guienne, his great grand-mother's inheritance, his chief ambition was to unite the whole island of Great Britain under one government. When Llewellyn, Prince of Wales, had refused to do the customary feudal homage to the English king, Edward I. sent an English army into Wales in 1277; and Llewellyn, deserted by most of his chieftains, was forced to sue for peace and to acknowledge Edward's sovereignty over Wales.

In 1282 the Welsh, incited by their patriotic bards, whose inspiring songs kept alive the love of liberty, rose in revolt against the English dominion. Edward I. again led an irresistible English army into Wales, and Llewellyn was soon defeated and slain in a battle; whereupon the Welsh chieftains quietly submitted, and the principality of Wales was formally annexed to the realm of England, A. D. 1282. Irritated at the determined resistance of the Welsh, King Edward I. caused Llewellyn's brother David and the Welsh bards to be massacred.

Edward I. wisely gave the Welsh people the English system of courts and laws, and for a century they remained at peace, with a single exception. In a conference with the Welsh chiefs at Caernarvon, Edward I. promised to given them a prince born in their own country, a prince who could not speak a word of French or English; and then introduced his infant son Edward, who was born in Caernarvon Castle the day before, as the prince whom he meant. By the death of his elder brother, little Edward became the heir to the English crown; and ever since that time the eldest son of the British sovereign has been styled *Prince of Wales*.

After thus effecting the conquest of Wales, which Saxons and Normans for eight centuries had failed to subdue, King Edward I. returned to England and devoted himself to the administration of government and the restoration of public order. His strong hand soon put an end to the robberies which had become disgracefully frequent during his father's weak reign.

Edward's chief severity was visited upon the Jews. A common crime in that turbulent and corrupt age was "clipping the coin;" and the Jews were accused of having a principal share in that transaction. Two hundred and eighty Jews were hanged in London alone. Eight years later, A. D. 1292, all the Jews in England were ordered to be cast into prison, and were kept there until they had paid a heavy ransom. Finally, for no apparent cause, the entire Hebrew population of England, more than sixteen thousand in number, were forced to leave the kingdom. They were permitted to take their money and jewels; but these treasures increased their perils, as very many were murdered by sailors and others in their passage over the seas. In those ages of bigotry a crime against a Jew was regarded by many as no crime at all. But Edward I. was more just, and ordered the murderers to be hanged whenever they could be convicted.

Edward's next great object was the union of England and Scotland under one dominion. King Alexander III. of Scotland, whose wife was Edward's sister, died in 1286, leaving the Scottish crown to his only surviving descendant, his little granddaughter, Margaret, daughter of King Erik II. of Norway, and grandniece of the King of England. This princess, then three years old, and known as the *Maid of Norway*, was soon afterward betrothed to Edward's son, Edward the Prince of Wales. On her voyage from Norway to Scotland, the princess died on one of the Orkneys, from the fatigue of the rough voyage; and thus the plan for uniting England and Scotland under one sovereign was for the time frustrated, and the way opened for three centuries of bitter strife between the two kingdoms.

Among the Scots many rival competitors now appeared for the crown of Scotland, the chief of whom were John Baliol, Lord of Galloway; Robert Bruce, Lord of Annandale; and John Hastings, Lord of Abergavenny—all of whom were of Norman descent. The Scottish Parliament, unable to choose among the competitors, referred the decision to the King of England as umpire. At the head of a large English army Edward I. met the Scottish Parliament and all the rival claimants at Norham on the Tweed, May 10, 1291; and having them in his power, he declared that he, not as an umpire freely chosen, but as lord-paramount of Scotland, should appoint a vassal monarch for that kingdom. This suzerainty had been exercised by Henry II. after the capture of King William the Lion of Scotland at Alnwick Castle in 1174, but had been freely surrendered by Richard the Lion-hearted in 1190, for himself and his successors.

Being in no condition to resist Edward's claims, the Scots had no alternative than to submit; and Edward I. decided in favor of the claims of John Baliol to the crown of Scotland, with the understanding that he should do feudal homage to the King of England for his crown. Baliol was King of Scotland in little else than in name. On trifling pretexts he was six times summoned to London to appear before the English Parliament. Edward's apparent design was to vex Baliol into rebellion, and then to confiscate his kingdom as a punishment.

When Edward I. became involved in a war with King Philip the Fair of France, Baliol formed an alliance with the French monarch, thus causing a furious war between England and Scotland. Forty thousand Scots made a sudden raid across the border into Cumberland. Edward I. was prepared for them, and repulsed them at Carlisle; after which he drove them into Berwick, which he besieged by land and sea and finally captured. Edward entered the town at the head of his assaulting column, and a frightful slaughter of two days only ended when every inhabitant of the town had been slain. The English king then advanced into Scotland, and defeated Baliol in the battle of Dunbar, A. D. 1296. Roxburgh, Jedburgh and Dumbarton received English garrisons. Edinburgh was besieged, and Stirling was taken.

Finally at Montrose Abbey, in 1296, Baliol appeared in penitential garments before the Bishop of Durham, confessed his sins against his sovereign lord, King Edward I., and surrendered the Scottish crown into his hands. The English king then took possession of Scotland as a forfeited fief. He was acknowledged King of Scotland by the Scottish Parliament, and filled the offices in Scotland with Englishmen. Edward I. carried to London the Scottish crown, scepter, and the sacred stone at Scone, called the *Stone of Destiny*, on which the Scottish kings had been crowned for centuries. There was a Scottish tradition that this sacred stone was the pillow of stone used by the patriarch Jacob at Bethel and it was popularly believed that the Scots would reign wherever that stone might be. Edward I. had the stone placed in Westminster Abbey, then just completed, and put beneath the Coronation Chair, in which all the Kings of England are crowned.

The fierce and bloody wars between England and Scotland which began in the reign of Edward I. lasted two centuries, and desolated the border lands of the two kingdoms throughout successive reigns. "The earlier ballad and legend, wild and wierd like the Scotch character itself, and the later song and tale with their warp of fact and woof of fiction, have involved the whole story of the struggle between England and Scotland in the fascinations of romance."

The war which had arisen between England and France in the meantime was caused by a quarrel between some English and French sailors. This struggle greatly encouraged the Scots and led to that close alliance which united France and Scotland in common enmity to England for centuries.

As Duke of Guienne, King Edward I

was a vassal of the King of France, who delighted to treat him as Edward I. had treated John Baliol. King Philip the Fair summoned Edward I. to appear at Paris to answer for the misconduct of his subjects. The King of England appeared by his brother, Edmund Plantagenet, Earl of Lancaster, who acted as his proxy. The French king demanded that Aquitaine should, as a mere matter of form, be given into his hands until the matter could be settled; but when he had once obtained possession of the chief towns of Guienne he declared that duchy annexed to the French crown as a forfeited fief of the English king. Edward I. took the field to uphold his rights, and was supported by the Duke of Brittany, the Count of Flanders and Adolf of Nassau, King of Germany. The war commenced in Gascony in 1294, and lasted two years, with the general advantage on the side of the French; Edward 1. being hampered by his war with Scotland.

The wars of Edward I. in Continental Europe, though disastrous to the English, afforded the English people an opportunity to secure their rights through the king's necessities. Edward's subjects well knew that by holding the purse-strings of the nation they had a check upon their sovereign. In 1297 Edward's demand for money was answered by a demand on the part of the barons and the representatives of the people for the renewal of the Great Charter, with an additional clause, "that no tallage or aid should be levied without the assent of the peers spiritual and temporal, and the *knights, burgesses and other freemen in Parliament assembled.*" Edward I. very reluctantly signed this document, which made it forever illegal for a King of England to levy any tax upon his subjects without their own consent, through their legally elected representatives. Parliament willingly voted a large subsidy to Edward I. as the price of this concession.

At one time, under the pressure of want, Edward I. levied money in violation of the Great Charter; but, convinced of his error, he acknowledged it with tears in his eyes, in the presence of Parliament, and repented. In his reign Parliaments became more regular, and from this time met permanently at Westminster; but the Commons did not yet have any voice in matters of legislation, simply voting money.

Among the wise laws of Edward I. was one basing the defense of the kingdom more thoroughly than ever on an armed militia, ever at the king's immediate call. Another law ensured the freedom of elections against menace or forcible interference. Another forbade judges and officers to receive rewards for official services, lawyers to use deceit to beguile the court, persons to utter slanders, or jurors to render a false verdict. Another required the gates of walled towns to be kept closed from sunset to sunrise, and a watch to be set. Another required every man to cut away the bushes and undergrowth on his own land, two hundred feet on each side of the principal roads, to render an ambush by highwaymen difficult. A statute for London forbade armed men to appear in the streets, or taverns to sell ale or beer, after Curfew.

Edward I. greatly improved the courts, rendering the administration of justice more certain and equal. The ecclesiastical courts were confined to strictly spiritual matters. The county court was undisturbed; but its business was restricted, and the people in the rural districts better accommodated, by the appointment of *Justices of the Peace* as local magistrates. From the Court of Appeal sprang the Court of Chancery, with the Chancellor at the head—a court governed by the principles of equity, not by common law, and designed to have jurisdiction when the administration of exact justice was prevented by the technicalities of law and by the inability of the other courts to vary from the established modes of procedure.

A treaty of peace was finally made between England and France in June, 1299. In accordance with this treaty, Edward I. married Marguerite, the eldest sister of King Philip the Fair; his first wife, Eleanor of Castile, having died in the meantime; and his son Edward, the Prince of Wales, was affianced to the French king's daughter Isabella, then only six years old. This last marrage was the source of centuries of war between England and France. By this treaty the King of England abandoned his ally, the Count of Flanders; while the King of France left his allies, the Scots, to the vengeance of Edward I.

Edward's first conquest of Scotland was of short duration. The Scots found a heroic champion in the valiant patriot William Wallace, a gallant knight, a man of no high rank, but distinguished by extraordinary patience and determination, as well as by his remarkable strength. The great nobles of Scotland mostly held aloof from the struggle, or gave Wallace a very feeble support; but the common people considered him their hero and deliverer.

The great nobles of Scotland, like those of England, were mainly of Norman descent, and cared very little for the country or the people where their estates lay. John Baliol did homage to King Edward I. for lands in France and England, as well as for Scotland; and the real Scots of the Highlands preferred the King of England to either John Baliol or Robert Bruce.

Wallace secretly collected an army of stalwart peasants and a band of desperate outlaws, and attacked and defeated the English under Earl Warrenne, Edward's governor of Scotland, with great slaughter at Stirling, in September, 1297. Wallace took castle after castle, and liberated all Scotland from English rule; after which he pushed his victorious arms across the border into England, and ravaged Cumberland and Northumberland. His countrymen chose him for their ruler, with the modest title of *Guardian of the Realm of Scotland*.

The warlike Edward I., who had been in Continental Europe when this revolt of the Scots broke out, now returned to England with a great train of knights and archers, to which he added the forces of England, Ireland and Wales. Enraged at the new outbreak of Scottish patriotism, Edward I. led his forces into Scotland and annihilated the Scottish army under Wallace at Falkirk, July 22, 1298; the valiant Scottish patriot being forsaken by the proud Scottish lords, who scorned to serve under a leader of humble birth.

The victorious King of England was soon obliged to retire for want of food; and in 1303 the Scots were again in the field, under the leadership of John Comyn of Badenoch, son-in-law of John Baliol. This time Edward I. was invincible. A formidable English fleet laden with provisions sailed along the coast, almost abreast of Edward's land force. The English king marched in triumph through Scotland from south to north, through Lowlands and Highlands, reducing all the castles and forcing all the Scottish chiefs to do him feudal homage.

In the meantime the valiant Wallace waged a relentless war against the English for seven years, disdaining to accept the mercy of his country's conqueror. Outlawed and with a price set upon his head, and hiding in the mountains, he was at last basely betrayed into Edward's power by a Scottish noble; and, with a cruelty disgraceful to the memory of Edward I., the patriot leader was taken in chains to London, where he was tried as a traitor, with a crown of oak leaves upon his head, to indicate that he was king of outlaws. He was condemned to death for treason, simply because he defended the independence of his native land with indomitable heroism, and was hanged at Tyburn, August 24, 1305. His head, crowned in mockery with a circlet of laurel, was placed on London Bridge. His countrymen considered him a martyr, and he has ever since been honored as the national hero of Scotland.

The story of Wallace's martyrdom sped through Scotland, from Lowland moor to Highland glen, from peasant cot to lordly castle; and the dead Wallace achieved what the living Wallace had failed to accomplish. Scottish jealousies ceased; and the fierce resentment that united all Scottish hearts in the stern resolve to avenge the valiant patriot's cruel death also united them in the nobler resolve to liberate their country from the hated English yoke.

Robert Bruce, Earl of Carrick—grandson of the Robert Bruce who had been a competitor with John Baliol for the Scottish crown in 1292—lived at Edward's court, petted and favored, but closely watched. He conceived the design of freeing his country from English rule, and communicated his plans to his rival, John Comyn of Badenoch, John Baliol's son-in-law. Comyn at first agreed to Bruce's plans, but finally betrayed his design to the English king. A friend of Bruce at the English court, hearing of his danger and not daring to communicate with him personally, sent him a purse of gold and a pair of spurs; and the sagacious Bruce, rightly interpreting the friendly warning, secretly hastened to Scotland without a moment's delay. As the ground was then covered with snow, he had the precaution to order his horse to be shod with the shoes reversed, that he might deceive those who should track his path over the open fields and cross-roads through which he proposed to travel.

In a few days Bruce reached Scotland; and at Dumfries, in Annandale, the chief seat of his family interest, he fortunately found many of the Scottish nobility assembled, the traitor Comyn being among them. They were surprised at Bruce's unexpected arrival among them, and readily agreed to sustain him in his efforts for the deliverance of Scotland, with the exception of Comyn, who strenuously sought to induce the Scottish nobles to submit to English rule. To punish him for his treachery, and to prevent him from doing any mischief in future, Bruce drew his dagger and stabbed Comyn where he stood, before the high altar of the church at Dumfries.

Bruce then proceeded to Scone, and was crowned King of Scotland by the Bishop of St. Andrews, in the abbey which had been the scene of the coronation of so many Scottish kings; after which he published a defiance to the King of England, no longer as Robert Bruce of Annandale, but as King Robert I. of Scotland. The Scots rose bravely at the call of their second champion, and in about four months all the clans were in arms under Bruce's standard, resolved to recover their country's independence; and the English garrisons were driven from all but a few of the strongest castles.

Edward I. was greatly enraged when he heard of Bruce's proceedings in Scotland. He saw that his second conquest of Scotland was no more permanent than the first had been, and that he must begin the task anew. Bowed with years, but still resolute, he took the field against the Scots for the third time. Before starting on his expedition to Scotland, he assembled all his barons in Westminster Abbey, and took a solemn oath by two live swans, adorned with bells of gold, that he would invade Scotland and never return until he had completely subjugated that country. He kept his vow, but not in the way he intended. He did not subdue Scotland, and he never returned.

In the meantime Edward's son Edward, Prince of Wales, had advanced into Scotland and opened the campaign with such cruel devastations that his father was obliged to stop him. Bruce and his followers were driven about from place to place by Edward's advance troops under Sir Aymer de Valence, who defeated Bruce at Methven, in Perthshire, and forced him to take refuge in the Hebrides.

King Edward I., who was then in Cumberland with an army of a hundred thousand men, sinking under exertion and excitement, was overcome by illness near Carlisle, and died at Burgh-on-the-Sands, July 7, 1307, in the sixty-ninth year of his age, just as his army came in sight of the blue hills of Scotland. With his dying breath he enjoined his son to prosecute the war until he had completely conquered Scotland, and even desired that his dead body should be carried at the head of the invading army as it marched into that country.

EDWARD II., the son and successor of Edward I., was twenty-two years of age when he became King of England in 1307. His first act was to disobey his father's dying injunction to prosecute the war for the conquest of Scotland. He had advanced but a little way into Scotland when he ordered a retreat, abandoned the enterprise and disbanded his army ; thus disgusting his barons.

Edward II. was a weak prince, the slave of worthless favorites, and entirely lacked the knightly qualities which so distinguished his illustrious father. He was destitute of vigor or virtue sufficient to be just to himself, or to enforce justice among his subjects. His only aim was indulgence in sensual pleasures. The barons, seeing that he was too weak to hold the reins of government as firmly as his renowned father had done, soon began to entertain little respect for the royal authority, and to practice every form of insolence with the utmost impunity.

Edward II. also violated another promise which he had made to his father. In his early youth his father had assigned him for a companion a Gascon knight of good family, named Piers Gaveston. This Frenchman was a man of elegant manners and many accomplishments, and excelled in all the knightly and courtly graces of the time; but his character was wholly dissolute, and he exercised a most corrupting influence over the young prince, leading him into such wild and lawless courses that Edward I. banished Gaveston from England, after vainly striving to check his son's frivolous career. Edward I., on his death-bed, made his son swear that he would never recall Gaveston ; but no sooner had Edward II. ascended the English throne than he summoned Gaveston back to England and loaded him with honors, wealth and estates—a proceeding which greatly offended the English barons, who resented the inferior birth and the haughty and insolent bearing of the king's French favorite.

Early in 1308 King Edward II. went to France and married the Princess Isabella, the daughter of King Philip the Fair, to whom he had been affianced since 1299. He left Gaveston in charge of the kingdom during his absence—an act which excited the disaffection of the barons to the highest degree. The new queen, who desired to rule her husband herself, became jealous of Gaveston's influence, and joined the English barons against the king's insolent French favorite.

Soon after the king's coronation the barons demanded the banishment of the haughty Gaveston. Edward II. consented to this demand with great reluctance; but, instead of sending the favorite out of the English dominions entirely, the king turned his punishment into a promotion by appointing him Lord Lieutenant of Ireland, going with him as far as Bristol, and bestowing upon him new estates in England and Gascony. Gaveston was a brave and energetic man, and his administration in Ireland was, on the whole, creditable.

Anxious for the recall of his favorite, King Edward II. softened the hostility of the barons by making concessions to them, and obtained from the Pope a dispensation absolving Gaveston from the oath he had taken never to return to England; and the favorite was recalled. Gaveston was just as arrogant and insolent as ever, and continued the same course as before, thus exciting a fresh outbreak of the barons.

In 1310 the barons forced the weak king to relinquish the royal authority for one year into the hands of a committee of twelve barons, styled *Ordainers*, who instituted a series of measures, some of which were useful and praiseworthy, because they diminished the arbitrary powers of the crown. The Ordainers banished Gaveston from England, though the king begged piteously that he might be permitted to remain. The exiled favorite retired to Flanders, and in less than a year Edward II. removed the court to York and recalled Gaveston.

The barons now determined to get rid of the king's insolent favorite forever. They took up arms, under the leadership of the king's cousin, Thomas Plantagenet, Earl of Lancaster, the most powerful baron in England. The rebel barons captured Scarborough Castle, in which Gaveston had taken refuge. Gaveston was conducted to Warwick Castle, where he was beheaded without trial, by order of his enemies, June 19, 1312. Edward II. was furious with rage at the death of his favorite, and swore vengeance on all who had been concerned in the murder; but he lacked the energy to hold a purpose requiring such efforts, and soon agreed to a reconciliation with the barons, thus restoring tranquillity to the kingdom.

In the meartime, while Edward II. and his barons were engaged in their petty quarrels, the Scots, under King Robert Bruce, were regaining their national independence. The Scots recovered Linlithgow, Roxburgh, Edinburgh and Perth in succession. The accounts of the sieges of castles held by English garrisons are full of romantic interest. Linlithgow was taken very much like ancient Troy was captured by the Greeks. A Scottish peasant had been in the habit of supplying the English garrison with forage. One day he came with a load of hay in which were concealed Scottish soldiers. After crossing the drawbridge he placed his load of hay in such a position that the gates could not be shut. The concealed soldiers suddenly made their appearance, and held the gates until reinforcements lying in ambush came up, when the garrison was overpowered.

The only fortress in Scotland that still held out for the English king was Stirling Castle, which was vigorously besieged by Edward Bruce, King Robert's brother. The governor of the castle, reduced to desperate straits by want of provisions, agreed to surrender on the day of the Feast of St. John the Baptist, if not relieved by the English in the meantime. Edward II., roused from his lethargy, speedily collected an army which the Scottish writers estimated at a hundred thousand men, and hastily marched to the relief of Stirling Castle.

Edward II. was confronted by thirty thousand Scots under King Robert Bruce at Bannockburn, two miles from Stirling, June 24, 1314. The English king attacked the Scots, but suffered the most disastrous defeat in the history of English warfare, considering the disparity of the forces engaged —the greatest reverse which the English had sustained since the battle of Hastings. The English army fled from the field in utter dismay; and King Edward II. himself fled in hot haste to Dunbar, closely pursued by some Scottish knights, and from that town he returned to England by sea. The English camp, with all its treasures and supplies, fell into the possession of the victorious Scots, while the panic-stricken English soldiers were slaughtered without mercy. The battle of Bannockburn secured the independence of Scotland, and King Robert Bruce retaliated by invading England and ravaging Cumberland and Northumberland.

Encouraged by his success in Scotland, King Robert Bruce made an effort to wrest Ireland from the English, sending his brother Edward into that island with a Scottish army to accept the Irish crown, which had been offered to him by the O'Neil and other chiefs of Ulster. Edward Bruce landed in Ulster in 1315 and achieved some successes, after which he was crowned King of Ireland at Carrickfergus. The English and their Irish supporters rallied for a supreme effort, and inflicted a crushing defeat upon Edward Bruce at Athenree, August 10, 1316. Edward Bruce was defeated and slain in the battle of Dundalk in 1318, thus ending this effort to liberate Ireland from the English dominion.

In the meantime King Edward II. had found a new favorite, Hugh Spenser, a young Welsh gentleman of noble birth, who was a man very much like Gaveston; but his father, whom the king also took into his favor, was deservedly honored for his wisdom and valor, his fidelity in many high offices, his integrity and pure life. The elder Spenser was a man of advanced age, and was well adapted to be the counselor to such a king as Edward II.

The king's favoritism for the two Spensers, father and son, provoked another outbreak of the barons, who again took up arms under the Earls of Hereford and Lancaster.

The rebellious barons were defeated at Boroughbridge. The Earl of Hereford was slain, and the Earl of Lancaster was taken prisoner and beheaded. Roger Mortimer, one of the same party, who was also the queen's paramour, was likewise taken prisoner, and was condemned to death; but his sentence was afterwards commuted to imprisonment in the Tower.

King Charles the Fair of France, brother-in-law of Edward II., took advantage of the domestic troubles of England, to make an effort to obtain possession of the English monarch's territories in France; and in 1325 Edward II. sent his wife Isabella to Paris to arrange matters with her brother. Queen Isabella was soon joined in France by her young son Edward, Prince of Wales, and also by her lover Roger Mortimer, who had escaped from the Tower. Isabella had no love for her husband, her affections being wholly centered on Mortimer; and, instead of endeavoring to bring about a peace between her brother and her husband, she plotted for her husband's overthrow, being aided by her brother with men and money. She affianced her son to the Princess Philippa, daughter of Count William of Hainault.

In 1326 Queen Isabella returned to England, landing in Suffolk with an army consisting mainly of foreigners. She at once raised the standard of revolt against her husband, ostensibly to overthrow the Spensers, but really to acquire the supreme power for herself and Mortimer. She was joined by the discontented barons, and was hailed as a deliverer by all classes, so that she soon had an overwhelming force at her command.

King Edward II., deserted and helpless, was obliged to flee from London. He embarked for the Isle of Lundy, off Bristol Channel; but was driven upon the coast of Wales, landing at Swansea. The queen's troops took Bristol; and the elder Spenser, an old man of ninety, who commanded there, was barbarously put to death. King Edward II. and Hugh Spenser were captured in Glamorganshire. Hugh Spenser was crowned with nettles and hanged, while the king was imprisoned in Kenilworth Castle.

In the meantime Edward, Prince of Wales, a boy of fourteen years, had been made regent by his mother and Mortimer; but, as the young prince possessed no authority, the kingdom was in a deplorable condition. The mobs of London and other cities committed robberies and murders with impunity, and were called *Rifters*.

In 1327 a Parliament summoned by the queen assembled at Westminster, revived the constitutional usage of the earlier English freedom and asserted the right of Parliament to depose the king, by declaring Edward II. unworthy to rule and proclaiming his son Edward king by acclamation. Queen Isabella, the real author of her husband's misery, burst into a flood of hypocritical tears at this announcement; and her son Edward, Prince of Wales, was so affected by her feigned sorrow that he swore that he would never reign in his father's life-time without his consent.

To satisfy the pretended scruples of the queen, Parliament sent a deputation to Kenilworth Castle to procure a formal abdication of the English crown from the dethroned king in favor of his son. As soon as the discrowned sovereign saw the deputies he fainted; and when he recovered and was informed of their errand he told them that he was in their power and must submit to their will. Sir William Trussel, in the name of the people of England, then renounced all fealty to "Edward of Caernarvon," so styled from the place of his birth, in Wales; and Sir Francis Blount, High Steward, broke his staff and declared all the king's officers discharged from his service.

Thus ended the reign of Edward II., which had lasted twenty years (A. D. 1307-1327); but his own miseries were not yet ended. The dethroned king was committed to the custody of some wretches, who did all in their power to kill him by ill usage. They hurried him like a common felon from castle to castle in the middle of the night, only half clothed. One day for sport they ordered him to be shaved in the open fields, with water out of a dirty ditch, and refused to let him have any other. The unhappy monarch shed tears at this treatment; and, while the tears were trickling down his cheeks, he said, with a smile of grief: "Here is clean warm water, whether you will or no."

But this method of killing the deposed king proved too slow, and compassion for his sufferings was working a reaction in his favor among the people. Finally he was lodged in Berkeley Castle, which he never left alive. By Mortimer's orders the unfortunate Edward II. was horribly murdered one autumn night, the gloomy walls of Berkeley Castle resounding with the most heart-rending shrieks, September 21, 1327; and the next day the distorted features of the dead king told only too well the story of his cruel murder, in the forty-third year of his age.

The chivalrous EDWARD III., the son and successor of Edward II., became a powerful monarch; and his reign of fifty years was one of the longest and most brilliant in the annals of England. Unlike his father, he was an energetic and vigorous sovereign, and was one of the greatest of the Plantagenets. He was an able statesman, a great warrior and a gallant knight.

As Edward III. was only fourteen years of age when he became King of England in 1327, a Council of Regency composed of twelve of the principal lords was appointed to administer the government during the king's minority; but the real power was exercised by his mother Isabella and her paramour Roger Mortimer, who controlled the Council of Regency. Mortimer soon assumed the title of Earl of March.

The Scots under James, Earl of Douglas, continued their raids across the border, and young King Edward III. led an English army against them; but the light-armed and well-mounted Scots skillfully avoided battles and eluded pursuit, and the young English king was obliged to retire for want of supplies. Finally, England acknowledged the independence of Scotland by the Treaty of Northampton, in March, 1328; and a sister of King Edward III. was betrothed to David Bruce, the son and heir of King Robert I.

Mortimer, who felt sure of his power, conducted himself with such insolence and such reckless disregard of the rights of others that he soon raised a determined opposition to his supremacy. His infamous course in causing the king's uncle, the Duke of Kent, to be executed, and the Earl of Lancaster to be imprisoned, aggravated the hostility with which he was threatened; and finally the young king's eyes were opened to the ambitious schemes of his mother's arrogant favorite.

When Edward III. was eighteen years of age he resolved to take the government into his own hands and be his own master. Isabella and Mortimer then occupied Nottingham Castle. Every night the keys of the castle gates were brought to the suspicious queen-mother's bed-side, while guards were stationed at every avenue of approach. Under the guidance of the governor of the castle, a small but trusty band of the young king's friends entered the castle at night, through a subterranean passage, and, being joined by King Edward III. himself, took the garrison utterly by surprise. Mortimer was seized in Isabella's presence and borne away to prison; the queen-mother piteously entreating her son to "spare the gentle Mortimer."

Thenceforth Edward III. was king in fact as well as in name. He at once summoned a Parliament, before whom Mortimer was brought charged with various offences and crimes, one of which was the murder of King Edward II. He was pronounced guilty, and was hanged on an elm at Tyburn, in 1330; and the king's mother was consigned to life-long imprisonment in Castle Rising, where she lingered in hopeless captivity for the remaining twenty-seven years of her life, visited once a year by her son.

In 1331 King Edward III. settled colonies of Flemish weavers in the counties of

PILLAGING A TOWN IN THE MIDDLE AGES.

Norfolk, Suffolk and Essex, thus laying the foundation of one of England's greatest industries. These foreign settlers introduced into England the manufacture of the finest woolen cloths. The wool of England was then the finest in Europe, and was the principal article of export from the kingdom. The English people, fearing that the establishment of home manufactures would ruin their commerce, treated the Flemish immigrants with such hostility that King Edward III. was put to much trouble to protect them.

England was now in terrible disorder. Robbery and all manner of violence had increased without check, under the weakness of Edward II. and the crimes of Isabella. Edward III. devoted himself with vigor and energy to the restoration of order and justice, and put down many gangs of robbers by his own personal presence. By a series of wise and heroic measures he reëstablished the royal power and the supremacy of the law throughout the kingdom.

Edward III. next turned his attention to Scotland. King Robert Bruce died in 1329, and the Scottish crown passed to his son David, then only seven years old. Scottish history repeated itself in this instance. Edward Baliol, son of John Baliol who figured so prominently in the reign of Edward I., now asserted his right to the Scottish throne, as his father had done before him. After defeating the forces of David Bruce, near Perth, in 1332, Edward Baliol seized the crown of Scotland; and David Bruce fled to France. To gain the support of King Edward III., Edward Baliol, like his father before him, agreed to reign as a vassal of the English crown. The indignant Scots flew to arms and drove him from the country in 1333.

The exiled Edward Baliol sought refuge in England; and, after a show of reluctance because of the treaty still in force between England and Scotland, Edward III. declared in Baliol's favor, led a large army into Scotland, and defeated the Scots in the great battle of Halidon Hill, in 1333, thus restoring Edward Baliol to the Scottish throne and compelling David Bruce to take refuge in France a second time. Edward Baliol ceded the fortresses of Berwick, Dunbar and Edinburgh, and all the south-eastern counties of Scotland, to England; while he and many of the Scottish lords swore fealty to Edward III.

The very name of Baliol was repugnant to the Scots, and after the withdrawal of the English army he was driven from Scotland a second time. The Scots were encouraged and aided by France, and they made Sir Andrew Murray regent for David Bruce, who was still in France. The King of England again marched into Scotland to restore Edward Baliol to the throne of that kingdom; and the Scots, unable to cope with Edward III. in the Lowlands, retreated into the Highlands, where they kept alive their hostility to the usurper Baliol and his master, the English king.

The cause of David Bruce had been warmly supported by King Philip VI. of France, the first of the Valois branch of the royal race of Capet. This conduct of the King of France deeply offended King Edward III., who retaliated by giving a cordial reception to the French king's inveterate enemy, Count Robert of Artois, who fled to England in 1333. King Philip VI. endeavored to force Edward III. to send the Count of Artois away, and also committed many aggressions upon Edward's duchy of Guienne, although the English king had consented to do homage to the King of France for that province.

In 1336 the French king brought matters to a crisis by an insolent demand that the English monarch should give up the Count of Artois, threatening the confiscation of his duchy of Guienne in case of refusal. Edward III. instantly began preparations for war; and, acting on the advice of Jacques van Artevelde, the famous brewer of Ghent and the leader of the Flemings, he claimed the French crown because his mother Isabella was a daughter of Philip the Fair, and assumed the title of King of France; but his pretensions were invalidated by the Salic Law, which prevailed in France, and which prevented females from inheriting the French crown.

The basis of the claim of Edward III. to the crown of France will be best seen in the following statement: Philip the Fair's three sons, who reigned over France in succession, left only female issue; while his daughter Isabella, who was excluded from the French throne by the Salic Law, married King Edward II. of England and left only male issue, King Edward III. of England. Thus Edward III. claimed to be the nearest male heir; but the French maintained that the Salic Law, which prohibited female inheritance of the French crown, debarred Edward's claim. Edward III. sought to evade the force of the Salic Law by asserting that, though a female could not inherit the French crown, she could transmit it to her male descendants; but the French replied that a female could not transmit a right which she did not herself possess. It was in accordance with the French view of the Salic Law that on the extinction of the direct male line of the House of Capet, in 1328, the French crown passed to Philip the Fair's nephew, Count Philip of Valois, who then became King Philip VI. of France.

Edward III. had powerful adherents in Germany, as well as in Flanders, and the Emperor Louis the Bavarian appointed him Imperial Vicar in the Netherlands; while Jacques van Artevelde, the brewer of Ghent already alluded to, acknowledged him King of France.

The great struggle that now began between England and France is known as the *Hundred Years' War*, because it lasted more than a century, with intervals of peace. During this long struggle English kings achieved a world-wide renown and English soldiers covered themselves with glory, but the final result was the loss of all the English possessions in France except Calais.

The Hundred Years' War commenced in 1339. The next year the English fleet destroyed the French navy in the great battle of Sluys, or Helvoetsluys, off the coast of Flanders, June 24, 1340. But the English king's unjust wars with Scotland and France had exhausted his treasures. The clergy and people of England refused more taxes, except upon the concession of greater privileges; and thus Edward III. was obliged to conclude peace with the King of France for the time.

A disputed succession to the duchy of Brittany again involved Edward III. in the affairs of France. He invaded France with thirty thousand men, landing at Cape La Hogue, in Normandy, June 12, 1346; and, accompanied by his eldest son, Edward, he marched almost to the gates of Paris, ravaging the country with fire and sword. Upon being pursued by King Philip VI. with an army of one hundred thousand Frenchmen, he retreated to the Somme and crossed that stream, taking position on the edge of the forest of Creçy, about twelve miles from Abbeville, where he was attacked by the French king with his superior army, August 26, 1346; thus bringing on the great battle of Creçy, in which the English, although only one-third as numerous as the French, won a glorious victory.

The French advance troops came up with the English about three o'clock in the afternoon. The engagement was delayed by a short but severe thunder-storm; but in half an hour the sun shone out brightly, darting his rays on the backs of the English, but full in the eyes of the French. The battle began with the archers on both sides, and the superior discipline of the English at once became apparent. Their bows had been carefully secured in their cases during the recent storm, and their arrows fell like hail and with terrible execution among the French; while the arrows of the French fell short of their mark, because their bow strings were wet and slackened.

The battle soon became general. The English employed the new invention of gunpowder by using several pieces of cannon—the first instance of such engines of warfare being used in any great European battle. The front ranks of the French were thrown into confusion; and Prince Edward, with remarkable valor, led a charge right into the disordered mass. King Edward III., who was watching the field from the top of a windmill, was importuned to send him help. He asked: "Is my son dead, wounded, or felled to the ground?" He was answered: "Not so, thank God!" The king then said: "Nay, then, he has no aid from me; let him bear himself like a man; in this battle he must win his spurs."

The King of France fought with great valor, but without success. His entire army fled in dismay in the evening, and were pursued and slaughtered without mercy. Among the slain was the blind old King John of Bohemia, a singular soldier of fortune, who had fought on most of the battle-fields of Europe in his day. He had ordered his horse to be tied to those of two knights of his retinue, who rode one on each side. All three knights lay dead together, while the three horses stood unhurt beside the bodies of their dead masters. The Prince of Wales is said to have adopted the dead Bohemian king's crest and motto; the crest consisting of three ostrich feathers surmounting the motto in German, *Ich dien*, meaning "I serve." This crest and motto has been borne by every Prince of Wales ever since. This young Prince of Wales, the hero of Creçy, was ever afterwards known as *Edward the Black Prince*, from the color of the armor which he wore on that memorable field.

The Scots took advantage of the war between England and France to recall King David Bruce and form an alliance with France. Instigated by the King of France, David Bruce led an army of fifty thousand Scots across the border into the North of England, ravaging the country as far as Durham. With great energy, Edward's heroic queen, Philippa of Hainault, raised an army of twelve thousand men, placing it under the command of Lord Percy, who won a great and decisive victory over the Scots in the battle of Neville's Cross, near Durham, October 10, 1346, taking King David Bruce prisoner. The King of Scots was carried a captive to London and confined in the Tower.

In her campaign against the Scots, Queen Philippa ascertained that there were rich deposits of coal about Newcastle, and perceiving their vast importance she obtained permission from Parliament to open the mines. England's coal is, directly and indirectly, one of the chief sources of her wealth.

After his great victory at Creçy, Edward III. laid siege to Calais, the key to France. The city was stubbornly defended by the French for nearly a year, when, reduced by famine, Calais was obliged to surrender. It is said that the English king agreed to spare the inhabitants of Calais, whose long resistance exasperated him, if six of the leading citizens should be sent to him, with ropes about their necks, ready for hanging. The unfortunate inhabitants gave way to despair at these hard conditions; but Eustace St. Pierre, a wealthy merchant of Calais, offered himself as one of the victims. Inspired by his noble example, five others followed him. The entreaties of the English nobles, of Edward's queen, Philippa, and of his heroic son, Edward the Black Prince, finally prevailed over the king's obstinate temper and saved the lives of the six noble-hearted citizens. After the surrender of Calais, Edward III. expelled its French inhabitants, and peopled the city with English; and for two centuries that important town remained in the possession of England.

After the capture of Calais a truce of ten months was concluded; but hostilities were not renewed for eight years, as both England and France were frightfully ravaged by the *Black Plague*, which commenced in Western Asia and swept over Europe during the four years beginning with 1348, destroying one-third of the population. It is said that over half the inhabitants of England perished from this dreadful plague.

Hostilities between England and France were renewed in 1355, when King Edward III. invaded the North of France; while his chivalrous son, Edward the Black Prince, hastened to Guienne. Both these English armies ravaged the French dominions.

The next year, A. D. 1356, the Black Prince advanced into the county of Poitou with only eight thousand English and Gascon troops; but at Poitiers he found himself confronted by a French army of sixty thousand men under King John the Good, the successor of Philip of Valois on the throne of France. The English, by the skill and discipline of their archers, won as brilliant a victory in the battle of Poitiers, September 19, 1356, as they had achieved at Creçy ten years before.

Two days before this battle the Black Prince encamped near Poitiers. The same evening the King of France encamped a mile away. When the Black Prince saw the French army advance upon him so unexpectedly, he exclaimed: "God help us! it only remains for us to fight bravely." The Cardinal of Perigord, who was with the French army, desired peace very much, and rode backwards and forwards between King John the Good and the Black Prince several times for the purpose of effecting a treaty. The Black Prince said to him: "Save my honor, and the honor of my army, and I will readily listen to any reasonable conditions." But the French king would consent to nothing unless the Black Prince and a hundred of his knights would surrender themselves prisoners of war. The Black Prince replied to this demand thus: "I will never be made a prisoner but sword in hand."

Finding his efforts unavailing, the Cardinal of Perigord retired to Poitiers, and both armies prepared for the decisive battle which ensued. King John the Good fought bravely, though deserted by most of his knights. His son Philip, afterwards Duke Philip the Bold of Burgundy, fought gallantly by his father's side, though scarcely fourteen years old. The French king, wearied and overwhelmed by numbers, might easily have been slain; but every English knight was ambitious to take him alive, and he was exhorted on all sides to surrender. King John still cried out: "Where is my cousin, the Prince of Wales?" He seemed unwilling to surrender to any person of inferior rank; but, being told that the Black Prince was at a distance, he finally surrendered to a French knight named Morbec, who had been obliged to leave his country for murder. The French king's heroic son Philip, who acquired the surname of *the Bold*, on account of his gallantry in this battle, likewise surrendered.

The Black Prince, who was reposing in his tent from the fatigues of the battle, displayed anxiety for the fate of the King of France, and sent the Earl of Warwick to bring him intelligence. That nobleman found the captive king at a fortunate moment, as his life was exposed to more danger than during the battle. The English had forcibly taken the royal prisoner from Morbec, and quarreled among themselves for the custody of his person. Some brutal soldiers, rather than yield the prize to their rivals, had threatened to put their illustrious captive to death; but the Earl of Warwick overawed all parties, rescued the captive monarch from their turbulence, and led him to the Black Prince.

The Black Prince treated the captive French king with every mark of respect and sympathy, seeking to soothe and comfort him. He ordered a magnificent supper to be prepared, and himself served at the table, as if he had been one of the retinue. He stood behind the captive monarch's chair, refusing to be seated in his presence, saying: "I know too well the difference of rank between a subject and a sovereign prince." King John the Good was much affected by the Black Prince's generous treatment, so little to be expected from so youthful a conqueror; and he burst into tears, declaring that though it was his fate to be a captive he rejoiced that he had fallen into the hands of the most generous and valiant prince then living.

After returning thanks to God for his victory, the Black Prince praised his troops for their valor, and gave rewards and dignities to such as had especially distinguished themselves. On April 24, 1357, he sailed for England with his royal prisoners. On approaching London they were met by a thousand citizens in their best array, who conducted them with great state to Westminster. The Black Prince, in a plain dress and on a little palfrey, rode beside the captive King of France, who was attired in royal robes and mounted on a stately war horse. When they arrived at Westminster, King Edward III. met them and embraced King John the Good with every mark of respect and affection. The French king and his son were sumptuously lodged in the old palace of the Savoy, and during their three years' captivity in England they were treated more like guests than like prisoners.

Edward III. now had two kings in captivity; but King David Bruce, who had been a prisoner in England eleven years, was soon released, upon the payment of a large ransom by the Scots. After being a captive in England for three years, King John the Good was released by the Peace of Bretigny, in May, 1360, upon the payment of a ransom of three million gold crowns. By this treaty Edward III. renounced his claim to the French crown and to the French provinces of Normandy, Brittany, Maine, Touraine and Anjou; but he retained the town of Calais, the county of Ponthieu, and the duchy of Guienne with Poitou and Gascony, no longer as a vassal, but as an independent sovereign. Edward III. promised to give no more assistance or encouragement to the rebellious Flemings, and John the Good agreed to abandon the cause of the Scots.

Edward III. accompanied King John the Good to Calais, on his return to France; and the two king's parted with many expressions of affection and regard, October 24, 1360. King John gave forty hostages to Edward III. for the payment of the ransom, among whom were two of the French king's sons. These princes violated their parole by escaping from England; whereupon King John the Good, thinking that his own honor was impeached by this breach of faith on the part of his sons, voluntarily returned to captivity in London, where he died in 1364.

The government of the English provinces in France was conferred on the Black Prince, who, with his wife, the *Fair Maid of Kent*, established their court at Bordeaux. In a few years he was called upon to interfere in the affairs of Castile, one of the Christian kingdoms in Spain. King Pedro the Cruel of Castile had so disgusted his subjects that they dethroned him, with the aid of the French under Du Guesclin, and conferred the Castilian crown upon his halfbrother, Henry of Trastamara. The deposed Pedro the Cruel appealed to the Black Prince, who led his army into Spain and defeated Henry of Trastamara at Navarette, April 3, 1367. Thereupon all Castile submitted, and Pedro the Cruel was restored to his throne, but he proved a worse tyrant than before. Henry of Trastamara, with military aid from France, again dethroned the tyrant, and murdered him with his own hand. John of Gaunt, Duke of Lancaster, the Black Prince's brother, married a daughter of Pedro the Cruel, and claimed the Castilian crown in her name.

A change was gradually taking place in the methods of warfare. Hitherto mail-clad knights had been the chief reliance in battle; but Edward III., by following the example of William Wallace at Falkirk, had achieved his most brilliant triumphs with English archers, whose volleys of arrows discharged with unerring aim threw the knights of France into hopeless confusion at Creçy and Poitiers. Although Creçy was the first great European battle-field in which cannon were used, heavy cannon which hurled stones were used before for siege purposes.

During the reign of Edward III., Chivalry was at its height, and his court was Chivalry's capital, whither gallant knights had been in the habit of gathering from all portions of Europe, to mingle in the scenes of feudal splendor that constantly dazzled the eyes of the wondering and admiring people. His plume was always preëminent, alike in the friendly lists of the tournament or in the deadly shock of battle.

Edward III. made the English name

glorious by his victories over the French and the Scots, and his fame was worthily sustained by his gallant son, Edward the Black Prince. As King of England, Edward III. proved himself worthy to rule a great nation. By the vigor and wisdom of his administration, he forced all classes to acknowledge the supremacy of the law; and by his affability and generosity, and his earnest desire for the welfare and happiness of all his two million subjects, he attached both nobles and commons to his rule, and won their hearty support in all his enterprises.

Though the foreign wars of Edward III. were unjust, they served to occupy the turbulent spirits of the great nobles with adventures adapted to their tastes, and kept England at internal peace. The laws were well administered, and the common people enjoyed greater prosperity than for several centuries before or after.

The national animosity engendered between England and France by the wars of Edward III. made the feeling of nationality stronger in England. Hitherto feelings of jealousy and antipathy had existed among the people of the different nationalities in England. The native Briton could not forgive his Saxon conqueror, and both Briton and Saxon detested the proud and domineering Norman. During the reign of Edward III. these discordant nationalities were blended into one harmonious nation. They then ceased to be any longer Britons, Anglo-Saxons, or Normans; but all became Englishmen. They fought side by side at Creçy and Poitiers, and the animosities of the hitherto discordant nationalities melted away amid the rejoicing of victory over a common enemy of all. National hatred toward the French blended these different nationalities into one people. Thenceforth they looked back with a common pride to a glorious past, and forward with a common hope to a more glorious future.

As a result of the blending of the different nationalities into Englishmen, the English language began to assume its present form during the reign of Edward III. The Anglo-Saxon peasantry had always adhered to their own language; while Latin was the language of business and of the graver literature, and French the language of society and the lighter literature. But during this reign the Anglo-Saxon, or Old English, with an admixture of both Latin and French, was slowly becoming the national tongue by developing into the modern English. This result was greatly accelerated by the mighty impetus which it received from the writings of the renowned Oxford professor and reformer, John Wickliffe, which were extensively circulated throughout England. In 1357 Parliament enacted a statute requiring the use of the English language in the courts of justice and in the public deeds, instead of the French. Late in the reign of Edward III. the English tongue was taught in the schools, instead of the French. Even the French romances began to be translated into English.

The earliest writer of English prose whose work remains was Sir John Mandeville, who is supposed to have been born about A. D. 1300, and who died in 1372. He left England in 1327, the year of the accession of Edward III., and spent thirty-four years in visiting Palestine, Egypt, India and China. On his return to his native land, he published an account of his travels, in Latin, which was afterwards translated into French, and from French into English. His work, full of the most entertaining details, freely interspersed with many wonderful and incredible tales, acquired for him an extraordinary reputation among his contemporaries, and was soon circulated over Europe translated into various languages.

The king's urgent need of money for his wars with Scotland and France made him dependent upon Parliament, and thus the English people's representatives acquired greater dignity and power. Forced by his necessities during his French wars, Edward III. confirmed the Great Charter thirteen times.

Edward III. increased the number of towns allowed to send representatives to Parliament, making the legislative body so

HOUSES OF PARLIAMENT, LONDON.

large that it was found necessary to divide it into two distinct branches. The branch composed of the nobles, or Lords Temporal, and the bishops, or Lords Spiritual, was thenceforth called the *House of Lords*. The other branch, consisting of the representatives of the cities, boroughs and counties, has ever since been styled the *House of Commons*.

Thus was perfected the legislative department of the English Government. The Witenagemote of the Anglo-Saxons had developed into the Great Council of the Normans; the Great Council had given place to the single Parliament of Simon de Montfort during the reign of Henry III.; and this single Parliament prepared the way for the Parliament in its perfect form of two independent Houses during the reign of Edward III. Thenceforth the Commons, or people's representatives, who had been overawed in the presence of the Lords, assumed a more independent character.

In 1352 Parliament passed the *Statute of Treasons*, by which the crime of high treason was clearly defined. Edward III. enlarged and improved Windsor Castle, and founded the order of the *Knights of the Garter*.

At this time the Romish Church owned about one-third of the real estate of England, and the taxes for church purposes exceeded all the other taxes in the kingdom combined. Although more money was annually raised in England for the Pope than for the king himself, the Pope had demanded the payment of the tribute money, one thousand marks a year, promised by King John to Pope Innocent III. when he made England a papal fief—a tribute now in arrears thirty-three years.

Edward III. and Parliament firmly maintained the independence of England against the papal encroachments; and in this they were ably sustained by the Oxford professor and reformer, John Wickliffe, who boldly denied the pope's assumptions, and maintained that no man could be excommunicated by the Pope "unless he first excommunicated himself." Wickliffe defended Parliament's indignant refusal to pay the tribute demanded by Pope Urban V.—a demand which the Pope was unable to enforce.

During this and the preceding reigns the English serfs had in various ways gradually risen to the condition of freemen. The work of emancipation had been accelerated by the necessities of the lords themselves, who resorted to every expedient to obtain money to maintain the pomp and splendor of Chivalry, which was expensive in time of peace, and doubly so in time of war. To commute the services of the serfs for their estimated value in money was a ready and productive way with the nobility. Edward III. himself sent agents all over the royal estates to sell to the serfs their freedom, in order to raise funds for his wars with France. Thus, by the middle of the fourteenth century, slave labor had largely given place to free labor, which was then abundant and cheap.

The Black Plague, which swept England with the besom of destruction in 1348, carrying off more than half the inhabitants, was especially malignant among the lower classes. At its close labor was scarce and high; and, as it naturally sought the best market, harvests in some parts of England could not be gathered for want of help.

The landowners appealed to Parliament for relief; and an act called the *Statute of Laborers* was passed in 1350, restoring the old price of labor, and compelling the laboring classes to seek employment within the limits of their own respective parishes; thus practically reviving the old and odious system of serfdom, and creating the most intense discontent among the peasantry. The peasants assembled at the various centers to listen to the harangues of their leaders, who depicted in bitter language the wretched condition of the poor and the luxurious estate of the rich. The oppressed peasantry were ready for revolt by the close of the reign of Edward III.

The repeated reënactment of the Statute of Laborers shows how ineffectual was its enforcement and the stubborn resistance of the peasantry, who found ready allies among the villains, or the very lowest serfs. Throughout Kent and the eastern counties the gatherings of the "fugitive serfs" were supported by an organized resistance and by contributions of money from the wealthier tenantry. In the towns, where the system of forced labor was also rigorously applied, strikes and combinations among the craftsmen became frequent. Imprisonment was the penalty for disobedience of the Statute of Laborers. So ineffectual were the punishments that at last the runaway laborer, who often became a beggar and an outlaw, was ordered to be branded on the forehead with a hot iron; and the harboring of serfs in towns and villages was rigorously suppressed.

After his return to Bordeaux from his Castilian campaign the Black Prince became subject to such continued ill-health that he was believed to have been poisoned. His illness had a most unhappy effect upon his temper; and, from being one of the most benevolent and generous of men, he became cruel and morose. After some months of constant suffering, he became so weak that he was unable to mount his horse, and was obliged to relinquish his command in the army.

Thus far the career of King Edward III. and Edward the Black Prince had been one of brilliant success, but after the retirement of the Black Prince the glory of England departed, and disasters fell thick and fast after the renewal of the war with France in 1368. King Charles the Wise of France—the son and successor of John the Good—slowly and steadily retrieved his father's losses, through the military talents of his great general, Du Guesclin, who deprived the English of all their possessions in France except the seaport towns of Calais, Bordeaux and Bayonne. Castilian fleets had well-nigh destroyed the navy of England and swept English commerce from the seas. Worn out with the struggle, Edward III. obtained a truce in 1375 for two years; and the Black Prince returned to England, as a last hope for the recovery of his health.

King Edward III. was now an old man, scarcely able to administer the government; and Edward the Black Prince, the heir to the throne, was slowly dying. The king's worthy wife, Philippa of Hainault, was dead; and the enfeebled old king fell under the influence of an infamous mistress, named Alice Perrers, who made use of the royal favors for unworthy purposes; while John, Duke of Lancaster, one of the king's sons—called John of Gaunt, or Ghent, from his birth-place, in Flanders—got control of the government and appointed unworthy men to office, so that England was in a deplorable condition. The people were burdened with oppressive taxation, the public funds were squandered, the courts of justice were overawed, and the elections were corrupted.

The *Good Parliament*, which convened at Westminister in 1376, proceeded to reform the abuses that had crept into the affairs of state, and was nobly supported by the Black Prince, who devoted his last remaining energies to the work of reform. The Commons impeached, or accused before the Lords, several of the corrupt officials appointed by the Duke of Lancaster—the first instance in which the Commons used their power to impeach ministers of the crown. The Duke of Lancaster was obliged to retire from the government, and Alice Perrers was forced by a threat of banishment to cease interfering with the administration of justice.

John of Gaunt, Duke of Lancaster, whose corrupt administration was the source of so many of the prevalent abuses, was in accord with the Good Parliament and the English people in resisting the Pope's demands for tribute from England. He was powerfully sustained in this course by John Wickliffe, the Oxford professor and reformer, who boldly denounced the exactions and corruptions of the Romish Church. The Duke of Lancaster, who was selfish and unscrupulous, cared little for the corruptions of the Church, but coveted its vast wealth, and planned a sweeping confiscation of Church property; but Wickliffe, who was of exalted purity of character, opposed the Church on account of its abuses and assumptions.

Edward the Black Prince died June 8.

1376, in the forty-seventh year of his age, amid the grief of all England; and he was buried in Canterbury Cathedral. His death was a public calamity, as it brought the reforms of the Good Parliament to a sudden close. His brother, John of Gaunt, Duke of Lancaster, at once returned to power, followed by the election of a new Parliament in his interest.

The death of the Black Prince broke the heart of poor old King Edward III., who survived his illustrious son but one year, dying at Shene, June 21, 1377, in the sixty-fifth year of his age, after a reign of fifty years. His last years were rendered gloomy by the disasters which had befallen him, and his death was peculiarly sad—a striking commentary on the vanity of human glory. As death drew near he was utterly forsaken, being deserted by all his attendants. Even his mistress, Alice Perrers, fled, after snatching a ring from his unresisting finger. A compassionate priest entered the deserted chamber at the last moment, and held a crucifix before the eyes of the dying king. Such was the melancholy end of Edward III., the very prince of the renowned royal race of the Plantagenets, the hero of the French wars, the pride of England.

RICHARD II., the son of the Black Prince, became King of England upon the death of his illustrious grandfather in 1377; but, as the new king was only a boy of eleven years at his accession, Parliament chose a Council of Regency to administer the government. The English people idolized their handsome boy king as they had his renowned father and grandfather, and his early years gave encouragement to their hopes. No king ever ascended the throne of England more heartily welcomed; as the very fact that he was the son of the Black Prince, that model of Chivalry and idol of the people, gave him a warm place in all English hearts. Though handsome, he was effeminate, a mere lover of pleasure and royal pomp. His retinue numbered ten thousand persons, and its passage through the kingdom was dreaded almost as much as an army of invasion.

We have already alluded to the discontent of the laboring classes at the close of the preceding reign. When Richard II. ascended the throne of England he was involved in wars with Scotland, France and Castile. One English fleet was beaten by the Castilians; another was lost in a storm; while a campaign in the heart of France terminated disastrously to the English.

To defray the expenses of these repeated disasters, Parliament in 1381 levied a tax of one shilling on every person in England over fifteen years of age. The injustice of imposing a tax to which the poorest man in the kingdom contributed as large a share as the richest threw all England into a violent ferment, and the insolence of the tax-gatherers fanned this flame of disaffection into open rebellion.

One of these tax-collectors insulted the daughter of Wat Tyler, a blacksmith at Deptford, in Kent; whereupon the enraged father knocked the ruffian down with his hammer. The plucky blacksmith's action was heartily applauded by the mob; and the peasants of Essex, Kent and the neighboring counties gathered together, armed with clubs, bows and rusty swords, under the leadership of Wat Tyler, Jack Straw, Hob Carter and Tom Miller. The royal commissioners who had been sent to repress the tumult were driven from the field; and a band of insurgents in Essex under Jack Straw crossed the Thames to summon the men of Kent to arms, but a hundred thousand Kentishmen were already rallying under Wat Tyler.

The cry of the poor and oppressed peasantry, who had thus risen in revolt, found a terrible utterance in the words of John Ball, "a mad priest of Kent," as the courtly historian Froissart called him. For twenty years this Kentish priest had preached a coarser and more popular type of reform than that of Wickliffe, and the stalwart yeomanry assembled in the Kentish churchyards to listen to his sermons, in defiance of interdict and imprisonment. Though the land-owners called John Ball "mad," his preaching was the first declaration of the rights of man in England—the death-knell of Feudalism. The tyranny of property then as ever roused the defiance of Socialism. John Ball's leveling doctrine breathed a spirit fatal to the entire system of the Middle Ages. His sermons set forth the popular grievances in words as extreme as those of any Communist or Chartist of our own time.

Said this Kentish priest: "Good people, things will never go well in England so long as goods be not in common, and so long as there be villains and gentlemen. By what right are they whom we call lords greater folk than we? On what grounds have they deserved it? Why do they hold us in serfage? If we all came of the same father and mother, of Adam and Eve, how can they say or prove that they are better than we, if it be not that they make us gain for them by our toil what they spend in their pride? They are clothed in velvet, and warm in their furs and their ermines, while we are covered with rags. They have wine and spices and fair bread; and we oatcake and straw, and water to drink. They have leisure and fine houses; we have pain and labor, the rain and the wind in the fields. And yet it is of us and of our toil that these men hold their state."

Ball expressed his leveling doctrines in the following rhyme which passed from lip to lip:

"When Adam delved and Eve span,
Who was then the gentleman?"

The following quaint rhymes passed through the revolted counties as the summons to the peasant revolt:

"John Ball greeteth you all,
And doth for to understand
He hath rung your bell.
Now right and might,
Will and skill,
God speed every dele."

"Help truth, and truth shall help you!
Now reigneth pride in price,
And covetise is counted wise,
And lechery withouten shame,
And gluttony withouten blame.
Envy reigneth with treason,
And sloth is take in great season.
God do bote, for now is tyme!"

"Jack Miller asketh help to turn his mill aright.
He hath grounden small, small;
The King's Son of Heaven he shall pay for all.
Look thy mill go aright with the four sailes,
And the post stand with steadfastness.
With right and with might,
With skill and with will;
Let might help right,
And skill go before will,
And right before might,
So goeth our mill aright."

"Jack Carter prays you all
That ye make a good end
Of that ye have begun,
And do well, and aye better and better;
For at the even men heareth the day."

"Falseness and guile have reigned too long,
And truth hath been set under a lock,
And falseness and guile reigneth in every stock.
No man may come truth to,
But if he sing 'si dedero.'
True love is away that was so good,
And clerks for wealth work them woe.
God do bote, for now is tyme!"

The revolt of the peasants spread like wild fire over England. From Kent, Sussex and Essex, the revolt spread over Norfolk, Suffolk, Cambridgeshire and Hertfordshire, and as far west as Somerset and Winchester. But the strength of the outbreak lay in the Kentishmen, who welcomed Jack Straw and his rebels from Essex, who plundered the archbishop's palace at Canterbury and liberated John Ball from its prison; while a hundred thousand Kentishmen under Wat Tyler marched to London, killing every lawyer who fell into their hands as they reached Blackheath, shouting: "Not till all these be killed will the land enjoy its freedom again." At the same time they fired the houses of the stewards and cast the records of the manor courts into the flames.

The whole population joined the insurgents as they marched along, while the nobles were paralyzed with fear. John of Gaunt, Duke of Lancaster, the head of the Council of Regency, fled before the popular fury, and took refuge in Scotland. Young King Richard II., but a boy of sixteen, addressed the insurgents from a barge on the Thames, June 14, 1381; but the Council of

Regency, under the guidance of Sudbury, Archbishop of Canterbury, refused to allow him to land, thus arousing the peasants to the greatest fury; and the great mass of rebels rushed on London, crying: "Treason! treason!" The great gates of the metropolis were flung open by the poorer artisans within the city; and the stately palace of the Duke of Lancaster at the Savoy, the new inn of the lawyers at the Temple, and the houses of the foreign merchants, were all soon in a blaze.

The next day, June 15, 1381, a daring band of the insurgent peasants, under Wat Tyler himself, forced their way into the Tower, took the panic-stricken knights of the garrison roughly by the beard, and promised to be their equals and comrades in the good time to come. The infuriated mob discovered Sudbury, Archbishop of Canterbury, and some of the ministers who had hindered the young king from a conference with them, in the chapel; whereupon the Primate was dragged from the sanctuary and beheaded on Tower Hill, while the same vengeance was wrecked on the treasurer and the chief commissioner in the levy of the obnoxious poll-tax.

In the meantime the young king found sixty thousand of the peasant mob waiting for a conference with him outside of the city, at Mile-End. Addressing the vast mob, Richard II. spoke thus: "My good people, what means this disorder? I am your king and lord, what will ye?" The peasants shouted: "We will that you free us forever, us and our lands; and that we be never named nor held for serfs." The boy king replied: "I grant it." He then requested them to retire to their homes, and pledged himself instantly to issue charters of freedom and amnesty. This promise was welcomed with a shout of joy. During the same day more than thirty clerks were busy writing letters of pardon and emancipation, and when these were handed to the rebels they dispersed quietly to their homes.

William Grindecobbe returned to St. Albans with one of these charters of freedom, marched at the head of the townsmen, and summoned the abbot to deliver up the charters which bound the town in serfage to his house. After a long suit at law, the millstones had been surrendered to the abbey, and placed within its cloister as a triumphant witness that no burgess held the right of grinding corn within the bounds of its domain. The men of St. Albans now burst open the cloister gates, tore the millstones from the floor, and broke them into fragments "like blessed bread in church," so that all might have something to show of the day when their freedom was again acquired.

Thirty thousand peasants under Wat Tyler, thinking the king's promise was only a stratagem to get them out of the city, still remained to see the royal pledge fulfilled; and the next day, June 16, 1381, Richard II., accompanied by William Walworth, Lord Mayor of London, and a retinue of sixty horsemen, met this part of the mob at Smithfield. Wat Tyler ordered his followers to remain at a distance, while he rode up to the king and behaved toward him with such insolence that Lord Mayor William Walworth struck the audacious blacksmith to the ground with his sword, whereupon Wat Tyler was slain by others of the king's retinue.

The enraged mob, infuriated by the loss of their leader, rushed forward and threatened to overwhelm the king's entire party, shouting: "Kill, kill. They have killed our captain." But the young king's presence of mind saved the lives of himself and his retinue. Riding boldly up to the mob before they had time to recover from their momentary surprise, Richard II. cried: "What need ye, my masters? Be not troubled for the death of your unworthy leader. I, your king, will be your leader! Follow me." Turning his horse, the boy king rode into the open field at the head of the mob, who followed him with a touching loyalty and trust to the Tower, believing that he had abused his youth under the influence of evil counselors.

The young king's mother welcomed her son with tears of joy. The boy king answered: "Rejoice and praise God; for I have recovered to-day my heritage which was lost, and the realm of England." The nobles had recovered from their panic, and six thousand knights gathered around the king, eager for the blood of the mob; but Richard II. was still true to his word, and contented himself with issuing the promised certificates of freedom and amnesty to the insurgents who dismissed to their homes.

But the peasant revolt was not yet over. A strong body of the mob still occupied St. Albans. In the eastern counties, fifty thousand rebels forced the gates of St. Edmundsbury and compelled the trembling monks to grant a charter of enfranchisement to the town. Littester, a dyer of Norwich, headed a strong mass of peasants, under the title of "King of the Commons," and forced the nobles whom he had captured to act as his meat-tasters and to serve him on their knees during his repast.

The death of Wat Tyler, however, encouraged the nobles, and deprived the revolted peasants of all decision and all concert of action. The warlike Bishop of Norwich with lance in hand attacked the rebel camp in his own diocese, and dispersed the peasants at the first onset. King Richard II., with forty thousand troops, spread terror by the ruthlessness of his executions as he marched in triumph through Kent and Essex; but the obstinate resistance which he encountered showed the temper of the people.

The villagers of Billericay demanded that the king should grant them the same liberties that their lords possessed, and when he refused their demand they occupied the woods and were only reduced to submission after two desperate conflicts. Verdicts of guilty against the leaders of the revolt could only be wrung from the Essex jurors by the threat of death. William Grindecobbe was offered his life if he would persuade his followers at St. Albans to surrender the charters of freedom which they had wrested from the monks. He turned bravely to his fellow-townsmen and bade them not to be concerned for his trouble. Said he: "If I die, I shall die for the cause of the freedom we have won, counting myself happy to end my life by such a martyrdom. Do, then, to-day as you would have done had I been killed yesterday."

But the resolute will of the conquered peasants encountered as determined a will in their lordly conquerors. The Royal Council, however, manifested its sense of danger by submitting the question of enfranchisement to the Parliament which had convened on the suppression of the revolt, with words which suggested a compromise. Said the royal message: "If you desire to enfranchise and set at liberty the said serfs by your common assent, as the king has been informed that some of you desire, he will consent to your prayer." But the reply of the land-owners showed their determination to consent to no compromise. They answered that the king's grant and letters of freedom were legally null and void; that their serfs were their goods, and that the king could not take their goods from them without their own consent. They closed by declaring: "And this consent we have never given and never will give, were we all to die in one day."

Though the revolts were quelled and the peasants nominally returned to a condition of serfdom, the newly awakened desire for personal liberty could not be extinguished; and the work of emancipation went on slowly but surely, until a century and a half later, when serfdom finally ceased in England.

Though Wat Tyler's Rebellion was little better than tumultuous gatherings of ill-organized mobs, whose subsidence was as sudden as their uprising, the social and political questions involved raise it to a plane of serious importance. It was a revolt based on social distinctions—the commencement of an irrepressible conflict between the poor and humble oppressed and the rich and noble oppressor—the beginning of an antagonism between labor and capital, that has continued unabated in one form or another to the present day. Wat Tyler is said to have been an ancestor of John Tyler, tenth President of the United States.

Wat Tyler's Rebellion, which the Church charged to the seditious and heretical teachings of John Wickliffe and his followers, was a serious blow to the *First Reformation*, as Wickliffe's religious movement was called. Wickliffe was forsaken by his most powerful friends, including John of Gaunt, Duke of Lancaster. Another reason for this defection was Wickliffe's extreme views concerning some of the tenets of the Romish Church. He was applauded by all classes so long as he merely exposed the corruptions of the Church; but he lost the sympathy of all good Catholics when he assailed its cardinal doctrines.

It was in this emergency that Wickliffe displayed the real grandeur and versatility of his genius. He no longer addressed scholarly arguments in classic Latin to the learned, but he thenceforth directed his appeals in plain Anglo-Saxon to the English masses. Pamphlet after pamphlet from his prolific pen denouncing the doctrines and practises of the Church alike was circulated broadcast over England. In these pamphlets the clergy were fearlessly assailed for their avarice and exactions, their sale of indulgences for sin, and the gift of Church benefices to foreign priests, "who neither see nor care to see their parishioners, convey away the treasure of the realm, and are worse than Jews or Saracens." These tracts, written in the strong, rough language of the plowmen and mechanics of the time, are the earliest specimens of English prose.

Like Roger Bacon a century before, John Wickliffe was surrounded by a throng of eager disciples; and an order of preachers, called the *Simple Priests*, was instituted to disseminate his doctrines among the English people. These earnest young men, who, scattering to their humble parishes, diffused Wickliffe's teachings throughout England, were derisively called *Lollards*, or "babblers," by their enemies; but the common people heard them gladly, and such progress was made that, in the bitter language of a careful observer of the times, "every other man you met was a Lollard."

The first wife of King Richard II., Anne of Bohemia, favored Wickliffe's doctrines; and many of her countrymen, who attended

JOHN WICKLIFFE AND HIS CHURCH AT LUTTERWORTH.

the University of Oxford, carried the great reformer's writings thence to the University of Prague, in Bohemia, where they kindled an extraordinary religious movement; so that Wickliffe was the "Morning Star of the Reformation" for Bohemia as well as for England.

The regency in England, under the influence of the Duke of Lancaster, came to the assistance of the Church in 1381, the very year of Wat Tyler's Rebellion; and Wickliffe was banished from the University of Oxford, while his writings were condemned as heretical and sentenced to the flames. He then retired to Lutterworth, where he devoted the remaining three years of his life to the humble duties of a parish priest, and to the last and greatest work of his life—the complete translation of the Bible into English, for the instruction of the common people. He had a stroke of paralysis while attending mass in the parish church, and died peacefully the next day, December 31, 1384, at the age of sixty years.

Thirty years after Wickliffe's death the rage of his enemies invaded his tomb, burned his bones, and scattered his ashes upon a little brook which flowed through the village. Says Fuller: "Thus the brook conveyed his ashes into Avon; Avon into Severn; Severn into the narrow seas; they into the main ocean; and thus the ashes of Wickliffe are the emblem of his doctrine, which is dispersed over all the world."

During the reign of Richard II. flourished Geoffrey Chaucer, the "Morning Star of English Poetry." Chaucer was born in 1328, and died in 1400. Many causes operating through five centuries had so changed the language of England that the prose of Alfred the Great and the poetry of Cædmon required as much special study to be read in Chaucer's day as in ours.

Of Chaucer's numerous works the most celebrated is his *Canterbury Tales*, which is still read with delight, and in which thirty pilgrims from all classes are represented as traveling together from London to Canterbury to visit the shrine of St. Thomas à Becket, and as whiling away the tedium of the journey by telling tales, which present lively descriptions of the men and women of his time, in all ranks from sailor to baron, and from doctor to plowman.

Chaucer's sympathy with Wickliffe is expressed in his praise of the poor parson—who followed "Christ's lore and his Apostles'" before he taught it to his flock—and in his ridicule of the seller of indulgences with his wallet "full of pardons come from Rome all hot."

Chaucer was a favorite with the king and the nobles, and his poetry breathes the perfumed elegance and luxury of the royal court. William Langland, who styled him-

GEOFFREY CHAUCER.

self Piers the Plowman, was the people's poet of the time. He sang in ruder and sadder lines the hunger, the toil and the misery of the poor man's life, made dark by his own ignorance and the remorseless oppressions which he suffered from his lords.

John Gower, called "Moral Gower," was born in 1320, and died in 1402. He was the author of three great poetical works—*Speculum Meditantis*, written in French; *Vox Clamantis*, written in Latin; and *Confessio Amantis*, written in English. The English poem begins by introducing the author himself in the character of an unhappy lover in despair. Venus appears to him; and appoints her priest, called Genius, to hear the lover's confession. This priest plies him with moral tales, the most extraordinary of which is the tale of the Caskets in the fifth book. This is the tale from which Shakespeare is believed to have taken the hint of the incident of the caskets in his Merchant of Venice. Near the end of his English poem, Gower represents Venus as paying a glowing compliment to Chaucer, his friend and brother poet.

The war with France and Scotland still continued; and Richard II. invaded Scotland with the design of conquering that kingdom, but failed in that undertaking, though the invasion was conducted with great cruelty. The English arms suffered many disasters in other quarters. The immense English trade with Flanders was cut off by the submission of Ghent and the whole of Flanders to a brother of King Charles the Wise of France. A French army landed in Scotland and threatened an invasion of England. The border lands of England and Scotland were wasted by hostile raids; and in 1388 occurred the battle of Otterburn—a mere border-fight between two hostile noblemen, the English Percy and the Scottish Douglas, and their vassals —which has been commemorated by the famous ballad of *Chevy Chase.*

The men and means which Parliament voted for the common defense were squandered in Spain by John of Gaunt, Duke of Lancaster. who was seeking to obtain the crown of Castile in his wife's name. The hopes which the decisive conduct of Richard II. had raised during Wat Tyler's Rebellion were soon dispelled. He was fond of shows and pageants, and was profligate and dissipated. He abandoned himself to the influence of favorites, who were as obnoxious to the English people as Gaveston and the Spensers had been during the reign of his great-grandfather, Edward II. The chief of these worthless favorites was Michael de la Pole, a London merchant's son, who was created Duke of Suffolk.

The king's profligacy and dissipation, and his partiality for his worthless favorites, made him so unpopular that his youngest and ablest uncle, the Duke of Gloucester,

8—37.-U. H.

contrived to vest the whole sovereign power in a Council of Regency, consisting of fourteen noblemen, with himself at the head. Richard II. resisted, but was compelled to submit by force of arms in 1387; and his favorite minister, Michæl de la Pole, Duke of Suffolk, only saved his life by flight from the kingdom, while many others of the king's favorites were doomed to exile and death.

The Duke of Gloucester then resolved to destroy all the friends of his royal nephew. The venerable and respected Sir Samuel Burleigh, the young king's tutor, was also condemned on a pretended charge of high treason, through the instrumentality of the king's tyrannical uncle; and he was executed like a common traitor, although the young monarch's good wife, Anne of Bohemia, remained on her knees three hours before the inexorable Duke of Gloucester, begging for the old man's life.

After Richard II. had submitted to his uncle's tyranny for about a year and a half, he suddenly asserted his own right to the sovereign power, and removed the officers appointed by the Duke of Gloucester, filling their places with men of ability. He acted with such prudence and vigor that the Duke of Gloucester and his party were thunderstruck and at once relinquished their authority.

During the reign of Richard II. the effort to maintain the independence of England against papal aggressions was continued with firmness. In 1393 a powerful blow was struck in defense of the liberties of England by Parliament's passage of the *Statute of Præmunire,* "which enacted that whoever should procure from Rome or elsewhere, excommunications, bulls, or other things against the king and his realm, should be put out of the king's protection, and all his lands and goods forfeited."

Richard II. conducted the government himself for nine years and ruled well. His first wife, Anne of Bohemia, who endeared herself to her husband and to the English people, died in 1394; and in 1396 Richard II. affianced the Princess Isabella, the daughter of King Charles VI. of France, then only eight years old. This marriage, and the peace which Richard II. concluded with France, were unpopular with the English people.

The opposition of the Duke of Gloucester to the peace with France induced the king to free himself from the danger with which he was menaced by his uncle's ambition. Hearing that the Duke of Gloucester was conspiring against him, Richard II. caused his uncle to be seized by surprise, hurried to Calais and imprisoned in the castle of that city. The imprisoned nobleman was charged with high treason, and a Parliament was summoned at Westminster, September 17, 1397, to try him. So many nobles came to London to attend this trial that every lodging place in the city and for ten miles around was filled. On the arrival of the day of trial the Governor of Calais was summoned to bring his illustrious prisoner before Parliament. The governor sent word that the Duke of Gloucester had suddenly died in prison of apoplexy, but it was generally believed that he had been murdered by the king's order. The duke's friends were terrified into submission by the king's bold stroke, and none dared to oppose the king's will.

Pleased with his new taste of power, and unable to brook opposition, Richard II. endeavored to reign without a Parliament; that body being virtually abolished by a cunningly devised statute, which placed the legislative power in a select number of lords and burgesses, and which granted him a life income and enabled him to resort to forced loans to defray the expenses of government.

The good and bad impulses by which Richard II. was controlled were both fatal to his power, which, though now apparently more secure than ever, was approaching its downfall. The war-loving barons were offended by the peace with France; the landowners by the protection of the serfs; the merchants by the king's demands for money; and the clergy by the favor which the king showed to Wickliffe's followers and their doctrines.

Some of the nobles openly accused the king of the murder of the Duke of Gloucester. One day Thomas Mowbray, Duke of Norfolk, expressed this opinion in the presence of the king's cousin, Henry Plantagenet, Duke of Hereford—called Henry of Bolingbroke, from his birth-place, or Henry of Lancaster, he being a son of John of Gaunt, Duke of Lancaster. This young nobleman was an able and valiant knight, who had become celebrated as a good soldier and a zealous Christian by fighting in the cause of Christ against the heathen tribes on the eastern shores of the Baltic. He was a great favorite with the soldiers, possessed immense wealth, and was related to all the great families of England.

Henry of Lancaster, Duke of Hereford, was highly indignant at the charge made by the Duke of Norfolk against Richard II., and accused that nobleman in Parliament of having spoken seditious words against the king in a private conversation. The Duke of Norfolk indignantly denied the charge, called Henry of Lancaster a liar, and offered to prove his innocence by an appeal to Wager of Battle. As there were no proofs for a legal trial, the Lords in Parliament readily assented to that mode of settling the controversy. The time and place for the duel were appointed, and all England awaited the event with anxious suspense.

On the day when this personal combat between the two noblemen was to take place, and in the presence of the vast multitude assembled to witness it, just as the trumpets had sounded the charge and the combatants, mounted on their horses, rushed at each other with fixed lances, King Richard II., who appeared upon the scene, threw down his scepter, which was a signal for the heralds to stop the combat. The king then ordered the lances of the combatants to be taken away, and banished the Duke of Hereford for ten years, and the Duke of Norfolk for life.

Thus one of the combatants was condemned to exile without being charged with any offense, and the other without being convicted of any crime. The king's action gave general dissatisfaction. There was a feeling of disappointment at being deprived of the pleasure of seeing a combat, and of indignation at the injustice done to the duelists themselves.

The Duke of Norfolk, overwhelmed with grief and despondency at the judgment awarded against him, retired to Venice, where he soon died of a broken heart. Henry of Lancaster, Duke of Hereford, behaved on this occasion with such submission and resignation that the king consented to shorten his banishment four years, and granted him letters-patent insuring him the enjoyment of any inheritance which should fall to him during his exile; but upon the death of Henry's father, John of Gaunt, Duke of Lancaster, in 1399, Richard II. seized all the great estates of the Lancaster family.

Roused to intense indignation by the king's outrage, the exiled Henry of Lancaster sailed from France for England to reclaim his rights, embarking at Nantes with a small retinue, and landing at Ravenspur, in Yorkshire, with about twenty followers, July 4, 1399; Richard II. being then in Ireland. Henry of Lancaster immediately raised the standard of revolt, and was joined by the Earl of Northumberland, who had long been disaffected toward Richard II., and by that powerful nobleman's son, Henry Percy, surnamed *Hotspur*, from his fiery temper and his ardent valor. In a few days Henry's army numbered sixty thousand men, and was soon increased by the royal forces under the king's uncle, the Duke of York, who deserted the king's side when Henry of Lancaster persuaded him that he had come only to claim his inheritance, and not to seize the crown.

In the mean time Richard II. remained in Ireland in perfect security. Contrary winds for three weeks prevented him from receiving any news of the rebellion against his authority in England; and when he landed at Milford Haven, in Wales, on his return, with a force of twenty thousand men, he found himself in a dreadful situation, in the midst of an enraged people, without any friend on whom he could rely, and forsaken by those who had been instrumental in encouraging his follies in the time of his prosperity. His little army gradually deserted him, until at last he discovered that he did not have over six thousand men who followed his standard.

Not knowing whom to trust, or where to turn, Richard II. saw that his only hopes of safety lay in throwing himself upon the generosity of his enemy and in obtaining by pity what he could not win by force of arms. He therefore sent word to Henry of Lancaster that he was ready to submit to whatever terms he deemed proper to impose, and that he earnestly desired a conference. For this purpose Henry of Lancaster requested Richard II. to meet him at Flint Castle, about ten miles from Chester, and there Henry with his army appeared the next day to meet the king.

Richard II., who had been brought thither by the Earl of Northumberland the day before, seeing his rival's approach from the walls, went down to receive him; while Henry of Lancaster, after some ceremony, entered the castle in full armor, only his head being bare in compliment to the fallen king. Richard II. received his triumphant rival with that open air for which he had been remarkable, and kindly bade him welcome. Said Henry of Lancaster, with a respectful bow: "My lord king, I am come sooner than you appointed, because your people say that for one and twenty years you have governed with rigor and indiscretion. They are very ill satisfied with your conduct; but, if it please God, I will help you to govern them better for the time to come." To this declaration Richard II. only replied: "Fair cousin, since it pleases you, it pleases us likewise."

After a short conversation with some of the king's attendants, Henry of Lancaster ordered the king's horses to be brought out of the stable; and when the wretched animals were produced Richard II. was placed on one, while his favorite, the Earl of Salisbury, was placed upon the other. In this humble equipage they rode to Chester, and were conveyed to the castle with a great noise of trumpets, through an immense multitude of people, who were unmoved by the sight. In this manner Richard II. was led from town to town amid crowds of people, who scoffed at him and extolled his rivals, exclaiming: "Long live the good Duke of Lancaster, our deliverer!" In the poet's pathetic words concerning the king, "None cried God bless him!"

Thus, after repeated indignities from Henry of Lancaster and from the populace, Richard II. was conveyed to London and lodged in the Tower as a close prisoner, where he underwent a still greater variety of studied insolence and flagrant contempt. Humiliated in this manner, the wretched king began to lose a monarch's pride with the splendors of royalty, and his spirit sunk to his circumstances. He therefore willingly signed a deed by which he abdicated the crown of England.

Upon the abdication of Richard II., Henry of Lancaster founded his principal claim to the English throne; but, in order to secure his pretensions with every appearance of justice, he convened a Parliament, which was readily induced to approve and confirm his claim. A frivolous charge of thirty-three articles was drawn up and found valid against Richard II., whereupon he was solemnly deposed by act of Parliament; and that body unanimously chose Henry of Lancaster to the English throne with the title of HENRY IV., the new king being conducted to the vacant throne by the Archbishops of Canterbury and York, September 30, 1399. Thus began the royal House of Lancaster, which furnished England with three kings, whose aggregate reigns numbered sixty-two years (A. D. 1399-1461.)

When Richard II. was deposed, the Earl of Northumberland made a motion in the House of Lords demanding the advice of Parliament concerning the future treatment of the discrowned king. Parliament decided that he should be imprisoned in some secure place, where his friends and partisans would be unable to find him; and Richard II. was accordingly confined in Pontefract Castle. But the usurper could not hope to remain in safety while the deposed monarch was still living, and some plots and commotions which occurred soon afterward induced Henry IV. to desire the death of his dethroned cousin; and Richard II. was found dead in Pontefract Castle in the beginning of the year 1400, at the age of thirty-three years and after a reign of twenty-two years, believed to have been murdered or starved by the new king's order.

Some writers say that an assassin agreed to murder the fallen king for a reward, and that he took eight companions with him for the purpose. When the assassins rushed into the king's apartments in Pontefract Castle the deposed king knew that their design was to murder him, and he determined to sell his life as dearly as possible; wherefore he wrested a pole-ax from one of the murderers and soon laid four of them dead at his feet, but was finally overpowered and struck dead by a blow from a pole-ax.

Though elected King of England by Parliament, Henry IV. was not satisfied to rest his claim on the national will; but asserted that he held the throne by right of his birth, he being the son of John of Gaunt, Duke of Lancaster, and the grandson of Edward III. But, according to the strict principles of hereditary succession, the nearest heir to the English throne was Edmund Mortimer, Earl of March, who was a lineal descendant of Lionel, Duke of Clarence, John of Gaunt's elder brother, and whom Parliament had declared heir to the English crown. The young Earl of March was a child of seven years, and Henry IV. sought to avoid a conflict with his claims by keeping him in a sort of mild captivity at Windsor Castle.

As the English crown had always been in some degree elective, Henry IV. no doubt had all the claim that could be derived from the national will. The conflict between the elective and hereditary principles was not settled until several centuries afterward.

Henry IV. soon found that the throne of

a usurper is a bed of thorns; as conspiracies and rebellions were still undertaken in the interest of Richard II., who, some of the enemies of Henry claimed, was not dead, and whom some one tried to personate. The nobles taken in arms were beheaded; and, to prevent any more rebellions in the dead king's interest, Henry IV. caused the body of Richard II. to be brought from Pontefract Castle to London, and to be publicly exposed at St. Paul's Cathedral, with the face uncovered for three days; after which it was buried at Langley. Still some of the enemies of Henry IV. claimed that Richard II. was still alive and in exile in Scotland, and that the body shown at St. Paul's Cathedral was that of another person.

The very first Parliament that convened under Henry IV. gave evidence of the unsettled condition of the kingdom. The House of Lords broke up in a furious quarrel, and forty challenges were given and received, and forty gauntlets were thrown down as pledges of the sincerity of the resentment of the angry barons. Some of the disaffected nobles endeavored to seize King Henry IV. at Windsor; but the king withdrew to London, where he raised an army of the citizens and quelled the outbreak of the discontented lords. The Earls of Kent and Salisbury, and some of the other leaders of the outbreak, were beheaded for their rebellion. A rebellion against the authority of Henry IV. in Gascony was also suppressed.

Still one plot after another disturbed the usurping king. One night he found a steel instrument with three sharp points, concealed in his bed, just as he was about to lie down.

The most serious of the rebellions against Henry IV. was that of the Welsh, under Owen Glendower, who claimed descent from the royal race of Llewellyn and the ancient Princes of Wales. As in the time of Edward I., patriot bards, who journeyed from place to place with song and story of the ancient heroes of Welsh history, fired the Welsh heart afresh with its old love of liberty. After being defeated in the open field, Owen Glendower retired to the fastnesses of Mount Snowdon, and defied the whole power of England throughout the reign of Henry IV. For some years after this reign he lived as a wanderer and an outlaw, rejecting all overtures of peace, and sojourning in hidden caves among his native hills. His fate has never been known. A cave still called *Owen's Cave* can be seen on the coast of Merioneth.

In one of his raids into England, Owen Glendower captured Sir Edward Mortimer, the uncle of the young Earl of March, and carried him a prisoner into Wales. Henry IV., dreading and hating the whole of the Mortimer family, allowed Sir Edward Mortimer to remain in captivity, and refused to permit Mortimer's kinsman, the Earl of Northumberland, to treat with Owen Glendower for his ransom; thus offending the family of the Percies, who were the king's most powerful partisans.

In 1402 a Scottish army of twelve thousand men, under Archibald, Earl of Douglas, invaded England. The Earl of Northumberland and his son, Henry Percy, surnamed *Hotspur*, took the field against the Scots and defeated them at Homildon Hill, in Northumberland, September 14, 1402, taking the Earl of Douglas and many of the leading nobles of Scotland prisoners. Henry IV. sent the victorious Earl of Northumberland strict orders forbidding him to admit any of his prisoners to ransom, as he desired to make better terms with Scotland by the possession of one of the great Scottish nobles. According to the laws of war in that age of Chivalry and Feudalism, the captor had the right to the ransom of his prisoner; and the proud Earl of Northumberland considered himself both insulted and robbed by the king's demand.

The angry Earl of Northumberland now rebelled against King Henry IV., thus seeking to overthrow the monarch whom he had been chiefly instrumental in raising to the throne of England. He instantly released his Scottish captives, and made an alliance with the Earl of Douglas and with the Welsh leader, Owen Glendower. The

Earl of Westmoreland, the brother of the Earl of Northumberland, joined in the rebellion against Henry IV.; and the rebels openly avowed their purpose to dethrone Henry IV. and to place the young Edmund Mortimer, Earl of March, upon the English throne.

Henry IV. had raised a small army, with which he intended to invade Scotland, when he was astounded by the news of the rebellion of the Percies. This rebellion was wholly unexpected by the king, but he was not disconcerted thereby. He fully appreciated the importance of swift and decisive movements in civil wars, and accordingly he at once marched against the rebels. The rebel forces under the Percies and the Scots under the Earl of Douglas marched southward into Shropshire, where they effected a junction with the Welsh under Owen Glendower.

Henry IV. encountered the combined forces of his enemies at Shrewsbury, July 21, 1403. Each army numbered about twelve thousand men. The battle which ensued was desperate and sanguinary, and the animosities on both sides were inflamed to the highest pitch. Great bravery was displayed by the commanders on both sides. The Earl of Northumberland being absent through illness, the command of his forces devolved on his fiery-tempered son, Henry Percy, Hotspur. Henry IV. displayed great valor, being in the thickest of the fight; while his valiant son Henry, the Prince of Wales, fought gallantly by his father's side, and performed astonishing feats of valor even after he had been wounded in the face with an arrow. The daring Hotspur also sustained his renown for bravery, and sought to engage the king in person, but could not distinguish him from others who wore the same armor. The death of Hotspur from an unknown hand finally decided the victory in favor of Henry IV. The Scottish Earl of Douglas was taken prisoner.

The king's victory in the battle of Shrewsbury put an end to the rebellion of the Percies. The Earl of Northumberland threw himself upon the generosity of Henry IV., who, remembering the former services of this powerful baron, and pitying the old man's bereaved condition, pardoned him, and soon afterward restored to him almost all of his honors and estates.

Two years later, A. D. 1405, another rebellion broke out against Henry IV., headed by Scrope, Archbishop of York, and Thomas Mowbray, Earl Marshal of England; and the rebels were joined by the Earl of Northumberland, who had again taken up arms against the king; but the outbreak was quickly quelled, and Archbishop Scrope was beheaded as a traitor—the first instance of a bishop being punished with death in England. This was considered a sacrilegious act, and Henry IV. was soon afterward afflicted with a loathsome eruption in the face, which was believed to be a direct punishment from Heaven. After several years of exile and wandering, the Earl of Northumberland finally lost his life in a last effort to overthrow Henry IV.

By accident Henry IV. got the heir to the Scottish throne into his possession. King Robert III. of Scotland stood in deadly fear of his violent and unscrupulous brother, the Duke of Albany, who had already caused the heir-apparent to be starved in a dungeon, and who appeared resolved to make his way to the throne of Scotland by destroying the lives of all the legitimate heirs. To save his only surviving son's life, King Robert III. sent this son, Prince James, to France, in 1406; but the vessel in which the Scottish prince sailed was seized by an English cruiser, although a state of peace then existed between England and Scotland; and the prince, then nine years of age, was detained by Henry IV., and remained a state prisoner in England for over eighteen years, two of which were spent in the Tower, and sixteen in Windsor Castle.

Upon being brought before Henry IV., the Earl of Orkney, who accompanied the young prince, told the English king that the prince was going to France to learn French; whereupon Henry IV. replied: "I understand French, and therefore ought to be intrusted with his education." Henry IV. then committed Prince James and the Earl of Orkney to the Tower. Grief at his son's capture broke the heart of poor old King Robert III., who died three days after he had received the news. His brother, the Duke of Albany, ruled Scotland as regent for the remaining eighteen years of his life, but would do nothing to obtain the release of Prince James.

Henry IV. made some amends for his injustice by giving the captive Scottish prince the best education afforded by the times. The prince was provided with good instructors, and became the famous "Poet-King of Scotland." He was a poetic genius, and some of his ballads continue to be popular to the present day. He was released upon the death of the Duke of Albany in 1424, when he became King James I. of Scotland. He married Lady Joanna Beaufort, an English princess, for whom he had formed an attachment while in prison. James I. was the best king that ever reigned over Scotland, and his name is reverenced by his countrymen to this day.

Henry IV. sought to please the clergy by persecuting the Lollards, and the fires of persecution were kindled in England for the first time in her history. As the Archbishop of Canterbury had given Henry IV. valuable aid in his efforts to secure the English crown, the king in his turn assisted the Romish Church with all his power to root out Wickliffe's doctrines, which had taken a strong hold upon the English people.

An act of Parliament, passed in 1401 and called the *Statute of Heretics*, empowered the bishops to imprison all writers, teachers and preachers of heresy, and, if they refused to abjure their heretical doctrines, to hand them over to the civil authorities to be burned. Under this cruel law, William Sawtre, a London preacher, was the first martyr at the stake in England. After being condemned by the bishops, he was handed over to the civil authorities and burned to death, in accordance with the Statute of Heretics, February 12, 1401.

Thus Henry IV. has the infamous reputation of being the first King of England who imposed by statute the awful penalty of death by fire upon his subjects simply on account of religious belief. Thus was commenced the system of horrible religious intolerance that blackens the pages of English history for so long a period—an intolerance whose only palliation is the spirit of the age.

But the Commons in Parliament were not as subservient to the priests as the Lords. When it was found that the clergy were resolved to resist the payment of their share of the taxes of the kingdom, notwithstanding their vast wealth, the Commons sided with the Lollards in order to check the power of the priesthood. The Commons asked the king for a mitigation of the law of burning, and advised him to seize the wealth of the Church and employ it as a permanent fund to serve the necessities of the state. They even framed a bill for this purpose.

But Henry IV. refused to mitigate the law against heretics, saying that he wished one more severe had been passed, and to show the Commons that he was in earnest he immediately signed the death-warrant of John Badbie, a poor tailor, for holding Wickliffe's doctrines; and thus another martyr perished at the stake. Instead of checking the growth of Lollardism, these barbarous measures only served to extend the new doctrines.

The position of Henry IV. as King of England was an unenviable one. He lived in constant dread of the Lollards, who were known to be active in inciting insurrections. He was also conscience-smitten at the part he had taken in the persecution of that sect, as well as at the means which he had employed to obtain the English crown. He was obliged to be ever on the alert against the friends of the murdered Richard II. and those of the living Edmund Mortimer, Earl of March. His consciousness of the irregular manner of his own accession made him suspicious of his own son Henry, Prince of Wales, of whose constantly growing popularity he was morbidly jealous. This feeling made the king stern and cruel to all whom he suspected of plotting against him.

Henry IV. was also a sufferer from ill health, and was distressed at the wild and reckless conduct of his son Henry, the Prince of Wales, called *Madcap Harry*. This prince led a most disorderly life. One of his companions was arrested for a highway robbery, and was brought before Chief Justice Gascoigne for trial. The evidence was strong against the prisoner, but the prince demanded that he should be released. The Chief Justice refused to comply with the prince's insolent demand; whereupon the prince became so angry as to forget himself, and he actually struck the Chief Justice as he sat upon the bench. The judge vindicated the dignity of his office by sending Prince Henry to prison. The prince at once acknowledged the impropriety of his conduct toward the judge and submitted to the punishment. Upon hearing of this, the king exclaimed: "Happy the monarch who possesses a judge so resolute in the discharge of his duty, and a son so willing to submit to the law!"

The king's health now rapidly declined. He was shattered mentally and physically by epileptic fits, which hurried him to a premature grave. As his strength declined his fears of conspiracies and insurrections increased even to childish anxiety, and he could not sleep unless the royal crown was laid upon his pillow. One day, when he had fallen down in a fit of epilepsy, the Prince of Wales, believing him actually dead, took the crown from his pillow and carried it away. When the king recovered his consciousness he instantly missed his crown, and sternly asked who had dared to remove it. Prince Henry made a dutiful apology, thus pacifying the king, who said with a sigh: "Alas! fair son, what right have you to the crown when you know your father has none?" The prince replied: "My liege, with your sword you won it, and with the sword I will keep it." The king replied: "Well, do as you please; I leave the issue to God, and hope he will have mercy on my soul."

Soon afterward Henry IV. died in a fit of epilepsy, while kneeling in prayer before the shrine of Edward the Confessor in Westminster Abbey, March 20, 1413, at the age of fourty-four years, and after a reign of thirteen years. Shakespeare's sage reflection on the stormy years of the reign of Henry IV. was: "Uneasy lies the head that wears a crown." The Commons greatly increased their power during his reign—a natural result when the king's best title to his crown rested upon their consent.

HENRY V., the son and successor of Henry IV., had a short but brilliant reign. As soon as he heard of his father's death he retired to his own chamber and spent the remainder of the day in prayer. The next morning he sent for the companions of his youthful follies and told them that he was going to reform and lead a better life, and forbade them to come again into his presence until they should follow his example by reforming their habits of life. He then sent for his father's wise ministers who had checked his wild and reckless conduct, and retained them in office. Among these was Chief Justice Gascoigne, who had sent Henry to prison for interfering with the course of justice, as we have observed.

Thus Henry V. happily disappointed those who feared that the reckless prince would make a reckless king. He did much to conciliate the enemies of the House of Lancaster by several just and noble acts at the very beginning of his reign. He pacified the House of York by releasing the imprisoned Edmund Mortimer, Earl of March, and honoring the bones of Richard II. with a truly royal burial among the remains of the Kings of England in Westminster Abbey. Mortimer showed his gratitude by disclosing to the king a plot formed by some nobles to place him on the English throne. Henry V. won the support of the powerful family of the Percies by recalling the son of Hotspur and restoring to him all the honors and estates of his family.

Henry V. was the idol of his subjects, for his extraordinary talents in war and government, and also for his gay and genial disposition, which formed a strong contrast to his father's gloomy temper. He possessed in a great degree the qualities which were most calculated to make him a favorite with the English people. His person was tall and slender, his hair was dark, and his features were exceedingly beautiful. His accession to the English throne was hailed with general joy.

But Henry V. stained his character by a cruel persecution of the Lollards, whose doctrines had been gradually spreading, not only in England, but also in Continental Europe. Through the influence of Wickliffe's writings, John Huss, Rector of the University of Prague, in Bohemia, had become a convert to Lollardism, and openly preached it until he was silenced at the stake by command of the Council of Constance in 1415.

Early in the reign of Henry V., Arundel, Archbishop of Canterbury, perceived the necessity of acting more vigorously and rigorously toward "the new heresy." The leader of the Lollards in England was Sir John Oldcastle, who was created Lord Cobham, and whose castle was a place of refuge for the Lollards. Sir John Oldcastle had been an old friend of Henry V., and had formerly been very wicked, but from the time that he adopted Wickliffe's doctrines he had lived a moral and religious life. The king, inspired by his old friendship for Sir John Oldcastle, and thinking him a very wise and virtuous man, sought to convince him of the fallacy of his new opinions. After a long conversation, Henry V. became so shocked at Oldcastle's obstinacy in defense of his faith that he turned him over to the vengeance of the Romish Church.

Oldcastle, or Lord Cobham, was imprisoned in the Tower; and, after being tried and condemned by the bishops for disbelieving the doctrine of transubstantiation and other Catholic dogmas, he was delivered into the hands of the civil authorities to be burned to death. The king again interposed, granting him a respite of fifty days, during which Lord Cobham escaped from the Tower, and was suspected of planning a Lollard insurrection against the king. This act added treason to heresy; and the king dreaded to see Lord Cobham, who was an experienced soldier, at the head of the movement.

Henry V. at once took a decided stand against the First Reformation, and the most violent persecution followed. The severest statutes were enacted by Parliament, ordering the arrest of all persons, even if only suspected of heresy, and entailing forfeiture of estate and blood on all who were convicted. A price was set on the head of Lord Cobham, and many of his followers suffered martyrdom. Lord Cobham concealed himself for four years, but was finally captured, and was first hanged at London as a traitor, after which his body was burned as a heretic, to combine the punishments due to the two crimes of treason and heresy. The charge of treason did much to bring the Lollards into disrepute, and the First Reformation was soon at an end in all that was outward and visible.

The First Reformation had declined among the influential classes on account of its connection with Wat Tyler's Rebellion during the reign of Richard II. Some of the leaders of the Lollards, lacking the singleness of purpose that inspired Wickliffe, sought to bring about the abolition of social distinctions and the equalization of property —our modern Communism. In addition to this, the First Reformation, at the time of its suppression during the reign of Henry V., rested under the odium of conspiring to subvert the government. Thus branded as Communistic and dangerous to society, and as revolutionary and destructive to public order, the First Reformation had arrayed the rich and powerful, also the more thoughtful and conservative, against itself.

Though the Reformation ceased to exist outwardly, there was all the time a simple and a purer faith taking root in the hearts of many—a faith based on the open Bible that Wickliffe had placed in their hands. Charles Knight, the popular English historian, has truly said: "Out of Wickliffe's rectory, at Lutterworth, seeds were to be borne upon the wind which would abide in the earth till they sprang up into the stately growth of other centuries."

It was in the early part of the reign of Henry V., thirty years after Wickliffe's death, that the Council of Constance, which condemned John Huss and Jerome of Prague to suffer the death of martyrs at the stake, caused Wickliffe's remains to be disinterred and burned, and his ashes to be cast into a little brook that runs past Lutterworth into the Avon. The following beautiful lines concerning the scattering of Wickliffe's ashes are from Wordsworth:

"As thou these ashes, little brook, wilt bear
Into the Avon—Avon to the tide
Of Severn—Severn to the narrow seas—
Into main ocean they—this deed accurst,
An emblem yields to friends and enemies,
How the bold teacher's doctrine, sanctified
By truth, shall spread throughout the world dispersed."

Henry IV. on his death-bed had charged his son not to let the English remain long at peace, as foreign wars alone could save England from internal troubles; and Henry V. followed his father's advice by renewing the Hundred Years' War with France, reviving the old claim of Edward III. to the French crown. The title of Henry V. to his English crown required to be strengthened by military renown. His barons' thirst for stirring adventures might have made trouble at home if it had not been gratified abroad. Henry V. renewed the attack on France at an opportune moment. King Charles VI. was insane; and his son, the Dauphin, was too young to rule; while the Dukes of Burgundy and Orleans had involved France in a sanguinary civil war concerning the regency during the Dauphin's minority.

When the demand of Henry V. that the French should acknowledge his claim to the crown of France and that the Princess Catharine should be given in marriage to him was rejected, he assembled a fleet and army at Southampton and crossed the English Channel and invaded France, landing at Harfleur, in Normandy, with a well equipped and powerful army of thirty thousand men, in August, 1415. He captured that place in September, 1415, after a siege of five weeks, but lost two-thirds of his army by sickness and death.

Henry V. was now in a perilous situation. He sent his ships away with his sick and wounded, and he had no means of returning to England but by marching to Calais with his remaining ten thousand troops. The whole distance lay through the enemy's country. There were strong towns to pass, and deep rivers to cross; while a French army of a hundred thousand men was already in the field to oppose his progress. Against the advice of his nobles he undertook his march for Calais, starting from Harfleur in October, 1415, and following the old route of Edward III.

Henry V. proceeded by easy marches and enforced the strictest discipline. He paid the country people liberally for everything that he obtained from them, and they accordingly brought him supplies of provisions, in spite of the orders that they received not to do so. During the march the young king fared no better than the meanest soldier, and he encouraged his troops by the cheerful and familiar manner in which he conversed with them.

The French army, one hundred thousand strong, was drawn up to oppose the English king's little army of ten thousand men at the village of Agincourt, in the county of Artois, not far from the famous field of Creçy. In the battle of Agincourt, October 25, 1415, although the French army was ten times as large as his own, the superior skill and efficiency of the English archers prevailed, and Henry V. won as brilliant a victory over the flower of the chivalry of France as those of Edward III. and the Black Prince at Creçy and Poitiers.

The day before the battle Henry V. took his position on a rising ground, surrounded by trees and brushwood. He placed guards and lighted fires; and the army, excepting some who passed the night in prayer, retired to rest. As some of the English nobles were conversing together, one of them said that he wished all the brave men in

England were there to help them. The king answered: "No! I would not have one more here. If we are defeated, we are too many; but if it please God to give us the victory, as I trust He will, the smaller our number, the greater our glory." The French passed the night in noisy festivity; and, confident of victory on the morrow, they agreed among themselves to put all the English to the sword, excepting the king and the principal nobles, who were to be spared for their ransoms.

Heavy rains had made the ground difficult for cavalry, while the English light-armed archers were able to move with ease. These opened the battle with one well-aimed volley of arrows; after which they seized the hatchets which hung from their necks, and rushed forward with a deafening shout, thus increasing the confusion of the wounded Frenchmen and horses before them. The gallant knights and gentlemen of France, weighted with their steel armor, sank to their saddle-girths in mud and marsh.

Henry V. displayed a valor worthy of the Black Prince. Arrayed in shining armor, with a gold crown adorned with precious gems on his head, he was easily to be distinguished in the thickest of the conflict. Eighteen French knights had made a vow to kill or take the English king, and they all lost their lives in attempting to fulfill their vow, being all slain by David Cam, the English king's faithful squire, and two other Welshmen, who lost their own lives in defending their king. Henry V. knighted these brave men on the battle-field, as their life-blood was ebbing away at his feet.

The French lines gave way one by one, and after a battle of three hours the English victory was won. The French left ten thousand dead upon the field; among whom were seven princes of the blood royal, over a hundred noblemen, and eight thousand knights. The Constable d'Albret and the Dukes of Alençon and Brabant were among the slain, while the Dukes of Orleans and Bourbon were among the fourteen thousand prisoners taken by the victorious English. This battle destroyed the old nobility of France, and left the French throne unsupported. The English loss was only about forty men.

When this remarkable battle was ended, Henry V. called upon the French herald, who was named *Mountjoy*, and asked him what was the name of a neighboring castle, to which he pointed with his finger. The herald replied: "It is called Agincourt." Then said the English king: "This action shall henceforth be called *the Battle of Agincourt.*"

Considering all the circumstances, the battle of Agincourt, which added new glory to the English arms and new laurels to the English kings, was the most brilliant victory ever gained by English soldiers over the soldiers of France. Agincourt at once took its place beside Crecy and Poitiers, but outshone both those famous conflicts. But the expense of maintaining a modern army made the victory almost useless to the English; and Henry V., after making his way to Calais unopposed, crossed the Strait of Dover to England, "covered with glory and buried in debt."

The English people gave their warrior king a joyful welcome when he returned from his brilliant campaign. They rushed into the water as he approached the land, and bore him on their shoulders to the shore. Throngs of delighted people from all the towns went out to meet him, strewing flowers in his path. His entrance into London finds a parallel in the magnificent Triumphs which the people of ancient Rome gave to their returning victors.

All efforts at a permanent peace failed; and in August, 1417, Henry V. again invaded France, landing in Normandy with a well-equipped army of forty thousand men, when France was once more distracted by the quarrels of its own nobles and princes. Towns and castles in Normandy surrendered at the summons of Henry V., or fell before his assaults. The siege of Rouen lasted six months. Its two hundred thousand inhabitants refused to open their gates until reduced to the most desperate extremities by famine. Said Henry V.: "War has three handmaidens—Fire, Blood and Famine; and I have chosen the meekest maid of the three." While the merciless English king was drawing his lines closer around the devoted city, Famine was doing its terrible work within its walls. One-half of the inhabitants of Rouen had perished; and the survivors, in despair, had resolved to burn the city and die in battle before its walls, when Henry V., fearing that Fire and Blood would finally deprive him of his coveted prize, offered the inhabitants terms of capitulation, January, 1419.

By the capture of Rouen, Henry V. completed the conquest of Normandy; and an event that occurred soon afterward hastened and completed the conquest of France. After a solemn treaty of peace between Duke John the Fearless of Burgundy and the Dauphin Charles, the former was assassinated by a servant of the latter, A. D. 1419. The murdered Burgundian duke's son and successor, Philip the Good, in revenge, formed an alliance with the King of England; and the entire Burgundian party threw itself into the scale against the Dauphin, offering to do all in their power to make Henry V. King of France.

By the Treaty of Troyes, in May, 1420, concluded with Henry V. of England by Duke Philip the Good of Burgundy and Isabella of Bavaria, the wife of the poor old crazy King Charles VI. of France, it was agreed that Henry V. should marry the Princess Catharine, the daughter of the French king; while the English king's brother, the Duke of Bedford, was to marry a sister of the Duke of Burgundy. Charles VI. was to remain King of France during his life-time; but Henry V. of England was invested with the regency of France for the same period, and was to receive the French crown upon the death of the crazy French king, to the exclusion of the latter's son, the Dauphin Charles. The States-General of France solemnly ratified this treaty.

Kings Henry V. and Charles VI. made a triumphal entry into Paris in May, 1420, just after the Treaty of Troyes had been agreed to; and the union of the crowns of England and France was celebrated with great outward demonstrations of joy. In accordance with the Treaty of Troyes, Henry V. married the Princess Catharine, June 2, 1420; and the next year she bore him a son, an event celebrated with equal rejoicings in the capitals of England and France. But the Dauphin Charles refused to submit to the loss of his inheritance, and held that part of France south of the Loire, while the King of England was in possession of almost all of the French kingdom north of that great river.

While engaged in the task of establishing his authority in France, in the very prime of life and the very midst of his power and glory, Henry V. was suddenly attacked with a painful and incurable illness, of which he died at Vincennes, August 31, 1422, at the age of thirty-three years, and after a reign of nine years; after appointing his brother, the Duke of Bedford, regent of France, and his other brother, the Duke of Gloucester, regent of England, while committing the guardianship of his infant son to the Earl of Warwick. His body was conveyed to England with great pomp and buried in Westminster Abbey. Tapers were kept burning on his tomb day and night for almost a century. His widow married Owen Tudor, a Welsh gentleman, and from them was descended the renowned Tudor dynasty of England.

The first ship of war ever owned by the English government was built during the reign of Henry V. Previous to this period the maritime towns had furnished all the ships required for war or national purposes. During the reign of Henry V. it was settled that no laws should be valid without the assent of the House of Commons.

HENRY VI., the infant son of Henry V., was proclaimed King of England, upon his father's death; and, upon the death of the poor old crazy King Charles VI. two months later, he was also proclaimed King of France, and was crowned at Paris as King of England and France, being then only nine months old, A. D. 1422. The infant king's uncles—the Duke of Gloucester, regent of England, and the Duke of Bedford, regent of France—were men of integrity and excellent virtues; the Duke of Gloucester being called the "Good Duke Humphrey."

The Dauphin, the son of Charles VI., had never consented to the Treaty of Troyes, which set aside his claims to the French throne; and, upon the death of his father, in 1422, he assumed the title of Charles VII., King of France. The English wittily called him "King of Bourges," that city being the extent of his actual dominion, though the sovereignty of France was his birth-right. For six years the English were constantly victorious, taking town after town, until in 1428 they laid siege to Orleans, the only important stronghold yet remaining in the possession of the Dauphin's troops. The capture of that city by the English would have exposed to them the whole of France south of the Loire, and the cause of Charles VII. would have been irretrievably ruined. This danger filled the French with consternation.

At this darkest hour in the fortunes of France and her legitimate, native king, when no gleam of hope appeared visible, Orleans was relieved and the deliverance of Charles VII. effected by one of the most extraordinary occurrences in history. In the history of France we have related the remarkable career of Jeanne d'Arc, the poor peasant girl of Domremy, in Lorraine; her visions of angels and "Voices," which she declared told her to raise the siege of Orleans and have Charles VII. crowned at Rheims; the faith of the French king and people in her mission; her commission from Charles VII. to command the French armies; her appearance at the head of the army destined to raise the siege of Orleans, when she was clad in armor and mounted on a snow-white horse, with her consecrated banner borne before her; the irresistible enthusiasm which she inspired among the French and the dismay which she caused among the English; her rescue of Orleans by entering the city and compelling the English to raise the siege; her repeated victories over the English; her capture of Rheims, in which city Charles VII. was then crowned; her expressed desire to return to her father's home to take care of his flocks; the French king's refusal to consent to her retirement from the army; the jealousy of the French officers on account of her fame; their treacherous abandonment of her at a sally from the town of Compèigne, where they allowed her to be taken prisoner by the Duke of Burgundy, who sold her to the English; and the base conduct of the English, who caused her to be tried, condemned and burned by a court of bishops as a witch and a heretic, at Rouen, May 30, 1431.

Though her ungrateful king made no effort to rescue the valiant *Maid of Orleans*, as the heroine was called, and took no interest in her fate, her name is held in grateful remembrance by her countrymen, and excites a tender respect and admiration wherever the strange, sad story of her wonderful career is told; and this is a far nobler and more enduring monument to her than the one erected to her memory on the spot where she suffered a martyr's death.

Although the Maid of Orleans no longer led the French armies, victory still perched upon the French banners, the spell of English ascendancy was broken, and the English dominion in France was fast hastening to a close. All France submitted to her hereditary and legitimate king when a reconciliation was effected between Duke Philip the Good of Burgundy and King Charles VII., who then hurled their united forces against the English invaders. The Duke of Bedford soon afterward died of vexation at the disasters which had befallen the English cause. Paris opened her gates to Charles VII., and the English power gradually grew weaker and weaker during the remaining twenty years of the war.

The English fought bravely, but were defeated on every side, and finally retired into Normandy in the hope that they might at least save that province. A truce and a treaty both failed to stop the war. Normandy in the North of France, and Guienne in the

South, both revolted from the English dominion. The English were steadily driven toward the sea-board, though they fought with desperate valor, and they finally sought refuge within the walls of Calais, which was the only place in France that remained in their possession by 1453, when the Hundred Years' War finally closed, and the dream of an English empire in France was over.

The campaigns of Edward III. and the Black Prince, and those of Henry V., were brilliant, but unsubstantial, gratifying the national pride of the English, but exhausting their national resources. As soon as those great warriors retired from the scenes of their triumphs and conquests, those conquests melted away like mist before the rising sun.

Henry VI. was a man of weak intellect and of gentle and amiable disposition. He was a most insignificant character, and would have been satisfied to remain in the background his entire life, as his timid and quiet disposition entirely unfitted him for the cares of royalty. He inherited neither the fine qualities nor the majestic figure of his father, nor any of the delicate beauty of his mother. His personal appearance was inelegant, and his countenance was dull and unmeaning. An old historian thus describes his character:

"There never was a more holy, nor a better creature, a man of a meek spirit and a simple wit, preferring peace to war, and rest to business, and honesty before profit. He was governed of those he should have ruled, and bridled of those he should have sharply spurred."

When Henry VI. was only eight months old he was kept quiet in his mother's lap to listen, or rather to appear to listen, to a long address from Parliament, in which he was called a "most toward prince and sovereign governor." When he was eight years old he was solemnly crowned at Paris as King of France.

But Henry VI. was very fortunate in having a wise and sincere friend in the good old Beauchamp, Earl of Warwick, who reprimanded the king when he was eleven years old, and desired that the Royal Council would in a body admonish him of his faults.

The death of the Duke of Bedford produced effects in England almost as disastrous as in France. England was divided between two parties, led respectively by the Duke of Gloucester, the king's uncle and the regent of the kingdom, and by this duke's uncle, Cardinal Beaufort, a son of John of Gaunt. One great object of rivalry between these two men was the choice of a wife for the young king.

As Henry VI. was of a gentle and harmless disposition, and resembled his imbecile maternal grandfather, King Charles VI. of France, rather than the three great Kings of England from whom he was more immediately descended, it was hoped that a spirited wife of masculine qualities would supply his defects; and the Beaufort party selected a French princess, Margaret of Anjou, reputed to be the most beautiful, clever and accomplished princess of her time, though she was then only fifteen years old. The Beaufort party succeeded in their plan, and a secret article of the marriage contract ceded England's province of Maine, in France, to Margaret's uncle, Duke Charles of Anjou. The marriage between Henry VI. and Margaret of Anjou occurred in 1445.

The new queen became a warm adherent of the Beaufort party, which had secured her marriage. She never forgave the Duke of Gloucester for opposing it, and she came to England vowing vengeance against him in her heart. Cardinal Beaufort and William de la Pole, Duke of Suffolk, were her willing allies in her opposition to the good Duke of Gloucester, who had tried to prevent the marriage because he foresaw the miseries that it would entail upon the kingdom.

Cardinal Beaufort and the Duke of Suffolk commenced their machinations by accusing Eleanor Cotham, the wife of the Duke of Gloucester, of witchcraft. She was charged with having caused a waxen image of the king to be made and laid before a gentle fire, and as the wax dissolved the king's strength was wasted, so that his life would become extinct upon the total dissolution of the waxen image. The Duke of Gloucester's wife was found guilty upon this absurd charge, and was condemned to do public penance and then to be imprisoned for life on the Isle of Man. To prove that she was a witch a paper of mathematical figures written by her priest was produced, and the ignorance of the people who found it believed it to be some magical incantation.

Supported by the queen, Cardinal Beaufort and the Duke of Suffolk next sought the ruin of the Duke of Gloucester himself. They accused him of high treason; but the council, though composed wholly of his enemies, was obliged to pronounce him innocent of this charge. Nevertheless, he was imprisoned, and soon afterward found dead in his bed, believed to have been murdered by his enemies. His wicked uncle, Cardinal Beaufort, died several weeks afterward in agonies of remorse.

Queen Margaret was unpopular with the English people. When her kinsman, King Charles VII. of France, reconquered Normandy and Guienne from the English, they suspected the same kind of treachery that had deprived them of Maine; and though they were generally unwilling to vote money for the king's wars in France, which were really opposed to their interests, they considered the loss of any conquered territory as a national disgrace.

Poor King Henry VI. was then at a low ebb in his fortunes. The crown-lands and revenues had been squandered during his minority, and his household was only maintained by a system of robbery politely styled the "royal right of purveyance."

The popular indignation at this state of affairs, and at the loss of the English possessions in France, forced Parliament to bring charges of high treason against the Duke of Suffolk in 1450. Queen Margaret hoped to save him from summary vengeance by inducing the king to banish him for five years. But his enemies, fearing that Margaret would recall him, caused him to be pursued on the high seas by a large vessel, called *Nicholas of the Tower*. He was overtaken and ordered on board this ship, and as he reached its deck he was greeted with the salutation: "Welcome, traitor." He was brought to Dover, and two days later he was let down into a small boat and beheaded with a rusty sword on a block of wood, his body being cast into the sea.

Edmund Beaufort, Duke of Somerset, a relative of the king and a favorite of the queen, was held responsible for the more recent losses of English territory in France; but he continued to defy his enemies and remained in office a while longer.

In 1450, soon after the murder of the Duke of Suffolk, several insurrections broke out in various parts of England, but these were all soon suppressed. The most formidable of these revolts was that of Jack Cade, an Irishman, who assumed the more dignified name of John Mortimer, intending to pass himself off as a son of Sir John Mortimer, who had been sentenced to death by Parliament at the beginning of this reign, without any trial or evidence, merely upon an indictment of high treason. Sir John Mortimer had been popular in Kent, the seat of Jack Cade's Rebellion; and his name gave Jack Cade his chief strength.

Jack Cade's Rebellion grew out of the general discontent at the mismanagement of affairs at home and in France. It is an interesting fact that Jack Cade's Rebellion had its chief seat in Kent, the old home of Wat Tyler, and among the very classes which had been implicated in Wat Tyler's Rebellion.

Jack Cade led twenty thousand Kentishmen to London, defeating the royal forces under Sir Humphrey Stafford on the way, at Sevenoaks. The victorious rebels encamped on Blackheath, whence Jack Cade sent to the Royal Council his "Complaint," embodying a statement of grievances, chief of which were maladministration in the government, the king's favoritism to his evil counselors, the interference of the nobles in the county elections, the extortions of the tax-collectors, and the hardships imposed on the peasants by the Statute of Laborers.

Appreciating the fact that Jack Cade's demands were reasonable, the Royal Council removed the king to Kenilworth Castle, whereupon Jack Cade entered London. He held the city for three days, and caused Lord Say and Seal, the treasurer, and that official's son-in-law, Cromer, the Sheriff of Kent, to be beheaded at Cheapside for their extortions. Cade then exclaimed: "Now I am master of London!"

Cade's followers now plundered private property, in disobedience of his orders. The citizens then rose against Cade, and when he retired at night to Southwark they held London Bridge with the aid of some soldiers from the Tower, thus preventing his return. After a conflict of six hours the Royal Council granted Jack Cade's demands, and most of the insurgents dispersed and returned to their homes upon being promised a pardon for their rebellion. Jack Cade, with a price on his head, fled almost alone into Sussex, but was pursued and killed by a Kentish gentleman named Iden; and many of his followers were executed.

The loss of the English possessions in France compelled the English nobles to confine their ambitious schemes at home, and these nobles were divided into two parties which contended for supremacy in the nation. The party which adhered to the reigning family, the House of Lancaster, was headed by Edmund Beaufort, Duke of Somerset, the representative of the illegitimate branch of the House of Lancaster. The other party, which adhered to the rival House of York, was under the leadership of Richard Plantagenet, Duke of York, who aspired to the English throne, which he claimed as a descendant from Edward III. both on his father's and his mother's side. By his father he was descended from the youngest son of Edward III. From his mother, who was the last of the Mortimers, he inherited the claim of that family from Lionel, second son of Edward III.

Although it was believed that the Duke of Somerset aspired to the English throne, his influence was all powerful at court; but he was unpopular with the English people, because he was considered responsible for the loss of Normandy by the English. The Duke of York, who had commanded with credit both in France and in Ireland, was very popular with the English people. He was a brave, able and generous man, and was closely related by marriage to the Earls of Salisbury and Warwick, the most powerful noblemen in England.

If Henry VI. had been an able man like his father his subjects might have forgotten by this time that his grandfather was a usurper; but his incapacity reminded them of the imperfection of his royal title and of the superior claim of the Mortimers, who, though extinct in the male line, had their rights to the English crown transferred by marriage to the House of York.

The birth of a Prince of Wales, instead of strengthening the cause of the imbecile King Henry VI., removed all hope of the peaceable succession of the Duke of York to the English throne, and thus hastened the approaching civil war. In 1454 the king sunk into a condition of total bodily and mental weakness, so that he was unfit to govern. Queen Margaret and her council were obliged to yield to the popular will, and Parliament appointed the Duke of York to the office of Protector of the kingdom. The first use that the Duke of York made of his power was to send the Duke of Somerset to the Tower; but Henry VI. soon recovered his reason, whereupon the Duke of York was removed from the Protectorship, and the Duke of Somerset released from prison and restored to power in the government.

The quarrel between the Dukes of Somerset and York soon threw all England into a violent ferment. Both assembled their partisans and vassals, and in the first battle of St. Albans, May 3, 1455, the Duke of Somerset was defeated and killed. King Henry VI., whom the Duke of Somerset had dragged into the battle much against his will, was wounded, and took refuge in the house of a tanner, where the victorious Duke of York found him. The Duke of York fell upon his knees before the king, declared himself his loyal subject, and ready to obey his commands; to which the king replied: "If so, stop the pursuit and slaughter."

Thus began the *Wars of the Roses*—the badge of the House of Lancaster being a red rose, and the badge of the House of York a white rose. This civil war for thirty years deluged England with the blood of her own people, destroyed eighty princes of the blood royal, and almost annihilated the ancient nobility of England.

The victorious Duke of York conducted Henry VI. to London and treated him with great respect; but, notwithstanding his professions of loyalty to the king, he continued the civil war against the queen and her party, under the pretense of freeing the king from evil counselors. At last the Duke of York threw off the mask in the House of Lords by boldly declaring Henry VI. a usurper and claiming the English crown as his own by right of inheritance; whereupon many of his supporters, who had joined him because they had supposed that he was only contending for the public welfare, deserted his standard.

Seeing himself thus abandoned, the Duke of York retired into Ireland; but he left a very able and zealous friend in England—his wife's brother, Neville, Earl of Warwick; afterwards called the *King-maker*, because he was able to raise up and pull down kings at will. The Earl of Warwick was the richest nobleman in England, and was the last of the great barons who held their broad lands on the feudal tenure of military service. This powerful nobleman maintained thirty thousand persons on his various estates and manors—a very great number when the whole kingdom had a population of less than two and a half millions. He was idolized by the soldiers and the people as the greatest representative of the national aristocracy of England.

Stow, a writer of that day, describes the great Earl of Warwick coming to London with a retinue of six hundred men, all in red jackets, embroidered on the sleeves with the "bare and ragged staff," the badge of the Warwick family. He lodged in his house on Warwick Lane, and six fat oxen were frequently consumed in one breakfast. All his own people were fed at his cost, and even all who were acquainted with his household were permitted to carry away as much boiled or roasted meat as they could take on their dagger; so that it is no wonder that he was extremely popular.

The Yorkists were victorious at Bloreheath, in Staffordshire, in 1459; and the Earl of Warwick defeated the Lancastrians at Northampton, July 10, 1460, compelling them to flee in all directions. Queen Margaret and her son fled to Scotland. King Henry VI. was found sitting alone in his tent by the Earl of Warwick, who carried him a prisoner to London.

When Parliament convened in the fall of 1460 the Duke of York returned from Ireland and presented his claim to the English crown. There was no doubt that he was the direct heir of Edward III., but Parliament was unwilling to dethrone the reigning king. Parliament therefore decided that Henry VI. should remain King of England during his life, but that on his death the Duke of York and his heirs should succeed to the throne.

But Queen Margaret was not disposed to see her son thus set aside. By great exertions she raised an army of twenty thousand men, whom she induced to enter her service by promising them the plunder of the fertile lands of England. With this army Margaret advanced toward London, and encountered the Duke of York at the head of only five thousand men at Wakefield, in Yorkshire, where he was defeated and slain, December 30, 1460. The spot where he fell is still fenced off in a corner of a field near Sandal. His death was sincerely lamented by his partisans. The cruel Margaret caused his head to be cut off and fixed on the gate of York with a paper crown, in derision of his claim. His son Edmund,

Earl of Rutland, a handsome boy of twelve years, was murdered in cold blood by Lord Clifford on Wakefield hedge, where a small chapel, afterward erected, still commemorates the bloody deed. The cruel queen also caused the most noble and valiant of her prisoners to be beheaded without trial.

The Duke of York left three sons and three daughters. The sons were Edward, Duke of York, afterward King Edward IV.; Richard, Duke of Gloucester, afterward King Richard III.; and George, Duke of Clarence. His eldest daughter became the wife of the renowned Duke Charles the Bold of Burgundy.

Edward Plantagenet, the young Duke of York, took up the cause and claim of his lamented father, defeated the Lancastrians in the battle of Mortimer's Cross, in Herefordshire, early in 1461, and followed up his victory by the bloody execution of the Lancastrian nobles who fell into his hands. After her victory in the battle of Wakefield, Queen Margaret resumed her advance toward London; her followers fully availing themselves of the liberty to plunder by pillaging and burning every church and dwelling, marking their way by fire and devastation. The Earl of Warwick led an army against her, taking the poor passive king with him.

In the second battle of St. Albans, February 17, 1461, Margaret won a victory over the Earl of Warwick, who fled, leaving behind him the king, who was rejoiced at being restored to his wife and son. But the queen's triumph was of short duration. The city of London was firm in the interests of the Yorkists, while the citizens also feared to admit Margaret's tumultuous army and refused to open their gates. The queen was therefore again obliged to retreat northward.

The young Duke of York, with the remains of the army of the Earl of Warwick, entered London amid the acclamations of the populace, March 3, 1461. The Earl of Warwick then assembled the people, presented the young duke to them, and asked whether they would have him or Henry VI. for their king. The multitude shouted: " A York! a York! Long live King Edward!" The young Duke of York was that day proclaimed King of England with the title of EDWARD IV. The next day he went in solemn procession to Westminster Hall, took his seat on the throne, and received the homage of a large assemblage of nobles, bishops and magistrates, March 4, 1461. Thus ended the reign of the poor idiotic Henry VI., the last of the three English kings belonging to the House of Lancaster; and thus began the royal House of York, which also furnished three kings to England, whose united reigns aggregated twenty-four years (A. D. 1461-1485).

Edward IV. was only in his nineteenth year when he found himself so unexpectedly seated on the throne of England. He was brave, active and enterprising, with a capacity far beyond his years. Comines, the contemporary French historian, says that "he was tall of person, fair of face, of a most princely presence, and altogether the goodliest man that ever mine eyes beheld." But these brilliant qualities were blackened by the darkest vices. In peace Edward IV. reveled in all kinds of self-indulgence, and in war he was sanguinary beyond all who had preceded him. He was willing to wade through seas of blood to secure possession of his throne.

Immediately after his accession the new king mustered an army of sixty thousand men, which he led northward in pursuit of the Lancastrian army of sixty thousand men under the deposed Henry VI. and Margaret. Edward IV. overtook the fleeing Lancastrians at Towton, about eight miles from York, in the midst of a severe snow storm, about four o'clock in the afternoon of Palm Sunday, 1461. The Yorkists had their backs toward the storm, while the Lancastrians faced it and were thus greatly incommoded by it. The sanguinary battle raged all that night and part of the next day, until finally the Lancastrian army fled in a panic from the bloody field, leaving thirty-three thousand men dead in the snow. Henry VI. and his wife and son awaited the result at York, and when they were informed of the defeat of their army they fled with the utmost haste to Scotland.

It had been the practice from the beginning of the war for either party, when victorious, to execute the nobles of the other party and to confiscate their estates. After the battle of Towton there was a sweeping confiscation of Lancastrian estates, many of which were conferred on the Earl of Warwick, the main pillar of the House of York. Edward IV. also satiated his revengeful temper by many bloody executions, and every Lancastrian who fell into his hands was condemned as a traitor. He strengthened his own party by conferring titles and honors on all his friends. It was very necessary to create new peers, as the numbers of the nobility had been vastly reduced by the recent exterminating battles and by the sanguinary executions which followed them. Thus some of the noblest heads in England fell upon the scaffold, and their confiscated wealth went to build up the despotic power on which Edward IV. had set his heart, as it enabled him to support the expense of his government without having recourse to Parliament.

Margaret's energy was only increased by these reverses of fortune. She made two voyages to France, in hopes of receiving assistance from there. Finally, by her untiring exertions, she raised an army, with which she invaded England by way of Scotland. After some slight successes, she was defeated by King Edward IV. at Hedgley Moor, April 25, 1464, and three weeks later at Hexham.

This last defeat was so decisive that Henry VI. only escaped capture by the swiftness of his horse. Margaret and her eleven-year-old son sought a hiding place in the woods, but there they fell among robbers, who took all their valuables from them. Fortunately, the robbers then quarreled about the division of the plunder, thus giving Margaret and her little boy an opportunity to escape. As she and her son were wandering about in the woods they met another robber. Margaret boldly approached him with her boy, saying: "Behold, my friend, the son of your king. I commit him to your protection." This appeal aroused the pity of the robber, who accordingly led the fallen queen and her little son to a hiding place, where they remained until the pursuit was over. The robber then led them to the sea-coast, whence they escaped to France.

The unfortunate Henry VI. wandered from one hiding place to another for the space of a year, suffering many hardships. While sitting at dinner at Waddington Hall, in July, 1465, he was betrayed by a monk to Sir James Harrington, who conveyed him to London and turned him over to his great enemy, the Earl of Warwick. The Earl of Warwick treated the fallen king with the utmost indignity; tying his feet under his horse's belly, as if he had been a criminal, and thus compelling him to ride round the pillory three times, while the populace were forbidden to show him any respect or compassion. The poor ex-king was then imprisoned in the Tower.

The partisans of Henry VI. were now reduced to such distress that many of the most distinguished Lancastrian nobles were actually begging their bread in foreign lands, while the triumphant Yorkists were reveling in their estates. Says Comines: "I have seen the Duke of Exeter, barefooted and barelegged, begging from door to door; but becoming known, the Duke of Burgundy bestowed on him a pension."

With savage ferocity, Edward IV. did all in his power to exterminate the Lancastrian nobles, and those remaining in England could only save themselves by hiding. The son of that Lord Clifford who murdered young Edmund, Earl of Rutland, the brother of Edward IV., on the bloody field of Wakefield, was brought up as a shepherd. Another Lancastrian was hidden for five years in a cave on the banks of the river Derwent. The Countess of Oxford supported herself and her family for some time by working with her needle, and when that failed she was obliged to beg about the streets of London.

The Earl of Warwick very much desired that Edward IV. should marry into some powerful foreign family. The great earl was accordingly sent abroad to negotiate a match, and was successful in procuring for the king the hand of Bona, sister to the wife of King Louis XI. of France. In the meantime, Edward IV., while one day hunting in Witchwood Forest, happened to stop at the manor of Grafton, where he met Lady Elizabeth Gray, daughter of Sir Richard Woodville and widow of Sir John Gray, a Lancastrian knight, who was slain at St. Albans. This lady became a suitor to the king for some lands which had been confiscated for the part that her husband had taken in the civil war.

Edward IV. was so much charmed by the grace and beauty of Lady Elizabeth Gray that he in turn became a suitor to her. She received his addresses favorably, and he presently married her. The new queen claimed all the gifts and honors of the court for her kinsmen, and improved every opportunity to thwart and injure the Earl of Warwick. The king, who was deeply in love with his wife, filled the court with her kindred, showering riches and honors upon them. Her father, Sir Richard Woodville —whom her mother, the Duchess of Bedford, had married after the death of her first husband, the Duke of Bedford—was raised to the rank of nobility; as were also the queen's three brothers and her five sisters, all of whom married into the greatest families. Her eldest son, by her first husband, Sir John Gray, was married to the king's niece, the daughter of the Duke of Exeter. Edward IV. abandoned himself to pleasure, and the court was one continued scene of revelry; but under this external gayety and amusement was hidden a smothered fire of hatred and envy, as the sudden advancement of the new queen's family made them objects of jealousy to all the old nobility.

The king's marriage with an English subject led to his estrangement from the Earl of Warwick, whose indignation was aroused by the removal of his friends from office in rapid succession; and from being the best friend of Edward IV. the Earl of Warwick soon became his most powerful enemy, but concealed his resentment until the most favorable opportunity arrived for taking revenge.

The king's brothers—George, Duke of Clarence, and Richard, Duke of Gloucester —were likewise affronted at beholding themselves supplanted by the new royal favorites. The Duke of Clarence had married the daughter of the Earl of Warwick, and in 1469 the two conspired against the king. To further their designs, they proceeded to France, where they were joyfully welcomed by all the Lancastrians in that country. The exiled Queen Margaret hastened to secure the friendship of the Earl of Warwick by marrying her son to his daughter Anne. Duke Charles the Bold of Burgundy, whose wife was the English king's eldest sister, warned Edward IV. of the coming storm; but the king, heedless of his brother-in-law's admonition, continued to pass his time in idle diversions.

The Earl of Warwick returned to England, landing with a few followers on the Kentish coast, September 13, 1470. No preparations had been made to oppose him, and he was at once joined by many nobles and by a great army, so that he was master of England in eleven days. Edward IV. and his brother, Richard, Duke of Gloucester, fled on horseback and escaped from the kingdom by taking passage on a trading vessel to Friesland, embarking so hastily that they had no money to pay their passage, so that the fugitive king was obliged to reward the captain of the vessel by giving him his cloak.

Edward's queen took refuge in a sanctuary at Westminster, where her son, afterward King Edward V., was born. The Earl of Warwick, the King-maker, dragged the poor forgotten Henry VI. from the Tower and replaced him on the English throne. But the Yorkists, who had been stunned by so sudden a blow, soon recovered from their momentary consternation. Edward IV., with the aid of his brother-in-law, Duke

Charles the Bold of Burgundy, soon mustered a small fleet and army, with which he returned to England, effecting a landing in Yorkshire. He soon had possession of the two great cities of York and London, and returned the poor helpless Henry VI. to his prison in the Tower, after which he rallied all his forces to oppose the Earl of Warwick, who was marching against him.

The hostile armies met at Barnet, near London, April 13, 1471. During the night the fickle Duke of Clarence deserted with twelve thousand men from the army of his father-in-law, the Earl of Warwick, and joined his brother, King Edward IV. The battle of Barnet was fought the next day, when the great Earl of Warwick, the Kingmaker, was defeated and slain while fighting bravely for the Lancastrians, many of the nobles perishing with him on that fatal field, April 14, 1471.

Queen Margaret and her son had been detained by contrary winds, and did not land in England until the evening of the day on which the battle of Barnet was fought. Finding all her hopes blasted by the fatal result of that day, Margaret's undaunted spirit forsook her for the first time, and she sank fainting to the ground. When she revived she fled with her son to a sanctuary, with the intention of returning to France; but some of the Lancastrians gathered around her and persuaded her to stay and make one more effort to recover the kingdom for her son. In the bloody battle of Tewkesbury, in Gloucestershire, May 4, 1471, the Lancastrians were again defeated, and Margaret and her son were taken prisoners.

Margaret's son, young Prince Edward, was brought into the presence of King Edward IV., and was asked how he dared to come into his kingdom in arms. The prince boldly replied: "I came to recover my father's kingdom." Thereupon Edward IV. struck him a brutal blow on the face, which was a signal for further violence; and the young prince was dragged out of the room by the king's brothers, the Dukes of Clarence and Gloucester, who murdered him with their daggers. Edward IV. returned in triumph to London, and the next day the poor helpless Henry VI. was found dead in his bed in the Tower, supposed to have been murdered by the Duke of Gloucester.

The high-spirited Margaret, who had been the very soul of the Lancastrian cause, was detained a state prisoner for five years in the Tower, and was then ransomed by her kinsman, King Louis XI. of France, when she returned to that country, dying four years later in her native county of Anjou, broken-hearted on account of the disasters which had befallen her family.

The triumph of Edward IV. was now complete, and the Lancastrian cause was irretrievably ruined. The principal Lancastrian nobles died on the scaffold as traitors. The triumphant Edward IV. now led a life of luxury and indulgence, and the remainder of his reign was inglorious. Having established his power at home, he prepared to punish Louis XI. of France for the aid which that king had given Margaret in her last effort to recover the English kingdom for her son. Parliament granted Edward IV. a large sum for this purpose, and he obtained more money from the wealthy citizens of London, who feared to refuse his request. These loans were called *benevolences*.

In 1475 Edward IV. revived the old worn-out claim of the English kings to the crown of France, and invaded that country by way of Calais with an army of thirty thousand men. His brother-in-law, Duke Charles the Bold of Burgundy, failed to join him; and Edward IV., who had grown indolent and who preferred pleasure to war, suffered himself to be outwitted by the crafty Louis XI., who bribed the English king to consent to the disgraceful Treaty of Pequigny, by which the wily French king agreed to pay an annual pension to Edward IV. and betrothed the Dauphin Charles to the English king's eldest daughter, Elizabeth.

The failure of Edward IV. to accomplish anything in France was a sore disappointment to the English people, who had expected a renewal of the glories of Crecy,

Poitiers and Agincourt. The venal conduct of the English king and nobles excited the contempt even of the French. All the while that Louis XI. was treating Edward IV. with the most profound respect to his face, he ridiculed him and his courtiers behind his back for being so mercenary and greedy.

Although the Duke of Clarence had rendered such great service to his brother, King Edward IV., in the battle of Barnet, the king had never forgiven him for his aid to the Earl of Warwick just before that battle ; and the Duke of Clarence now had the misfortune to gain the enemity of the queen and of his youngest brother, Richard, Duke of Gloucester.

The Duke of Gloucester very much desired to marry Anne Neville, the widow of the murdered Prince Edward of Lancaster and the daughter of the great Earl of Warwick, the King-maker. The Duke of Clarence had married Anne's eldest sister, and wished Anne to remain a widow, so that he might secure to himself her inheritance, and thus come into possession of the whole of the Warwick estates. As the Duke of Gloucester was not very attractive, the Duke of Clarence very easily persuaded Anne Neville to reject the addresses of the murderer of her husband. But the Duke of Gloucester did not have any scruples about resorting to violence for the accomplishment of that which he was unable to effect by persuasion, and Anne was obliged to resort to many artifices to conceal herself. Finally he discovered her, disguised as a cook in London, and immediately married her.

The Duke of Gloucester sought in every way to excite the king's jealousy of the Duke of Clarence, and at length a trifle afforded an opportunity of gratifying his malice. One day, as Edward IV. was hunting in the park of Thomas Burdet, who was a friend of the Duke of Clarence, it happened that the king killed a white buck, a great favorite of the owner. Burdet, vexed at his loss, fell into a violent passion, during which he expressed the wish that the horns of the buck might cause the death of the person who had advised the king to kill the animal. As no one had advised the king to kill the buck, it was agreed that these words could apply to none but the king himself; and Burdet was accordingly tried, condemned and executed for wishing the king's death.

The Duke of Clarence was very free in expressing his opinion of the injustice of this act. The Duke of Gloucester reported these expressions to Edward IV., whereupon the Duke of Clarence was arrested; and Parliament, which then dared not oppose the king's wishes, condemned the arrested brother to death. As a royal and brotherly favor, Edward IV. permitted the Duke of Clarence to choose the manner of his death. The condemned duke desired to be drowned in a butt of Malmsey wine, and his wish was gratified. He had a son, who inherited his grandfather's title of Earl of Warwick, and a daughter, afterwards Countess of Salisbury; both of whom died violent deaths.

Edward IV., so sagacious and unscrupulous in matters of state, became a tyrant and established a despotism. He introduced the odious spy system into England, and made it so thorough that the lightest court gossip, as well as the most serious state intrigue, reached the king's ear. He also instituted the system of *benevolences*, which were gifts of money which he invited his wealthy subjects to make to him, and which none dared to refuse—an ingenious method of observing the letter, while violating the spirit, of the law against arbitrary taxation.

The greatest event of the reign of Edward IV. was the introduction of the new art of printing into England by William Caxton, a worthy London merchant, who had retired from trade and become a copyist in the service of the king's sister, the wife of Duke Charles the Bold of Burgundy. When Caxton heard of the invention of this art in Germany, which was rapidly multiplying the number of books, he learned to be a printer in his sixtieth year ; and three years later, A. D. 1476, he carried his press and types from Burgundy to England. The old man toiled in London until his eightieth year; and his industry and zeal is attested by the sixty-five books which he printed, of many of which he was the author and translator as well as the printer.

In the Treaty of Arras, December 23, 1482, Louis XI. of France offered a mortal insult to Edward IV. by setting aside the marriage engagement of his son, the Dauphin Charles, to the English king's daughter Elizabeth, and betrothing the Dauphin to Anne, the daughter of the Archduke Maximilian of Austria, afterwards the Emperor Maximilian I. Edward IV. prepared to avenge the French king's insult by a fresh invasion of France; but he died in the midst of his warlike preparations, April 9, 1483, at the age of forty years, and after a reign of twenty-two years, his life being shortened by his excesses.

We now come to the shortest and most pathetic reign in English history. Edward IV. left two sons and five daughters. The sons were Edward, Prince of Wales, thirteen years of age, and Richard, Duke of York, ten years old. The eldest of these was proclaimed King of England with the title of EDWARD V. The public in general acknowledged his title; but his uncle, Richard, Duke of Gloucester, had long intended to put the innocent boy king out of the way, for the purpose of usurping the English crown for himself.

The Duke of Gloucester profited by the jealousy which the nobles felt for the widow of Edward IV. and her relatives. The young king had been intrusted to the care of his maternal uncles, Lords Rivers and Gray. Richard's first step was to remove these noblemen from about the person of Edward V.; and in this he was willingly assisted by Lord Hastings, a loyal and honest man, but a bitter enemy of the queen-mother and her relatives.

Richard, Duke of Gloucester, and Lord Hastings set out to meet the boy king, who was on his way from Ludlow Castle to London to be crowned, being accompanied by his maternal uncles. The two parties met at Stony Stratford, where Lords Rivers and Gray passed the evening with the Duke of Gloucester in mirth and pleasantry, wholly unsuspicious of their impending fate. The next morning these two noblemen were seized and sent to Pontefract Castle, and all the rest of the youthful king's attendants were dismissed and forbidden to come near the court on penalty of death.

Little King Edward V. was struck with grief and terror upon finding himself alone and in the power of his wicked uncle Richard, whom he had early been taught to dread; but the Duke of Gloucester fell on his knees, and assured his royal nephew, with strong professions of loyalty and affection, that all that he had done was for his preservation. After being soothed into composure, the boy king proceeded with his uncle Richard to London, where the news of these violent acts had arrived before them and caused great alarm. The king's mother instantly fled into the sanctuary at Westminster, taking with her her younger son, Richard, Duke of York, and her five daughters. Rotherham, Archbishop of York, a faithful servant of the crown, hastened to comfort the alarmed and distressed queen-mother.

The Duke of Gloucester conducted his royal nephew into London, May 4, 1483, riding bareheaded before him, and frequently calling out to the people: "Behold your king!" A great council was held two days afterward, which appointed the artful Duke of Gloucester to the office of Protector of the kingdom. To keep up the deception, a day was appointed for the little king's coronation, and the preparations were immediately commenced for that event.

In the meantime, those to whom the Duke of Gloucester had disclosed his design to seize the English crown were actively employed. Sir Thomas Ratcliffe, one of the duke's chief confidents, entered Pontefract Castle with five thousand men, May 13, 1483, and beheaded the imprisoned Lords Rivers and Gray without any trial. The death of Lord Rivers was deeply lamented, as he was the most accomplished English nobleman of his time.

Catesby, another creature of the Duke of Gloucester, had sought to win the support of Lord Hastings to the duke's schemes; but Hastings was firm in his devotion to the boy king, whereupon it was resolved to put him out of the way. On the very day that Lords Rivers and Gray were murdered in Pontefract Castle, the Duke of Gloucester summoned the council to meet in the Tower. The duke seemed to be remarkably gay and good-natured, but left the council-chamber as if called out upon business.

He soon returned with an angry countenance and demanded the punishment of those who plotted against his life. Lord Hastings, who was president of the council, replied that they should be treated as traitors. Said the Duke of Gloucester: "These traitors are the sorceresses, my brother's wife and another of his late friends. See to what they have reduced me by their witchcraft." Thereupon the Duke laid bare his withered arm. The councilors looked at one another with amazement, well-knowing that Richard's arm had been withered from his birth. Lord Hasting's ventured to defend the late king's friend, Jane Shore, against the charge of witchcraft. Thereupon the duke exclaimed: "And do you reply to me with your *ifs* and your *ands*? You are yourself the chief traitor; and I swear by St. Paul I will not dine before your head be brought to me!" Thereupon Richard struck his hand upon the table as a signal; and armed men rushed into the chamber, seized Hastings and instantly beheaded him in the presence of the council.

The next object of the Duke of Gloucester was to get the little king's brother, the youthful Duke of York, into his power; declaring that it would be highly improper to permit the boy to remain in the sanctuary, because thieves and murderers found refuge therein. The Duke of Gloucester according sent the Archbishop of Canterbury, who had no suspicion of Richard's evil designs, to persuade the queen-mother to surrender her little son. She had begun to suspect the ambitious designs of the Duke of Gloucester, although she had not heard of the murder of Lords Rivers and Gray. She knew that her little boy would be taken from her by force if she refused to consent to let him go. She clasped him to her breast and took leave of him with a flood of tears. Little King Edward V. was delighted to see his brother, and hoped long to enjoy his company.

After getting both his little nephews in his power, the Duke of Gloucester commenced acting more openly. He employed a popular preacher to harangue the people in his favor, but he met with little success. The Duke of Buckingham next addressed them; describing the miseries of the reign of Edward IV., dwelling upon the unfitness of the boy king to govern, and enlarging upon the virtues of the Duke of Gloucester. The Duke of Buckingham expressed his apprehension that the Protector could not be induced to accept the English crown, but he hoped that the people would do all in their power to persuade him to do so. He concluded by desiring every man to speak his real sentiments and to declare without fear whether they would have little Edward V., or his virtuous uncle, for their king.

After a short silence some of the servants of the Duke of Gloucester slipped in among the multitude and exclaimed: "Long live King Richard!" A few of the mob joined in the cry, and the duke induced the Lord Mayor and the Aldermen of London to accompany him to the Protector's palace and to offer him the English crown. The Duke of Gloucester pretended to be very much surprised at seeing such a concourse of people. When he was informed that their design was to offer him the royal crown he declined accepting it, saying that his love of his brother's children was greater than his love of a crown; but he finally allowed himself to be persuaded by the Duke of Buckingham and announced his acceptance.

The Duke of Gloucester was at once proclaimed King of England with the title of RICHARD III., June 22, 1483; and the preparations which had been made for the coronation of Edward V. served for that of his uncle, who was crowned at Westminster,

July 6, 1483, and who repeated the ceremony at York in order to please the people in the North of England. Richard III. claimed that the English crown was rightfully his, on the ground that his nephews were illegitimate on account of a marriage of Edward IV. contracted before his union with Lady Elizabeth Gray. In order to strengthen his claim he did not hesitate to insult his own mother, who was still living, by declaring that he was the only one of all her sons who was legitimate. Edward V. had reigned about two months and a half (April 9-June 22, 1483).

The fate of Edward V. and his little brother, the Duke of York, was unknown for a long time with certainty; but they were never seen again. Some years afterward several persons confessed themselves to have murdered them, and said that their bodies were buried at the foot of a staircase in the Tower. The story was not credited at the time, it being believed to have been fabricated for political effect; but it was confirmed in an extraordinary manner two centuries later, when a staircase in the Tower was altered. Then a chest was found buried under that staircase, and in that chest were the bones of two children corresponding in size to the ages of Edward V. and his brother.

No sooner had Richard III. obtained the crown of England than he sought to secure the future support of those who had aided him, by conferring liberal rewards upon them. The Duke of Buckingham, who had the largest claim, received the largest share of the royal favors. But even this ample compensation failed to satisfy the avarice or ambition of this nobleman; and he was soon engaged in a conspiracy to depose Richard III. and to place on the throne Henry Tudor, Earl of Richmond, a grandson of the Welshman Owen Tudor and his wife Catharine, the widow of Henry V. Henry Tudor was thus, through his paternal grandfather, a descendant of Llewellyn and the ancient Princes of Wales; and through his paternal grandmother he was the only remaining heir of the House of Lancaster. He was then an exile in France under the protection of the Duke of Brittany, who had brought him up and secured him against every attempt of Edward IV. to get him into his power.

In order to supply the defects of Henry Tudor's title to the crown, it was agreed that he should marry the Princess Elizabeth, the eldest daughter of Edward IV., and therefore the heiress of the House of York. The vigilance of Richard III. never slept, and when he perceived the impending storm he raised an army and summoned the Duke of Buckingham to attend him. This nobleman answered the summons by taking the field against the king, at the head of a military force which he had raised in Wales and with which he advanced into England.

When the Duke of Buckingham had arrived near the river Severn an extraordinary flood, long known as *Buckingham's Flood*, prevented his crossing. His Welsh troops, influenced by superstition and suffering from hunger, deserted his standard and returned to their homes. Their deserted officers fled from the kingdom or took refuge in sanctuaries. The Duke of Buckingham sought refuge in the house of a dependent of his own named Bannister, on whose fidelity he thought he could rely; but this man was unable to resist the temptation of the large reward offered for his master's apprehension, and betrayed him to the Sheriff of Shropshire, who found the duke in the disguise of a peasant hidden in an orchard behind Bannister's house, and took him to London, where he was executed.

Richard III., whose heart appeared callous to the sufferings of others, was vulnerable in one point. His only child, Edward, died April 9, 1484; and it is said that the king's grief was so intense that he almost "run mad." The queen's grief was just as violent, and her death several months later is usually ascribed to it, though some assert that she was poisoned by her husband. Richard III. now sought to win the favor of the widowed queen of Edward IV.; and in this he was so successful that he induced her to consent to his own marriage with her

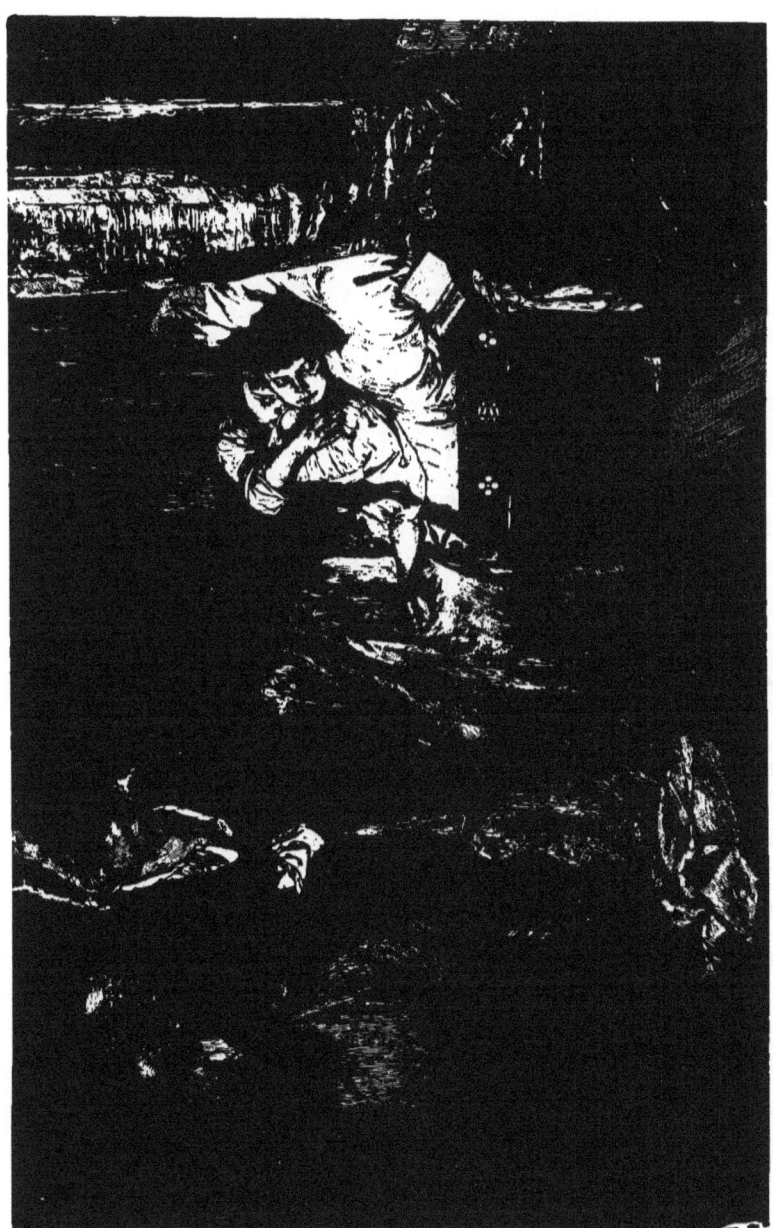

MURDER OF THE PRINCES IN THE TOWER.

daughter, the Princess Elizabeth, although he was the paternal uncle of the princess and had murdered her two brothers and her two maternal uncles.

Notwithstanding all his spies, Richard III. did not appear to have been aware that Henry Tudor, Earl of Richmond, who was supposed to be all the while in France, had actually passed much of his time in Wales, gaining adherents among his own countrymen. Once the young earl came so near being discovered by the king's spies that he only escaped by jumping out of a back window and getting through an opening, which is still called the *King's Hole*. On his return to France, Henry Tudor heard the report of the intended marriage of Richard III. with the Princess Elizabeth of York. He therefore hastily raised an army of three thousand men, consisting of English exiles and a few French troops, and with this small force he landed at Milford Haven, in Wales, August 7, 1485.

When Richard III. heard how small an army Henry Tudor had with him, and what a ragged, beggarly crowd they were, he despised so weak an enemy. But when the king discovered that the young earl's force was fast increasing in numbers, and that some Welsh troops who had been sent against Henry Tudor had actually joined him, he began to perceive the danger by which he was threatened. Richard III. might still have quelled the rising against him had he known in whom to confide.

The chief agents in the king's wicked schemes were Ratcliffe, Catesby and Lovel, which gave rise to the following verses, which an old chronicler says passed for excellent wit in those times:

"The Cat, the Rat, and Lovel the Dog,
Rule all England under the Hog."

The term *Hog* referred to Richard III., whose badge was the white boar.

Richard III. knew that these three men were not the friends on whom he could rely in the time of his own need. With good reason, he distrusted all around him; as Lord Stanley, to whom he had assigned the chief command of his army, was secretly in league with the Earl of Richmond, whose mother he had married.

Richard soon aroused himself to action, quickly raised an army and marched with great pomp against the Earl of Richmond, wearing a crown on his helmet. The two armies met on the field of Bosworth, in Leicestershire, August 22, 1485, where they were that day drawn up in line of battle, Lord Stanley drawing up the royal troops under his command a short distance away from the rest of the king's army. The Earl of Richmond, who was no soldier, sent a request to Lord Stanley to aid him in forming his troops in line; but Stanley replied to the earl that he must form them himself, and that he would come to him at a convenient moment.

Richard III. was very angry when he saw how Lord Stanley had drawn up his troops; but it was then too late to do any more than to summon Stanley's instant attendance—a summons which Stanley disobeyed. When the battle began no vigor or spirit was displayed in the king's army. When Lord Stanley suddenly turned and attacked the royal troops under the king's immediate command, Richard III. saw that all was lost. In the courage of despair, he plunged into the thickest of the fight, crying: "Treason! treason!" Hewing down all before him, the desperate king made his way to the Earl of Richmond, who shrank back at his approach. The earl's attendants gathered around Richard III., who fought like a lion at bay until he fell covered with wounds and expired. His helmet was so beaten in by the blows it had received that its form was quite destroyed. The royal crown, which had rolled under a hawthorn-bush when the king fell, was placed upon the head of the victorious Earl of Richmond, who was crowned on the battle-field by Sir William Stanley, brother of Lord Stanley, and was hailed from all parts of the field with shouts of "God save King Henry VII.!"

There was unbounded rejoicing throughout England because of the defeat and death of the royal murderer and usurper, who had committed so many crimes to obtain the English crown.

Most of the English nobles had deserted Richard III.; but the Duke of Norfolk was one of the few who had remained loyal to him. Some friend had tried to save him from his impending fate, and had that morning thrown an admonitory letter into his tent, which read thus:

"Jockey of Norfolk, be not too bold,
    For Dickon, thy master, is bought and sold."

Richard III. had reigned little more than two years (June 22, 1483–August 22, 1485); and was thirty-four years of age when he was slain. He fell near a brook which runs through Bosworth-field, the water of which long remained stained with blood; and it is said that the people in the vicinity are averse to using it even at the present day. After suffering many indignities, the body of Richard III. was finally buried in a church at Leicester; but his bones were not permitted to rest even there. At the time of the destruction of the religious houses, during the reign of Henry VIII., they were torn from their grave; and his stone coffin was converted into a watering-trough for horses at an inn at Leicester.

The battle of Bosworth—the most important in English history since that of Hastings—ended at once, not only the House of York and the Wars of the Roses, but also the renowned royal race of the Plantagenets and the Feudal System in England; and with HENRY VII., the first Tudor who occupied the English throne, began modern England. The Tudor dynasty furnished five sovereigns to England, whose aggregate reigns amounted to one hundred and eighteen years (A. D. 1485–1603.)

The great results of the Wars of the Roses were the destruction of the ancient nobility of England and the overthrow of the Feudal System, the loss of constitutional liberty, and the decline of civilization.

The Wars of the Roses were peculiarly the wars of the English nobles. All the great feudal families, gathered around the rival standards of the Houses of York and Lancaster, were hurled against each other in battle after battle with terrible loss. Confiscations, executions and exile still further diminished the numbers and power of the nobility, until at the end of these bloody civil wars the ancient baronage of England was left in a hopeless wreck. It is said that at some time during these civil wars the crown held one-fifth of all the real estate of England as its share of the spoils. Both lands and titles remained, some of them to return to their former owners or their kindred, but more went to enrich the king and to ennoble the king's favorites.

The nobility, which was thus reëstablished by royal clemency and royal bounty, was deprived of its traditional power and independence. It very little resembled the grand feudal race that, descending from William the Conqueror, was as old and as proud as the throne which he reared. It little resembled the lordly race that had stood so firmly between the throne and the people for centuries, the support of the throne against faction, and the defense of the people against tyranny.

It is impossible not to feel an admiration for the old-time baron of England, whether we think of him in time of peace, in the old ancestral castle, extending a hearty though rude hospitality, or in time of war, closing his gates and bidding defiance to all his foes. He feasted and fought with the same relish, and was no respecter of persons, as he buckled on his armor with the same readiness for a tilt with the king's forces as with those of his quarrelsome neighbor. Said Earl Warrenne, upon flinging his sword upon the table before the commissioners which Edward I. had sent to examine his title-deed: "That, sirs, is my title-deed." Said Henry III. to Earl Bigod, who had refused the king's demand for aid: "I will send reapers and reap your fields for you." The fearless earl replied: "And I will send you back the heads of your reapers."

We must honor the patriotism of these old-time barons of our mother country, as well as admire their fearlessness. They came to the front in periods of national peril time and again. The barons of England wrested the Great Charter of English freedom from the tyrant King John. History is silent as to which of the immortal twenty-four was the Thomas Jefferson who originated and framed that wonderful instrument—the origin and basis of all English and American liberty. But history is sufficiently definite as to the name of Simon de Montfort, the leader of that other immortal twenty-four who founded the House of Commons, the republican portion of the English system, in the very face of the throne itself.

The Feudal System fell with the ancient baronage. Feudalism, as a power in England, expired in a bright but lurid flame, when the great Earl of Warwick, after towering high above the throne itself for a short time, suddenly fell on the bloody field of Barnet. We can only regret that the Earl of Warwick, "the Last of the Barons," was not the best as well as the last of his race.

From Magna Charta to the Wars of the Roses there was a slow but real development of constitutional freedom, almost every reign being signalized by either a limitation of the royal prerogative or an enlargement of popular rights.

When the Wars of the Roses commenced, the following principles had been established, so far as the intelligence of the people and the arbitrary dispositions of kings permitted: The king had lost the right to levy taxes, to make or alter the laws, and imprison or punish subjects arbitrarily. Parliament had gained, in addition to the control of laws and taxes, the right to impeach and remove the ministers of the crown, the right to direct and investigate expenditures, to depose the king, and to settle questions of peace and war.

All these great principles and guaranties, won through centuries of toil and suffering, were rudely swept away during the Wars of the Roses; and the English nation did not sufficiently recover itself to reassert and reëstablish them for more than a century later. When the king lost the right to levy taxes without the consent of Parliament, during the reign of Edward I., England passed from an absolute to a limited monarchy. Edward IV. reëstablished absolute monarchy in England, which continued growing more and more absolute, until, during the reign of Henry VIII., it became a despotism as unmitigated as that of the Czar of Russia.

This will not appear so strange when we consider that the English nobility, so shattered and dependent, were without power or prestige, and were no longer able, if willing, to stand between the English people and royal oppression. The Church, which had so frequently stood side by side with the nobility in the struggle with tyranny, was infected with heresy and paralyzed through fear of another reformation. The people of England were not yet sufficiently enlightened to understand or maintain their own rights. Thus the English crown was left with little or no restraint, and the descent in the direction of absolutism was easy and rapid. Charters, statutes and human rights were trodden under the sovereign's feet with perfect impunity. In the language of Green: "The crown, which only fifty years before had been the sport of every faction, towered into solitary greatness."

Although constitutional liberty appeared to have been lost to England after the Wars of the Roses, none of the great statutes which had advanced the cause of human rights were ever abrogated. Kings and ministers recognized Magna Charta as the supreme law of the land, even while they trampled its provisions under their feet. The House of Commons was never abolished, though the Monarchy and the House of Lords once were. The popular branch of the English Parliament never ceased to exist for a moment, though hated by tyrants, and thus prorogued, dissolved, overawed and ignored.

The barbarous manner in which the Wars of the Roses were conducted was most debasing, to the people who were spectators in the horrible drama, as well as to the soldiers who were the actors. The savage order in many of the battles of these sanguinary civil wars was: "No quarter." But the cold-blooded executions which followed almost every battle were still more demoralizing. The hideous and sickening spectacle of ghastly heads and limbs of human bodies, impaled on stakes and placed on walls in public places, and constantly staring the people in the face, had a most brutalizing effect.

The Wars of the Roses had a most pernicious and debasing influence upon the young. The fierce animosities which these destructive civil wars engendered consumed the nobler qualities of individual character. During the entire gloomy period there is scarcely a chivalrous deed to be found recorded. War need not be necessarily demoralizing to either national or individual character. It may ennoble both when waged in the cause of truth and justice. In the midst of conflict and carnage a Washington or a Hampden may become great and good. But there was no principle at stake in the Wars of the Roses. It was simply a struggle for power between two rival families. The welfare of the English nation was sacrificed to the interests of the rival Houses of York and Lancaster. The patriot was sunk in the partisan. The baser passions reigned supreme, and civilization was on the decline.

Henry VII. was formally crowned at Westminster, and was married to Elizabeth of York, the daughter of Edward IV., January 18, 1486. His hatred of the House of York was so great that he was very much averse to this marriage, and he is said to have treated his wife with great coldness as a result of this feeling. The throne of Henry VII., under ordinary circumstances, would have been imperiled, from the fact that he was the heir of the House of Lancaster ; but his marriage with the heiress of the House of York, by uniting the claims of the two rival families which had for thirty years drenched England with the blood of her own people, entirely appeased all jealousies ; while the universal national joy and general satisfaction at the overthrow and death of the infamous Richard III. fully reconciled all parties of the English people to Henry Tudor's usurpation. The union of the Red and White Roses, in the marriage of Henry VII. with Elizabeth of York, was a source of great strength to all the Tudor sovereigns of England.

Henry VII. was only thirty years of age when the victory of Bosworth-field made him King of England. He was of a tall and slender physical form, a pale complexion, and of a grave, sedate deportment. He was cold, cautious and designing, and was without a single amiable quality. He did not possess any brilliant natural abilities, but he made up for want of quickness by the most diligent application, and was rewarded for his perseverance by gaining a reputation for wisdom which he lacked. He was an unkind husband, a careful though not an affectionate father, a rigorous master and a bitter enemy.

His whole conduct and policy, from the beginning to the end of his reign, were swayed by two ruling passions—his avarice, and his hatred of the House of York. The first command that he issued, even before he had left the bloody field of Bosworth, where he had been proclaimed king, was that persons should be sent into Yorkshire to seize young Edward Plantagenet, Earl of Warwick, son of the Duke of Clarence.

Henry's avarice was not without its advantages to his kingdom, though an odious vice in itself, and particularly obnoxious in a king. It led him to encourage commerce, and to lay the foundations of the English navy. The *Great Henry*, a four-masted ship which he caused to be built, was, properly speaking, the first ship in the English navy ; as hitherto, when the king wanted a fleet, his only expedient was to hire or purchase ships from foreign merchants.

The harshness of Henry VII. toward the House of York naturally irritated the members of that family against him, and thus gave rise to two Yorkist insurrections, headed by two impostors who claimed the English crown. The first of these risings was in 1487, when an Oxford priest, named Simon, instructed Lambert Simnel, an Oxford baker's son, to personate the young Earl of Warwick, the son of the Duke of Clarence. This young earl had been imprisoned in the Tower by Henry VII., and it was now pretended that he had escaped therefrom.

Lambert Simnel, the pretended Earl of Warwick, was furnished with troops by Margaret, the widow of Duke Charles the Bold of Burgundy and the sister of Edward IV., for the purpose of enforcing his pretensions to the English throne. He was joined by the Earl of Lincoln and Lord Lovel. When Henry VII. heard of this false Earl of Warwick he caused the real earl to be taken from the Tower and carried in procession through London, permitting all to converse with him who so desired. This proceeding satisfied the people of England; but it did not convince those of Ireland, who were warmly attached to the House of York, and especially to the Duke of Clarence, who had been Lord Lieutenant of Ireland. When Lambert Simnel landed in Dublin as Edward Plantagenet, Earl of Warwick, all Ireland greeted him with loyal acclamations as "King Edward VI."

With the few nobles who joined him, and some troops which he had raised in Ireland, Lambert Simnel invaded England, landing in Lancashire, where he expected to be joined by the inhabitants; while the dowager Duchess of Burgundy, who had been so easily convinced or so willingly deceived by the imposture, sent over a German army to invade England in concert with the impostor's Irish forces. Simnel was disappointed in his expectations of an English rising in his favor, and he had advanced as far as Stoke-upon-Trent without receiving any reinforcements from the inhabitants. He was utterly defeated and his cause irretrievably crushed by the royal army under King Henry VII. in the battle of Stoke-upon-Trent, August 16, 1487. Simnel was taken prisoner in this battle, and was punished with less severity than he could have expected under the circumstances, as the king contented himself with degrading the impostor by making him a scullion in the royal kitchen. Simnel was subsequently promoted to the office of falconer to the king.

Most of Simnel's followers lost their lives in the battle of Stoke-upon-Trent, among them the Earl of Lincoln; while Lord Lovel fled, and was no more seen afterward.

The notorious avarice of Henry VII. was so far a benefit to England that it restrained the king from engaging in expensive foreign wars. In 1487 he availed himself of a quarrel with France about the duchy of Brittany to fill his own coffers. Under the pretense of aiding the young Duchess Anne of Brittany, he obtained liberal supplies of money from Parliament, and extorted a forced loan called a *benevolence* from the rich merchants. In 1492 he invaded France and besieged Boulogne for a few days, after which he suffered himself to be bought off by King Charles VIII. of France for the sum of one hundred and forty-nine thousand pounds sterling, and returned to England. Thus, like a shrewd merchant, Henry VII. made a double profit out of friends and foes by filling his coffers at the expense of both the English and French nations.

The dowager Duchess of Burgundy, seeing how easily many people in England had been deceived by the fraud of Lambert Simnel, resolved upon a new project, contrived with more art and plausibility. She first caused a rumor to be circulated that the young Duke of York, the brother of Edward V., was alive and had escaped from the Tower after his imprisonment there by Richard III. She then found a youth, named Perkin Warbeck, son of a Jewish merchant of Tournay, in Flanders. This youth, with his courtly manners and speech, with his intellectual gifts and accomplishments, made him more presentable as a prince than poor Lambert Simnel, the Oxford baker's boy, had been. Perkin Warbeck bore a strong resemblance to the Plantagenets; and his winning manners and demeanor, his princely and dignified bearing, fascinated all who conversed with him and persuaded them that he was a prince.

Perkin Warbeck first presented himself at the court of France, and was well received by King Charles VIII. He was dismissed at the demand of Henry VII., but with courtesy; after which he sought the protection of his "aunt," as he called the Duchess of Burgundy. She received him as if he had been a complete stranger to her, and pretended to disbelieve his story; after which, as if suddenly convinced by his answers to her questions, she embraced him with a transport of joy, declaring that he was actually her long-lost nephew, and giving him the title of the "White Rose of England."

Henry VII. was now anxious to convince the world that the real Duke of York had been murdered in the Tower by the secret orders of Richard III., and he obtained the confession of two persons who acknowledged that they had been concerned in putting him to death. But these confessions received little credit at the time, though they were corroborated two centuries later, as we have before remarked.

Henry VII. also sought to ascertain the true story of Perkin Warbeck; but the secret was kept so well, and his origin was so obscure, that this was no easy matter. Finally the king won over one of the impostor's confidents, and from this individual Henry VII. obtained a knowledge of almost the entire history of the conspiracy, with the names of all those in England who favored it. The story was published for the information of the English nation; and those concerned in it were all seized in one day, and were immediately tried, condemned and executed. Sir William Stanley, who had saved the life of Henry VII. in the battle of Bosworth, and who had also crowned the king on that famous field, was beheaded for having been heard to say that if he were sure that Perkin Warbeck was the real Duke of York he would never bear arms against him. As Sir William Stanley was one of the richest gentlemen in England, it was believed that the king had put him to death for the purpose of confiscating his vast wealth to the crown.

After two unsuccessful efforts to effect a landing in England, Perkin Warbeck proceeded to Scotland, in 1496, where he was kindly welcomed by King James IV., who espoused the impostor's cause with the utmost warmth. The Scottish king also gave to Warbeck in marriage the Lady Catharine Gordon, one of the noblest and most accomplished ladies of the time. James IV. did not content himself with simple promises; but in October, 1496, he invaded England with a Scottish army for the purpose of placing Perkin Warbeck on the English throne, inviting all the people of England to rally to the standard of their rightful sovereign, "King Richard IV." The Scots immediately commenced plundering, in accordance with their usual custom; and Warbeck expostulated with King James IV. on this barbarous manner of conducting the war, declaring that he would rather lose a crown than to obtain it by the ruin of his subjects.

It was expected that upon Perkin Warbeck's first appearance in England all the partisans of the House of York would rise in his favor, but in this he was disappointed. None came to his assistance, and he was obliged to retreat toward Edinburgh. King Henry VII. was always a better diplomat than soldier, and preferred concluding a treaty with King James IV. to meeting him on the battle-field, and a truce was made between the two sovereigns.

In consequence of the treaty between the Kings of England and Scotland, Perkin Warbeck went to Ireland with about one hundred and twenty followers, and with his devoted wife, who would not forsake her husband. The next year, A. D. 1497, the impostor returned to England, landing in Cornwall, where the poor miners had in the meantime been driven to rebellion by oppressive taxation. The pretended Duke of York was soon at the head of seven thousand Cornishmen, and besieged Exeter; but on the approach of the royal forces, Warbeck, seeing that all resistance would be in vain, deserted his companions and fled for refuge by night to the sanctuary of Beaulieu, in the New Forest. This unkingly cowardice satisfied the English people that the pretended Duke of York was no Plantagenet.

The king's troops soon surrounded the sanctuary, and Henry VII. would have gladly forced open its gates and seized his victim, but was persuaded to attempt to entice the impostor out by a promise of sparing his life. On receiving this pledge, Warbeck surrendered himself to the king, and was conveyed a prisoner to the Tower. He escaped from that prison, but was soon recaptured and brought back; after which he was exposed upon a scaffold, and forced to read aloud a written paper in which he confessed himself to be an impostor.

Perkin Warbeck afterwards found means to have some communication with his fellow-prisoner, Edward Plantagenet, Earl of Warwick; and the two contrived a plan for their escape, the discovery of which was followed by the execution of both. Perkin Warbeck was hanged at Tyburn, the place of execution for common malefactors, November 23, 1499; while the Earl of Warwick, from the respect due to his undoubted rank, was beheaded on Tower Hill a few days later.

After Perkin Warbeck had been taken a prisoner to the Tower, his young and beautiful wife was sent for by King Henry VII., who, notwithstanding the hardness of his heart, appears to have been touched by her youth, her beauty, her grief, and her devotion to her husband. The king said some kind and soothing words to her, and presented her to his queen, with whom she remained as an attendant. She had an adequate allowance conferred on her, and was much beloved at the English court, where she was called the "White Rose of England."

The king's revengeful act in executing the Earl of Warwick destroyed whatever love the English people may have felt for their king. The young earl was not executed because he was guilty of any offense deserving death, but because he was the last male Plantagenet, and, as such, was a source of possible danger to the throne of Henry VII.

The attempts of the impostors, Lambert Simnel and Perkin Warbeck, caused Parliament to pass the *Statute of Allegiance*, providing that none should be punished for allegiance to the reigning king, whether he be king *de jure* (by right), or king *de facto* (in fact). This statute was intended to guard against such wholesale executions, in case of a change of dynasty, as followed the fortunes of the Red and White Roses, when men were pronounced traitors one day for adhering to the House of York, and beheaded the next day for supporting the House of Lancaster.

As we have already remarked, the reign of Henry VII. was the beginning of the modern era. The fall of the ancient baronage of England was a great benefit to the nation, as their iron hand had rested heavily upon the English people; though the immediate effect was to increase the power of the king, thus giving the Tudors greater power than the Plantagenets had possessed. Nevertheless, the diffusion of intelligence through printed books, the revival of learning and the new enthusiasm awakened in the study of Greek and Roman literature, the numerous cheap editions of the printed Bible, and the mental excitement caused by the stirring events in general which ushered in the modern era, led to great progress in art, science, literature and the refinements of home-life.

During this period the Greek and Hebrew languages began to be studied in the great universities of England and throughout Europe. Mediæval superstitions were passing away; and men were beginning to think for themselves, in philosophy and science, also in politics and religion. Here began modern civilization, based not on the essential slavery of the Feudal System, as was the mediæval, but on the growing intelligence and increasing importance of the masses.

It was during this time that the great Portuguese navigators discovered the sea-passage to India around Southern Africa; that Columbus, in the service of Spain, made his voyages of discovery, which opened the New World to the eyes of Europe. England had her share in these maritime enterprises, as it was under the auspices of Henry VII. that John and Sebastian Cabot made their several voyages which revealed the existence of the North American continent to European eyes; and the brave and hardy English, inclined to the sea, both from their Saxon and Norman blood and from their island home, were soon to be found in the remotest quarters of the globe.

Henry VII. had always been avaricious and miserly, but in the latter part of his reign his exactions caused him to be cordially hated by his subjects, from whom he extorted money by many unlawful devices. His chief instruments in these extortions were two lawyers, Richard Empson and Edmund Dudley, who searched out obsolete statutes to enable the king to impose unjust fines and penalties for the most trifling offenses; and forgotten tenures and petty violations of law were so many traps to bring multitudes of men into the courts of justice, and the fines exacted from these filled the royal treasury with a constant stream of wealth.

The royal miser also increased his wealth by means of taxes and benevolences. A benevolence originally meant a voluntary contribution for the king's expenses, made among his immediate vassals. Edward IV. extended it to the entire kingdom; and, though the name implies a free gift, a benevolence became a very arbitrary tax, as the king could quarter soldiers on those who refused to contribute, and could annoy them in many other ways, for which reason the people called these benevolences *malevolences*.

Edward IV. had exacted benevolences from the rich only, but Henry VII. extorted them from the poor as well. By a crafty device, called from its author, *Morton's Fork*, the king extorted money from those who made a display in their style of living, as display was evidence of wealth; and from those who made no display he exacted gifts, on the ground that they must have become rich by their economy.

Henry VII. neglected no opportunity to seize the estates of those attainted, and acquired a large income by the rigid execution of the *Statute of Liveries*. In feudal times castles of the barons resembled armed camps. Crowds of idle vassals, supported by the bounty of their lords, were always ready, at their bidding, to storm a castle or menace a throne. The Statute of Liveries, which had been enacted in a previous reign, was intended to break up these great military establishments. This statute had fallen into disuse, but was revived and executed by Henry VII. with fine and forfeiture.

A new court, called the *Star Chamber*, was appointed to have special reference to cases coming under the Statute of Liveries. This court, which received its name from the star decorations of the room in which the sessions were held, was solely under the king's control, and became an instrument of great oppression in subsequent reigns.

By sharp practice and rigid economy, Henry VII. amassed a fortune equal to ten million pounds sterling. Though avaricious and miserly by nature, there was policy in his desire for wealth. The one grand purpose which he had in view was the establishment of the throne of the Tudors on a solid and secure basis. He knew very well that the great power of the Commons lay in their control of the public funds, and that the possession of adequate means on the king's part was the royal road to independence. He therefore exerted himself to obtain money without having recourse to Parliament, and in this he succeeded so well that there was but one session of Parliament during the last thirteen years of his reign.

Henry VII. also endeavored to strengthen the Tudor dynasty by marriage alliances with other reigning families of Europe. In 1501 his eldest son, Arthur, Prince of Wales, was married to Catharine of Aragon, daugh-

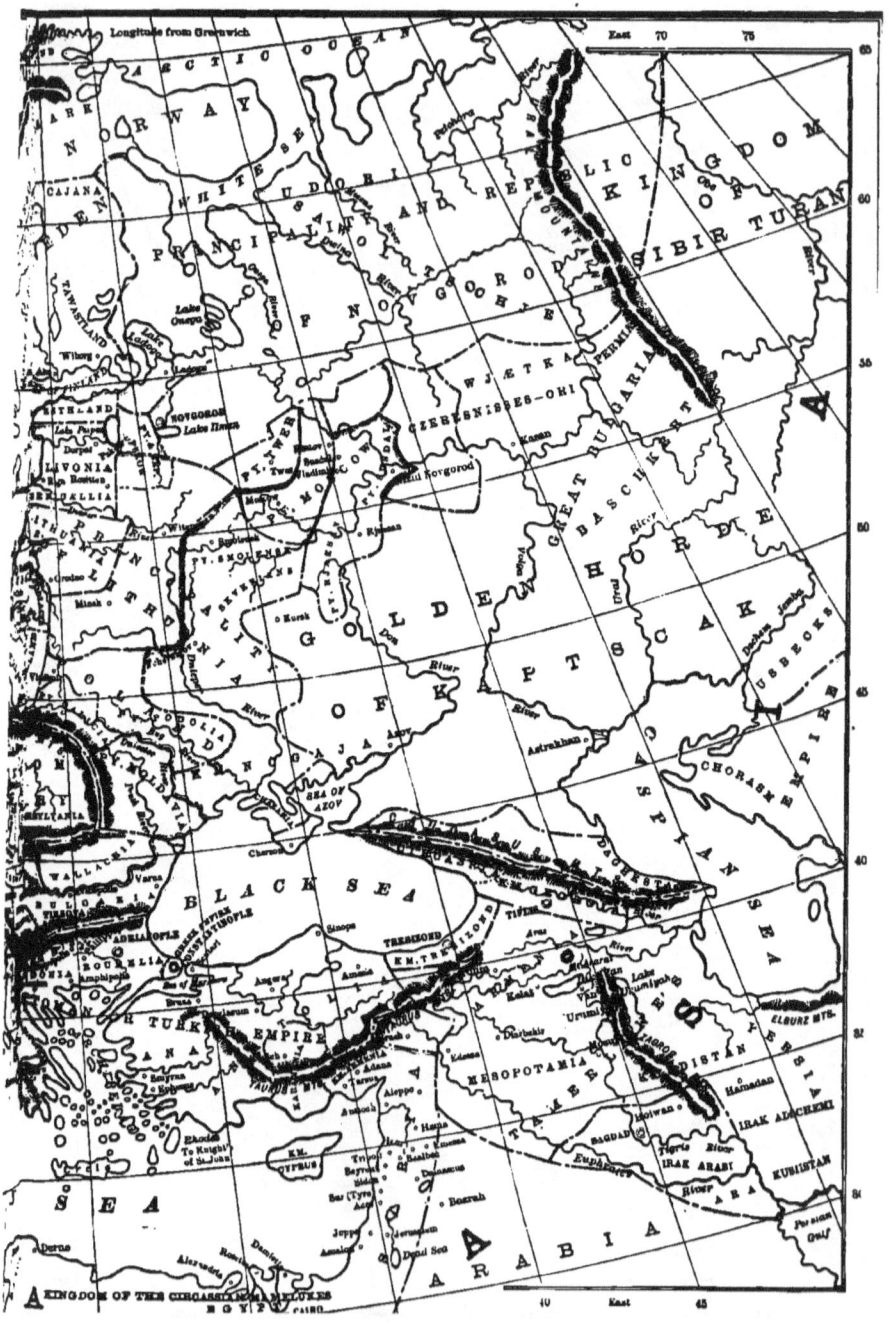

ter of Ferdinand and Isabella, the reigning sovereigns of Spain, then the most powerful kingdom in Europe. The young prince died five months after his marriage; and Henry VII., unwilling to part with the rich dowry of the Spanish princess, obtained a dispensation from Pope Alexander VI. permitting his next son Henry, who then became the heir to the English crown, to marry the young widow. Prince Henry, who was then only twelve years of age, and therefore much younger than his bride, was very much opposed to the match; but his father forced him into it. In 1503 the Princess Margaret, the eldest daughter of Henry VII., was married to King James IV. of Scotland—a marriage from which the Stuarts derived their title to the crown of England.

In 1506 the Princess Catharine had a forced visit from her eldest sister, the wife of the Archduke Philip of Austria. The archduke's vessel was driven by a storm into an English harbor; and Henry VII. refused to allow his guests to depart until he had wrested from them a new treaty of commerce with the Netherlands, and some other concessions equally as advantageous to himself.

The only feeling which was strong enough to overcome the avarice of Henry VII. was his ambition to have a splendid tomb. With this view he erected what is known as the Chapel of Henry VII., at Westminster Abbey. He called upon the best architects of the time to furnish designs for this magnificent structure, on which the king did not grudge the expenditure of large sums of his hoarded wealth. This chapel is still one of the most beautiful edifices in England.

A violent attack of the gout warned Henry VII. that his end was approaching, and he devoted his remaining days to preparations for the next world. Even his dying acts were tinctured by that calculating, money-loving spirit which had been the ruling passion of his life. He ordered two thousand prayers to be said for the repose of his soul, and for these prayers sixpence a piece was to be paid.

Several of his bequests, however, showed that he still had some conscience. He ordered that restitution should be made to those persons from whom Empson and Dudley had extorted more than the law would warrant. He also ordered the payment of the debts of all persons who were imprisoned in London for sums less than forty shillings. He died at his new palace of Richmond, April 21, 1509, in the fifty-fourth year of his age and the twenty-fourth of his reign, and was buried in the magnificent chapel which he had built for his tomb at Westminster Abbey.

SECTION IV.—ITALIAN STATES.

AFTER the Partition Treaty of Verdun, in 843, Italy remained under the weak Carlovingian dynasty a half century. In 962 A. D. the Emperor Otho the Great of Germany annexed Italy to the Holy Roman Empire of Germany. For three centuries Italy was distracted by the civil wars between the Guelfs and the Ghibellines—the former the adherents of the Popes, and the latter the supporters of the Emperors of Germany. During the whole period of the Middle Ages, Italy was the seat of European civilization, wealth, culture and refinement. The most important states of mediæval Italy were the papal state of Rome; the duchy of Milan; the duchy of Savoy; the kingdom of Naples and Sicily; and the famous republics of Venice, Genoa, Pisa and Florence—noted for their extensive commerce and maritime power, and for their political freedom and high state of civilization, thus recalling the glories of the ancient Grecian republics.

REPUBLIC OF VENICE.

During the Middle Ages, a number of small republics arose in Italy, the most prominent of which were Venice, Genoa, Pisa and Florence. The most famous of these Italian republics was Venice, which was founded in the year 452 A. D., by the Veneti, a people of Northern Italy, who fled in terror from their homes during the frightful ravages in Italy by Attila and his Hunnic followers. The fugitive Veneti took refuge among the small islands at the head of the Adriatic sea, and there founded a settlement called Venezia, or Venice.

Venice—which dated its existence from the time of Attila the Hun's invasion of Italy—excelled other Italian republics in the extent of its commerce and its naval power; and was for centuries the mistress of the Mediterranean, and controlled Europe's commerce with the East. The magnificent works of Venice—such as the cathedral of St. Mark, the palace of the Doge, the place of St. Mark, and the bridge of the Rialto—made this city of islands, with bridges and canals instead of streets, the admiration and wonder of the world.

For more than two centuries, Venice was a simple republic; but in the year 697 A. D., its form of government was changed by the election of a Doge, or Duke, who was vested with almost absolute power. In the beginning of the ninth century, the central island, Rialto, was connected with the other islands by bridges; and this city became a great commercial power.

ST. MARK'S, VENICE.

In the ninth century, the Venetians adopted St. Mark as their patron saint, having brought, as it is said, his body from Alexandria, in Egypt, to Venice (A. D. 829). During the seventh, eighth and ninth centuries, Venice greatly increased in wealth, commerce and naval power; and its territories were enlarged by the annexation of Dalmatia and other provinces. Later Venice acquired possession of many rich towns in Lombardy, and also of Crete, Cyprus, the Peloponnesus, and the little islands

MARRIAGE OF THE DOGE OF VENICE WITH THE SEA.

of the Archipelago (the ancient Ægean sea.)

In the First Crusade, the Venetians aided Godfrey of Bouillon with a fleet of two hundred vessels; and during the period of those Holy Wars, Venice was the great commercial center and emporium of the trade between the nations of Europe and those of the East.

In the twelfth century, the ceremony of "wedding the Adriatic" was instituted, the Pope presenting the Doge of Venice with a ring for the purpose. The ceremony was annually performed with great pomp, and consisted in casting a ring into the

MARCO POLO.

Adriatic by the Doge, to indicate that the sea was subject to Venice as a bride is to her husband. While casting the ring into the sea, the Doge exclaimed : "We betroth thee, O Sea, in sign of our lawful and perpetual dominion!"

In the latter part of the thirteenth century, Marco Polo, the great Venetian traveler, visited China and the far East, bringing home a knowledge of the countries of Eastern Asia.

Venice—at first a perfect democracy, celebrated for its political freedom—at length became torn by internal dissensions; and the introduction of luxury and wealth brought their attendant evils—political corruption and the loss of civic virtue. In the fourteenth century the government became an aristocracy under the *Doges* (Dukes) and the *Council of Ten*, which, with its secret spies and its dungeons, was enabled to exercise a most unmitigated tyranny, and to suppress every effort to restore the democratic constitution.

At the commencement of the fifteenth century, Venice attained the highest pitch of greatness and prosperity, and was for more than a century the chief commercial and maritime power of the world. Venice did very important service to all Christian Europe by checking the naval power of the Ottoman Turks in the Mediterranean sea; but her long maritime wars finally exhausted her resources.

The discovery of a sea-passage to India by way of the Cape of Good Hope in 1497 sealed the fate of Venice, and her commercial and maritime glory, in a great measure, departed from her; but for several centuries longer Venice continued formidable, and her fleets contended successfully against the Ottoman Turks, who endeavored to secure the control of the Mediterranean sea.

When, at the beginning of the sixteenth century, Venice attempted to extend her territorial possessions in Italy, the powerful *League of Cambray* was formed against her by Pope Julius II., King Ferdinand the Catholic of Spain, King Louis XII. of France, and the Emperor Maximilian I. of Germany (A. D. 1508). The Venetians soon succeeded in winning the Pope and the King of Spain to their interest, and so contrived to dissolve the league; and the French, who had threatened the independence of Venice, were soon expelled from Italy.

REPUBLIC OF GENOA.

The republic of Genoa—also a flourishing commercial and maritime power—was the great rival of Venice for the control of the Eastern commerce; but in the many wars between the two republics, Genoa had to yield the supremacy to her great rival. The

contests between the democracy and aristocracy and political corruption led to the decline of Genoa, and the republic was con-
quered by the French early in the sixteenth century, but its independence was reëstablished in 1528 by the great Genoese admiral,
Andrea Doria, "the Father of his Country and the Restorer of its Liberties." In 1547, Fiesco attempted to deprive the family of
Doria of the office of Doge, but the conspiracy failed by the unexpected death of Fiesco. Pisa—a flourishing city of Tuscany, cele-

PALAZZO DARIO, VENICE.

CATHEDRAL AND LEANING TOWER OF PISA.

brated for its leaning tower—was also a prosperous commercial republic, but was conquered by Genoa, and finally by Florence in 1406.

REPUBLIC OF FLORENCE.

Florence—the most flourishing republic of Middle Italy and the seat of mediæval Italian literature—rivalled ancient Athens in the freedom of her political institutions, and in her patronage of literature and the fine arts. The great poets, Dante and Petrarch, and the great novelist, Boccaccio, flourished at Florence. The commercial spirit of her citizens made Florence a wealthy and powerful republic. The Florentines wove in silk and wool, made jewelry, and were the leading bankers of Europe. The gold *florin*—first coined in 1252—became the standard currency of Europe.

The inland republic of Florence has left a deeper impress upon the Italian character and upon the art and literature of the world than Venice or Genoa. The Florentine government was far more democratic than that of Venice, and rested upon the industries of the citizens. Chief magistrates could be chosen from members of the *Arts*, or trades' unions, which resembled the Guilds of England and the Netherlands. These officers were chosen every two months, and the Council of State every four months; so that the whole mass of citizens were qualified for office, and were elevated in turn to public trust. No magistrate received any reward for his services. During the Guelfic supremacy Florence conquered the ports of Pisa and Leghorn and half of Tuscany; while the wealth of her bankers, merchants and woolen manufacturers established her commercial fame in Europe.

Florence—at first a model democracy—in the fifteenth century passed under the absolute rule of the illustrious family of the Medici; and under Cosmo de Medici (1428-1464) and his renowned grandson, Lorenzo the Magnificent (1472-1492), Florence enjoyed a high degree of prosperity, as the seat of European civilization, culture and refinement.

Cosmo de Medici, who had been a prosperous merchant, who ruled Florence so wisely and well for thirty-six years, simply exercised the power of a citizen among equals; and his power appeared to rest on the esteem and affection of his countrymen, though it was supported by the control which a rich money-lender exercised over needy borrowers. Cosmo de Medici was a man of lofty mind and patriotic spirit, and without assuming either rank or title he governed Florence with almost unlimited power, and rendered the republic flourishing and powerful by successful wars abroad and by encouragement of the arts and sciences at home, so that he was justly called "Father of his Country."

Lorenzo the Magnificent, trod the same path as his renowned grandfather, and made his name illustrious by rendering Florence the seat of every art and science and a university for all Europe. His court was ornamented with artists, poets and writers; and learned men from Constantinople, fleeing from the sword of the conquering Turks, taught the Greek language and literature in Florence. Under his rule the arts of sculpture, painting and music commenced unfolding their choicest blossoms.

The power of Cosmo de Medici and Lorenzo the Magnificent resembled that of Pisistratus in Athens. They so well succeeded in winning the affection of their fellow citizens by their benevolence and their kindness to the poor, and by their friendly affability toward the illustrious, that their power was securely established. The public entertainments which they gave rendered life in Florence a perpetual scene of gay and brilliant festivity. Their policy exalted the intellectual fame of Florence at the expense of her freedom, and their influence among the Italian states was frequently exerted on the side of despotism, as in the case of Milan. Still Florence largely owes her title of "Mother of Modern Art" to their liberal and enlightened tastes.

After Lorenzo's death, the earnest discourses of the Dominican monk and reformer, Savonarola, induced the Florentines to drive out the Medici and to restore the democratic republic; but the "bold prophet of Florence" was excommunicated by Pope Alexander VI., and, at the instigation of the clergy, was tried, convicted, and burned to death as a disturber of the Church and a corrupter of the people. The Medici returned and recovered their power, and after being again banished were restored by the forcible intervention of Pope Clement VII.

DUCHY OF MILAN.

As we have seen, after many bloody wars with Frederick Barbarossa, Milan and the Lombard League won their independence of the German Emperor by the battle of Lignano in 1176, and the Peace of Constance in 1183. The Duchy of Milan, under the renowned families of Visconti and Sforza, afterward became powerful in Northern Italy.

DEATH OF SAVONAROLA.

and the Emperor Charles V., who besieged and took Florence, and placed Alexander de Medici as Duke over the conquered republic. Alexander's tyranny caused his assassination, but Florence remained under the Medici until 1737. Among the great men who ornamented the court of the Medici were the artist, Michael Angelo, and the historian and statesman, Macchiavelli.

Milan, which was ruled by the family of Visconti, in the process of time acquired nearly the whole of Lombardy. The ruler of Milan and its territory received the title of Duke from the Emperor of Germany. On the death of the last Milanese duke of the family of Visconti, in 1450, the government of the duchy was bestowed on Francisco Sforza.

ITALIAN STATES.

In 1500, the Duchy of Milan was subdued by Louis XII., King of France, and the Milanese duke, Louis Moro, was kept a prisoner for ten years; but the French were finally driven away and Moro was restored to his dukedom. In 1515 King Francis I. of France conquered Milan by defeating the Swiss and Milanese in the battle of Marignano, "the Battle of the Giants"; but in 1525 Francis I. was defeated and taken prisoner by the Spaniards, who governed Milan thereafter for two centuries, until 1714, after which the House of Austria held possession of the duchy until 1866.

DUCHY OF SAVOY.

The western part of Northern Italy fell gradually under the control of the powerful Counts of Savoy, who eventually erected their territory into the *Duchy of Savoy*, which lost many of its territories in subsequent wars with Burgundy, Milan and France; and Geneva was lost in the sixteenth century; but the Dukes of Savoy eventually conquered Sardinia and Genoa, and in 1720 the Duchy of Savoy became the Kingdom of Sardinia; and the Savoyard dynasty now occupies the throne of the Kingdom of Italy, formed in 1861.

PAPAL ROME.

From the time that Pepin the Little bestowed Rome and its adjacent territory on Pope Adrian I., Rome was governed by the Popes, with several interruptions, until 1870. During the seventy-two years' residence of the Popes at Avignon, in France (1305-1377), Rome was a prey to the violence of domestic factions, and suffered greatly from the lawlessness of the nobles. Out of these intestine disorders and quarrels of the families of Orsini and Colonna arose the fiery orator, Cola di Rienzi, the "Last of the Tribunes," who was imbued with the spirit of the ancient Roman republicans, and who sought to restore Rome to its former glory and preëminence. Having gained the support of the Roman people by his fiery addresses, Rienzi was made a Tribune of the People; and he seized the supreme power in Rome in 1347, expelled the lawless nobles and established a new *Roman Republic;* but he soon lost his popularity by his impolicy in loading the Roman people with the most oppressive taxes, and, after a brief existence of seven months, his government was overthrown and he was driven into exile. Rienzi afterwards returned to Rome, and was assassinated during a tumult in the city, in 1354.

After the return of the Popes to Rome, a few Popes—such as Nicholas V., the founder of the Vatican library, and Pius II. (Æneas Silvius), a clever and versatile writer—endeavored to reform Church and State, and patronized literature and science; but Alexander VI., who bought his election, was the worst Pope that ever occupied the Chair of St. Peter, frequently poisoning his political rivals and wealthy cardinals to secure their estates, and his death was caused by accidentally drinking poisoned wine intended for another. Alexander's successor, Julius II. (1503-1513), was a warlike Pope, and enlarged his dominions by conquering Bologna, Ancona, Ferrara and other towns. Leo X. (1513-1521)—the accomplished son of Lorenzo de Medici of Florence—was a great patron of men of genius; and the great artist, Raphael, "the Divine Painter," flourished at his court. One of his great objects was the completion of St. Peter's Church at Rome. The Popes now ranked more as Italian princes than as Heads of the Christian Church.

KINGDOM OF NAPLES AND SICILY.

The foundations of the kingdom of Naples and Sicily were laid by the Norman chief, Robert Guiscard, who, in 1060, conquered Southern Italy, and whose nephew, Roger II., became the first King of Naples and Sicily. After the extinction of the Norman dynasty upon the death of William II., the grandson of Roger II., in 1186, the Kingdom of Naples and Sicily fell to the German House of Hohenstaufen by the marriage of the Emperor Henry VI. with the Norman heiress; but during the contests between the Guelfs and Ghibellines, the Hohenstaufens were overthrown, Manfred being defeated and killed in the battle of Benevento in 1266, by his rival, Charles of Anjou, the brother of St. Louis, King of France; Pope Urban IV. having bestowed Naples and Sicily, as papal fiefs, upon the House of Anjou; and Manfred's brother and successor, Conradine, being defeated, taken prisoner and beheaded. The House of Anjou then ruled Naples and Sicily, but the tyranny of Charles of Anjou led to the massacre of eight thousand French in Sicily on Easter day, 1282—the *Sicilian Vespers*—by which the House of Anjou lost Sicily, which fell to the Kings of Aragon.

CHARLES I. of Anjou, at his death in 1285, was succeeded by his son CHARLES II. Charles II. died in 1309 and was succeeded by his son ROBERT THE WISE, who died in 1343 and was succeeded by his granddaughter JOANNA I., who was then only sixteen years old and already married to her cousin, Andrew of Hungary. The boorish manners of Andrew and his Hungarian attendants shocked Joanna's elegant court, while his assumed claim to the crown of Naples in his own right alarmed her counselors. Andrew was murdered in 1345 by his wife's adherents. His brother, King Louis the Great of Hungary, avenged his death by invading Naples, while Joanna I. fled for refuge to the States of the Church.

In revenge for the aid which Joanna I. had given to the election of Clement VII. as Antipope, Pope Urban VI. bestowed the Kingdom of Naples upon Charles of Durazzo, nephew of King Louis the Great of Hungary, and crowned him at Rome in 1381. Charles had a hereditary claim to Naples, as the old Angevin line was to expire with Joanna I.; but the childless queen, exasperated at the disposal of her kingdom before her death, adopted Louis of Anjou, uncle of King Charles VI. of France, as her heir.

Pope Clement VII. at Avignon hastened to crown Louis of Anjou as King of Naples, and to assign him a new "Kingdom of Adria" from the States of the Church. But Charles of Durazzo was first in the field, and took Joanna I. prisoner and caused her to be murdered—a long cherished revenge on the part of King Louis the Great of Hungary for the murder of his brother Andrew. In order to enforce his pretensions to Naples, the Duke of Anjou seized the treasures of the French kingdom immediately upon his brother's death; but his great preparations ended only in failure and humiliation. Most of his army fell victims to the plague, and he himself died near Bari in 1384. French claims upon Naples caused more than a century of war without effecting any permanent conquest.

JOANNA II., daughter of Charles of Durazzo, called to her assistance Alfonso V. of Aragon and Sicily, who received the title of Duke of Calabria as heir-expectant of the Italian crown. But Joanna II. changed her mind and adopted Louis III. of Anjou as her heir. Louis III. died in 1434, and Joanna II. in 1435. Count Réné of Anjou, brother of Louis III., had been named in Joanna's will, but he was captured and detained in France by a rival claimant to the duchy of Lorraine; and the Neapolitan nobles again called in Alfonso V. of Aragon.

The forces of Genoa and Milan fought for Réné of Anjou, and gained a most bloody victory over the Aragonian fleet in the Mediterranean, taking Alfonso V., his brother and many of their attendant nobles, prisoners; but the King of Aragon finally triumphed, and the amiable and accomplished Réné of Anjou turned his attention to the more congenial pursuits of poetry and painting. Two of Réné's children strongly contrasted with their father in energy of character—Margaret, the wife of Henry VI. of England, who so long and valiantly maintained the Lancastrian cause against the House of York; and John, Duke of Calabria, who displayed the same genius and resolution in the pursuit of his lost inheritance.

Thus the Kingdom of Naples also came under the dominion of the Kings of Aragon, but a strong party in the kingdom adhered to the French claimant of the Neapolitan throne, thus distracting the kingdom until the end of the fifteenth century. In 1493

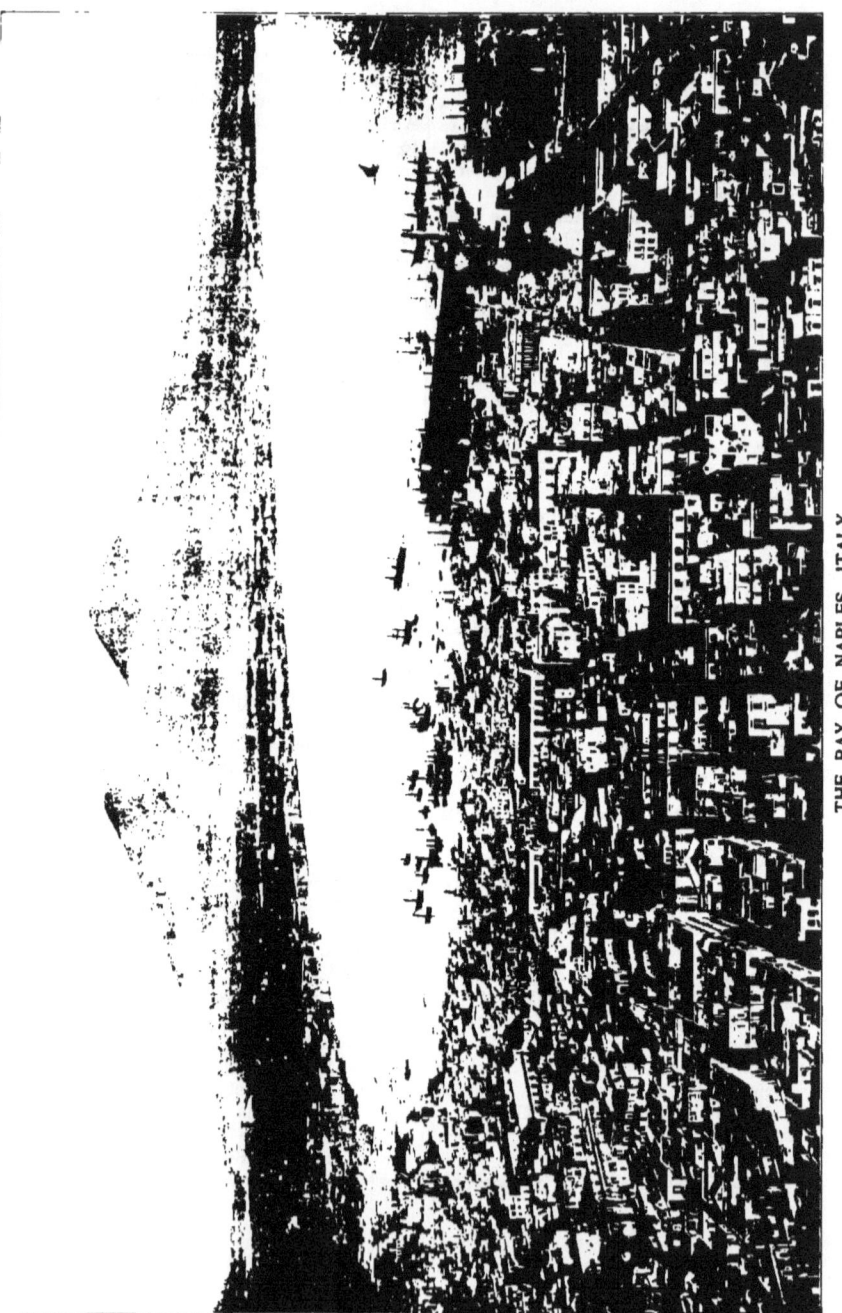
THE BAY OF NAPLES, ITALY.

King Charles VIII. of France conquered and lost Naples, and only effected his safe retreat to France by his victory at Fornovo in 1494. In 1500 his successor, King Louis XII. of France, conquered Naples, but was driven away in 1504 by the Spaniards, who retained possession of Naples for more than two centuries.

SECTION V.—SPAIN AND PORTUGAL.

FOR a period of eight centuries, the Saracens and Moors, after establishing themselves in the Spanish peninsula, were engaged in constant wars with the Christian Spaniards, who, in the course of time, erected the powerful Christian kingdoms of Asturias and Leon, Aragon, Castile, Navarre, and Portugal. The wars with the Moors produced a spirit of romantic chivalry and love of freedom among the Christian Spaniards.

ASTURIAS AND LEON, NAVARRE, CASTILE, ARAGON AND GRANADA.

As we have seen, the *Kingdom of Asturias* was founded by the Christian Spaniards under the Gothic prince PELAYO, who fled into the mountains in the North of Spain at the time of the Saracen conquest of Spain in 711. This Christian kingdom flourished in spite of all the Saracen efforts to conquer it. It was at first confined to the district of Ovieda. Constant war was waged against the Saracens and Moors, and in the course of time the Christians were enabled to extend their territories southward. ALFONSO I., THE CATHOLIC—the third prince of Asturias, and Pelayo's son-in-law—ascended the throne in 739, conquered and annexed Galicia and parts of Leon and Castile, and assumed the title of King of Asturias. ALFONSO III., who became King of Asturias in 866, conquered all of Leon, and removed his capital to the city of Leon; and during his reign, in A. D. 873, *Navarre* became independent of Asturias, and eventually grew into a powerful kingdom.

Castile, which had been subject to Leon, recovered its independence about A. D. 982, and was erected into a kingdom early in the next century. In 1037 FERDINAND I., THE GREAT, of Castile, united the Kingdom of Leon with Castile, which was thenceforth the strongest power in Spain. Ferdinand the Great died in 1065, assigning Castile to his eldest son, SANCHO II., and Asturias and Leon to his other son, ALFONSO VI., THE VALIANT. There was almost constant war between these two brothers; and on the death of Sancho II., in 1071, Alfonso the Valiant obtained the crown of Castile, thus reuniting the two kingdoms; but at his death, in 1109, his dominions were divided among his children. Alfonso the Valiant recovered Toledo, the old capital of Spain, from the Moors, whom he came near driving from Spain. He destroyed the old Moorish kingdom of Toledo, made that city his capital, and named the territory which he had thus acquired *New Castile*. In 1095 Alfonso the Valiant erected *Portugal* into a separate earldom, and in 1139 that country renounced its allegiance to Leon and Castile and became an independent kingdom.

Aragon, hitherto a part of the Kingdom of Navarre, became an independent kingdom under RAMIRO I., in 1035, and rapidly grew in strength and importance during the next century. In 1118 ALFONSO I., THE WARRIOR, took Saragossa, the principal city in the North-east of Spain, from the Moors.

In the meantime all the Christian kingdoms in the North of Spain had been pressing the Moors farther southward. The growing weakness of the Khalifate of Cordova enabled the Christians to drive back the Moors with comparative ease; and the condition of affairs that followed the fall of the Khalifate gave the Christians an opportunity to vastly increase their territories—an opportunity of which they readily availed themselves.

During this period flourished the chivalrous Cid, Rodrigo Diaz, the great hero of Spanish history, whose career belongs to the realms of romance rather than to actual history. This legendary warrior is represented as having struck terror into the hearts of the Moors by his numerous victories; and it is said that having been killed in an engagement, in 1099, he was set on his steed at the head of his troops, and that when the Moors beheld him thus leading his warlike hosts, they were seized with superstitious awe and fled in consternation, so that the Cid won a victory even in death.

Gradually the Christians pushed the Moors southward and made themselves masters of Spain. Towards the middle of the twelfth century the Spanish peninsula contained the Moorish kingdoms of Cordova and Granada and the Christian kingdoms of Aragon, Navarre, Castile, Leon, and Portugal. The Christian kingdoms were generally divided against each other; but the Moors, though divided among themselves, were firmly united against the Christians, and maintained their hold upon Andalusia with the aid of recruits from their brethren in Africa.

Near the end of the eleventh century the Moorish sect of the Almoravides, who had established their dynasty in Morocco, invaded Spain, conquered the Moorish kingdom of Seville, and speedily reduced the other Moorish territories in Spain under their dominion. Near the latter part of the twelfth century the dynasty of the Almoravides was overthrown in Africa by the Almohades, who reduced Moorish Spain to subjection. The dissensions among the Christian kingdoms in the Spanish peninsula enabled the dynasty of the Almohades to recover some of the territory that the Moors had lost.

The death of Yacub Ben Yussef, the greatest of the Almohade Khalifs, in 1198, relieved the Christians of Spain of a formidable enemy. The Christian kingdoms laid aside their quarrels, and their united armies broke the power of the Moors by a great victory in the battle of the Navas de Tolosa, in the Sierra Morena, in 1212; after which the Moorish power in Spain steadily declined; but the final overthrow of the Moslems was delayed by the rise of the Moorish kingdom of Granada and by wars among the Christian kingdoms.

The Moorish kingdom of *Granada* was founded in 1238 by Mohammed Ben Alhamar, a great and warlike sovereign, who collected in his new realm most of his Moorish countrymen who had been steadily driven southward by the advancing arms of the Christian kingdoms. The Kingdom of Granada remained prosperous and powerful for two and a half centuries, and was inhabited by a numerous population. This Moorish kingdom became celebrated for its culture and refinement, of which the beautiful castle of the *Alhambra* is a permanent monument. Art and science flourished, and the kingdom was adorned with many noble and useful public works.

Every Moorish town was divided into wards, with an inspector over each, patrols guarding the streets at night, and the gates of the cities being closed at a certain hour of the evening. Courts of justice were held every day by an impartial sovereign. Charity was practiced, the poor being well provided for, and the sick well cared for. Every Moor was a soldier. A regular standing army was kept on pay, and each soldier had a lot of land on the frontier large enough to maintain himself, his family and his horse. These little farms served as a barrier against the Christian enemy, more effectual than walls, as each soldier fought to protect his own family and hearthstone.

Thus secured externally, Granada soon became as renowned as Cordova had been for agriculture, commerce, arts, manufactures, especially silk, and for wealth and industry. Prizes were awarded to stimulate all the mechanical arts, and especially to the best weavers of silk and growers of wool. Warehouses, hospitals, almshouses, markets with fixed prices, schools, colleges

THE CID.

and good inns were seen on every hand. Besides the famous Alhambra, the Moorish capital, Granada, was also beautified with baths, fountains, delightful public walks, gardens, and every convenience, all paid for from the king's gold and silver mines.

The wars between the Moors and the Christians had the greatest influence upon the history and character of the Spanish nation. These struggles produced a love of war and a chivalrous turn of mind, and caused the Christian Spaniards to take de-

CORDOVA.

light in contests and arms, in tournaments and knightly exercises, and in romantic poetry and minstrelsy. These wars also preserved the zeal for religion, and were the foundation of that predominance of the clergy which has always been characteristic of Spain. Lastly, these wars aroused a feeling of liberty and self-reliance among the Christian Spaniards, and led to the establishment of the *Cortes*, or national legislative assembly, which possessed the law-making power in both Aragon and Castile, and which was composed of the Estates in both kingdoms—the nobles, the clergy, and deputies of the towns. The royal power in Aragon was more limited than in Castile; and the Cortes of Aragon possessed not only the power of legislation and of consenting to the levying of taxes, but the king was obliged to consult it in the choice of his council. The *Justitia*, an independent chief justice, decided quarrels between the king and the Cortes.

FERDINAND III., THE SAINT, who became King of Castile in 1217, and who died in 1252, permanently united the crowns of Castile and Leon in 1230, and extended his dominions southward at the expense of the Moors, recovering a large part of Spain from them, including the cities of Seville and Cordova. The famous ALFONSO X., THE WISE, the son and successor of Ferdinand the Saint, reigned from 1252 to 1284. He occupied himself with astronomy and astrology, with music and poetry, enlarged the University of Salamanca, encouraged the development of the Spanish language, and had works prepared on history and jurisprudence; but he lacked in the practical wisdom of life. He was elected King of Germany by one faction in that country, but never visited his new dominions. To gain the shadow of the imperial crown he loaded his Castilian subjects with oppressive taxes, and plunged the kingdom into confusion by his extravagance and by debasing the coinage.

ALFONSO XI., who reigned over the united Kingdom of Castile and Leon from 1324 to 1350, defeated the Moors on the river Salado, and took from them the strongly fortified town of Algeciras, in Andalusia. To defray the expenses of the war with the Moors, the Castilian Cortes introduced the tax, called *alcavala*, which was levied upon all movable and immovable property; every time it was sold or exchanged, and which was extremely detrimental to commerce. This impost has remained in Spain to the present day.

PEDRO THE CRUEL, the son and successor of Alfonso XI., reigned from 1350 to 1369. His cruelties made him odious to his subjects; while his murder of his wife, Blanche of Bourbon, drew the hostility of the French upon him. At length his half-brother, Henry of Trastamara, took up arms against him, but was driven from the kingdom. Henry fled to the French court, and solicited the aid of King Charles the Wise of France. The French king sent his great general, Du Guesclin, with an army to aid Henry of Trastamara; and Pedro the Cruel was driven from his kingdom, whereupon Henry became King of Castile and Leon. Pedro the Cruel fled to Bordeaux and obtained the aid of Edward the Black Prince, the famous English warrior, who led an army into Castile, defeated Henry of Trastamara and the French under Du Guesclin at Navarette, in April, 1367, and restored Pedro the Cruel to the throne of Castile. Pedro had promised to pay the expenses of the war, but when he recovered his throne he broke his promise, and left the Black Prince to bear the burden alone, thus alienating his ally. The next year the King of France sent Du Guesclin into Spain a second time; and Pedro the Cruel was again driven from the Castilian throne, and was soon afterward slain by HENRY of Trastamara, who was formally acknowledged King of Castile and Leon.

During the long minority and reign of JOHN II. (1406-1454) the Kingdom of Castile and Leon was ruled by the Constable Alvaro de Luna, the most powerful noble of the kingdom, as regent. His administration was so oppressive that the nobles, headed by King John II. himself, rose against him and caused him to be executed at Valladolid. HENRY IV., the son and successor of John II., died in 1474; and, as he left no male heirs, his sister ISABELLA became Queen of Castile and Leon. Isabella's marriage with Ferdinand the Catholic of Aragon in 1471 united the two kingdoms.

While the united Kingdom of Castile and Leon, the largest and most powerful of the Spanish kingdoms, was extending its power and dominion, Aragon in the East and Portugal in the West of the Spanish peninsula were steadily pushing their conquests. Castile and Portugal were the Spanish kingdoms chiefly engaged in the task of redeeming the Spanish peninsula from the Moors, who, in their kingdom of Granada, protected on their northern frontier by a chain of high mountains, maintained themselves for two and a half centuries against the attacks of the Christians, whose superiors they were in civilization, culture and refinement.

Aragon was the only one of the Spanish kingdoms that concerned itself with European affairs at that period. By the annexation of Catalonia, in 1137, Aragon had become the third naval power in Europe, being excelled only by Venice and Genoa. The Catalans were a hardy and adventurous race, and were the best of sailors, their bravery contributing largely to the extension of the Aragonian dominions.

GIRALDA OF SEVILLE.

JAMES I., THE CONQUEROR, who reigned over Aragon from 1213 to 1276, was the greatest of Aragonian kings. His son and successor, PEDRO III., who reigned nine years (A. D. 1276-1285), married the daughter of Manfred, the Hohenstaufen King of Sicily, thus giving rise to the connection between Aragon and the Kingdoms of Naples and Sicily.

ALFONSO V., THE WISE, who became King of Aragon and Sicily in 1416, and who died in 1458, also became King of Naples in 1435, and resided chiefly in his Italian kingdom; while his brother, JOHN II. of Aragon, governed his Spanish dominions as viceroy, and at his death in 1458 became King of Aragon, Naples and Sicily. John II. acquired the Kingdom of Navarre by marrying its queen, Blanche, but this increase of dominion occasioned many crimes.

Charles, the son by this marriage, was the rightful heir to the crown of Navarre upon the death of his mother; but his father, jealous of his popularity, refused him the crown. Charles took refuge with his uncle Alfonso the Wise in Naples, and after Alfonso's death in 1458 he went into studious retirement in Sicily, but was recalled to Spain by false promises that he would be allowed to ascend the Navarrese throne without opposition. He died soon after his return to Spain, believed to have been poisoned by his step-mother, Joanna, the second wife of King John II. of Aragon.

The rightful heir to the Navarrese crown was Charles's sister Blanche; but the Kingdom of Navarre had been promised by treaty to the Count of Foix, who had married Eleanor, the next younger sister of Charles. Blanche was betrayed into the power of her sister, who caused her to be poisoned in 1464. The brave and freedom-loving Catalans, believing that the queen-mother Joanna, the second wife of John II., was the real author of the crimes just mentioned, refused to take the oath of allegiance to their son Ferdinand; and a civil war of eleven years ensued. The Catalans were finally reduced to submission; and upon the death of John II., in 1479, his son FERDINAND V., THE CATHOLIC, became undisputed King of Aragon. As before remarked, Ferdinand the Catholic had married Queen Isabella of Castile and Leon in 1471, thus uniting the crowns of the two most powerful Spanish kingdoms.

KINGDOM OF PORTUGAL.

Portugal, the ancient Lusitania, had been recovered from the Moors by King Alfonso the Valiant of Castile and Leon near the end of the eleventh century. In 1095 that monarch granted the territory between the Minho and the Douro to his son-in-law, Henry of Burgundy, who assumed the title of Count of Portugal, from *Portus Cale*, the ancient name of the town of Oporto. Count Henry established his capital at Guimaraens, and extended his territories southward by several vigorous campaigns against the Moors.

Count Henry died in 1112, and was succeeded by his son Alfonso Henry, who also achieved great victories over the Moors. He defeated them in the great battle of Ourique, near the Tagus, in 1139; after which he assumed the title of ALFONSO I., King of Portugal. Thus was founded the Kingdom of Portugal, which was liberated from Castilian supremacy. The title of Alfonso I. as King of Portugal was acknowledged by Alfonso VII., Raymond, of Castile and Leon. Alfonso I. continued his wars against the Moors, and took Lisbon by storm, October 25, 1147. He extended his dominion over at least one-half of the modern Kingdom of Portugal, and laid the foundations of his country's greatness. In 1143 he convened a Cortes, or assembly of the Portuguese Estates, at Lamego, which framed the first code of laws for Portugal.

On the death of Alfonso I., in 1185, his son, SANCHO I., became King of Portugal. Sancho I. continued his father's wars against the Moors. He removed his capital to Coimbra, and raised Portugal to a high degree of prosperity and power. Sancho II. died in 1211, and was succeeded by his son ALFONSO II., who suffered many reverses in a war with Castile and Leon.

Alfonso II. died in 1223, and was succeeded by his son SANCHO II., who won several important successes over the Moors, and conquered a large part of Algarve, the extreme southern province of Portugal; after which he became involved in a quarrel with the Church. He was never very scrupulous in his dealings with the clergy, and now he seized their revenues and their property without the least compunction, at the same time appointing his favorites to the vacancies in the Church. He was deposed by the Council of Lyons in 1245, and retired to Castile, where he died in 1248.

Sancho II. was succeeded by his son, ALFONSO III., who extended Portugal to its present limits by the annexation of Algarve, the most southern province, which he had conquered from the Moors. He drew upon himself the censure of the Church by marrying a second wife while his first wife was still living. Pope Alexander IV. pronounced the second marriage invalid, but on the death of the first wife he issued a bull declaring the second marriage legitimate, also the issue resulting from this marriage.

Upon the death of Alfonso III., in 1279, his son DINIS became King of Portugal. Like his predecessors, Dinis soon became involved in a quarrel with the Church, but contrived to effect a reconciliation with the Pope on terms advantageous to himself. Dinis was one of the greatest of the Kings of Portugal. He founded more than forty cities, and was a liberal friend of learning, industry and commerce. During his reign Portugal commenced that career of navigation and commercial enterprise which afterward rendered her illustrious and wealthy. He united a truly royal liberality and a truly comprehensive capacity of mind with great zeal in the administration of justice. His subjects called him the "Father of his Country."

Dinis died in 1325, and was succeeded by his son, ALFONSO IV., THE BRAVE. The only important event of his reign was the war which he waged with Alfonso XI. of Castile to avenge the wrongs of his daughter, who was the Castilian king's wife.

Pedro, the son and heir of the King of Portugal, had held guilty relations with Iñes de Castro, a lady of his court. Fearing that Pedro would attempt to marry Iñes after his first wife's death, King Alfonso the Brave caused Iñes to hold a child of Pedro over the baptismal font; thus forcing her to contract what was believed to be too close a spiritual affinity to Pedro to permit him to marry her. Pedro paid no attention to this, and after his first wife's death he privately married Iñes, January 1, 1354; she having already borne him four children. When questioned by his father, Pedro denied the marriage, but firmly refused to desert Iñes or to marry again.

King Alfonso the Brave feared that Pedro's infatuation for Iñes would cause him to set aside his son by his first wife, the legitimate heir, in favor of one of his children with Iñes. He consulted his courtiers, who were already jealous of the favor shown by Pedro to the Castros, and was advised to put Iñes to death. The king consented to this with reluctance. Pedro was warned of the plot by his mother and by the Archbishop of Braga, but he disregarded their warnings, because he was unable to believe that his father would even for a moment contemplate such a crime. Several months afterward, while Pedro was absent on a hunting excursion, Alfonso the Brave proceeded to the convent of St. Clair at Coimbra, where Iñes was residing, to put her to death; but he was so moved by the tears, the youth and the beauty of Iñes, and by the sight of her little ones, his own grandchildren, that he left without doing her any harm.

After the king's departure his attendants reproached him for what they called his weakness, and procured an order from him to carry out the plan themselves. They at once returned to the convent, and murdered the unfortunate Iñes with their daggers. Soon after the departure of the assassins Pedro returned from his hunting expedition. He manifested the wildest grief and rage when he found his wife barbarously murdered. Being unable to take revenge on the persons of the assassins, as his father protected them, he took up arms and ravaged with fire and sword the provinces where their principal estates lay. The king was greatly alarmed by his son's outbreak and sought to pacify Pedro, agreeing to banish the murderers of Iñes from Portugal as the price of peace, though he refused to deliver them up to Pedro. Pedro then agreed to a reconciliation, waiting until he should have become king to take full revenge on the murderers of Iñes.

Alfonso the Brave died in 1357, two years after the murder of Iñes, and his death is said to have been hastened by remorse for his part in that tragic deed. His son, PEDRO I., THE SEVERE, then became King of Portugal. He at once demanded of his namesake, Pedro the Cruel, King of Castile, that he should surrender the murderers of Iñes, who had taken refuge in Castile, offering to surrender certain Castilian nobles who had found an asylum in Portugal, and whom Pedro the Cruel was anxious to get into his power. The Portuguese king's offer was accepted by the King of Castile. One of the murderers of Iñes escaped, but the other two were arrested and delivered to the King of Portugal, who on his part seized the Castilian refugees and surrendered them to their king. After thus getting the assassins into his power, Pedro the Severe put them to death with horrible torments, which he helped to inflict with his own hand.

Pedro the Severe now caused his marriage with Iñes to be made public, and the Portuguese Cortes solemnly declared that Iñes was entitled to the honors usually paid to the wives of the Kings of Portugal. He next caused the body of his murdered wife to be disinterred and arrayed in royal robes, with crown and scepter, and seated on a magnificent throne in the Church of St. Clair, at Coimbra. He then took his stand beside the corpse, and compelled his nobles and clergy to do homage to the dead body, sternly eying each one as he approached, to see that he did not fail to fulfill a subject's duty to his queen. Pedro the Severe then buried the remains of Iñes with solemn pomp in the monastery of Alcobaça.

The reign of Pedro the Severe lasted ten years. He executed the laws sternly and mercilessly, and his principal wrath was aimed at those who were guilty of the excesses that had disgraced his own youth.

Pedro the Severe died in 1367, and was succeeded by FERDINAND I., his son by his first wife. Ferdinand I. was cruel and licentious. He compelled one of his nobles to divorce his wife, so that he might marry her himself; and he was under this unprincipled woman's influence during his entire reign. This marriage greatly offended his subjects. Ferdinand I. did some worthy things, though his reign was infamous on the whole. He suppressed the bandits who caused much trouble in some of the Portuguese provinces. He prohibited the clergy from succeeding to landed property by testamentary bequest. He improved the government of the cities. He brought the Portuguese navy to a higher degree of efficiency, and rebuilt the walls of Coimbra and Lisbon. His only child, a daughter, was the wife of the King of Castile.

The death of Ferdinand I., in 1383, was followed by an interregnum of two years, during which Portugal was distracted by the violence of the contending parties, the result of which was that John, the illegitimate son of Pedro the Severe by a lady of Galicia, who had made himself regent, seized the Portuguese throne and was proclaimed king, April 6, 1385, and is known as JOHN I., THE BASTARD.

John the Bastard was an able, crafty and unscrupulous king. He defeated the efforts of the King of Castile to conquer Portugal, the crown of which was claimed by that monarch in right of his wife, a daughter of Ferdinand I. John the Bastard administered justice faithfully, and did much for the suppression of brigandage. He married Philippa, the daughter of the English Duke of Lancaster, John of Gaunt, by whom he had five sons and several daughters. For the purpose of affording these sons an opportunity of distinguishing themselves he undertook a war against the Moors on the African side of the Strait of Gibraltar, his forces taking the fortified city of Ceuta in 1415. The Moors made repeated and desperate efforts to recover the city, but the Portuguese garrison held it against all their attacks. This fortress remained in the possession of Portugal until the seizure of the kingdom by King Philip II. of Spain in 1580, when it became a possession of that kingdom, which still retains it.

It was in the reign of John the Bastard that the Portuguese commenced their wonderful career of maritime discovery under the patronage of his fourth son, Prince Henry.

John the Bastard died in 1433, and was succeeded by his son DUARTE, or EDWARD, who reigned five years, and undertook an unsuccessful war against the Moors of North-western Africa. His army was defeated; and his brother, Dom Fernando, or Ferdinand, was taken prisoner and treated with great cruelty by the Moors, so that he died from the severities imposed upon him during a captivity of several years.

Duarte died of the plague in 1438, whereupon his son ALFONSO V. became King of Portugal. As the new king was a minor, his mother, Queen Leonora, claimed the regency; but she was driven from Portugal by the boy king's uncle, Dom Pedro, Duke of Coimbra, and forced to retire into exile in Castile. Dom Pedro governed Portugal wisely during the eight years of his regency, and the grateful people of Lisbon would have erected a statue to him had he not forbidden them to do so.

In 1446 Alfonso V., being fourteen years

CASTLE BELEM, PORTUGAL.

old, was declared of age. He retained Dom Pedro at the head of the state for some time, and married his daughter Isabel. The king's favorites finally succeeded in influencing their sovereign against Dom Pedro, and Alfonso V. came to regard his uncle and father-in-law as his most dangerous enemy. When Dom Pedro perceived this change in his royal nephew and son-in-law's mind he requested permission to resign his place in the government and to retire to Coimbra. The king granted this request, but Dom

Pedro was soon horrified by being accused by his enemies of having poisoned the king's father and mother.

Alfonso V. accepted the accusation against Dom Pedro as true, ordered him to remain on his estates, and forbade his subjects to have any communication with him. Dom Pedro was subjected to other insults and persecutions, and was finally obliged to take up arms in self-defense, as it was evident that his choice lay between death on the battle-field or on the scaffold; but he was defeated and slain in battle with the royal army.

Alfonso V. brutally refused to honor Dom Pedro's body with burial, and it was privately interred by some peasants. Five years afterward Alfonso V. was brought to his senses by the indignant remonstrances of the Pope and the European sovereigns, and he acknowledged Dom Pedro's innocence and interred his remains with great pomp in the burial-place of the Portuguese kings.

In revenge for the cruel fate of the unfortunate Dom Fernando, Alfonso V. renewed the war against the Moors of North-western Africa, and invaded their country in 1471. He took Tangier, and that post was held by the Portuguese until 1662, when it was ceded to England as a part of the dowry of Catharine of Braganza, the Portuguese bride of King Charles II. of England. Alfonso V. was next involved in a war with Castile, in the hope of obtaining the Castilian crown by marrying Joanna, the reputed daughter of King Henry IV. of Castile; but he was forced to make peace in 1479 and to relinquish his pretensions to the Castilian crown.

Alfonso V. died in 1481, and was succeeded by his son, JOHN II., THE PERFECT, the greatest of the Portuguese kings, and whose reign was the most brilliant in Portuguese

PUERTO DEL SOL.

history. John the Perfect was a sovereign of broad and liberal views. He was vigorous in the execution of his designs, though he was politic and cautious. He loved justice, and sincerely desired to promote the prosperity and happiness of his subjects.

Upon his accession to the Portuguese throne John the Perfect found the royal revenues so much exhausted by his father's extravagance that the kingdom was almost bankrupt. He immediately introduced reforms which replenished the royal treasury without oppressing his subjects. He next inaugurated a series of measures by which he broke the power of the feudal nobility and rendered them wholly dependent upon the crown.

He deprived the Portuguese nobles of the power of life and death over their vassals, and restricted that power to himself and to the royal courts—a great gain for the Portuguese people. He compelled all who had obtained grants of land or dignities from his predecessors to produce their title-deeds and other legal documents. In cases in which there was a defective title the claimant was deprived of it, and in cases in which there was extravagant concession it was very much modified. He also deprived his nobles of the right to nominate the local magistrates, who had hitherto been chosen from the nobility, and vested the nomination in the crown, making all classes eligible to these offices, the only qualifications required being learning and merit.

These reforms, so essential to the welfare of the masses of the Portuguese people and of the whole kingdom, greatly offended the Portuguese nobles, who formed several conspiracies against their king. The Duke of Braganza headed the first of these plots, but it was detected and the duke was beheaded. Some of the principal nobles organized another conspiracy, having for its object the elevation of the Duke of Viseo, the king's cousin, to the Portuguese throne; but the mistress of the Bishop of Evora, one of the chief conspirators, betrayed the plot to the king, who slew the Duke of Viseo with his own hand, and caused the other conspirators to be beheaded and imprisoned.

John the Perfect prosecuted the war against the Moors of North-western Africa with vigor, and his generals achieved many brilliant victories over them. He introduced industry and comfort among his subjects, and vastly increased the wealth and resources of his kingdom. In his reign the maritime enterprises of the Portuguese were vigorously pushed forward; and these undertakings, which the king encouraged, contributed largely to the prosperity and greatness of Portugal. The African coasts were explored, and in 1486 Bartholomew Diaz discovered the Cape of Good Hope.

The last years of the reign of John the Perfect were rendered melancholy by the death of his only son in 1491. The king survived this affliction only a few years, dying in 1495, sincerely mourned by all classes of his subjects.

MANUEL THE GREAT, the brother of the Duke of Viseo, then became King of Portugal. He was also a great sovereign, and maintained the prosperity of his kingdom at home and its renown abroad. He vigorously continued his illustrious predecessor's policy of establishing Portuguese influence in Africa, and in 1497 Vasco da Gama doubled the Cape of Good Hope and discovered the sea-passage to India, thus opening the way for the establishment of Portuguese influence in Southern Asia; while Cabral discovered Brazil in 1500.

Manuel the Great died in 1521, and was succeeded by JOHN III., THE GREAT, during whose reign Brazil was colonized by the Portuguese and Portuguese influence extended in India. John the Great introduced the horrible tribunal of the Inquisition into Portugal against the protests and entreaties of his subjects, but his reign was a good one on the whole.

John the Great died in 1557, and was succeeded by his grandson SEBASTIAN, then only three years old. The regency was first exercised by his grandmother, the widow of John the Great, but after her resignation by the king's uncle, Henry. King Sebastian assumed the government himself in 1568, when he was fourteen years of age. Against the desires of his subjects and the advice of his counselors, Sebastian engaged in an ill-advised war against the Empire of Morocco, oppressing his subjects with heavy taxation for its support. In 1578 he invaded Morocco with fifteen thousand men, but was defeated and slain by the Moors in the battle of Alcazarquivir, August 4, 1578.

HENRY, Sebastian's uncle, then became King of Portugal, but died in 1580 without heirs; whereupon a number of pretenders appeared for the Portuguese crown, the most powerful of whom was Philip II. of Spain, whose mother was the daughter of Manuel the Great, and whose first wife was Maria, the eldest daughter of John the Great. Philip II. triumphed over his rivals, and for the next sixty years Portugal constituted a part of the Kingdom of Spain (A. D. 1580-1640).

RISE OF THE MODERN KINGDOM OF SPAIN.

The modern Kingdom of Spain was formed by the marriage of FERDINAND THE CATHOLIC of Aragon with ISABELLA of Castile in 1471. This was the beginning of the real greatness of Spain, and the new kingdom at once came into prominence as the leading power of Europe. The reign of Ferdinand and Isabella was signalized by the restoration of order and justice throughout Spain, in place of the lawless violence of the Spanish nobles. According to the good old custom of Aragon and Castile, the new king and queen presided in person once a week in courts of law, in which the poor, who could not afford to employ counsel, might plead their own cause.

The joint reign of Ferdinand and Isabella is tarnished by the establishment of the infamous court of the Inquisition, which was established in Spain in 1480, as a royal tribunal for the punishment of heresy and kindred offenses. The Dominican Inquisition had been merely an ecclesiastical court, and both Jews and heretics had been treated with more clemency in Spain than in any other European country. Many of the Jews had been elevated to the highest offices in the state, being even intrusted with the education of royal princes; and their wealth as bankers rendered them indispensable to many a necessitious Aragonian or Castilian king. The just and merciful Queen Isabella for a long time resisted her husband's arbitrary policy and her confessor's bigotry, but she finally yielded, and obtained a bull from Pope Sixtus IV. for the establishment of the horrible tribunal in her own kingdom of Castile. In 1481 two thousand persons were burned to death in Spain, and seventeen thousand others were subjected to fine, imprisonment, or other lighter penalties.

Ferdinand and Isabella were engaged in a nobler enterprise in their wars with the Moorish Kingdom of Granada. The Moors still far surpassed their Christian neighbors in the arts and sciences, and the greatest European scholars had studied at Cordova, while Arab physicians were still in demand at many European courts. Architecture was developed in the Moorish cities earlier than in Christian Europe, and travelers at this day are struck with wonder at the airy grace of the ruined arches of the Alhambra at Granada.

The fall of the Moorish Kingdom of Granada was hastened by domestic dissensions among the Moors themselves. Abu Abdallah, or Boabdil, rebelled against his aged father, MULEY ALI, King of Granada, thus involving the Moorish kingdom in a disastrous civil war; but, after making peace with the Spaniards, ABU ABDALLAH was in turn opposed by his uncle, ABDALLAH THE VALIANT. The King and Queen of Spain took advantage of this civil war among the Moors, and the Spanish armies steadily advanced into the Kingdom of Granada, thus weakened by domestic dissensions. In 1487 the Spaniards took Malaga after a three months' siege; and in January, 1492, they also took Granada, the capital of the Moorish kingdom, after a siege of little more than ten years, thus putting an end to the Moorish power in

SURRENDER OF GRANADA.

ITALIAN SCHOLARS—GERMAN WOMEN (CITY BURGESSES).

KNIGHT—DUKE—KNIGHT TEMPLAR.

MOORISH KINGS (14TH CENTURY).

THE CID CAMPEADOR ON HIS HORSE "BABIECA."

MOORISH KINGS—14TH CENTURY.

Spain, which had lasted almost eight centuries. Many of the conquered Moors passed over to Africa and joined their countrymen in Morocco; and all Spain, except the little Kingdom of Navarre in the North, was united under the dominion of Ferdinand and Isabella.

The union of all Spain under Christian rule by the conquest of Granada was hailed with joy throughout Christendom, and was regarded as an offset to the overthrow of the Eastern Roman Empire and the establishment of the Ottoman Turkish Empire in the South-east of Europe.

Ferdinand and Isabella tarnished their triumph by an act of persecution. In spite of the dreadful warnings of the Inquisition, the great body of the Jews in Spain still firmly adhered to their national religion. The clergy now induced the covetous Ferdinand and the pious Isabella to issue an order banishing the nine hundred thousand Jews in Spain from the kingdom, although they and their ancestors had lived in Spain for centuries. The Jews heroically refused to barter their religion for the privilege of remaining. The heart-rending incidents of this sudden and compulsory emigration were numerous. Thousands perished from shipwreck, from starvation, and from diseases produced by the fatigues and exposures of the voyage. A Jewish mother was observed killing her little child rather than endure the sight of its misery. This expulsion of the most enterprising of Spanish subjects inflicted a mortal blow upon the wealth and prosperity of the Spanish nation.

Some of the more hardy and enterprising of the exiled Jews found new homes in other lands, where they soon acquired wealth by their industry or achieved fame by their learning. Sultan Bajazet II. of Turkey spoke thus derisively of Ferdinand: "You call this a wise sovereign, who impoverishes his own kingdom to enrich mine!"

The example of the King and Queen of Spain was followed by their son-in-law, the King of Portugal, who, in addition to his edict banishing the Jews from his kingdom, issued a still more barbarous decree that all Hebrew children under fourteen years of age should be wrested from their parents and dispersed throughout his kingdom.

In the very year that the arms of Ferdinand and Isabella were crowned with the conquest of Granada, A. D. 1492, the great Genoese navigator, Christopher Columbus, under the patronage of Queen Isabella, discovered America. An account of these voyages of discovery will be given more fully in a subsequent portion of this volume.

Ferdinand's dominions were increased by the expulsion of the French from Naples by the Spanish forces under Gonsalvo de Cordova, *the Great Captain*, in 1503, thus giving the crown of Naples and Sicily to the King of Spain. Queen Isabella died in 1504, thus removing the last check upon her husband's meanness and selfishness.

Joanna, the daughter of Ferdinand and Isabella, was married to the Archduke Philip of Austria, the son of the Emperor Maximilian I. of Germany and his wife, the Duchess Mary of Burgundy. Philip and Joanna succeeded Isabella in the sovereignty of Castile, while Ferdinand continued to reign over Aragon and over Naples and Sicily. Philip died in 1506; and, as Joanna was insane, Ferdinand again became the actual sovereign of all Spain except the little kingdom of Navarre in the North, which was yet independent. Joanna's son Charles remained under the guardianship of his paternal grandfather, the Emperor Maximilian I. of Germany.

The part which Ferdinand played in the affairs of Italy and France is related in other parts of this volume. Spain was extended to its present limits by Ferdinand's conquest and annexation of the little kingdom of Navarre, on the south side of the Pyrenees, in 1512. The Kings of Navarre were thenceforth restricted to the little kingdom of Bearn, or French Navarre, on the north side of the Pyrenees. Ferdinand died in 1516, and was succeeded by his grandson, CHARLES I., who also inherited the Netherlands and the Austrian states, and became Charles V., Emperor of Germany, in 1519.

SARACEN AND MOORISH RULERS IN SPAIN.

Saracen Emirs.

A.D.	
712	TARIK and MUSA.
714	ABDELASIS.
715	AYUB, ALHAUR.
721	ALSAMA.
722	ABDERRAHMAN.
724	AMBISA.
726	HODEIRA, YAHIA.
727	OTHMAN, HODEIRA BEN ALHAUS, AL-HAITAM.
728	MOHAMMED.
729	ABDERRAHMAN restored.
733	ABDELMELIC.
736	OCBA.
741	ABDELMELIC restored.
742	BALEG, THALABA.
743	HUSAM.
744	THUEBA.
746	YUSSUF (to 755).

Caliphs of Cordova.

A.D.	
755	ABDERRAHMAN I.
787	HIXEM I.
796	ALHAKEM I.
821	ABDERRAHMAN II.
852	MOHAMMED I.
886	ALMONDHIR.
888	ABDALLA.
912	ABDERRAHMAN III.
961	ALHAKEM II.
976	HIXEM II.
1012	SULEYMAN.
1015	ALI.
1017	ABDERRAHMAN IV.
1018	ALCASSIM.
1023	ABDERRAHMAN V., MOHAMMED II.
1026	HIXEM III. (Caliphate ended in 1031).

Reguli of Cordova.

A.D.	
1031	GEHWAR.

A.D.	
1044	MOHAMMED BEN GEHWAR.
1060	MOHAMMED ALMOATEDED.
1069	MOHAMMED ALMOSTADIR.

Almoravide Dynasty (African).

A.D.	
1094	JUSEF.
1107	ALI.
1144	FAXFIN.

Almohade Dynasty (African).

A.D.	
1147	ABDELMUMEN.
1163	JUSEF.
1178	YACUB.
1199	MOHAMMED.
1213	ABU YACUB.
1223	ABULMELIC, ABDELWAHID.
1225	ALMAMON, ABU ALI (to 1238).

Moorish Kings of Granada.

A.D.	
1238	MOHAMMED I.
1273	MOHAMMED II.
1302	MOHAMMED III.
1309	NASSIR.
1313	ISMAIL I.
1325	MOHAMMED IV.
1333	JUSEF I.
1354	MOHAMMED V.
1359	ISMAIL II.
1360	ABU SAID.
1391	JUSEF II.
1396	MOHAMMED VI.
1408	JUSEF III.
1423	MOHAMMED VII. (deposed).
1427	MOHAMMED VIII.
1429	MOHAMMED VII. restored.
1445	MOHAMMED IX.
1454	MOHAMMED X.
1463	MULEY ALI.
1483	ABU ABDALLA.
1484	ABDALLA EL ZAGAL (his kingdom conquered in 1492 by Ferdinand V. of Aragon and Isabella of Castile).

MEDIÆVAL SPANISH CHRISTIAN KINGS.

Kings of Asturias and Leon.

A.D.	
718	PELAYO.
737	FAVILA.
739	ALFONSO I., THE CATHOLIC.
757	FROILA I.
768	AURELIO.
774	MAUREGATO, THE USURPER.
788	BERMUDA I.
791	ALFONSO II., THE CHASTE.
842	RAMIRIO I.
850	ORDONO I.
866	ALFONSO III., THE GREAT.
910	GARCIAS.
914	ORDONO II.
923	FROILA II.
925	ALFONSO IV., THE MONK.
930	RAMIRIO II.
950	ORDONO III.
955	ORDONO IV.
956	SANCHO I., THE FAT.
967	RAMIRIO III.
983	BERMUDA II., THE GOUTY
999	ALFONSO V.
1007	BERMUDA III. (to 1037).

Kings of Castile and Leon.

A.D.	
1035	FERDINAND I., THE GREAT.
1065	SANCHO II., THE STRONG.
1072	ALFONSO VI., THE VALIANT.
1109	URACA and ALFONSO VII.
1126	ALFONSO VII., RAYMOND.
1157	SANCHO III., THE BELOVED.
1158	ALFONSO VIII., THE NOBLE.
1157	FERDINAND II., King of Leon, which is separated from Castile from 1157 to 1188.
1188	ALFONSO IX. of Leon.
1214	HENRY I.
1217	FERDINAND III., THE SAINT.
1252	ALFONSO X., THE WISE.
1284	SANCHO IV., THE BRAVE.
1295	FERDINAND IV.
1312	ALFONSO XI.
1350	PEDRO THE CRUEL.
1369	HENRY II., THE GRACIOUS.
1379	JOHN I.
1390	HENRY III., THE SICKLY.
1406	JOHN II.
1454	HENRY IV., THE IMPOTENT.

MEDIÆVAL SPANISH CHRISTIAN KINGS.

A. D.		A. D.	
1474	ISABELLA (married to Ferdinand V. of Aragon, thus uniting Aragon and Castile, 1479).	1035	GARCIAS III.
		1054	SANCHO III.
		1076	SANCHO IV. (Ramirez of Aragon).
	Kings of Aragon.	1094	PEDRO of Aragon.
		1104	ALFONSO I. of Aragon.
1035	RAMIRO I.	1134	GARCIAS IV., RAMIREZ.
1065	SANCHO RAMIREZ, (IV. of Navarre.)	1150	SANCHO V., THE WISE.
1094	PEDRO of Navarre.	1194	SANCHO VI., THE INFIRM.
1104	ALFONSO I. THE WARRIOR (Navarre).	1234	THEOBALD I. (Count of Champagne).
1134	RAMIRO II., THE MEEK.	1253	THEOBALD II.
1137	PETRONILLA, AND RAYMOND OF BARCELONA.	1270	HENRY CRASSUS.
		1274	JOANNA I. (married to Philip the Fair of France).
1163	ALFONSO II.		
1196	PEDRO II.	1305	LOUIS X. OF FRANCE.
1213	JAMES I.	1316	JOHN.
1276	PEDRO III.	1316	PHILIP V. (Philip the Tall of France).
1285	ALFONSO III., THE BENEFICENT.	1322	CHARLES I. (Charles IV, of France).
1291	JAMES II., THE JUST.	1328	JOANNA II. AND PHILIP, COUNT D' EVREUX.
1327	ALFONSO IV.		
1336	PEDRO IV., THE CEREMONIOUS.	1343	JOANNA II. alone.
1387	JOHN I.	1349	CHARLES II., THE BAD.
1410	AN INTERREGNUM.	1387	CHARLES III., THE NOBLE.
1412	FERDINAND I., THE JUST (King of Sicily).	1425	BLANCHE AND HER HUSBAND, JOHN II.
1416	ALFONSO V., THE WISE.	1479	ELEANOR DE FOIX.
1458	JOHN II., (of Navarre).	1479	FRANCIS PHŒBUS DE FOIX.
1479	FERDINAND II., THE CATHOLIC (married Isabella of Castile, thus uniting the two kingdoms).	1483	CATHARINE AND JOHN D' ALBRET (Navarre annexed to Spain, 1512).
	Kings of Navarre.		*Lower Navarre (in France).*
885	GARCIAS I. (son of Count Sancho Inigo, who founded Navarre, 873).	1516	HENRY D' ALBRET.
		1555	JANE D' ALBRET (and her husband ANTHONY DE BOURBON, who died in 1562).
905	SANCHO GARCIAS.		
924	GARCIAS II., THE TREMBLER.	1572	HENRY III. (became Henry IV. of France in 1589, to which Lower Navarre was annexed in 1609).
970	SANCHO II., THE GREAT (King of Castile).		

SECTION VI.—KINGDOM OF SCOTLAND.

ROM the earliest period, the northern part of the island of Britain—anciently called *Caledonia* (now Scotland)—had been occupied by two wild Celtic tribes, known as *Scots* and *Picts*, whom the Romans could not subdue, and who made plundering raids into Britain. Bands of Scots continued their migrations from Ireland to Scotland as late as the sixth century. The Scots settled along the western shores of Caledonia, to which they gave their name. They were led by Fergus Mac Erc, who founded a kingdom.

In the sixth century hordes of Angles from Germany settled in the south-eastern part of Caledonia, which constituted a part of the Angle kingdom of Northumbria; while the Celtic or British kingdom of Strathclyde embraced South-western Scotland and the modern English counties of Cumberland and Westmoreland.

Christianity was introduced into Scotland in the sixth century by St. Columba, an Irishman, who was welcomed by Conal, the King of the Scots, who gave him the island of Iona, west of Mull. There St. Columba and his comrades erected a church and several dwellings, and converted the Picts; the Scots having been converted before their migration from Ireland. From the school of theology established at Iona zealous missionaries were sent to Britain, Gaul, Germany, Helvetia and Italy.

Says D'Aubigné: "The free church of the Scots and Britons did more for the conversion of Central Europe than the half-enslaved Church of Rome." The same writer says: "The sages of Iona knew nothing of transubstantiation, or of the withdrawal of the cup in the Lord's Supper, or of auricular confession, or of prayers for the dead, or tapers, or incense. They celebrated Easter on a different day from Rome. Synodal assemblies regulated the affairs of the Church, and the papal supremacy was unknown."

The Angles of Northumberland were converted to Christianity in the seventh century. Oswald, King of Northumbria, extended his conquests beyond the Friths of Forth and Clyde; and his son and successor, Oswin, reduced the Scots to tribute; but the Angles were routed in the next reign, their king was slain, and the Picts and Scots recovered their independence.

In 843 KENNETH MAC ALPIN, King of the Scots, reduced the Angles, or English, north of Adrian's Wall under his dominion. He also extended his authority over the Picts, and thus founded the *Kingdom of Scotland.*

The reigns of Kenneth's brother DONALD (A. D. 854-858) and his son CONSTANTINE I. (A. D. 858-874) were passed in struggles with the Northmen, who ravaged Scotland, as well as England and Ireland. Harald Fairhair, King of Norway, conquered the Orkney and the Shetland Isles. A Danish chief named Cyric, or Grig, seized the throne of Scotland and reigned eighteen years.

CONSTANTINE II., the great-grandson of Kenneth Mac Alpin, reigned over Scotland from A. D. 900 to 943. He placed his kingdom under the protection of Edward the Elder, King of England. In 937 he joined the Danes in an effort to recover Northumberland, from which they had been driven by the English king Athelstan, but the allies were beaten by the English in the bloody battle of Brunanburgh. Constantine II. abdicated in 943, and became a monk in the monastery of St. Andrews.

MALCOLM I. was the next King of Scotland (A. D. 944-954). He obtained the Kingdom of Strathclyde from the English king as a fief. During the reign of INDUFF (A. D. 954-961), Edinburgh, or Edwin's Burgh, founded by King Edwin of Northumberland, came into the possession of the Scots. The reigns of DUFF, COLIN, KENNETH II., CONSTANTINE III. and KENNETH III. were passed in wars with the Kingdom of Strathclyde or with their own rebellious subjects, and all of them died in battle.

MALCOLM II. (A. D. 1003-1033), the grandson of Malcolm I., was the last of the dynasty of Kenneth Mac Alpin. He wrested Lothian from the Earl of Northumberland in 1018, and annexed it to Scotland. In 1031 Malcolm II. acknowledged Canute the Great, King of England and Denmark, as his suzerain. Malcolm II. died in 1034, transmitting the Scottish crown to his grandson DUNCAN, after having caused the legitimate heir, the grandson of Kenneth III., to be murdered.

Gruach, the murdered prince's sister, was married to Macbeth, Earl of Moray, one of the most powerful of the Scottish chiefs. Duncan took the field against the rebellious Highland clans. Macbeth determined to avenge the murder of his brother-in-law, and now attacked Duncan in his province and defeated him in battle, and afterward killed him, A. D. 1040.

MACBETH then made himself King of Scotland, and reigned seventeen years (A. D. 1040-1057). He governed with firmness and wisdom, and Scotland prospered under his rule. He and his queen were very kind to the poor, and sent alms to the poor at Rome. Crinan, Abbot of Dunkeld, Duncan's father, instigated Siward, Earl of Northumberland, to take up the cause of Malcolm and Donald Bane, Duncan's sons. Macbeth was driven from the Scottish throne, but recovered it immediately after Siward's withdrawal. Siward again invaded Scotland some years later in behalf of Duncan's sons, whereupon a struggle of four years followed, ending in Macbeth's defeat and death in the battle of Lumphanan, in Aberdeenshire, A. D. 1057.

MALCOLM III., CANMORE, "the Great Head," then became King of Scotland. The Norman Conquest of England drove many Anglo-Saxons into Scotland, and these were kindly welcomed by Malcolm Canmore. Among these English refugees were Edgar Atheling, his mother and his two sisters, Margaret and Christina. Immediately after the Norman Conquest of England, Malcolm Canmore had sent in his nominal homage to William the Conqueror. The Scottish king now espoused the cause of Edgar Atheling as the rightful King of England, and made a bloody raid into England, in the districts of Cleveland and Durham. Soon afterwards Malcolm Canmore married Edgar Atheling's sister Margaret.

In 1072 William the Conqueror invaded Scotland with an Anglo-Norman fleet and army to chastise Malcolm Canmore for his raid into England. The Norman King of England advanced as far as Abernethy, on the Tay, where Malcolm Canmore met him and did homage to him as his vassal, and placed his son Duncan, the child of his first wife, in William's hands as a hostage for his good behavior.

When William the Conqueror was absent in Normandy several years afterward, Malcolm Canmore made another raid into England, ravaging the country as far as the Tyne. William's eldest son, Robert, marched towards the Scottish border to repel this invasion, but the matter was settled by negotiation between Malcolm Canmore and Robert.

In 1092, during the reign of William Rufus in England, Malcolm Canmore invaded England a third time. The English king marched into Scotland, and Malcolm Canmore averted his wrath by renewing his homage as a vassal monarch of the English sovereign. As William Rufus failed to fulfill his part of the agreement, Malcolm Canmore invaded England a fourth time in 1093, with a powerful Scottish army, but was defeated and slain in a battle at Alnwick Castle. His son and heir Edward also perished on this fatal field. Malcolm Canmore's queen, Margaret, died of grief upon hearing of the death of her husband and son. She had used her influence over her husband to reform many abuses in the kingdom, and had introduced more refinement and civilization into Scotland than the Scots had ever known before.

DONALD BANE, Malcolm Canmore's brother, was elected King of Scotland by the chiefs of the Scottish clans. Duncan, Malcolm Canmore's eldest son, who had been kept in England as a hostage, induced the English king to aid him with an army to recover the Scottish throne, which he promised to hold as a vassal of the English crown. With this aid DUNCAN drove Donald Bane from the Scottish throne and reigned for a few months, A. D. 1094.

Donald Bane, aided by Edmund, Malcolm Canmore's eldest surviving son by his marriage with Margaret, renewed the civil war, defeated Duncan, put him to death, and exiled the other members of his family. Donald Bane then reigned three years (A. D. 1094-1097), at the end of which he was defeated by an English army under Edgar Atheling, who placed his nephew EDGAR upon the throne of Scotland, and put out Donald Bane's eyes and cast him into prison. Edmund took refuge in an English monastery, where he died.

Edgar, who was the son of Malcolm Canmore and Margaret, carried out the reforms commenced by his mother; and during his reign the people of the Lowlands of Scotland generally adopted the Anglo-Saxon civilization, and the old Celtic customs disappeared. This change in the customs and manners of the Southern Scots widely separated them from the real Scots of the Highlands, who thenceforth were considered the natural enemies of law and order, and the perpetual disturbers of the peace and prosperity of the Scottish kingdom.

Edgar reigned over Scotland ten years (A. D. 1097-1107). In the early part of his reign, Magnus Barefoot, King of Norway, seized the Orkneys and the Scandinavian earldom on the mainland of Scotland, placing them under the government of his own son, Sigurd; after which he invaded and ravaged the Hebrides. At the death of Magnus Barefoot the Orkneys and the Hebrides again fell into the possession of the Scots. The chiefs of these islands, called *Lords of the Isles*, thenceforth had a convenient way of declaring themselves vassals of the Kings of Norway whenever they desired to evade their feudal obligations to the Kings of Scotland.

During Edgar's entire reign the relations between Scotland and England were friendly, and Edgar's sister Edith was married to King Henry I. of England. She took the Norman name of Matilda, or Maud, and was very much beloved by her husband and by the English people. On his death-bed, in 1107, Edgar separated Strathclyde from the rest of Scotland, bestowing it upon his brother David.

Edgar was succeeded on the throne of Scotland by his brother, ALEXANDER I., a man of great energy and of strong, unyielding will. He was involved in constant trouble with his unruly subjects by his efforts to govern them. In the early part of his reign Alexander I. was confronted by a formidable revolt of the men of Merne and Moray. Alexander I. promptly marched against the rebels and defeated them in a battle on the northern shore of the Frith of Moray. He took a bloody vengeance on the rebels, and founded the Abbey of Scone to commemorate his victory.

Alexander I. vigorously maintained the independence of the Church of Scotland against the Archbishop of York, who claimed ecclesiastical jurisdiction over the entire Kingdom of Scotland. Alexander I. would not permit any appeal to the Pope, and refused to listen for a moment to any claim of the Northern Metropolitan of England to ecclesiastical authority in Scotland.

Alexander I. died in 1124, and, as he was childless, his brother, DAVID I., ascended the Scottish throne; whereupon Strathclyde again became a part of the Scottish kingdom. In the early part of David's reign a rebellion broke out in Moray, but it was suppressed by the king with the assistance of some Norman knights whom he had gathered about him when he was Prince of Strathclyde. He declared Moray forfeited, and divided it among his Norman knights.

David I. took part in the civil war in England between his niece Matilda and Stephen of Blois, in behalf of his niece. Stephen forced the Scottish king to retire from the struggle. David I. would not violate his oath of fealty to Matilda, but evaded it by investing his son Henry with the Honor of Huntingdon, an English barony which he had previously held. The English king conferred Carlisle and Doncaster on Prince Henry, who went to London with Stephen, and took precedence of the English barons at Stephen's court. Jealous of this honor to the Scottish prince, the English barons left Stephen's court in a body. David I. resented this insult by recalling his son to Scotland and preparing to invade England.

In 1138 David I. ravaged the northern counties of England, but was defeated by the English in the great Battle of the Standard, at North Allerton. Peace was concluded at Durham the next year. David's son Henry was invested with the English earldom of Northumberland. In 1141 David I. again took up arms in Matilda's behalf, and was almost taken prisoner when her army was defeated in the battle of Winchester.

David I. was one of Scotland's greatest, as well as one of her best kings. He labored to promote the welfare of his subjects at home, and firmly upheld the honor and renown of Scotland abroad. He steadily promoted the civilization of Scotland, introduced many foreign manners and customs, and induced many Norman barons to settle in his kingdom and granted them estates. He was a warm friend of the commons, and promoted the growth of the Scottish towns, conferring many important privileges upon them. He was always accessible to the poorest of his subjects, patiently listened to their complaints, and promptly redressed their grievances.

David I. founded Holyrood palace, and made Edinburgh the Scottish capital. He founded many abbeys, and also the bishoprics of Dunblane, Brechin, Aberdeen, Ross, Caithness and Glasgow. He also made many reforms in the government of the Church in Scotland. During his reign Scotland made wonderful progress in civilization, wealth and fertility. His last years were rendered sad by the death of his only son, Prince Henry, who was greatly beloved by the Scottish nation. David I. died in 1153, after a reign of twenty-nine years.

MALCOLM IV., the eldest son of Prince Henry, became King of Scotland upon his illustrious grandfather's death. He was less than twelve years of age at his accession, but the principle of hereditary succession had gained such a foothold in Scotland that his accession was generally acquiesced in. When he was nineteen years old a rebellion broke out in Galloway, but was suppressed, and that district was reduced to direct dependence on the Scottish crown. Several years afterward the Lord of Argyle revolted against the Scottish king, but was slain by treachery, and his estates were annexed to the royal territories. But Henry II. of England forced Malcolm IV. to relinquish the sovereignty of the northern English counties which David I. had held. Malcolm IV. was then invested with the Honor of Huntingdon, as a fief of the English crown.

Malcolm IV. died in 1165, and was succeeded on the Scottish throne by his brother WILLIAM THE LION, whose reign is the longest in Scottish history, lasting almost half a century (A. D. 1165-1214). At the beginning of his reign William the Lion demanded that Henry II. of England should restore to him the earldom of Northumberland, which his father had held and which his brother had lost. Henry II. refused to grant it, whereupon William the Lion invaded England while the English king was absent in France, and overran a large part of the northern English counties; but the Scottish king was taken prisoner with several of his chief nobles near Alnwick Castle in the summer of 1174, and was sent into captivity to the Castle of Falaise, in Normandy.

At the end of the year William the Lion was released, upon agreeing to hold the Scottish crown as a vassal of the English monarch, and requiring his nobles and clergy to do homage to the same king. The chief strongholds of Scotland were garrisoned with English troops, and William the Lion and his nobles and clergy did homage to Henry II. of England at York as their feudal lord. This humiliating treaty remained in force until the death of Henry II. in 1189.

Richard the Lion-hearted, the next King of England, released William the Lion from his obligations and restored the Scottish castles upon the payment of a ransom of ten thousand marks; but he refused to restore the earldom of Northumberland to the Scottish king. When John became King of England, William the Lion did such homage as the Scottish kings had formerly paid to the King of England for their fiefs in that kingdom. The two kings thoroughly distrusted each other; and for several years William the Lion was under the necessity of keeping a considerable force on the border to protect Berwick, the largest trading town of Scotland, from King John's efforts to ruin its commerce.

In 1176 the Archbishop of York again claimed ecclesiastical jurisdiction over Scotland. The Scottish clergy appealed to Pope Clement III., who confirmed their claim of independence in 1188, and declared Scotland subject to the Holy See only in matters of religion. During the captivity of William the Lion a formidable revolt had broken out in Galloway, but had been suppressed by his nephew Roland, who was confirmed in the possession of the district.

William the Lion died at Stirling in 1214, and was succeeded on the throne of Scotland by his only son, ALEXANDER II. Alexander II. took part in the civil war in England between King John and his barons, espousing the cause of the barons, in the hope of recovering the earldom of Northumberland. The Scottish king received the homage of the barons of the North of England, united his forces with theirs, and marched to Dover to welcome and do homage to Prince Louis of France, whom the English barons had invited to come to England and assume the English crown. The struggle was ended by King John's death in 1216 and the acceptance of his son Henry III. as their king by the English barons.

Alexander II. did homage to Henry III. of England in 1217, and was invested with the Honor of Huntingdon. In 1221 the Scottish king married the Princess Joanna, the sister of the King of England. This marriage was followed by a peace of almost a century between Scotland and England. Alexander II. consented to renounce his claim to the earldom of Northumberland in return for a grant of the lands of Penrith and Tynedale. The relations between the Scottish and English kings were so cordial that when Henry III. of England went to France he left the border under the protection of Alexander II. In 1222 the two kings appointed a joint commission to settle the boundary between Scotland and England. The result of their labors was the boundary line which still divides the two countries. A wide district on both sides was left as a neutral ground.

Alexander II. died in 1249, while engaged in an expedition against the Hebrides, and was succeeded as King of Scotland by his son, ALEXANDER III., who was then only eight years of age. Alexander III. was solemnly crowned at Scone, and was married to the Princess Margaret, the daughter of King Henry III. of England, at York, on Christmas day, A. D. 1251. On this occasion Alexander III. did homage to the English monarch for the lands which he held in England. Henry III. demanded that the Scottish king should also do homage for Scotland, but Alexander III. evaded this by declaring that he must consult the Scottish lords on a question of such importance.

In 1278 Alexander III. went to Westminster to do homage to Edward I. of England. Edward I. renewed the claim of Henry III. to the homage of the King of Scotland, but Alexander III. refused to acknowledge the English king's claim. Edward I. forbore to enforce his claim then.

In 1262 Hakon IV., King of Norway, with a large fleet, attempted the conquest of the Orkneys and the Hebrides, after which he ravaged the western coast of Scotland. The Norwegians gained no permanent advantages in this expedition; but in 1281 Margaret, the eldest daughter of the Scottish king, was married to Erik, the heir to the crown of Norway. Margaret died two years afterward, leaving a daughter also named Margaret. Alexander, the only son of the Scottish king, died several months afterward; whereupon the infant Margaret, the *Maid of Norway*, became the heir to the crown of Scotland. Alexander III. was killed by a fall from his horse in 1286.

The second period of Scottish history ended with the death of Alexander III. This period commenced with the dethronement of Donald Bane, the last Celtic King of Scotland, almost two centuries before; and during that period the boundary of Scotland had been extended by the annexation of Argyle and of the Isles, while the two dependencies of Galloway and Lothian had been more closely drawn to the Scottish kingdom, though they yet remained separate and distinct.

During this period the influence of England, though peaceable, had been stronger in Scotland than it was ever to be afterward. English laws and English customs had been introduced into Scotland, and had taken the place of the old Celtic usages in many cases. The old Celtic *Maers* had been removed to give place to the sheriffs of the Scottish crown; but, as Scotland was not divided into counties, the sheriffs in Scotland were not, like those in England, the reeves of the already existing shires, being officers placed over certain districts by the king. These districts, or sheriffdoms, became the Scottish counties of later times.

Feudalism, after the Norman model, with all its burdensome exactions and oppressions, had been introduced into Scotland, and had taken firmer root in that kingdom than it ever did in England. The native chiefs of Scotland had been displaced by foreign nobles, and thus a purely Norman baronage had come into possession of the Scottish lands, whether occupied by a Celtic or an Anglo-Saxon peasantry. In some cases the Norman landlords founded feudal families afterward known under Celtic names, as the Normans took the names which the Celts had given to the lands and adopted them as their own

The long peace between Scotland and England, which remained unbroken for almost a century, had been marked by great social progress in Scotland. The large proportion of land now under tillage proves that agriculture must have thriven during this troubled time. Roads and bridges were numerous and in good repair, while the trading towns had made great progress in wealth and power. Hitherto no town had taken its place distinctly as the capital of Scotland. Perth, or St. John's Town, had some claim to the first rank because of its connection with Scone; but the Scottish king held his court or his assize indifferently at any of the great royal burghs.

These burghs were of great importance in the Scottish kingdom; and, as the burgesses of the royal burghs were all vassals of the Scottish crown, they acted as some sort of a check upon the increasing power of the nobles. The burghers possessed the right to govern themselves by their own laws, and were divided into two groups. Those north of the Frith of Forth were united by a league like the Hanse towns of Continental Europe, and were known by the same name; while those in Lothian, represented by the four leading towns among them—Edinburgh, Roxburgh, Berwick and Stirling—held their *Court of the Four Burghs*, still represented by the *Convention of Royal Burghs*, which convenes once a year at Edinburgh.

None of the Scottish towns were in any way behind the cities of Continental Europe. Berwick, the richest and the greatest, was said to rival London. Inverness was celebrated for shipbuilding. A ship built there aroused the envy and wonder of the French nobles of that time.

But this condition of things was ended by the death of Alexander III.; and the long period of war and misery that ensued did much to wipe out every vestige of the high degree of civilization and prosperity that had been reached in that golden age of Scottish history.

Within the month following the death of Alexander III. the Scottish estates assembled at Scone and appointed a council of six regents to govern the Scottish kingdom for Margaret, the Maid of Norway, who was then only three years of age, and who had succeeded her grandfather on the throne of Scotland. Robert Bruce, a Norman baron, whose ancestors had settled in Annandale in the preceding century, attempted to seize the Scottish crown by force. He was the son of Isabella, the second daughter of David, Earl of Huntingdon, the brother of William the Lion. He appealed to Edward I. of England, as lord-paramount of Scotland, to sustain his claim.

The Scottish estates opposed Robert Bruce; and a treaty was negotiated with the King of England for the marriage of Margaret, the Maid of Norway, with the son and heir of the English sovereign. In this treaty it was stipulated that Scotland should remain a distinct and separate kingdom, and that England should respect her independence after the union of the English and Scottish crowns by the proposed marriage. The death of Margaret in 1290, while on her way from Norway to Scotland, broke off the arrangement.

The dynasty founded by William the Lion ended with Margaret's death. Several claimants for the crown of Scotland now appeared, who based their claims upon their descent from David, Earl of Huntingdon. The two principal ones were Robert Bruce and John Baliol, the latter of whom was the grandson of David's daughter Margaret. Both appealed to Edward I. of England, who decided in favor of Baliol, on condition that he should do homage to the English monarch for his crown; and near the end of 1292 Baliol was crowned at Scone as King JOHN of Scotland.

The English king had just conquered Wales, and ardently desired to unite the whole island of Great Britain under the English dominion. Immediately after his coronation John Baliol summoned the Scottish estates, now for the first time called a Parliament, to meet at Scone. Baliol was a weak, incompetent sovereign, and his subjects generally considered him a mere instrument of the King of England.

Roger Bartholomew, a burgess of Berwick, dissatisfied with an unfavorable decision of a Scottish court, appealed to Edward I. of England, who ordered a hearing of the case before an English council at Newcastle, thus directly violating his treaty with Scotland, but he forced the vassal King of Scotland to submit to it. Several months afterward Macduff, the granduncle of the Earl of Fife, appealed to the King of England from a decision of the estates concerning the lands of the families of Bruce and Douglas. Edward I. summoned Baliol to appear before the English Parliament, but even the submissive King of Scotland revolted against so abject a surrender of his country's freedom.

The English monarch thereupon declared Baliol a contumacious vassal, and ordered him to surrender three of the principal fortresses of Scotland into his hands until he should give satisfaction. Baliol replied by entering into an alliance with King Philip the Fair of France and King Eric II. of Norway against Edward I. of England. Baliol was heartily supported in this action by the nobles and people of Scotland. Thenceforth until the Reformation Scotland was the faithful ally of France. Immediately after the conclusion of this alliance a Scottish army crossed the border and ravaged the northern counties of England.

Having thus the pretext for the conquest of Scotland, for which he had long been watching, Edward I. immediately led a large English army into Scotland and inflicted a punishment upon the citizens of Berwick. He then defeated the Scots at Dunbar, A. D. 1296, besieged and took Edinburgh Castle, seized the crown jewels of Scotland, captured Stirling and Perth, and took the Stone of Destiny from Scone and sent it to Westminster Abbey, where it still remains.

As the Scots had regarded that sacred stone as in some way connected with their country's destiny they considered its capture a national misfortune. The English king marched as far north as Elgin and returned to Berwick in 1296, having thoroughly subdued Scotland. John Baliol was compelled to surrender his crown, and was sent a prisoner to England. He was afterward permitted to retire to his estate in the county of Picardy, in France, where he died in 1315.

The Scottish nobles were forced to swear fealty to Edward I. of England, who treated Scotland as a confiscated fief. All the Scottish castles were garrisoned with English troops. The Scots were not allowed to hold any important offices, and were treated with great severity. Scotland was governed by English officials, as an integral portion of the English kingdom. The Earl of Warrenne and Surrey was appointed guardian of Scotland, and administered the government in the English king's name. The Highlanders, who had not been directly molested by Edward I., paid no attention to the change in the government of Scotland, and the Norman nobles quietly accepted it; but English tyranny soon produced a Scottish revolt.

William Wallace, a gentleman of Clydesdale, killed an English officer who had inflicted a grievous injury upon him, and escaped to the woods, calling on his countrymen to assist him to liberate Scotland from English rule, A. D. 1297. With a band of devoted followers, he cut to pieces the English garrison at Lanark, and killed Haselrig, the newly appointed Sheriff of Ayr. After other successes, he attacked Scone, where Warrenne's justiciary, Ormesby, was holding his court. Ormesby escaped, but Wallace captured many prisoners and much booty. Wallace next attacked Glasgow, compelling Anthony Beck, Bishop of Durham, to take flight to England. All the English officials, except those in the fortified places, now abandoned their posts and fled into England.

Wallace, whose successes had again aroused the spirit of Scotland, was now joined by Lord William Douglas and Robert Bruce, Earl of Carrick, a grandson of the Robert Bruce who had been John Baliol's competitor for the Scottish crown; but the Scottish nobles looked upon Wallace's movement with coldness, and when an English army under Lord Percy marched into Scotland in the summer of 1297 they renewed their allegiance to Edward I.

Lord Percy soon retired to England, believing the Scottish outbreak over; but Wallace again took the field at the head of many Lowlanders. He soon made himself master of the fortresses north of the Tay. Earl Warrenne marched against him with forty thousand men, but was utterly routed at Stirling, September 11, 1297; Cressingham, the English treasurer of Scotland, being among the slain, and his body being flayed by the Scots, who made saddles and girths of the skin. Warrenne retreated into England, and Wallace crossed the border and ravaged the northern counties of England with great cruelty, carrying much plunder with him to Scotland. All the strongholds south of the Frith of Forth came into the possession of the Scots, and Wallace was made guardian of Scotland.

Edward I., who had been absent in Flanders, now returned to England, led almost a hundred thousand men into Scotland, and defeated Wallace at Falkirk in 1298. Wallace now resigned the guardianship of Scotland, and the English monarch returned to Carlisle. Edward I. reduced the Northern Lowlands to submission in 1303. Edward I. granted an amnesty to all the Scottish leaders except Wallace, who was required to submit unconditionally to the English king's clemency. Wallace, who had been absent in Continental Europe since the battle of Falkirk, now returned to Scotland; but was soon afterward betrayed to Edward I. by his trusted friend, Sir John Monteith, and was taken to London, where he was hanged as a traitor. The Scots have always honored him as a martyr to their cause, and his memory is still cherished as the greatest of Scottish heroes.

The English were now supreme in Scotland, and that kingdom was governed by a lieutenant of the King of England, aided by a council of barons and bishops. Scotland was allowed a representation by ten deputies in the English Parliament, and English officials were appointed in every department of the Scottish government. Edward I. sought to conciliate the Scots to English rule by just treatment, but he was unable to suppress the natural longings of the Scots for national independence.

Scottish discontent soon produced another revolt. Robert Bruce, Earl of Carrick, who had taken part in Wallace's insurrections, had been pardoned by the English monarch and received into his favor. Bruce intended to renew the effort for his country's liberation, and when Edward I. discovered his plotting for that purpose he was obliged to save himself by flight from the English court.

Bruce hastened to Scotland, and murdered his rival, John Comyn of Badenoch, who opposed his plans, in an interview in the Grey Friars' Church at Dumfries, being aided in the act by Sir Roger Kirkpatrick. By this act, combining murder and sacrilege, Bruce aroused the vengeance of the English king and the Church. But it made him the legitimate heir of the Scottish throne, thus arousing the sympathy and support of his countrymen, who were very restless under the English yoke. Bruce at once put forward his claims, and was solemnly crowned King of Scotland at Scone, March 27, 1306, with the title of ROBERT I.

Edward I. made vigorous preparations to crush this new Scottish outbreak, and made Aymer de Valence governor of Scotland. King Robert Bruce was declared a traitor, and was excommunicated by a special bull from the Pope, while all who had aided him were punished with great severity as fast as they fell into the power of the English. Nigel Bruce, Robert's brother; Christopher Seton, his brother-in-law; and three other Scottish nobles, were executed. The execution of these leaders contributed much to alienate the nobles of Scotland from the English dominion, and to induce them to second the efforts of the Scottish people.

Edward I. led an army of a hundred thousand men northward for a third invasion of Scotland, but died at Burgh-on-the-Sands, July 7, 1307. His son and successor, Edward II., disregarded his father's dying injunction to prosecute the war for the subjugation of Scotland, and abandoned the struggle and disbanded his army, thus giving Scotland several years to prepare for the decisive blow for her deliverance.

As King Robert I. was not acknowledged by the whole Scottish nation, his prospects were so desperate for several years that he was a wanderer and an outlaw. During this time he maintained an irregular warfare with the English, in which he very much increased his reputation for good generalship and personal bravery. His principal enemies were the Earl of Buchan and Macdougal of Lorn, who had been gained over to the English interests.

At length Bruce was obliged to seek refuge in the island of Rachrin, off the northern coast of Ireland. According to a tradition, he had almost resolved to give up the struggle in Scotland. As he lay in bed one morning in the hut in which he had found shelter he observed a spider vainly endeavoring to throw its web across from beam to beam in the roof above him. The insect failed in six attempts. Said Bruce to himself: "Six times have I failed in my efforts against the English." He watched with renewed interest to see if the spider would repeat the effort. Said he: "If it does, I will take it as an encouragement to try again." To his delight, the spider made another effort and succeeded.

Greatly encouraged, Bruce returned to Scotland, joined some of his followers in the isle of Arran, and passed over to the mainland. He had a small force, and was confronted with many perils. He bore his trials manfully, and infused his patience and hopefulness into his followers, whose numbers increased slowly; and he finally defeated his old foe, the Earl of Buchan, near Inveraray; after which he ravaged the lands of the Earl of Buchan with fire and sword.

Bruce's cause steadily gained ground, and the Scottish clergy soon acknowledged him as their king, thus virtually relieving him of the ban of excommunication. This was a great gain for him. The Scottish strongholds came into his possession one by one, until finally Stirling was the only post in Scotland remaining in the possession of the English, and even that place was so hard pressed that the governor agreed to surrender it if not relieved by the day of the Feast of St. John the Baptist, in 1314. Edward II. of England led an army of a hundred thousand men into Scotland to the relief of Stirling, but was utterly routed by thirty thousand Scots under Bruce at Bannockburn, within sight of Stirling, June 24, 1314. The English king and his army fled to their own country, and the independence of Scotland was virtually secured.

During this period Lord James Douglas, the son of the Douglas who had sustained Wallace, achieved so many victories over the English that his name became a terror to them. He was called the "Black Douglas," from his swarthy complexion and his black hair, to distinguish him from the "Red Douglas."

Although the battle of Bannockburn virtually established the independence of Scotland, England still refused to acknowledge that independence, and the struggle went on, producing much suffering to the borders of both kingdoms. Edward Bruce, Robert's brother, invaded Ireland and tried to wrest that dependency from the crown of England. With Robert's assistance, Edward Bruce was crowned King of Ireland at Carrickfergus, but was defeated at Athenree, August 10, 1316, and was finally defeated and killed at Dundalk in 1318, thus ending this effort to liberate Ireland from English rule, King Robert Bruce having in the meantime returned to Scotland.

In the meantime war between the English and the Scots went on along the border. The Scots recovered Berwick and held it against all the efforts of the English to recapture it. In 1328 the long struggle was ended by the Treaty of Northampton, by which England formally acknowledged the independence of Scotland, and Kings Robert I. and Edward II. pledged themselves to be faithful allies and to refrain from instigating each other's subjects to rebellion. Edward's sister Joan was betrothed to Robert's infant son, David Bruce.

The Treaty of Northampton did away with all former Scottish submissions to England, and Lothian and Strathclyde became wholly independent of England and integral portions of Scotland. The struggle for Scottish independence tended to the consolidation of all the hitherto discordant races in the Scottish kingdom, and thus to develop a feeling of nationality among the Scottish people, making them a united and compact nation.

A less fortunate result of the struggle was the deep-rooted hatred of England and everything English that had grown up among all classes of Scots—a feeling which drove the Scots into an alliance with France, which shaped the future destiny of Scotland. King Robert I. entered into a treaty with France by which he bound himself to invade England whenever France should declare war against that kingdom.

In 1318 the Scottish Parliament settled the succession to the Scottish crown—first, on the direct male heirs, in the order of seniority; next, on the direct female heirs; and, in case of the failure of both the direct lines, on the next of kin. This Parliament likewise forbade the holders of Scottish estates residing in England from taking any produce or revenues of those lands out of the Scottish kingdom. This was done in order to force the landholders of Scotland to be Scots only. The Scottish Parliament of 1326 admitted representatives from the burghs, and acknowledged the Third Estate, or the commons, as an essential part of the Scottish Parliament.

King Robert I. died at Cardross in 1329, and was greatly mourned by the Scottish nation. His only son, DAVID II., then only eight years old, succeeded him on the throne of Scotland. David II. was crowned at Scone, and was likewise anointed, the latter ceremony being performed in Scotland for the first time, it being considered the exclusive right of independent sovereigns. Lord Randolph, a nephew of Robert Bruce, was made regent of Scotland during the young king's minority.

In the early part of the reign of David II. the English barons who had been dispossessed of their estates in Scotland by the law passed by the Scottish Parliament of 1318, invaded Scotland with the avowed intention of placing Edward Baliol, son of John Baliol, on the throne of Scotland. In this emergency Lord Randolph died; whereupon Donald, Earl of Mar, also a nephew of Robert Bruce, was made regent of Scotland.

The English invaders landed on the coast of Fife and defeated the Scottish army under the regent Donald, who was killed in the battle. The English victors then occupied Perth, and crowned EDWARD BALIOL King of Scotland at Scone, September 24, 1332. Edward Baliol acknowledged himself a vassal of King Edward III. of England.

The Scots were so incensed at this English invasion that they made war on the English border counties, thus giving Edward III. of England a pretext for invading Scotland. He besieged Berwick in the spring of 1333. Archibald Douglas, the new regent of Scotland, marched to relieve the beleaguered town, but was defeated by the English king in the great battle of Halidon Hill, and Berwick was forced to capitulate to Edward III. Edward Baliol ceded Berwick to the English, and surrendered to them all the Scottish fortresses south of the Frith of Forth.

The war between Scotland and England continued three years longer with varying success. At length, when Edward III. of England was occupied with his war with France, the national party in Scotland, under Robert Stuart, the high steward of the Scottish kingdom, who became regent in 1338, recovered the Scottish fortresses which Edward Baliol had surrendered to the English king, and drove Edward Baliol from Scotland in 1341. David Bruce, and his wife, Joan of England, who had been sent to France to insure their safety, were immediately brought back to Scotland; and David at once resumed the government of his kingdom. A truce was concluded with England, and a period of peace ensued for five years, broken only by raids along the border.

In 1346, when Edward III. of England was engaged in the siege of Calais, King David Bruce broke the truce in the interest of France by invading England; but he was defeated and taken prisoner in the battle of Neville's Cross, near Durham, October 10, 1346. He remained in captivity in England for eleven years, during which time Scotland was governed by the former regent, Robert Stuart, or the Steward. The Scots recovered Berwick, but again lost it. Upon returning from France, Edward III. of England marched with his army into Scotland as far as the Frith of Forth, the Scots retreating before him and devastating the country. David Bruce was released in 1357 upon the payment of a ransom of a hundred thousand marks.

Upon the death of David Bruce in 1370, without children, Robert Stuart, or the Steward, became King ROBERT II. of Scotland; and thenceforth the Stuart dynasty occupied the Scottish throne. The office of Steward was hereditary, having descended from Walter Fitz-Alan, upon whom David I. had conferred it; and from this the family took the name of Stewart, or Stuart, by which it is known in Scottish history. The accession of Robert II. was undisputed.

The truce with England expired in 1385, whereupon Robert II. renewed the war with that kingdom. King Charles VI. of France sent two thousand troops, with arms and money, to his Scottish ally. Richard II. of England invaded Scotland and destroyed Melrose Abbey, while the Scots and their French allies ravaged the northern counties of England with fire and sword. Upon the English king's retreat from Scotland the French troops returned to their own country. A few years afterward the war between the Scots and the English was renewed on the border; and in August, 1388, the Scottish Earl of Douglas was slain in the hard-fought battle of Otterburn, in Northumberland—a combat so celebrated in the famous ballad of *Chevy Chase*. Peace was made between Scotland and England in 1389.

King Robert II. died in 1390, and was succeeded on the throne of Scotland by his eldest son, ROBERT III. Robert III. was weak in mind and body, and the government of Scotland fell under the control of his brothers, the Duke of Albany and the Earl of Buchan. The Duke of Albany was the real ruler. Scotland was in a condition of anarchy, and lawless violence distracted the whole kingdom. The Scottish nobles and chieftains fought out their quarrels, and some of their combats assumed the proportion of battles. They also robbed and maltreated the peasants and burghers.

In 1400 a border war broke out with England, in consequence of the English claim to the crown of Scotland by Henry IV. of England; and Archibald, Earl of Douglas, was defeated and taken prisoner in the battle of Homildon Hill, in 1402, by the English under the Earl of Northumberland and his son Henry Percy, Hotspur; but peace was made soon afterward.

The Duke of Albany caused the king's eldest son, the heir to the Scottish throne, to be starved in a dungeon; and in 1406 the king's remaining son, James, Earl of Carrick, then the heir to the crown, was captured by an English cruiser, while on board a Scottish vessel sailing for France, where the prince was being sent to be educated.

KINGDOM OF SCOTLAND.

Although a state of peace then existed between Scotland and England, King Henry IV. retained the Scottish prince a prisoner in England; and for eighteen years Prince James remained in captivity, two years in the Tower and sixteen in Windsor Castle. King Robert III. died of grief three days after hearing of his son's capture, A. D. 1406.

The Duke of Albany as regent at once proclaimed JAMES I. King of Scotland, although he was a captive in England, and administered the Scottish government in his name. Peace was nominally maintained with England, but the border war still continued, and the Scots recovered many of the frontier fortresses. They retook Jedburgh, and destroyed it for the purpose of preventing the English from occupying it in future invasions of Scotland.

In 1411 the Highlanders, under Donald, Lord of the Isles, burst into the Lowlands north of the Frith of Forth, for the purpose of ravaging that part of the kingdom; but they were defeated by the Lowlanders, under Alexander Stewart, Earl of Mar, at Harlow, in Aberdeenshire, July 24, 1411, thus delivering Scotland from a terrible danger.

The Duke of Albany died in 1419, and was succeeded in the regency and in his dukedom by his son. The Scottish kingdom was so distracted with anarchy that the regent exercised but nominal power. The real remedy for the disorders which afflicted Scotland was to place the king, who was still a captive in England, on the throne. Douglas and some of the other Scottish nobles obtained the release of James I., who returned to Scotland in 1424, when the Scots paid a ransom of forty thousand pounds, to defray the expense of his maintenance and education during his captivity of eighteen years in England.

During his captivity James I. married the Lady Joanna Beaufort, daughter of the Duke of Somerset, and she came with him to Scotland. James I. was well aware that the new regent, the young Duke of Albany, and his partisans had sought to prevent his release, because they were reluctant to relinquish the government of Scotland; but he did not manifest any sign of displeasure for eight months. He then arrested the Duke of Albany, his two sons, and twenty-six other Scottish noblemen, during the session of the Scottish Parliament at Perth. The Duke of Albany and his sons were tried before a jury of twenty-one peers, over which the king presided; and they were convicted of treason, and were executed at Stirling.

James I. then summoned the chiefs of the Highland clans and of the Hebrides to a Parliament at Inverness in 1427. They were instantly arrested upon their arrival, and were imprisoned. Three of them were hanged immediately, and several others afterward. Others were detained in prison, and only a few were permitted to return to their estates. James I. hoped to strike terror into these barbarous chiefs by his stern proceedings, but in this he failed.

Alexander, Lord of the Isles, was of the few who were allowed to return home. He at once rallied his vassals, marched to Inverness, and destroyed that town. The king hastened to the Highlands and defeated Alexander in Lochaber. The chieftain surrendered unconditionally to the king, and was imprisoned in Tantalion Castle. His kinsman, Donald Balloch, called the Highland clans to arms and defeated the royal troops. The king thereupon led a formidable army into the Highlands, resolved to crush the power of the clans forever. Perceiving their weakness, the Highland chieftains submitted and did homage to the king.

James I. then proceeded to deprive some of the most powerful and dangerous nobles of their estates, which he conferred upon others; thus arousing the vengeance of the nobles, who formed a conspiracy against him and assassinated him in the monastery of the Black Friars at Perth, on Christmas, in 1436.

The reign of James I. was one of the most celebrated in Scottish history. The Scottish Parliaments during his reign enacted many laws for the advancement of the best interests of the Scottish people.

The king caused a collection of the statutes of his kingdom to be made, in which he set aside all laws that were obsolete and retained only those that were then in force. He established a definite standard of weights and measures, and caused the coinage of the kingdom to be regulated upon a scale which made it equal to the money of England in fineness and weight. He created the office of treasurer; caused the acts of the Scottish Parliament to be published in the language of the Scottish people; and instituted schools of archery for the purpose of training the bowmen of Scotland to be as efficient as those of England. James I. was a learned man himself and also a patron of learning. He was the famous poet-king of Scotland, and such of his poems as still remain show him to have possessed real genius.

JAMES II. was only eight years of age when he succeeded his murdered father as King of Scotland in 1436. After he had been proclaimed king a short struggle for the guardianship of the king's person ensued between the queen-mother and two others, William Crichton, the Chancellor and Governor of Edinburgh Castle, and Archibald Livingstone, Governor of Stirling Castle. The struggle was ended by the queen-mother's withdrawal and by an agreement between Chrichton and Livingstone to share between them the power which the possession of the king's person gave them.

Archibald, Earl of Douglas, the most powerful noble of Scotland at that time, possessed Galloway, Annandale and other estates in Scotland, and also the duchy of Touraine in France. He had been made lieutenant-governor of Scotland, and might easily have obtained possession of all the power in the kingdom had he so desired. He died in 1439, and his son William, a youth of seventeen, succeeded to his estates. This new Earl of Douglas maintained an almost royal state, and was accused of many acts of violence and oppression. The king's guardians resolved to get rid of him, and invited him and his brother David to visit James II. at Edinburgh. When they arrived there they were seized and were beheaded in the castle-yard after a mock trial.

The estates of the Douglas family were divided; a portion being assigned with the title to James, the grand-uncle of William and David, the male heir; while their sister Margaret obtained Galloway. At the death of James, his son William married his cousin Margaret of Galloway, thus reuniting the Douglas estates. William then proceeded to court, and there contrived to get most of the power of the government into his possession. He openly defied the king's commands; and, as he was able to put a force of five thousand of his own vassals into the field, the king dared not punish him. When King James II. once ordered William to release a prisoner whom he held unlawfully, William caused the man to be beheaded, and then notified the king that he could have the body.

When James II., upon coming of age, assumed the government of Scotland, he resolved to get rid of William Douglas, whom he invited to Stirling, receiving him cordially. The king then urged the earl to break off his "bonds," or alliances with the Highland chiefs, which menaced the power of the Scottish crown. As Douglas refused, the king stabbed him. The wounded earl fell, and was killed with a pole-ax by Sir Patrick Gray, one of the king's attendants.

James Douglas, the brother and heir of the murdered Earl William, cast off his allegiance to King James II. and took up arms against him, being joined by the Earls of Ross and Crawford. As the king was too weak to defeat the rebels in the field he undertook to break up their union by diplomacy, in which he was so successful that he defeated James Douglas in the battle of Arkinholm in 1454 and forced him to take refuge in England.

The Scottish Parliament passed an act of forfeiture against the fugititve Douglas, and Galloway and certain other estates of the exiled earl were declared inalienable possessions of the Scottish crown. Most of the remainder of the Douglas estates was conferred upon the Earl of Angus, the head of the Red Douglases, the rivals of the Black Douglases. Some of the former possessions of the Black Douglases were bestowed upon Sir James Hamilton. These vigorous measures humbled the proud family of Douglas, and firmly established the royal power in Scotland.

James II. took part in the Wars of the Roses in England on the side of the House of Lancaster, and sought to take advantage of the occasion to recover from the English the towns which they still held in Scotland. He besieged Roxburgh, and was killed by the bursting of a cannon while directing the operations, A. D. 1460. After his death Roxburgh was taken and destroyed. This was the first siege in which the Scots used artillery.

JAMES III. was only eight years of age at the time of his father's death. The Bishop of St. Andrews governed the Scottish kingdom for six years as regent. At his death, Lord Boyd obtained the regency and possession of the king's person. In 1469 James III. was married to Margaret, daughter of King Christian I. of Denmark and Norway. As security for her dowry, the Orkney and Shetland Isles were placed by Norway in the care of Scotland. As the dowry was never paid, the islands remained in the possession of the Scots and became a part of the Scottish kingdom.

James III. now turned upon the Boyds and punished them for their seizure of his person by executing the regent's younger son and confiscating the family estates, which were now declared the inalienable possessions of the Scottish crown. Lord Boyd and his eldest son, the Earl of Arran, escaped to England. The king's brother, the Duke of Albany, being suspected of conspiring against James III., was arrested and imprisoned in Edinburgh Castle. He escaped to France, whence he went to England.

King Edward IV. of England agreed to aid him to dethrone James III., and the Douglases and the Lord of the Isles pledged themselves to support the English monarch. James III. declared war against England, placed himself at the head of a large army, and advanced as far as the Lauder. There the Scottish nobles, under the leadership of the Earl of Angus, resolving to get rid of certain of the king's favorites who had incurred their hostility, seized them and hanged them over Lauder bridge, in spite of the king's entreaties. This ended the expedition, and the nobles returned in triumph to Edinburgh, with the king a virtual prisoner in their possession, A. D. 1482.

The Duke of Albany returned to Scotland soon afterward and obtained the release of his brother, King James III. The two brothers lived together amicably for a while, until the Duke of Albany went back to England. Before he left Scotland he showed his treasonable design by placing Dunbar Castle in the possession of the English. The king's unpopularity continued increasing; and the Lowland nobles conspired against him, raised a large army, and proclaimed his son king in his stead. James III. was defeated in the battle of Sauchieburn, and fled from the field, being thrown from his horse during his flight and carried to a mill at Bannockburn, where he was assassinated by some unknown person, A. D. 1488.

The assassination of James III. left the government of Scotland in the hands of the rebellious nobles; and the murdered king's son, JAMES IV., ascended the Scottish throne, at the age of sixteen years. For the next few years the victorious nobles governed the Scottish kingdom for him. When James IV. became of age and assumed the government he soon gave evidence of being an able and vigorous ruler. He maintained a splendid court, and promoted the civilization of his subjects. He constantly sought to curb the power of the Lowland nobles and the Highland chiefs, and to increase the royal authority. This aroused the animosity of some of his nobles, and they laid plans to make him a prisoner.

Henry VII. of England, who was prevented by the condition of affairs in his own kingdom from making open war against

Scotland, secretly encouraged the conspiracies of the Scottish nobles against their king. Upon discovering this, James IV. retaliated by espousing the cause of Perkin Warbeck, whom he welcomed at his court as Richard, Duke of York, the son of King Edward IV. The Scottish king gave Warbeck his relative, Lady Catharine Gordon, in marriage, and led an army in his behalf into England. James IV. finally grew tired of Warbeck, sent him off to Ireland, and renewed the truce with Henry VII. In 1502 James IV. married Margaret, the eldest daughter of Henry VII.

For the purpose of curbing the power of the Highlanders and the Lord of the Isles, James IV. placed royal garrisons in the castles and fortresses of that portion of his kingdom and erected other strongholds. He was unable to carry the plan as far as he desired, and thus resorted to the policy of using the feuds of the Highland chieftains as a means of destroying them. The Earl of Huntly, the head of the Gordon family, was made Sheriff of Inverness, Ross and Caithness, on condition that he erected and maintained a castle at Inverness. The Earl of Argyle, the head of the Campbells, was assigned the task of maintaining order in the Hebrides. James IV. also endeavored to divide the islands into sheriffdoms.

The Highland clans rallied under Donald Dhu, an illegitimate descendant of the last Lord of the Isles, to resist the king's measures. After a struggle of three years, Donald Dhu was brought a prisoner to Edinburgh, and was deprived of his Lordship of the Isles, his dominions being confiscated to the Scottish crown, A. D. 1504.

In 1513 James IV. unwisely renewed the old alliance between Scotland and France, and declared war against Henry VIII. of England. He led a splendid army across the border into England, but committed so many blunders that he wholly destroyed every prospect of success, and was defeated and slain by the English army under the Earl of Surrey ir the battle of Flodden Field, September 9, 1513. The flower of the Scottish nobility perished with their king on this fatal field, and all Scotland was plunged into mourning.

James IV. was one of the most popular of the Scottish kings, and his reign was one of the most prosperous that Scotland had ever known. Trade improved rapidly, and the exports of Scotland to other countries vastly increased. In the reign of James IV. the art of printing was introduced into Scotland, and the first printing-press was set up by Walter Chapman under the king's patronage.

SECTION VII.—THE SCANDINAVIAN KINGDOMS.

WHILE the Northmen from Scandinavia were committing their ravages throughout Europe, the three Scandinavian kingdoms took their rise. Denmark was founded by Gorm the Old, and Norway by Harald Fairhair, about A. D. 875; while Sweden was founded by the royal race of the Ynglingar about A. D. 900.

KINGDOM OF DENMARK.

GORM THE OLD, who reigned over Denmark from 860 to 936, ravaged the northern coast of Germany with fire and sword, plundered Charlemagne's chapel at Aix la Chapelle, took part in the first siege of Paris by the Northmen in 885, and was overwhelmingly beaten by the German king Arnulf in the battle of Louvain in 891.

During Gorm's absence on his inroads into Germany and France, his kingdom was ruled by his queen, Thyra, a woman of more than ordinary vigor of mind. Gorm the Old was a fierce pagan, but Thyra was favorably disposed toward Christianity. She caused the immense rampart of the Dannevirke to be erected across the peninsula of Denmark at the southern end of Schleswig. This rampart was eight miles long and from forty-five to seventy feet high, and was intended to protect Denmark from German invasions.

On the death of Gorm the Old, in 936, his son HARALD BLUETOOTH became King of Denmark. Harald Bluetooth was a cruel and crafty king, and by treachery he succeeded in making Norway tributary to him for a time, but Norway soon regained its independence. Harald Bluetooth professed Christianity, and was baptized, along with his wife and his son Sweyn, by a German monk named Poppa, who also converted a considerable portion of the Danish people. Harald Bluetooth led several expeditions to France to aid young Richard the Fearless, Duke of Normandy.

Harald Bluetooth lost his life in battle in 985, and was succeeded on the throne of Denmark by his son SWEYN I., who invaded England in 994, during the reign of Ethelred the Unready, and conquered a large portion of that kingdom. This conquest occupied some years, and in 1014 Sweyn I. died at Gainesborough, in England. Though Sweyn had been baptized in childhood, he relapsed from Christianity into paganism when he attained maturer years.

Sweyn I. left two sons. One of these was HARALD II., who was elected King of Denmark. The other was CANUTE THE GREAT, who was then but fourteen years of age, and was assigned the crown of England. Canute the Great soon conquered the whole of England. Upon the death of Harald II., in 1018, Canute the Great also became King of Denmark. Canute the Great had been converted to Christianity in England, and he abolished the worship of Odin in Denmark, making Christianity the state religion. Canute the Great resided chiefly in England, and his reign belongs more to English than to Danish history. He conquered Sweden in 1025 and Norway in 1027, so that before his death he wore the crowns of four kingdoms, and had founded a great Scandinavian empire.

Canute the Great died in 1036, at the age of thirty-six years; and was succeeded on the throne of Denmark by HARDICANUTE, his son by his second wife, and on the throne of England by HARALD HAREFOOT, his son by his first wife. On the death of Harald Harefoot, in 1039, Hardicanute also became King of England, after which he passed most of his time in that kingdom.

Upon the death of Hardicanute, in 1041, MAGNUS THE GOOD, King of Norway, obtained the crown of Denmark. This was a great gain for the Danes, who enjoyed the benefits of the wise rule of Magnus the Good for five years. On the death of Magnus the Good, in 1047, SWEYN II., the nephew of Canute the Great, became King of Denmark, so that the crowns of Denmark and Norway were again separated.

Harald Hardrada, King of Norway, sought to defeat this arrangement, and for seventeen years he maintained a constant war with Denmark, inflicting great suffering upon that kingdom, until peace was made in 1064. Sweyn II. was a good sovereign and a good man, and his reign was one of great prosperity for Denmark. In 1069 he endeavored to wrest England from William the Conqueror, but failed. This was the last of the Danish attempts upon England. Sweyn II. was an ardent friend of Pope Gregory VII. (Hildebrand), with whom he maintained a constant correspondence; but when Gregory VII. ordered this Danish king to acknowledge himself a vassal of the Pope he refused to do so and resolutely maintained the independence of Denmark.

Sweyn II. died in 1076, and five of his fourteen sons reigned over Denmark in succession. The eldest of these, HARALD THE SIMPLE, reigned from 1076 to 1080; CANUTE IV., from 1080 to 1086; OLAF THE HUNGRY, from 1086 to 1095; ERIK THE GOOD, from 1095 to 1103; and NIELS, from 1103 to 1134. The reigns of these five kings were distracted by internal dissensions.

The death of Niels was followed by a troublesome period, during which Denmark was successively ruled by ERIK HAREFOOT, from 1135 to 1137; ERIK THE LAMB, from 1137 to 1147; SWEYN III. and CANUTE V., from 1147 to 1154; and Sweyn III. alone, from 1154 to 1157.

This distracted period was ended when WALDEMAR THE GREAT became King of Denmark, in 1157. This sovereign found his kingdom poor, without an army and in great distress; but he left it a prosperous, well-defended and busy nation. He achieved great victories over the heathen Wends and Esthonians, on the southern and eastern shores of the Baltic, compelling them to accept Christianity. Waldemar the Great died in 1182, and was succeeded by his son, CANUTE THE PIOUS, who reduced all of Pomerania and a part of Eastern Prussia under the dominion of Denmark.

On the death of Canute the Pious, in 1202, his brother, WALDEMAR THE CONQUEROR, became his successor. Waldemar the Conqueror was one of Denmark's greatest kings. He conquered and annexed the whole of Pomerania, and in 1217 the German Emperor granted to him and his successors all the territories north of the Elbe and the Elde, thus making Waldemar the Conqueror the actual master of most of Northern Germany.

With the sanction of Pope Honorius III., Waldemar the Conqueror undertook to compel the Esthonians to embrace Christianity in 1219, undertaking this task with an army of sixty thousand men and a fleet of fourteen hundred ships. He soon overran all of Esthonia, forcing many of the inhabitants to accept baptism. The Livonian Knights of the Sword bitterly opposed this Danish conversion of Esthonia, declaring that they alone had the right to convert the heathen of that region to Christianity. These knights took up arms to drive out the Danes, and in the several battles which followed between the contending forces the Danes were generally the victors.

When Waldemar the Conquerer returned from Esthonia to Denmark he seemed to be at the height of his power and greatness; but in 1223, while sleeping in his tent during a hunting expedition, he was seized, gagged and bound, along with his eldest son, Prince Waldemar, by Count Henry of Schwerin, who conveyed his captives in a swift sailing vessel to Germany and imprisoned them in a dungeon in the Castle of Danneberg, in Hanover. Waldemar the Conqueror and his son were detained in this shameful captivity for several years, and were only released upon the payment of a ransom of forty-five thousand silver marks.

Waldemar the Conqueror's vast empire fell to pieces during his captivity, his German provinces reverting to the dominion of their Emperor. Waldemar was unable to avenge himself upon Count Henry of Schwerin, and he applied himself to the improvement of his kingdom. In 1241 he gave Demark her first uniform code of laws —a code which remained in force for almost four and a half centuries, and was not wholly abolished even then. Waldemar the Conqueror died three days after the Danish Diet had adopted his code, at the age of seventy-one years, A. D. 1241.

As Prince Waldemar had died before his father, Waldemar the Conqueror's second son, ERIK IV., succeeded his father on the throne of Denmark. Eric IV. was assassinated in 1251 by his brother ABEL, Duke of Schleswig, who then acquired the Danish crown. During Abel's short reign of less than two years, the burgher class were first allowed representation in the *Danehof*, the yearly national assembly of Denmark. The burghers were also then granted important municipal privileges which they had not previously enjoyed. King Abel was assassinated in 1252 by a man whom he had wronged, and was succeeded by his brother CHRISTOPHER I.

On the death of Christopher I., in 1259, his son ERIK GLIPPING, a child of ten years, became King of Denmark. On the death of Erik Glipping, in 1286, his son ERIK MENVED, also a child of ten years, succeeded to the Danish throne, and reigned until his death in 1319. Under Erik Glipping and Erik Menved the royal power in Denmark rapidly declined, and the Hanseatic League dictated the terms upon which

WALDEMAR ATTERDAG SACKING A SWEDISH TOWN.

the Danes should engage in the fisheries.

Upon the death of Erik Menved, in 1319, his brother CHRISTOPHER II. ascended the throne of Denmark. After electing Christopher II. king, the Danish nobles compelled him to sign a charter rendering them almost independent of the Danish crown and entirely exempting them from royal taxation, thus reducing vastly the royal revenues.

The efforts of Christopher II. to release himself from these hard conditions involved his kingdom in many civil wars. In 1325 the Danish nobles obtained the assistance of Count Gerhard of Holstein, who defeated Christopher II. and induced the Danes to dethrone their king. Count Gerhard then made his nephew, WALDEMAR of Schleswig, King of Denmark; but Count Gerhard was himself the real ruler of Denmark for fourteen years (A. D. 1326-1340), greatly oppressing the Danish people and thus incurring their bitter hatred. The deposed Christopher II. failed in many efforts to recover his throne, and died in 1332.

In 1340 Count Gerhard of Holstein was assassinated in the midst of his nobles and his troops by a Jutlander of rank named Niels Ebbesön. The Jutlanders instantly rallied under this intrepid leader and drove the German troops from Denmark. Count Henry of Holstein, Gerhard's son and successor, took up arms to avenge his father's murder, and defeated the Danes in the battle of Skandersborg, in which Niels Ebbesön was slain. Count Henry then retired to Holstein with his troops, leaving the Danes to manage their own affairs.

The Danish nobles elected WALDEMAR ATTERDAG, the youngest son of Christopher II., King of Denmark. Waldemar Atterdag revived the power and credit of the Danish kingdom, and was successful in a war with the Hanseatic League. Desiring to secure the marriage of his daughter Margaret with the Crown Prince of Sweden and Norway, he seized the Princess Elizabeth of Holstein Gottorp, who was betrothed to that prince, and detained her in captivity until he had effected his daughter's marriage with the heir to the Swedish throne. This proceeding involved Waldemar Atterdag in a war with the Counts of Holstein, who formed an alliance with the Hanseatic League and some of the German princes against the Danish king. Waldemar Atterdag was defeated with the loss of a large part of his kingdom, and was obliged to flee from Denmark in 1368. The Hanseatic League managed the affairs of Denmark for four years, but permitted Waldemar Atterdag to return to the Danish throne in 1372 on condition that the Hanseatic League should have a voice in the election of the Danish kings in the future.

Waldemar Atterdag died in 1375, whereupon the Danish nobles chose to the Danish throne OLAF V., the son of Margaret, Queen of Sweden and Norway, Waldemar Atterdag's daughter. Upon the death of Olaf V., in 1387, at the age of seventeen, the Danish nobles elected his mother MARGARET, "the Semiramis of the North," to the throne of Denmark. Soon afterward Margaret was crowned Queen of Norway, thus uniting Denmark and Norway under one crown.

KINGDOM OF NORWAY.

HARALD HARFAGER, or HARALD FAIRHAIR, the founder of the Kingdom of Norway, reigned from A. D. 863 to 933. The high-spirited Norse chieftains whom he reduced under his dominion could not endure their subjugation, and embarked with their followers in piratical expeditions against the coasts of all Europe.

Upon Harald Fairhair's death, in 933, his son ERIK THE CRUEL became King of Norway, and reigned five years. Exasperated by his tyranny, his subjects rose against him in 938 and drove him from Norway, after which they conferred the Norwegian crown upon his brother HAKON THE GOOD, who had been educated in England at the court of King Athelstan, from which circumstance he was called "Athelstan's foster son." Hakon the Good was a wise and good monarch, and the Norwegian people justly cherish his memory to this day. He gave Norway a code of laws, and also endeavored to introduce Christianity into his kingdom, but his subjects were staunch pagans, and it required three centuries for their conversion. The sons of Erik the Cruel, aided by Denmark, made repeated efforts to seize the Norwegian crown; and Hakon the Good lost his life in battle with them in 963.

ERIK GRAAFELL, Erik the Cruel's son, and his cousin, HAKON JARL, divided Norway between them until Hakon Jarl's death, in 995, when the Norwegians revolted, and placed OLAF TRYGVÆSON on the throne of Norway. Olaf Trygvæson is one of the great heroes of Norwegian romance, and his exploits constitute a fruitful theme for the songs of poets. He destroyed the pagan temples, and founded the city of Drontheim. He was defeated by the Danes in a great naval battle in the year A. D. 1000, and when all was lost he sprang overboard in full armor to escape capture, and was drowned. For the next fifteen years Norway suffered severely from Danish and Swedish attacks.

OLAF THE SAINT drove out the Danish and Swedish oppressors of Norway in 1015, thus restoring the independence and unity of Norway. Olaf the Saint completed the establishment of the Christian religion in Norway, but accomplished this result in so harsh and cruel a manner that all classes of his subjects were aroused against him. In 1027 Canute the Great of Denmark and England invaded Norway, defeated Olaf the Saint and drove him from his kingdom, and annexed Norway to his own dominions. Olaf the Saint afterward returned and made an effort to recover the Norwegian crown, but was defeated and slain in the battle of Stikklestad.

Canute the Great then assigned Norway to his son SWEYN II.; but in 1035 Sweyn II. was driven out by MAGNUS THE BASTARD, the illegitimate son of Olaf the Saint. Magnus the Bastard lost his life in battle with the Danes in 1047, and was succeeded on the throne of Norway by his uncle HARALD HARDRADA, who inflicted great suffering upon Denmark in a war of seventeen years. In 1066 Harald Hardrada invaded England for the purpose of wresting that kingdom from Harold, the last of its Saxon kings, but was defeated and killed in the battle of Stamford Bridge, in Yorkshire, September 25, 1066.

OLAF III., the eldest son of Harald Hardrada, then became King of Norway. His reign was peaceful and prosperous, and he won the affection of his subjects. He endeavored to introduce European civilization into his kingdom. Olaf III. died in 1093, and was succeeded on the throne of Norway by his son MAGNUS BAREFOOT, who invaded and conquered the Isle of Man, the Hebrides, the Orkneys and the Shetlands. Magnus Barefoot also invaded Ireland, but was defeated and killed in battle with the Irish, A. D. 1103.

Upon the death of Magnus Barefoot the Norwegians made his three sons, EJSTEN I., SIGURD I. and OLAF IV., joint Kings of Norway. Olaf IV. died when a child, and Ejsten I. followed him in 1123, leaving Sigurd I. sole sovereign. Sigurd I. is one of the great heroes of Norway. He fought against the Moors, made a pilgrimage to Jerusalem and there joined his arms with those of King Baldwin, and captured and plundered Sidon.

After the death of Sigurd I., in 1130, Norway was afflicted with anarchy and civil war for fifty-four years, various princes contending for the Norwegian crown. MAGNUS IV. and HARALD IV., the sons of Sigurd I., first rent the kingdom with turmoil. In 1136 SIGURD II., INGE I., EJSTEN II., HAKON III. and MAGNUS V. claimed the sovereignty.

SVERRE restored order and tranquillity to Norway in 1184. He pretended to be a son of Sigurd II., but was generally believed to be the son of a brushmaker. On Sverre's death, in 1202, his only son, HAKON III., became King of Norway. Hakon III. died in 1204, and was succeeded on the Norwegian throne by GUTHRUM, a grandson of Sverre. Guthrum was a mere child, and died after a reign of a few months; after which the Norwegian crown passed to INGE BAARDSEN, a nephew of Sverre.

Inge Baardsen's entire reign was passed in civil wars with rival claimants for the Norwegian crown.

Upon Inge Baardsen's death, in 1217, HAKON IV., the son of Hakon III., ascended the throne of Norway. Hakon IV. was a wise and powerful monarch, and conquered Iceland in 1261. He made an effort to subdue Scotland in 1262, but was defeated in a battle at the mouth of the Clyde, and soon afterward died in the Orkneys. MAGNUS VI., the son and successor of Hakon IV., sold the Hebrides to Scotland; and his son Erik married the daughter of the Scottish king, Alexander III. Magnus VI. was a good king, and greatly improved the laws of Norway.

On the death of Magnus VI., in 1280, his son ERIK THE PRIEST-HATER became King of Norway. Erik the Priest-hater died in 1299; and, as he left no sons, he was succeeded by his only brother HAKON V., who was a good sovereign, and so won the affections of his subjects that at his death in 1319 they conferred the crown of Norway on MAGNUS SMÆK, King of Sweden, who was the son of Ingeborg, the daughter of Hakon V., by her marriage with Erik, the brother of one of the previous Kings of Sweden.

In 1350 Magnus Smæk abdicated the crown of Norway in favor of his second son HAKON VI., who had married Margaret of Denmark. Upon the death of Hakon VI., in 1380, his son OLAF V., Olaf II. of Denmark, became King of Norway, under the regency of his mother Margaret. Upon the death of Olaf V., in 1387, MARGARET of Denmark also became Queen of Norway.

Norway had steadily declined since the death of Hakon VI. in 1380. The kingdom was exhausted by the constant wars with Denmark, and the monopoly of trade which the Hanseatic League enjoyed interfered with the industry of the Norwegian people. The Black Plague, which spread over Europe in 1348, scourged the kingdom for two years, destroying more than two-thirds of its people; and Norway did not recover from its effects for centuries.

KINGDOM OF SWEDEN.

The authentic history of Sweden begins with OLAF THE LAP-KING, who began to reign A. D. 993, and who received his surname from the circumstance that he had received the homage of his princes while he was an infant in his mother's arms. St. Ansgar, "the Apostle of the North," had introduced Christianity into Sweden in 829; but it had made slow progress. Olaf the Lap-king embraced the new religion and founded a bishopric at Skara, but he could not induce his subjects to accept Christianity, and they continued pagans for over a century longer.

Olaf the Lap-king died in 1024, and was succeeded as King of Sweden by his son EDMUND COLBRENNER, who died in 1052, when his brother EDMUND SLEMME ascended the Swedish throne. Edmund Slemme was the last of the Upsala line of Swedish sovereigns, and died in 1055. His reign was mainly signalized by a great persecution of the Christians.

After the death of Edmund Slemme, in 1055, a fierce war broke out between the Goths and the Swedes, the two chief races in the kingdom; and the Goths succeeded in placing STENKIL, one of their own chiefs, upon the Swedish throne as King of the Goths and the Swedes. Stenkil was a Christian. Anarchy prevailed in the Swedish kingdom for the next century, and the period was signalized by the incessant struggles between the Swedes and the Goths. Stenkil's successors on the Swedish throne were HALSTAN, from 1066 to 1090; INGO THE GREAT, from 1090 to 1112; PHILIP, from 1112 to 1118; and INGO II., from 1118 to 1135.

SVERKER I., a Christian, became King of Sweden in 1135. He made great exertions for the establishment of Christianity in his kingdom, and erected many churches and monasteries. He restored order and prosperity to Sweden, and vastly improved the administration of justice. Sverker I. died in 1155, and was succeeded on the Swedish throne by his cousin ERIK THE SAINT, who improved the laws of his kingdom and promoted the spread of Christianity. Erik the Saint conquered a large portion of Finland and forced it to accept the Christian religion. He died in 1160.

During the reigns of CHARLES SVERKERSSON (A. D. 1160-1167), CANUTE ERICSSON (A. D. 1167-1195), SVERKER II. (A. D. 1195-1210), ERIK CANUTESSON (A. D. 1210 -1216), JOHN SVERKERSSON (A. D. 1216-1222), and ERIK LÆSPE (A. D. 1222-1250) Christianity spread rapidly in Sweden, and the clergy became the most powerful order in the kingdom. During this entire period of ninety years the only things to record in the affairs of Sweden are the dissensions, civil wars and assassinations of kings, and the disorder and misery of the entire kingdom. The Benedictine monks were the only class of men who did anything to lessen these evils, and many of them had come from England. These zealous men first taught the Swedes how to till the soil and plant gardens, to prepare salt, to build and work water-mills, and to make roads and bridges.

A more certain period of Swedish history commenced in 1250. WALDEMAR, the son of the chief of the powerful family of the Folkungar, was elected King of Sweden; and with him began the dynasty of the Folkungar. Waldemar died in 1275, and was succeeded on the Swedish throne by his brother, MAGNUS BARNLOCK, so called because he protected the granaries of his subjects from the rapacity of the nobles. He was a wise king, and greatly increased the royal power. After the death of Magnus Barnlock, in 1290, a long period of civil war ensued between his three sons.

MAGNUS SMÆK, the grandson of Magnus Barnlock, became King of Sweden in 1319, at the age of only three years. In 1320 he became King of Norway by right of his mother. He afterward married his son Hakon to Margaret of Denmark, as already noticed, and placed him on the throne of Norway. As the three Scandinavian kingdoms were now so closely allied, Magnus Smæk undertook to abolish the Swedish Senate. but was dethroned; and in 1363 ALBERT of Mecklenburg was elected King of Sweden.

THE UNION OF CALMAR.

We have now reached an important epoch in the history of the three Scandinavian kingdoms. Queen Margaret of Denmark and Norway, "the Semiramis of the North," was one of the most remarkable women in history. She was a wise and good sovereign to both Denmark and Norway, and greatly endeared herself to her subjects. She adopted as her heir Erik of Pomerania, the grandson of her sister Ingeborg, and earnestly sought to render him worthy of his destiny. She made peace with her old enemies, and maintained good order among her subjects, winning both nobles and peasants to her side. She proceeded from castle to castle, and received the homage and faithful service of the great. She went from province to province, and looked well into matters of law and of right, until all obeyed and served her. Justice was done in her two kingdoms; and even the high-born sea-robbers, who had plagued the kingdoms and defied the laws for so long a period, were seized with terror and were glad to come forward and give surety in money for their future good behavior.

Not satisfied with her two kingdoms of Denmark and Norway, Margaret also claimed the crown of Sweden in right of her husband. In 1389 she invaded that kingdom and defeated its king, Albert of Mecklenburg, and kept him a prisoner for six years. She assumed the government of Sweden immediately after her victory. In 1397 she proclaimed an act of union, known as the *Union of Calmar*, uniting the three Scandinavian kingdoms under one scepter, the king to be elected conjointly by the three nations. On this occasion Margaret caused her grandnephew, ERIK of Pomerania, to be crowned with great state at Calmar as King of Denmark, Norway and Sweden.

After the Union of Calmar the Norwegians entirely lost their independence, and the Danish influence became supreme in Norway. The Norwegian nobles were de-

MARGARET OF DENMARK.

stroyed as an order, and were obliged to give way to Danish immigrants. For several centuries after Margaret, Norway had no separate existence, being little more than a province of Denmark.

The Union of Calmar was distasteful to the Swedes, but remained in force for more than a century. This union might have been productive of good to the three Scandinavian kingdoms if Margaret's successors had been as good and as just as she had been. It was true, as Margaret said, that each one of the three kingdoms alone was a poor, weak state, exposed to danger on all sides, but that the three united would make a monarchy sufficiently strong to defy the attacks and schemes of the Hanseatic League and all foes from the side of Germany, and would keep the Baltic clear of danger from foreigners. But none of Margaret's successors were equal to her, as none of her predecessors could be compared to her. After Margaret's sudden death, in 1412, Erik remained sole sovereign of Scandinavia.

Erik was a weak and incompetent monarch. During Margaret's last years he had exhibited signs of incapacity, but her abilities had saved him from the consequences of his blunders. He devoted his chief energies to the conquest of Holstein, but his operations were generally unsuccessful. He married Philippa, the daughter of King Henry IV. of England, and her abilities had much to do with prolonging his reign.

In 1435 the Swedes rose against Erik to resist his oppression of them, and in 1439 a council of state declared him deposed in Sweden. The Danes followed the example of the Swedes by deposing Erik in Denmark. Erik was then absent in the island of Gothland, and sought to return to Denmark, but was not permitted to land, and died in 1459, poor and neglected.

CHRISTOPHER III., the son of the Duke of Bavaria and the nephew of Erik, was elected King of Denmark, and was crowned the same year, A. D. 1439. In 1442 he was also proclaimed King of Sweden and Norway. He died in 1448, and CHARLES CANUTESSON became King of Sweden.

3—42.-U. H.

The Danish nobles then conferred the crown of Denmark on Count Christian of Oldenburg, a descendant of the ancient Danish kings, with the title of CHRISTIAN I. He married the widow of Christopher III., and was readily acknowledged king by the Danes, thus establishing the House of Oldenburg, which has ever since occupied the throne of Denmark. In 1450 Christian I. was crowned King of Norway, and he also claimed the crown of Sweden and strove hard to obtain it, but was unable to obtain a firm footing in that country. In 1469 Christian I. married his daughter Margaret to the young King James III. of Scotland, and ceded the Orkney and Shetland Isles to that kingdom in lieu of her dowry.

Christian I. died in 1481, and was succeeded by his eldest son JOHN, who only obtained the crown of Denmark by making hard terms with the Danish nobles, with whom he was unpopular. John failed in his efforts to obtain the crown of Sweden; but he defeated the Lübeck traders, and greatly restrained the insolence of the Hanseatic League. John died in 1513, and was succeeded on the thrones of Denmark and Norway by his only son, CHRISTIAN II.

After the death of Charles Canutesson, in 1471, Sweden came under the government of STENO STURE I., a valiant and sagacious ruler, who curbed the insolence of the Swedish nobles, elevated the peasant and burgher classes, founded the University of Upsala, and invited learned men and printers from other countries into Sweden. Steno Sture I. governed Sweden with almost absolute power, and died in 1504. His second successor, STENO STURE II., who became ruler of Sweden in 1512, quarreled with the Archbishop of Upsala; whereupon the tyrannical Christian II. of Denmark reëstablished the Danish supremacy over Sweden, Steno Sture II. being defeated and mortally wounded in battle, A. D. 1520; but the cruel massacre of ninety-four Swedish nobles at Stockholm led to Sweden's liberation by the valiant Gustavus Vasa in 1523, of which we shall give a more full account in a subsequent part of this volume.

SECTION VIII.—RUSSIA, OR MUSCOVY.

N A. D. 862 RURIK, a Varangian or pirate chief of the Norman or Scandinavian tribe of Russ, received the invitation of the people of the powerful commercial city of Novgorod, on Lake Ilmen, the capital of a Slavonic principality, to become their ruler. Rurik accepted the invitation and founded the *Grand Duchy of Great Russia*, with Novgorod for its capital. This Norman Varangian chieftain is therefore considered the founder of the Russian Empire.

The Slavic cities of Novgorod and Kiev had each already for several centuries been the capital of an independent Slavic principality. Novgorod had become so powerful that it was commonly said among its neighbors: "Who can resist God and the Great Novgorod!" Kelly says that its commerce extended to Persia and even to India, and from Constantinople to Vineta, a commercial city at the mouth of the Oder. The surrounding nations were its tributaries, from Lithuania to the Ural mountains, and from Bielo Ozero and Lake Rostof to the White Sea. The most active commerce of Novgorod was carried on through the Baltic, for a long time held by the Russian Varangians, a Scandinavian tribe of warriors, who several times reduced Novgorod to tribute.

The old Russian chronicle says that Rurik and his two brothers were invited to serve as auxiliaries of the republic of Novgorod for its defense against foreign aggression. After accepting the invitation the three brothers established themselves on the three principal frontiers of the republic—Rurik at Old Ladoga, near the Volkhof; Sinaf at Bielo Ozero, on the northern bank of the lake of the same name; and Truvor at Izborsk, near Pleskof. These positions enabled the Varangian princes to secure the republic against external attacks and likewise to extend their power over it, as they held the chief outlets of its foreign trade. Novgorod was obliged to submit to Rurik and his brothers to save its commerce; and in A. D. 864 Rurik took peaceable possession of this city of wooden huts and barbarian traders, and established his authority over its territories.

As Rurik's two brothers died childless, his rule was undisputed. He was joined by hordes of his Scandinavian countrymen, and bestowed upon them the other Slavic cities, one of his followers taking possession of Kiev, which traded with Constantinople. Rurik gave his Slavonic subjects Scandinavian laws, reigned fifteen years at Novgorod, and died in 879.

As Igor, Rurik's son, was a child four years of age at the time of his father's death, Rurik bequeathed his crown to his cousin OLEG, whom he appointed guardian of his son. This was a wise choice, as Oleg proved to be a great sovereign and a great conqueror. He was also a faithful guardian of the young prince, and while he held the crown of Great Russia during his life-time he was careful to secure the succession of Igor.

Oleg vastly extended the Russian dominion. He took Smolensk in 882; and shortly afterward he seized Kiev by a bold stratagem, and made that city one of the capitals of his empire. Kiev had previously been converted to Christianity, and Oleg wisely tolerated and protected that religion, though he was himself a pagan. He next conquered the region between Novgorod and Kiev, thus uniting his two capitals; after which he subdued the Khazars, a Turanian nation that had established a powerful kingdom between the Dnieper and the Caspian Sea in the seventh and eighth centuries. Oleg then drove the Magyars beyond the Russian frontiers into the valleys of the Theiss and the Middle Danube, where their descendants still remain, and firmly established his authority in the conquered lands.

Oleg had always desired to extend his dominion at the expense of the Eastern Roman Empire. When he had settled the domestic affairs of his kingdom he descended the Dnieper to the Black Sea with an army of eighty thousand men and a fleet of nine hundred galleys, and attacked Constantinople, fixing his shield on the gate of that city as a trophy, and compelling the Greek Emperor to agree to a humiliating treaty and to pay an immense ransom; after which he returned to Kiev with a vast amount of booty, A. D. 911.

Karamsin, the great Russian historian, says that Oleg "is to be regarded as the founder of the empire's greatness, for to him it owes its finest and richest provinces. Rurik's sway extended from Esthonia, the Slav sources, and the Volkhof, to Bielo Ozero, the mouth of the Oka, and the city of Rostof. Oleg subjugated all the countries from Smolensk to the Sula, the Dniester, and probably to the Carpathian mountains."

Oleg died in 913, after a reign of thirty-three years, and was succeeded on the Russian throne by IGOR, Rurik's son. Igor was thirty-eight years old at his accession, and proved to be an able sovereign. At the beginning of his reign the Drevlians, encouraged by Oleg's death, revolted against Russian rule, but were reduced to submission by Igor, who likewise conquered the Petchenegs, who occupied the Black Sea coast from the mouths of the Danube to the mouths of the Dnieper.

Igor led an expedition against Constantinople in 941, but was driven back with the loss of two-thirds of his force. He was not discouraged by this reverse, but prepared to avenge it, and for this purpose he led a second expedition against the Greek capital in 944. His march was stayed at the mouths of the Danube by the Greek Emperor's offers to pay him the same tribute that Oleg had received. Igor accepted the offer, and concluded a treaty with the Emperor Constantine VIII, in 945, similar to the treaty which Oleg had imposed upon the Emperor.

Igor was now an old man, and desired to pass the remainder of his life in peace, but the insatiable cupidity of his followers obliged him to undertake new wars, one being with the Drevlians, whom he plundered without mercy. They surprised him near Korosten and massacred him and his entire guard, A. D. 945.

SVIATOSLAF, Igor's only son, and the first sovereign bearing a Russian name, was very young at the time of his father's death; and the government fell into the possession of Olga, Igor's widow, who acted as regent for her son. Olga took a frightful vengeance on the Drevlians for the murder of her husband, but her rule was as wise as it was firm in other respects.

Thus far Kiev was the only part of Russia that had been converted to Christianity, and the Christians had been protected in their civil and religious privileges. Olga now embraced the Christian religion, and proceeded to Constantinople in 955, where she was baptized by the Patriarch of the Greek Church with great pomp, receiving the Greek name of Helena. Few of Olga's subjects followed her example. She earnestly entreated her son to be baptized, but he replied: "Would you have me be a laughing-stock to my friends?" He sternly refused to be baptized, though he offered no opposition to those who desired to espouse the faith of Christ, for which he openly expressed his contempt, saying that as Christianity taught love and forgiveness it was a religion fit only for women, and not for warriors.

Sviatoslaf achieved victories over the Khazars, and those people disappeared from Russian history thereafter. He also subdued the Petchenegs and the Bulgarians, and extended his dominion to the Sea of Azov. In 970 he divided his empire among his three sons, giving Kiev to Yaropolk I., the country of the Drevlians to Oleg, and Novgorod to Vladimir.

Soon afterward Sviatoslaf undertook another war against the Bulgarians, and quickly overran their country. The Greek Emperor became alarmed at the proximity of the Russians to Constantinople, and summoned the Grand Duke of Great Russia to evacuate the territories which he had conquered. The Grand Duke's refusal to comply with this demand led to war. The Russians were defeated in every battle, and were obliged to sue for peace. They retired from Bulgaria and started for Kiev; but Sviatoslaf was waylaid by the Petchenegs, while passing through their country, being murdered near the cataracts of the Dnieper, A. D. 972.

After the death of Sviatoslaf a war ensued between his three sons. Oleg was killed, and Vladimir fled across the Baltic sea to the Varangians, so that all the Russian dominions were reunited under YAROPOLK I. But Vladimir never relinquished his design of recovering his lost power; and in 980, after an absence of two years, he returned with a horde of Varangian adventurers, conquered Novgorod and Kiev, put his brother to death, and thus became the sovereign of all Russia, being known in history as VLADIMIR THE GREAT.

Vladimir the Great was one of the greatest of Russian monarchs. His efforts were directed at ridding himself of his Varangian warriors, who had begun to give him trouble, and also to the consolidation of his authority in his empire. He succeeded in both undertakings. He was a pagan when he ascended the Russian throne, and he manifested intense zeal in behalf of his gods, but his religion was very lax. He had six wives, who bore him twelve sons, among whom he subsequently divided his dominions; and he maintained about eight hundred concubines in several of the Russian cities. No woman in his dominions was safe from his violence.

Vladimir the Great was a great warrior and statesman. He conquered Red Russia and Lithuania, and rendered Livonia tributary. After completing his conquests he resolved to show his gratitude to his gods by offering a human sacrifice to them, and for this purpose he set apart the captives whom he had taken in war; but his courtiers persuaded him that the gods would be better pleased by the sacrifice of one of his own subjects, and therefore he selected a young Varangian, the son of a Christian, and who had been educated in his father's religion. The father refused to give up his son; and the populace, enraged at what they considered an insult to their religion and to their sovereign, attacked and murdered both father and son. The Russian Church has canonized both as its only martyrs.

The fame of Vladimir the Great as a conqueror had by this time spread into the neighboring countries, and the four great religious bodies of the world made efforts to convert him to their respective faiths. The Eastern Bulgarians recommended to him the conquering religion of Mohammed, and his voluptuous imagination was excited by the description of its paradise and its lovely maidens, but his repugnance to circumcision and the interdiction of wine could not be overcome. Said he: "Wine is the delight of the Russians; we cannot do without it." He disliked Roman Catholicism, which the Germans offered him, because of its Pope, an earthly deity, which seemed to him a monstrous thing. He disliked Judaism, because it had no country, and he did not regard it as either rational to take advice from wanderers under the ban of heaven or desirable to be punished with them.

The Greek religion which Olga had professed had been expounded to Vladimir by a learned man from Constantinople, and he embraced it after due deliberation and was baptized. He at once overthrew the idols and closed their temples. His example was speedily followed by his subjects, who said: "If it be not good to be baptized, the prince and the boyars would never submit to it." Thus the Greek Christian Church was established in Russia in A. D. 988. Vladimir the Great founded churches, schools and new towns during the remainder of his reign, and energetically applied himself to the work of establishing civilization and Christianity among his subjects.

Vladimir the Great was successful in several wars with the Petchenegs in the latter part of his reign. Domestic troubles embittered his last days. He had divided his dominions among his twelve sons, who soon became involved in civil war with each other. He had granted Novgorod to his son Yoraslav, but this son refused to pay the tribute due him as his vassal, and applied to the Varangians for assistance against his father. Vladimir, who was now an old man, took the field against his unnatural son, but died of grief in consequence of being under the necessity of so doing, A. D. 1015.

Concerning Vladimir the Great, Kelly says: "This rough-hewn colossus had great qualities. If he was not always able to repress his turbulent neighbors, he generally frustrated their incursions. He caused deserts to be cleared by colonies established for that purpose. He built towns, and while he was rendering his country more flourishing he thought it his duty to provide for its embellishment, and invited from Greece architects and workmen eminent for their skill. By their means he raised convenient and substantial churches, palaces and other buildings. The young nobles were brought up in seminaries endowed by the prince, to which his bounty had attracted able masters from Greece. Parents saw with horror these strokes aimed at ignorance, and the honors that were paid to foreign services. It was necessary to use violence in taking their children to place them in the new establishments, where they were to be taught reading and writing, unholy arts, identified with sorcery. Vladimir, who waded through the blood of his brother to the throne of Kiev, received from his nation the surname of the Great, was advanced to the rank of a saint, and is recognized by the Russian Church as coequal with the Apostles."

The civil wars which Vladimir's sons had commenced during their father's lifetime were continued after his death, with the result that SVIATOPOLK, the son of Vladimir's brother Yaropolk I., whom Vladimir had adopted as his own son, seized the Russian throne after murdering three of his brothers. Yaroslav, another brother of Vladimir the Great, entered into an alliance with the German Emperor Henry II. against Sviatopolk and his father-in-law, Boleslas I., King of Poland. This war was ended in 1019 by a three days' battle, in which Yaroslav and his ally won the victory. Sviatopolk fled to Poland, but died on the journey.

YAROSLAV thus became the sole sovereign of Russia. He destroyed the Petchenegs in a vigorous campaign, and caused his power to be dreaded by Finland, Livonia, Lithuania and Bulgaria. In 1026 he was defeated in a war with his brother MSTISLAV, Prince of Tmutarakan, by whom he was defeated. Mstislav had conquered the Crimean remnant of the kingdom of the Khazars in 1016, and had subdued the Circassians in 1022. He dealt generously with his brother, leaving him half of his dominions.

After Mstislav's death, in 1036, Yaroslav again became sole sovereign of Russia. After securing his power he engaged in the work to which he is indebted for his real fame. He was an ardent friend of education, and caused numerous Greek works to be translated into the Russian language. He erected schools and churches, increased the number of the towns, and caused many waste tracts to be settled with colonies. He caused the Scriptures to be translated into the Russian language, and transcribed several copies of them with his own hand. He likewise kept the Russian Greek Church independent of the Greek Church at Constantinople, and appointed its bishops without reference to the Greek Patriarch.

Yaroslav's three daughters married respectively the Kings of Norway, Hungary and France; his sons married Greek, German and English princesses; and his sister married the King of Poland. These marriage alliances brought Russia into more intimate relations with the other European nations.

The greatest work of Yaroslav's reign was the preparation of the *Russkaya Pravda*, the first Russian code of laws. This was a rude and barbarous code, but it was an effort to establish the reign of justice in Russia, and to afford protection to the weak against the strong. This code recognized the right of private vengeance, but restricted it to the relations of the man who had been murdered. If none came forward to avenge the murder, the murderer could atone for his crime by paying to the state a fixed price, regulated by the code according to the victim's rank. Judges were appointed, and circuits were assigned to them; while trial by a jury of twelve respectable persons was secured.

Several days before his death, in 1054, Yaroslav divided his dominions among his four sons, on condition that the younger ones should obey their eldest brother, IZASLAV, to whom he assigned Novgorod and Kiev. This arrangement failed to preserve peace, as the younger sons rejected their eldest brother's control over them, and civil war ensued. The result was that the Russian dominions were divided into a number of principalities, which were united in a kind of confederation, but which were constantly quarreling and fighting with each other. During this period of confusion the Poles, the Lithuanians, the Danes and the Teutonic Knights seized large parts of Western Russia.

VLADIMIR II., who succeeded to the Russian throne in 1114, was a great and wise sovereign; and Russia made great progress during his reign. He died in 1125, and was succeeded by his eldest son MSTISLAV II., who reigned only six years. At his death, in 1131, Russia became a prey to anarchy, and very soon the dominion of the Russian sovereign embraced only the city of Kiev and its vicinity.

In 1155 IGOR of Susdal obtained the ascendency, and for a while it appeared that he would reunite Russia under one scepter. His principality of Susdal comprised the territory included in the present governments of Yaroslav, Kostroma, Vladimir and Moscow, and a portion of Novgorod, Tver, Nijni Novgorod, Tula and Kaluga, or almost all of Central Russia. He had founded the city of Moscow in 1147 and granted it important privileges. He made Kiev his capital, and under his rule that city made rapid progress in wealth and prosperity. He died in 1157, whereupon the struggle between the various Russian princes was renewed.

Igor's son ANDREW at first took part in this struggle, but retired into his principality of Susdal, and made Vladimir his capital. He energetically applied himself to the civilization and advancement of his dominions. He greatly improved Moscow, founded a number of other cities and peopled them with the Bulgarians of the Volga, and fairly established the civilization of Central Russia. He was repulsed in an attempt to take Novgorod in 1168, after which he marched against Kiev and took that city by storm, plundering it and forcing it to acknowledge the supremacy of Vladimir.

In 1169 Andrew sent an army under his son against Novgorod, which was then at the height of its power,' having recently been admitted into the Hanseatic League. The attack was repulsed, but Novgorod was forced to acknowledge the supremacy of Vladimir. Andrew's principal object was to destroy the numerous petty princes which ruled in Russia and to consolidate the entire power of the various Russian principalities in the hands of the Grand Prince of Vladimir or Susdal. But these various Russian princes united against him and defeated his armies, thus ending his attempts at consolidation. Andrew was assassinated by his subjects in 1174. His successor was unable to hold the vast domain of Vladimir or Susdal together, and the next Grand Prince relinquished all claim to the homage of the petty princes.

The internal dissensions which weakened Russia rendered her an easy prey to a foreign foe. The Mongol or Tartar hordes under Zingis Khan, which had overrun Hungary and Poland, made a resistless irruption into Russia in 1221, defeated the united forces of the Russian princes in the bloody battle of Kalka, ravaged all of Southern Russia, and then returned to Asia.

No sooner had the Mongols retired from Russia than the internal wars were renewed between the Russian princes, accompanied this time by famine and pestilence. In 1230 Smolensk and Novgorod were scourged by the plague, thirty thousand persons dying in the former city, and forty-two thousand in the latter.

In 1237 the Mongols again invaded Russia, being that time under the leadership of Batou, the grandson of Zingis Khan and the Great Kahn of the Golden Horde of Kipzak. The Mongols quickly overran Russia and laid the country waste from the present city of Kazan to Vladimir. The Mongols proceeded to establish themselves in the country after they had conquered it. They founded the cities of Sarai and Kazan, and forced the Russian princes to pay tribute.

The Mongol conquerors themselves collected the tribute of each district; they received the homage and the appeals of every Russian prince; and when they established a Grand Prince they permitted several rivals to claim the feudal supremacy, made them wait for their decision, and sometimes detained them at their horde for two years. They also prevented the settlement of any order of succession. In short, they made themselves lords-paramount; as they adopted the plan of not permitting any Russian prince, great or small, to assume the government of his states before he had journeyed to the Great Khan of the Golden Horde to solicit the investiture. These journeys usually required a year for their accomplishment, and their effect was to leave the Russian principalities without native chiefs, and under the authority of the Tartar governors, or *Baskaks*. Other effects of these journeys were to prove the supremacy of the Great Khans; to disclose to the Mongols what kind of men they had to deal with; to ruin the Russian rival princes by the customary presents; and to make the Russian princes dread the terrible vengeance of the Great Khan in case they even sighed for independence.

Several Russian princes were summoned to the Great Khan of the Golden Horde and executed. But the Mongols, who punished the insubordination of the Russian princes so cruelly, united with them in their foreign wars, and even served them in their civil wars. A Russian prince would journey to the Great Khan of the Golden Horde to impeach the Grand Prince and to petition to be substituted in his place, and he would return with a Mongol army, which permitted him to reign over ashes and blood.

Russia was under the Tartar supremacy for two and a half centuries. In 1245 ALEXANDER NEVSKI became Grand Prince of Novgorod. He was a great statesman and warrior, and gained many victories over the Teutonic Knights and the Lithuanians, and recovered the Neva from the Swedes, this latter success giving rise to his surname. He secured the good-will of the Tartars. About this time the Grand Prince of Kiev was considered guilty of an act of rebellion in the eyes of the Great Khan, because he recognized the Pope as Head of the Christian Church, instead of the Greek Patriarch. The Grand Prince's sister was married to the Grand Prince of Vladimir, who refused to pay tribute. This enraged the Great Khan, who sent his armies to dethrone both the Grand Princes, and granted the principalities of Kiev and Vladimir to Alexander Nevski with the title of *Grand Duke of Russia*.

Alexander Nevski thereafter kept Russia at peace, and employed his wealth in rebuilding the Russian towns and encouraging every good enterprise. His grateful subjects rewarded him with their affection. He died suddenly in 1262, believed to have been poisoned by the Great Khan of the Golden Horde, who had begun to suspect him of aiming at independence. At his death he was canonized. He is still revered as a saint, and festivals are yet held in his honor.

For many years after the death of Alexander Nevski the petty Russian princes kept up a constant warfare among themselves, each aspiring to the sovereignty of the entire Russian nation, and each seeking to supplant the others with the Great Khan of the Golden Horde and to gain his favor; so that there was as much political intrigue and party feeling at the barbarous court of the Golden Horde as there was in the palaces of the Christian princes of Russia. In the meantime Moscow became the Russian capital, and the Grand Duchy of Russia was named *Muscovy*, whence the Russians are called *Muscovites*.

Kiev fell into the possession of the Lithuanians, while the Poles also wrested several states from Russia. During these wars many Russians deserted their homes, taking their wives and children into portions of the country hitherto uninhabited; and, as their numbers were increased by fresh refugees, they built villages, cultivated the land, and formed themselves into military republics. These people were called *Cossacks*, from Asiatic tribes of that name, with which they intermingled. The Cossacks themselves are a mixed race of Caucasian and Tartar origin.

Commerce flourished in Russia under the Tartar sway; and great fairs were held, which were attended by merchants from Greece, Italy and Asia.

IVAN I., surnamed KALITA, "the Purse," because he always carried a purse of money with him to distribute to the poor wherever he went, became Grand Duke of Moscow in 1328. He annexed the principality of Tver to the Grand Duchy of Moscow, adorned his capital with many new churches, and began the erection of the Kremlin in 1339. He induced the Head of the Russian Church to remove his residence from Vladimir to Moscow, and purchased the favor and protection of the Tartars by means of his immense wealth. He was a statesman of the Macchiavellian sort; and the result of his tortuous policy was the establishment of his authority over the Russian princes, whom he kept down with a firm hand, with the aid of his influence with their Tartar masters. He restored tranquillity to Russia, thus enabling the country to revive and increase its commercial prosperity, and to acquire the means to resist its barbarian oppressors in the future.

Ivan I. died in 1340, leaving to his son SIMEON the means to purchase his throne from the Golden Horde, thus securing the direct succession to the throne of Russia. Simeon vigorously carried out his father's policy, and died in 1353; whereupon his brother IVAN II. succeeded him, being also obliged to purchase the sanction of the Golden Horde to his accession. The regular order of succession thus maintained was vastly beneficial to Russia, as it gave the country half a century of repose and prosperity. The Grand Duke's throne became the rallying point of the Russians, and its strength and stability inspired them with a patriotism and courage which clearly indicated an early effort to recover their country's independence.

In 1359 DIMITRI II., the son of Ivan II., ascended the Russian throne. His first act was the establishment of the natural order of succession to the Russian crown from father to son. The Russian nobles, or *boyars*, had recognized the advantages held out to them by this mode of succession, and readily agreed to it. Dimitri II. then established his power over the minor Russian princes, making them his vassals. Moscow became the Russian capital in a truer sense than it had ever been before; and it was very evident that at Moscow was the only protecting power, and that it was a matter of necessity to have recourse to its support. The petty Russian princes could only obtain this support by sacrificing their independence, and thus all of them became vassals to the Grand Duke of Moscow.

From 1362 to 1380 the dissensions of the Tartars, who had by this time split up into several hordes, enabled the Grand Duke Dimitri II. to carry out his project unmolested by them. He was likewise able to beat back the Lithuanians, who thrice besieged Moscow and threatened to put an end to his reign. After driving away these enemies and securing his power at home, Dimitri II. felt himself strong enough to cast off the Tartar yoke. In 1378 he refused the customary tribute to the Great Khan, and put to death the Tartar ambassador sent to demand the tribute. The Great Khan burst into a storm of rage when he was informed of the murder of his ambassador, and summoned his hitherto invincible warriors to assist him in the conquest and destruction of Moscow.

Russia was thus threatened with a great danger, and all the Russian princes united under the Grand Duke Dimitri II. for the common defense. In 1380 the Great Khan advanced into Russia at the head of all his warriors. He encountered the Grand Duke of Moscow and his army on the banks of the Don, and was routed with the loss of one hundred thousand killed. This memorable victory acquired for Dimitri II. the surname of DONSKOI.

In 1382 the Tartars returned, and took and burned Vladimir and Moscow, massacring twenty-four thousand persons in the latter city. Dimitri II. was under the necessity of purchasing peace by making large sacrifices. The defection of the vassal Russian princes had been the cause of his defeat, and he now proceeded to wreak his vengeance upon them and to reduce them to their former vassalage. Dimitri II. passed his last years in consolidating his power in his dominions.

Dimitri II. died in 1389, and was succeeded as Grand Duke of Moscow by his son VASSILI III. Vassili III. treated his vassal princes with severity; but by timely submissions and presents he gained the good-will of the Great Khan, who conferred upon him the principalities of Susdal, Tchernigov and Nijni Novgorod, which were thenceforth inalienably united with Moscow. Vassili III. sought to render the Great Novgorod tributary to Moscow, but failed in that undertaking. Money was first coined in Russia during the reign of Vassili III.

Vassili III. died in 1425, leaving to his son and successor, VASSILI IV., the most compact and powerful of the Russian states. Vassili IV. was only five years old at his accession; and his uncle IGOR, taking advantage of the Grand Duke's youth, usurped the Muscovite throne. Vassili IV. appealed to the Golden Horde, who ordered the usurper to relinquish the Muscovite throne. Igor raised an army, took Moscow by surprise, and banished Vassili IV. to a remote part of the Grand Duchy. But in a moment of apparent triumph the usurper found himself abandoned. The whole population of Moscow followed their young Grand Duke into his exile, and Igor was left literally alone with his troops in the city. He was struck with dismay, so that he descended from his solitary throne and restored it to Vassili IV.

Vassili IV. greatly extended the Muscovite dominions by annexing Galicia, Mozhaisk and Borousk to his Grand Duchy. During his reign, Isidore, the Metropolitan of Kiev, took part in the general council of the Christian Church at Florence in 1439, and signed the act of union of the Greek and Roman Catholic Churches. Vassili IV. disapproved of this act of union, and imprisoned Isidore, who escaped some years later to Italy.

Vassili IV. became involved in a war with the Tartars, who deprived him of his throne, but afterward restored it to him. He was afterward taken prisoner by his cousin, Igor's son, who put out his eyes and seized his throne. The Russian nobles, or boyars, rallied to the support of their blind sovereign; the usurper was overthrown and poisoned; and Vassili IV. was restored to his throne.

Vassili IV. died in 1462, and was succeeded by his son, the illustrious IVAN THE GREAT, who was twenty-two years old at his accession, and who reigned forty-three years (A. D. 1462-1505). The two great objects of the life of Ivan the Great were to liberate Russia from foreign influence, and to make himself the autocrat of his own dominions. He succeeded in both undertakings.

In 1469 Ivan the Great conquered the Tartar Khan of Kazan and made him tributary. In the next ten years he conquered and annexed the republics of Novgorod, Perm and Pskov. Novgorod was conquered early in this reign. A rich widow of Novgorod, desiring to raise her Lithuanian lover to the head of the republic, bribed a strong party to revolt and to dethrone the reigning Prince of Novgorod, who applied to Ivan the Great for aid. Ivan entered Novgorod with a large army, in violation of the chartered rights of the citizens, seized merchandise, jewels and money, and sent the insurgent nobles to Moscow.

When the citizens of Novgorod revolted a second time, Ivan the Great besieged and took the city, forced the citizens to surrender their charter of liberties and to acknowledge him as their sovereign. He removed the great bell to Moscow in 1477. This conquest sealed the fate of Novgorod. Its commerce declined, and its prosperity vanished. Before its conquest by Ivan the Great it is said to have had a population of four hundred thousand souls, but after its conquest it dwindled into a second-rate town of the Russian Empire.

When an ambassador arrived from the naughty court of the Golden Horde of Kipzak with despatches from the Great Khan to the vassal Grand Duke of Russia, Ivan the Great, like his predecessors, had to ride out to meet him and to conduct him with all possible respect to the hall of state at Moscow, where the most costly furs were spread for his seat, while the vassal Grand Duke and his boyars were on their knees around the ambassador, listening in profound silence to their Tartar master's letters.

But Ivan the Great was too proud to continue this humiliating state of vassalage; and when the Great Khan's messengers arrived he took the papers from their hands, tore them in pieces and trampled them under his feet. He then declared to the Tartar envoys that he would no longer pay tribute to the Great Khan, expelled the Tartar merchants from his capital, and prepared for war. He defeated the Great Khan's troops repeatedly, destroyed their head-quarters and all their settlements, and drove them from his dominions in about twenty years from his accession to the Muscovite throne. Thenceforth the Grand Duke of Moscow ceased to be a tributary of the Great Khan of the Golden Horde of Kipzak.

Ivan the Great next subdued Tver and several other Russian principalities and annexed them to his dominions. He also conquered portions of Siberia in 1499; but was totally defeated in a war with the Livonians and the Teutonic Knights, with whom he was obliged to make peace in 1501.

As Constantinople had been taken and the Eastern Roman Empire overthrown by the Ottoman Turks in 1453, Ivan the Great desired to become the successor of the Greek Emperors; and, for the purpose of accomplishing this object, he married the Princess Sophia, the heiress of the Byzantine imperial dynasty ; his first wife having died some years previous to this. Immediately after his second marriage, Ivan the Great adopted as his insignia the double-headed eagle of the Greek, or Eastern Roman Emperors.

The appearance of the beautiful and highly-educated Sophia at the Russian court, with a numerous retinue of Greeks and Italians, made Ivan the Great emulous to introduce the useful and elegant arts of Greece and Italy into Russia. He sent for architects, founders and miners, thus beginning that system of improvement which Peter the Great afterwards carried out so energetically and successfully.

Ivan the Great was a master of statecraft, and some of his most important successes were achieved by the exercise of this talent as much as by force of arms. He was a stern despot in his government of his subjects. He broke the power of the petty Russian princes and boyars, and had them beheaded at his pleasure. He was the first who assumed the title of *Autocrat of all the Russias*—a title borne by all his successors on the Russian throne. He inaugurated many important reforms, improved the laws, regulated the public taxes, and reformed the manners of the Russian clergy.

The rightful heir of Ivan the Great was Dimitri, the child of his eldest son by his first wife; but Ivan arbitrarily thrust this prince aside, and finally cast him into prison. Ivan then appointed Vassili, his son by his second wife Sophia, his heir. When remonstrated with for thus arbitrarily changing the succession, Ivan exclaimed sternly: "Am I not, then, at liberty to act as I please! I will give Russia to whom I think proper, and I command you to obey!" The stern tyrant imprisoned the remonstrants. Ivan the Great died in 1505, at the age of sixty-seven years, leaving to his successor a stronger and more compact empire than had ever been ruled by his predecessors.

SECTION IX.—KINGDOM OF POLAND.

THE lands of the Vistula and the Oder were inhabited by tribes of the Slavonic race, known as Poles, or Slavonians of the Plain. In the year A. D. 840 a simple peasant, named PIAST, was chosen duke of the Polish territories. About the middle of the tenth century the Poles embraced Christianity, after the conversion of their duke, MICISLAS, by German missionaries.

The numerous Polish principalities were first united into one kingdom under BOLESLAS I., who was crowned King of Poland in 1025; but the Polish kingdom was subsequently subdivided among the family of the Piasts; and Poland was claimed as a fief of the German Empire, until during the reign of the Emperor Frederick II. of Germany, in the first half of the thirteenth century, when it secured its complete national independence.

Poland first rose to consideration in the fourteenth century, when King LADISLAS IV. united Great Poland with Little Poland, and was crowned at Cracow. The son and successor of Ladislas IV., CASIMIR THE GREAT, who obtained the Polish crown in 1333, added Galicia and Red Russia to the Polish dominions, founded the University of Cracow, and showed himself to be a wise legislator; but his efforts to diminish the power of the Polish nobility, and to establish a powerful citizen and burgher class, proved futile; and the Polish peasants, or serfs, continued to live in the most abject servitude.

King Casimir the Great died in 1370; and, as he was the last of the male line of Piast, the Polish nobles, or *voiwodes*, bestowed the crown of Poland on King LOUIS THE GREAT of Hungary, who proved to be a wise and able monarch. Louis the Great of Hungary (1370-1382) was the first elective King of Poland, whose sovereigns were thenceforth chosen by the Polish nobles, or voiwodes, in the Polish Diet; and Poland was thereafter called a *republic*.

Louis the Great's son-in-law and successor, the Grand-Duke Jagello of Lithuania, was LADISLAS V. of Poland (1382-1434), and was the first of the famous race of the Jagellos, which occupied the elective throne of Poland two centuries (1382-1572); during which Poland was one of the most extensive and powerful monarchies in Europe, stretching from the Baltic to the Euxine or Black Sea, along the whole frontier of European civilization, thus forming an effectual barrier to Germany and the states of Western Europe against barbarian invasion.

LADISLAS VI. (1434-1444), King of Poland and Hungary, was defeated and killed by the Turks at Varna in 1444. CASIMIR IV., who reigned from 1444 to 1492, subdued the Teutonic Knights, who had for a long time warred against the Poles; but he was obliged to make many concessions to the voiwodes, thus diminishing the royal power. It was the Polish aristocracy, who alone were represented in the Polish Diet, who had a voice in legislation, the raising of taxes, and the levying of troops. The nobles, or voiwodes, only were regarded as citizens in Poland. The reigns of the next two Kings of Poland—JOHN ALBERT (1492-1501) and ALEXANDER (1501-1506)—were unimportant. Thus at the close of the Middle Ages, Poland was at the zenith of its glory, and thus remained almost a century longer.

SECTION X.—KINGDOM OF HUNGARY.

THE Tartaric tribe of Magyars, or Hungarians, who had settled in the valleys of the Theiss and the Danube, in the beginning of the tenth century, and who made plundering incursions into Germany, were ruled by a number of princes, the chief of whom was Duke Arpad, whose descendants subsequently became the only rulers of Hungary. Duke GEISA I., who ruled Hungary in the latter half of the tenth century, received the doctrines of Christianity, and employed German missionaries to teach the gospel of a crucified Savior to his savage people. At the same time, the Magyars abandoned their nomadic habits, and applied themselves to agriculture.

Geisa's son, STEPHEN THE PIOUS, who assumed the title and dignity of King of Hungary in the year A. D. 1000, conquered Transylvania, repressed the insolence of the Hungarian nobility, defended the royal power against all encroachments, and reigned with vigor and wisdom. King Stephen founded monasteries and invited Benedictine monks into Hungary. He was the founder of the political institutions of Hungary, and did much to civilize his barbarous subjects and to accustom them to the arts of peace; but the progress of Christianity and civilization in Hungary was retarded by civil wars among the Magyars after Stephen's death.

During the reign of GEISA II., in the twelfth century, Flemings from Flanders and Saxons from Germany migrated to, and settled in, Transylvania; and their descendants still retain the manners and customs of their ancestors. The Flemings and Saxons in Transylvania built many towns, and converted a desert land into a blooming region.

In the year A. D. 1222 the Magyar nobles, or *magnates*, compelled their king, ANDREW II., to grant a charter called the *Golden Privilege*, which conceded great privileges to the nobility and the clergy, and was the foundation of the free constitution of Hungary. Any encroachment by the king on the rights secured to the magnates by the Golden Privilege justified the Hungarian nobles in armed rebellion against their sovereign. The magnates in Hungary, like the voiwodes in Poland, became the actual ruling class; while the Hungarian peasants, or serfs, pined in a condition little better than abject slavery.

ANDREW III.—the last of the royal race of Arpad—died in 1302; whereupon Hungary became an elective kingdom, whose sovereigns were thenceforth chosen by the magnates in the Hungarian Diet. Under LOUIS THE GREAT (1342-1382)—of the royal House of Anjou in Naples—Hungary attained its highest point of power and prosperity. Louis received the crown of Poland in 1370, extended the Hungarian kingdom to the Lower Danube, and made Venice tributary. He also protected the peasant class of Hungary from the tyranny of the magnates, improved the administration of justice, and established schools of education throughout the Hungarian kingdom. He also conducted many wars in Italy.

After the death of Louis the Great, in 1382, disputes and contests for the Hungarian crown arose, which for many years distracted the Hungarian kingdom with civil war; and tranquillity was only restored when SIGISMUND, afterward Emperor of Germany, was King of Hungary (1392-1437). The valiant John Hunnfyades of Transylvania saved Hungary from the dominion of the Ottoman Turks by his great victory at Belgrade in 1456.

In gratitude to the memory of John Hunnfyades, the Hungarian Diet in 1457 bestowed the crown of Hungary on his son, MATTHIAS CORVINUS, who proved to be one of the greatest and best of Hungarian sovereigns. He successfully defended his kingdom against the Ottoman Turks, and

BAPTISM OF STEPHEN THE PIOUS BY POPE SYLVESTER II.

extended its frontiers on the side of Austria. He established a university and a library at Buda, and invited learned men, artists, mechanics and agriculturists, into Hungary, to advance the civilization of his subjects.

After the death of King Matthias, in 1490, Hungary rapidly declined. The kingdom was invaded by the Ottoman Turks; and the royal power was diminished by the nobility, who made the raising of taxes. the declaring of war, and the making of peace, privileges of the Hungarian Diet. Finally the nobles, or magnates, usurped the whole royal authority. When King LOUIS II. of Hungary was defeated and killed by the Turks in the battle of Mohacz, in 1526, a dispute for the Hungarian crown arose, which was finally settled by leaving Transylvania and East Hungary in the possession of the mighty Turkish Sultan, Solyman the Magnificent, while West Hungary reverted to the sovereignty of the Archduke Ferdinand I. of Austria. Long and bloody wars between the Austrians and the Turks resulted in favor of the House of Hapsburg; and ever since that period the sovereign prince of Austria has borne the title and dignity of King of Hungary.

SECTION XI.—BULGARIA, SERVIA AND BOSNIA.

IN connection with the Eastern Roman Empire we have alluded to several conquering races that at times invaded that empire; such as the Bulgarians, Magyars or Hungarians, Russians, Servians and Bosnians. These established independent states, some of which had but a temporary existence; and the most important of these were Bulgaria, Servia and Bosnia. We will now give a brief sketch of these three states.

KINGDOM OF BULGARIA.

The Bulgarians were a Turanian people who emigrated from their original seats near the Caspian Sea, in two divisions—one founding *Great*, or *White Bulgaria*, on the Volga river; and the other passing to the West in the fifth century, and establishing the kingdom of Black Bulgaria, north of the Lower Danube, in A. D. 680. This latter branch of the Bulgarian nation had come into collision with the Avars and Slavonians, and had been assimilated by the Slavonians so largely that this western Bulgarian kingdom is historically Slavic, or Slavonic.

Says Charles Freeman, the English historian, in his *Historical Geography of Europe*: "The modern Bulgarians bear the Bulgarian name only in the way in which the Romanized Celts of Gaul bear the name of their Frankish masters from Germany, and in which the Slavs of Kiev and Moscow bear the name of their Russian masters from Scandinavia. In all three cases the power formed by the union of conquerors and conquered has taken the name of the conquerors, and has kept the speech of the conquered."

Christianity was introduced into this Bulgarian kingdom in the middle of the ninth century, and in the latter part of the same century the kingdom was conquered by the Russians. In the middle of the tenth century there was a great revival of the power of the Greek Empire; and Bulgaria again became a part of that empire, making the Danube its southern boundary once more, thus remaining for more than two centuries. A revolt then occurred, which led to the establishment of a second Bulgarian kingdom, extending southward as far as Thessaly and Epirus; but this kingdom was again subdued by the Byzantine Empire in 1018. The Bulgarian kingdom was revived a third time by a revolt against the Eastern Empire in 1187, and remained independent until it was conquered by the Ottoman Turks after their great victory at Cossova in 1390.

KINGDOM OF SERVIA.

Servia was a part of the Eastern Roman Empire until the early part of the seventh century, when it was ravaged by the Avars, who were afterward driven out by the Serbs, or Servians, a Slavonic people, who had hitherto occupied the region north of the Carpathian mountains, which they had abandoned at the instigation of the Eastern Emperor, to aid him against the Avars. Servia remained in vassalage to the Byzantine Empire for some time; but afterward it became dependent on Bulgaria, until the conquest of that kingdom by the Eastern Empire in 1018.

Servia became an independent principality in 1043, and formed an alliance with Hungary against the Greek Empire; but its prince was not crowned king until 1217. About the middle of the next century Servia made extensive conquests, and soon included in its dominion Macedonia, Albania, Thessaly, Northern Greece and a part of Bulgaria. The Servian king at that time assumed the title of *Emperor of the Serbs and the Greeks*. This was the zenith of Servian power and glory; as the Servian dominion fell to pieces under subsequent sovereigns, and was absorbed by the Ottoman Turks after their great victory of Cossova in 1390, though Servia was not permanently annexed to the Ottoman Empire until 1521.

KINGDOM OF BOSNIA.

Bosnia took its rise as an independent kingdom in consequence of an irruption of the Bosnians, a Slavonic people, who had migrated from the east in the seventh century; but the new state maintained an uncertain and changeable independence for a considerable time. In the twelfth and thirteenth centuries Bosnia was under the dominion of Hungary; and in 1339 it became a part of the Servian Empire, to which it belonged until 1370, when it again became independent.

Bosnia acquired a real position among the European powers under its last dynasty, beginning in 1376, upon the dissolution of the Servian Empire; and it seemed likely at one time to take the place of that fallen empire. But Bosnia's greatness was shattered, along with that of Bulgaria and Servia, by the Turkish victory at Cossova in 1390; and it finally yielded to Turkish sway, becoming a province of the Ottoman Empire in 1463, though not permanently annexed to that empire until 1528.

SECTION XII.—END OF THE EASTERN EMPIRE.

E have traced the history of the Eastern Roman Empire to the time of its temporary subversion by the leaders of the Fourth Crusade in 1204. The Crusaders had assembled at Venice, and were provided with shipping to be tranported to the Holy Land. As they were unable to raise the entire sum demanded by the Venetian republic, they were allowed by the Venetians to postpone its payment on condition of conquering for them some towns on the coast of Dalmatia, which had revolted from the Venetian republic. The Crusaders complied with this condition, and captured the town of Zara, where they passed the winter.

The young Greek prince Alexis proceeded to the camp of the Crusaders and solicited their assistance in recovering his throne. The blind old Doge Dandolo of Venice sustained the Byzantine prince's appeal, and the Crusaders finally resolved to aid him, as he promised them ample compensation for their services in the event of success. The Crusaders besieged Constantinople in the summer of 1203, and took the city by storm after a stubborn conflict.

ALEXIS was thus established on the Byzantine throne through the aid of the French Crusaders and the Venetians; but, as he had lost the confidence of his subjects by abandoning the Greek religion for the Roman Catholic, he was killed in a revolt of the people of Constantinople the next year, A. D. 1204. The Crusaders were so enraged by this revolt that they stormed and took Constantinople a second time, and put an end to the Eastern Roman Empire for fifty-seven years (A. D. 1204-1261).

On the ruins of this Greek Empire the Crusaders founded a Latin Empire under Count BALDWIN of Flanders, the leader of the Fourth Crusade. The Crusaders divided among themselves as much of the Eastern Empire as they could secure and hold. Baldwin received only about a fourth of the Empire, which was now split up into a number of petty states, some of which were Greek and others Latin. The remaining European possessions of the Empire were divided between the Venetians, the Lombards and the French; the Venetians receiving a disproportionately large share. The Venetians established a chain of factories or trading-posts along the coast from Constantinople to Venice. Boniface, Marquis of Montferrat, became King of Macedonia.

The dominions of the Greek Empire in Asia which had not passed into the possession of the Seljuk Turks were divided between the two Greek sovereigns reigning respectively at Nice and Trebizond, each claiming the title of Emperor. The Emperors of Nice were able and prudent sovereigns, and their dominions became powerful and prosperous under their rule.

The Latin Empire of Constantinople had no hold on the Byzantine people, and therefore only lasted fifty-seven years, the attempt to Latinize it having failed, so that it fell before the conquering arms of the Emperor MICHAEL PALÆOLOGUS of Nice, A. D. 1261. The restored Greek Empire under the dynasty of the Palæologi lasted almost two centuries.

As the Greek Empire of Nice had claimed to be the legitimate successor of the Eastern Roman Empire, the conquest of Constantinople by Michael Palæologus may be regarded as a revival of that state to some extent; but it never recovered its former power, as the Ottoman Turks pressed upon its eastern border, and the Greek Emperor of Trebizond and some of the Greek and Latin princes continued to rule their territories independent of the Greek Emperor at Constantinople. The restored Greek Empire of Constantinople was merely the most powerful of the various Greek states, which continued to to exist without attracting much attention, until they were all finally conquered by the Ottoman Turks in the fifteenth century.

Michael Palæologus, alarmed by the Pope's threat to arouse Western Europe to a crusade against him, sought to force his subjects into a union with the Romish Church; but his efforts in this direction brought only suffering and sorrow to his dominions, though his violence and cruelty were insufficient to satisfy the Pope, great as they were. Gibbon says that at Rome "his slowness was arraigned and his sincerity suspected."

On the death of Michael Palæologus, in 1282, his son ANDRONICUS II. became his successor on the Byzantine throne. Andronícus II. put an end to the outrages which his father inaugurated, dissolved the union with the Romish Church, and restored the Greek religion in his Empire. About twenty years after his accession a band of Catalan adventurers, reinforced by men from all portions of the world and known as the *Great Company*, having rendered good service to the Empire by defeating the Ottoman Turks in two bloody battles, imagined that they had a right to the property of the Empire which they had saved, and commenced such a series of arbitrary exactions upon the Byzantine provinces that the Emperor was put to great exertions to resist them. After their leader had been assassinated, they seized the strong fortress of Gallipoli, on the Hellespont, and defeated the forces of the Eastern Empire twice by sea and land. These successes brought many recruits to their ranks, and they continued their outrages upon the Empire until they were obliged to disperse on account of the lack of provisions and the dissensions of their leaders.

Andronícus II. associated his son Michael

with him in the government at the age of eighteen. Michael's son Andronícus shared the imperial honors at an early age, and soon began to wait impatiently the removal of the obstacles in the way of his sole possession of the Byzantine throne. One of these obstacles was removed by his father's premature death; but then, to the surprise of the younger Andronícus, his grandfather transferred his hopes and affections to another grandson. The younger Andronícus fled from Constantinople in 1321, and began a civil war against his grandfather. After a struggle of seven years the younger Andronícus triumphed in 1328, and the Emperor Andronícus II. retired to a monastery, where he died in 1332.

ANDRONICUS III. thus became sole Emperor, and soon afterward he attempted to check the progress of the Ottoman Turks, but was beaten badly and wounded in his only campaign. His early intemperance brought him to a premature grave, and he died in 1341, at the age of forty-four. His son JOHN IV. by his second wife, the Empress Anne, sister of the Count of Savoy, was a child of nine years; and Andronícus III. in his will appointed his old and tried friend, John Cantacuzene, guardian of his son.

During the Emperor John's minority John Cantacuzene was the real ruler of the Eastern Empire. He ruled with wisdom and firmness, and recovered the isle of Lesbos and the principality of Ætolia by his valor and prudence. One of his rivals instigated the young Emperor and his mother to cast off John Cantacuzene's rule, and the able minister was declared an enemy of the Empire and of the Church. He at once appealed to arms to recover his power, thus beginning a civil war of six years.

In 1343 John Cantacuzene solicited the assistance of the Ottoman Turks, who were thus admitted into Europe, where they obtained a permanent footing, thus sealing the doom of the Eastern Roman Empire. With the aid of his Turkish allies, John Cantacuzene reduced the young Emperor to submission, returned to Constantinople in

triumph, ascended the Byzantine throne with the title of JOHN V., and acknowledged the son of Andronícus III. as associate Emperor with the title of JOHN VI.

John VI. made two efforts to overthrow the elder Emperor by force, but was defeated both times. The second time he fled to the Latins of the isle of Tenedos for refuge. With the hope of ending these civil wars, John V. deposed his younger colleague John VI., associated his own son Matthew in the government, and established the Byzantine succession in his own family; thus bringing on a revolution which restored John VI. to the Byzantine throne with the aid of some Genoese troops. John V. retired to a cloister and passed the rest of his life in literary pursuits, A. D. 1355.

The reign of John V., like that of Andronícus III., had been distracted by the fierce quarrels of the Venetians, the Genoese and the Pisans, who contended with each other for the monopoly of the Eastern commerce. The Emperor was unable to enforce peace, and the imperial and Venetian forces were several times defeated by the Genoese. John V. was obliged to sign a humiliating treaty, by which he bound himself to expel the Venetians from Constantinople and to grant the desired monopoly to the Genoese. These troubles continued in some degree during the early part of the reign of John VI., who remained on the Byzantine throne until 1391.

The Eastern Empire now began to be afflicted with a most serious evil. The Ottoman Turks, whom John V. had admitted into Europe, had seized the city of Andrianople and made it their capital. They were fully resolved to extend their European dominion to the Hellespont, and the capture of Constantinople was a foregone conclusion. The Turks treated the Greek Emperors as their vassals, and the Emperors were unable to offer any resistance to such formidable foes. The Turkish Sultan Bajazet I. deprived his own son of his eyes for conspiring against him. The Greek Emperor's son John was an accomplice in the plot, his object being to dethrone his father. Sultan Bajazet I. sternly demanded that the Greek Emperor should blind his own son, and the Emperor was obliged to comply with the Sultan's demand.

Upon the death of John VI., in 1391, his second son, MANUEL II., ascended the Byzantine throne. The Turkish Sultan Bajazet I. immediately espoused the cause of the blind prince John. Manuel II. left Constantinople and hastened to France to solicit assistance, and his blind competitor occupied the Byzantine throne. Sultan Bajazet I. now threw off the mask, and claimed Constantinople as his own capital. Prince John refused to submit, whereupon the Turkish Sultan invested Constantinople and compelled the city to undergo the horrors of a siege and famine. The Byzantine capital would undoubtedly have fallen into Turkish hands at that time had not the Sultan been suddenly called into Asia Minor to defend his dominions against the Tartar conqueror Tamerlane.

The Turkish Sultan's retirement from the siege of Constantinople gave the Greek Emperor a brief respite, and the Emperor Manuel II. took advantage of it to visit the courts of Western Europe to solicit assistance; but none of the European sovereigns were in a condition to afford him any aid. The death of Sultan Bajazet I. was followed by quarrels among his sons, thus preventing the Turks from exerting their united strength against Constantinople.

JOHN PALÆOLOGUS II., the son and successor of Manuel II., ascended the Byzantine throne in 1425. He entertained the idea of effecting a union of the Greek and Romish Churches, and accepted the Pope's invitation to visit Italy to bring about such a consummation. In 1438 John Palæologus II. visited Ferrara, where a general council of the Romish Church was then in session. Pope Eugenius IV. summoned a council at Florence, and a reunion of the Greek and Latin Churches was formally proclaimed in July, 1438. But the Greek Church had no sympathy with this reunion, and the Greek Emperor had only planned it in order to secure the aid of Western Christendom in his efforts to maintain his Empire against the Ottoman Turks.

In the latter days of the Eastern Roman Empire, whenever the Greeks were in any difficulty, their Emperors always made a show of ending the division between the Eastern and Western Churches; but these schemes never took any real root, because the Greeks were fully resolved never to acknowledge the Pope's authority.

The Pope manifested a disposition to aid his Greek brethren, and sought to excite a crusade of Western Christendom in their behalf, but he found this a difficult task. The English, French and Germans took no part in the affair; but Hungary and Poland, which were more directly interested by being in constant danger of a Turkish invasion, gave a favorable response to the appeal of Pope Eugenius IV. The crowns of those two kingdoms were worn by the same monarch, Ladislas VI. Recruits were obtained from other lands by "an endless treasure of pardons and indulgences, scattered by the legate;" and a Christian army of a hundred thousand men was assembled under the command of Prince John Hunniyades of Transylvania, one of the most renowned warriors of the time. An alliance was made with the Turkish Sultan of Caramania, in Asia Minor; and a fleet was collected from Burgundy, Genoa and Venice. After gaining some advantages, the Christian army was defeated by the Turkish army under Sultan Amurath II. in the bloody battle of Varna in 1444, King Ladislas VI. of Poland and Hungary being among the slain.

Sultan Mohammed II., who succeeded Amurath II. on the Turkish throne in 1451, commenced fortifying the Hellespont, thus bringing on a war between himself and CONSTANTINE PALÆOLOGUS, the last Greek Emperor. In the spring of 1453 a Turkish army of two hundred and sixty thousand men invested Constantinople, and carried the city by storm on May 29, after a siege of fifty-three days. The Emperor Constantine Palæologus died sword in hand, in a gallant effort to save his capital. In this siege the Turks used cannon, which is the first use of such engines of warfare in so important an operation. Sultan Mohammed II. made Constantinople the capital of over a thousand years (A. D. 395-1453). The conquering Turks soon absorbed the remaining territories of the Greek Emperors. Sultan Mohammed II. treated the vanquished Greeks with great liberality, pro-

DEFENSE OF CONSTANTINOPLE AGAINST SULTAN MOHAMMED II.

the Ottoman Empire, and converted the Church of St. Sophia into a Mohammedan mosque.

The capture of Constantinople ended the Eastern Roman Empire, which had existed tecting them in their lives and liberties, and permitting them the free exercise of their religion, leaving them one-half of the churches of Constantinople—a toleration the benefits of which they enjoyed for sixty years.

GREEK EMPERORS.

Different Races.

A.D.	
364	VALENS.
379	THEODOSIUS THE GREAT.
395	ARCADIUS.
408	THEODOSIUS II.
450	MARCIAN.
457	LEO I., THE THRACIAN.
474	LEO II., THE YOUNGER.
474	ZENO THE ISAURIAN.
491	ANASTASIUS I., THE ILLYRIAN.
518	JUSTIN I.
527	JUSTINIAN I.
565	JUSTIN II.
578	TIBERIUS II.
582	MAURICE THE CAPPADOCIAN.
602	PHOCAS.
610	HERACLIUS.
641	CONSTANTINE III., HERACLEONUS.
641	CONSTANS II.
668	CONSTANTINE IV., POGONATUS.
685	JUSTINIAN II. (deposed).
695	LEONTIUS.
698	TIBERIUS III., ASPIMAR.
705	JUSTINIAN II. (restored).
711	PHILIPPICUS BARDANES.
713	ANASTASIUS II.
716	THEODOSIUS III.

Isauric Race.

718	LEO III., THE ISAURIAN.
741	CONSTANTINE V.
775	LEO IV.
780	CONSTANTINE VI. and IRENE.
792	IRENE, EMPRESS.
802	NICEPHORUS I., LOGOTHETES.
811	STAURACIUS.
811	MICHAEL I.
813	LEO V., THE ARMENIAN.
820	MICHAEL II., THE STAMMERER.
829	THEOPHILUS.
842	MICHAEL III., PORPHYROGENITUS.

Macedonian Race.

867	BASIL I., THE MACEDONIAN.
886	LEO VI., THE PHILOSOPHER.
911	ALEXANDER and CONSTANTINE VII., PORPHYROGENITUS.
919	ROMANUS LECAPENUS AND HIS SONS.
920	CHRISTOPHER AND HIS SONS.
928	STEPHEN and CONSTANTINE VIII.
945	CONSTANTINE VIII., (alone).
959	ROMANUS II.
963	NICEPHORUS II., PHOCAS.

A.D.	
969	JOHN I., ZIMISCES.
976	BASIL II. and CONSTANTINE IX.
1028	ROMANUS III., ARGYROPULUS.
1034	MICHAEL IV., THE PAPHLAGONIAN.
1041	MICHAEL V., CALAPHATES.
1042	CONSTANTINE X., MONOMACHUS, and ZOE.
1054	THEODORA.
1056	MICHAEL VI., STRATIOTES.

The Comneni.

1057	ISAAC I., COMNENUS.
1059	CONSTANTINE XI., DUCAS.
1067	EUDOCIA and ROMANUS DIOGENES.
1071	MICHAEL VII., PARAPINACES.
1078	NICEPHORUS III.
1081	ALEXIS I., COMNENUS.
1118	JOHN COMNENUS.
1143	MANUEL I., COMNENUS.
1180	ALEXIS II., COMNENUS.
1183	ANDRONICUS I., COMNENUS.
1185	ISAAC II., ANGELUS COMNENUS.
1195	ALEXIS III., ANGELUS, THE TYRANT.
1203	ISAAC II., and ALEXIS IV.
1204	ALEXIS V., DUCAS.

French or Latin Emperors.

1204	BALDWIN I. (of Flanders).
1206	HENRY I.
1216	PETER DE COURTENAY.
1221	ROBERT DE COURTENAY.
1228	BALDWIN II. (Latin dynasty ended in 1261).

Greek Emperors at Nice.

1204	THEODORE LASCARIS I.
1222	JOHN DUCAS VATACES.
1255	THEODORE LASCARIS II.
1259	JOHN LASCARIS.
1260	MICHAEL PALÆOLOGUS.

The Greek Empire Restored at Constantinople Under the Palæologi.

1261	MICHAEL VII., PALÆOLOGUS.
1282	ANDRONICUS II., THE ELDER.
1328	ANDRONICUS III., THE YOUNGER.
1341	JOHN PALÆOLOGUS I. (deposed).
1347	JOHN CANTACUZENUS.
1355	JOHN PALÆOLOGUS restored.
1391	MANUEL II., PALÆOLOGUS.
1425	JOHN PALÆOLOGUS II.
1448	CONSTANTINE PALÆOLOGUS XIV. (killed and empire ended by the Turks, 1453).

GREEK EMPERORS OF TREBIZOND.

A.D.	
1204	ALEXIS COMNENUS.
1222	ANDRONICUS I.
1235	JOHN I.
1238	MANUEL I.
1263	ANDRONICUS II.
1266	GEORGE.
1280	JOHN II. (deposed).
1285	THEODORA.
1285	JOHN II. restored.
1297	ALEXIS II.
1330	ANDRONICUS III.

A.D.	
1332	MANUEL II.
1332	BASIL.
1340	IRENE.
1341	ANNA.
1343	JOHN III.
1344	MICHAEL.
1349	ALEXIS III.
1390	MANUEL III.
1417	ALEXIS IV.
1446	JOHN IV., CABO JOANNES.
1458	DAVID. (Empire conquered by Turks, 1461).

SECTION XIII.—ZINGIS KHAN'S TARTAR EMPIRE.

INGIS KHAN, or TEMUJIN, the chief of a small tribe of Mongols, or Moguls, founded a vast Tartar empire in the early part of the thirteenth century —an empire which under his successors embraced almost the whole of the vast continent of Asia and the eastern half of Europe, and was thus the most extensive empire that the world has ever seen.

The Mongols were originally a tribe of Tartars who spread themselves south and east of Lake Baikal, in Southern Siberia, and between the rivers that form the Upper Amoor. Even in Zingis Khan's time they numbered about four hundred thousand tents. After his time many nations adopted the name that he had made illustrious by his conquests.

Thirteen Mongol hordes, who had obeyed Temujin's father, refused to obey the son, who was thirteen years old at the time of his father's death in 1167. The youthful Temujin fought them and reduced them to their allegiance. This was the first military exploit of the great Mongol conqueror, who was destined to conquer five or six million square miles of territory. Though this achievement acquired fame and prestige for the youthful Temujin, he was afterward obliged to seek aid from the Great Khan of the Kin Empire of Tartary, of which he was a vassal. The Great Khan, who had been under obligations to Temujin's father, showed his gratitude for the father and his esteem for the son by reinstating Temujin in his paternal inheritance, and gave him his daughter in marriage.

Temujin had been carefully educated, and a very able minister had been intrusted with the care of his childhood. He was well versed in all the exercises constituting a Tartar education. He could shoot his arrow or strike his lance with unerring aim, either when advancing or retreating. He could endure hunger, thirst, fatigue, cold and pain. He managed his fierce and heavy war-horse, or his light and impetuous courser, with such consummate skill, by word, or look, or touch, that man and beast appeared as but one animal swayed by one common will.

After gaining some successes for his father-in-law, jealousies were excited in his family and in the empire by the high favor with which Temujin was regarded at court. Temujin had rendered himself further unpopular by inducing the Khan to assume more authority than the vassal princes were willing to submit to. The princes therefore revolted against the Khan and defeated him in battle; but Temujin replaced his father-in-law on the throne by winning a brilliant victory over the revolted princes. Temujin tarnished his victory with great cruelty, scalding seventy of his enemies to death by flinging them alive into seventy caldrons of boiling water.

At length the Khan's jealousy was excited against his famous son-in-law. After exhausting every conciliatory method, Temujin thought himself justified in building up a party of his own in self-defense. At last recourse was had to arms, and Temujin defeated his father-in-law, who was slain in the battle. After some further struggles with his enemies, Temujin succeeded to his father-in-law's throne, A. D. 1205.

Temujin was then forty years old, and he convoked all the princes of his empire to do him homage. The Mongol princes all assembled on the appointed day, clothed in white. Temujin advanced into their midst, with the diadem upon his brow, seated himself upon his throne, and received the congratulations and good wishes of the assembled Mongol princes and Khans, who then confirmed him and his posterity in the sovereignty of the Mongol Empire, declaring themselves and their posterity vassals of the Great Khan.

After some additional victories, Temujin

repeated the ceremony in a still more simple and signal manner. He stood on a plain mound of turf near the banks of the Selinga, where he harangued the assembled Mongol Khans and princes with an eloquence natural to him, after which he sat down on a piece of black felt which was spread upon the earth. This felt was revered as a sacred relic for a long time afterward. An appointed orator then addressed Temujin thus: "However great your power, from God you hold it. He will prosper you if you govern justly. If you abuse your authority you will become black as this felt, a wretch and an outcast." Seven Khans then respectfully assisted him to rise, conducted him to his throne, and proclaimed him lord of the Mongol Empire. A relative, a saint and a prophet, approached naked, and said: "Brethren, I have seen a vision. The great God of Heaven, on his flaming throne, surrounded by the spirits on high, sat in judgment on the nations of the earth. Sentence was pronounced, and he gave the dominion of the world to our chief, Temujin, whom he appointed Zingis Khan, or Universal Sovereign." He said to Temujin: "Welcome, with God's order that you henceforth take the name of Zingis Khan." The Mongols ratified this name with extravagant joy, considering it a divine title to the conquest of the world, and regarded opposing nations as God's enemies. Thus early were the great Mongol leader and his followers inspired with fanaticism.

Zingis Khan, as Temujin was thereafter called, thus finding himself at the head of many Mongol tribes of nomads, proceeded to organize his vast dominions into a well-regulated empire, and to establish a powerful army consisting of the various Mongol elements, but mainly officered by Tartar chiefs. At this time Zingis Khan promulgated his celebrated civil and military code for his empire, under the sanction of monotheism, and in perfect toleration of all religions. He likewise afterward caused the best Arabic, Persian, Chinese and Thibetan books to be translated into the Mongol language, and this had a powerful tendency to elevate his subjects above their inherited barbarism. Roads were built and fortifications were constructed.

Zingis Khan then began his wonderful career of conquest, which made him master of a large part of the Eastern Continent from the Pacific ocean on the east to the frontiers of Germany on the west. His first great conquest was in the far East.

A demand from the Chinese Emperor upon Zingis Khan for the customary tribute from the Mongol tribes brought on a war between the Mongols and the Chinese; and very soon Zingis Khan's well-disciplined Mongol hordes broke through the Great Wall and reveled in the spoils of the Celestial Empire. Though the Chinese used in their defense some substance like Greek-fire and bombs filled with gunpowder, which appears to have been used by them for centuries before its invention in Europe, they were unable to withstand the Tartar hosts. The Mongols took Pekin in 1215; and all of Northern China, a part of the Kin Empire, was annexed to Zingis Khan's dominions.

After the conquest of China, Zingis Khan turned westward at the head of seven hundred thousand warriors, with the intention of making himself master of every nation from Orient to Occident. With this immense host the great Mongol conqueror overran the Korasmian Empire, the seat of which was in the region east of the Caspian Sea, in the modern Turkestan. The war between Zingis Khan and the Sultan of Korasm was brought on by the aggressions of the Sultan's subjects, who plundered some Tartar merchants.

After collecting his seven hundred thousand warriors, and ordering recruits to be raised throughout his dominions and sent after him, Zingis Khan advanced against the Korasmians. During his march he disciplined and regulated his army in the most efficient manner, and gave the following despotic general order: "If a soldier fly without having fought, whatever the danger or resistance, he shall die; if from a company of ten, any one or more shall separate, he or they shall die without mercy; if any of the company see their comrades engaged, and do not try to succor or rescue them, they shall die." The Korasmian Empire embraced Korasm, Great Bucharia, Persia, Persian Irak, and much of India. The Sultan of Korasm raised an army of half a million men to oppose the invading hosts of Zingis Khan.

The great Mongol conqueror overran all parts of the Korasmian Empire at once, and one hundred and sixty thousand Korasmians were slain in the first battle. The Mongol invaders swept from city to city like a devouring conflagration, leaving behind them only blackened heaps of ruins. Samarcand, Bokhara, Balkh and other flourishing cities, the seats of learning and Central Asian civilization, filled with the treasures of art, and celebrated for their commerce and wealth for centuries, were mercilessly sacked. The country was frightfully devastated, and the inhabitants were barbarously massacred or enslaved. The Korasmian armies were uniformly defeated. The Sultan of Korasm himself, driven to extremity, came to the shores of the Caspian, embarked in a boat amid a volley of arrows, and escaped to an island, where he died of sickness and despair, after enjoining his son Jelaleddin to avenge him.

The dauntless and persevering Jelaleddin did all that was possible to obey his father's dying injunctions, but fortune was always against him. He lost city after city, and finally sought refuge in an island of the Indus, where he burned his ships, except one for his family. His soldiers were slain around him while defending themselves like tigers at bay. The Korasmians sought refuge in the rocks where the Mongol cavalry could not penetrate, but as they were reduced to seven hundred men the Sultan disbanded them.

The unfortunate Jelaleddin, after embracing his family and tearing himself away from them, took off his cuirass, stripped himself of all his arms but his sword, bow and quiver, mounted a horse and plunged into the river, in the midst of which he turned around and discharged his arrows in defiance at Zingis Khan, who stood on the bank. The ship in which Jelaleddin's family had embarked split as it left the shore of the river, and the whole family fell into the Mongol conqueror's power, and were afterward murdered.

The fugitive Korasmian prince passed the night in a hollow tree, from fear of wild beasts. He then collected all the fugitives he could muster; and, after being joined by an officer of his household, with a boat laden with arms and provisions, money and clothing, he established himself in India; but after many misfortunes he returned to his native country, where he died in obscurity shortly after his conqueror.

A Turkoman horde of Jelaleddin's army engaged in the service of the Sultans of Iconium, or Roum, and from this horde sprung Othman, the founder of the Ottoman Turkish Empire. It is said that the ravages of the four years of Zingis Khan's Korasmian war were so great that five centuries were not sufficient to repair its ravages.

In his camp on the Indus, Zingis Khan—who was now master of Persia and all the other territories of the Korasmian Empire—yielded to the desire of his soldiers for repose and for the enjoyment of the wealth which they had acquired through so much toil and blood. Returning slowly, encumbered with spoil, he viewed with regret the desolation around him, and expressed his intention to rebuild the cities which he had reduced to ruins.

As Zingis Khan passed the Jaxartes he was met by two of his generals, whom he had sent around the southern shore of the Caspian with thirty thousand men, and who had fought their way through the passes of the Caucasus, traversed the marshy regions near the Volga, crossed that and the desert, and returned to Asia by a route north of the Caspian and Aral Seas.

When the Mongol princes and generals had returned from their several expeditions, Zingis Khan assembled them in a large plain twenty-one miles in extent, his own quarters occupying a circuit of six miles. Over his throne, on which lay the black bit of felt used at his coronation, was spread a white tent capable of sheltering two thousand persons. Instead of the primitive simplicity of the nomadic Tartars, all the luxury of Asia glittered in the dress, horses, harness, arms and furniture of the assembled multitude. The great Mongol conqueror received the homage of his powerful vassals with majesty, and that of his children and grandchildren with tenderness as they were introduced to kiss his hands. He graciously accepted their presents, and distributed magnificent donations among them in return. One of the presents offered by a vassal prince was a herd of a hundred thousand horses.

The mighty Zingis Khan, who was fond of public speaking, now delivered an oration, commending his code of laws, to which he ascribed all his success and all his conquests, which he enumerated minutely. The envoys of his vassal Khans were then admitted to an audience, and were dismissed well satisfied. The entire ceremony was ended with a grand festival, lasting many days. Everything most exquisite in fruits, game, liquors and edibles was served up at the daily banquets.

These festivals were followed by new triumphs, and prosperity seemed always to attend the great Mongol conqueror's military enterprises. Pillage and massacre followed in the course of his conquering hosts. Zingis Khan is said to have destroyed fifty thousand cities and six million human lives in building up an immense empire, six thousand miles in extent from east to west, from the Sea of Japan to the steppes of Russia.

Zingis Khan was characterized by qualities fitting him for a conqueror—a genius capable of conceiving great and arduous designs, and a prudence equal to the execution of these designs. He was endowed with a persuasive eloquence, a degree of patience enabling him to endure and overcome fatigue, an admirable temperament, a superior understanding, and a penetrating mind that instantly seized the measure proper to be adopted. His military talents were conspicuous in his successful enforcement of a strict discipline and the introduction of a severe police among the Tartars, who had never before submitted to such restraint.

He regulated everything, whether service, recompense or punishment. Intoxication was no excuse for wrong doing; neither were rank or power. Zingis Khan was a monotheist, believing in a deism; but his subjects were individually permitted to embrace any religion which they preferred, providing that they believed in but one God; and every one was protected against persecution for his religious belief. Some of his children and princes of the blood royal were Christians, some were Jews, and some were Mohammedans, with his full consent.

Zingis Khan's code of laws was simple. Murder, adultery, perjury, the theft of a horse or an ox, or making a Mongol his servant by another Mongol, were all punished with death. No Tartar was permitted to give a slave meat or drink without his master's consent. Every one was required to serve the public according to his ability. All servile labor was prohibited to the victorious nation, and was abandoned to slaves and strangers. All labor was servile except military labor.

The service and discipline of the troops were the institutions of a veteran commander. The Mongol troops were armed with bows, cimeters and iron maces; and were divided by hundreds, thousands and tens of thousands.

Zingis Khan was unable to read or write, and most of his Mongols and Tartars were as illiterate. Neither he nor his generals left any written memorials of his achievements, and the traditions of these were not collected and transcribed until sixty-eight years after his death; but, as the Mongols mingled in the destinies of so many nations, full accounts of their exploits are given by the Chinese, the Persians, the Armenians, the Syrians, the Arabs, the Greeks, the Russians, the Poles and the Hungarians.

Zingis Khan died A. D. 1227, at the age

of seventy years, and after a reign of twenty-two years, preserving to the last his complete ascendency over the vassal nations and his own Mongols. He was honored with a magnificent funeral; and his simple sepulcher, beneath a tree whose shade he had loved, became an object of veneration to his people, who loved fondly to embellish it.

Zingis Khan left a numerous offspring; and during his lifetime four of his sons, illustrious by birth and merit, had held the chief offices under their father, and their names and deeds are frequently conspicuous in the history of his conquests. These four sons were Toushi, his great huntsman; Zagatai, his judge; Oktai, his minister; and Tuli, his general.

Upon the death of his renowned father, OKTAI was proclaimed Great Khan of the Mongols and Tartars, with the general consent. His three brothers and their families, firmly united for their own and the public interest, were content with dependent scepters. According to the father's direction, Tuli ruled the empire as regent while his brother was absent on a military expedition; and Oktai was only confirmed by a general council of the Mongols after the lapse of two years.

Zingis Khan had selected his ministers and generals with so much judgment that Oktai did not find any change necessary. Oktai placed his chief confidence in Yelu, who had also enjoyed the implicit confidence of Zingis Khan. Yelu was a man of integrity, learned in the laws, of consummate prudence, and entirely devoted to the welfare of the vast Mongol Empire. Oktai placed his brother Tuli, to whom he was sincerely attached, at the head of his armies, and never had any cause to regret his choice.

Oktai resolved to carry the renown of his arms to the far West. We are told that one and a half million Mongols and Tartars were inscribed on his military roll. The Great Khan selected a third of these, and assigned them to the command of his nephew Batou, Tuli's son, who reigned over his father's conquests north of the Caspian. After a festival of forty days,

Batou set out on his expedition; and the speed and ardor of his innumerable hosts were such that in less than six years they had measured a line of ninety degrees of longtitude, or a fourth part of the earth's circumference.

The great rivers of Eastern Europe—the Volga, the Don, the Dnieper, the Dniester, the Vistula and the Danube—they either swam with their horses, or passed on the ice, or traversed in leathern boats, which they also used to transport their wagons and artillery across the streams. Batou's victories eradicated every vestige of national freedom in the vast steppes of Turkestan and Kipzak. Batou overran the Tartar kingdoms of Kazan and Astrakhan in his rapid march, and the troops which he sent against Mount Caucasus explored the innermost recesses of Georgia and Circassia.

The civil dissensions of the Russian princes betrayed their country to the Tartars, whose conquering hordes spread from Livonia to the Black Sea. The two great Russian capitals—Kiev and Moscow—were reduced to ashes. After effecting the conquest of Russia, the Tartar hordes made a brief but destructive inroad into Poland as far as the frontier of Germany, burning the cities of Lublin and Cracow, and approached the Baltic shores. They defeated Duke Henry of Lower Silesia, the Polish Palatines, and the Grand Master of the Teutonic Knights, in the terrible battle of Liegnitz, in Silesia, and laid Breslau, the Silesian capital, in ashes. After the battle of Liegnitz, in which Duke Henry of Lower Silesia was killed, the victorious Mongols filled nine sacks with the right ears of the slain, that the number of victims might be counted, in barbarous triumph.

The Tartar host, numbering half a million men, then turned southward into Hungary, piercing the Carpathian mountains; and the entire country north of the Danube was "lost in a day, was depopulated in a summer." The ruins of cities and churches were overspread with the bones of the inhabitants, who thus "expiated the sins of their Asiatic ancestors." Miserable refugees, enticed from the woods under a promise of peace and pardon, were barbarously slaughtered as soon as they had performed the labors of the harvest and the vintage.

The Mongols crossed the Danube and besieged Gran, planting thirty engines against the place, and filling the trenches with sacks of earth and corpses. After they captured the town a promiscuous massacre followed, during which three hundred noble matrons were slain before the victorious Tartar general. Europe was in fear that her cities, her arts and her institutions would be extinguished. The Pope sent monks to convert the barbaric invaders to Christianity, but the Tartars astonished him by answering that the sons of God and of Zingis Khan had a divine right to subdue and extirpate the nations, and invited him to submission by means of threats. Frederick II., of Germany, sought to unite Germany, France and England in a league against the common foe. The Tartars were awed by the fame and valor of the French. Neustadt, in Austria, was gallantly defended by fifty knights and twenty cross-bows; and the siege was raised on the approach of a German army.

After ravaging Servia, Bosnia and Bulgaria, Batou slowly retreated from the Danube to the Volga, to enjoy his victories at Sarai, in latitude 48°—a city which sprang up from the desert as if by magic. This was the beginning of the empire of the Great Khan of the Golden Horde of Kipzak, under Zingis Khan's descendants, and which had Sarai for its capital. In 1242 Batou's brother led a horde of fifteen thousand families into Siberia, and his descendants reigned at Tobolsk for more than three centuries.

Though Zingis Khan and Oktai were not Mohammedans they tolerated Islam the same as they did Christianity, Judaism and every other religion. A foreigner once told Oktai that Zingis Khan had appeared to him in a dream and had ordered a general massacre of Mohammedans throughout the empire. Oktai asked the man if he knew the Mongol language; and, when the man replied that he did not, Oktai said: "My father spoke no other; how then could you understand him?" Having thus detected the man's falsehood, Oktai punished him with death.

At Oktai's death his wife set aside her grandson, whom her husband had intended should be his successor, and contrived to keep the regency. In two years she induced the Couroultai, or general council of the Mongols, to name her own son KAYUK as her husband's successor. Her course displeased the good minister Yelu, and she managed gradually to deprive him of power, and he is said to have died of grief.

Yelu appears to have been the perpetual good genius of the Mongol court, always ready to suggest or forward anything that might have a tendency to elevate the barbarian's views or soften the conqueror's heart —anything to civilize or humanize the rough natures with which he was associated. Yelu was extremely learned in Chinese science, and was the author of numerous volumes on history, astronomy, agriculture, government and commerce. He also had a taste for collecting antiquities and curiosities.

Yelu was eminently endowed with all the qualities of a great minister—an inflexible steadiness, extraordinary presence of mind, a perfect knowledge of the countries under his master's dominion, judgment in the selection of the individuals whom he employed, and certain resources of money and provisions in case of emergency. He expended vast sums to draw artificers, officers, engineers and learned men from all quarters of the Mongol dominions. He was constantly laboring to inspire the princes with a love for their subjects, and the people with an abhorrence of carnage and rapine. During the sacking of Pekin and the palaces he took only some maps, books, paintings, and a few parcels of rhubarb; the last of which he used to cure the soldiers of a malignant epidemic fever.

Yelu was the first teacher of the Mongols, and also their first lawgiver by the advice he gave to Zingis Khan. He arranged a calendar for their use, and instituted wise and beneficial regulations concerning the finances, commerce, duties, the public granaries, and the subordination of officers, both civil and military. His designs encountered opposition from the natural ferocity of the Mongols, from their ignorance and defective early education; but his energy overcame all obstacles.

Kayuk's reign lasted eight years, during which the Mongols conquered Corea and some countries on the Caspian. Kayuk was priest-ridden, and his prodigality was excessive. His subjects complained of having to furnish horses to the nobles, who were always riding post. They were also offended at the sums which the court expended for jewels and precious stones, while the soldiers received scarcely any payment, or their dues were left long in arrears.

At Kayuk's death his mother and wife sought to place Oktai's former choice upon the Mongol throne; but the great council chose MANGOO, a grandson of Zingis Khan, but not belonging to the reigning branch. His firmness and celerity, and the well-regulated army that he kept at Karakorum, quelled any tendency to disturbance. Mangoo adopted the religion of the Grand Lama of Thibet, and became somewhat of a devotee. He portioned off the well-deserving of the royal family with fiefs in China, the largest and best of which was granted to his brother Kublai Khan, his successor on the Mongol throne. These Tartar lords had Chinese ministers, or stewards, who essentially modified and softened the barbarism of the Mongol government.

Kublai Khan's minister was Yansheu, who was one of these useful officers, and who suggested many wise and profitable measures to repair the ravages of war in his fief, thus causing Tartars and Chinese to be well pleased with each other. This sagacious prime minister, on Mangoo's jealousy of his brother, followed by injustice, advised Kublai Khan to go immediately, throw himself on his brother's neck, and thus disabuse him of his suspicions. Mangoo's tenderness was at once revived, and he repeatedly embraced his brother, while tears flowed down his cheeks. Mangoo assigned his brother still more important trusts.

Hoolagoo had been appointed by his brother Mangoo, the Great Khan, in 1251, to govern Persia. Hoolagoo cleared the North of Persia from the Ismaelians, or Assassins, whom he exterminated in 1255. He subjected Iconium, took Bagdad in 1258, capturing the last Khalif, took the cities of Mosul, Aleppo and Damascus, and conquered a large part of Syria. Hoolagoo threatened to march on Constantinople with four hundred thousand men, but was turned aside by the siege of Bagdad. Two hundred thousand Moslems perished in the defense of Bagdad.

When Bagdad was taken by the Mongols its was the richest city in the world. After plundering every part of Persia and Irak, the Tartar hordes hovered around this famous city like a hunter around his prey. The weak Khalif was betrayed by his own Vizier, who encouraged him in a false confidence, grateful to his avarice and indolence, until the Mongols took the city by assault; an army which had been hastily collected for the defense of the city having been lost by an inundation caused by the Tartars. The last Khalif presented himself to his Tartar conquerors with the vases containing diamonds and jewelry of incalculable value, hoarded by his ancestors for many years. Hoolagoo immediately distributed these valuables among the leading officers of his army.

Al Mostasem, the last Khalif, was the most abstentious and inaccessible of all the Bagdad sovereigns, the most chary of his august presence, and was in the habit of appearing veiled, as he deemed the sight of his countenance too great a boon to his people. On such occasions the abject populace so thronged the streets of the city that the windows and balconies were hired at extravagant prices to see him pass. Through these same streets, which witnessed his insane pride, exposed to the view of the same multitude, did the cruel Tartar conqueror drag the vanquished Khalif, confined in a leather sack, until his life was extinct. Thus perished Al Mostasem, the last of the Khalifs of Bagdad; and that city was pillaged by the conquering Tartars for a full week, A. D. 1258.

Mangoo perished in the siege of a city of the Song Empire in Southern China, A. D. 1259, thus leaving to his brother KUBLAI KHAN the Grand Khanate of the Mongols, and also the legacy of a war with the Song dynasty in South China, a war which Zingis Khan had almost with his dying breath enjoined upon his successors. But Kublai Khan was obliged to put down another brother, who aspired to the Mongol crown. After defeating this brother and routing his army, Kublai Khan selected wise and able counselors, and these aided in rendering his name illustrious.

Kublai Khan's great achievement was the conquest of Southern China, in which he employed European and Mohammedan engineers. The engines of antiquity, such as the balista and catapult for throwing stones and darts, the battering-ram, etc., were used; as were also Greek-fire, gunpowder, cannon and bombs. The Mongol troops, drawn along canals, lay siege to Hanchow, on the coast, in the most delightful climate of China. The Song Emperor, a mere youth, surrendered, put his head to the earth nine times in token of homage, and then went into exile in Tartary.

The last champion of the Song dynasty endeavored to escape by sea, but was surrounded by the Mongol fleet, whereupon he exclaimed: "It is more glorious to die a prince than live a slave!" He then leaped into the sea with his infant Emperor in his arms. His example was followed by a hundred thousand Chinese; and Kublai Khan reigned over all China, founding the Yuen dynasty.

After the conquest of South China, Kublai Khan desired to conquer Japan, but after losing a hundred thousand men by shipwreck and other disasters he relinquished the hopeless enterprise. His conquering arms reduced Pegu, Tonquin, Cochin China, Bengal, Thibet and Corea to different degrees of tribute and subjection. He explored the Indian Ocean with a fleet of a thousand ships for sixty-eight days, during which he visited and subdued portions of the large islands of Borneo and Java, but found nothing worth retaining in those remote islands.

Under Kublai Khan letters, commerce, peace and justice flourished; and the great canal of China, five hundred miles in length, was opened from Nankin to Pekin, his capital, where he displayed all the wealth and magnificence of Asia.

Yelu, the Chinese mandarin, the minister and friend of Zingis Khan and his sons and successors, had labored incessantly, during a spotless administration of thirty years, to mitigate or suspend the horrors of war; to save the monuments and to restore the preëminence of science; to restrain the military commander by restoring the civil magistrates; and to instill into the minds of the Mongols the love of industry, justice and peace. He struggled with the barbarism of the first Mongol conquerors, but his salutary lessons produced abundant fruits in the second generation.

Kublai Khan had been educated in Chinese manners and customs, and he inspired the loyalty of his Chinese subjects by restoring the forms of their venerable constitution, as it was easier to adopt than to invent, and as the conquering Mongols gradually submitted to the customs, manners, habits, fashions, laws and prejudices of the vanquished Chinese. The numbers, servitude, steady sense and impregnability of character of the Chinese were such that their Mongol conquerors appear repeatedly to have been absorbed and dissolved in the vast homogeneous mass of the teeming millions of the population of China. Marco Polo, the great Venetian traveler, visited Kublai Khan's court at Pekin.

After the death of Kublai Khan, in 1294, the Khans of Kipzak and Russia, the Khans of Zagatai or Transoxiana, and the Khans of Iran or Persia, although they received investiture from the Mongol Emperor of

China, threw off the supremacy of Zingis Khan's degenerate posterity, who reigned at Pekin for three quarters of a century after Kublai Khan's death. In 1368 the Mongol or Yuen dynasty, founded by Kublai Khan, was expelled from China; and the native Ming dynasty then occupied the Chinese throne until 1644.

Kublai Khan was succeeded on the Mongol throne by TIMOUR, the youngest of his brother's three sons, A. D. 1294. Timour's clemency and regard for his subjects endeared him to the Chinese, who extol him as a model of perfection. He often visited the needy and unfortunate, and frequently sent his almoners and agents into the provinces to search out objects of charity. No sovereign ever displayed better judgment in the choice of his ministers and generals, and none ever exhibited a more marked contempt for flattery and luxury. Timour died without children, and did not appoint a successor.

The Mongols and Chinese desired that Hayshan, Timour's brother, should be his successor; but another brother claimed the Chinese throne against a faction, as if for himself, and then resigned the scepter to Hayshan, surprising his brother with the grateful assurance that he acted only in his interest. HAYSHAN thus ascended the Chinese throne. He was fond of the writings of Confucius, and caused them to be translated into the Mongol language. He was licentious and intemperate, but was equitable and generous. He died after a reign of three years.

Hayshan was succeeded by his noble-minded brother, AYYULIPALIPATA, whose virtues were rather passive. During his reign China was afflicted by drought, famine, pestilence, inundations and earthquakes. These, together with eclipses, struck terror into the hearts of the Chinese. The famine which began in 1342 carried off thirteen millions of the population of China. The Emperor revived the literary examinations for office, and associated Tartar mandarins with Chinese. He sought to abdicate his throne in favor of his son, but the son would not agree to this.

The next Mongol Emperor of China was SHOTEPALA, who ascended the throne in 1350, and who governed with consummate wisdom, though he was but nineteen years of age at his accession. He reformed the luxury, debauchery and avarice of the Mongol court, but was assassinated after a reign of four years by the friends of a wretch whom he had justly punished.

The next Mongol Emperor was indolent, but punished the assassins who had elevated him to the Mongol Chinese throne. He was exhorted to banish from the palace the host of eunuchs, astrologers, physicians, women, and other idlers, whose maintenance required vast sums. His death in 1352 was followed by plots, assassinations and cabals, which continued through several short and worthless reigns.

An Empress, who was permitted to choose a sovereign, set up TOUHAN, Hayshan's grandson, who was noted for his luxury, indolence, dissipation, timidity and cruelty. His artful minister persuaded him that every official duty was a great burden for his august majesty; and while the minister was embroiling his sovereign in a thousand blind cabals, the Emperor's ambitious and licentious wife involved him in a disastrous war with Corea, which completed the ruin of the Mongol Chinese Empire.

To add to the Emperor's troubles, a bloody revolution broke out, under the lead of a Buddhist monk named Chu Yuen-chang, who proclaimed to his followers the following phrase, which aroused the Chinese nation: "It is the Chinese who should govern the Tartars, not the Tartars the Chinese." In 1368 he succeeded in overthrowing the Mongol dynasty, and ascended the throne of China with the name of HUNG-WU, thus founding the Ming dynasty, which ruled the Celestial Empire from 1368 to 1644—a period of two hundred and seventy-six years. The sixteen Chinese Emperors belonging to the Ming dynasty were generally able sovereigns.

THE KIPZAK EMPIRE.

The Kipzak Empire, in the basin of the Volga, was one of the fragments of Zingis

Khan's vast empire, and included Russia in Europe, taking tribute of the republic of Novgorod and of the other Russian principalities. The Kipzak Empire was bounded on the south by the Danube, the Euxine, the Caucasus and the Zagatai Empire; and on the north by the republic of Novgorod and the Kingdom of Sibir on the Irtish. This empire included but very little of Tartary. It was at first a subordinate government under a grandson of Zingis Khan, but it soon became independent. About twenty warlike sovereigns reigned over it in succession. At the end of the thirteenth century it was converted from Deism to Mohammedanism. Its sovereign was styled the *Great Khan of the Golden Horde of Kipzak*. After several centuries it was broken into fragments, the most important of which were the Khanates of Kazan, Astrakhan, and the Crimea, or Crim Tartary.

THE ZAGATAI EMPIRE.

The Zagatai Empire, another fragment of Zingis Khan's vast dominion, was founded by that great conqueror's eldest son ZAGATAI, who had received the government of a territory which in 1290 included Transoxiana, or the region north of the Oxus, together with Balkh, Kashgar, Khotan, and the Punjab, or region of the Indus and its five tributaries. A part of this empire took the name of *Uzbeck*, because of the fondness of the people there for their Khan of that name. One of these Uzbeck Khans invaded Persia, and carried away four hundred camel-loads of gold and jewels, along with other valuables, giving all of it to his soldiers.

The Punjab was lost to the Zagatai Empire in 1368, but the empire was extended on the north. Twenty-five sovereigns, the descendants of Zingis Khan through Zagatai, successively reigned over this empire, which lasted one hundred and seventy years, until 1402, when it was ended through dissensions among relatives whose ambition was active in expelling each other from the throne. The last sovereign of the Zagatai Empire was a monarch only in name, who held a command in Tamerlane's army. Like the Kipzak Empire, the Zagatai Empire was also converted from Deism to Islam.

THE MONGOL PERSIAN EMPIRE.

The Mongol Persian Empire, a third fragment of Zingis Khan's dominion, was founded by HOOLAGOO, a brother of Kublai Khan.

In 1282 AHMED succeeded to the Mongol Persian throne, being chosen thereto by the grandees; but he lost their esteem by embracing Islam, and was killed. His nephew then usurped the sovereignty. ALJAPTU, who came to the Mongol Persian throne in 1303, was distinguished for his love of justice and religion, which he caused to flourish throughout his dominions. He had founded the city of Sultania and made it his capital. He was succeeded in 1313 by his son ABUSAID, who was disturbed by court cabals, and was poisoned by his wife Khatun in 1337. Fresh plots and disorders followed; and the nobles fortified themselves in the different provinces which they ruled, or plundered and took up arms against each other. All these petty sovereignties were finally absorbed in Tamerlane's vast Tartar dominion, of which we shall now proceed to give an account.

SECTION XIV.—TAMERLANE'S TARTAR EMPIRE.

AMERLANE, or TIMOUR THE LAME, a famous Tartar conqueror, who claimed to be a descendant of the great Zingis Khan, entered upon a career of conquest, and built up a Tartar Empire that vied with that of his illustrious ancestor, embracing the greater part of Central, Southern and Western Asia.

A Persian writer tells us that Tamerlane's father was the wise and virtuous Emir, Tragai, and his mother was the chaste and beautiful Tekine Khatun, the Emir's lawful wife. Timour, as Tamerlane was most generally called by his Tartar countrymen, was born near Tashkend, his father's capital, in 1336, during the reign of Sultan Kazan of Zagatai.

It is said that Timour's birth had been foretold to one of his ancestors in a dream wherein eight stars appeared to shoot out of the sleeper; and the eight cast so great a splendor that it enlightened the four quarters of the globe. This was interpreted to signify that a prince of his race should be born in the eighth generation, who should fill the world with the splendor of his virtues and conquests. Timour's horoscope was drawn at the moment of his birth, and predicted to him the crown and the empire, with all manner of prosperity and a numerous issue.

It is also related that Timour gave indications during his childhood that he was likely to verify the predictions of the horoscope. As soon as he had reached the age of reason something in all his actions appeared to indicate an air of sovereignty. He would talk only of thrones and crowns. His favorite diversions were such as represented the military art; and in this he disposed of the youth who attended him like a sovereign disposes of his subjects, raising those who seemed most deserving to the highest degree, and conferring the bare title of soldiers upon others. He made figures of canes to represent the enemy's armies, and then attacked them with his troops, among whom he enforced a military discipline.

When Timour had attained a more advanced age, and was capable of applying himself to the sterner exercises of the body, he devoted himself to military science. His principal diversions were riding, racing, fencing, and the like. He was also frequently engaged in the pastime of the chase, and that was the only recreation that he took after his constant fatigues.

In these exercises Timour passed that part of his life which preceded his great and wonderful military achievements, or the period from his tenth to his twenty-fifth year. At the latter age his heart gave way to ambition, and he began to despise dangers, to win victories and to acquire the name of a great conqueror and a famous hero.

Timour was driven from his inheritance, the principality of Tashkend, while yet a youth; but he distinguished himself by his bravery in several petty conflicts as an adventurer, following his fortunes from place to place. He did good service to his country by expelling from its soil a formidable army of the Getes, who had invaded it from the north. At the head of an insignificant force, aided by the stratagem of many camp-fires on the mountains, he defeated the vast army of these invaders in a desperate battle. At another time he struck terror into his foes and took a fortified city, at the head of a small body of troops whom he had ordered to tie long branches to the sides of their horses. The dust thus raised made the enemy think that Timour had a large army, and he took advantage of the dismay thus excited in the ranks of the foe by making a bold and vigorous charge. The fertilities of his expedients gained the confidence of his followers, and this with his other qualities acquired for him the strong personal affection of his troops.

To secure his inheritance, Timour was under the necessity of making an alliance with Hussein, a neighboring chieftain. Both encountered extreme perils in the constant wars which disturbed the empire through the feuds and the ambition of the various chiefs. Timour heroically exposed his life in every encounter, but knew as well how to command as how to fight. He underwent every vicissitude of fortune—victorious, defeated, a captive, released, wounded, a fugitive in the deserts, reappearing with a few vagabond troops, increasing his forces, welcomed in the great cities, or shut out with indignities, at one time on friendly terms, at another time at bitter feud with his ally, Hussein.

It is said that on one occasion, after Timour had suffered three disastrous defeats, fleeing for his life and deserted by all, he had taken refuge in a ruined building, in utter despair. Almost hopelessly despondent, Timour was brooding over his misfortunes, when his eyes caught an ant that was striving to carry a grain to her magazine, up the opposite side of the wall. The insect failed ninety-nine times in her efforts, but accomplished its task at the hundredth attempt. The indomitable patience and perseverance of so small an insect for a paltry grain gave Timour fresh courage. He rose from the ground, braced up with new energy, a new man, hazarded another engagement and came forth victor.

In one of his contests he received a severe wound in the hand, and in another action he was wounded in the foot, from which circumstance he received the name of Timour Lenk, meaning Timour the Lame, which was corrupted into Tamerlane, by which name he is generally known. At length Tamerlane grew more powerful than his ally, Hussein, who lost the affection of his officers and troops through his jealousy, avarice and other bad qualities; while Tamerlane captivated the hearts of all by his valor, affability and equity.

Hussein, who became jealous and sought in every way to put Tamerlane in the wrong, finally adopted such outrageous measures that Tamerlane was obliged to declare war against him. Hussein was taken prisoner at Balkh and led to Tamerlane, who was melted to tears by the recollections of their former friendship, and could only say: "I renounce my right to his life." Some of Tamerlane's courtiers, without waiting for his words, followed Hussein out and killed him.

The Khan of Zagatai finally confirmed Tamerlane in his hereditary principality of Tashkend, and assigned him a battalion of ten thousand cavalry. Soon afterward Tamerlane was elected Khan by the general council of his nation, and found himself at the head of an empire which he afterward enlarged by victories that ranked him among the most renowned conquerors, A. D. 1370.

Like all semi-barbarians and great conquerors, Tamerlane displayed the highest virtues along with the most horrible vices; sublime justice along with the most atrocious oppression; winning and simplehearted benevolence with the cruelty of a fiend; the most tender natural affection with the most revolting and hard-hearted disregard of all domestic and social ties; a deep sense of humility, dependence and piety with the utmost arrogance toward his fellow-creatures—trampling on everything that they held dear, and causing by his selfish ambition the violent deaths of millions of mankind, with more or less misery. These "scourges of God" have no orderly, proportionate and harmonious characters; and their mission is to destroy, overturn, unsettle, to reduce to chaos, so that the foundations of future progress may be laid broader, deeper and better. The elements are more diverse, embrace a greater multitude of particulars, and may thus contribute to a wider harmony and a higher order of things.

Tamerlane asserted that it was neither consistent nor proper that the earth should be shared between two monarchs. His first aim was universal dominion. His second object was to live in the memory and esteem of posterity; and this appears to have been associated in his half-enlightened mind with the view of propagating Islam, which he regarded as the true religion.

It is said that among Tamerlane's early exploits, after vainly waiting for allies who failed to join him, he fled from the hills of Samarcand into the desert with only sixty horsemen. He was overtaken and attacked by a thousand Getes, whom he repulsed with frightful slaughter, and caused his enemies to remark: "Timour is a wonderful man; fortune and the divine favor are with him." His little band being reduced to ten men, lost three more by desertion. Tamerlane wandered in the desert, was plunged in a dungeon sixty-two days, swam the Oxus and led the life of an outlaw; but adversity taught him salutary lessons.

After Tamerlane had returned to his native country certain of his adherents eagerly sought him, to join him in the desert. He presented himself as a guide to three chiefs, and he described this recognition in the following words: "When their eyes fell upon me they were overwhelmed with joy, and they alighted from their horses, and they came and kneeled, and they kissed my stirrup. I also came down from my horse, and took each of them in my arms. And I put my turban on the head of the first chief; and my girdle, rich in jewels and wrought with gold, I bound on the loins of the second; and the third I clothed in my own coat. And they wept, and I wept also, and the hour of prayer was arrived, and we prayed. And we mounted our horses, and came to my dwelling; and I collected my people and made a feast."

Tamerlane conducted thirty-five campaigns, and placed the crowns of twenty-seven kingdoms on his head. Soon after he had been chosen Khan by the Couroultai of his nation, he annexed the dependent countries of Korasm and Kandahar to the patrimony of Zagatai, after which he turned to Persia. That unhappy country had been without a lawful sovereign since Abusaid's death, and had not witnessed peace or justice for forty years. Tamerlane conquered its petty tyrants in detail. One of them brought his peace-offering of silks, horses and jewels, each consisting of nine pieces, in accordance with the Tartar custom. There being only eight slaves in the present, the servile prince said: "I myself am the ninth." The Tartar conqueror rewarded this orientalism with a smile.

In a battle under the walls of Shiraz, the valiant prince of Fars, the ancient Persia proper, at the head of three or four thousand troops, broke the main body of Tamerlane's cavalry, thirty thousand strong. Tamerlane remained near the standard with only fifteen of his guards, where his helmet was twice struck by a cimeter, but he was not beaten down. His Mongols rallied, and were victorious after a desperate conflict. The valliant prince of Fars was slain, and his head was thrown at Tamerlane's feet. The Tartar conqueror afterward extirpated

the prince's family, putting every male of that formidable princely race to death. Tamerlane advanced to the Persian Gulf, and compelled Ormuz, the island queen of commerce, to pay an annual tribute of six hundred thousand dinars of gold. He subdued the plains and valleys of the Tigris and the Euphrates, and the country as far north as the Caucasus and as far west as Mount Lebanon and the territories of the Ottoman Turks.

In Tartary, Tamerlane crossed the Jaxartes, and annexed the broad belt of territory north of that stream to his dominions by conquering a large part of the Kipzak Empire. He also subdued Kashgar, marching into the heart of that country seven times, once almost fifteen hundred miles to the north-east of Samarcand. On that side the kingdom of the Oigurs, and that of Thibet south of it, separated Tamerlane's empire from the Ming Empire of China and from the remnant of the empire of the Mongols to the north of China.

Tamerlane's struggle with the Kipzak Empire is interesting. Tamerlane had protected the fugitive Kipzak prince and had restored him to his throne; but ten years afterward the restored Kipzak prince forgot Tamerlane's benefits, and marched against the "usurper of the rights of the house of Zingis," as he called Tamerlane. He entered Persia on the west side of the Caspian, through the gates of Derbend, at the head of ninety thousand cavalry. On the east side of the Caspian and Aral Seas he crossed the Jaxartes with the countless hosts of Kipzak, Bulgaria, Circassia and Russia, burned Tamerlane's palace, and compelled the Tartar conqueror to struggle for Samarcand and for his life amid the snows of winter.

After a mild expostulation and a glorious victory, Tamerlane sought revenge, and twice invaded Kipzak on the east and west side of the Caspian and the Volga with so mighty an army that thirteen miles were measured from his right to his left wing. His soldiers seldom beheld the footsteps of man during a march of five months, and they depended only on the chase for their daily subsistence.

At length the armies of Tamerlane and the Great Khan of the Golden Horde of Kipzak encountered each other. The standard-bearer of Kipzak treacherously reversed the imperial standard, thus discouraging his troops, and giving Tamerlane the victory. In Tamerlane's words, the Great Khan of the Golden Horde of Kipzak gave the tribe of the son of Zingis Khan "to the winds of desolation." Tamerlane's victorious army burned several capitals, took a Russian prince into captivity, terrified Moscow and Novgorod, reduced Azov to ashes, and then returned home, laden with an enormous spoil of precious furs, linens, and ingots of gold and silver, A. D. 1383.

In 1398 Tamerlane planned an invasion of India. His troops murmured against the dangers and hardships of such a campaign, and talked with fear of the "rivers, mountains, deserts, soldiers in armor, elephants, destroyers of men." But the conqueror's frown was more terrible than all these, and Tamerlane was well aware of the real weakness and anarchy of Hindoostan. His invading army contained ninety-two squadrons of cavalry, and marched in three divisions. While crossing the Hindoo Koosh mountains, at their terrible pass, thousands of the Tartar conqueror's troops and horses perished in the snow. At five places Tamerlane was let down a precipice on a portable scaffold by means of ropes one hundred and fifty cubits long.

Tamerlane crossed the Indus at Attok, and advanced by a circuitous rout to the great city of Delhi, which had flourished under Mohammedan Sultans for three centuries. The weak Sultan was enticed from his strong castle and city, and came out into the plain with ten thousand cuirassiers, forty thousand foot-guards, and one hundred and twenty elephants, whose tusks were armed with sharp and pointed daggers. Tamerlane employed fire, a ditch of iron spikes and a rampart of bucklers against the enemy, to allay the uneasiness of his troops; but the Tartars soon learned to smile at their own fears, and as soon as they routed the elephants the enemy's troops disappeared from the field. Delhi was taken by Tamerlane's victorious troops, and was given up to pillage and massacre. The great Tartar conqueror advanced one hundred miles to the north-east and crossed the Ganges, and returned along the northern hills of India.

During this wanton inroad into India millions of human beings perished. A city of the Ghebers, or fire-worshipers, was negotiating for its ransom; but during the delay a breach in the walls was effected, through which the ruthless Tartars entered the city. The dispersed Ghebers set fire to their own houses, threw their wives, their children and all their wealth into the flames, and perished to the last man, heroically defending themselves on the smoking ruins. Those who sought refuge in mountains and caverns were appalled at seeing wooden trunks suspended to iron chains at the entrance of their retreats, from which soldiers issued who pursued them into the darkness of their caves with relentless carnage.

Before his victory at Delhi, Tamerlane was told that his camp was filled with captives, mainly Ghebers and idolaters, the garrisons of the cities he had taken, who might escape to the enemy during the battle. The fanatical conqueror ordered them to be put to death, and over a hundred thousand wretched victims were massacred in less than an hour. The conquering Tartars obtained an immense booty by the plunder and devastation of the richest country in the world; and every Tartar soldier was loaded with diamonds and jewels, and carried off vast numbers of slaves.

Tamerlane was called away from the further prosecution of the *Ghazi*, or "holy war," as he called it, by insurrections in Persia. After suppressing these revolts, he marched into Georgia, where he perpetrated other religious massacres, his victims there being Christians. His soldiers scoured the rocks and caverns of Georgia in pursuit of the Christians, with the same success that they had hunted down the Ghebers in India. Wearied with their murderous brutality, the Tartars finally accepted tribute, instead of exterminating the Christians. Tamerlane would have subjected all of Georgia to his sway had he not turned his attention in another direction by taking the field against the Ottoman Turkish Sultan Bajazet I.

Before marching against Bajazet I., Tamerlane invaded Syria, where he massacred hundreds of thousands of human beings and destroyed Damascus. He also took and destroyed Bagdad. Tamerlane ordered each of his soldiers to bring him a head, and caused a pyramid of ninety thousand human heads to be erected on the ruins of Bagdad. This was in accordance with his custom during his career. In one instance he caused four thousand soldiers with their horses to be cast into the moat of a city that he had taken, and these were all buried alive. In an expedition against the Getes he once took two thousand prisoners, and caused them to be heaped upon one another alive, with bricks and mortar between them, to construct towers or pyramids. These horrible scenes of cruelty were frequent with him.

When the Persian city of Ispahan, which had a population of a million, revolted against Tamerlane, he ordered all the inhabitants to be massacred, except such as had saved the lives of some of his soldiers. To insure the execution of this atrocious decree, he required each company of his army to furnish him a specific number of human heads. His troops bought these heads from each other to finish their contingent. So many were slaughtered that finally the heads were sold for a trifling sum. The Divan's register states that seventy thousand heads were obtained in this manner, and were used with stones and mortar as building materials for towers or pyramids in different parts of the city.

At Tamerlane's capture of the Syrian city of Aleppo the streets of that city streamed with blood, and reëchoed to the shrieks of violated maidens and the cries of mothers and children, while towers or pyramids of human heads were also constructed.

At Tamerlane's capture of Damascus all the inhabitants of that city were massacred, except one family and a colony of artificers sent to Samarcand. Ten millions of gold were exacted from Damascus, and the city was reduced to ashes.

But Tamerlane was not altogether savage. A certain historian says that he greatly delighted to see his soldiers enjoying themselves in games and festivals for whole days together, after a victory. He would then reward his generals with vests of honor and jewels, warmly interest himself in their happiness, be present at their weddings, and receive their felicitations with marks of sensibility in any prosperity which attended himself. He gave a splendid feast at his capital, Samarcand, when his sister congratulated him on the birth of a grandson. The tents occupied a space of six miles; and his pavilion, which was placed near a canopy supported by forty columns, was as spacious as a palace. When all was ready Tamerlane advanced, with the crown encircling his brow and the scepter in his hand, and seated himself on the throne erected in the middle of the tent and ornamented with precious stones.

The two sides of the throne were filled by a vast number of the most beautiful females of Asia, shaded with veils of gold brocade studded with jewels. Two rows were occupied with musicians; and nine stewards holding golden maces preceded the courses, and were followed by cupbearers holding decanters containing various kinds of wine and brandy. The many lovely women, whose braided hair extended to the ground, gave additional luster to the brilliant assemblage. The festival ended with shows and dances.

While the Tartar arms had been employed in Syria and Mesopotamia, after the destruction of the Ottoman Turkish Sultan's city of Sivas, Sultan Bajazet I., who had been besieging Constantinople, had two years to prepare for the final encounter with Tamerlane. In Tamerlane's first expedition the Tartar conqueror and the Ottoman Sultan had addressed a great deal of princely billingsgate and bravado to each other. Tamerlane called Bajazet I. "nothing but a Turkman," and himself a Turk, bidding him "be wise in time, reflect, repent, and avert the thunder of our vengeance." He exclaimed: "Thou ant! why wilt thou seek to provoke elephants? They will trample thee under their feet!" Bajazet replied still more indecorously, and made domestic allusions considered the most degrading insults and unpardonable offenses. The two barbarian conquerors were very much alike in their arrogance and in their ruthless ambition.

Sultan Bajazet's army numbered four hundred thousand infantry and cavalry, among whom were forty thousand Janizaries, a large force of national cavalry, twenty thousand European cuirassiers clad in black and impenetrable armor, troops of Asia Minor, and a colony of Tartars whom Tamerlane had driven from Kipzak. This army was posted in the plain near Sivas. Tamerlane moved through Armenia from the Araxes. His boldness was secured by the wisest precautions. His speed was guided by order and discipline. The flying squadrons which marked his road and preceded his standard diligently explored the woods, the mountains and the rivers. He moved on, marched into the very heart of the Ottoman Empire, and besieged Angora. Sultan Bajazet I. hastened to oppose him. The impatient rivals engaged in battle in the plains around the city of Angora, and after a mighty struggle Tamerlane was victorious, July 28, 1402.

Tamerlane owed his signal victory to himself, the genius of the moment, and the military discipline of thirty years. He had improved the tactics, without violating the manners of the Tartars, whose force still consisted in the missile weapons and the rapid evolutions of a numerous cavalry. The mode of attack was the same, from a single troop to a great army. A foremost line advanced to the charge, and was supported by the squadrons of the great vanguard in proper order. The general's eye watched over the field, and, at his command, the front and rear of the right and left wings successively advanced in their respective divisions, and in a direct or oblique line. The enemy was pressed by eighteen or twenty attacks, each of which afforded a chance of victory. But in the battle of Angora the main body itself was supported, on the flanks and in the rear, by the bravest squadrons of the reserve, under the command of Tamerlane's sons and grandsons.

Sultan Bajazet I. displayed the qualities of a soldier and a chief on that memorable day, but his genius was no match for his invincible adversary, and from various causes most of his troops failed him at the decisive moment. The European cuirassiers, who formed part of his right wing, charged with faithful hearts and irresistible arms; but these men of iron were soon broken by an artful flight and a headlong pursuit. The Janizaries alone, without cavalry or missile weapons, were encompassed by a circle of Tartars; but their valor was at length overcome by heat, thirst, and the superior numbers of their foes. The unfortunate Sultan Bajazet I., afflicted with the gout in his hands and feet, was transported from the field on the fleetest of his horses. He was pursued and taken prisoner by Tamerlane's victorious troops.

Tamerlane was playing chess with his son when the captive Turkish Sultan was brought to his tent, and he kept his illustrious prisoner standing at the door until the game was finished. Bajazet I. was then courteously received and treated with princely generosity by his Tartar conqueror; but when he afterwards attempted to escape he was loaded with chains and thrust into an iron cage, against the bars of which he dashed out his brains.

After the battle of Angora the Turkish kingdom of Anatolia submitted to Tamerlane, who enacted his usual scenes of rapine and destruction on every side. The spoils of the palace and city of Brusa were enormous, but one of Sultan Bajazet's sons carried the royal treasury into Europe, and the inhabitants had fled. The buildings, which were mainly of wood, were burned.

Tamerlane took Smyrna by storm, after an obstinate defense by the Knights of St. John, and massacred all the garrison, beheading the Christian heroes on board two great ships in the harbor. The two straits of the Dardanelles and the Bosphorus were defended by the Turks and the Christians, who combined in this emergency to prevent Tamerlane from crossing over into Europe; but he was master of all of Western and Central Asia, from the Archipelago on the west to the Ganges and the frontiers of Mongolia on the east.

Solyman, Bajazet's son—then King of Roumania—and the Eastern Roman Emperor, both paid tribute and swore allegiance to the conquering Tamerlane. The Sultan of Egypt submitted, and coin was struck and prayers were said for the great Tartar conqueror at Cairo. The indefatigable Tamerlane, in his camp at Smyrna, now meditated the conquest of China, and thus making himself master of the East of Asia as well as of the western portion of that great continent. The fanatical Tartar conqueror hoped to atone for the Moslem blood that he had shed, and to smooth his way to the joys of Paradise, by forcing the Chinese to embrace Islam, by filling China with Mohammedan mosques and drenching that land with heathen blood. While he was still in Asia Minor he sent pioneers beyond the Jaxartes to subdue the pagan Kalmucks and Mongols, to found cities and magazines in the desert, and to open a way through Central Asia to China.

Tamerlane returned to Samarcand after his triumph over the Turkish Sultan; and there, during a brief rest, he displayed his magnificence and power, listened to the complaints of his subjects, distributed a just proportion of rewards and punishments, employed his wealth in erecting palaces and temples, and received ambassadors from Egypt, Arabia, India, Tartary, Russia and Spain, A. D. 1404, 1405.

Tamerlane now occupied himself with the marriage of six of his grandsons; and, as this was considered an act of religion, no less than of paternal tenderness, the pomp of the Saracen Khalifs was revived in these nuptials. On this occasion the nobility and the people of Asia crowded to Samarcand. The nuptials were celebrated in the gardens of Carighul, decorated with a countless number of tents and pavilions, displaying the luxury of a great capital and the spoils of a triumphant army. Entire forests were cut down to supply fuel for the kitchens. The plain was spread with pyramids of meat and vases of every liquor, to which thousands of guests were courteously invited. The orders of the state and the nations of the world, including the European ambassadors, were marshaled at the great Khan's banquet. Illuminations and masquerades testified the public joy. The trades of Samarcand passed in review; and every trade was emulous to execute some quaint device, some marvelous pageant, with the materials of its peculiar art.

After the marriage contracts had been ratified by the cadis, the bridegrooms and their brides retired to their nuptial chambers. In accordance with the Asiatic fashion they were dressed and undressed nine times; and at each change of apparel pearls and rubies were showered on their heads, and were abandoned to their attendants with surprising indifference. A general indulgence was proclaimed; and every law was relaxed, and every pleasure permitted. The Great Khan's proclamation was in these words: "This is the season of feasts, of pleasure and of rejoicing. No one is allowed to dispute or reprimand. Let not the rich exult over the poor, nor the powerful over the weak. Let no one ask his neighbor, Why hast thou acted thus?" The festival lasted two months, during which the people were free and the sovereign was idle.

But after these two months of festivity Tamerlane returned to the cares of government and war. His standard was unfurled for the invasion of China. The Emirs reported two hundred thousand men under arms, and these were the select and veteran soldiers of Persia and Turkestan. Their baggage and provisions were transported on five hundred wagons and an immense train of horses and camels. The troops were prepared for a long absence, as it required six months for a caravan journey from Samarcand to Pekin. It is said that Tamerlane had raised an army of one million two hundred thousand troops for the conquest of China.

Tamerlane's impatience was not retarded by age or the rigor of winter. He mounted on horseback, crossed the Jaxartes on the ice, marched three hundred miles from his capital, and pitched his last camp in the vicinity of Otrar, "where he was expected by the angel of death." He was seized with a fever, the progress of which was accelerated by fatigue and by the indiscreet use of ice water; and the great Tartar Khan who had conquered half of Asia died in the seventieth year of his age, A. D. 1405—thirty-five years after he had ascended the throne of Zagatai. His death put an end to his enterprise, his armies were disbanded, and China was saved from another great Tartar conquest.

Tamerlane was fond of chess, and invented a new game. He was likewise fond of reading, particularly history. His custom was to converse awhile every evening with learned and literary men, whose society he prized. He looked after all details, leaving to others nothing that he himself was able to attend to. He had so retentive a memory that those who knew the vastness of his affairs were astonished at his minute questionings as to different circumstances and persons on revisiting the great variety of places through which he passed. He neglected no opportunity to do honor to the tomb of a saint or to a relic, either from policy to secure the veneration of his subjects for himself, or from a strong native tinge of superstition in his own mind.

Tamerlane was corpulent and robust in person, and was rather tall and well formed. He had a high forehead, a large head, a ruddy and fair complexion, a long beard, broad shoulders, thick fingers, long legs, eyes full of fire, a loud and piercing voice, and an engaging air. His right hand and right foot were lame from wounds. His biographer says: "Never a prince carried a more majestic and terrible air in his wrath, nor yet a more sweet and agreeable one when he was pleased to bestow his favors."

Even in old age Tamerlane retained a sound mind, a strong body, a great degree of firmness and an unshaken constancy. He had the greatest veneration for Zingis Khan, and the judicial formula which he adopted was: "By virtue of the laws of Zingis Khan." Tamerlane loved the truth without disguise, even if it was to his disadvantage. The motto of his seal was: "I am simple and sincere." Neither prosperity nor adversity disturbed his equality of soul. Though he was a scourge to mankind, and though his ambition and cruelty brought twelve million human beings to violent deaths, he put an end to the anarchy and rapine to which Asia had been a prey at his accession; and it is said that under his vigorous and prosperous rule a child might carry a purse of gold from one end of his dominions to the other without fear or without being molested.

But the blessings of Tamerlane's administration ended with his death. Not one of his thirty-six sons and seventeen daughters and their children was found equal to the task of governing the empire which he had founded. His son CHAROC alone maintained the glory of the empire for a time; but after his death there was a renewal of those scenes of darkness and bloodshed that have involved the destinies of Tartary from time immemorial. In less than a century after Tamerlane's death Transoxiana and Persia—Turan and Iran—were ravaged by the Uzbecks and the Turkomans.

Tamerlane's race was saved from extinction by his descendant in the fifth generation, the hero Baber, who fled before the Uzbeck conquerors of Turkestan, and himself effected the conquest of Hindoostan in 1525, founding an empire which under his successors, the *Grand Moguls*, embraced all of Hindoostan, Afghanistan and Beloochistan. The history of this Mongol, or Mogul, Empire in India will be related in subsequent portions of this volume.

SECTION XV.—RISE OF THE OTTOMAN TURKISH EMPIRE.

OLYMAN, the chief of a Turkish tribe called *Oguz*, perhaps the same as the ancient Oigurs and the modern Ogres, had attached himself to the fortunes of Korasm. When the Korasmian power was overthrown by the victorious Mongol hordes under Zingis Khan, Solyman fled westward with his followers, taking with them their wives and children, their sheep and cattle. They first sought an asylum in Armenia, but after a residence of seven years in that country they returned to their native land. Their leader Solyman was drowned in crossing the Euphrates, and his four sons divided the leadership of the tribe between them.

Many of the tribe dispersed into the deserts, but about four hundred families remained attached to ORTHOGRUL, one of Solyman's four sons. Orthogrul immediately marched westward to seek his fortune in Asia Minor, where the chieftains who ruled the fragments of the dismembered Seljuk Turkish dominions were harassing each other with mutual wars, and could not be induced to unite against the Mongols or the Crusaders. While the Korasmian Turkish tribe under Orthogrul was on its journey to Asia Minor it fell in with two armies engaged in a fierce struggle. Orthogrul joined the weaker party, and thus changed the fortune of the day. The victorious chief was Aladdin, a Seljuk chieftain, who rewarded Orthogrul for his aid by the present of a rich silk robe, which was a gift of honor in the East, and also with the grant of a mountainous district on the frontiers of Bithynia and Phrygia, where there was sufficient pasturage for the flocks and herds of the nomad followers of Orthogrul.

The first settlement of Orthogrul's tribe was a camp of four hundred tents at Surgut, on the banks of the river Sanjar, on the frontier of the Eastern Empire, A. D. 1280. Orthogrul made constant raids into the Byzantine territories; and, as the Seljuk Sultan of Iconium had appointed him commander-in-chief of his armies, he maintained and extended his conquests in that quarter for half a century.

OTHMAN I., or OSMAN I., the youngest of Orthogrul's three sons, gave his name to this Turkish tribe, which was thereafter known as the *Ottoman Turks*; and he is considered the founder of the Ottoman Empire, which has existed for six centuries and has been steadily declining for the last two centuries. On the death of his father, Othman was chosen his successor, in preference to his two elder brothers, because of his superior bravery and enterprise, A. D. 1299.

Othman I. was in high favor with Aladdin II., the last Seljuk Sultan of Iconium, who gave him a castle and additional territory, and granted him the privilege of holding as his own any Christian states that he might conquer. The young Emir of the Ottoman Turks profited by this permission, and gradually extended his conquests on all sides until he was master of a large extent of territory. The neighboring Emirs grew jealous of the growing power of Othman I., and they contrived many stratagems to destroy him.

On the death of the Seljuk Turkish Sultan Aladdin II. of Iconium, without children, his dominions were seized and divided by his Emirs. Nearly all of Bithynia came into the possession of Othman I. He was fortunate in obtaining the friendship of a young Greek who espoused the Moslem faith to please his patron, and who instructed the Turkish Emir in the art of government. This renegade Greek Christian was the ancestor of the family of the Michaelogi, so frequently conspicuous in Turkish annals. Othman I. was chiefly indebted for the supremacy which he speedily obtained to the information which he received from this apostate Greek. His proximity to Constantinople opened to him a wide field of enterprise, and the civil wars between the elder and younger Andronícus, which then distracted the Eastern Empire, left the Asiatic subjects of the Empire to their own feeble resources, in consequence of which they fell an easy prey to the first invaders.

The Christian princes of Asia Minor, alarmed at the progress of Othman I., united their forces and sought to crush the rising power of the ambitious Turk by one decisive effort; but Othman I. gained the victory in a battle on the frontiers of Phrygia and Bithynia, and took Prusa, the ancient capital of Bithynia, and made it his capital, slightly altering its name to *Brusa*, which it retains at the present day. Othman's policy was equal to his military skill, and what he won by his valor he secured by wise and salutary regulations. He reconciled his Christian subjects to his government by his impartial administration of justice and mercy, and many who fled before his arms returned to enjoy safety and repose under his powerful protection.

Othman I. died in 1326, and was succeeded by his son ORKHAN, who prosecuted his father's ambitious designs with vigor. He defeated the Christians under the Eastern Emperor Andronícus III., captured Nice and Nicomedía, and extended the Ottoman dominion to the Hellespont. During the civil war which distracted the Eastern Empire after the death of Andronícus III., concerning the regency, John Cantacuzene solicited the aid of the Turkish Emir against the Empress Anne, and secured his friendship and assistance by giving him his daughter Theodora in marriage. Orkhan aided John Cantacuzene with a force of ten thousand Turkish cavalry, which, under the command of his son Solyman, crossed the Hellespont in 1358, and obtained possession of Gallipoli.

The admission of these Turkish auxiliaries into Europe gave a deep and mortal wound to the Eastern Empire, which succeeding Emperors vainly endeavored to heal. The Ottoman Turks, as allies of John Cantacuzene, seized the fortresses of Thrace, and held on to the most important of those strongholds, even after their restitution was demanded and a ransom paid therefor; and Gallipoli, the key of the Hellespont, was peopled by a Turkish colony.

While Solyman was securing a foothold for the Ottoman Turks in Europe, his father had compelled many of the neighboring Emirs, by force or fraud, to seek his protection and to acknowledge his supremacy. In the midst of his triumphs he suffered a misfortune in the death of his son, who was killed by a fall from his horse while hunting. Orkhan did not long survive this loss, and died in 1360.

Orkhan is extolled by the Turks for his justice, clemency, and liberality to the poor. He adorned the city of Brusa, his capital, with a splendid mosque, a hospital and an academy. He was the first of the Turkish sovereigns who assigned regular pay to the troops while they were on duty. There was a great variety of costume and weapons in the Ottoman armies at that period. Some of the Turkish soldiers wore iron helmets, and coats of armor made of felt or cloth, quilted and stuffed with cotton, with shoulder and neck pieces of iron. Gunpowder was then scarcely known.

On the death of Orkhan, in 1360, his son, AMURATH I., ascended the Ottoman Turkish throne, and became one of the most famous of Turkish sovereigns. He wielded his father's cimeter with terrible effect. He carried his arms into Europe, overran all of Thrace, and made Adrianople the capital of the rising Ottoman Empire. He was recalled from his European conquests by disturbances in Asia Minor.

Aladdin, the Seljuk Turkish Emir of Caramania, who had married Amurath's daughter, and who was the most powerful of the Turkish chieftains in that region, had taken advantage of his father-in-law's absence to invade his Asiatic territories. Amurath I. hastened to repel his son-in-law's aggression. The two armies engaged in battle on the plains of Dorylæum, and Aladdin fled after a stubborn conflict, taking refuge in the city of Iconium. He was pardoned at his wife's intercession, and his possessions were restored to him by his father-in-law.

Amurath I. now devoted his entire energies to the extension of the Ottoman dominion in Europe, which already extended within sight of the capital of the Eastern Roman Empire. Amurath I. next subdued the Slavonic nations of Bulgaria, Servia, Bosnia and Albania.

From the multitudes of his Christian captives Amurath I. selected the strongest and most beautiful youths, and caused them to be trained for his service. They became the famous body-guard of the Turkish Sultans, and were called *Janizaries*. They were reared in the Mohammedan faith in early childhood, and were treated with great favor by the Sultan, so that they became his most devoted subjects. They constituted the flower of the Turkish army, and were considered the most formidable body of troops in the world.

In the military colleges in which they were instructed in the Moslem religion they were likewise trained in the Turkish military discipline. In order to increase their number, a law was promulgated that the Christian subjects of the Sultan should give up all their male children born in every fifth year, to be educated in the military schools, where they were taught to speak the Turkish language, to shoot with the bow and to wrestle. As they grew to manhood some were appointed to attend the Sultan and guard the palace. The rest were formed into companies, and constituted a disciplined army.

They were called *Janizaries*, from a dervish, whom the Sultan ordered to bless and consecrate the new army. As they were drawn up in order, this dervish threw the sleeve of his gown over the foremost soldier's head, and said: "Let them be called *Janizaries*—a word signifying *new soldiers*. May their countenances be ever bright, their hands victorious and their swords keen. May their spears hang always over the heads of their enemies, and wherever they go may they return with a shining face."

The Janizaries wore long gowns and tunics, which were common among the Turks. They also wore a red cloth cap, the back of which was formed like a sleeve, and hung down behind, in memory of the dervish from whom they received their name. When they were on duty the gown of the Janizaries was changed for a jacket, which was worn over large trowsers. Their boots were of red leather. All of them wore long beards, except the cavalry, who shaved their chins and wore mustaches. All the Turks from the time of Othman I. shaved their heads, with the exception of a single lock on the crown. This custom has given adequate employment to the barbers, who are very numerous in all the Turkish towns.

The Turkish institutions were well calculated to nourish the military spirit. The laws of Mohammed make every true Mussulman a soldier, and a third of all the conquered land belonged to the army. In the time to which we here allude the Turkish conquests had become so extensive that every Turk held an estate of his own directly from the Sultan, who now claimed a right over all property. He granted these lands under a kind of feudal title, each proprietor being obliged to keep a horse and a number of men for military service, in proportion to the size of his estate.

The lands were usually tilled by the conquered people, mainly Greeks, who paid a certain proportion of their produce—generally one-tenth—to their landlords. This practice was so general that a Turkish soldier would not accept land in a province where the population had been exterminated or driven out, as the people were more valuable than the land. These estates were not hereditary, and the Sultan might at his pleasure take them away from the holder.

At length the Servians, Bosnians and Bulgarians revolted against Amurath I., and were aided by the Hungarians and the Wallachians Amurath I. took the field against his enemies, and a terrible battle was fought at Cossova, in Servia, in 1389. The conflict was long doubtful, until the Turks, by pretending to give way, threw the Christian ranks into disorder. A frightful slaughter ensued, and the allied Christian hosts fled, leaving the field to the victorious Ottomans. The Servian prince Lazarus, who had instigated the revolt, was among the slain. But the triumph of Amurath I. was cut short in a most unexpected manner. As he was walking over the battle-field he stopped to look at some wounded men, when one of them, a fierce Croat, among the Hungarian wounded, just breathing his last, made a sudden plunge at the Turkish sovereign, and with a short sword which he still held in his hand he gave Amurath I. a mortal wound, causing almost instant death.

Amurath I. was succeeded by his son BAJAZET I., who secured himself on the Turkish throne by murdering his brother, an unnatural custom which became the settled policy of his successors. Bajazet I. was the first of Ottoman rulers who assumed the title of *Sultan*. He was ferocious and cruel by nature, and crushed all the petty Turkish Emirs of Asia Minor, either putting them to death or driving them into exile.

During the whole of his reign Bajazet I. was incessantly engaged in wars in Asia and Europe, and he was named *Ilderim*, "Lightning," from the rapidity and energy of his movements. His victories in Europe left to the Greek Emperor very little but his capital, which was several times besieged by the Turkish armies. Bajazet I. secured uninterrupted communication between his European and Asiatic dominions by stationing a fleet of galleys at Gallipoli, so that he was able to command the Hellespont and to intercept the expeditions sent from Western Europe to the relief of Constantinople.

Bajazet I. filled Europe with terror, and made a strenuous effort to conquer Hungary. All Western Europe sent aid to Hungary, whose cause was that of all Christendom; but the great warrior Sultan defeated the allied Christian army of one hundred thousand men under the command of King Sigismund of Hungary and Duke John the Fearless of Burgundy in the bloody battle of Nicopolis, on the Danube, in Bulgaria, in 1396.

Sultan Bajazet I. invariably treated the Greek Emperors as his vassals. He enclosed the Eastern Empire, which by this time consisted of but little more than Constantinople and its suburbs, by surrounding it on all sides with his extensive dominions; and the capture of the Byzantine capital was only a question of time. Bajazet I. took advantage of the death of John Palæologus I. and the accession of Manuel II. to the Byzantine throne to claim Constantinople as his own capital, and when his demand was rejected he besieged the city, which would have speedily fallen into his possession had he not been called to Asia Minor to save his dominions there from falling into the power of the great Tartar conqueror Tamerlane.

The Seljuk Turkish Emirs who had been driven from Asia Minor by Sultan Bajazet's usurpations fled to Turkestan and found refuge at Samarcand, Tamerlane's capital. These refugee Emirs solicited the assistance of the great Tartar chieftain to recover their dominions. Tamerlane at first refused to interfere with the Ottoman Turkish Sultan in his pious task of humbling the Christians and extending Islam; but he was at length persuaded to aid the fugitive Emirs.

Tamerlane sent an ambassador to Sultan Bajazet I. to demand the restoration of the exiled Emirs to their respective possessions. He also required that the Ottoman Sultan should become his vassal, and that the Sultan should testify his submission by substituting the name of Tamerlane for his own upon the Turkish coinage and in the public prayers in the Ottoman dominions. The haughty Turkish Sultan, who acknowledged none as his suzerain or superior, rejected the great Tartar Khan's degrading demand with scorn, hurling his defiance in the most insulting terms that his pride and indignation could dictate. Bajazet I. and Tamerlane were equally confident of success, and each prepared for the decisive struggle.

Manuel Palæologus, the reigning Greek Emperor at Constantinople, who was then engaged in a civil war with his nephew who claimed the Byzantine throne, proposed terms of peace to the Turkish Sultan. Bajazet eagerly embraced the proposal; and a treaty of peace was accordingly concluded, by which one of the streets of Constantinople was appropriated for the residence of Turkish merchants, who were permitted to carry on their trade with the Genoese and the Venetians. A mosque was also erected for the Turkish residents in the Byzantine capital at the Byzantine Emperor's expense, and they were allowed to have a cadi among them to settle their differences according to the Mohammedan laws. All these terms of the treaty were fulfilled.

The progress of Tamerlane's fierce barbarian warriors was irresistible. They overran the greater part of Asia Minor with scarcely any resistance; and, before Sultan Bajazet I. could lead his army to the scene of action, most of his Asiatic dominions had been ravaged with fire and sword by the fierce Tartar invaders. At the capture of Sivas, the ancient Sebaste, the bravest of the Turkish garrison were buried alive by the ferocious victors.

Finally the armies of Bajazet I. and Tamerlane encountered each other on the plains of the city of Angora, the ancient Ancyra, in Galatia; and after a desperate and bloody battle Sultan Bajazet I. was defeated and taken prisoner, July 28, 1402, and was confined in a cage by his Tartar conqueror, where he dashed out his brains; as already related.

Bajazet I. had five sons. Of these, Mustapha was slain on the bloody field of Angora; Solyman escaped from Tamerlane's pursuing cavalry, fled to Adrianople, and preserved the Ottoman power in Europe; Musa retained the sovereignty of the small kingdom of Anatolia, in Asia Minor, having Brusa for its capital; Isa reigned over a small territory in the vicinity of Angora, Sinopé and the Black Sea; and Mohammed retained the government of Amasia, which his father had assigned to him.

Ten years of civil war ensued between these five brothers, A. D. 1403-1413, and this period is known in the Turkish annals as an interregnum. Solyman drove Musa from his throne, and united the governments of Adrianople and Brusa for a time; but Solyman was afterwards surprised by Musa in his capital, and was overtaken and slain while fleeing toward Constantinople. Musa and Isa both fell before the valor and policy of their younger brother, who thus reunited the Ottoman dominions under his own scepter, and was recognized by the entire Turkish nation as Sultan MOHAMMED I.

The eight years of the reign of Mohammed I. were peaceful, and were passed in the consolidation of his power and in restoring the reign of law which had been overthrown by the civil war. The only disturbance was by an impostor who pretended to be Mustapha, that son of Bajazet I. who was killed at Angora, but whom the impostor pretended had escaped alive from that fatal field. The impostor's pretensions were supported by the Wallachians, but Sultan Mohammed I. routed the Wallachians and forced them to pay an annual tribute, while the impostor sought refuge at Constantinople.

Mohammed I. faithfully observed his friendly engagements with the Eastern Empire during his entire reign. His treatment of the Christian ambassadors from Servia, Wallachia, Bulgaria and Greece showed his earnest desire to cultivate a good understanding with his neighbors. These ambassadors were permitted to eat at the Sultan's table, and after being entertained with great kindness and hospitality they were dismissed by Mohammed I., who addressed them in these words: "Tell your masters that I offer them peace, that I accept of that which they offer me, and I hope that the God of peace will punish those who violate it." His last care was to provide two able counselors to guide the youth of his eldest son Amurath, and he consigned his two youngest sons to the guardianship of the Greek Emperor Manuel II.

Mohammed I. died in 1421, and was succeeded on the Turkish throne by his eldest son AMURATH II., whose reign was soon disturbed by the impostor who had disturbed the preceding reign. The impostor's pretensions were supported by the Greek Emperor Manuel II., and his career was successful for a time. The army of Sultan Amurath II., commanded by his Grand Vizier, Bajazet, was defeated, and the Grand Vizier himself was slain. The pretended Mustapha entered Adrianople in triumph, and seized the vast treasures which Amurath II. had collected in that city. He passed a short time in riotous pleasures, but was soon aroused from his revels by the Sultan's approach at the head of an army. The impostor's career was ended after a short campaign, and Mustapha was deserted by his friends and ended his life on the scaffold.

The Greek Emperor raised up another claimant for the Ottoman throne in the person of the brother of Sultan Amurath II., a child of only six years, who had escaped from Amurath's hands when his other brother was murdered. His standard was set up at Nice, but Sultan Amurath II. soon obtained possession of that city, and caused his little brother to be strangled with the bowstring.

Amurath II. renewed the attack upon Constantinople, but retired after a siege of two months. He was a sovereign of singular moderation and justice for an Ottoman Turk, and preferred the repose of private life to the cares of sovereignty. His reign was perpetually disturbed by the rebellions of the Emirs of Asia Minor, and by the invasions of the Hungarians under John Hunníyades. The Emirs were easily quelled, but the Hungarians proved a more formidable foe. After concluding a ten years' truce with the Hungarians, Amurath II. resigned the Turkish scepter to his son Mohammed, then only fifteen years of age, and retired to Magnesia, near Smyrna, in Asia Minor.

No sooner had Amurath II. begun to taste the sweets of repose than the restless Caramanians, who had repeatedly rebelled against him, and who had been as often subdued and pardoned, took advantage of his retirement and again took up arms. The Hungarians also, instigated by the Pope, and in violation of a solemn treaty, crossed the Danube into Bulgaria with a large army, composed of various Christian nations, being under the command of King Ladislas VI. of Poland and Hungary and John Hunníyades of Transylvania.

The young Mohammed, thus surrounded with enemies, and destitute of experience, yielded to the advice of his counselors and entreated his father to resume the throne. Amurath II. reluctantly complied, hastened to Adrianople, took command of the Ottoman armies, and saved the Ottoman Empire from ruin by his great victory over the Christian army under King Ladislas VI. of Poland and Hungary and John Hunníyades of Transylvania, at Varna, in Bulgaria, on the Black Sea coast, in 1444, King Ladislas VI. himself being slain, and his head being carried about on a spear, while the papal legate Julian was overtaken by death during the flight from the fatal field. Soon afterward Amurath II. again retired from the cares of government to the solitude of his beautiful residence at Magnesia; but his son's feeble hand was unable to restrain the licentiousness of the Janizaries. Adrianople became a prey to domestic faction, and the aged Sultan again resumed the scepter.

Amurath II. has been praised by both Turkish and Greek writers. He was a just and valiant prince, moderate in victory, and always ready to grant peace to the vanquished. He was a learned man himself, and encouraged learning in others. Says the historian Cantemir: "Every year he gave a thousand pieces of gold to the sons of the Prophet, and sent twenty-five hundred pieces to the religious persons at Mecca, Medina and Jerusalem." He founded many colleges and hospitals, built many mosques and caravanseries, and added much to the magnificence of the cities and towns of the Ottoman Empire.

HUNYADY IN BATTLE WITH THE TURKS.

Amurath II. died in 1451, and was succeeded by his son MOHAMMED II., who was then twenty-one years of age, and who was one of the most famous of the Turkish Sultans. He had been educated by his father with the greatest care, and is said to have been able to speak in the Arabic, Persian, Hebrew, Greek and Latin languages, in addition to his native Turkish tongue. But, in spite of his training, he was a cruel and lustful tyrant; and began his reign by putting his two infant brothers to death.

From the beginning of his reign Mohammed II. was resolved upon taking Constantinople and making that city the capital of the Ottoman Empire. Constantinople and its suburbs were now all that remained of the Eastern Roman Empire. The inhabitants of Constantinople were but ill prepared to withstand the attack of an enemy. They were distracted with religious feuds. Some desired a union with the Romish Church, but others declared that they would rather see the turban of Mohammed in their cathedral than the tiara of the Pope. The Christian nations of Western Europe refused to send relief to their Greek brethren of the East, and Constantinople was left to its fate. In 1452 Sultan Mohammed II. commenced fortifying the Bosphorus, to prevent the passage of European fleets to the relief of the Byzantine capital; and in the spring of 1453 he advanced to Constantinople with an army of two hundred and sixty thousand men, invested the city and took it by storm, after a siege of fifty-three days, May 29, 1453. The last Greek Emperor, Constantine Palæologus, was slain while gallantly defending his capital. Constantinople became the capital of the Ottoman Empire, but the triumphant Sultan Mohammed II. treated the vanquished

MOSQUE OF ST. SOPHIA AT CONSTANTINOPLE

Greeks with liberality, and encouraged them to remain in the conquered city. Thus ended the Eastern Empire of the Romans; the last remnants of Roman and Greek civilization in the East were now extinguished; the Greek Christian Church of St. Sophia became a Mohammedan mosque; the crescent supplanted the cross in the city of Constantine; and a Moslem monarch occupied the throne of the first Christian Roman Emperor.

The capture of Constantinople and overthrow of the Greek Empire by the arms of Sultan Mohammed II. alarmed all Europe and caused Italy to tremble for its safety. Pope Nicholas V., and his second successor, Pius II., sent the most urgent appeals to all the monarchs of Western Christendom, entreating them to combine their forces against the conquering Turks. Pius II. even resolved to animate this new crusade by his own presence, but death prevented him from executing his purpose. But two Christian princes arrested the progress of the Ottoman arms, as we shall now see.

Sultan Mohammed II. sought to follow up the capture of Constantinople by the conquest of Hungary. He advanced to the Danube and laid siege to the important fortress of Belgrade, but was defeated and driven back with heavy loss, after a siege of six months, in 1456, by the Hungarians under the valiant regent, John Hunnfyades of Transylvania. According to a Greek writer, the Sultan lost many troops "not only by the plague, but by engines cast in the form of tubes, which, by means of a dust, composed of nitre, sulphur and charcoal, shot out balls of lead, five or ten together, each as big as a walnut." This is one of the earliest descriptions of gunpowder to be found in any history.

The victory of Hunnfyades at Belgrade saved Hungary's independence. The renewal of these efforts at conquest by Sultan Mohammed II. met with no better success, and the Ottoman arms made no further progress in that quarter for many years. The voiwodes of Moldavia defended themselves with such valor that the Sultan was content with their nominal submission.

Mohammed II. turned his arms against the remaining Greek states. He conquered Greece proper and annexed it to the Ottoman Empire in 1460; and the next year Trebizond, at the east end of the Black Sea, surrendered to his arms, and the Greek dynasty of the Comneni, which had reigned there for two and a half centuries, came to an end.

In the mountainous region of Albania, the ancient Epirus, the valiant prince, Alexander Castriota, better known as Scanderbeg, which in Turkish signifies *Alexander the Great*, defended himself. In 1467 the Turks invaded his territory; but Scanderbeg, at the head of a small but faithful band of followers, resisted the mighty Ottoman hosts with success and forced them to raise the siege of his capital. Thenceforth until his death Scanderbeg maintained the independence of his little principality.

In 1481 Sultan Mohammed II. sent an army across the Adriatic, and this Turkish force stormed and sacked the town of Otranto, on the eastern coast of Lower Italy. After securing this important footing in Italy, the Turkish Sultan prepared to follow it up by the conquest of that entire peninsula; but, in the midst of the general alarm which his movements occasioned throughout Europe, Mohammed II. died the same year, A. D. 1481.

A dispute for the succession to the Turkish throne arose between the two sons of Mohammed II., Bajazet and Zizim, each of whom had partisans among the Janizaries. BAJAZET II. prevailed in Constantinople, and seized the throne. Zizim raised an army in Bithynia, and took possession of Brusa. Bajazet II. sent his Grand Vizier, Ahmed, against his brother with a strong force; and Zizim was forced to seek refuge with his mother and his two children in Syria, and afterward in Egypt, both of which countries were then under the dominion of the Mameluke Sultans.

The Sultan of Egypt and Syria received Zizim with great hospitality and endeavored to persuade him to relinquish his ambitious schemes, but without success; and Zizim next resorted to the Emir of Caramania, in Asia Minor, the petty province which had so long been hostile to the Ottoman Sultans. Zizim and the Emir of Caramania took the field against Bajazet II., but were defeated; and Zizim fled to the island of Rhodes, where he sought an asylum with the Knights of St. John, who were then at war with Bajazet II.

Zizim was favorably received at Rhodes by the Knights of St. John. Sultan Bajazet II. made advantageous offers of peace to the Knights of St. John, on condition that they should deliver his brother into his power. They refused this condition; but, as they were anxious to conclude a treaty with the Sultan, they persuaded Zizim to retire to Italy. The Pope kept him a prisoner at Rome for several years, assigned him elegant apartments at the Vatican, and treated him with all the respect due to his rank, but refused him his liberty.

Several Christian kings desired to have the custody of the captive Turkish prince, as a check upon the Sultan. At length King Charles VIII. of France, while passing through Rome, on his expedition against Naples in 1494, caused Zizim to be released; but the exiled Turkish prince died several days afterward, believed to have been poisoned through the instrumentality of the wicked Pope Alexander VI. at the instigation of Sultan Bajazet II. Being thus relieved of a dangerous competitor, Bajazet II. devoted himself to the cultivation of literature. During his reign the Turkish power declined.

The last days of Sultan Bajazet II. were embittered by the unfilial treatment which he received from his son Selim, who was fierce and warlike, and a great favorite with the Janizaries, by whose aid he forced his father to abdicate the Turkish crown in his favor, in preference to his elder brother, Achmet. Bowed down with age and infirmities, Bajazet II. retired from Constantinople with about five hundred domestics, but died on his way to Adrianople, supposed to have been poisoned by his physician at the command of his son and successor, SELIM I., A. D. 1512.

The Turkish conquerors did not attempt to impose their religion on the people whom they conquered. They even left the conquered race in the enjoyment of their own political institutions. They contented themselves with levying a tribute on every Greek town and village, according to its population. So long as the inhabitants paid their tribute regularly they were left at liberty to worship in their own churches, to elect their own magistrates, and to be governed by their own municipal laws. Although the conquered people were subject to a heavy contribution for the benefit of the Sultan's treasury, this tribute was collected in the least oppressive manner by their own magistrates, whose duty was to tax all persons, without distinction, according to their means. Not many people who have been subjected to foreign dominion have been left in possession of so many political privileges as were the Greeks by their Ottoman conquerors.

FLYING WALDENSIANS.

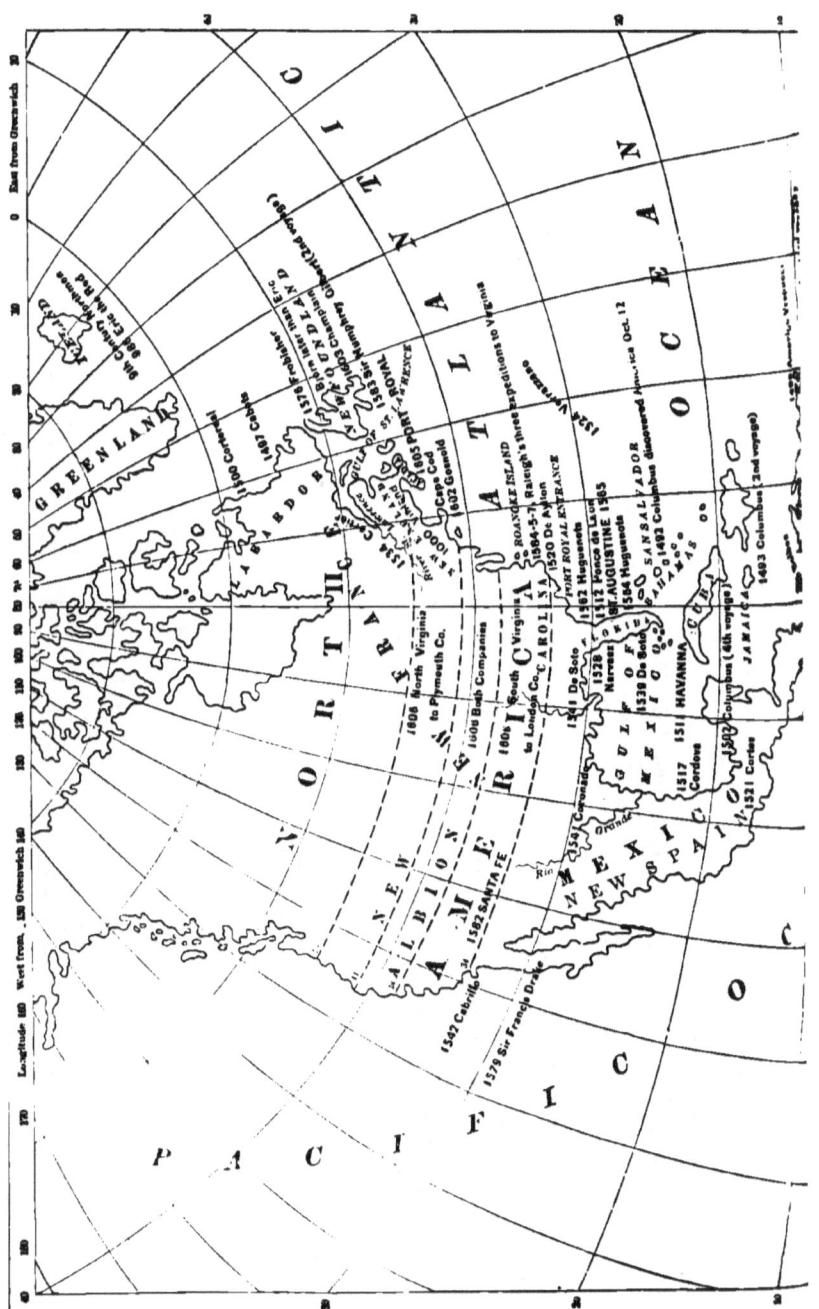

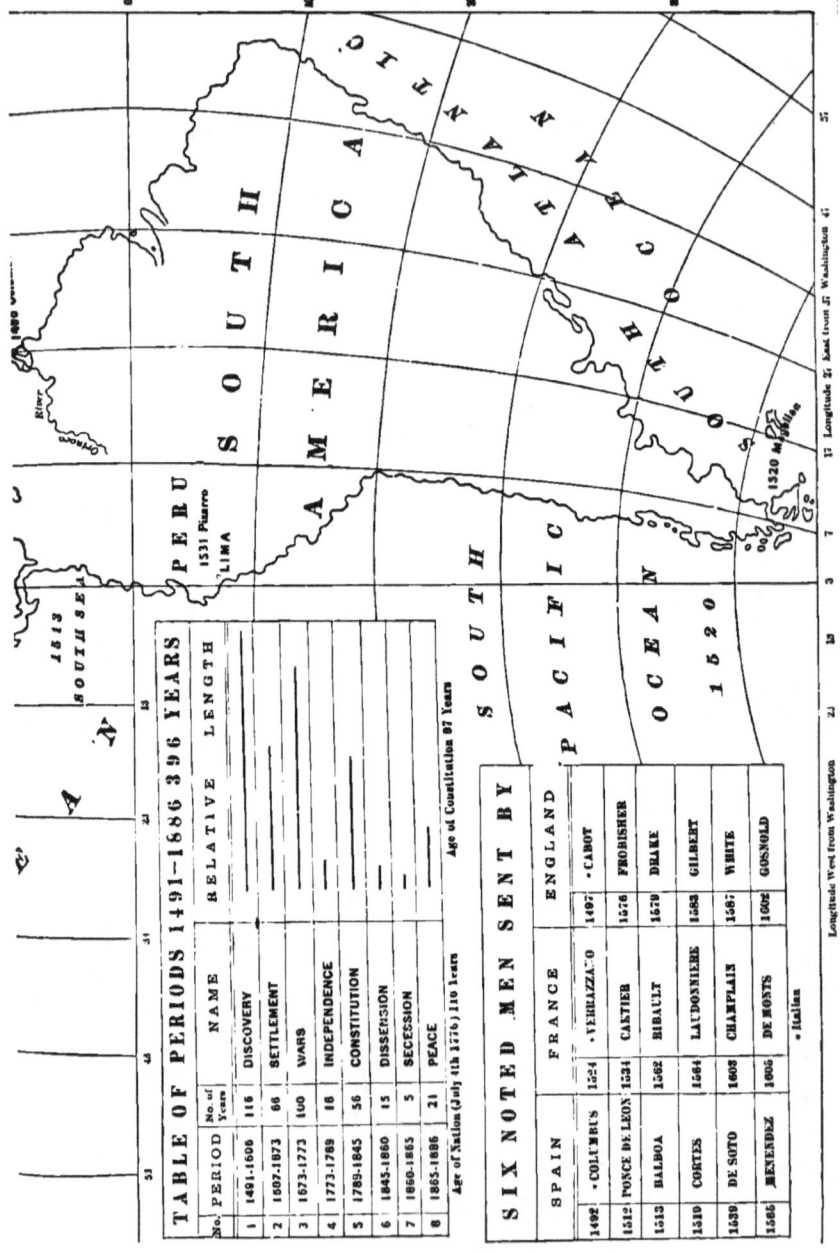

TABLE OF PERIODS 1491–1886 396 YEARS

No.	PERIOD	No. of Years	NAME	RELATIVE LENGTH
1	1491-1606	115	DISCOVERY	
2	1607-1673	66	SETTLEMENT	
3	1673-1773	100	WARS	
4	1773-1789	16	INDEPENDENCE	
5	1789-1845	56	CONSTITUTION	
6	1845-1860	15	DISSENSION	
7	1860-1865	5	SECESSION	
8	1865-1886	21	PEACE	

Age of Nation (July 4th 1776) 110 Years   Age of Constitution 97 Years

SIX NOTED MEN SENT BY

	SPAIN		FRANCE		ENGLAND
1492	•COLUMBUS	1524	•VERRAZANO	1497	•CABOT
1512	PONCE DE LEON	1534	CARTIER	1576	FROBISHER
1513	BALBOA	1562	RIBAULT	1579	DRAKE
1519	CORTES	1564	LAUDONNIERE	1583	GILBERT
1539	DE SOTO	1603	CHAMPLAIN	1587	WHITE
1565	MENENDEZ	1605	DE MONTS	1602	GOSNOLD

• Italian

PART THIRD.

MODERN HISTORY.

(1913)

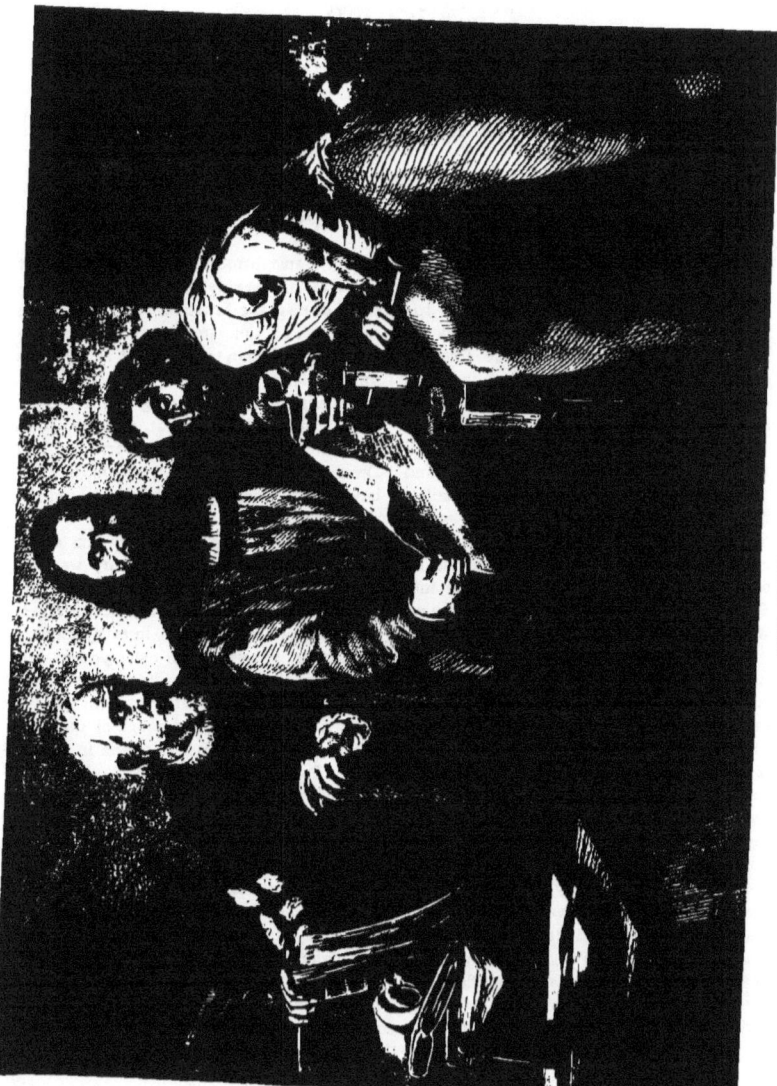

THE FIRST PROOF.

CHAPTER I.

DAWN OF THE MODERN ERA.

SECTION I.—PROGRESS OF CIVILIZATION AND INVENTION.

ANY useful inventions during the fourteenth and fifteenth centuries aided vastly in the return of European civilization at the close of the fifteenth century. The most important of these inventions was that of the art of printing, about the year 1440 A. D., by Laurence Koster, of Haarlem, in Holland, and John Gutenberg, of Mayence, in Germany, and Gutenberg's assistants, Faust and Schœffer. The result of this useful invention was a great increase in the number of books, which now, for the first time, were attainable by all classes. Printing was introduced into England by William Caxton, in 1476, as we have already remarked.

The invention of gunpowder by the German monk, Berthold Schwarz, prepared the way for the downfall of Chivalry, by the substitution of fire-arms for the old weapons of warfare. The invention of the *mariner's compass* by the Italian, Flavio Gioja, gave a fresh impulse to navigation; and very soon the gallant Portuguese navigators ventured out farther and farther from the coast than had been hitherto attempted by any mariner.

In the fifteenth century the long night of barbarism which had hung over Europe since the fall of the Western Roman Empire was rapidly passing away. The invention of the art of printing, and the flight of learned Greeks, with their valuable manuscripts, to Western Europe, upon the capture of Constantinople by the Turks, led to a revival of learning and the arts and sciences during the latter part of the fifteenth century; and the Greek and Hebrew languages now began to be studied in the great universities of Europe. Among those most instrumental in introducing the study of Greek were the two great scholars, John Reuchlin, of Pförzheim, in Germany, and Desiderius Erasmus, of Rotterdam, in Holland—both of whom flourished early in the sixteenth century.

The decay of the Feudal System about the close of the fifteenth century was followed by a change in the condition of the European states. During the Middle Ages, the great barons, or nobles, in every country of Europe, possessed the chief power; but about the close of the mediæval period the royal power became supreme in all the countries of Europe, and much of the freedom which the cities and towns in Spain, Italy, France, Germany and England had enjoyed was taken from them. Absolute monarchy was established in England by Henry VII., the first of the Tudor kings; in France by the crafty and cruel Louis XI.; in Austria by Maximilian I.; and in Spain by Ferdinand and Isabella. Chivalry had also decayed; and the knights, who at first had defended the weak and the oppressed, became highway robbers, especially in Germany, where they plundered and waylaid inoffensive peasants and merchants.

SECTION II.—THE SEA-PASSAGE TO INDIA.

HE Portuguese under Prince Henry—son of King John the Bastard (1385-1433)—took the lead in maritime discovery. This enlightened prince established an observatory near Cape St. Vincent, and gathered around him eminent astronomers and navigators from all quarters, and discussed with them his favorite project of finding a sea-passage to India by sailing around Africa. Under Prince Henry's patronage, the bold Portuguese navigators discovered and explored the western coast of Africa as far south as Cape de Verde; while the Madeira, the Azores and the Cape de Verde Islands were discovered and taken possession of by the Portuguese.

Under the patronage of King John the Perfect (1481-1495), the Portuguese crossed the equator for the first time, and the coast of Guinea was discovered and settled by the enterprising Portuguese. In 1486 Bartholomew Diaz, a daring Portuguese navigator, discovered the southern point of Africa, which was named the *Cape of Good Hope*, because there was now good hope of finding a sea-passage to India.

In 1497—during the reign of King Manuel the Great (1495-1521)—Vasco da Gama, another bold Portuguese navigator, sailed round the Cape of Good Hope to India; thus discovering the sea-passage to the East Indies—a discovery which revolutionized the world's commerce, by diverting the trade of the East from the Venetians to the Portuguese. Vasco da Gama landed at Calicut, where was planted a Portuguese colony—the first European settlement in the East Indies. In 1500 Cabral, another Portuguese navigator, discovered Brazil, which was occupied and settled by the Portuguese.

SECTION III.—DISCOVERY OF AMERICA.

MONG others who were attracted to Lisbon was Christopher Columbus, a Genoese sailor. Columbus believed the earth to be round, and that India could be reached sooner by sailing westward than by making the long voyage around Africa. He vainly endeavored to procure aid, first from his native city, Genoa, and afterward from the Kings of Portugal and England; but he finally obtained assistance from the noble-hearted queen, Isabella of Castile, who fitted out several vessels for him, and appointed him admiral and viceroy of all the lands he might discover.

On August 3, 1492, Christopher Columbus, with three Spanish vessels, left the harbor of Palos, in South-western Spain; and after a voyage of seventy days, he discovered, October 12, 1492, Guanahani, or Cat Island, which he named *San Salvador* (Holy Savior), and of which he took possession in the name of Ferdinand and Isabella—the joint sovereigns of Spain. Columbus found the inhabitants of a copper color and of savage manners; and, supposing he had only discovered the coast of India, he called the people *Indians*—a name ever since very inappropriately applied to the aborigines of the Western Continent. In 1493 he discovered the large and important islands of Cuba and Hayti, and founded the town of St. Domingo—the first European settlement in the New World. Several other large islands were discovered, and Columbus named the whole group the *West Indies*. When Columbus returned to Spain he was treated with great honors by the ruling sovereigns, and his progress from Palos to Barcelona was a triumphal procession.

After the great discovery of Columbus an

COLUMBUS BEFORE THE COUNCIL OF SALAMANCA.

India-house was established at Seville and a custom-house at Cadiz, under the direction of a new board of trade. Pope Alexander VI. conferred upon the King and Queen of Spain all the lands then or thereafter to be discovered in the New World, and these territories were to be divided from those of Portugal by an imaginary line passing due north and south, a hundred leagues west of the Azores.

Columbus made three other voyages across the stormy Atlantic. On his second voyage, in 1493, he discovered Jamaica and the Caribee Islands. On his third voyage, in 1498, Columbus discovered the great continent of South America, at the mouth of the great river Orinoco. On his fourth and last voyage — during which he discovered Central America (A. D. 1501) — his enemies caused him to be sent back to Spain in irons. He died at Valladolid, in Spain, in 1506. Ferdinand ordered the following inscription to be put upon his tomb at Seville: "To Castile and Leon, Columbus gave a New World." His remains were afterwards conveyed to Havana, in Cuba, where, it is said, they still remain.

Columbus did not know that he had discovered a new continent, but thought that he had only reached the eastern shores of Asia. This secret was revealed to Amerigo Vespucci, a Florentine navigator, who explored the eastern coast of South America in 1498, and published a glowing description of that vast continent. In his honor, the new world was named *America*.

CHRISTOPHER COLUMBUS.

In 1496 John Cabot — a native of Venice, but at that time a merchant of Bristol, in England — obtained the aid of King Henry VII. of England in fitting out an expedition for the discovery of a North-west passage to India. The next year (1497), the expedition — commanded by John Cabot's son Sebastian — sailed westward and discovered the coasts of Labrador and Newfoundland. Thus Sebastian Cabot was the first discoverer of the continent of North America. In 1498 Sebastian Cabot again sailed westward and explored the greater part of the Atlantic coast of the present United States. In 1517 he made a third voyage to the polar seas; and in 1526 — while in the service of Spain — he discovered the great river Rio de la Plata, in South America.

The aborigines, or first inhabitants, of the American continent when discovered by Europeans were a race of copper-colored savages, whom Columbus called *Indians*. The Indian is often spoken of as the *Red Man*, in contradistinction from the European, or White Man. The Indians were divided into a number of nations with distinct languages, and subdivided into numerous tribes with various dialects. These nations and tribes were very much alike in color, size, moral character, religion and government. Their rulers were called *sachems*, and their military leaders were called *chiefs*. They engaged in war, hunting and fishing. War parties would often seek renown in mortal combat. Their weapons were bows and arrows, tomahawks, or hatchets of stone, and scalping-knives of bone. They tortured their prisoners and scalped their enemies. Their women were called *squaws*, their rude the *calumet*, or pipe of peace. The Indians of Mexico and Peru were highly civilized. From ruins and mounds found in various

THE NIGHT OF OCTOBER 11, 1492.

huts *wigwams*. They believed in a Great Good Spirit and a Great Evil Spirit. Sachems in council, in making peace. smoked parts of the present United States, it is believed that the Indians displaced a highly-civilized ancient race.

MAGELLAN AT THE STRAITS.

CHAPTER II.

SIXTEENTH CENTURY.

SECTION I.—DISCOVERIES AND EXPLORATIONS IN AMERICA.

THE great discoveries of Columbus and the Cabots having revealed to Europeans the existence of a new continent a spirit of maritime enterprise was excited, which led other navigators to make voyages to the New World for purposes of discovery and exploration. We will now briefly allude to these.

We have already alluded to the discovery of Brazil by the Portuguese navigator Cabral in 1500. In 1501 Gaspar Cortereal, another Portuguese navigator, who had been commissioned by his king to make discoveries in the New World, touched at several points on the Atlantic coast of North America between Labrador and the present New Jersey, and kidnapped fifty natives for slaves. He made a second voyage, from which he never returned. As successful adventures in Africa and Asia engaged the entire attention of the Portuguese they attempted no further discoveries in America. In 1509 Diego Columbus, the son of the great discoverer, having become hereditary viceroy of Spain in the New World, undertook the conquest and colonization of Cuba, which were accomplished in 1511.

In the year A. D. 1512 John Ponce de Leon, a Spaniard, sailed from Porto Rico, in search of a "fountain of youth," which was said to exist on the neighboring continent. This fountain was said to restore youth and to perpetuate it. On the 27th of March (1512), Ponce de Leon reached the North American continent at the great peninsula between the Atlantic Ocean and the Gulf of Mexico, and named the domain *Florida*, because its banks were laden with flowers, and because the discovery was made on Pasquas de Flores, or Easter Sunday, when the Spanish churches were decorated with flowers. Ponce de Leon was afterward killed in a contest with the natives of Florida.

In 1513 the Spaniard Vasco Nuñez de Balboa crossed the Isthmus of Darien, or Panama, and discovered the Pacific Ocean, which he called *South Sea*. He waded into its waters in full costume, and took possession of sea and land in the name of his sovereign, the King of Spain. Balboa was put to death by order of the Spanish governor of Darien.

In 1517 Cordova, also a Spanish adventurer, discovered Mexico, the seat of the flourishing empire of the Aztecs, a highly civilized America Indian race, who had populous cities and towns, a regular government, and the various arts and customs of civilized life. In 1521 this empire was conquered by the Spaniards under Fernando Cortez, of which we shall give a fuller account in another section.

The name *Pacific Ocean* was given to the South Sea by Ferdinand Magellan, a Portuguese navigator, who, in the service of the King of Spain, sailed through the straits, in the southern part of South America, which bear his name, in 1520, and who, several years afterward, was killed on the Philippine Islands by the natives, and whose followers returned to Spain by way of the Indian and Atlantic Oceans, thus completing the first circumnavigation of the globe.

In 1520 Vasquez de Ayllon, a Spanish

adventurer, visited the coast of the present South Carolina, then called *Chicora*, and enticed a number of unsuspecting natives on board his two vessels and sailed with them for Hayti, but one of his vessels foundered and all on board perished, while many on board the other ship absolutely refused food and died of starvation.

Stephen Gomez, a Spaniard, who had accompanied Magellan on his search for a North-west passage to India, sailed on a voyage in 1525 for the purpose of discovering such a passage, and touched at various points on the Atlantic coast of the present United States from Delaware to New England. As he failed in the great object of his expedition he kidnapped many Indians on board his vessels for the purpose of selling them into slavery.

In 1528 Pamphilo de Narvaez, a Spanish adventurer, attempted the conquest of Florida, but failed, and lost his life in a conflict with the natives.

In 1524 Francis I., King of France, employed John Verrazzani, a Florentine, to make discoveries in the New World. Verrazzani explored the Atlantic coast of North America, from the mouth of the Cape Fear River to the Gulf of St. Lawrence, and named the region *New France*. In 1534 the French king sent Jacques Cartier, a Frenchman, on an expedition to New France. Cartier discovered the mouth of the great river which he named St. Lawrence. In 1535 Cartier sailed up the St. Lawrence, exploring the country to Montreal.

In 1539 Ferdinand De Soto, then the Spanish governor of Cuba, landed in Florida, and, proceeding westward, discovered the great river Mississippi, and explored the continent as far west as the Rocky Mountains. De Soto died on the banks of the Mississippi river in 1541; and the remnant of his followers, having suffered terribly, found their way to a Spanish settlement in Mexico. In 1539 the great Amazon river, in South America, was first explored by Orellana, a Spaniard.

The Spaniards were the first to make discoveries on the Pacific shores and in the interior of North America. In 1541 Alarçon sailed north along the Pacific coast almost to the site of San Francisco. In 1542 De Cabrillo explored the same coast almost to the mouth of the Columbia river. The same year Coronado sailed up the Gulf of California and discovered the Gila river.

SECTION II.—THE SPANISH EMPIRE IN AMERICA.

AVING given an account of the discoveries of the Spaniards, Portuguese, English and the French in America, we will now proceed to a view of the Spanish conquest and colonization in America. The Spaniards made settlements in various parts of North and South America; and their greatest exploits were the conquest of two civilized Indian empires—that of Mexico in North America and that of Peru in South America. Before proceeding with the Spanish conquest of these countries, we will give a brief historical sketch of Mexico.

The history of Mexico goes back as far as the sixth century of the Christian era. The native Mexican traditions, and the remains of ancient structures which are still to be found in the country, make it evident that the primitive inhabitants were possessed of a civilization equal to that of the Aztecs, who occupied the country when it was conquered by the Spaniards; but those aborigines of Mexico are a wholly prehistoric race.

The Toltecs entered the valley of Mexico early in the seventh century and built the city of Tollan, or Tula, and made it their capital. Some writers believe these people to have come from Central America, while others think them to have migrated from Asia by way of Behring Strait. The Toltecs are said to have been an agricultural people, and to have understood the mechanical arts. Their cities were of the cyclopæan character, and these people originated the system of astronomy which the Aztecs afterward adopted. Early in the eighth century a Toltec kingdom is said to have been founded by Icoatizin; and this kingdom lasted five centuries, at the end of which time it fell in consequence of a long period of pestilence and civil war, and the greater portion of the Toltecs migrated southward.

In the thirteenth century, soon after the Toltecs had emigrated from Meico, the Chichimecs, a fierce savage tribe who are said to have worshipped the sun as their father and the moon as their mother, migrated from the north into Mexico. The few Toltecs who remained in the country submitted to the invading Chichimecs, who settled peacefully in the country and became amalgamated with the Toltecs. From this amalgamation sprang the Colhuis, or Culhuas, who founded the kingdom of Colhuaca.

After the immigration of the Chichimecs into Mexico a number of other tribes entered the country, the most powerful of whom were the Tepanecs, who established their capital at Atzcapozalco, and founded one of the most powerful of the Mexican states. Another of these tribes were the Techichimecs, who founded the republic of Tlascala. All these tribes spoke the Nohoa, or Nahuatl, language. Another tribe were the Alcolhuis, who were considered the most refined, and were of the same race as the Toltecs. The Alcolhuis taught the Chichimecs agriculture, the mechanical arts, and the manners and customs of city life. In the course of time the Alcolhuis became amalgamated with the Chichimecs, and the two races founded the kingdom of Tezuco, or Acolhuacan.

The Aztecs, or Mexicans, were the last of the tribes who permanently settled in the valley of Mexico. They had been in the country as long as the other tribes, but had not chosen any permanent abode. They migrated from Azatlan, a region of the North whose location is unknown, and they seem to have made several prolonged halts on their journey southward. The first of these halts seems to have been on the shores of the Great Salt Lake in Utah. Another halt appears to have been at the Gila river, and a third in the vicinity of the Presidio de los Llanos.

About A. D. 1195 the Aztecs arrived in Anáhuac, or the valley of Mexico, where they led a nomadic life for the next one hundred and thirty years, during which they waged an almost constant war with the other tribes, in which their numbers were vastly diminished. In 1325 the Aztecs founded the city of Tenochtitlan on the islands of Lake Tezuco. The name of this city was afterward changed to Mexico, in honor of the Aztec god of war, Mexitli.

The other tribes bitterly hated the Aztecs, who had a severe struggle to found their kingdom; but the Aztecs persevered, and finally increased in wealth and power to such an extent that they were enabled to reduce their enemies to subjection. The conquering Aztecs subdued the surrounding country and established garrisons at commanding points; and finally all of Central and Southern Mexico, and a part of the country to the north, were included in the Aztec Empire. As the Aztecs grew more powerful they enlarged and improved their capital until its magnificence and extent excited the wonder and admiration of the Spanish conquerors, who were familiar with the splendors of the Old World.

STATUE OF COLUMBUS AT GENOA.

For twenty-seven years after the founding of their capital the government of the Aztecs was administered by a council of twenty nobles. In 1352 they changed their government to an elective monarchy, and chose ACAMAPITZIN, or ACAMAPICHTLE, for their first king. At first the royal power was limited, but it increased with the Aztec nation's conquests and wealth.

The Aztecs made rapid progress in civilization, and soon became the most highly civilized nation in Mexico. Their peculiar civilization was of a high order. The king was elected by the nobles. The candidate for the throne was required to be at least thirty years of age, and to have been a general in the royal armies. Military service was the basis of all rank in the Aztec state, and the nobles were the officers of the army. The Aztec king was vested with very great authority, but his powers were regulated by a fixed code of laws. The priests ranked next to the king and the nobles, and their power was restricted to spiritual matters. The priests exercised great influence, as they had charge of the education of the young, and were consulted in domestic affairs.

A system of rigid morality prevailed among all classes of Aztecs. Murder, theft, adultery and drunkenness were punished with death. Their civil code was as mild as their penal code was severe. A well-arranged system of courts existed in the capital and the provincial towns, at which complaints were heard and justice was administered. Marriage was encouraged, and the family relations constituted a prominent and favorable feature of Aztec life. Only the men were allowed the right to hold property.

The crown derived its revenues from state lands set apart in certain provinces, and from a tax upon agricultural products and a tribute consisting of articles of food and manufactured wares. The Aztec army was regularly organized, and its discipline was firm and well planned. The towns of the kingdom were connected with the capital by well-built roads, which the government kept in good repair, and an active commerce was carried on between the different parts of the kingdom. Large fleets of boats engaged in this traffic covered the lakes. No beasts of burden were used, and the Aztecs looked with wonder upon the horses which the Spaniards introduced into the country.

The Aztecs carried on mining very successfully and were skillful in metallurgy. They were likewise well versed in astronomy; knew the true length of the year, the nature and cause of eclipses, the period of the solstices and the equinoxes, and the

AMERIGO VESPUCCI.

transit of the sun across the zenith of Mexico; and had a calendar which was ingenious and accurate. They possessed a remarkable knowledge of medicine, surgery, botany and natural history; and had made a wonderful progress in the science of geography at the time of their conquest by the Spaniards. Their agricultural and military implements were made of copper, bronze and obsidian. Agriculture was carried on by means of irrigation.

The Aztecs were a deeply religious people, and were extremely zealous in the practice of the rites and ceremonies of their religion. Their religion was a polytheism. They believed in a Supreme Being, invisible, but omnipresent, omnipotent and omniscient, and requiring numerous assistants in the performance of his will, each of whom presided over some special natural phenomenon or phase of human existence.

SEBASTIAN CABOT AT LABRADOR.

Huitzilopochtli, the god of war, was the chief deity and the patron divinity of the Aztec nation. Next was Quetzalcoatl, the "white god" of Mexican mythology, who taught the Aztecs the arts of peace and good government, and forbade human sacrifices. All the Aztec gods were represented by idols of clay, wood, stone or precious metals. Great numbers of priests were attached to the temples, and the religious ceremonies were conducted on a scale of the greatest magnificence.

The Aztecs had two kinds of temples, low and circular, or high and pyramidal, on the tops of which the sacrifices took place. Torquemada estimates that there were forty thousand of these temples throughout the Aztec Empire. There were hundreds of them in each principal Aztec city, besides the great temple with several smaller ones within its precincts. There were other small courts with as many as six temples in each outlying quarter of the city, and there were temples on the mountains and along the public highways.

The Aztec temples were solid pyramidal masses of earth cased with brick or stone, many of them being more than one hundred feet square and of a still greater height. The ascent was by flights of steps on the outside; and on the broad, flat summit were sanctuaries which contained the idols of the deities and the altars on which fires were constantly burning. The principal religious ceremonial of the Aztecs were human sacrifices; and twenty-five hundred persons, mainly captives taken in war, are said to have been annually sacrificed on the altars of the capital.

At the time of the Spanish conquest of Mexico, Tenochtitlan, or the city of Mexico, the capital of the Aztec Empire, was a large and splendid city, being nine miles in circumference, and having about sixty thousand houses and probably a population of half a million. Most of the streets were short and narrow, and were lined with mean houses. The large streets were intersected by many canals crossed by bridges. The royal palace near the center of the city was a pile of low, irregular stone edifices of en-

THE STONE OF THE SUN, MEXICO.

RUINS OF THE PALACE OF THE NUNS, YUCATAN.

ormous size. Another palace, which was assigned to Fernando Cortez when he entered the city, was large enough to accommodate his entire army.

The most remarkable building of the entire city was the great Teocalli, or temple, completed in 1486; which was encompassed by a stone wall about eight feet high, orna-
of earth and pebbles, coated on the outside with hewn stone. It was square, its four sides facing the cardinal points of the compass; and it was five stories high, each story receding so as to be smaller than the one below it.

The ascent to the temple was by a flight of one hundred and fourteen steps on the

BALBOA TAKING POSSESSION OF THE PACIFIC OCEAN.

mented on the other side by figures of serpents in bas-relief, and pierced on its four sides by gateways opening on the four main streets. Over each gate was an arsenal; and near the temple were barracks, which were garrisoned by ten thousand soldiers. The temple was a solid pyramidal structure
outside, so arranged that it was necessary to pass around the whole edifice four times to reach the top; and the base of the temple is believed to have been three hundred feet square. The summit of the temple was a large area paved with broad, flat stones; and on it were two towers or sanctu-

aries, before each of which was an altar on which a fire was kept constantly burning. The top of this remarkable edifice commanded a splendid view of the city, the lake, the valley and the surrounding mountains.

The lake that surrounded the city was very brackish, and pure water was supplied to the inhabitants by means of an aqueduct from the neighboring hill of Chapultepec,

FERDINAND MAGELLAN.

The capital had an efficient and vigilant police, and a thousand men were employed daily in watering and sweeping its streets. where Montezuma had a summer palace surrounded by vast and magnificent gardens.

The Aztec king AHUITZOTL was succeeded on the Mexican throne by his nephew

FERDINAND CORTEZ.

MONTEZUMA II., in 1502. Montezuma II. was an active and warlike sovereign, and made conquests as far south into Central America as Honduras and Nicaragua. He made numerous changes in the internal administration of his kingdom, and was distinguished for the strictness and stringency with which he executed the laws. He liberally rewarded those who served him faithfully, and expended vast sums on the public works. He maintained his court on a scale of magnificence never before equaled in Mexico. Heavy taxes were imposed upon his subjects to provide for these expenditures, and these caused frequent insurrections.

As we have seen, the Spaniard Cordova discovered Mexico in 1517. In 1519, when King Montezuma II. was at the height of his power and glory, Fernando Cortez, a Spanish adventurer, at the head of five hundred and fifty Spaniards, and with ten pieces of cannon and about a dozen horsemen, invaded the Aztec Empire for purposes of conquest, landing on the eastern coast. Cortez defeated the natives who endeavored to prevent his landing, founded the city of Vera Cruz (True Cross), burned his ships, left a small garrison to defend his new conquest, and advanced into the interior.

Cortez first subdued the warlike republic of Tlascala, defeating the Tlascalans in four battles and entering the city of Tlascala on September 18, 1519. The natives were astonished at the fair skin and the martial prowess of the Spanish invaders, and believed them to be beings of divine origin, so that a rumor was circulated that the gods had undertaken the conquest of the country. Cortez vainly endeavored to persuade the Tlascalans to abjure their religion and to accept Christianity, but he succeeded in inducing them to acknowledge themselves vassals of the King of Spain.

Cortez remained at Tlascala twenty days; after which he resumed his march toward the city of Tenochtitlan, or Mexico, accompanied by a force of several thousand Tlascalans who had espoused his cause. His route lay through Cholula, the inhabitants of which were induced by the Aztecs to attempt a treacherous attack upon the Spanish invaders. Cortez severely punished the Cholulans for their intended attack, after which he resumed his march to the city of Mexico, before which he arrived November 8, 1519.

King Montezuma II. had already sent ambassadors to Cortez to warn him not to approach the capital. The Aztec king now changed his policy, received the Spanish invaders with great pomp, and assigned them one of the largest and strongest palaces in the city for their quarters. The Spaniards soon converted this palace into a fortress. They were very much surprised at the extent and magnificence of the Aztec capital, and from the very beginning they prepared to conquer it.

The Aztecs strongly disapproved of their king's course in permitting the Spaniards to enter the capital, and manifested their hostility to the invaders on every possible occasion. At length a party of seventeen Aztecs attacked a Spanish detachment. Cortez thereupon sought an interview with Montezuma II. in the Aztec monarch's own palace, seized him and conveyed him a captive to the Spanish quarters, and threatened him with instant death if he should give any sign to the multitude in the streets that he was a prisoner. The Aztecs would have attempted to rescue their captive king had he not assured them that he was going of his own free will to visit the Spanish commander.

When Cortez arrived at his quarters he put his royal captive in irons, and captured and burned to death the seventeen natives who had attacked the Spaniards. He then forced Montezuma II. to take an oath of allegiance to the King of Spain, and to induce his nobles to do the same; after which he obtained from the captive monarch a sum of gold equal in value to one hundred thousand ducats.

In this emergency Cortez was informed that an expedition from Spain had landed on the eastern coast of Mexico, under the command of Narvaez, who had come to take from Cortez the command of the Spanish troops in Mexico. Cortez left two hundred of his troops to hold the Spanish position in the city of Mexico, and hastened with seventy troops to Cholula, where he was reinforced by one hundred and fifty troops whom he had left there, after which he marched against Narvaez, who was encamped in one of the Cempoallan cities with nine hundred Spanish soldiers, eighty horses, and a dozen pieces of artillery. By a bold stroke Cortez captured Narvaez and his entire force. The vanquished troops of Narvaez readily enlisted in the service of their captor, and with this reinforcement Cortez returned to the city of Mexico.

Upon his return to the Aztec capital Cortez found the inhabitants in open rebellion against his troops. He brought out Montezuma and forced him to address his subjects; but the enraged Aztecs discharged a volley of missiles at their captive king, who thus received a mortal wound, of which he died several days afterward, June, 1520.

The Aztecs now assailed the Spaniards with desperate fury, drove them from the city, and literally annihilated their rear-guard in their retreat across the causeway leading to the mainland. The retreat lasted six days; but at length Cortez halted on the plain of Otumba, where an overwhelming Aztec force attacked him July 7, 1520, but he came forth victorious. This battle settled the fate of Mexico. Cortez instantly proceeded to Tlascala, where he collected an auxiliary force of natives, after which he

SLAUGHTER OF THE MEXICANS AT CHOLULA.

speedily reduced the neighboring provinces, and again appeared before the city of Mexico, April 28, 1521.

GUATEMOZIN, the new Aztec king, the nephew and son-in-law of the ill-fated Montezuma II., was a man of firmness and decision. He held his capital against the Spanish invaders for seventy-seven days, during which the city was literally reduced to ruins by the Indian allies of Cortez. By the final assault, August 15, 1521, the Spaniards captured what was left of the

MONTEZUMA.

beautiful capital of the Aztec Empire. King Guatemozin sought to escape with his family by the lake; but was pursued and taken prisoner by the Spaniards, who treated him with great cruelty, putting him on a bed of fiery coals, from which he was at once released by Cortez. But Cortez soon put Guatemozin and many of his nobles to death.

With the conquest of the remainder of the country the same year the Aztec Empire ended, and for three centuries (A.D. 1521–1821) Mexico was a province of Spain. After effecting the conquest of the country, Cortez rebuilt the city of Mexico upon its present plan, employing a large force of natives for that purpose. He exerted himself to introduce European civilization and Roman Catholic Christianity into the country. He established a military government in the conquered land with himself as its chief. In October, 1522, King Charles I. of Spain, Emperor Charles V. of Germany, issued a decree naming the conquered country *New Spain*, and appointed Cortez governor of the new province. The Spanish conquerors enslaved the natives, and compelled them to work in the mines and to till the soil.

In 1528 the Spanish king suppressed the system set up by Cortez, and made New Spain a Spanish viceroyalty, which it remained during the entire subsequent period of the Spanish dominion, during which period there were sixty-four viceroys, all but one of them being natives of Spain. The province continued to improve, in spite of the policy pursued by Spain, which aimed at little besides extracting as much treasure from the province as it would yield.

Notwithstanding all his services to the Spanish crown, Cortez was treated with ingratitude by his sovereign, and he died in comparative obscurity. It was with great difficulty that he could obtain an audience from the Emperor Charles V. When one day the conqueror of Mexico rushed through the multitude which surrounded the Emperor's coach, and placed his foot on the step of the door, Charles inquired who this man was. Cortez replied: "It is he who has given you more kingdoms than your ancestors left you cities."

The Spanish conquerors devoted their first efforts to propagating the Christian religion in Mexico, and for this purpose they invited missionaries from Europe. Between the years 1522 and 1545 numbers of monks came into Mexico from various parts of

MONTEZUMA II., THE LAST KING OF THE AZTECS.

Europe to assist in the conversion of the natives; and to conciliate the Mexicans many practices hitherto unknown to the Roman ritual were admitted and consecrated.

The missionaries honorably exerted themselves to protect the Mexicans from the sanguinary cruelty of the Spaniards. Among these Sahagun and Las Casas were especially distinguished for their benevolent exertions in behalf of the conquered Mexicans. These two humane missionaries obtained bulls from the Pope and edicts from the Spanish government fully recognizing the claims of the Indians to the rights of humanity, and they saved the native Mexicans from the wretched fate which swept away the native population of almost every other Spanish American colony, though they failed to obtain a full measure of justice. The protection thus accorded by the regular and secular clergy to the native Mexicans caused them to be more ardently attached to the Roman Catholic Church than were the Spaniards themselves; and this attachment is still felt by the Mexicans, though their country has recovered its independence. But the native Mexicans were reduced to a condition of abject serfdom, differing little from that of the serfs of Russia or Poland.

Peru, which was conquered by the Spaniards under Francisco Pizarro in 1532, was originally inhabited by several Indian tribes who possessed a high degree of civilization, a simple but just code of laws and a well-arranged system of government under a sovereign called the *Inca*. The Peruvian government was an absolute despotism mildly administered, and the military class was the most favored, as the great aim of the state was territorial expansion. The civilization of the ancient Peruvians, though vastly superior to that of the Indian nations around them, was inferior to that of the Aztecs in Mexico. Education was restricted to the ruling class, and there were laws which compelled a son to pursue his father's occupation, prohibiting him from receiving an education superior to his station in life.

The religion of the ancient Peruvians consisted in worshiping the sun, from which the Inca claimed descent. The Inca's person was considered divine. He had numerous wives, the chief one of which was required to be his eldest sister. He also had as many concubines as he desired. His son by his principal wife, his eldest sister, was the heir to the throne. When the Inca died he was supposed to have been called home to the mansion of his father, the sun.

In 1512 Vasco Nuñez de Balboa, the governor of the Spanish colony of Darien, on the Isthmus of Panama, was informed by the Indians that there was a country far south of the isthmus where gold was as commonly in use as iron was with the Spaniards. Balboa vainly endeavored to find this rich land.

In 1524 Francisco Pizarro, a Spanish adventurer, made a voyage to the coast of Peru, but failed to accomplish anything. In 1531 the King of Spain granted Pizarro the titles of Governor and Captain-General of all the countries that he should conquer; and that adventurer sailed for Peru with his four brothers and a few followers, arriving in that country late in January, after a voyage of fourteen days from Panama. Pizarro captured and plundered a town in the province of Coaque, and was soon afterward reinforced by the arrival of one hundred and thirty Spaniards under Almagro, his second in command. The Spanish adventurers then laid the foundations of the town of San Miguel in the valley of Tangarala.

At that time the empire of the Incas was distracted by a civil war. HUAYNA CAPAC, the late Inca, had divided his dominions between his two sons, HUASCAR and ATAHUALPA. In the civil war which had broken out between the two brothers Atahualpa had defeated his brother and taken him prisoner. He now encamped with his army at Cajamarca, whither Pizarro hastened to meet him in September, 1532, with a force of one hundred and seventy-seven men, with the professed design of acting as mediator between Atahualpa and his brother.

FRANCISCO PIZARRO URGING HIS COMRADES TO THE CONQUEST OF PERU.

but with the perfidious purpose of seizing the victorious Inca in the same manner that Cortez had seized the unfortunate Montezuma II. in Mexico. The Inca received Pizarro with great kindness and readily consented to an interview. The Inca visited the Spanish invaders with a barbarous magnificence and an ostentatious display of wealth which inflamed the cupidity of Pizarro and his followers.

On reaching the Spanish camp the Inca was addressed by Valverde, the chaplain of the invaders, in a long discourse. After a brief notice of the mysteries of creation and redemption, the priest proceeded to explain the doctrine of the Pope's supremacy. He dwelt upon the grant which Pope Alexander VI. had made to the Spanish crown, and by virtue of that grant he called upon Atahualpa to embrace Christianity at once and to acknowledge himself a vassal of the King of Spain. The Inca was utterly perplexed, and inquired where Valverde had learned such wonderful things. The priest, showing his breviary to the Inca, replied: "In this book." Atahualpa took the book, turned over the leaves, and then put it to his ear to hear what the book had to say. He suddenly flung the breviary to the ground, exclaiming: "This tells me nothing!" Valverde exclaimed: "Blasphemy! blasphemy! to arms, to arms, my Christian brethren! avenge the profanation of God's word by the polluted hands of infidels!"

This solemn farce seems to have been preconcerted. Before Valverde had ceased speaking, the trumpets sounded a charge, and a dreadful fire of musketry and artillery was opened on the defenseless Peruvians. In the midst of their surprise and consternation, they were charged by the Spanish cavalry; and, as the Peruvians had never before seen a horse, the appearance of the Spanish cavalry seemed like something supernatural, and increased their dismay to utter helplessness. Atahualpa was seized and carried a prisoner to the Spanish camp, while the triumphant invaders satiated themselves with the rich spoils of conquest.

The unfortunate Inca endeavored to obtain his release by paying a ransom of gold equal in value to seventeen and a half million dollars. The cruel and treacherous Pizarro accepted the offer; but when he had received the gold he refused to release Atahualpa, and caused him to be tried under the most iniquitous pretenses and sentenced to be burned to death. When the Inca consented to receive baptism from Valverde his sentence was so far mitigated

ATAHUALPA, THE LAST INCA OF PERU.

that he was first strangled at the stake, after which his body was burned, August 29, 1533.

The victorious Pizarro then marched upon Cuzco, the ancient capital of the Incas; and, as Huascar had been slain by order of Atahualpa, the Spanish conqueror proclaimed MANCO CAPAC, a half-brother of Atahualpa, Inca. For the purpose of establishing a new capital for Peru near the Pacific coast, Pizarro founded the city of Lima, in the valley of the river Rimac, January 6, 1535.

The Spanish conquerors treated the vanquished Peruvians with the most barbarous cruelty. At last the oppressed Peruvians, driven to despair, rose in arms under Manco Capac to recover their independence, took and burned Cuzco, and massacred such of the Spaniards as they took prisoners.

The Spanish robbers quarreled among themselves about the division of the spoils of conquest; and a civil war broke out between Pizarro and Almagro, in which Almagro was defeated, taken prisoner and executed. The triumphant Pizarro then crushed the outbreak of the Peruvians, whom he treated with the most fiendish cruelty and reduced to abject slavery. He set up a military government and ruled the province with merciless rigor. For almost three centuries Peru remained a Spanish province (A. D. 1532–1821).

When the King of Spain was informed of Pizarro's tyranny in Peru he sent Vaca de Castro over in 1540 to investigate the matter. Before Castro arrived at Lima the cruel Pizarro was assassinated by Almagro's son, who proclaimed himself governor of Peru. The younger Almagro took up arms to resist Castro, who had orders to assume the governorship in case of Pizarro's death; but Almagro was defeated, taken prisoner and executed. Castro was recognized as governor of Peru, and devoted his attention to a settlement of the affairs of the province.

Castro was superseded by Blasco Nuñez Vela, who had been appointed viceroy of Peru by the King of Spain, and who came charged with the duty of inaugurating a new and better system of government, and especially to liberate the Indians from slavery and to impose a fairer system of taxation upon them. These measures produced a civil war in Peru, in which the rebels were under the leadership of Gonzalo Pizarro, son of the conqueror of Peru. This civil war lasted several years, and ended in the defeat of the insurgents and the capture and execution of Gonzalo Pizarro in 1548. The government of Peru was then established on a more solid and permanent basis, and for almost three centuries Peru remained tranquil as a Spanish province.

The government which the Spaniards established in Peru was far more oppressive and iniquitous than that which they introduced into Mexico, because the Peruvian mines were almost the only objects which engaged the attention of the Spaniards from the time of their conquest of the country. The Spaniards devised a horrible system of conscription for working the mines; and all the Indians between the ages of eighteen and fifty were enrolled in seven lists, the persons on each list being obliged to work in the mines for six months, so that this forced labor came on the unfortunate Indians at intervals of three and a half years. Four out of every five were supposed to perish annually in these deadly labors; and, to add to the misery of the natives, they were not permitted to purchase the necessaries of life from any except privileged dealers, who remorselessly and unscrupulously robbed them of their earnings.

At the time of the Spanish conquest of Peru, Chili was occupied by a number of kindred Indian tribes who called themselves *Alapu-che*, "the people of the land," and who spoke a common language. The northern part of Chili had been conquered by the Inca of Peru about the middle of the fifteenth century, but the Incas were never able to subdue the southern tribes.

After the Spanish conquest of Peru, the Spaniards, finding that Northern Chili had been subject to the Incas, resolved to conquer that country likewise. A Spanish

CHARLES V. AND PIZARRO.

expedition under Diego Almagro entered Chili from Peru in 1535, and advanced southward into the territories of the Purumancian Indians, who drove them back to Peru.

In 1540 Pedro de Valdivia, an able and prudent Spanish officer, led an expedition against Chili, defeated the Indians, and founded the city of Santiago, named in honor of the patron saint of Spain. The Indians made a desperate effort to destroy the town, but were defeated. After receiving a reinforcement from Peru, Valdivia advanced southward into the country of the Araucanian Indians, who attacked and almost annihilated his army, thus compelling him to retreat to Santiago. He returned to Peru for reinforcements; and in 1550 he came back to Santiago with a large and well-armed force, and marched southward and founded the city of Concepcion, on the present site of Penco. Four thousand Araucanians attacked Concepcion, but were defeated with great slaughter, their chief being among the slain. The war proceeded with terrible fury; and in 1559 Valdivia was captured and put to death by the Indians, who then took and destroyed Concepcion, and even marched upon Santiago, but were driven back.

For more than a century after their arrival in Chili the Spaniards made persistent efforts to conquer the Araucanians, but always failed. In 1665 they concluded a treaty with the Indian tribes south of the Bobio, acknowledging their independence; but the war was renewed in 1723, and lasted for half a century with brief intervals of peace, until 1773. The Spaniards made Chili a viceroyalty.

The Indian kingdom of Quito, which had also been subdued by the Incas of Peru and made a part of their empire, also came under the Spanish dominion, and was made a presidency of the viceroyalty of Peru, being ruled by Spanish governors from 1553 to 1822. The towns of Quito and Guayaquil were founded by the Spaniards in 1535, the same year as the founding of Lima.

The coast of Venezuela had been discovered by Columbus during his third voyage, in 1498. In 1499 Ojeda and Amerigo Vespucci explored the coast of Venezuela and Colombia; and, finding an Indian village built on piles over the water on the shore of Lake Maracaybo, they named it *Venezuela*, or Little Venice—a name eventually applied to the entire territory of the present republic. The Spaniards soon took possession of both Venezuela and Colombia, and gold was discovered in the coast range in 1540. They founded the colony of New Granada in 1510, which became a separate viceroyalty in 1718. In the territory of Venezuela the Spaniards founded some flourishing towns—Cumana in 1520, Coro in 1527, Tocuyo in 1545, Barquisemeto in 1552, Valencia in 1555, Carácas in 1567, and Porto Bello in 1584.

The discovery of silver in the territory of Bolivia and Buenos Ayres quickened Spanish enterprise in South America. Bolivia, or Upper Peru, which had also formed a part of the empire of the Incas of Peru, came into the possession of the Spaniards after their conquest of Peru, and formed part of the viceroyalty of Peru until 1776, when it became a part of the viceroyalty of Buenos Ayres. Buenos Ayres was founded by the Spaniards in 1535. The colony was a part of the viceroyalty of Peru until 1776, when the viceroyalty of Buenos Ayres was created, which included Buenos Ayres, with Uruguay, Paraguay and Bolivia.

The first Spanish settlement in Paraguay was Asuncion, founded in 1536. The colony prospered wonderfully, and was erected into a bishopric in 1555. In 1557 Jesuit missions were established in Paraguay, and these met with wonderful success in the Christianization and civilization of the neighboring Indians, so that two centuries later there were one hundred and fifty thousand civilized Indians in Paraguay.

While the Spaniards had thus been taking possession of and colonizing Mexico and South America during the sixteenth century, the oldest towns within the limits of the present United States were also founded by the Spaniards. In 1565 Pedro

Melendez de Avilez, after massacring a colony of French Protestants that had attempted to settle on the St. John's River in Flordia, founded the city of St. Augustine, on the eastern coast of Florida. In 1582 De Espejo founded Santa Fé, in New Mexico.

Thus, in the sixteenth century, Spain obtained possession of Florida, Mexico, Central America, and all of South America except Guiana and Brazil, the latter of which was claimed by the Portuguese. The precious metals which Spain obtained from her American possessions contributed to make her for a time the leading power of Europe, but an inordinate thirst for the gold and silver of America caused the Spaniards to neglect agriculture and manufactures. The Spanish American colonies increased very slowly in population, and none of these were as prosperous as the Philippine Islands, which had been taken possession of by the Spaniards and settled by a colony from Mexico in 1564.

SECTION III.—PORTUGUESE EMPIRE IN ASIA AND AMERICA.

 THE great voyages of Bartholomew Diaz and Vasco da Gama, which, at the close of the fifteenth century, made known to Europe the existence of a sea-passage to India by way of the Cape of Good Hope, led to the founding of a great Portuguese colonial empire in Southern and Eastern Asia. The founding of Calicut, on the Malabar coast of India, in 1498, was the first step in the establishment of such a dominion.

Vasco da Gama's successor was Cabral, who discovered Brazil in 1500, during his voyage to India. The Portuguese power in India was extended by the gallant Almeida, Cabral's successor, who reduced many of the native princes of Hindoostan to tribute and forced them to consent to the establishment of Portuguese factories in their principal cities, and who was killed by the savage Hottentots of Southern Africa while on his return to Portugal.

The illustrious Dom Alfonso Albuquerque, the next Portuguese viceroy in the East, notwithstanding the hostility of the Mohammedan rulers of India, obtained a grant of ground from one of the Hindoo princes, and founded a strong fort at Cochin in 1503, where the Portuguese had established factories; and this stronghold became the cradle of the great commercial empire of the Portuguese, whose power was felt from China to the Red Sea. The Mohammedans, who had hitherto engrossed the entire commerce of India, formed a league to expel the Portuguese, and were encouraged therein by the Venetians, who purchased Indian spices and other goods from the Arabs, with which they supplied the principal markets of Europe; but this enterprise was defeated.

In 1510 Albuquerque conquered the city of Goa, on the western coast of India, which afterwards became the capital of the Portuguese empire in the East, and was erected into an archbishopric by the Pope. Goa, which still belongs to the Portuguese, displays in its stately churches, warehouses and deserted dwellings a vestige of that magnificence which acquired for it the title of "Goa the Golden." The reduction of Goa was the first instance of territorial acquisition in India by European powers—a system strongly deprecated by Vasco da Gama, and which cannot be defended on any principles of national justice, but which Albuquerque declared absolutely necessary for Portugal to command the trade of the East.

Albuquerque also subdued the city of Malacca, the emporium of the trade of Farther India. He also reduced the isle of Ormuz, in the Persian Gulf, to subjection; and when the King of Persia, to whom the isle belonged, demanded tribute from the Portuguese viceroy, Albuquerque pointing to his cannon and balls, replied: "There is the coin with which the King of Portugal pays tribute." Albuquerque caused the name of King Manuel the Great to be feared and respected throughout the East; but the illustrious viceroy was only rewarded with his sovereign's ingratitude, and died of grief because of this treatment.

During the next ten years the Portuguese established colonies and factories on the island of Ceylon and on the Coromandel coast of Hindoostan, and subjected the spice-bearing Molucca and Sunda Islands to tribute. In 1517 the Portuguese were granted a trading-station at Macao, in China, which remained in their possession until 1846, when it was opened to all nations. They also obtained a free trade with the Empire of Japan.

All the islands in the Persian Gulf acknowledged the dominion of the Portuguese. Some of the Arabian princes became their tributaries, while others became their allies; and throughout the entire Arabian peninsula none dared to show them any hostility. In the Red Sea they were the only power that commanded any respect, and they also had considerable influence over the Negus of Abyssinia and the other sovereigns of Eastern Africa.

The most remarkable of the Portuguese settlements was the isle of Ormuz, which, although a salt and barren rock in the Persian Gulf, was rendered the most flourishing commercial mart in the East, on account of its commodious situation. Its roadsteads were frequented by shipping from all parts of the East Indies, from the coasts of Africa, Egypt and Arabia; and it possessed an extensive caravan trade with Central Asia through the opposite ports of Persia. The semi-annual fairs held at Ormuz transformed this salt and barren rock into almost the fabled splendor and luxury of an Oriental palace. The wealth, the splendor, and the concourse of traders at Ormuz during its flourishing condition furnished a striking example of the almost omnipotent power of commerce.

During the semi-annual fairs, which lasted from January to March, and from the end of August to the beginning of November, there was, besides the display of luxury and magnificence, an almost unparalleled activity. The salt dust of the streets was concealed and kept down by neat mats and rich carpets. Canvas-awnings were extended from the roofs of the houses to exclude the scorching rays of the sun. The rooms next to the street were opened like shops, adorned with Indian cabinets and piles of porcelain, intermixed with odoriferous dwarf trees and shrubs, set in gilded vases, elegantly adorned with figures. At the corners of all the streets stood camels laden with water-skins; while the richest wines of Persia, the most costly perfumes and the choicest delicacies of Asia, were poured forth in lavish profusion.

The efforts of Albuquerque's successors were directed chiefly to the maintenance of his acquisitions and to checking the power of the Turks, who, after conquering Egypt and Syria in 1517, made strenuous efforts to establish themselves on the Malabar coast of India.

Thus, early in the sixteenth century, the Portuguese had established a colonial and commercial empire which embraced the western, southern and eastern coasts of Africa, from Guinea to the Red Sea, and which extended along the shores of Southern and Eastern Asia from the Red Sea to China; although throughout this vast extent of territory they had little more than a chain of factories and forts. Lisbon, the capital of Portugal, became the seat of the world's commerce; but the nobler emotions in the hearts of the Portuguese were stifled by avarice and selfishness.

On the union of Portugal with Spain in 1580 the Portuguese East India possessions also came into the possession of the Spaniards; but when Spanish tyranny and cruelty caused the Dutch to revolt, the Dutch extended their commerce to the East Indies, and at the close of the sixteenth century they had possession of the once-flourishing Portuguese colonial empire. In 1622 Ormuz was wrested from the Portuguese by the English and the Persians. The glory and splendor of that famous emporium soon departed, and it relapsed into its original condition of a barren and desolate rock, so that not a vestige of its former grandeur remains.

After Pedro Alvarez Cabral, while on his voyage to India to continue the discoveries of Vasco da Gama, had accidentally discovered the coast of Brazil by being driven westward by adverse winds, April 22, 1500, he anchored in the large and excellent harbor of Porto Seguro, April 25, 1500, and took possession of the country in the name of his sovereign, King Manuel the Great of Portugal; after which he resumed his voyage to the East Indies, having sent a vessel back to Portugal with the news of his discovery.

Upon receiving intelligence of Cabral's discovery, the King of Portugal sent an expedition under Amerigo Vespucci to visit and explore the new country. Upon his return to Europe, Amerigo Vespucci published an account of the country, together with a map. He brought back a cargo of dyewoods, of which he said that whole forests were to be found in Brazil; and an active and profitable trade in these woods at once sprang up. Other nations commenced to take part in this traffic, and the King of Portugal determined to put a stop to this intrusion.

Accordingly, in 1531, King John III. caused a number of Portuguese colonies to be planted on the coast of Brazil. These settlements were called *Capitanias*, and were founded by Portuguese nobles, to whom the King of Portugal granted absolute powers over their settlements on the sole condition that they should bear the expense of colonization. This system worked admirably for several years, but at length it caused so much trouble that the Portuguese government determined to establish a permanent colonial system directly dependent on the Portuguese crown.

In 1549 a Governor-General was appointed for Brazil, and was made the direct representative of the King of Portugal, being vested with absolute jurisdiction in civil and criminal matters. The first Governor-General of Brazil was Thomé de Souza, and the success of the new system was due to his wisdom and good government. He founded the town of Sao Salvador da Bahia, and made it the capital of Brazil. A colony of French Protestants settled on an island in the bay of Rio de Janeiro in 1555, but were expelled ten years later. The Portuguese founded Rio de Janeiro in 1567.

The forcible annexation of Portugal to Spain in 1580 made Brazil a Spanish dependency for the time, and Brazil suffered much from the attacks of Dutch, French and English fleets; but after Portugal had regained her independence in 1640 she recovered Brazil from the Dutch, who had in the meantime occupied the country, and Brazil was made a principality for the heir-apparent of the Portuguese crown.

SECTION IV.—RISE OF THE EUROPEAN STATES-SYSTEM.

E NOW return to resume the narrative of European history, which we left off at the close of the Middle Ages and the beginning of the modern era. The common interests of the several states of Europe had been vastly multiplied by the progress of civilization. Certain events were perceived to affect all European nations alike, particularly the progress of the Ottoman Turks and the rapid growth of opinions in every European country contrary to the doctrines of the established Church. The new art of printing increased the interchange of ideas, and the founding of European colonies in America and Asia led to more intimate commercial relations between the European states. All these causes

Duke—Page—Nobleman (14th Century).

Nobleman—English Duchess (14th Century).

French Lady and Gentleman (Middle 14th Century).

Family of German Knight.

THE 14th CENTURY.

tended to develop the *European States-System*—a league of independent powers widely different in their respective constitutions, but whose relations are determined and maintained by diplomacy or by the science of international law.

The preservation of the *Balance of Power* —the independence of all the European states by preventing any one of them from acquiring such a preponderance that would menace the general security—became the chief object, and demanded from every European government a vigilant attention to the affairs of other nations, thus giving rise to many alliances and counter-alliances and much diplomatic activity. States of inferior rank—like Savoy, Lorraine and the Swiss Republic—were protected by their more powerful neighbors as convenient smaller weights in the balance.

At the beginning of the sixteenth century, Spain, under Ferdinand and Isabella, was the most powerful monarchy in Europe; while France, under Louis XII., the first of the Orleans branch of the Valois dynasty, was also a powerful monarchy; and England, under Henry VII., the first of the Tudor dynasty, had also risen into importance; but the Empire existed only in theory, the Emperor Maximilian I. being a powerful prince only as the head of the House of Hapsburg, and Archduke of Austria, Count of the Tyrol, Duke of Styria and Carinthia, and Regent of the Netherlands. In Italy the republics of Venice, Genoa and Florence were preëminent; while the Duchy of Milan and the Kingdom of Naples and Sicily were contested between the French and the Spaniards. Scotland and the Scandinavian kingdoms occupied a secondary place; Poland was a half-barbarous kingdom on the eastern frontiers of European civilization; Hungary was a bulwark against the Ottoman Turks, whose continuous progress, under warlike Sultans, alarmed all Christendom; and Russia ranked more as an Asiatic power than a European one.

During the last years of the fifteenth century King Charles VIII. of France undertook to enforce the claim to Naples which he inherited through his father from Charles of Maine. He wasted in tournaments and festivities the entire sum provided for the prosecution of his grand schemes of conquest, and he was only enabled to proceed by borrowing fifty thousand crowns from a Milanese merchant. After entering Italy he borrowed and pawned the jewels of the Duchess of Savoy and the Marchioness of Montferrat, for the prosecution of his enterprise.

Ludovico Sforza, the uncle of the reigning Duke of Milan, had invited the French king into Italy for the purpose of obtaining his protection in the usurpation of the duchy. This prince was one of the most unscrupulous plotters of the age, and he was suspected of having poisoned his nephew, who died about that time.

Florence was the old ally of France; but Piero de Medici, who was then the ruler of that republic, was bound by a treaty to King Alfonso II. of Naples. A tumult which arose against Piero de Medici drove him to the opposite extreme of offering to put the King of France in possession of all the fortresses of Tuscany and to furnish him with a loan of two hundred thousand florins. The Florentines were so enraged at this humiliating subserviency of their ruler that they drove the Medici into exile, confiscated their goods and set a price on their heads.

The Dominican monk and reformer Savonarola, who had foretold the coming of the French as ministers of divine vengeance for Italian corruptions—especially the notorious wickedness of Pope Alexander VI. and his family, the Borgias—now came to the head of affairs in Florence. He appeared before Charles VIII. at Lucca, and predicted for him an earthly victory and a heavenly glory on condition that he protected the liberties of Florence. The French king took up his residence in Florence, but when he proposed to tax the city and recall the Medici the Florentines rose en masse in defense of their rights and drove him from the city.

Charles VIII. entered Rome with an army of fifty thousand men and a train of artillery. The personal wickedness of Pope Alexander VI. was intensified in the opinion of his contemporaries by his unnatural alliance with Sultan Bajazet II. of Turkey. Zizim, the Sultan's younger brother and hated rival, who had sought refuge with the Knights of St. John at Rhodes, was sent to France for greater security in 1483, and remained in various fortresses belonging to the order for several years; while Bajazet II. paid a liberal annual allowance for his maintenance, in order to keep him out of the way. The unfortunate Zizim was afterward committed to the Pope's keeping, and Alexander VI. made use of so valuable a prize in his negotiations with the Sultan.

It was well known that the King of France designed to conquer the Turks and to restore the Eastern Empire, the title to which he had purchased from Andrew Palæologus, nephew of the last reigning Greek Emperor. Pope Alexander VI. informed the Sultan that the French king was scheming to acquire possession of Zizim to further his plans against the Ottoman Empire. Bajazet II. then offered three hundred thousand ducats for the murder of his brother; and, as Zizim died within a few months, it was generally believed that his death was caused by a slow poison administered by the Pope's order.

As soon as the French army entered the Kingdom of Naples the Neapolitans rose in revolt against their king, Alfonso II., a cruel and detested tyrant. Seized with remorse and terror, Alfonso II. abdicated in favor of his son Ferdinand II.; but the new king's virtues were unable to retrieve his family's desperate fortunes. His infantry threw down their arms at the approach of the French; while one of his principal officers betrayed Capua to King Charles VIII., and the city of Naples rose in revolt. Ferdinand II. burned or sunk most of his fleet, placed his available troops in the fortresses near the city of Naples, and fled to Sicily with fifteen ships. The King of France entered the city of Naples the next day amid the acclamations of the people. The Neapolitan fortresses soon surrendered, and in the course of several weeks the entire Kingdom of Naples had come into the possession of Charles VIII. almost without a blow.

The triumphant French king treated the Neapolitans as a conquered people. Instead of rewarding their nobles and generals, whose influence had mainly secured his triumph, he confiscated their hereditary lands and offices to grant them to his own idle followers.

The first great coalition known in European history was now formed against Charles VIII. by the arts of his former ally, Ludovico Sforza, who had gained all that he had hoped for by the French invasion of Italy, and who was alarmed by the nearness of the Duke of Orleans, the rightful heir of the Visconti to the Duchy of Milan. In March, 1495, a treaty of alliance was signed at Venice by the envoys of Pope Alexander VI., the Emperor Maximilian I., King Ferdinand the Catholic of Spain, the Venetian Republic, and the Duke of Milan. A Spanish army was soon landed in Sicily, and a Venetian fleet appeared on the coast of Apulia.

Charles VIII. made a magnificent entry into Naples, clothed in the robes of an Eastern Emperor, carrying a globe in one hand and a scepter in the other. In the following week he fled from that city, leaving its treasury without money and its fortresses without food or ammunition, and took with him in his march northward an immense baggage-train loaded with treasure. He was encountered by an army of the allies four times as numerous as his own, at Fornovo, in Lombardy, in July, 1495, and was victorious. The French army was saved from defeat and ruin by their rich plunder, which diverted the attention of the enemy, whose disorderly ranks were easily put to flight. Charles VIII. then concluded a new treaty with Ludovico Sforza, who acknowledged himself a vassal of the French king for Genoa, and promised to take no part in the movement of the allies against France.

The French dominion in Naples was short-lived. King Ferdinand of Spain sent an army to assist King Ferdinand II. of Naples, who landed at Reggio within a week after the French king's retreat from Naples. His forces were defeated at Seminara; but the people of the city of Naples, weary of the French, rose in revolt against them and welcomed their lawful sovereign with joyful acclamations. The entire Southern coast of Naples declared for Ferdinand II.

The French king's cousin and viceroy, the Duke of Montpensier, made some efforts to continue hostilities; but, as he received no assistance from France, he was obliged to conclude a treaty in which the French obtained little more than permission to return home. While waiting for transports a pestilence broke out, in which the viceroy and many of his troops perished. The Constable d'Aubigny was defeated in Calabria about the same time, by Gonsalvo de Cordova, the *Great Captain*, so called because of his career of uninterrupted victories. Ferdinand II. died in 1496, and was succeeded by his uncle Don Frederick, a prince of great talents and popular disposition, who soon wiped out every remaining vestige of French domination.

The principal result of the wild expedition of Charles VIII. into Italy was the fatal desire for distant conquests which it excited in the sovereigns and people who had become involved in his wars; and unfortunate Italy, weakened by her own dissensions, suffered for many years from the display of her wealth and helplessness. To the refined and enervated Italians the invasion of the French seemed like a new inroad of Northern barbarians; as the carnage wrought by the well-served artillery of Charles VIII. presented a destructive contrast to the Italian battles of the time, in which "the worst that a soldier had to fear was the loss of his horse or the expense of his ransom."

During the fourteenth and fifteenth centuries the manufacture of defensive armor so far excelled that of destructive weapons that war became almost as safe as the peaceful contests of the chess-board. War was carried on in Italy mainly by mercenary companies of adventurers, who were hired out by their captains to any prince or city that offered the most pay or plunder; and it was the evident policy of the leaders to keep their forces undiminished, as the material for subsequent bargains. Macchiavelli mentions a decisive battle in which no man suffered any injury, and another in which one was killed by accidentally falling from his horse and being smothered in the mud.

Several marriages negotiated by Ferdinand and Isabella of Spain about this time had a controlling influence upon future history. The Princess Margaret, daughter of the Emperor Maximilian I. and the discarded bride of Charles VIII. of France, was married to John, Prince of Asturias, the eldest son of the King and Queen of Spain; while her brother Philip, the heir to the Netherlands, married Joanna, the second daughter of the same king and queen. The Princess Isabella, the eldest daughter of King Ferdinand and Queen Isabella, was espoused to King Manuel the Great of Portugal; and the Princess Catharine, the youngest daughter of the Spanish sovereigns, was betrothed to Prince Henry, the heir to the English crown, afterward King Henry VIII. By the premature deaths of the Infant of Spain, the Queen of Portugal and her only son, the whole Spanish inheritance fell to Charles, the eldest son of Philip and Joanna, who ranks as the great central figure in the history of the first half of the sixteenth century.

The crimes and vices of the Borgia family gave resolute energy to the preaching of Savonarola, who earnestly called upon the European sovereigns to convene a council of the Church to depose Pope Alexander VI. The Pope replied by excommunicating the "bold prophet of Florence" and all the members of his government. The fanaticism of the *Piagnoni*, or Weepers, who followed Savonarola, had strengthened two other parties in Florence; and Pope Alexander VI. took advantage of the dissensions of these parties to cause his bold antagonist to be put to death. Savonarola and two of his disciples were burned to death in the market-place of Florence, May 23, 1498.

But Pope Alexander VI. did not escape the natural result of his crimes. His eldest son, the Duke of Gandia, had already been murdered by Cæsar Borgia, his own brother, who was Cardinal of Valencia. For several days even the Pope was struck with remorse. He openly confessed his sins and promised to reform, but he soon plunged more deeply than ever into violent and degrading courses. He pardoned the murderer, and even released him from his vows as a prelate for the purpose of making him a great secular prince.

Charles VIII. of France was suddenly hurried to his grave while preparing for another invasion of Italy, A. D. 1498. Louis XII., the next King of France, proceeded to enforce his hereditary claim on Milan; and in 1499 a French army of twenty-three thousand men was sent into Italy under three experienced commanders. Venice was in alliance with the King of France. The success of this expedition was as sudden as that of Charles VIII. against Naples had been. The Milanese were disaffected toward their duke, who was in such fear of popular violence that he fled into the Tyrol to solicit the assistance of the Emperor Maximilian I. While the duke was absent from Milan the Milanese declared for the French, and their example was followed by all Lombardy, which was annexed to the French dominions without a battle having been fought.

Louis XII. crossed the Alps into Italy and entered Milan in triumph. He pleased the Lombards with fair promises of a mild, paternal government; but no sooner had he returned to France than the extortions of Trivulzio, his lieutenant, and the rudeness of his soldiery, exasperated the Milanese and revived the party of the exiled duke. Ludovico Sforza now approached with an army he had raised in Switzerland, and the French retreated to Mortara.

In April, 1500, the two armies encountered each other near Novara; but the infantry on both sides was Swiss—that in the French army obtained by treaty with the Swiss government, and that in Sforza's force enlisted man by man. Sforza's recruits had received orders from the Swiss Diet not to fight their countrymen in the French army; and as soon as the battle of Novara began they retreated into the town, where they commenced a secret agreement with the French, promising to desert the Duke of Milan and to return to their homes, on condition of a safe-conduct, which was readily granted.

One private soldier betrayed Sforza as he was trying to pass out of the ranks of his perfidious Swiss in the disguise of a monk. He was conveyed a captive to France, and passed the remainder of his life in a dungeon. In spite of the perfidious crimes which condemn him, Ludovico Sforza had been a wise and beneficent sovereign in many respects. The great plain of Lombardy to this day is indebted for much of its productiveness to the canal by which he completed its system of irrigation. Leonardo da Vinci, the greatest artist of the time, selected Sforza for his patron and friend, and contributed much to the splendor of the Milanese court by his genius as a painter, sculptor and poet.

By a counter-revolution the King of France now again came into possession of the Milanese duchy, and opened the way for his march upon Naples. King Ferdinand of Spain—the cousin and natural ally of King Frederick of Naples—had secretly turned against him, and entered into a treaty with Louis XII. to divide the Kingdom of Naples and Sicily between them. Under the pretense of a crusade against the Turks, which was duly proclaimed by the infamous Pope Alexander VI., Ferdinand of Spain had a fleet and an army ready in the ports of Sicily before the French had arrived. The Spanish king kept possession of several towns and fortresses which his cousin had entrusted to him as a friend and ally.

When Frederick became aware of the disgraceful plot he abandoned Naples and Sicily rather than to subject his people to a useless war, and surrendered himself to Stuart d'Aubigny, who conveyed him a captive to France. The military renown of Gonsalvo de Cordova, the Great Captain, is sullied by his obedience to a faithless monarch. By a false oath, that great general obtained possession of King Frederick's son and heir, and sent him a prisoner to Spain. Thus ended the Neapolitan branch of the House of Aragon, which had reigned over Naples and Sicily sixty-five years.

The perfidious conquerors of Naples and Sicily qurrelled about the division of the spoils. The French gradually became masters of the entire kingdom, excepting Barletta and several towns on the south-western coast; but the Spaniards again came into possession by a new fraud. The Archduke Philip, on returning from Spain to the Netherlands, was commissioned to conclude a treaty with Louis XII. of France at Lyons. By that treaty it was agreed that the Kings of France and Spain should confer the Kingdom of Naples and Sicily upon two children, Charles of Austria and Claude of France, who were to be married when they became of age.

In the meantime Philip was to be regent for his infant son and to rule at Naples, jointly with a commissioner appointed by the King of France. Relying on this treaty, Louis XII. had ordered his commanders in Italy to suspend hostilities; but Ferdinand of Spain had resolved not to be bound by the treaty, and sent secret orders to his Great Captain, who by a sudden and rapid movement surprised the French in their inaction. By their victories in the two decisive battles of Seminara and Cerignola, the Spaniards secured possession of the Kingdom of Naples and Sicily. The city of Naples and most of the other towns of the kingdom opened their gates to Gonsalvo de Cordova, and the last Frenchman had retired from the Neapolitan kingdom within three months.

Taking advantage of the French invasion of Italy, the Borgias conquered many small sovereignties in Central Italy by force or fraud, and they intended to form a new and powerful "Kingdom of Romagna" from these conquered sovereignties. But Pope Alexander VI. was destined to perish by his own wicked devices. Most of the forty-three cardinals whom he appointed bought their dignities with vast sums of gold; but after they had become enriched by employments in the Church the wicked Pope caused many of them to be poisoned, so that the papal coffers might again be replenished by the confiscation of their estates and the sale of their high offices.

The Pope designed such a fate for the Cardinal of Corneto, whom he invited with Cæsar Borgia, the Pope's son, to the Belvedere, a favorite retreat of the Pope near the Vatican. The Pope had instructed one of his servants to serve the visiting cardinal with poisoned wine. The bottles were interchanged by mistake, and Pope Alexander VI. and his son partook of the poisoned wine, as well as their unsuspecting victim. The more vigorous constitutions of Cæsar Borgia and the Cardinal of Corneto conquered the violent illness with which the poisoned wine attacked them; but the aged Pope, then in his seventy-third year, died within a week, A. D. 1503.

The Cardinal d'Amboise, the famous prime minister of Louis XII. of France, now proved the worthlessness of the friendship purchased with worldly favors. While marching to Naples, a French army halted near Rome, to influence the election of a new Pope; but, as the Cardinal d'Amboise perceived that the election would nevertheless be against him, he gave the votes of his party to the Cardinal of Siena, who thus became Pope Pius III. The new Pope was a good old man, but his election was mainly owing to a mortal disease with which he was already prostrated, and which terminated fatally in less than a month, A. D. 1503. He had during his brief pontificate planned a general council for the reform of the Church.

The next papal election was still more fatal to the ambition of Cardinal d' Amboise. The votes of the conclave were given to Cardinal Julian della Rovera, an active and powerful man, who thus became Pope Julius II. This warlike pontiff's reign was absorbed by two objects—the expulsion of the French from Italy, and the recovery of the alienated estates of the Church. His attention failed to be attracted by the spiritual dangers which menaced the papal supremacy more and more. He soon deprived Cæsar Borgia of his ill-gotten possessions, and immured him in the same tower in Rome where he had incarcerated many prisoners. When Borgia was released he availed himself of the safe-conduct given him by Gonsalvo de Cordova, and proceeded to Naples, where he was betrayed by that great Spanish general to King Ferdinand, who confined him in a Spanish prison for three years. He made his escape therefrom, and perished in one of the civil wars of Navarre.

Indignant at the ill-faith of King Ferdinand of Spain and his Great Captain, Louis XII. of France hastily fitted out three expeditions—one against Naples and two against Spain. The expedition against Naples was delayed by the ambitious designs of Cardinal d' Amboise, until all its efforts were rendered futile by the lateness of the season. The valley of Garigliano had been converted into a noisome swamp by heavy rains. Hundreds of French soldiers died of malaria; but the Spanish army under Gonsalvo de Cordova, better posted and more thoroughly fed and equipped, was able to profit by the misfortunes of the French. The battle of Garigliano, December 29, 1503, in which the French were utterly routed, completed the conquest of Naples by the Spaniards. The two French expeditions against Spain met with no better success, and the deposed and captive King Frederick of Naples and Sicily negotiated a treaty of peace between France and Spain.

The good Queen Isabella of Spain died in 1504, overwhelmed with grief for the loss of her family, and especially for the insanity of her daughter Joanna, the wife of Philip of Austria. King Ferdinand became Regent of Castile, in his daughter's absence, though he caused Philip and Joanna to be proclaimed sovereigns of Castile. Encouraged by a party among the Castilian nobles opposed to Ferdinand, Philip wrote a discourteous letter to his father-in-law, demanding that he retire into his own kingdom of Aragon. Ferdinand replied by inviting Philip to Spain; but he sought revenge by entering into a close alliance with Louis XII. of France, and marrying Germaine de Foix, the French king's niece, who received the French claims upon Naples as her dowry.

Philip and Joanna sailed for Spain early in 1506; but their Netherland fleet was dispersed by a storm, and they were obliged to take refuge in an English port. Henry VII. of England took advantage of their misfortune to extort a commercial treaty from Philip, favoring England at the expense of the Netherlands, and promising the close alliance of their families by two marriages, which, however, never occurred.

After being detained in England several months Philip and Joanna were allowed to proceed to Spain, where they received the allegiance of the Castilian Cortes. Ferdinand resigned all authority in Castile, retaining only the West Indian revenues and the grand-masterships of the three military orders, which Isabella's will secured to him, and sailed with his new queen for Italy. Before he arrived at Naples he was informed of Philip's sudden death. But Ferdinand was willing to have his absence regretted by the ungrateful Spaniards, who were overwhelmed with confusion and alarm by the unexpected event. Ferdinand proceeded to regulate the affairs of his Neapolitan kingdom at leisure, and did not return to Spain until the summer of 1507.

The unfortunate Joanna's mental malady was aggravated by excessive grief for her husband's sudden death. She submitted herself entirely to her father's control, and never consented to take any part in public affairs during the remaining forty-seven years of her life. Her son Charles remained

LOUIS XII. AT THE BATTLE OF AGNADELLO.

in the Netherlands, under the guardianship of his paternal grandfather, the German Emperor Maximilian I. Maximilian's daughter Margaret, who was then a widow for the second time, was appointed regent for the Netherlands. Her skillful diplomacy led to the *League of Cambray*, which she negotiated with the Cardinal d' Amboise, the great French prime minister, and which was signed in the cathedral of Cambray, December 10, 1508; thus uniting King Ferdinand of Spain, King Louis XII. of France, the Emperor Maximilian I. and Pope Julius II. in a coalition against the Venetian Republic.

The wealth and power of Venice, which had recently been confirmed by the capture of several Greek islands from the Ottoman Turks, excited the fears and the jealousy of her neighbors. Louis XII. of France, as Duke of Milan, desired to reclaim several Lombard towns which had been secured to Venice by treaty during his wars with Ludovico Sforza. Pope Julius II. insisted upon the grants of Pepin the Little and Charlemagne, securing Rimini, Faenza and some other towns to the dominion of St. Peter.

Ferdinand of Spain desired the possession of Brindisi and other maritime cities which his cousin and predecessor, King Frederick of Naples, had pledged to Venice as security for the expenses of the Venetian Republic in his cause. Padua, Vicenza and Verona were claimed as belonging to the Germano-Roman Empire by ancient right. Roveredo, Treviso and Friuli were claimed as belonging to the Austrian House of Hapsburg. The Duke of Savoy, as lineal descendant of Guy of Lusignan, the King of Jerusalem before the Third Crusade, claimed the isle of Cyprus, which had been bequeathed to Venice by Catharine Cornaro, the widow of the last reigning sovereign of the island. The King of Hungary desired to reannex the lands which Venice had conquered in Dalmatia and Slavonia.

Florence was induced to join the League of Cambray by an act of the basest perfidy on the part of Kings Ferdinand of Spain and Louis XII. of France. Ever since the expedition of Charles VIII. of France into Italy, Pisa, which had previously been the unwilling subject of Florence, had been bravely struggling for independence. Maximilian I., as Emperor, and therefore as nominal sovereign of Italy, had been implored to espouse the cause of Pisa; but his movements were delayed so long that "succor for Pisa" had become a proverb and a by-word in Germany.

The Kings of France and Spain now agreed to put a garrison in Pisa, which would be readily received as friendly, but which should be instructed to open the gates of the city to the Florentine army at an appointed time. Louis XII. was to receive one hundred thousand ducats, and Ferdinand fifty thousand, for this act of royal treachery. The troops of Florence entered the half-starved city of Pisa, June 8, 1509, and, by a liberal distribution of food, exhibited greater generosity than their allies.

The League of Cambray was the first great European coalition since the Crusades; and it laid the foundation of public law by raising the question whether ancient and hereditary right, the faith of treaties, or general considerations of the common good shall have precedence in controlling the affairs of nations. The text of the treaty is strongly tinged with the hypocrisy of the time; as it declares the principal object of the alliance to be a war against the Ottoman Turks, and that, as a preliminary to such a war, it was necessary to put an end to the rapine, the losses and the injuries caused by the insatiable cupidity and the thirst for domination which were characteristic of the Venetian Republic. Venice was really the strongest barrier of Europe against the Turks, and was best able by her maritime power to oppose them in the seat of their dominion.

Pope Julius II. began hostilities by a decree of excommunication against the Venetians, expressed in the bitterest terms of reproach. Louis XII. was the first to take the field; and, by a victory which he won over the Venetians at Agnadello in 1509, he gained more than had been assigned to him by the Treaty of Cambray, as he was able to send the keys of Verona, Vicenza and Padua to the Emperor Maximilian I.

Reduced to desperate straits by the number and strength of their enemies, the Venetians adopted the masterly plan of freeing all their Italian dependencies, thus throwing upon the subject cities the burden of their own defense, and narrowing the frontiers of the Venetian Republic to the islands at the head of the Adriatic which had been the Republic's original territories. They also surrendered to Ferdinand of Spain the towns which he had demanded in Apulia, and made dutiful professions of submission to the Emperor and the Pope.

The barbarities which the French and the Germans committed aroused the peasantry of all North-eastern Italy to espouse the cause of Venice. A Venetian force retook and garrisoned Padua. Maximilian I. besieged that town with an army of forty thousand men, but was finally forced to retire and to disband his army, after which the Venetians recovered many cities.

Pope Julius II. had now gained all that he desired for the territories of the Church, and he turned his attention to the expulsion of the French from Italy. He relieved Venice from the interdict, and concluded an alliance with the Swiss Republic, which had quarreled with the King of France, and which now agreed to furnish more than six thousand of their best halberdiers to the Pope's service.

The Pope propitiated the King of Spain by the feudal investiture of the Kingdom of Naples, and commuted the tribute formerly received from that realm into an annual offering of a white horse and an aid of three hundred lances in case of an actual invasion of the States of the Church. The Duke of Ferrara had incurred the Pope's wrath by yielding in everything to the counsels of the King of France, and the ambassadors of France and Ferrara were at once dismissed from the papal court.

The allied French and German armies were still prosecuting hostilities in Northern Italy in the most cruel manner. Vicenza had speedily returned to its alliance with Venice after the repulse of the Emperor Maximilian's army at Padua, and was now exposed to the vengeance of the Germans. All its inhabitants who were able to do so removed their families and their property to Padua, but the remainder took refuge with the peasantry in a vast cavern in the mountains near the city. The French soldiery filled the entrance to the cave with light wood, to which they set fire, thus smothering all who were in the cave, six thousand in number.

Just when the two fortified towns of Porto Legnano and Monselice had yielded to the allied French and German armies, the scale was turned against the Germans by the Pope's declaration of war against the Duke of Ferrara, and by a simultaneous attack by his Roman and Swiss forces upon Genoa and Milan. The Venetians promptly took advantage of the changed situation, and recovered Vicenza and many other towns; but the papal officers failed to excite a revolt in Genoa against the French; and the Swiss who had entered the plain of Lombardy found themselves entrapped among the many rivers and harassed by the movements of their foes, and were thus obliged to retreat hastily to their own country.

After the death of the Cardinal d'Amboise the French clergy assembled at Lyons and called upon Pope Julius II. to lay down weapons so inconsistent with his spiritual dignity and to submit his complaints to a general council of the Church. A new treaty signed at Blois between King Louis XII. of France and the Emperor Maximilian I. provided for the sending of French troops into the field.

Pope Julius II. was enraged by these movements of his enemies, and pushed his warlike operations with increased vigor. He was almost taken prisoner by the French at Bologna, while prostrated by a dangerous illness; but he contrived to occupy their general by negotiations until a Venetian army, including a detachment of Turkish cavalry, arrived. The fiery old pontiff laid siege to the fortresses of Concordia and Mirandola amid the snows of a most rigorous winter. Encased in armor, his white hair covered by a steel helmet, he appeared on horseback among his troops, sharing all their hardships and perils, and encouraging them with promises of rich plunder. When the fortress finally surrendered, he entered by a ladder at the breach which his guns had effected, being too impatient to wait for the opening of the gates.

In a congress which the Emperor Maximilian I. had opened at Bologna the warlike Pope made an unsuccessful effort to detach the Emperor from his alliance with the King of France, and the haughty demeanor of the imperial secretary rendered peace impossible. Being seized with a panic the Pople fled from Bologna; and the French pursued his army, and captured its great standard, twenty-six cannon and an enormous quantity of baggage. The Bolognese received back the Bentivoglios, their former masters, and destroyed the bronze statue of Pope Julius II., which was regarded as one of Michael Angelo's greatest works.

A new coalition, called the *Holy League*, was now formed against the French by Pope Julius II., King Ferdinand of Spain, and the Venetian Republic; while King Henry VIII. of England and the Emperor Maximilian I. were secret parties to the alliance, but did not openly avow their designs until the interests of each could be best secured. The King of England was promised the Duchy of Guienne, along with the title of "Most Christian King," which were to be taken from the King of France. The Emperor Maximilian's romantic mind was now occupied with an unusually visionary scheme. The Pope's illness had inspired the Emperor with the idea of taking holy orders and becoming the successor of Julius II. in the Chair of St. Peter, assuming in advance the title of Pontifex Maximus, which the Popes had inherited from the Cæsars.

Pope Julius II. united in his person the

genius of a military commander with the ambition of a temporal sovereign; while Louis XII. of France was holding ecclesiastical councils, and the Emperor Maximilian I. in his old age commenced sighing for the dignity of a Pope and the life of a saint. Louis XII., the object of the jealousy of Julius II., was the only one who scrupled to fight against the Pope, and voluntarily relinquished advantages which he had acquired, rather than to do injury to Christ's Vicar on earth; while Henry VIII. of England, who afterward destroyed the papal supremacy in his own realm, was on this occasion won to the Pope's side by the artful flatteries of Julius II.

The French armies in Italy were under the command of Gaston de Foix, nephew of Louis XII. and brother-in-law of Ferdinand of Spain—a young nobleman of remarkable talents, whose short and brilliant career astonished Europe and acquired for him the title of the *Thunderbolt of Italy*. By a swift and determined movement he threw his army into Bologna, which the allies were then besieging. The forces of the Holy League at once fled; and Gaston de Foix strongly guarded Bologna and then rapidly marched into Lombardy, where he ascertained that two cities had driven away their French garrisons or taken them captive. He defeated the Venetians near Isola della Scala before dawn by the light which the stars reflected from the snow. He took Brescia by storm and gave the city up to plunder and massacre. Bergamo escaped a similar fate by prompt submission and the payment of a ransom.

The King of France now ordered his victorious commander to fight one decisive battle, and, if victorious, to march upon Rome, depose Pope Julius II. and dictate terms of peace. In executing this plan, Gaston de Foix marched toward Ravenna, driving the allied army before him. The great battle of Ravenna, which was fought April 11, 1512, has been described as "one of those tremendous days into which human folly and wickedness compress the whole devastation of a famine or a plague."

The French general, who claimed the Kingdom of Navarre, and who considered the King of Spain his personal enemy and rival, bared his left arm so that he might bathe it in Spanish blood. The artillery of the Duke of Ferrara, from one end of the crescent-shaped line of the French army, kept up a destructive cross-fire, mowing down entire ranks of the Spanish and papal troops. The French were victorious in the cavalry charge which followed; but the serried ranks of the Swiss, bristling with the points of their long lances, like a Macedonian phalanx, had to sustain a harder struggle with the short swords and the Roman drill of the Spanish infantry. The Swiss columns were only rescued from destruction by the French cavalry, led by the gallant Gaston de Foix himself, who won the victory by the sacrifice of his life. On receiving the fatal tidings, Louis XII. exclaimed: "Would to God that I had lost all Italy, and that Gaston were safe!"

In the midst of the panic of the allies all Romagna fell into the power of the victorious French. Rome trembled, and the iron-hearted Pope Julius II. was ready to accept the French king's conditions of peace. But in a few weeks the entire situation was changed. The French soldiery were dispirited by the death of their gallant commander. The German lancers were withdrawn, and the Duke of Ferrara negotiated a separate peace with the Pope. The Council which convened at Rome three weeks after the battle of Ravenna opposed the terms of peace offered by France. Pope Julius II., the Emperor Maximilian I. and the Swiss Republic united in making Maximilian Sforza, Ludovico's son, Duke of Milan. The French forces, under La Palisse, fled before the allies to Pavia, and thence, after a sanguinary battle, into their own country. At the close of June, 1512, only three towns and three fortresses in Italy remained in the French king's possession.

But, after the expulsion of the French from Italy, the Holy League fell to pieces from its own dissensions. Pope Julius II., who was resolved upon enlarging the States of the Church to their former limits, wrested the cities of Parma and Piacenza from the new Duke of Milan, and sent his nephew to occupy the Duchy of Ferrara, while he kept the now pardoned and reconciled Alfonso a prisoner at Rome. The Emperor Maximilian I. sent a German army to prey upon the territories of his new allies, the Venetians; while the Swiss kept possession of the three districts of the Valtelline, Locarno and Chiavenna, and levied forced contributions upon the Milanese and deposed their new duke, Maximilian Sforza.

The late allies agreed upon the necessity of chastising Florence for her neutrality during their wars, by bestowing power in the Florentine Republic upon the party which was able to pay the highest price. Cardinal John de Medici had been taken prisoner in the battle of Ravenna, but he escaped in the confusion during the French retreat from Milan. He was now sent with a Spanish army to revolutionize Florence and to restore the dominion of his family. This force took the suburban village of Prato and subjected it to a brutal massacre and pillage.

The Florentine government, in utter dismay, deposed its chief magistrate, and accepted all the terms of the allies, including the payment of a vast sum of money to the Emperor Maximilian I. and King Ferdinand of Spain, and the restoration of the Medici as private citizens only. Julian de Medici, the youngest son of Lorenzo the Magnificent, entered Florence, followed soon afterward by his brother, the cardinal, who, in a packed assembly of the citizens, procured a thorough reversal of the Republic and the establishment of a narrow oligarchy headed by Julian.

Upon the death of Pope Julius II., the next year, A. D. 1513, John de Medici was elected Pope by the conclave of cardinals, with the title of Leo X. Leo X. had derived from his illustrious father and the brilliant freethinkers of the New Academy as much regard for pagan mythology as for the Christian religion, but his mind had been improved by travel and the conversation of the greatest and wisest men of his time.

He had an excellent taste in art. His court was celebrated for the highest elegance and the most profuse magnificence. He had remarkably charming and amiable manners.

Leo X. differed from his stern and warlike predecessor in governmental principles as much as in manners. He dissolved the Holy League and made peace with France. He pursued his predecessor's policy of expelling all foreigners from Italy, for the purpose of uniting the entire peninsula under the rule of the Medici. His brother Julian was unfitted by his imbecile character for administering the government of a freedom-loving people, and therefore abdicated in favor of his nephew, Lorenzo II., and accepted the office of Captain-General of the Church, which his brother, the Pope, conferred upon him; and thus Florence became the slave of a despotic master.

In the meantime the English army which was to have been transported to the coast of Guienne in Spanish vessels had been landed in Spain by the order of King Ferdinand, who sought to enlist the English commander, the Marquis of Dorset, in his own schemes against the Kingdom of Navarre. The English declined to engage in actual hostilities against Navarre; but their presence as allies of Spain so overawed the Navarrese that the Duke of Alva, the Spanish general, was able to conquer the entire Kingdom of Navarre. That little kingdom was annexed to Spain; while its native sovereigns, who still retained their royal titles, only kept possession of the little principality of Bearn, on the north side of the Pyrenees.

In April, 1513, Margaret, regent of the Netherlands, concluded a new treaty at Mechlin between her father the Emperor Maximilian I., Ferdinand of Spain, Henry VIII. of England, and Pope Leo X., by which the contracting parties bound themselves to invade France from four different points, while still pursuing their combined hostilities against the French king in Italy.

Louis XII. hastened his preparations; and in May, 1513, his generals subdued all of Lombardy, except two towns, by a series of brilliant victories. The Italians, who were by this time equally disgusted with the inefficiency of Maximilian Sforza and the brutality of the Swiss, welcomed the French on every side. But the reaction was as sudden and rapid as the advance. The French were obliged to raise the siege of Novara in consequence of fresh arrivals of Swiss, and were defeated and driven beyond the Alps within a few days.

The English army under King Henry VIII. arrived at Calais, and was joined by the Emperor Maximilian I. in the siege of Terouenne; but the English victory in the "Battle of the Spurs," in which the French cavalry fled at the first onset, decided the fate of Terouenne, which surrendered and was destroyed, to the dismay of the Parisians. Several weeks after the Battle of the Spurs, September 9, 1513, King James IV. of Scotland, the generous ally of Louis XII. of France, was defeated and slain by an English army under the Earl of Surrey at Flodden Field, in the North-east corner of England.

The invasion of Burgundy by German and Swiss troops in the Emperor Maximilian's pay was defeated by bribery. This was the most disgraceful period in the history of the Swiss Republic, when the brave Swiss mountaineers successively sold themselves to the highest bidders, not content with once exchanging their blood for the gold of their purchasers.

The eventful year 1513 was signalized by still greater changes. Before it ended, Louis XII. had become reconciled with Pope Leo X., and sought the friendship of the Emperor Maximilian I. and King Ferdinand of Spain, for the purpose of furthering his designs upon Milan. As Anne of Brittany, the consort of Louis XII., died in January, 1514, he became the ally of Maximilian I. by engaging to marry the Emperor's granddaughter, Eleanora of Austria; while his own daughter Renée was affianced to the Archduke Charles, the heir to the sovereignty of Spain and the Netherlands, as the grandson of Ferdinand and Isabella, and of the Emperor Maximilian I. and the Duchess Mary of Burgundy.

This projected alliance of families alarmed Pope Leo X. by its threatened union of Austria, France, Spain and the Netherlands into one vast dominion, which would have, inevitably destroyed the newly cherished balance of power in Europe. With the support of two English prelates, the Pope arranged a new marriage-treaty, by which Louis XII. espoused Mary, the sister of Henry VIII. of England. This royal wedding occurred at Abbeville, in October, 1514; but the festivities in honor of the marriage proved fatal to the already failing health of Louis XII., who breathed his last January 1, 1515.

The Princess Claude, the eldest daughter of Louis XII., was already married to Duke Francis of Angoulême, the representative of the younger branch of the House of Orleans. As Louis XII. left no son, this prince at once became King of France with the title of FRANCIS I.; and the duchy of Brittany, or Bretagne, thenceforth remained a part of the Kingdom of France.

SECTION V.—FRANCIS I., CHARLES V. AND HENRY VIII.

FRANCIS I. the new King of France, was twenty-one years of age, gay, brilliant and equally fond of pleasure and military glory. The cares of government in France fell into the hands of his mother, whom he made Duchess of Angoulême and Anjou. The queen-mother gathered the ladies of the noblest families around her, and under her auspices the French court first became noted for its elegance and extravagant gayety. The penetrating wit of French women, veiling profound art with consummate grace, has ever since exerted a good or evil influence in the affairs of France.

The Chancellor Duprat and the Constable de Bourbon—both of whom had been raised to their dignities by the queen-mother's favor—acted very conspicuous parts in the history of the reign of Francis I. Pedro Navarro, a famous military engineer, who had long been in the service of King Ferdinand of Spain, having been wronged by that sovereign, entered the armies of France; and from the recruits which he raised among the mountaineers of the Cevennes and the Pyrenees he presented Francis I. with the powerful assistance of regiments organized upon the model of the Spanish infantry.

The new French king at once assumed the title of Duke of Milan, and prepared to prosecute the claims of his dynasty in Northern Italy. A Swiss army guarded the passes of Mont Cenis and Mont Genèvre—the only western Alpine passes considered practicable—and was stationed in the Italian plain near the exits from the valleys.

In this emergency the French forces, numbering sixty-four thousand men, with seventy-two great and three hundred smaller cannon, performed one of the most remarkable transits mentioned in history. Guided by chamois-hunters, the two great French generals, Trivulzio and Lautrec, with the engineer Navarro, pioneered a more southerly route over the Col d' Argentière. This path, which was scarcely passable by the sure foot and the practiced eye of the mountaineer, was prepared by the skill and genius of Navarro for the transportation of heavy artillery. Bridges were placed across from one dizzy height to another. Masses of solid rock were disposed of by charges of gunpowder. Cannon were swung from peak to peak by means of ropes. The French army suddenly surprised the enemy by appearing on the Lombard plain.

A small division of cavalry, which had crossed the Alps by another route never before trodden by horses, had in the meantime surprised Prosper Colonna, the Pope's general, at Villa Franca, with seven hundred of his troops. The main army proceeded

ALBRECHT III. (ACHILLES).

BURGUNDIANS (1470).

KNIGHT IN FULL ARMOR AND LADY (MIDDLE OF 15TH CENTURY).

CITIZENS AND PEASANTS (15 CENTURY).

THE 15TH CENTURY.

by way of Turin, the Swiss retiring before them to Milan and Novara; while a detachment marched southward and recovered Genoa and the entire region south of the Po by a bloodless victory.

A decisive battle fought at Marignano, about ten miles from Milan, September 14-15, 1515, transferred the Duchy of Milan from Maximilian Sforza to King Francis I. of France. The Swiss, after being reinforced by twenty thousand of their countrymen, burst upon the French quarters unexpectedly late in the afternoon. The fierce onset and the furious resistance rendered the result doubtful, and at midnight the exhausted combatants took a rest until daybreak. The French king slept on a gun-carriage, and rallied his troops at dawn with sound of trumpet. The Swiss retired in good order when a Venetian detachment appeared upon the scene. Francis I. was knighted on the battle-field by the Chevalier Bayard, "the knight without fear and without reproach."

Maximilian Sforza retired to France on a pension. Francis I. now entered into a close alliance with the Medici, the oppressors of Florence; thus sacrificing most of the advantages of his great victory at Marignano, and allowing himself to be persuaded by Pope Leo X. to postpone his attack upon Naples until the death of its sovereign, King Ferdinand of Spain. The French king made a treaty of peace and alliance with the Swiss at Geneva, thus gaining the important right to levy troops in Switzerland. He then disbanded most of his army, and appointed the Constable de Bourbon his viceroy in Milan, after which he retired into France.

Before the French king had left Italy, Pope Leo X. was conspiring with the Emperor Maximilian I., and with Kings Henry VIII. of England and Ferdinand of Spain, to invest Francisco Sforza with the Duchy of Milan, notwithstanding the fact that the Pope's recognition of the title of Francis I. to that duchy had been almost the only article in the Treaty of Bologna that favored the French king. But the coalition against Francis I. was disconcerted by the sudden death of King Ferdinand of Spain, in January, 1516.

The friends and enemies of Ferdinand expressed their various estimates of his character in his titles. "Spain called him the Wise; Italy, the Pious; France and England, the Perfidious." We can not help regarding the last of these epithets deserved when we are reminded of his ingratitude toward Columbus and Gonsalvo de Cordova, or the base deception by which he deprived his cousin Frederick of the crown of Naples. But he was the most successful sovereign of his time, and even his avarice and duplicity laid the foundation for the ascendency of Spain during the sixteenth century, while his bigoted and intolerant policy introduced the elements of the sudden and fatal decline of that kingdom.

The Emperor Maximilian I. fulfilled his part of the treaty by invading Lombardy in March, 1516, with a large force of German, Swiss and Spanish troops. The French general, Lautrec, was obliged to retire to Milan; while the other French commander, the Constable de Bourbon, burned the surrounding villages, for the purpose of depriving the enemy of all shelter.

Thirteen thousand Swiss in the French army refused to fight their countrymen in the Emperor Maximilian's army, which was now approaching; and the Constable de Bourbon was reluctantly obliged to dismiss them. But the Emperor's good fortune deserted him when it seemed within his grasp. His coffers were empty and his troops unpaid, as usual; and the Swiss colonel entered his bed-chamber one morning and bluntly told him that he would lead his followers over to the service of the French if their pay was not forthcoming.

Maximilian then left his army and made a hasty journey to Trent under pretense of collecting money; but he failed to return, whereupon his army disbanded, and its dispersed companies consoled themselves for their arrears of pay by pillaging several unoffending towns. The menacing war cloud disappeared; and Maximilian I., conscious of the ridicule which he had incurred, never again led an army into the field.

Upon the death of King Ferdinand of Spain, in January, 1516, his celebrated prime-minister, Cardinal Ximenes, proclaimed his grandson, the Archduke Charles of Austria, as King of Spain, at Madrid, which had recently become the capital of Spain. Thus the Archduke Charles, who was also the grandson of the Emperor Maximilian I., and lord of the Netherlands, became CHARLES I. of Spain.

The Navarrese made an unsuccessful effort to restore the House of Albret; and Cardinal Ximenes wreaked a terrible vengeance upon the conquered kingdom, destroying its towns, villages and castles, two thousand in number, reserving only Pampeluna and a few places on the Ebro as military posts from which he might hold the Navarrese in awe. The exposed situation of Navarre and the Netherlands induced King Charles I. of Spain to cultivate the friendship of King Francis I. of France. By the Treaty of Noyon, Charles agreed to marry the infant daughter of Francis I., who was to have all her father's claims to Naples as her dowry; and already the Spanish monarch addressed the French sovereign, who was scarcely older than himself, as "My good father."

The Peace of Brussels, in December, 1516, closed the wars arising from the League of Cambray and the Holy League. In the fall of 1517 King Charles I. visited his Spanish kingdom for the first time since his accession to the Spanish throne, and the cloud which rested upon the mind of Queen Joanna was dispelled for a moment by the unexpected meeting. But the Spaniards were disgusted with the insolent rapacity of the Flemish courtiers who accompanied their new king and absorbed his confidence. A constant stream of gold flowed from Spain into the Netherlands, drawn from the Spanish offices and pensions.

The aged minister, Cardinal Ximenes, from his sick-bed addressed a letter to King Charles I., soliciting a personal interview.

The Flemings feared the great minister's influence, and persuaded the king to reply in terms which veiled the coolest and basest ingratitude under the forms of courtesy, dismissing Ximenes from all his offices except that of bishop. This ungrateful treatment from a sovereign whom Ximenes had served so well and faithfully brought on a relapse of the fever which had already conquered the great minister's iron frame; and he died at the age of eighty, with his last breath commending his university at Alcala to the king's favor.

Cardinal Ximenes rendered his name illustrious by his Polyglot edition of the Bible—the greatest literary work of his time, and one of the greatest glories of the University of Alcala. This work was the production of nine scholars, deeply learned in the ancient languages, and sustained by the patronage and guided by the counsel of Ximenes. The Old Testament contained the original Hebrew, with Chaldaic, Greek and Latin versions. The New Testament contained the Greek and Vulgate versions. The type was cast at Alcala under the eye of Ximenes, as none yet existed in the Oriental character. The most ancient Hebrew texts were discovered among the confiscated property of the exiled Jews.

Besides his zeal for learning and his great ability as a statesman, Cardinal Ximenes possessed military talents. In 1509 he undertook to chastise the Moors of Africa for their depredations on the coast of Spain. He himself captured Oran by storm, and in pursuance of his plans several important Moorish fortresses became permanent possessions of Spain. The darkest side of his character belongs more properly to the age in which he lived. During his eleven years' presidency of the Inquisition, he "permitted," in the language of Llorente, two thousand five hundred and thirty-six persons to be burned to death, while fifty-one thousand one hundred and sixty-seven endured less severe punishments.

The Chancellorship of Spain, thus made vacant by the death of Cardinal Ximenes, was conferred upon a Fleming; and his Primacy was bestowed upon another Fleming. The Castilian cities, which had been early given a voice in national affairs, now united in defense of their rights and addressed a petition to King Charles I., complaining of the illegal appointment of foreigners to high offices in Spain, and also of the increase of taxes and the exportation of coin. The king paid no attention to their complaints, but the Junta afterward threatened to overthrow the monarchy in Spain.

Upon the death of the Emperor Maximilian I., in 1519, three kings became candidates for the imperial throne—Charles I. of Spain, Francis I. of France and Henry VIII. of England. The seven Electors of the German Empire chose the King of Spain, who thus became Emperor with the title of CHARLES V. As Maximilian's grandson and as Archduke of Austria and lord of the Netherlands, Charles had the best claim to the imperial dignity. Conscious of the vast powers they were bestowing, the seven Electors required Charles V. to give a solemn guarantee of all their privileges; and the Elector-Palatine, with the Archbishops of Mayence, Trèves and Cologne formed the *Electoral Union of the Rhine* for common defense.

The Emperor Charles V. was the most powerful monarch that had reigned in Christendom since the time of Charlemagne, and his dominions were far more extensive than those of Alexander the Great or those of Augustus Cæsar. As we have seen, while yet a youth he was lord of the rich and flourishing Netherlands, which he inherited from his father Philip, the son of the Emperor Maximilian I. and the Duchess Mary of Burgundy. As we have also seen, on the death of his maternal grandfather, King Ferdinand of Spain, in 1516, he obtained the crown of Spain with Naples, Sicily, Sardinia and the Spanish possessions in America; inheriting these through his mother Joanna, the daughter of Ferdinand and Isabella. And lastly, as we have just noticed, on the death of his paternal grandfather, the Emperor Maximilian I., in 1519, he succeeded by inheritance to the hereditary Austrian territories, and by election to the imperial throne of Germany. His Spanish dominions were enlarged by the conquest of Mexico by Cortez in 1521, and by the conquest of Peru by Pizarro in 1532. He soon bestowed his hereditary Austrian estates on his brother Ferdinand, who, as we shall presently see, added the Kingdom of Bohemia and a large part of Hungary to the possessions of the House of Hapsburg, A. D. 1526.

Charles V., having been born in 1500, was therefore only nineteen years of age when he became the leading prince of Christendom upon his election to the imperial throne in 1519. At this early age he gave but little promise of the commanding character by which he was subsequently distinguished. He was sluggish in mind and weak in body; but his motto "*Non Dum*" (Not Yet), which he assumed at his first tournament, expressed some consciousness of unawakened power. His Spanish subjects were extremely offended by his acceptance of the imperial crown; and the Spanish Cortes very reluctantly voted him a grant of money, to enable him to make a suitable appearance in his new dignity.

Francis I. was deeply offended by the election of Charles V. to the imperial throne, and became his rival and enemy. Four wars arose between the two monarchs, caused by the conflicting claims of each to the possession of Milan, Naples, Navarre and Burgundy. Charles V. demanded the restitution of Burgundy, which had been confiscated from his grandmother, the Duchess Mary, by Louis XI. of France. He inherited the right of the Hohenstaufen and Aragonian dynasties to the Kingdom of Naples, while Francis I. represented the House of Anjou. As Emperor, Charles V. became sovereign of the imperial fiefs in Italy, including the Duchy of Milan, which Francis I. claimed as head of the House of Orleans. All these rival claims of Charles V. and Francis I. afforded so many pretexts for indulging their ambition and jealousy.

Charles V. and Francis I. each wished to secure the favor of the vain and capricious

Henry VIII., who had ascended the throne of England upon the death of his father, Henry VII., in 1509, and who was, like themselves, a candidate for the imperial throne. On his way to Germany, after his election to the imperial throne, Charles V. visited Henry VIII. in England, for the purpose of diverting him from any alliance with Francis I. The Emperor won the English king's favor by gifts and promises to his celebrated Prime Minister, Cardinal Wolsey, while Henry VIII. was already opposed to Francis I. by his desire to renew the conquests of Henry V. in France.

Henry VIII. nevertheless proceeded to that celebrated interview with Francis I. at Calais, during the splendid festival of two weeks in June, 1520, known as the *Field of the Cloth of Gold*, because of the magnificence displayed on that occasion. In reading aloud his state-paper, prepared for the occasion, Henry VIII. is even said to have dropped his own customary title of "King of France." The Emperor Charles V. waited at Gravelines for the meeting of the Kings of England and France to be over; and afterwards passed some days with Henry VIII. at Calais, for the purpose of removing any favorable impression which the French king might have made upon him.

Charles V. was crowned as Emperor-Elect at Aix la Chapelle, in October, 1520; and in January following he held his first Diet at Worms, where events of the most momentous importance were transacted, which will be fully related in the next section.

SECTION VI.—CHARLES V. AND THE REFORMATION.

HE great religious Reformation, which caused the separation of most of the Teutonic nations from the Romish Church, was one of the most important events connected with the opening of the modern era.

For several centuries the Chair of St. Peter had been occupied by Popes whose vices and crimes were a reproach to Christendom; and men doubted whether such creatures were God's agents upon earth. The pious and eloquent St. Bernard—although a staunch adherent of the Church—had as early as the twelfth century condemned the vices of the Popes and clergy. Monks and nuns disgraced themselves by their shameful vices. All attempts at reformation were sternly suppressed by the Popes, backed by the whole power of the Church. We have noticed the extinction of the unfortunate creed of the Albigenses in blood; the bold denial of the papal assumptions by Wickliffe and Huss, the martyrdom of Huss, and the suppression of their attempts at reformation; and the bold denunciation of the wickedness of Popes and clergy by the pious Florentine, Savonarola, and his consequent martyrdom.

After the Councils of Constance and Basle, the Church continued to grow more and more corrupt. Seventy great crimes had been proven against Pope John XXIII. Alexander VI. (1492-1503), the worst of the Popes, poisoned political opponents and cardinals to obtain their wealth; and, as we have seen, his death was caused by accidentally drinking poisoned wine which he had intended for another. Julius II. (1503-1513), the warlike Pope, swore at God for giving the French the victory; and his military ambition and desire to extend his dominions ill accorded with his spiritual office. Pope Leo X. (1513-1521)—John de Medici, the accomplished but dissolute son of Lorenzo the Magnificent, the illustrious ruler of Florence—disgraced his station by his vices and his skepticism; although he was a great patron of literature and the arts.

As we shall presently see, the great Reformation was begun in Germany in 1517 by Dr. Martin Luther's bold opposition to the papal assumptions. Luther was the son of a miner, and was born at Eisleben in Saxony, November 10, 1483. His father had destined him to study. Like other poor scholars, he earned his daily bread by singing from door to door, and in this way he cultivated that love and talent for music which afterward enabled him to move the German heart by his hymns.

Luther had studied jurisprudence for four years at the University of Erfurt, when anxiety for the salvation of his soul, and the sudden death of a friend, caused him to enter an Augustinian monastery in 1507; and he was finally admitted as a monk, but he obtained no alleviation of his melancholy. His experience in the monastery at Erfurt caused him to regard the rites of the Church as insufficient to give peace to his soul, and only when he devoted himself diligently to the study of a Latin Bible which he found chained in the library did he obtain any comfort to his conscience.

In 1508 Luther was appointed Professor of Theology in the new University of Wittenberg, founded by Frederick the Wise, Elector of Saxony. His appointment was made on the recommendation of Staupitz, the chief of the Augustinian order. His clear and vigorous style caused multitudes of students to throng to his lectures. The Elector Frederick the Wise was a devout member of the Church, but also a firm friend and protector of Luther, whom he highly appreciated as the main ornament of his favorite university; and the esteem in which the Saxon Elector was held throughout Germany secured a respectful hearing for Luther's doctrines.

The insight which Luther had gained during his monastic life, and which made him doubt the efficacy of some of the doctrines and practices of the Church, was strengthened by a journey to Rome in 1510 on business connected with his Augustinian order, when his suspicions were fully confirmed. The warlike pomp and ambition of Pope Julius II., the avowed skepticism of the clergy, and their sacrilegious contempt for the mysteries of the faith, shocked his religious nature. While ascending the Holy Staircase he was reminded of the words "The just shall live by faith;" and these became the watch-word of the Reformation. He said in after years: "I would not for a hundred thousand florins have missed seeing Rome. I should always have felt an uneasy doubt whether I was not, after all, doing injustice to the Pope. As it is, I am quite satisfied on the point."

The sale of *indulgences*, or licenses to sin, by which past and future sins might be pardoned, brought matters to a crisis, and was the immediate cause of Luther's separation from the Church of Rome. The traffic in indulgences had risen from apparently innocent beginnings, by successive degrees, until it became the chief source of income to the papal treasury. At first, the remission of temporal penalties for sin was promised to all who took part in the Crusades; then to those who founded churches or monasteries, or to those who paid a certain sum of money as a commutation for personal service; and afterwards to those who performed pilgrimages, especially by visiting Rome during the years of Jubilee.

Pope Alexander VI. first assumed the right to remit the penalties of sin in a future life, in consideration of money paid or penances performed in this life. These indulgences soon became very popular; and people sought by their means to deliver the souls of their departed friends from the pains of purgatory, and to secure the same immunities for themselves hereafter.

Germany was the great market for the sale of indulgences, either from the credulity or piety of its people; and the large sums annually remitted to Rome on this account were there styled "the sins of the Germans." The management of this revenue was so open that the Popes farmed it out to the great Augsburg bankers, the Fuggers, and sometimes granted parts of it to temporal princes for limited times. Thus Frederick the Wise had himself obtained the sale of indulgences in Saxony for the purpose of building a bridge over the Elbe. In 1508 the King of Hungary received two-thirds of the proceeds in his kingdom for the prosecution of his wars against the

Turks. The Emperor at one time permitted the sale only on condition of the payment of one-third into his treasury.

In order to defray the expenses of building the great Cathedral of St. Peter's at Rome, which had been commenced by his famous predecessor Julius II., Pope Leo X. pushed the sale of indulgences with increased energy. The Elector Albert, Archbishop of Mayence and Primate of Germany —a young and immoral churchman—had bought his ecclesiastical dignity at an enormous price; and the Pope aided him to pay for it by a special dispensation of indulgences.

INTERIOR OF ST. PETER'S CHURCH AT ROME.

The archbishop employed John Tetzel, a Dominican monk of infamous and immoral character, as his agent for the sale of these indulgences throughout Germany. Tetzel traveled over the country selling for a fixed price remission for past and future sins. Cried he: "Pour in your money, and whatever crimes you have committed, or may commit, are forgiven! Pour in your coin, and the souls of your friends and relations will fly out of purgatory the moment they hear the clink of your money at the bottom of the box!"

The following was Tetzel's form of absolution: "May our Lord Jesus Christ have mercy upon thee, and absolve thee by all the merits of his most holy passion; and I, by his authority, that of his blessed apostles, Peter and Paul, and of the most holy Pope, granted and committed to me in these parts, do absolve thee first from all ecclesiastical censures, in whatever manner they have been incurred, and then from all thy sins, transgressions and excesses, how enormous soever they may be, even from such as are reserved for the cognizance of the Holy See; and as far as the keys of the Holy Church extend I remit to you all punishment which you deserve in purgatory on their account; and I restore you to the holy sacraments of the Church, to the unity of the faithful, and to that innocence and purity which you possessed at baptism; so that when you die the gates of punishment shall be shut, and the gates of the paradise of delight shall be opened; and if you shall not die at present this grace shall remain in full force when you are at the point of death. In the name of the Father, and of the Son, and of the Holy Ghost."

A gay young knight, who saw an opportunity for sport, bought an indulgence permitting him to beat and plunder a man for whom he said that he had a thorough contempt. After the paper had been duly signed and a liberal price paid for the indulgence, the knight with a band of his men-at-arms waylaid Tetzel himself in a wood, robbing him of the chest of gold which he had gained by the sale of his indulgences.

This disgraceful traffic shocked many good men, and Tetzel's overbearing conduct aroused great indignation in Germany. Animated by his new and ardent belief in justification by faith alone, Dr. Martin Luther preached vigorously and energetically against the traffic in indulgences, and refused absolution to any of his hearers who should buy the indulgences from Tetzel. On October 31, 1517, Luther nailed to his church-door his *ninety-five theses*, boldly denying the Pope's right to sell indulgences, and declaring that remission of sins is from God alone. This was the beginning of the great *Reformation*, which rapidly spread and which ended in the withdrawal of the Teutonic nations from the Church of Rome.

Tetzel and others of the clergy published replies to Luther's theses, and the matter was finally reported at Rome. Pope Leo X. paid little attention to this at first, saying: "It is a quarrel of the monks." He also said that Luther wrote well, and was evidently a man of genius. Dr. John von Eck, or Eckius, Chancellor of the University of Ingolstadt, a learned man and skillful in argument, was one of the first to oppose Luther in Leipsic. He composed a book in which he undertook to show that Luthers's heresy was identical with that of Huss, but Luther replied with such overwhelming force that Eck sought revenge by inducing the Pope to interfere and silence the audacious Reformer of Wittenberg.

In his disputation with Eck, Luther maintained that the Bishop of Rome was made Head of the Church by human and not by divine ordination, and expressed doubt of the infallibility of Councils and of the Pope himself. It was these bold avowals that caused Eck to compose his learned work called *The Obelisks*. Luther had urged that the Bishop of Rome became Head of the Church by a human arrangement, made some centuries after the rise of Christianity. Eck endeavored to prove that such was not the case, and proceeded to Rome with his book.

Luther's ninety-five theses had created great excitement in Germany, and a party had rapidly been formed about him which demanded a thorough reform in the doctrines and discipline of the Church. This party was very strong in the German cities.

Luther advanced steadily in his opinions and promulgated his views more boldly, thus driving forward the movement which he had begun with every advance of his own.

Pope Leo X. finally aroused himself to the significance of the movement in Germany, and summoned Luther to appear at Rome; but the Elector of Saxony was well aware of what would be the Reformer's fate if he obeyed the Pope's summons, and therefore interposed as Luther's sovereign by forbidding him to go to Rome and demanding that he should be tried for his doctrines in Germany.

In 1518 the Pope sent Cardinal Cajetan, or Cajetanus, into Germany as the papal legate, to examine Luther. Luther was summoned before Cajetan in the imperial Diet at Augsburg. Provided with a safe-conduct, Luther obeyed the summons, and declared his willingness to recant if it could be shown to him that his doctrines were contrary to the Holy Scriptures; but the cardinal refused to allow any discussion. Luther then offered to submit his doctrines to the four universities of Basle, Freiburg, Louvain and Paris; but Cajetan rejected the proposition with scorn. When Luther saw that he would not receive justice from the papal legate he drew up an appeal to the Pope, and affixed it to the door of Augsburg Cathedral, after which he fled from Augsburg by night and returned to Saxony. The Elector refused to banish him at the legate's demand.

The great majority of the German people were now on Luther's side, and his party was growing stronger every day. The most enlightened men of the time—poets, painters and scholars—united in doing honor to the great Reformer's piety and moral courage.

The death of the Emperor Maximilian I., in 1519, and the contest for the German imperial crown which followed, produced a lull in the conflict of religious opinions for several years. The imperial crown was offered to the Elector of Saxony, but he refused it and recommended the young King Charles I. of Spain, who was accordingly chosen and became the Emperor Charles V., as already noticed. Charles V. was very willing to help the Pope; but, as Luther was the friend of the Elector of Saxony, to whom the new Emperor was indebted for his German crown, Charles V. could not immediately offend the Elector by proceeding against the great Reformer.

In 1520 Pope Leo X. condemned Luther's writings to be burned, and threatened the great Reformer with excommunication unless he recanted within sixty days; and on December 11th of the same year (1520) Luther publicly burned the papal bull of condemnation and the volumes of the canon-law of the Romish Church in the public square of Wittenberg. The Pope punished Luther and his adherents by solemnly excommunicating them from the Church, but Luther replied by excommunicating the Pope. In 1521 Luther appeared before the Diet of Worms, at the command of the Emperor Charles V., who provided the Reformer with a safe-conduct. Luther's friends, fearing for his safety, had advised him not to go to Worms; but the daring Reformer replied: "I will go to Worms if there be as many devils there as tiles on the roofs of the houses."

Luther's journey to Worms resembled a triumphal procession, as the people of many towns came a distance of many miles to meet him and to escort him. When he arrived at Worms he was escorted to his lodgings by a multitude of nobles and citizens. The next day he appeared before the assembled Diet. As he entered the great hall where the Diet was in session, George Frundsberg, the famous general, who afterward embraced his opinions, tapped him on the shoulder and said to him earnestly: "Little monk, little monk, thou art doing a more daring thing than I or any other general ever ventured on. But if thou art confident in thy cause, go on, in God's name and be of good cheer, for He will not forsake thee."

Luther made an eloquent defense before the Diet, and when ordered to recant he refused unless convinced from Scripture that he was wrong, and concluded thus: "Here I stand; I cannot do otherwise; God help me—Amen!" Some of the Pope's adherents advised the Emperor to violate his solemn promise and mete out to Luther the fate of Huss; but Charles, true to his word, allowed Luther to depart, saying: "No, I will not blush like Sigismund at Constance!"

The Emperor permitted Luther to depart from Worms, but warned him that thenceforth he must expect the treatment due a heretic. Charles V. then issued an edict condemning Luther as a heretic and punishing all who should shelter the Reformer, or print, sell, buy or read his books, by putting them under the ban of the Empire.

Soon after Luther had departed from Worms he was seized by a company of masked horsemen sent by the Elector of Saxony to secure him from his enemies. Luther was at once stripped of his monkish dress, attired in military costume, with a false beard, mounted on a spare horse, and hurried away to the manorial castle of Wartburg, in Thuringia, which belonged to the Elector Frederick the Wise. The Reformer lived in that castle almost a year under the name of "Ritter George." It was generally believed that he had been murdered, and his friends were greatly alarmed for his safety, but soon received tidings setting at rest all fears.

During this period of seclusion in the

DR. MARTIN LUTHER.

Wartburg castle Luther passed his time in the most important of all his works—the translation of the Scriptures into the German language. He continued striking at the dogmas of the Roman Catholic Church, and his disciples and the press of Germany circulated his writings broadcast over the Empire. The art of printing aided vastly in spreading the tenets of the great Reformer, so that all classes were made acquainted with his doctrines.

Luther believed strongly in the Devil.

During his confinement in Wartburg castle he once threw his inkstand at the Devil's head, and the spot of ink is still shown on the wall. Said Luther: "Once, in our monastery at Wittenberg, I distinctly heard the Devil making a noise. As I sat down and began to study, the Devil came and made a noise behind my stove as though he would drag it away. At last, as he would not stop, I put my books by and went to bed. Another night I heard him overhead, but perceiving it was the Devil I paid no attention, and went to sleep again. This morning, when I awoke, the Devil said to me, 'Thou art a sinner.' I answered, 'Tell me something new, Devil, I knew that before.' He continued, 'What have you done with the monasteries?' I replied, 'What's that to thee? thy accursed worship goes on as ever.' The Devil sometimes casts me into such despair that I hardly know whether there is a God. He sets the law, sin and death before my eyes, compels me to ponder on this Trinity, and so torments me. He has sworn my death, but he will crack a hollow nut. When the Devil comes to me at night I give him these and the like answers, and say, 'Devil, I must now sleep, for this is God's command, to labor by day and sleep by night.' Then, if he charge me with being a sinner, I say, to spite him, 'Holy Satan! pray for me,' or 'Physician, heal thyself!' The Devil hates to be laughed at. He is of a melancholy disposition, and cheerful music soon puts him to flight."

During Luther's confinement in the Wartburg castle one of his earliest disciples, Dr. Carlstadt, began a series of hasty innovations at Wittenberg, abolishing the mass, extending the cup to the laity, and exercising his zeal against images and ceremonies with an eagerness equal to that of the Iconoclasts of the Byzantine Empire almost a thousand years before. Dr. Carlstadt was soon joined by the so-called Zurickhauer prophets, who denounced the baptism of infants, insisted upon the rebaptism of adults and were thus called *Anabaptists*, and believed in direct inspiration from God. These radical Reformers destroyed the robes used in celebrating mass, and also destroyed images in some churches; and monks fled in great alarm from their cloisters.

These hasty proceedings disturbed Luther's tranquillity of mind so that he could no longer remain at the castle of Wartburg. He therefore hastened to Wittenberg, preached against Dr. Carlstadt's innovations, pronouncing them over-hasty and uncharitable, and sought to bring about a more peaceful development of his views.

Wittenberg now became the seat of German culture. In its famous university Philip Melanchthon of Bretten had already occupied the chair of Professor of Greek at the age of twenty-two, and he was Luther's co-worker in the Reformation. This Reformer was of a pensive disposition, prone to mystical effusions of tender piety, while his mind was richly stored with classic lore. He had been captivated by Luther's eloquence; and, as he was of a timid disposition, he became one of the great Reformer's most zealous disciples and devoted friends. By his learned Latin writings Melanchthon endeavored to secure the doctrines of the new Church on a scientific basis.

Luther won the hearts of the people by his German writings and hymns; one of which—*Eine feste Burg ist unser Gott*, "A strong fort is our God"—became the battle hymn of the Reformation. His translation of the Bible into German begun at the Wartburg castle was completed at Wittenberg, and was first published in 1534. It was generally considered a masterpiece of the German language and an exponent of the German spirit.

The Lutheran doctrines soon spread from Saxony into other German states. The Landgrave Philip of Hesse, the founder of the University of Marburg, zealously supported the Reformation; while the educated burghers of the German imperial cities likewise distinguished themselves by their zeal in the same cause. For a long time the German nobility had coveted the Church property, and now they had a favorable opportunity to seize control over it. It appeared for the time as if all Germany was being carried away by the Lutheran movement, and a national Church was rising.

The Catholic princes of Germany were naturally alarmed, and felt that all their power was needed to resist the new Church movement. The Archduke Ferdinand of Austria, the brother of the Emperor Charles V., concluded a treaty of alliance at Ratisbon, or Regensburg, with Duke Louis of Bavaria, Duke William and several bishops and archbishops of Southern Germany, for the preservation of the Roman Catholic Church.

Landgrave Philip of Hesse and the Elector John of Saxony entered into an alliance with several German cities to uphold the Reformation.

The tranquillity of Germany was now disturbed by several causes. Notwithstanding the abolition of the right of private warfare, the country was still scoured by lawless knights and their men-at-arms, who robbed merchants and wealthy travelers, and even cut off the right hands of their captives. Franz von Sickingen, the greatest of the Rhenish knights, headed a league organized in hostility to the German princes. The knights professed an inveterate animosity toward the priests, and claimed Luther's support; but the great Reformer dreaded the propagation of his doctrines by the sword, and exhorted Franz von Sickingen and his followers to observe the peace of the Empire.

PREACHING THE REFORMATION.

At the Diet of the German Empire held at Nuremberg in 1524 most of the German princes favored the Reformation. The war which the Emperor Charles V., as King of Spain, was waging against King Francis I. of France in Italy, by diverting the Empereror's attention from Germany, gave the Lutherans additional power; and while the Catholic princes of Germany were forming the League of Ratisbon the Lutherans held a meeting at Torgau in 1526, at which the

In spite of Luther's efforts, Franz von Sickingen and his supporters declared war against the Archbishop of Trèves, who was aided by the Landgrave Philip of Hesse and Frederick the Elector-Palatine. Franz von

Sickingen was deprived of many of his castles, after which he was besieged in Landstuhl, the massive walls of which were reduced to ruins by artillery; and he was found mortally wounded in one of the inner apartments. The victorious Archbishop of Trèves, upon entering the vaulted chamber, exclaimed: "What have I done, that you should attack me and my poor people?" The Landgrave Philip of Hesse also asked: "Or I, that you should overrun my lands in my minority?" Franz von Sickingen replied: "I must answer to a greater Lord." When asked to confess his sins he answered: "I have already in my heart confessed to God." The princes knelt in prayer, while the chaplain administered the religious rites, and Franz von Sickingen's soul passed away. Twenty-seven castles belonging to him and his supporters, and most of the similar strongholds in Franconia, were dismantled or destroyed.

During the next three years (A. D. 1523–1525) Germany was distracted by a terrible revolt of the peasantry of Suabia, Franconia, Alsace, Lorraine and the Palatinate. The fanatical discourses of the fickle Anabaptist, Thomas Münzer, attracted crowds of idle and unprincipled people around him by proclaiming the principles of Communism and instigating these people to plunder churches, convents and castles. This leader talked of abolishing all temporal and spiritual power, and of establishing a heavenly kingdom in which all men should be equal, and in which every distinction between rich and poor, noble and peasant, should disappear.

Thomas Münzer's harangues confused the excited peasants, and very soon the populace from the Boden Lake to Dreisam followed the leadership of Hans Müller of Bulgenbach, who had formerly been a soldier. Attired in a red mantle and cap, Hans Müller marched from village to village, at the head of his followers. The chief banner was borne behind him on a carriage decorated with boughs and ribbons. The revolted peasants carried with them twelve articles, the importance of which they were ready to maintain with their swords. By these articles they demanded the liberty of hunting, fishing, cutting wood, etc.; the abolition of serfdom, tithes and soccage duties; the right of choosing their own preachers; and the free preaching of the Gospel.

The peasants of the Odenwald soon afterward rose in revolt, as did those on the Neckar and in Franconia, under the leadership of the audacious publican, George Metzler. These revolted peasants forced the Counts of Hohenlohe, Lowenstein, Wertheim and Gemmingen, the Superiors of the German Order in Mergentheim, and others to accept the twelve articles and to concede to their subjects the privileges demanded. Any one venturing to resist them was put to death, as in the case of Count Helfenstein von Weinsberg. They marched through the land burning and devastating. They destroyed the castles and monasteries, and took a bloody revenge on their foes and oppressors. Under the leadership of gallant knights, like Florian Geier and Götz von Berlichingen of the Iron Hand, the revolted peasants marched into Wurzburg, while other bands of insurgents ravaged the lands of Baden.

The peasant revolt soon spread over all of Suabia, Franconia, Alsace, Lorraine and the Palatinate. The spiritual and temporal princes of Germany became alarmed, and granted some of the exasperated peasants' demands. In Thuringia and the Hartz mountains the insurrection assumed more of a religious character. In Mühlhausen, Thomas Münzer had acquired great respect and the reputation of a prophet. He rejected Luther's moderate views, girded himself with the sword of Gideon, and desired to found a divine kingdom, with freedom and equality for all. The people were so excited by his preaching that they destroyed castles, convents and churches with the most barbarous fury.

In the beginning of the present revolt Luther attempted to restore peace. He represented to the German princes and nobles that they had been guilty of acts of

THE PEASANT WAR IN GERMANY.

violence, and he also exhorted the peasants to refrain from rebellion. But when the danger increased, when temporal and spiritual affairs were mingled together, he published a forcible tract "against the plundering and bloodthirsty peasants," calling upon the magistrates to attack them with the sword and to show them no mercy whatever.

In response to Luther's call, the German nobles and knights took the field against the rebel peasants. The Elector John of Saxony, the Landgrave Philip of Hesse and others marched into Thuringia, and gained an easy victory by means of their artillery over the half-starved peasants under Thomas Münzer, who was executed at Mülhausen after being subjected to the most horrible tortures.

The insurrection was suppressed in Suabia by Truchsess of Waldburg, the Captain of the Suabian League, who then marched with the Elector-Palatine and the warlike Archbishop of Trèves against the insurgent bands in Franconia, which were besieging the strong castle of Wurzburg, where the disorderly and disorganized populace were again subdued by superior military skill and better arms After a short resistance the rebels fled with precipitation, during which most of them were killed. Those who were taken prisoners were put to death, and the citizens of the Franconian towns who had sided with the insurgent peasantry were severely punished, many being beheaded by the ax of the executioner at Wurzburg.

The same scenes were enacted in Alsace, in the Palatinate and in Suabia, where the insurrection had continued longest. Order was finally restored by Truchsess of Waldburg and by the famous condottiere, George Frundsberg, who resorted to severe measures for the accomplishment of this result. The revolt was only quelled when one hundred thousand lives had been lost and many fertile fields reduced to desolation. In most places the peasants were again oppressed with all their former burdens, and in many localities the cry was loudly echoed: "If they have formerly been chastised with rods they shall now be scourged with scorpions."

The Reformation acquired additional strength in the midst of tumults and bloodshed, and Luther's energy increased with opposition. In 1524 he left the Augustinian cloisters, and in 1525 he married Catharine of Bora, who had formerly been a nun. He thereafter led a more domestic life, in the midst of a circle of princes, literary men and familiar friends. Neither poverty nor idleness affected his energy or zeal. He now devoted himself to framing a constitution for his Church and ordaining ministers for it. Having assailed the fundamental laws of the Romish Church, he was now obliged to substitute new laws in place of the old.

In a Diet of the German Empire assembled at Spires in 1526, presided over by the Archduke Ferdinand of Austria, the Emperor's brother, it was agreed to take no measures respecting religious affairs, but that each German state should regulate such matters at its own pleasure until a general council of the Church could be convened. The Elector John of Saxony, the Landgrave Philip of Hesse and other German Princes, thus encouraged, proceeded to make great changes in the Church in their respective dominions. The mass was abolished, and the church services were celebrated in the German language ; while new systems of church government were introduced, convents were suppressed, and the lands and revenues of the Church were restricted to ecclesiastical purposes. Preaching was made the main pursuit of the clergy.

The Landgrave Philip of Hesse called a synod, which convened in October, 1526, and gave Lutheranism the definitive organization which it has ever since preserved. The duty of visiting all the churches of Saxony devolved upon Melanchthon, who was as active as Luther. The combined efforts of these two active and able men gave the Reformation such a mighty impulse that the Catholic princes of Germany were seriously alarmed. The printed copies of the formula which Melanchthon had composed, and the two Catechisms which Luther had prepared, disseminated the Reformed doctrines among both old and young.

The Catholic German princes now combined to offer a more effectual resistance to the progress of the Reformation. In another imperial Diet convened at Spires in 1529, over which the Archduke Ferdinand of Austria also presided, the Catholic princes were in a majority. This Diet passed a decree "that the edicts of Worms should be observed in all the states in which they had been received; that the others should be free to continue in the new doctrines until the next general council. No one was allowed to preach in public against the mass, or to hinder its celebration."

This decree aroused the entire Lutheran party in the Diet, and the Lutheran princes and cities unanimously protested against this attack on the freedom of conscience and evangelical doctrine. This solemn *Protest*, duly signed by the Lutheran princes in the Diet, was sent to the Emperor Charles V.; and this circumstance gave the Lutherans the name of *Protestants*—a name ever since applied to all Christians outside of the Roman Catholic and Greek Churches.

These protesting princes at Spires were the Elector John of Saxony; the Landgrave Philip of Hesse; the Dukes of Grubenhagen, Celle and Mecklenburg; Prince Wolfgang of Anhalt; two Counts of Mansfeld; the Margrave George of Brandenburg; and the cities of Magdeburg, Strassburg, Nuremberg, Ulm, Constance, Reutlingen, Windsheim, Memmingen, Lindau, Kempten, Heilbronn, Issny, Weissenburg, Nördlingen and St. Gallen.

The Lutheran deputation met with a very cold reception from the Emperor Charles V., who refused to receive their protest. The protesting princes and cities would immediately have concluded a league for their mutual defense had not Luther and the other evangelical theologians forbidden it on the ground that "a magnanimous scrupulousness bade them reject the defense of the Word of God by worldly weapons."

Having driven the French out of Italy, and ended his second war with Francis I. of France by the Peace of Cambray in 1529, the Emperor Charles V. returned to Germany in 1530, and convened a Diet of the Empire at Augsburg the same year for the twofold purpose of suppressing the Reformation and adopting measures for the defeat of the Turks, whose invasions of Hungary and Austria had created serious alarm.

In this splendid imperial Diet at Augsburg, in 1530, the Lutheran princes who had protested in the Diet at Spires the preceding year presented the articles of their creed known as the *Confession of Augsburg*, which had been drawn up by the learned and peaceable Philip Melanchthon in both the German and Latin languages, and which had been approved by Luther. In this famous document the protesting princes claimed that they did not wish to found a new Church, but merely to reform and purify the old one.

After reading this document the Diet endeavored to effect a union of discordant elements in the Church by a conference of the men of moderate tempers selected by both parties. The Catholic theologians— Eck, Cochlaus, Wimpana, Faber and others —drew up a *Refutation* of the Confession of Augsburg, as it was called; and this was read to the assembled Diet. Melanchthon replied to the Catholic Refutation in a document of his own, called his *Apology*. The Emperor Charles V. afterward addressed the Diet, expressing his desire for the unity of the Church, and stating that otherwise he should be obliged to act in accordance with his oath as protector of the Holy Catholic Church.

The Diet of Augsburg was without results, as no reconciliation of opposing opinions could be effected, because Luther, who remained at Coburg during the sessions of the Diet, opposed the concessions required from the Reformed party. The protesting princes and the representatives of the principal imperial towns rejected the decisions of the Diet, and retired from Augsburg. The Emperor Charles V. declared that they must decide before the 15th of April upon the course that they would pursue. He called on the German princes to sustain him, declaring that he was bound by his oath and by his conscience.

The Emperor's edict condemned the Lutheran heresy, and commanded all who had accepted it to return to their allegiance to the Holy Catholic Church. All the Church property that had been seized was to be restored, and the suppressed convents were to be reopened. All who disobeyed the Emperor's mandate were subject to outlawry.

The Emperor's decree did not intimidate the Lutherans the least; and the Elector John of Saxony, the Landgrave Philip of Hesse and the other protesting princes met at Schmalkald, in the Thuringian forest, in March, 1531, and concluded a league, defensive and offensive, for six years. The Catholic German princes dreaded the effect of a civil and religious war, as the Empire was constantly menaced by Turkish invasions; and Charles V. was obliged to conclude the Peace of Nuremberg with the League of Schmalkald in 1532.

Fearing that a Protestant successor to Charles V. on the imperial throne of Germany would be chosen, the Catholic party in the Empire resolved to secure a Catholic successor at once; and the Catholic German princes accordingly elected the Emperor's brother, the Archduke Ferdinand of Austria, who was crowned at Aix la Chapelle in 1531.

The Protestant Church of Germany was even already divided. Ulrich Zwingli, a priest of Glarus, born in 1484, was the leader of the Reformation in Switzerland. He was a classically educated priest, of republican principles. As Canon of Zurich he exerted himself zealously against the doctrine of indulgences, as preached by Samson, a Franciscan monk. He labored against all kinds of abuses, and against the Swiss custom of engaging as mercenaries in foreign military service.

Ulrich Zwingli was a man of practical understanding, without Luther's depth of mind or disposition, and did not concern himself with the reform of doctrine or creed, but with the improvement of life and morals. He engaged in the Reformation with little ceremony, as he desired to restore primitive Christianity in its simplest form. As he was agreed with the Chief Council of Zurich, he set about a thorough reform of ecclesiastical doctrine and practice; banished all images, crosses, candles, altars and organs from the churches; and administered the Lord's Supper after the manner of the early Christian love-feasts, the communicants receiving the bread and wine while sitting.

Zwingli engaged in an irreconcilable controversy with Luther concerning the Lord's Supper. Zwingli recognized nothing but a token of remembrance and fellowship in that ceremony, and explained the words "this is my body" as meaning "this represents my body." Luther would not receive these words in such a sense, but maintained that Christ's blood and body were present in the bread and wine administered in the holy sacrament. The Landgrave Philip of Hesse sought to effect a reconciliation between the two sincere Reformers by means of a disputation between them at Marburg. Luther considered Zwingli's view a denial of Christ, and when Zwingli offered his brotherly hand with tears Luther drew back his own hand, thus refusing to receive the noble-hearted Zwingli as a brother. As Luther opposed any union with those German towns which had adopted Zwingli's doctrines, those towns presented their own confession of faith to the Diet of Augsburg.

Zwingli's appearance in Switzerland was followed by disturbances similar to those which followed Luther's appearance in Germany. The Church was reformed according to Zwingli's principles in Zurich, Basle, Berne, Schaffhausen, the Rhinethal and other cantons. The Catholics contended with the Zwinglians in Appenzell, the Grisons, St. Gall, Glarus and other cantons. In Zug, and in the four forest cantons—Uri, Schwyz, Unterwalden and Lucerne—the Catholic faith maintained its ascendency, because of the influence of the monks and clergy over the simple populace, and because the custom of engaging in foreign military service, which formed the chief means of support among these people, was opposed by the Reformers.

The five Catholic cantons concluded an alliance with Austria, and vigorously and sternly suppressed every innovation; while Berne and Zurich aided the Reformation in the frontier towns with bigoted zeal and violence. In this agitated condition of Switzerland a civil and religious war was inevitable, especially as Zwingli meditated such a revolution as would give the political supremacy in the Republic to the two most powerful cantons, Berne and Zurich.

Mutual revilings of the clergy, which proceeded with perfect impunity from punishment, increased the public irritation and provoked hostilities. Berne and Zurich blockaded the public roads, thus preventing the transportation of goods and the necessaries of life—a proceeding which exasperated the Catholic cantons. The Catholics made secret preparations and attacked the people of Zurich unawares. The Zurichers, surprised and irresolute, and forsaken by the Bernese, sent a force of two thousand men against double that number of Catholics, but were totally defeated in the bloody battle of Kappel, in 1531, in which Zwingli was slain.

The brave Zwingli had accompanied his followers as field preacher, and fell beside the banner of the city; and along with him perished the staunchest friends of the Reformation in Switzerland. His dead body was subjected to the insults of his indignant foes, after which it was burned and the ashes scattered to the winds. The Catholic triumph restored the Romish Church in many places in Switzerland that had seemed to favor the Reformation, thus producing the religious divisions that have prevailed in the Swiss Republic ever since.

SECTION VII.—CHARLES V., FRANCIS I. AND THE TURKS.

IN THE meantime, during the progress of the Reformation in Germany, the Emperor Charles V. was engaged in his wars with King Francis I. of France—the first of that long series of wars between Austria and France that lasted with but brief intervals of peace for almost two centuries (A. D. 1520-1714).

The war began on the side of Navarre, which little kingdom was invaded by a French army under Andrew de Foix, a relative of the deposed King of Navarre, who quickly and easily effected the conquest of the kingdom, as almost all of its fortresses had been destroyed. He then sought to join the insurgents in Spain, who had secured control of the imbecile Queen Joanna, and who in her name endeavored to expel the regent appointed by Charles V.

The Castilian Junta demanded that Charles V. should reside in Spain, not in Germany or in the Netherlands; that he should appoint no foreigner to any civil or ecclesiastical office in Spain; and that he should convene the Cortes once in three years. The independence of the Cortes was guarded by a rule that none of its members should receive any place or pension from the king. Judges were to be maintained by regular salaries, and were forbidden to receive any portion of the fines or forfeitures of persons whom they condemned; while bishops were to reside in their dioceses at least half the year; and indulgences were to be sold in Spain only with the consent of the Cortes, and the proceeds therefrom were to be applied entirely to wars against the Moslems.

Charles V. rejected this bill of rights, whereupon the Castilian Junta appealed to arms; but the insurgent army of twenty

CHARLES V. OF SPAIN.

thousand men was defeated, and its leader was executed. The king's army prevented a junction of the rebels with the French force under Andrew de Foix; but when this French commander laid siege to a Castilian town even the Castilian insurgents turned against him and drove him into Navarre, where he was defeated, mortally wounded and taken prisoner, dying several days later of his wounds; and the Spaniards rapidly recovered Navarre.

By successively allying himself with Charles V. and Francis I., Pope Leo X. obtained the duchy of Urbino and the lordships of Modena, Reggio, Perugia and Fermo. In 1521 he united with the King of France to expel the Spaniards from Southern Italy, which was to be divided between the Pope and the French king's second son. As Francis I. delayed the ratification of this treaty, Pope Leo X. made a counter alliance with the Emperor Charles V. to drive the French from Northern Italy. The Pope allowed the Emperor to seize the territories of Venice in return for promising to extirpate the Lutheran heresy in Germany—an agreement which was signed in the presence of the German Diet on the same day with the Edict of Worms issued by the Emperor against Luther and his supporters.

Three months afterward a conference was held at Calais between the envoys of the Pope, the Emperor and the Kings of France and England. Henry VIII. had offered his mediation between Francis I. and Charles V.; and his great Prime Minister, Cardinal Wolsey, was courted and flattered by the two rival sovereigns, each of whom desired to gain the English king's favor. The Emperor pledged his vast influence to secure the Papacy to Wolsey at the death of Leo X., having already granted the English Prime Minister an annual pension of ten thousand ducats. The Conference of Calais failed to accomplish anything, as the conflicting claims of the rival monarchs could not be reconciled. Francis I. demanded the two kingdoms of Naples and Navarre; while Charles V. insisted that the King of France should relinquish Milan and Genoa, restore Burgundy, and release the Emperor from homage for the Netherlands.

Immediately afterward the Emperor of Germany and the King of England concluded a treaty by which each agreed to invade France with an army of forty thousand men, while the Pope excommunicated the King of France and absolved his subjects from their allegiance. Another treaty was afterward concluded between the Emperor Charles V., King Henry VIII. and Pope Leo X., by which all three agreed to take rigorous proceedings against heretics in their respective dominions; and Leo X. conferred the title of *Defender of the Faith* upon Henry VIII., who had just written a Latin work against Luther and the Reformation.

The Albrets recovered all that part of Navarre north of the Pyrenees, and ever afterward retained possession of it. In the Netherlands, the French took the town and fortress of Hesdin, but lost Tournay. In Italy, the principal seat of the war, the able French general Lautrec, a cruel and rapacious tyrant, as viceroy of Milan, enriched himself at the expense of the inhabitants; but the French king soon lost Milan through the dissensions of his court.

One of the two hostile parties at the French court was led by Louisa of Savoy, the mother of King Francis I.; the other by the Countess of Chateaubriand, the sister of the great general, Lautrec. The twenty thousand Swiss troops in Lautrec's service, discontented for want of pay, either marched home or deserted to the Emperor Charles V. Lautrec was besieged in Milan, and when the Spanish infantry made a night attack upon the Roman gate of the city that gate was opened by the Emperor's partisans in Milan, whereupon Lautrec and his brother fled.

Francis I. severely reproached his general for the loss of Milan. Lautrec threw the entire blame on Semblançai, the French Minister of Finance, for having failed to send him money for the payment of his Swiss troops, thus causing them to desert his standard. Semblançai declared that he had paid the money to the king's mother, and offered to produce her receipt therefor; but the wicked Louisa, who had applied the money to her private use, had bribed a clerk in the treasury to steal the receipt; and the venerable Semblançai, respected for his years and his integrity, was sentenced to be executed, being thus sacrificed to screen the queen-mother's crime. The Chancelor Duprat, who was envious of Semblançai's influence over the king, who always called the aged minister "My father," was concerned in this crime. Duprat was then employed to raise money, which he effected by the most illegal and scandalous methods, alienating the royal domains, selling public offices to the highest bidder, and doubling the already oppressive taxes.

The fortress of Milan was still held by the French, but almost all the Lombard cities opened their gates to the Emperor's troops. The imperial troops also took Parma and Piacenza, and occupied them for Pope Leo X. according to treaty. Leo X. is said to have died of joy in consequence of these successes, but other accounts say that he was poisoned. He was forty-five years of age at his death, and had reigned eight years (A. D. 1513-1521). The victorious allies were thrown into confusion by this event. The papal army was disbanded for want of funds; and Urbino, Perugia and other places gladly received back their native rulers.

The next Pope, Adrian VI., who had been regent of Spain, was chosen to the Chair of St. Peter in 1522, after a long and violent contest in the conclave of cardinals. His scholastic education made him a bitter antagonist of Luther, but he was an honest man and deplored the corruptions of the Church. He began his reign with stern efforts at reform, entering Rome bare-footed, in scorn of the luxury of his predecessors, and turning with horror from the sculptures which Leo X. had collected in the Vatican, exclaiming: "These are pagan idols!" He kept but one old servant for his household. The elegant courtiers of Leo X. looked on with disgust, which was increased when the new Pope sought to replenish his exhausted finances by abolishing many useless and expensive offices; but the common people of Rome regarded his self-denying humility with enthusiastic reverence.

After being again defeated by the Emperor's troops, the French retired from Italy, surrendering all but the three citadels of Milan, Novara and Cremona. The Germans also took Genoa, of which Antoniotto Adorno became Doge.

The departure of the regent Adrian from Spain upon his election to the Papacy made it necessary for Charles V. to return to that discontented kingdom. He visited England on his way from Germany to Spain, and renewed his agreement with Cardinal Wolsey by fresh promises, at the same time flattering the English nation by making the Earl of Surrey his admiral and inducing Henry VIII. to declare war against the King of France.

Francis I. secured his eastern frontier by a treaty with Margaret, the Emperor's regent in the Netherlands, by which he promised not to invade or attack her territory of Franche-Comté for three years. The frequent renewal of this treaty left Burgundy and Franche-Comté in the enjoyment of peace, industry and prosperity for more than a century, while the Austro-French wars were raging around them. The three duchies of Savoy, Lorraine and Bar were likewise neutral territories; and these, along with Franche-Comté, thoroughly covered the eastern side of France.

For the next eight years (A. D. 1521-1529) Charles V. resided in his Kingdom of Spain, being absent all that time from his Empire of Germany. He won the hearts of his Spanish subjects by his lenity to those who had rebelled during his absence, by adopting the Spanish dress, language and manners, and by excluding all foreigners from civil or ecclesiastical offices. But he strengthened his own power at the expense of the popular liberties, by making the three estates of the Spanish Cortes meet in separate places, thus dividing their strength; by winning individual representatives of the commons to his interest, and by prohibiting all debate except in the presence of a presiding officer appointed by himself.

Charles's policy toward his Moorish subjects was as unjust as his grandfather Ferdinand's treatment of the Jews. The refined and industrious Moors contributed vastly to the prosperity of Spain, while being allowed toleration for their own religion, but living in obedience to Spanish laws. In 1525 Charles suddenly resolved to force them to accept Christianity, causing their copies of the Koran to be seized and their mosques to be closed, and exiling from Spain all who were not baptized before a specified date, but preventing them from reaching Africa by closing all the Spanish ports against them except Corunna in the extreme North-west of the kingdom.

Charles afterward issued a harsher edict, confiscating the goods of all Moors who refused to embrace Christianity, and selling them into slavery. This atrocious policy caused a revolt among the Moors, thousands of whom were slain, while a hundred thousand succeeded in escaping to Africa. Those remaining in Spain conformed with reluctance to the Spanish rites, customs and language, but were deprived of all privileges and reduced to the condition of beasts of burden.

Pope Adrian VI. formed a powerful coalition against Francis I., whom he held responsible for the failure of Christendom to unite in a crusade against the Ottoman Turks, who had resumed their career of conquest. In 1523 the King of France sent another army into Italy to recover Milan; but his undertaking failed, in a great measure through the conduct of his wicked mother, Louisa of Savoy, whose injustice toward the Constable de Bourbon made that powerful French nobleman the most bitter enemy of the French court, and caused him to enter the service of the Emperor Charles V. against his own king and country.

The Constable de Bourbon possessed by inheritance and marriage four duchies, four counties, two viscounties, and many smaller lordships in the center of France; and he might even have hoped to inherit the French crown itself in case his kinsman, King Francis I., died without sons. His great military services had been rewarded with the highest dignities and revenues, but his cold and haughty temper did not suit the king's jovial disposition, and the court favorites delighted to annoy so powerful a rival.

On the death of the Constable's wife Susanna, the heiress of the elder branch of the House of Bourbon, the king's mother desired to marry him; but the Constable, who utterly detested Louisa's vices, expressed his dislike for her in such strong language that the king was provoked to strike him. Louisa's love for the Constable was thenceforth turned to the most inveterate hatred, and she resolved to ruin him. She put in a claim to all the Bourbon possessions in right of her mother, who represented another branch of the House of Bourbon, and obtained a decision from the Parliament of Paris in her favor, also securing to herself the private revenues of his mother-in-law, Anne.

Thus deprived of everything and reduced to the verge of ruin, the proud heart of the Constable de Bourbon sought bitter revenge; and in a moment of desperation he opened negotiations with the Emperor Charles V. and with Henry VIII. of England to betray his country into their hands. An arrangement was effected for the partition of France between Charles V., King Henry VIII. and the Constable. The hereditary dominions of the Bourbons, with Lyonnois, Dauphiny and Provence, were to be erected into an independent sovereignty for the Constable himself.

The plot seemed about to succeed. The English army landed at Calais, and was joined by an imperial force from the Netherlands, after which the united forces marched to within thirty-three miles from Paris. But the invasions of France on the sides of Germany and Spain failed, and the French king's discovery of the conspiracy prevented the Constable de Bourbon's vassals and retainers from executing their part in the transaction. The Constable fled into Germany, and was received with open arms by the Emperor Charles V., who entrusted him with the command of his armies.

In this emergency Pope Adrian VI. died, A. D. 1523; whereupon the Cardinal Giulio de Medici was chosen by the conclave of cardinals, and assumed the title of Clement VII. Thus Cardinal Wolsey was a second time disappointed, and was obliged to content himself with the dignity of papal legate, or nuncio, in England, to which extraordinary powers were attached.

In the spring of 1524 the Constable de Bourbon entered Italy as the Emperor's Lieutenant-General. The allies forced the incompetent Bonnivet, the commander of the French forces, to retreat into France. In a battle near Romagnano, during this retreat, the Chevalier Bayard, *le chevalier sans peur et sans reproche*, "the knight without fear and without reproach," was mortally wounded. Unwilling that the retreating army should be delayed by his misfortune, he ordered himself to be placed against a tree with his face toward the enemy. In this condition he was found by the Constable de Bourbon, who lamented that the vicissitudes of war had reduced so noble a knight to such a fate; but the dying chevalier replied: "I am not an object of pity, Sir Duke. I die happy in having performed my duty to my king and country. It is you who deserve pity, who are bearing arms against your native land, forgetting that the death of every traitor is violent, and his memory detested."

This favorite hero of the age was the last model of chivalry that appeared in Europe. Though he held only the rank of captain, he really possessed more influence than any general, from the universal respect and admiration inspired by his high character. He had been taken prisoner by the English in the Battle of the Spurs in 1513. He was the ancestor of the Bayard family which has represented the State of Delaware in the United States Senate at different times for a century.

The German imperial army under the Constable de Bourbon and the Marquis Pescara now invaded France by the Cornice Road, captured Aix, Toulon and Frejus, and besieged Marseilles; but on the approach of Francis I. with a powerful army the Constable raised the siege and beat a precipitate retreat into Italy, pursued by the King of France with a well equipped army of thirty thousand men.

With characteristic imprudence, Francis I. laid siege to the strongly fortified town of Pavia, which was defended by a numerous garrison, under the command of Antonio de Leyva, an able general. The imperial generals, who were the viceroy Lannoy and the Constable de Bourbon, made the greatest efforts to collect a numerous army for the relief of the garrison of Pavia. The inactivity and indiscretion of the French king, who weakened his army by sending detachments against Naples and Savona, operated in favor of the imperialists.

Bourbon resolved to attack the French in their intrenchments; and on the night of February 23, 1523, Bourbon's army stormed the French camp, while at the same time the garrison of Pavia made a furious sally, thus placing the French between two fires. After a most sanguinary conflict, the French army was almost totally destroyed. Ten thousand brave warriors were either killed in the encounter, or drowned in the waters of the Ticino. The chivalrous Francis himself, after a gallant defense, was unhorsed and taken prisoner. He was recognized by an attendant of the Constable de Bourbon, who advised him to surrender. The chivalrous king scornfully refused to become the captive of his traitorous vassal, but called for Lannoy and surrendered his sword to that commander.

This was the greatest disaster that the French had suffered since the battle of Poitiers, as their king was a captive, and the flower of their nobility and soldiery was left dead on the sanguinary field. Bonnivet was among the slain, and when the Constable de Bourbon saw his dead body he exclaimed: "Unfortunate man, you have ruined France, yourself and me!" The

THE BATTLE OF PAVIA.

French army was permitted to retreat into France, and within a fortnight the last French soldier had recrossed the Alps. The captive Francis I. conveyed the sad intelligence of the great catastrophe to his mother in a single line: "Madame, all is lost but honor."

The battle of Pavia produced joy in Spain, terror in France, jealousy in England, and dissatisfaction in Italy. When the news reached Madrid, Charles forbade all public rejoicings, and sought to dissemble his natural exultation over the event. France was stricken with terror, and Paris was guarded as if the triumphant foe was already at its gates. The captive king's mother, who assumed the regency in this perilous crisis, had by her intrigues alienated those who should have been her best supporters.

Of the leading French princes of the blood royal, the Constable de Bourbon was declared a traitor; the Duke d' Alençon, the king's brother-in-law, had disgraced himself by cowardice in the battle of Pavia, and had since died of vexation and chagrin; and the Duke of Vendôme, an enemy to the queen-mother, was suspected of a secret understanding with the traitor Constable, but he silenced all suspicions by generously forgetting his grievances and joining the queen-mother at Lyons.

The Count of Guise, the founder of a family destined to act an important part in the future history of France, rendered good service by suppressing a peasant revolt which had spread from Germany into the French provinces of Lorraine, Champagne and Burgundy. The Parliament of Paris, which had assembled at once upon the sad tidings of the king's captivity, presented a long list of grievances, and demanded redress as a condition of granting supplies or adopting measures for the public defense. One of their demands was for the extermination of the Lutheran heretics, who were held responsible for all the calamities that had befallen France; and two of these pious and unoffending persons were soon burned to death at Paris.

Four months after the battle of Pavia the captive Francis I. was conveyed into Spain and incarcerated in the tower of the Alcazar at Madrid. He was attacked by a dangerous illness, brought on by mortification and anxiety; and Charles V., who had not hitherto deigned to visit his former "good father," "friend" and "brother," now feared that his royal prisoner would die without signing the severe conditions of peace which he desired to exact from him. He visited the captive monarch in prison, and a few words from the triumphant Emperor so raised the spirits of his illustrious prisoner that his health commenced improving.

The recently widowed Duchess of Alençon, the favorite sister of Francis I., undertook an embassy to Spain, with full authority to negotiate a treaty of peace between the two sovereigns; but she did not succeed in obtaining easy terms for her royal brother. Charles V. insisted upon a partition of France, by which he was to have Burgundy, Picardy and all the other territories of Charles the Bold of Burgundy; while Provence and all the Bourbon possessions were to be formed into a new kingdom for the Constable de Bourbon; and Normandy, Guienne and Gascony were to be bestowed on Henry VIII. of England. Thus the dominions of Francis I. would have been reduced to the territorial extent of the possessions of the first Capets.

In January, 1526, Francis I., worn out with his incarceration in the gloomy tower of the Alcazar at Madrid, swore to the Peace of Madrid "on the word and honor of a king." By this treaty the King of France agreed to cede the duchy of Burgundy and the counties of Flanders and Artois to the Emperor Charles V., renounced all claim to Naples and Milan, and restored to the Constable de Bourbon all his former possessions. He had previously told his ambassadors that he had acted under compulsion, and that he had no intention of executing the conditions which he was about to sign. Nevertheless, the treaty was confirmed by his betrothal with the Emperor's sister Eleanora, the widowed Queen of Portugal. Two of the French king's sons were then delivered to Charles V. as hostages for the fulfillment of the treaty, and Francis I. bound himself to return to captivity if he did not relinquish Burgundy within four months.

Francis I. was then released and escorted to the French frontier, March 18, 1526. His joy at his release was unbounded. When he was once upon his own soil he mounted a Turkish horse; and, putting him at full speed and waving his hand over his head, he exclaimed aloud several times: "I am yet a king!"

No sooner had the King of France been again free and in his own dominions than he refused to ratify the treaty which had been extorted from him while a prisoner, on the plea that he must first consult the Estates of France and Burgundy on a matter of such importance. When the Burgundian Estates convened at Cognac they insisted, according to prearrangement, that the King of France could not annul his coronation-oath by any subsequent agreement. The Burgundian envoys likewise asserted that they would forcibly resist any effort to alienate the duchy of Burgundy from the crown of France.

Francis I. then offered the Spanish ambassadors, who were present, two million crowns as a compensation for Burgundy, and promised to fulfill every other condition of the treaty. When Charles V. was informed of this evasion he remarked that it was easy for the King of France at least to redeem his personal honor by returning into captivity in Spain; but the honor of Francis I. was not of the same kind as that of Regulus, or that of his own ancestor, King John the Good; and Pope Clement VII. soon absolved him from his engagements with the Emperor.

In the meantime the Italians had been thrown into consternation by the decisive victory of their powerful ally at Pavia, as all Italy appeared to be at the Emperor's mercy; and a *Holy League* was formed against Charles V. by Pope Clement VII., the Duke of Milan, the Venetian Republic and the King of France. Francisco Sforza had been restored to the Duchy of Milan only as a vassal; and his Chancellor, Morone, now contrived a plot to destroy the unity and freedom of Italy at one blow.

Pescara, who was an Italian by birth, but a Spaniard by descent, was known to be disaffected toward the Emperor. He ascertained through a trusty messenger that all the Italian states were ready to unite in making him King of Naples if he would disband the imperial army which he commanded, and thus aid in delivering Italy from the German and Spanish yoke. When Pescara discovered that this conspiracy was already known in Madrid he determined upon a counter-plot to meet the advances of the Milanese. He therefore invited Morone to a personal interview, and concealed the Spanish general, Antonio de Leyva, behind the tapestry. When the unsuspecting Chancellor had fully disclosed his master's plans he was seized, thus finding himself Pescara's victim rather than his partner.

Charles V. then deprived Francisco Sforza of the Duchy of Milan and bestowed it upon the Constable de Bourbon. Pescara died several weeks afterward. Morone remained a prisoner in Milan until the Constable de Bourbon, wanting money, first sentenced him to death, and then released him upon the payment of a ransom of twenty thousand ducats. The Milanese people, who had endured new miseries at every change of masters, hailed the Constable de Bourbon's arrival in the hope of a firm and settled government. The Constable promised to remove his army, which had been quartered upon the citizens of Milan, upon the payment of three hundred thousand crowns; but, when that sum was raised, the imperial troops still refused to evacuate the city, and some of the Milanese committed suicide in utter despair.

Pope Clement VII. soon endured greater misfortunes than the Milanese. Cardinal Colonna, a man of revengeful and lawless disposition, an old enemy of the Pope, but to whom he had been formally reconciled, suddenly raised an army of his own vassals and retainers, and marched against Rome. The Pope was besieged in the Castle of St. Angelo in September, 1526, and was forced to surrender in three days for want of provisions. Colonna's freebooters plundered the Vatican and St. Peter's Church. The Kings of France and England hastened to send money and troops to His Holiness; and Clement VII. was soon enabled to exact a terrible vengeance from the Colonnas, whose palaces in Rome were leveled with the ground, while their country estates were ravaged by the papal troops.

In May, 1527, Rome suffered a more serious calamity. Frundsberg, the celebrated Lutheran general, marched from Germany into Italy at the head of eleven thousand brigands, who had enlisted in his service in the hope of plunder rather than of pay. Frundsberg's force formed a junction with the Constable de Bourbon's unpaid and hungry troops at Milan, and this united German and Spanish army marched against Rome. On their way they were met by a papal embassy proposing a truce; but the soldiery, who were resolved upon their coveted prize, openly mutinied, and leveled their spears at their general's breast while he was seeking to pacify them. Frundsberg was so stung by their ingratitude that he fell into violent convulsions, from which he never recovered; and his soldiers, struck with remorse too late, subsided into order, only reiterating their cry of "Rome! Rome!"

On the evening of May 5, 1527, the German and Spanish army arrived before the walls of Rome, and the next day the Eternal City was taken by storm and plundered by the soldiers of the leading Catholic prince of Christendom. The assault began in the morning, and the Constable de Bourbon was shot in the side while placing a ladder with his own hands. When he found that he must die he covered his face with his cloak, so that he might not be recognized, and breathed his last while his victorious troops were entering the papal capital. The Spanish and German troops selected the Prince of Orange for their general.

For two weeks the German and Spanish soldiery filled the religious capital of Christendom with the horrid scenes of massacre, pillage and desecration, and seized the treasures which had been the accumulation of so many centuries. The pillage of Rome by the Germans and Spaniards on this occasion equaled that of the Goths and the Vandals, more than a thousand years before. Convents, churches and dwelling-houses were plundered; and nearly eight thousand Romans were massacred on the day of the capture of the city. Pope Clement VII. was besieged in his Castle of St. Angelo, and soon obliged to surrender himself a prisoner.

The Florentines took advantage of the presence of the German imperial army in Italy to expel the Medici and to place themselves under the protection of France, thus seeking to restore the republic which Savonarola had set up. Venice recovered Ravenna and Cervia, and the Dukes of Urbino and Ferrara took revenge for their former disasters by seizing several cities in the States of the Church.

Charles V. affected great sorrow and displeasure at the insults suffered by the Head of the Church, but was inwardly pleased at the Pope's humiliation; and, instead of ordering the release of the Holy Father, the hypocritical Emperor commanded prayers for the liberation of the Pontiff to be offered in all the churches in his dominions, and attired himself and his court in mourning. Clement VII. was liberated six months after the capture of Rome, upon the payment of a ransom of several hundred thousand crowns of gold. He promised to convene a general council to reform the Church and suppress heresy, and also engaged to cease meddling in the affairs of Milan and Naples.

A French army under Lautrec had already marched into Italy; and a French fleet commanded by Andrea Doria, the great Genoese admiral, besieged Genoa, expelled the Doge Adorno, and appointed a governor in the name of the King of France. Lautrec took Pavia by storm and sacked the town, in revenge for its resistance to Francis I. and his consequent disaster there in 1525.

As Pope Clement VII. was now liberated, Lautrec marched into Southern Italy, and laid siege to Naples in conjunction with a Genoese and Venetian fleet. Had not the French king withheld the necessary supplies for his army, and offended the Dorias of Genoa by unjust treatment, Naples would have been taken. Andrea Doria deserted Francis I. and entered the service of Charles V., and sailed to Naples and forced the French to raise the siege. Lautrec had already died of a pestilence which had carried off most of his army.

This fourth invasion of Italy by the armies of Francis I. was a failure. The Prince of Orange was made viceroy of Naples for Charles V. The French were driven from Genoa, and that republic was reorganized under the Emperor's protection. The old struggle of Guelfs and Ghibellines was ended by a more just and efficient constitution, by which public affairs were intrusted to a Council of Four Hundred; and Genoa was entirely free from revolutions thereafter until the French conquest of that republic in 1797.

Both the rival monarchs were by this time weary of the war. The King of France, disheartened by his losses and the enormous expenses of the contest, was willing to relinquish his claims to Milan and Naples, which he perceived that he was unable to maintain; while the Emperor, alarmed at the rapid progress of the Reformation in Germany, desired peace with his rival in order to devote his entire attention to that danger.

The second war between Charles V. and Francis I. was ended by the Peace of Cambray, in July, 1529—called the *Ladies' Peace*, because it was negotiated by the Emperor's aunt and the French king's mother. Francis I. retained the duchy of Burgundy, but relinquished all his pretensions to Italy, along with the feudal sovereignty of the counties of Artois and Flanders. Charles V. received an indemnity of two million crowns in lieu of his claims to Burgundy, and Francis I. was to aid him with a fleet and a subsidy of two hundred thousand crowns when called upon. The King of France also agreed to marry Eleanora, the queen-dowager of Portugal, the Emperor's sister. The sons of Francis I., who had been held as hostages at Madrid, were released, and accompanied the Emperor's sister from Spain. In July, 1530, she became the wife of the French king. Thus ended the wars which the French had waged in Italy during the reigns of three of their kings, and which embraced a period of thirty-six years (A. D. 1494–1529).

In the meantime, while the Emperor Charles V. was engaged in devising means to resist the progress of the Reformation in Germany, and in his wars with Francis I. of France, his attention was also occupied in opposing the alarming progress of the Turks under their mighty Sultan, Solyman the Magnificent, whose rapid conquests spread dismay throughout Christendom.

SELIM I., who had usurped the Turkish throne in 1512 by dethroning his father, whom he put to death along with his two brothers and his five nephews, waged frequent wars with the modern Persian kingdom under the Suffeean dynasty, subdued Kurdistan and Mesopotamia, conquered Syria and Egypt in 1517 and annexed them to the Ottoman Empire, and was the first of the Ottoman Sultans to assume the sacred title of Khalif, which has ever since been borne by his successors.

On the death of Selim I. in 1520, after a short but active and vigorous reign of eight years, his illustrious son, SOLYMAN THE MAGNIFICENT, the greatest of all the Turkish Sultans, ascended the Ottoman throne. In the summer of 1521 Solyman invaded Hungary, captured the strong fortresses of Sabatz, Semlin and Belgrade, and conquered and annexed the southern part of the Hungarian kingdom, along with the Banat.

In 1522 Solyman besieged the Knights of St. John in their stronghold, the isle of Rhodes, with an army of one hundred and ten thousand men and a fleet of three hundred ships. The Knights of St. John, under their renowned Grand Master, L'Ile Adam, were compelled to surrender to overwhelming numbers, December 21, 1522, after a long and valiant resistance. The Knights of St. John were then forced to retire from Rhodes, which they had held since the Crusades; and the Emperor Charles V. presented to them the isle of Malta, which they held until 1798.

In 1526 Europe was again thrown into the utmost consternation by the successes of Sultan Solyman the Magnificent. During the four years since his conquest of Rhodes, in 1522, he had completed the conquest of Egypt and shaken the very foundations of the Persian kingdom of the Suffeeans; after which he again turned toward Europe, declaring himself Emperor of the West as well as of the East, and designing to make Constantinople once more the capital of the civilized world.

Hungary was Solyman's first point of attack, and that kingdom had been reduced to the most deplorable weakness and poverty by the civil wars of its magnates. While the royal Council of Tolna was still wrangling about means to resist the Turkish invasion, the approach of the Turks was announced by the smoke of a burning town. Sultan Solyman the Magnificent, having crossed the Drave with three hundred thousand men, was in full march northward.

King Louis II. of Hungary, with only twenty thousand men, made a stand against the immense hosts of the Ottoman Sultan in the marshy plain of Mohacz, in August, 1526. His army consisted mainly of heavily armed cavalry; while the Grand Turk had availed himself of the latest improvements in firearms, and had a thoroughly disciplined infantry and three hundred well-mounted cannon in his camp. The dashing valor of the Hungarians was useless, as the flower of their nobility soon lay dead on the sanguinary field; and their young king perished in the marsh while seeking to make his escape, being then only nineteen years of age.

The triumphant Sultan marched toward Buda, burning towns and villages in his advance. After occupying the Hungarian capital for a fortnight he retired, taking with him the valuable library founded by Matthias Corvinus, and several works of art which were used to adorn Constantinople.

The death of King Louis II. at Mohacz left the crowns of Hungary and Bohemia vacant, and these were claimed by the Archduke Ferdinand of Austria, the brother of the Emperor Charles V., because he had married a sister of the unfortunate Louis II. Ferdinand was crowned at Prague as King of Bohemia, in February, 1527; but he found a formidable competitor for the Hungarian crown in John Zapolya, the greatest of the Hungarian magnates and the lord of seventy-two castles, and who was supported by the money and influence of Francis I. of France and Pope Clement VII. Zapolya received the crown of St. Stephen in November, 1526; but a party among the magnates pronounced in favor of Ferdinand, who marched with a large army from Bohemia into Hungary, won the battle of Tokay, and along with his wife was in turn crowned with the diadem of St. Stephen.

John Zapolya then entered into an alliance with Sultan Solyman the Magnificent, who had subdued most of Bosnia, Croatia, Dalmatia and Slavonia, and again advanced to the plain of Mohacz in 1529, where Zapolya did homage to the Sultan for the Hungarian crown. After that degrading ceremony Zapolya accompanied the Grand Turk to Buda and aided in the massacre of its garrison.

The entire Turkish army, with the coöperation of a Turkish fleet in the Danube, then laid siege to Vienna, A. D. 1529. Both Catholics and Lutherans in Germany united in this perilous emergency, and the defense of Vienna was as resolute as the attack on the city was formidable. The very number of the Turks rendered their maintenance in a hostile country extremely difficult. They raised the siege of Vienna by the middle of October, 1529, and began their retreat from the Austrian capital, thus leaving John Zapolya alone to prosecute his civil war with Ferdinand of Austria.

It was the progress of the Turks that

compelled the Emperor Charles V. to conclude the Peace of Nuremberg with the League of Schmalkald in 1532. Upon the conclusion of this religious peace with his Protestant German subjects, the Emperor was soon followed near Vienna by an army of eighty thousand men. Sultan Solyman the Magnificent invaded Hungary a third time, in 1532, with an army of three hundred and fifty thousand men, and with a dazzling display of Oriental magnificence. The garrisons of many of the Hungarian fortresses sent him their keys, and his march resembled a peaceful progress through his own dominions rather than a hostile invasion of an enemy's territory.

But when the Turkish Sultan attacked the little fortress of Güns he encountered so gallant a resistance that his pride was severely wounded. His entire army was detained for more than three weeks by a garrison of only seven hundred men, who repulsed his eleven assaults upon the fortress, and who finally only allowed ten Janizaries to remain in the place an hour to erect the Ottoman standard.

The Sultan was further discouraged by the operations of the Genoese admiral, Andrea Doria, in the Morea, the ancient Peloponnesus, and by the defeat of the Ottoman cavalry at the Sömmering Pass; and he therefore retreated hastily with the bulk of his mighty host, leaving only a force of sixty thousand men at Essek to support John Zapolya's interests. Peace was concluded between the Germano-Roman and Ottoman Turkish Empires the next year, A. D. 1533.

After his eight years' residence in Spain, the Emperor Charles V. visited Italy in 1529 to restore the order which had been interrupted so long by his wars with Francis I. of France. He completely subverted the freedom of Florence, which Pope Clement VII. had already sold to him in the Treaty of Barcelona. When the citizens of Florence refused to recall the Medici he ordered the Prince of Orange to lay siege to the city. Florence was fortified by the great artist, Michael Angelo, and the Florentine army outside the walls offered a valiant resistance to the Emperor's troops; but as the best Florentine general was slain in battle, and as another had proven a traitor, the city was forced to surrender and to receive an imperial garrison, to pay an enormous ransom, and to accept the hereditary rule of the Medici as dukes. The Prince of Orange was slain in the same battle; and, by his sister's marriage his titles and dominions came into the possession of the House of Nassau.

The Emperor Charles V. proceeded to Bologna, where he was invested by Pope Clement VII. with the iron crown of Lombardy and with the imperial diadem. The German Electors were not invited to take their hereditary parts in the ceremony. The Duke of Savoy carried the imperial crown, the Marquis of Montferrat the scepter, and the Duke of Urbino the sword. Charles V. was the last Emperor crowned in Italy.

Soon afterward Pope Clement VII., offended at the Emperor Charles V., courted the alliance of the King of France; and at Marseilles he negotiated the marriage of his niece, Catharine de Medici, with Henry, Duke of Orleans, the second son of Francis I. By the subsequent death of his elder brother, Henry became the heir to the French crown; and Catharine exerted a powerful and evil influence on the destinies of France during the reigns of her three sons.

Pope Clement VII. died in September, 1534. His pontificate had been signalized by losses and disasters which none of his predecessors had experienced. He had been taken prisoner, and Rome had been plundered and desecrated, once by one of the cardinals of the Church, and once by the Emperor's troops. Large parts of Germany and Switzerland had finally severed their connection with the Church of Rome, as had also England, Denmark and Sweden. His successor in the Papacy was Alexander Farnese, who, upon his election by the conclave of cardinals, assumed the title of Paul III.

At this time the coasts of the Mediterranean were infested by Mohammedan pirates, particularly by the "flying squadrons" of Hayraddin Barbarossa, who had become King of Algiers upon the death of his brother Horuc. Sultan Solyman the Magnificent appointed this daring freebooter his admiral. Such was the terror spread by his piracies that no man slept securely along the coasts of Spain, France and Italy; and multitudes of Christian captives on the African coast were reduced to the most degrading servitude, while waiting to be ransomed. Hayraddin Barbarossa had recently taken possession of the Kingdom of Tunis, after expelling its rightful sovereign, Muley Hassan; and the terror of his name was vastly heightened by this increase of his power.

In 1535 the Emperor Charles V. undertook a crusade against these Moslem pirates, and this was one of the most famous and successful of his enterprises. He mustered thirty thousand men at Cagliari, in the island of Sardinia, took command of the expedition in person, sailed to the African coast, and effected a landing near the site of the ancient Utica. He took by storm the fortress of Goletta, which protects Tunis; after which he routed Hayraddin Barbarossa in a pitched battle, and took Tunis itself with the aid of the Christian captives. He restored Muley Hassan to his throne on condition that he should suppress piracy, protect his Christian subjects in the exercise of their religion, and pay to the Emperor an annual tribute of twelve thousand ducats. The liberated Christian captives, whom Charles V. had caused to be clothed and equipped at his own expense, preceded him to Europe, and spread his fame with ardent gratitude through their respective countries. The number of liberated Christian captives was twenty-two thousand.

When Charles V. returned to Europe from his African expedition he became involved in his third war with Francis I. of France, caused by the French king's claim to the Duchy of Savoy. The reigning Duke of Savoy was the uncle of Francis I., but was closely allied with the Emperor by both marriage and interest. A French force overran Savoy early in 1536. As all efforts at negotiation failed, Charles V. declared war and assembled armies in Italy and the Netherlands to invade France from those two quarters.

In pursuance of the usual cruel policy of Francis I., the Constable de Montmorenci, the French commander, laid waste the region between the Rhone and the Alps, embracing Dauphiny and Provence. Towns, villages and mills were destroyed; crops were burned; and wells were poisoned. Charles V. invaded Provence by way of Italy and besieged Marseilles, but the destructive policy of the Constable de Montmorenci soon forced the Emperor to make a disgraceful retreat. The imperial army which invaded Picardy from the Netherlands met with no better success.

Elated by his rival's discomfiture, Francis I. now cherished new plans of conquest in Italy and in the Netherlands. He formed an alliance with Sultan Solyman the Magnificent, who continued his invasions of Hungary, and whose fleets swept the Mediterranean, carrying off captives from the shores of Italy. But the French king's great preparations came to naught. An armistice was signed in July, 1537; and the ten years' Truce of Nice in 1538 was followed by the Peace of Toledo in 1539, the "Perpetual Peace." Francis I. kept Savoy, Bresse and half of Piedmont; while Charles V. retained the other half of Piedmont and the Duchy of Milan. The Duke of Savoy, who had been thus robbed of his dominions, had to content himself with the little county of Nice.

Geneva, which had long been nominally subject to the Dukes of Savoy, but really ruled by its bishops, now became an independent republic, and was ruled for twenty-five years by John Calvin, through whose influence it became the stronghold of the Reformation in all French-speaking lands, and a great European center of religious, political and scientific progress.

Under the influence of the Constable de Montmorenci, King Francis I. broke off his friendship with Henry VIII. of England

and his alliance with the Turkish Sultan and with the Lutheran princes of Germany who had formed the League of Schmalkald, while he cultivated the Emperor's friendship. The French ambassador in England even proposed a scheme for the partition of that kingdom between Charles V., Francis I., and James V. of Scotland. When the English monarch was informed of this project he allied himself more closely with the League of Schmalkald by marrying Anne of Cleves, his fourth wife, the sister of the wife of the Elector John Frederick of Saxony, one of the most powerful of the Protestant princes of Germany.

Hayraddin Barbarossa's pirate fleet soon resumed its ravages in the Levant and wrested almost all the islands of the Archipelago from the Venetians, who also lost several places on the mainland, and were forced to pay a ransom which exhausted their resources and left the Venetian Republic dependent upon the protection of France.

Though the Emperor Charles V., as King of Spain, was master of the wealthy countries of Mexico and Peru, in the New World, he found great difficulty in meeting the expenses of his government ; and the Spaniards were so reluctant to be taxed for enterprises in which they had no interest that their Cortes refused to vote supplies. Charles revenged himself by ceasing to convene the Cortes. The grandees, thus deprived of political power, consoled themselves by maintaining all the ceremony of royal courts in their palaces and country-seats and by exercising sovereignty over thousands of vassals. When they had ruined their fortunes by their extravagance, and had lost all their warlike energy by a life of indolence, they were no longer formidable to their great sovereign.

The Emperor's subjects in the Netherlands likewise protested against the oppressive taxation with which he burdened them. His native city, Ghent, rose in revolt and sent envoys to the King of France, acknowledging him as its sovereign. As Francis I. was at that time on friendly terms with Charles V. he betrayed the confidence of the insurgents of Ghent, and even invited the Emperor to pass through France on his way to punish the rebels.

Francis entertained Charles with the greatest magnificence, but as soon as the Emperor had entered the Netherlands he received a demand from the King of France for the investiture of Milan as compensation for his safe passage through France. Charles V. refused this demand except upon conditions which Francis I. would not accept, and during the same year the Duchy of Milan was conferred on the Emperor's son Philip.

Charles V. entered the rebellious city of Ghent, his birth-place, on his birthday, when he was forty years of age, A. D. 1540. All the leading citizens, with bare heads and bare feet, implored pardon on their knees; but their sovereign's vengeance was not softened by submission. Twenty magistrates were beheaded. The old Abbey of St. Bavon and the Bell Roland, which, from its tower, had so often summoned a free people to arms, were destroyed ; and the fines of the citizens went to pay for the erection of a fortress on its site. Charles deprived Ghent of all its political privileges. Its commercial prosperity was transferred to Antwerp. The Northern provinces of the Netherlands inherited its brave enthusiasm for freedom, and afterward wrested their independence from Charles's son and successor, as we shall presently see.

Disappointed in his mercenary designs, Francis I. of France dismissed the Constable de Montmorenci, and renewed his alliance with the Lutheran princes of Germany and with Sultan Solyman the Magnificent. The death of King John Zapolya of Hungary was followed by a renewal of hostilities between the German and Ottoman Empires. Before the troops which the German Diet at Ratisbon had voted could take the field against the Turks, Solyman the Magnificent had entered Buda, the Hungarian capital, a third time, A. D. 1541 ; and that city remained under the

Turkish government and the Mohammedan religion for the next one hundred and forty-six years.

Ferdinand of Austria vainly sent ambassadors to the Grand Turk, offering to hold Hungary as a tributary of the Ottoman Porte. The haughty Sultan replied by demanding an annual tribute from Ferdinand for the Archduchy of Austria. The Elector Joachim II. of Brandenburg led a German army into Hungary and laid siege to Pesth, opposite Buda, but he failed; and the Turks took one town after another in Hungary until 1547, when Sultan Solyman the Magnificent consented to a truce for five years, as he desired to turn his arms against Persia. The Ottoman Porte appointed twelve officers to govern Turkish Hungary.

In 1541 the Emperor Charles V. led another expedition to Africa, for the purpose of thoroughly annihilating the power of the piratical Mohammedans of Algiers. But this expedition was a total failure. The fleet of Charles was destroyed by a terrible storm, and many of his followers died of a pestilential disease; and the Emperor, who had magnanimously shared all the sufferings of the humblest of his followers, was obliged to reëmbark and to return to Europe without effecting his object, landing at the Spanish port of Cartagena in December of the same year, A. D. 1541.

Francis I. of France received the news of the Emperor's calamities in Africa with unconcealed joy, and at once proceeded to enter into an alliance with the Sultan of Turkey, the Kings of Denmark and Sweden, the Duke of Cleves and the rebellious party in Naples, against Charles V.; but Henry VIII. of England, offended by the French king's intrigues with King James V. of Scotland, rejected the advances of Francis I.

In the summer of 1542 five French armies were in the field against the Emperor, three of which were to invade the Netherlands, one to operate in Italy, and one to threaten Spain. The French army under the Duke of Guise took many of the fortresses of Luxemburg; but the French king's second son, who nominally commanded this French army, disbanded his army and was to join his brother the Dauphin, who commanded the French army which operated against Spain, and who was planning a pitched battle; and the Regent of the Netherlands easily retook Luxemburg and Montmédy.

The Dauphin was unsuccessful in the siege of Perpignan, through the incompetency of his engineers and the violence of the autumnal rains. Perpignan was defended by the Spanish force under the Duke of Alva, with the coöperation of the Genoese admiral, Andrea Doria. Francis I. approached within forty miles of the beleaguered town, but when he perceived the hopelessness of the enterprise he ordered the raising of the siege. His vast preparations had been dissipated in trivial undertakings, and the results of his efforts were the capture of a few small towns in Picardy and in Northern Italy.

Charles V. now proceeded to Germany to chastise the Duke of Cleves for his alliance with the King of France. The Emperor took Düren, in the duchy of Jüliers, or Jülich, by storm, and caused the entire population of the town to be massacred; whereupon the duchy of Jülich immediately submitted to the Emperor, and the Duke of Cleves hastened to offer his submission to his offended sovereign. The Emperor refused to look at him for a time; but at length he granted very humiliating terms of peace to the humbled duke, who was obliged to give up the provinces of Guelders and Zutphen in the Netherlands, to renounce the Protestant worship and the alliance with France, and to transfer all the ducal troops to the imperial armies.

The Turkish freebooters, the most disgraceful allies of the French, ravaged Southern Italy, burning Reggio, destroying all vineyards and olive-orchards near the coast, carrying off many of the inhabitants, and appearing at the mouth of the Tiber and threatening Rome itself. When the French ambassador interfered in the Pope's behalf, Hayraddin Barbarossa sailed to Marseilles, where he found a ready market for his Italian captives, May, 1543. To pacify the Turkish admiral, Francis I. ordered an attack on Nice; and that stronghold of the Duke of Savoy was bombarded by the allied French and Turkish fleets, but was saved from capture by the opportune arrival of Andrea Doria's Genoese fleet and a Spanish army, which drove away the Franco-Turkish fleet. The French king assigned the city of Toulon to the Turks for winter-quarters, and for the time that French sea-port was a Mohammedan town. The disgraceful union of the Cross and the Crescent, in the alliance of the French with the Turks, shocked all Christendom.

The imminent peril with which the near presence of the Turks menaced the dominions of Charles V. induced the Emperor to renew his concessions to the Lutheran princes of Germany in the Diet of Spires in 1544; and the Lutherans in return vied with the Catholics of the German Empire in voting supplies for the war against the Emperor's foreign foes.

Hostilities were vigorously prosecuted in Piedmont during the winter of 1543-'44. The French under the Count d'Enghien defeated the imperialists at Cerisolles, in Savoy, April 14, 1544. As the King of France had secured the alliance of the Turks by sacrificing all other alliances, he was now obliged to get rid of these uncontrollable allies by the payment of almost a million crowns. The Turkish corsairs had conducted themselves at Toulon as if they had been in an enemy's country, seizing men even in the royal galleys for service in the Turkish fleet, and enslaving all whom they captured in the vicinity. Hayraddin Barbarossa had sailed for Constantinople in April, 1544, desolating the Italian coasts on his way.

In the meantime Charles V. had secured the alliance of Henry VIII. of England; and by a treaty which these two monarchs signed in February, 1543, they agreed to attempt the conquest of France, and, if successful, to partition that kingdom between them. In July, 1544, Henry VIII. landed at Calais with thirty thousand men, and took Boulogne after a siege of two months; while Charles V. led a large army into Champagne and besieged St. Dizier for six weeks, during which Francis I. was enabled to raise a large army to cover the approaches to Paris. When the Emperor had advanced to Chateau Thierry, within two days' march of Paris, he opened negotiations with the French king, without consulting his ally, the King of England.

By the Peace of Crespy between Charles V. and Francis I., September 18, 1544, each monarch relinquished the territory which he had taken since the Truce of Nice in 1538. The King of France once more renounced his claims to Naples and Flanders, and agreed to surrender Savoy on condition that his third son, the Duke of Orleans, should be invested with the Duchy of Milan, and should receive in marriage a daughter of the Emperor or of the Emperor's brother, the Archduke Ferdinand of Austria. The French king also agreed to coöperate with the Emperor in suppressing the Reformation and in defending Christendom against the Turks.

The premature death of the Duke of Orleans prevented the execution of the articles of the Treaty of Crespy concerning the Duchies of Savoy and Milan. Henry VIII. refused to take part in the Treaty of Crespy, and a desultory war went on between him and Francis I. until June, 1546, when peace was signed between them.

Both Charles V. and Francis I. at once proceeded to execute the article of the Peace of Crespy relating to the extirpation of heresy in their respective dominions. Charles ordered certain doctors of the University of Louvain to draw up a Confession of Faith, which he required all his subjects in the Netherlands to accept under penalty of death. To show that he was in earnest, he caused Peter du Breuil, a Calvinistic preacher, to be burned to death in the market-place of Tournay, February, 1545.

The King of France signalized his zeal for the Catholic faith by a persecution of the innocent Vaudois, or Waldenses, in the high Alpine valleys between France and Piedmont—a persecution so cruel that it would have disgraced the worst of the pagan Roman Emperors. The simple Vaudois had retained the purity of their Christian faith and worship from the earliest times, uncorrupted by the materialistic rites which had found their way into the wealthier and more elegant churches. They had recently hailed the doctrines of the Reformation as in accordance with their own faith—a circumstance which drew the attention of Europe to these hitherto-unnoticed and obscure heretics.

On New Year's Day, 1545, Francis I. addressed a letter to the Parliament of Provence, demanding the execution of the decree which it had passed in 1540 for the suppression of heresy, but which had been suspended hitherto by the intercession of the German Protestants. This atrocious edict required all fathers of families who persisted in heresy to be burned, their wives and children to be reduced to serfdom, their property to be confiscated, and their dwellings to be destroyed.

A Vaudois colony settled in the rugged mountain region north of the Durance, which their patient industry had converted into a fruitful garden, was the special object of the French king's persecution. The Baron d'Oppède, whose forces had been trained by the plundering and devastating campaigns of the French in Italy, was a fit instrument for this work of desolation. His bands soon overran the Vaudois country, laid waste the vineyards, orchards and grain-fields, and massacred the innocent inhabitants. The little town of Cabrières was induced to surrender by a promise that no one should be put to death—a promise that was violated as soon as the population were in the power of their cruel foes, who slaughtered their innocent victims without the least show of mercy. Those who had sought refuge in the mountains were hunted like wild beasts; and some of the strongest were chained to the galleys, while the others were butchered.

This cruel persecution of the simple Vaudois horrified most of Europe; but the French clergy, who had demanded it of their king, boldly avowed and sanctioned the atrocity. The fires of persecution were kindled throughout France, and Protestants were publicly burned at Paris, Meaux, Sens and Issoire. Briçonnet, the good Bishop of Meaux, had introduced the Reformed doctrines into that city twenty years before; and it became one of the centers of the Reformation in France. One of its martyrs was Stephen Dolet, a celebrated French scholar and author, who was highly esteemed by the literary men of that period.

Notwithstanding his many faults and vices, Francis I. was one of the greatest of the Kings of France. His great weakness was his subserviency to his wicked mother and mistresses, who ruled him thoroughly, and whose folly was accountable for most of the reverses which had befallen him. But his great sagacity clearly perceived the danger with which France and all Europe were menaced by the towering ambition of the illustrious royal Austrian House of Hapsburg. He struggled single-handed for thirty years against the most powerful monarch that had reigned in Christendom since the time of Charlemagne, and left France to his successor wholly unimpaired and even increased in territorial extent.

Francis I. was called the *Restorer of Letters and the Arts*, because of the wise and liberal encouragement and patronage which he gave to the revival of learning and the arts which distinguished his era; and many of the noblest monuments of France had their origin during his reign. He died March 31, 1547, of a painful malady from which he had long suffered, and which had been caused by his immoral life; and was succeeded by his son HENRY II. Henry VIII. of England died the same year.

Thus two of the six great contemporary European sovereigns of the first half of the sixteenth century passed from the world's stage. The four remaining were the Emperor Charles V., Sultan Solyman the Magnificent of Turkey, the Czar Ivan the Terrible of Russia, and King Gustavus Vasa of Sweden.

SECTION VIII.—WAR OF RELIGION IN GERMANY.

S THE Emperor Charles V., after the Peace of Cambray, in 1529, seemed determined to suppress the religious Reformation in his dominions, the Protestant princes of Germany, with the Elector of Saxony and the Landgrave of Hesse at their head, united in 1531 for their own protection, and formed an alliance, known as the *League of Schmalkald*, which was joined by the Kings of England, France, Denmark and Sweden.

The Emperor of Germany was obliged to avoid hostilities with his Protestant subjects at this time, in consequence of the formidable invasions of the Austrian territories by the Turks, who were then the most powerful people in Europe. Thus these constant Turkish invasions were highly favorable to the cause of the Reformation, as the Protestants of Germany refused to assist the Emperor in driving back the infidels, so long as the sword of Catholic vengeance was raised over their heads. The plans of Charles V. for the extermination of heresy were thus frustrated, and he found himself obliged to conclude with the League of Schmalkald the Peace of Nuremberg, in 1532.

The Peace of Nuremberg, which was confirmed by the German imperial Diet at Ratisbon, granted full liberty to preach and publish the doctrines of the Augsburg Confession. By this treaty both parties agreed to refrain from hostilities until a Council of the Church should be assembled to settle the division which thus distracted Christendom. Pope Clement VII. had been vehemently urged to convene such a Council. In the meantime the law proceedings were to cease. While the treaty bound the Protestants, it gave them no assurance for the future; but it afforded great opportunities for the diffusion of the Gospel throughout every portion of Germany.

The Lutheran form of worship was introduced into the Duchy of Wurtemberg. Duke Ulrich of Wurtemberg, a hot-tempered and cruel prince, had with his own hand murdered Hans von Hutten, a knight of his court, from motives of jealousy. He had so ill treated his wife that she fled from him, and he had conquered the imperial city of Reutlingen. He was at length outlawed for disturbing the peace of the country, and was driven from his land and his vassals by the Suabian League.

For fourteen years Ulrich was forced to lead a wandering life in exile from his dukedom, which meanwhile came under the dominion of Austria. At length the Landgrave Philip of Hesse resolved to restore Würtemberg to its exiled duke, who was then living at his court. Philip accordingly led a well-equipped army into Suabia, defeated the Austrian governor at Laufen on the Neckar, and reëstablished Ulrich in the government of his duchy. Ulrich was joyfully welcomed by his subjects, who had forgotten his former tyranny, and who were easily induced to accept the Lutheran doctrines, which Ulrich had embraced during his exile, and which he now caused to be disseminated by Brenz and Schnepf. The Lutheran Church was firmly established in the Duchy of Würtemberg, and the University of Tübingen was one of the most celebrated Lutheran seats of learning.

As we have seen, there were extremists in the new Church. Thomas Münzer's death had not suppressed the doctrines of the Anabaptists, who regarded their own passions as divine inspirations. In spite of the opposition of the leaders of the Reformation, and the discouragement given by all the lawful magistrates, the Anabaptists would make their appearance at various places in Germany. These fanatical doctrines displayed themselves in the most formidable manner in Münster, where the Reformation had made violent headway and driven the bishop and canons into exile.

GERMAN SOLDIERS.

GERMAN LANDSKNECHTS (16TH CENTURY).

GERMAN LANDSKNECHTS (16TH CENTURY).

MAJOR AND LIEUTENANT OF GERMAN LANDS-
KNECHTS.

THE AGE OF THE LANDSKNECHT.

It was soon apparent that Rottman, an influential preacher of the Reformation at Münster, was infected with Anabaptist ideas. He was at length aided by Jan Matthys and his countryman and disciple, the tailor, John Bockhold, called John of Leyden; whereupon the Anabaptists acquired such ascendency at Münster that they soon had possession of all the city offices, drove all such of the inhabitants who refused to accept their doctrines out of the city in the midst of winter, and divided their property among themselves. They then established a religious commonwealth in which Jan Matthys had absolute power, introduced the communistic plan of a community of goods, and conducted the defense of the city against the besieging force of the Bishop of Münster.

The fanaticism of the Anabaptists of Münster was heightened when Jan Matthys lost his life in a sally against the besiegers, when John of Leyden was placed at the head of the new commonwealth. John of Leyden selected twelve elders from the most violent of the fanatics, and entrusted them with the government of the city of Münster. Among these, Knipperdoling, who was burgomaster and executioner, acted the most conspicuous part. He introduced the practice of polygamy, and put to death without mercy all who denounced this outrage on Christian morality.

When the fanaticism of the Anabaptists of Münster had reached its height, John of Leyden assumed the title of "King of the New Israel," which he claimed by Divine inspiration. This "tailor king" had for his insignia a crown and a globe suspended by a golden chain. With this insignia, and magnificently attired, he set up the "Chair of David" in the market-place of Münster, where he sat for the administration of justice. He introduced a government in which tyranny and fanaticism were mingled, and in which spiritual pride and carnal lust were associated in the most repulsive manner.

The Anabaptists for a long time made a courageous and successful resistance to the attacks of their imperfectly armed foes. They still resolutely maintained their defense when the besieging army of the Bishop of Münster had been reinforced by imperial troops, and when the beleaguered city began to suffer the horrors of famine. They resisted with the courage of desperation even when the enemy were within the walls of the city. Rottman was slain while fighting. John of Leyden and Knipperdoling were put to death by torture, and their dead bodies were suspended in iron cages on the tower; while many were executed, and the rest were driven into exile. The bishop, the canons and the nobility returned; and Roman Catholicism, which was then reestablished in all its rigor, has ever since prevailed in Münster.

A few decades later the Anabaptists experienced a complete reformation of their doctrines and discipline under the direction and leadership of Menno Simon; and in that condition, under the name of *Mennonites*, they have continued to the present day, and have been distinguished for their simplicity of dress and manners, and for their rejection of a separate priesthood, of infant baptism, of oaths, of military service and the use of law. Under Menno Simon's direction they abandoned those principles of an earlier period which were in direct antagonism to Christian morality and the public welfare. In their old ancestral homes their descendants lead a quiet life as tenant farmers and peasants. Many are now living in the United States of America.

We have seen that the leading Protestant princes of Germany were the Elector John the Steadfast of Saxony and the Landgrave Philip of Hesse. The Elector John the Steadfast, who succeeded his father Frederick the Wise in 1525, died in 1532, and was succeeded by his son John Frederick. The Duke of Cleves was also one of the greatest of the Protestant princes of Germany; and inherited Guelders and Zutphen, in the Netherlands, through the extinction of the family of Egmont, as well as his father's duchy of Cleves and his mother's inheritance of Berg, Jülich and Ravensberg. His estates lay along the Rhine, from Cologne in Germany, to the vicinity of Utrecht, in the Netherlands, and from the Werre to the Meuse. At length Lutheranism was established in the Duchy of Saxony and in the Electorate of Brandenburg, after the death of their last Catholic princes.

The Margrave Albert of Brandenburg had become a Lutheran in the early part of the Reformation; but the *Electoral* branch of the Brandenburg House of Hohenzollern held fast to Roman Catholicism until after the death of the Elector Joachim I., in 1535. His son and successor, Joachim II., received the Eucharist under both Catholic and Lutheran forms at Spandau in 1539; whereupon the Electorate of Brandenburg embraced the Lutheran doctrine. The Roman Catholic Church in the whole North of Germany, and the Protestant worship now prevailed from the Rhine to the Baltic. Conferences between Romish and Protestant divines were held at Frankfort-on-the-Main in 1540, and before the German imperial Diet at Ratisbon in 1541, which brought the two religious parties nearer to agreement, but did not lead to peace.

Henry of Brunswick-Wolfenbüttel, a cruel and profligate prince, alone adhered to the Romish Church, more from his animosity to the Landgrave Philip of Hesse, the former friend of his youth, than from conviction; but the Protestant faith triumphed even in Wolfenbüttel, when Henry was overpowered by Hessian and Saxon troops and carried

THE REFORMATION—DECIMATING A REGIMENT.

The *Electorate* of Saxony, under the elder or Ernestine branch of the Saxon dynasty, had been the birth-place and early stronghold of the Reformation; but the *Duchy* of Saxony, under the younger or Albertine branch of the same dynasty, had adhered to the Romish Church until after the death of Duke George, in 1539. His brother and successor, Henry the Pious, who was devoted to the Reformation, as was also his son Maurice, established the Lutheran worship in Meissen, Dresden and Leipsic.

The conversion of the Duchy of Saxony and the Electorate of Brandenburg to the Lutheran faith sealed the fate of the Romish into captivity, after a fierce controversy, alike detrimental to the dignity of princes and to human nature.

Otho Heinrich ordered Osiander, the Nuremberger preacher, to teach the Lutheran doctrines in the Upper Palatinate; and a few weeks before Luther's death the Eucharist was administered in both the Lutheran and Catholic forms in the Palatinate of the Rhine, after the congregation which assembled to hear mass in the Church of the Holy Ghost on January 3, 1546, had sung the Lutheran hymn: "Salvation hath visited us."

Baden-Durlach likewise accepted the Reformed confession. Archbishop Hermann, Elector of Cologne, proposed to his Estates a moderate plan of reformation; and the Duke of Cleves seemed disposed to join the League of Schmalkald. The Roman Catholic Church now appeared doomed in Germany if the progress of the Reformation was not forcibly checked. The Emperor Charles V. was convinced that neither imperial Diets nor religious discussions could effect a restoration of the unity of the Church.

Importuned by the Emperor Charles V., Pope Paul III. summoned a Council of the Church to meet at Trent, in the Tyrol, for the purpose of effecting a reconciliation of opposing opinions and restoring the unity of the Church. The Protestants, foreseeing that their doctrines would be condemned in a Council held under the auspices of the Pope, rejected it as partial, and demanded, in its stead, a general synod of the Church of Germany. The Council, however, assembled at Trent, in December, 1545. Dr. Martin Luther died in his native city, Eisleben, in Saxony, on the 18th of February, 1546.

The very first decision of the Council of Trent rendered a reconciliation of opposing opinions hopeless. The Emperor, having concluded a disgraceful peace with Sultan Solyman the Magnificent, now determined to crush the Reformation by force of arms; and in the year 1546 the Religious War of Schmalkald broke out between Charles V. and his Protestant German subjects.

The Emperor had for some time been secretly preparing for war by mustering one army in Italy, another in Austria, and a third in the Netherlands. Pope Paul III. aided him by contributions of troops and money, and by authorizing the sale of monastic property in Spain and a tax upon the clergy in the same kingdom.

Though late in discerning the object of the Emperor's preparations, the League of Schmalkald determined to defend the Protestant cause, and promptly put its forces in the field under the command of the Elector John Frederick of Saxony and the Landgrave Philip of Hesse. The Lutheran cities of Germany also raised a large army, and placed it under the command of Sebastian Schärtlin, one of the ablest generals of his time.

Charles V. first broke his coronation-oath by bringing foreign troops into Germany, and then violated the imperial constitution by placing the leaders of the Schmalkald forces and their followers under the ban of the Empire—the highest penalty of treason. This sentence, which could not be legally published without the consent of the imperial Diet, declared the Protestant princes to be rebels and outlaws, absolved their subjects from allegiance, and confiscated all their territories.

The princes of the League of Schmalkald replied to the Emperor's sentence of outlawry by a declaration of war, in which they renounced all allegiance to "Charles of Ghent, pretended Emperor." The army of the Lutheran city of Strasburg hastened to occupy the forts of Ehrenberg and Kufstein, to prevent the Pope's forces from entering Bavaria through the passes of the Tyrol. Thus the Protestant forces were promptly in the field, and they were superior to the Emperor's armies. Both armies were in motion in the summer of 1546, but the first campaign was indecisive.

The hesitation and lack of vigor on the part of the Protestant princes enabled the Emperor to bring his auxiliaries from Italy and to move from his precarious situation at Ratisbon to a more secure position at Ingolstadt, where he was joined by his troops from the Netherlands, thus enabling him to assume the offensive. He marched into Suabia, and was followed thither by the Schmalkald army.

All the efforts of the Protestant princes of Germany were rendered fruitless by the perfidy of one of their own number—Duke Maurice of Saxony. This shrewd young prince had become the Duke of Albertine Saxony upon the death of his father, Henry the Pious, in 1541. Although a Lutheran in belief, Maurice had long withdrawn from the League of Schmalkald, because he envied and hated his cousin John Frederick, the Elector of Ernestine Saxony. Although the Landgrave Philip of Hesse was his father-in-law, Maurice formed a secret alliance with the Emperor Charles V., who had in the meantime reposed such confidence in the perfidious prince that he exempted him from the ban of the Empire.

The Lutheran princes had so little suspicion of the treachery of Maurice that his cousin, the Elector John Frederick, had during his absence entrusted him with the defense and administration of the Electorate of Saxony; but as soon as Maurice had been won over by the Emperor's flatteries and promises he betrayed his trust, and seized the Saxon Electorate for himself, with the aid of an army of Bohemians and Hungarians under the Emperor's brother Ferdinand, Archduke of Austria and King of Bohemia and Hungary.

The unexpected defection of Maurice of Saxony utterly ruined the Protestant cause in Germany, and the League of Schmalkald was at the Emperor's mercy. Their common treasury was exhausted; many of their troops deserted for want of pay; and their army was obliged to retreat from Southern Germany.

The triumphant Emperor now required the princes and cities of Southern Germany to submit to the imperial authority and to desert the League of Schmalkald, and the terrified imperial cities complied. Ulm, Heilbronn, Esslingen, Reutlingen, Augsburg, Frankfort, Strasburg and other cities surrendered their artillery, and obtained peace from the Emperor by the payment of heavy fines.

The old Duke Ulrich of Würtemberg humbled himself to the Emperor, paid his contributions of war, and surrendered his most important fortresses to the imperial troops. The old Archbishop Hermann, Elector of Cologne, anathematized by the Pope, threatened by Spanish troops, and finally abandoned by his Estates, relinquished his office in favor of a Catholic, who soon restored the Romish worship in place of Lutheranism. By the spring of 1547 all of Southern Germany was reduced to submission to the Emperor without a battle having been fought.

In the meantime victory had attended the Protestant arms in Northern Germany, where the Elector John Frederick had recovered his confiscated Electorate of Ernestine Saxony by repulsing and dispersing the army of Maurice, after which he overran and conquered Maurice's Duchy of Albertine Saxony as far as Dresden and Leipsic, being everywhere received with acclamations by the population, who were so unanimously on the Protestant side and against their perfidious duke that Maurice dared not levy an army among his own subjects.

Ferdinand of Austria, King of Hungary and Bohemia, met with as little success in raising an army among the Bohemians, whom he offended by his efforts to change the elective kingdom of Bohemia into a hereditary dominion for the Austrian House of Hapsburg. The Elector John Frederick might have raised a considerable army in both the Saxonies, bidden defiance to the whole Catholic power, and made himself Emperor of Protestant Germany, if his energy and enterprise had been equal to his general excellence of character.

The defeated Maurice, in his desperate extremity, invoked the Emperor's aid. Charles V. marched into Bavaria, although suffering from the gout, and effected a junction with the forces under Maurice and Ferdinand; after which he hastened into Saxony and came up with the Elector John Frederick, who was posted on the Elbe at Mühlberg, with six thousand troops. The Emperor with his army, twenty-seven thousand strong, crossed the Elbe almost before the eyes of the astonished Elector, who imagined the Emperor to be many miles distant. John Frederick's cavalry was surprised while engaged in a retreat, on a Sunday morning in April, 1547, while the Elector was attending Divine worship; and the Emperor Charles V. won a victory in the battle of Mühlberg, where the Elector John Frederick was wounded in the face and taken prisoner.

With the capitulation of Wittenberg, the

capital of the Saxon Electorate, all of John Frederick's electoral and princely rights were surrendered to the Emperor; but the vanquished Elector's possessions, except a few towns, were divided between his cousin, Duke Maurice, and the Emperor's brother, Ferdinand of Austria, King of Bohemia and Hungary. John Frederick remained in captivity at the Emperor's court, and his children became pensioners of their unfaithful kinsman.

In captivity John Frederick manifested the serenity of soul resulting from a good conscience and a firm trust in God. With the greatest composure he heard the sentence of death that the Emperor had pronounced against him, and without even interrupting the game of chess in which he was engaged. But Charles V. did not venture to carry this terrible sentence into execution. He changed the punishment to imprisonment for life, upon condition that John Frederick should surrender his fortresses to the Emperor and relinquish his electoral dignity and his dominions to Maurice, who was solemnly invested with his new dignity by the Emperor himself, while the deposed and captive John Frederick looked on the ceremony from the windows of his prison. Thus the Electorate of Saxony was transferred from the Ernestine to the Albertine branch of the Saxon dynasty, remaining thenceforth in the latter's possession.

During the spring of 1547 the imperial army under Duke Eric of Brunswick was forced to raise the siege of Bremen, and was defeated near Drachenburg; but the arms of the victorious Protestants were paralyzed by the news of the capitulation of Wittenberg, and all of Northern Germany except Magdeburg was soon reduced to submission to the Emperor.

Charles V. next proceeded to punish the Landgrave Philip of Hesse. The Electors Maurice of Saxony and Joachim II. of Brandenburg interceded for the unfortunate prince, and obtained from the Emperor the assurance "that if he would make an unconditional surrender, apologize for his proceedings and deliver up his castles, he should be punished neither with death nor with perpetual imprisonment." These conditions were subsequently modified during a personal interview, and Maurice of Saxony and Joachim II. of Brandenburg assured the Landgrave Philip of the safety of his person and possessions.

Relying on this assurance and provided with a safe-conduct, Philip of Hesse appeared before the Emperor Charles V. at Halle, begged pardon on his knees in the presence of the brilliant assembly of courtiers, promising to surrender his artillery, demolish all his fortresses but one, release the prisoners whom he had taken, and pay a considerable fine. Notwithstanding his humiliating submission, the terms of the treaty were evaded, and the Landgrave Philip was made a prisoner by the most shameful treachery. Being invited to supper with the Duke of Alva, the commander of the Spanish auxiliaries in the Emperor's service, Philip went to the Castle of Halle, where he was detained as a prisoner in spite of all protestations.

Charles V. could not deny himself the triumph of having the two leading Protestant princes of the Empire in his power. He soon afterward retired from Saxony, taking his two illustrious captives with him. The captivity of the two great Protestant princes of Germany only increased the complaints of the more honest portion of the German nation, and led to a coldness between Maurice of Saxony and the Emperor; but it contributed to overawe resistance in Bohemia, where the Protestant army was soon dispersed. The Bohemian nobles hastened to submit to King Ferdinand, and Prague itself surrendered after a short resistance. The Protestant rebellion in Bohemia resulted in a firmer establishment of the power of the Austrian House of Hapsburg in that kingdom and throughout the German Empire.

Pope Paul III. was alarmed at the Emperor's growing power too late, and had recalled the papal auxiliaries from Germany. By favoring the conspiracy of Fiesco at Genoa, the Pope endeavored to place that republic under French instead of imperial influence; but the death of the daring conspirator Fiesco, who sought to usurp the office of Doge, frustrated the Pope's design, and the Doria family remained in power in Genoa.

The dissension between the Pope and the Emperor was still more embittered by the murder of the Duke of Parma, a son of Pope Paul III. and an Italian tyrant of the most odious type. Instead of punishing this crime, Charles V. appeared to almost assume responsibility for it by occupying Placentia, the scene of the murder, with imperial troops, and refusing to invest the murdered duke's son, who was his own son-in-law, with the Duchy of Parma.

The Council of Trent assembled on the 13th of December, 1545. The division in the Church was made greater than before; and the Pope, suspecting the Emperor of a design to limit the papal power, removed the Council to Bologna, in Italy; but Charles V. forbade the clergy to leave Trent. The Spanish and Neapolitan prelates obeyed the Emperor by remaining at Trent, while the other thirty-four passed into Italy; and the two Councils, instead of restoring peace and unity to Christendom, began a war of words between each other.

For the purpose of bringing about a restoration of the unity of the Church, the Emperor Charles V. published an edict, which set forth how matters should be conducted until the termination of the Council of Trent. Accordingly three divines, representing respectively the Old Catholic, the New Catholic and the Lutheran parties, were appointed to draw up a Confession of Faith which should reconcile all religious controversies, at least until a more generally accepted Council than those of Trent and Bologna could be convened. This decree, which was called the *Augsburg Interim*, was at first designed for both religious parties, but was afterwards restricted to the Protestants. It permitted to the Lutherans the use of the cup and the marriage of the priests, and indefinite modes of expression were used to approach the Protestant opinions on the doctrines of justification, the mass, etc.; but the old usages were retained in the celebration of Divine worship and in the ceremonies.

In striving to please all parties Charles V. pleased none; and the Augsburg Interim encountered equally violent opposition from the Pope at Rome, from the Calvinists at Geneva, and from the Lutherans at Magdeburg. Nevertheless the Emperor submitted it to the German imperial Diet at Augsburg, in May, 1548, for acceptance without discussion. The Archbishop-Elector of Mayence immediately arose and thanked the Emperor for his efforts to restore peace to the Church, and declared the Interim to be fully approved by the Diet. This unauthorized assumption passed unchallenged on that occasion; but the Elector Maurice of Saxony and his deposed cousin John Frederick soon entered protests, as did also several imperial cities.

The Protestant preachers could not be induced to accept a religion that was offensive to their consciences, by being deprived of their offices, their property or their freedom. The preachers who were thus driven from their posts fled from their homes and firesides by secret paths to the North of Germany, where the Augsburg Interim was wholly rejected. Thus almost four hundred Lutheran preachers became exiles, and most of them found refuge at Magdeburg, which was under the ban of the Empire, as was also Constance, which was the chief center of opposition to the Interim in the South.

The Emperor's brother, Ferdinand of Austria, Bohemia and Hungary, attacked and captured Constance, and annexed it to the dominions of the Austrian House of Hapsburg, in defiance of its ancient privileges. Magdeburg sustained a longer resistance, and became the stronghold of Lutheranism.

Many Lutheran preachers also fled from their homes in Saxony, the cradle of the Reformation, because of their dislike to the Leipsic Interim, which was composed by Melanchthon, who thereby subjected himself to the imputation of weakness and cowardice. These also found refuge at Magdeburg, whence many pamphlets, satires, satirical poems and wood-cuts were issued, designed to bring hatred and contempt upon the Augsburg and Leipsic Interims and their authors.

After having, as he imagined, suppressed religious innovations by means of the Augsburg Interim, the Emperor Charles V. proceeded to reform the Catholic Church in Germany by a special edict remarkable for its great wisdom and moderation. The same Diet at Augsburg incorporated the seventeen provinces of the Netherlands with the Germano-Roman Empire under the name of the Circle of Burgundy.

Pope Paul III. died in November, 1549; whereupon the Cardinal Del Monte was elected Pope by the conclave of cardinals, and assumed the title of Julius III. The new Pope courted the Emperor's favor by reopening the Council of Trent, while Charles V. summoned a new German imperial Diet at Augsburg to devise means for compelling the Protestant party in Germany to submit to the Council's decrees.

As Charles V. advanced in years, and as his constitutional melancholy became settled more heavily over his mind, he more willingly engaged in the work of religious persecution. He had just introduced the Spanish Inquisition into the Netherlands; and his cruel Edict of Brussels threatened the death-penalty against all who should buy, sell, possess or read any Protestant book, or who should meet to study the Scriptures, or speak against any of the Roman Catholic doctrines. Men who were guilty of such offenses were beheaded, while women were either burned or buried alive.

When the Emperor Charles V. seemed to have attained the object of his desires; when everything seemed to insure his elevation to the position of temporal head of all Christendom; and when the Council of the Church had reassembled at Trent, Duke Maurice of Saxony, the prince to whom Charles V. was indebted for the overthrow of the League of Schmalkald, seeing to what dangers the civil and religious liberties of Germany were exposed by the ambitious schemes of the Emperor, and offended because of the captivity of his father-in-law, Philip of Hesse, suddenly formed a secret alliance with King Henry II. of France, the son and successor of Francis I., but concealed his designs until the most favorable time arrived for their execution.

The treaty between Maurice of Saxony and Henry II. of France provided for combined action against the Emperor Charles V. One of the articles authorized the French king to seize the towns of Metz, Toul, Verdun and Cambray, and to hold them as Imperial Vicar—an arrangement by which France held these towns until a recent date. This treaty was signed at the Castle of Chambord, near Blois, by Henry II. of France and the Margrave Albert of Brandenburg, January, 1552.

Maurice immediately granted freedom of religion to the Protestant city of Magdeburg, which he had been for some time besieging; and then, suddenly throwing off the mask, he published a manifesto announcing his intention to maintain the laws and constitution of the German Empire, to protect the Protestant religion, and to liberate the Landgrave of Hesse. In March, 1552, Maurice advanced into Southern Germany with three divisions of his army and took possession of Augsburg.

The Emperor was not alarmed by rumors of Maurice's proceedings, and had sent large detachments of his army into Hungary and Italy, while posting himself with a small guard at Innsbruck, in the Tyrol, to watch the proceedings of the Council of Trent.

Maurice marched into the Tyrol to make the Emperor a prisoner at Innsbruck. He put to flight a small force which the Emperor had collected upon the borders of the Tyrol, and took the pass and castle of Ehrenberg by storm. The Council of Trent was broken up in confusion; and Charles V., who was then afflicted with the gout, escaped with difficulty from Innsbruck in the cold and darkness of a rainy night, being carried in a litter over the snow-covered mountain roads into Carinthia. Before his hasty flight from Innsbruck, Charles

V. released the captive John Frederick of Saxony, whom he had kept a prisoner since the battle of Mühlberg. Maurice might perhaps have taken the Emperor prisoner, but desisted because he "had no cage big enough for such a bird."

In the meantime Maurice's ally, King Henry II. of France, invaded Lorraine and seized the strong towns of Toul, Metz and Verdun, according to treaty; after which he marched into Luxemburg, where he captured several towns, whose plunder he bestowed on his courtiers and higher officers.

Alarmed at the rapid advance of Maurice, the Emperor's brother, Archduke Ferdinand of Austria, immediately concluded with the Protestant princes the Religious Peace of Passau, by which the Protestants of Germany were allowed perfect religious freedom; the Landgrave Philip of Hesse was set at liberty; and a permanent peace and amnesty were decided upon, August, 1552. This was the first victory of the Reformation.

After the conclusion of the Peace of Passau, the forces of the Schmalkaldic League were either disbanded or enlisted in the war against the Turks, which had again broken out in Hungary, through an imaginary slight which the Sultan had inflicted upon Martinuzzi, Bishop of Waradin and guardian of the infant Zapolya. The restless and warlike bishop offered to betray the interests of his ward by securing the principality of Transylvania and the Hungarian crown to King Ferdinand on condition of being made a cardinal and governor of Transylvania.

The Turkish army at once invaded Transylvania, and was opposed by the united forces of Martinuzzi and Castaldo, Ferdinand's general; but the cardinal's arrogance became unendurable; and the general accused him of a secret understanding with the Turks, and caused him to be assassinated, with the consent of King Ferdinand, whose memory is stained with many similar crimes.

The Turks now overran all of Southern Hungary, and took possession of Temesvar and the other fortresses of the Banat; and their political and religious customs remained established there until 1716. The approach of Maurice of Saxony after the Peace of Passau forced the Turks to retire from Erlau, a little town in the North of Hungary, which had withstood three furious assaults from the Ottoman forces, thus holding them at bay until succor could arrive.

Late in 1552 the Emperor Charles V., at the head of an army of a hundred thousand men, undertook the recapture of Metz from the French. That strong fortress was gallantly defended by Francis, Duke of Guise, and all the chivalry of France. The Margrave Albert of Brandenburg, who had hitherto refused to accede to the Peace of Passau, and had been ravaging Western Germany as the French king's ally, now suddenly changed sides, defeated and captured the Duke d'Aumale, and made peace with the Emperor.

Metz was so skillfully and successfully defended by the French garrison under the Duke of Guise that the Emperor Charles V., after a siege of little more than two months, was obliged to raise the siege and to beat a disgraceful retreat, having lost about forty thousand men during the siege, his Spanish and Italian troops having suffered severely from the cold of winter and from the heavy rains which drenched their camp. Metz then became wholly French, and Lutheran books were burned and the Protestant worship was suppressed. That fortified town remained in the possession of France until 1870, when it was recovered by Germany.

In the meantime the Turkish corsair Draghut ravaged the Mediterranean coasts. From every cliff and castle along the Italian shores an anxious lookout was kept for the sails of this marauder, whose approach was too frequently signaled to the terrified inhabitants of the villages by columns of smoke. Besides capturing richly laden merchantmen at sea, the pirates frequently penetrated inland, carrying into slavery all whom they could seize. They attacked the island of Corsica, which then belonged to Genoa, and took several places; but there the Turks quarreled with their Christian allies, the French, and seized all the Corsicans who were fit to row in their galleys, along with several French nobles, whom they detained for ransom.

As the Margrave Albert of Brandenburg continued his wars and robberies in Lower Saxony, a new league of German princes was formed against him, and Maurice of Saxony marched against him to force him to accept peace. Maurice was victorious in the long and obstinate battle of Sievershausen, in 1553, but received a gun-shot wound, of which he died two days afterward, in the thirty-second year of his age, and in the flower of his manly strength. He was a man of rare qualities, "prudent and secret, enterprising and energetic." His brother Augustus succeeded him as Elector of Saxony; and the Electorate of Saxony remained in the possession of the Albertine branch of the Saxon dynasty until the dissolution of the Germano-Roman Empire in 1806, as did also the Kingdom of Saxony thereafter.

Albert of Brandenburg suffered another defeat near Brunswick, and passed the remaining years of his life as a dependent upon the French court or upon his brother-in-law, the Duke of Baden. Germany enjoyed tranquillity during the last half of the sixteenth century, during which it took little part in general European affairs.

In 1553 Charles V., after a vigorous siege, took the town of Terouenne from the French by assault, destroyed it, and massacred the entire garrison. Hesdin was also taken by the imperial forces; and during the siege of that fortress Emmanuel Philibert, eldest son of the exiled Duke of Savoy, exhibited those remarkable talents which regained for him his father's dominions in due time. The duke died a few months afterward at Vercelli, which the French seized and plundered almost immediately upon his death.

Pope Julius III., died in 1554, and his successor, Marcellus II., soon afterward also passed to his grave; whereupon John Peter Caraffa, who had been distinguished for his piety, learning, and simple and blameless life, was elected Pope by the conclave of cardinals, and assumed the title of Paul IV. The new Pope was a member of the Oratory of Divine Love, which had been instituted during the pontificate of Leo X. He was also one of the founders of the Theatins. He was seventy-nine years of age when he became Pope. He appeared in public in a magnificent array of velvet and gold, and his daily life was characterized by princely pomp and ceremony. His ruling passion was hatred of the Emperor Charles V., whose jealousy of the Popes he regarded as the cause of the alienation of the Germans from the Romish Church. Paul IV. accordingly hastened to enter into a close alliance with King Henry II. of France, and magnified all his causes of disagreement with the Emperor.

In 1555, in accordance with the terms of the Peace of Passau, Charles V. summoned a Diet of the German Empire at Augsburg; and, after much deliberation, this Diet concluded the *Religious Peace of Augsburg* the same year, by which the Protestants of Germany were allowed perfect liberty of conscience and full toleration for their religion, as well as equal civil and political rights with the Catholics, and to retain possession of the ecclesiastical property which they had seized. A free right of departure was granted to subjects who did not follow the religion of the Electors, and a free toleration was allowed those who remained. Each German state was secured in the right to maintain either the Protestant or the Catholic worship, or to tolerate both or prohibit whichever it pleased.

The demand which the Catholics made that those of the clergy who should in the future become Protestants should lose their offices and incomes occasioned the most vehement disputes. It being impossible to come to an agreement, the point was left undecided, and was admitted as a spiritual reservation into the laws of peace—"a seed of bloody contests."

MODERN HISTORY.—SIXTEENTH CENTURY.

The failure of the Emperor Charles V. to restore the unity of the Church made him lose his interest in the affairs of the world; and in 1555 and 1556, to the astonishment of the whole world, he followed the example of Diocletian by resigning the scepter of power, abdicating all his thrones and passing the remainder of his life in quiet retirement and monastic penance. The Emperor had this scheme in contemplation for a long time, and his failing health and recent political failures had made him more anxious than ever to carry it out. The recent death of his mother, Queen Joanna, whom the Spaniards had always regarded as their sovereign, made it possible for Charles to dispose of the Spanish crowns. In hours of prayer he imagined that he heard his mother's voice calling him away, and he determined to pass his remaining days in retirement.

With this object in view he called his son Philip, who had married Queen Mary of England, to Brussels and there invested him with the Grand Mastership of the Order of the Golden Fleece. Then, in the presence of all the Estates of the Netherlands, October 25, 1555, the Emperor abdicated the sovereignty of the seventeen provinces of the Netherlands, which he conferred upon his son PHILIP II., reviewed the events of his reign, implored the solemn assembly to pardon all the errors which he might have committed, and charged his son to defend the Catholic religion, to do justice and to love his subjects. His sister Mary, the widow of King Louis II. of Hungary, resigned the regency of the Netherlands at the same time; and Philip II. appointed the Duke of Savoy as her successor.

In the presence of all the Spanish nobles in the Netherlands, assembled in the same hall several weeks afterward, Charles V. abdicated the crowns of Spain, Naples and Sicily, and the sovereignty of Spanish America, all of which were also conferred upon Philip II.

In the autumn of 1556 Charles V. abdicated the German imperial crown in favor of his brother Ferdinand, Archduke of Austria, and King of Bohemia and Hungary. This latter abdication was addressed to the Electors, princes and Estates of Germany, and was formally accepted by the German imperial Diet at Frankfort in 1558, when Ferdinand was chosen Emperor, after pledging himself to observe the Peace of Religion —a pledge which he honestly fulfilled. Thenceforth the House of Hapsburg remained divided into a Spanish and an Austrian branch.

Immediately after committing to his most trusted friends, the Prince of Orange and Chancellor Seld, the document by which he abdicated the imperial crown of Germany, Charles proceeded to Spain, accompanied by his two sisters, the dowager queens of Hungary and France. He retired to the province of Estremadura, in the West of Spain, passing the remaining two years of his life in the residence which he had built near the monastery of San Yuste, on the pleasant declivity of a hill, surrounded by plantations of trees. He passed his retirement in religious devotion, in cultivating his own garden and orchard, and in mechanical inventions.

The ex-Emperor spent many hours with the Italian mechanician Torriano in making clocks and watches or in other delicate machinery. Having failed in repeated attempts to make two watches run exactly alike, he is said to have exclaimed: "I cannot make two watches run alike, and yet, fool that I was, I thought of governing so many nations of different languages and religions, and living in different climes!"

Two years after his abdication the ex-Emperor felt his end approaching, and was seized with a fancy for going through the ceremonies of his own funeral. He attired himself in monkish costume, and joined in the mournful chants of the brotherhood of monks around an empty coffin which was placed in the convent chapel. This solemn farce was turned into a reality in less than a month; as the great ex-monarch breathed his last September 21, 1558, at the age of fifty-eight, worn out by toils of state rather than by years.

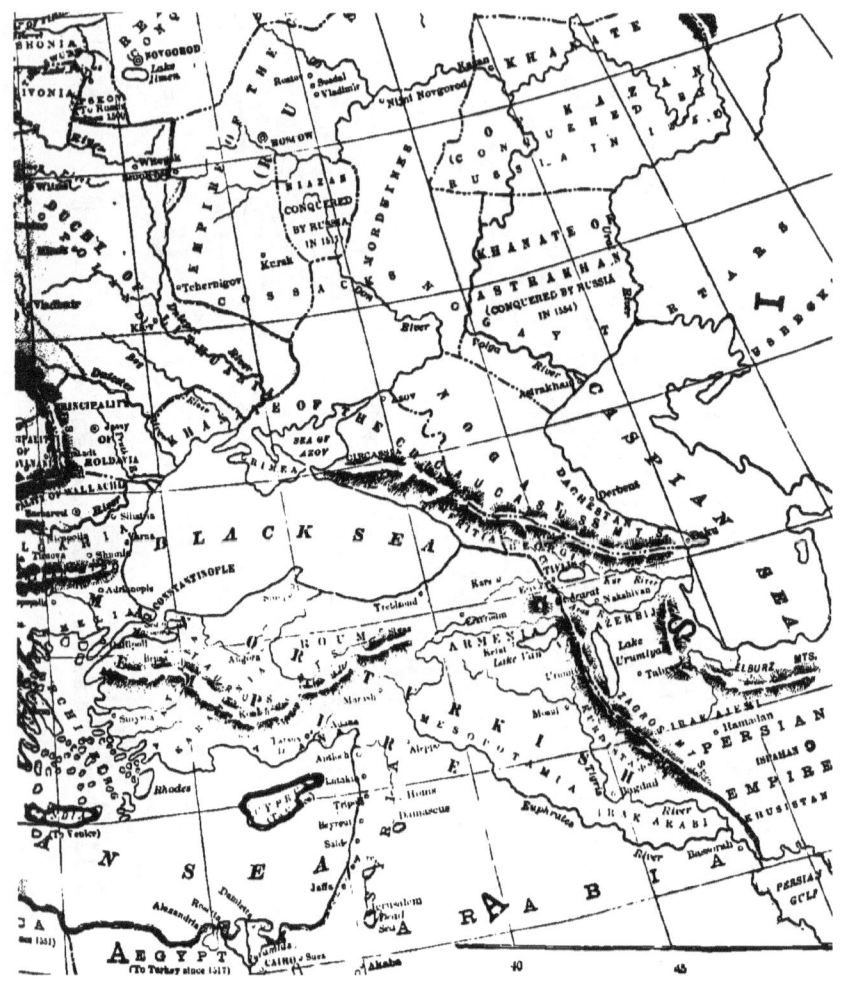

SECTION IX.—LUTHERANISM AND CALVINISM.

N GERMANY, the birth-place of the Reformation, the Lutheran form of worship strove long with the Catholic for the mastery. Lutheranism gradually spread from Saxony and Hesse over the neighboring counties, attained the ascendency in the North of Germany, gained great headway in Suabia and Franconia, and extended itself from Strasburg into Alsace and Lorraine.

In the early part of the Reformation the doctrines of Luther had penetrated to the region of the Vistula and the Baltic shores, where Albert of Brandenburg, the Grand Master of the Teutonic Order, pressed upon by the Poles and deserted by the Emperor and the Empire, had become a Lutheran, put an end to the Teutonic Order as a sovereign power by a treaty with King Sigismund I. of Poland in 1525, and received the eastern part of Prussia as a hereditary duchy under the suzerainty of the King of Poland. His children inherited the Prussian duchy, which finally came into the possession of the Electoral branch of the Brandenburg House of Hohenzollern, and became independent of Poland. In Courland and Livonia the same thing occurred with the Head of the Order of the Sword. Lutheranism was also established in the Scandinavian kingdoms, as we shall presently see.

The Catholic form of worship was zealously championed by the Dukes of Bavaria, by the royal Austrian House of Hapsburg, by the spiritual Electors of the German Empire, and by the prince-bishops. Ingolstadt was the great seat of Catholic learning in Germany. But the Emperors Ferdinand I. and Maximilian II. both sought not to offend the consciences of their subjects, thus allowing Lutheranism to gain many converts in the hereditary Austrian territories. The Protestants soon obtained religious toleration, and erected several churches in the archduchy of Austria and in the duchies of Carinthia and Styria. The Reformation made such rapid strides in Hungary and Transylvania that the Protestants outnumbered the Catholics, and acquired religious freedom and equal political rights with their opponents. The old Hussites of Bohemia mainly embraced the Lutheran doctrines. Notwithstanding the many treaties which guaranteed the rights of the Protestants in the Austrian dominions, those rights were disregarded by later rulers, who reëstablished the supremacy of the Catholic State Church.

The Reformed Church which Ulrich Zwingli originated in Switzerland also spread itself into Germany at an early period. Zwingli's doctrines were only accepted and supported by a few towns in the South of Germany, until John Calvin, the refugee French Reformer in Geneva, adopted Zwingli's principles and fashioned them into a complete system of doctrine by uniting them with his own views, after which the reformed Church in Germany obtained numerous accessions. Duke Frederick III. of Baden introduced this system into his own dominions from the Palatinate, and in 1559 he ordered Ursinus and Olevianus to draw up the *Heidelberg Catechism*, a widely extended compend of the Zwinglian and Calvinistic doctrines.

The Zwinglian and Calvinistic Church was also introduced into Hesse, Bremen and Brandenburg. Even Melanchthon and his disciples—called *Philippists* and *Cryptocalvinists*—inwardly accepted Calvin's views as correct. Melanchthon so embittered his last days by promulgating these opinions that he died calumniated and full of sorrow, in 1560, and his disciples in Saxony suffered persecution and imprisonment. An effort was made to restore harmony among the Protestants of Germany by the *Form of Concord*, a confession of faith subscribed by ninety-six of the Lutheran Estates of the Empire about the year A. D. 1580; but its only result was to confirm and aggravate the dissensions and animosities between the Lutheranists and Calvinists of Germany. Thus, in the century of the Reformation, German Protestantism was divided between the Lutheran and the German Reformed Church.

Switzerland was divided between Protestantism and Catholicism, and the Zwinglian system which prevailed in the greater German cantons very nearly resembled the Calvinistic doctrine which was supreme in French Switzerland; so that Zwingli is considered the founder of the German Reformed Church, whose creed is based on the Heidelberg Catechism, the same as the Lutheran creed is based on the Augsburg Confession.

John Calvin, or Jean Chauvin—the French Reformer—fled from persecution in France, to Geneva, in Switzerland; where he established a sort of theocracy, and endeavored to bring Christianity to its primitive simplicity in ceremonies and worship, excluding images, ornaments, organs, candles and crucifixes from the churches, and allowing no church feast but a rigorously-observed Sabbath, to be spent in prayer, preaching, and singing of Psalms, which Calvin's faithful fellow-minister, Theodore Beza, had translated into French. Calvin taught the creed of the great Christian Father, St. Augustine, that man is incapable of himself to do good and partake of salvation, and that the future destiny of every human creature is preordained from time of birth. Although Calvin had fled from persecution himself and had severely denounced religious intolerance on the part of the Catholics, he was very intolerant himself and became a violent persecutor, causing Servetus to be burned at the stake for denying the doctrine of the Trinity and Christ's divinity. Calvinism was generally rejected by the higher orders, because it opposed many prevalent amusements, such as the theater, dancing, and the more refined pleasures of society. Like the ancient lawgivers, Calvin exercised unbounded influence at Geneva, in civil and religious affairs, and in education and manners, until his death in 1564.

Calvin was a man of great intellect and

JOHN CALVIN.

moral power. He was severe to himself and to others, and hostile to all earthly pleasures. His doctrine is impressed with his character—severity and simplicity. He acquired a command over men by the reverence due to his strong and pure will.

The constitution of the Calvinistic Church is a republican synodical government. The congregation, represented by freely chosen *elders*, or *presbyters*, exercises the power of the Church, elects the ministers, watches over morals by means of the elders, administers the Church discipline and punishments, and attends to the distribution of alms. The ministers and a part of the elders form the synod, which gives the Church laws to the different congregations.

Calvinism spread rapidly from Geneva into the South of France, into Scotland, and into the Northern Netherlands. In France the Calvinists were called *Huguenots*, and were rigorously persecuted, their ministers being given to the flames. In Scotland they were called *Presbyterians*, because the affairs of their Church were managed by elders, or *presbyters*, elected by the congregations. The apostle of Calvinism in Scotland was the celebrated John Knox, who succeeded in establishing that faith as the state-religion of Scotland. In the Northern Netherland provinces Calvinism soon obtained a foothold, and became the state-religion of the new Duch Republic (Holland); and in 1618 the views of the Arminians, who did not fully accept Calvin's doctrine of predestination, were condemned as heretical by the Synod of Dort, which upheld St. Augustine's doctrine of man's inability of himself to do good and be saved, and punished the Arminian leaders by death or imprisonment.

SECTION X.—THE CATHOLIC CHURCH AND THE JESUITS.

THUS by the middle of the sixteenth century the Church of Rome had been repudiated by the Teutonic nations of Europe, except by Austria and some of the other German states. Such was the result of Tetzel's sale of indulgences, when the Romish Church and its agents sought to give practical force to the sentiment expressed in the following lines in German:

"*So wie das geld im kasten klingt,
Die seele aus dem fegfeuer springt.*"

"As in the box the money rings,
The soul from purgatory springs."

The Reformation was checked in Italy and Spain, partly by the character of the people, and partly by the severity of the Inquisition; many of the followers of the new doctrines dying in dungeons or at the stake, while many illustrious authors and scholars who advocated the new movement sought refuge in exile. Some embraced principles which even the Reformers rejected as heretical. The two Italian relatives Socinus denied Christ's divinity and the doctrine of the Trinity, views advocated by the Arians of the early Christian Church and by the modern Unitarians. The Spaniard Servetus held heterodox opinions respecting the Trinity; for which he perished at the stake at Geneva, through Calvin's instrumentality, in 1553, as we have noticed.

All the Popes during the Reformation made strenuous efforts to exterminate heresy; but the twice-interrupted Council of Trent, which first assembled in 1545, and which opened its third session in January, 1562, adjourned finally December 4, 1563, without effecting the desired result, although the Catholic Church was somewhat purified of its corruptions.

The Catholics regard the resolutions of the Council of Trent as their own Reformation, and these resolutions constitute the basis of the Roman Catholic Church. This ecclesiastical assembly recognized as infallible the religious doctrines that had hitherto been considered orthodox, and embodied these doctrines in carefully defined propositions. This Council established a purer code of morals, improved the Church discipline, and inaugurated a more stringent supervision of the clergy. The work of the Council of Trent was gradually accepted in all Roman Catholic countries, and is the final conclusion of the Catholic doctrine. In this manner every attempt at innovation was prevented, and Roman Catholicism was impressed with the character of stability; while development and progress is the essence of Protestantism.

Luther's work was followed by gratifying results even for the Romish Church. The Protestant Reformation was also a Catholic Reformation. The formidable and growing opposition from without forced the Church of Rome to reform itself within, in order to preserve its existence. Thus, while religious beliefs and principles had undergone a remarkable transformation, especially in Northern and Central Europe, a Catholic reaction, or counter-revolution, had already commenced, which arrested the progress of the Reformation, and neutralized its results in Austria, Bohemia, Hungary, Italy and Spain, or, in other words, in all the countries subject to either the Austrian or the Spanish branch of the House of Hapsburg. This result was partly due to the powerful moral reaction felt almost equally within and without the Romish Church against the old-time venality and corruption of the clergy. Many virtuous prelates—the greatest and best of whom was Charles Borromeo, Archbishop of Milan—restored the respectability of the Church; and ever since no Pope has disgraced his station by the shameful iniquities of Alexander VI. or the refined voluptuousness of Leo X. As the reforms for which Wickliffe, Huss, Luther, Melanchthon, Zwingli and Calvin had striven were thus effected, the necessity for a separation from the old established Church became less strongly felt.

The efforts of the Popes to suppress the Reformation, or to arrest its progress, found their chief support in the Order of Jesuits, which was founded in the year 1540 by the enthusiastic and chivalrous Ignatius Loyola, a Spanish nobleman. During the healing of the wound which he had received at the defense of Pampeluna in 1521, his mind was turned to serious reflection by reading the Lives of the Saints. He accordingly renounced the military profession, and with prayers and penance made a toilsome pilgrimage to the Holy Sepulcher at Jerusalem, but returned to his native land at the command of the papal legate.

So ignorant was Ignatius Loyola at the age of thirty-three that he then had to begin his elementary education. With incredible perseverance he acquired the education which he needed, beginning at a school at Barcelona, and completing his studies in the great universities of Alcala, Salamanca and Paris. At each of these places he labored to convert the students to a religious life. Among his early converts at Paris were Peter Faber, Francis Xavier and Peter Laynez.

These all went through the "Spiritual Exercises" with him, and he made them fast three days and three nights at a time. In 1534, when Loyola was in his forty-third year, he and six of his young disciples at Paris took upon themselves the three monastic vows of poverty, chastity and obedience, along with a fourth vow to devote themselves to the service of Christ by going as missionaries wherever the Pope might send them. They were to complete their studies first, and the vow was to take effect in three years.

In 1540 Ignatius Loyola and his disciples submitted to Pope Paul III. the rules which they had adopted and the purpose to which they had devoted their lives. The Pope approved the new institution, which became incorporated under the name of the *Society of Jesus*. In 1541 Ignatius Loyola was elected the first General of the Order; but his constitution was not approved until the election of his successor, Peter Laynez, one of his earliest disciples and also a Spaniard. The Pope endowed the *Jesuits*, as the members of the new Order were called, with great privileges.

The Jesuits adopted a monarchical and oligarchical government; and the General of the Order, residing at Rome, knew each member's qualifications and work. The Order was divided into provinces; and the provincial, as well as the local superiors, were appointed by the General, who was aided in the government of the Order by assistants. The Provincials who governed the districts or provinces made reports to the

BISHOP IN THE PLUVIALE—BISHOP IN THE CASULA.

PAPAL SWISS GUARD—POPE IN ORNATE—POPE IN HOUSE COSTUME.

AZTEC PRIESTS SACRIFICING A VICTIM.

GERMAN CITIZEN'S DRESS (FIRST THIRD OF 16TH CENTURY).

THE CHURCH.

General at regular intervals concerning the conduct and character of the members. In case the General proved unworthy of his trust, the assistants could convoke a general assembly of deputies to investigate charges, and even to proceed to depose or expel the offender.

The four classes into which this powerful religious association was divided were: 1. The Professed, who, after going through the other stages, had taken all vows; 2. The Coadjutors, who aided the Professed in teaching, preaching, and the direction of souls; 3. The Scholastics, employed in study or teaching; 4. The Novices, who passed two years in spiritual exercises, such as prayer and meditation.

Strict obedience and perfect subordination in everything compatible with the laws and precepts of Christianity became the soul of this famous religious society. Its members were obliged to disconnect themselves with the rest of the world, their families and friends. Those intending to enter the Order were required to pass through a long period of severe probation, during which their talents and dispositions were carefully examined. Every member of the Order was required to be in the hands of his superior "like a staff in the hands of an old man," or "as clay in the hands of the potter." The subordination was complete in all the gradations. Ignatius Loyola's military training caused him to constitute his society like soldiers in an army:

> "Not theirs to reason why,
> Not theirs to make reply,
> Theirs but to do and die."

The chief object of the Jesuits was to counteract Protestantism and to suppress the spirit of inquiry awakened by the Reformation. By persecution and seduction they endeavored to win Protestants over to Catholicism; and, by getting the education of youth into their hands, they sought to bring up the young in the doctrines of the Romish Church. The Order acquired immense wealth by donations and legacies, and was thus enabled to establish schools and colleges in every Catholic country of Europe, which attracted the necessitous by imparting instruction gratuitously.

The outward and immediate success of the Society of Jesus justified the hopes of its founder and the wisdom of his plans, as the Order soon spread over Catholic Europe, and many of its members were engaged in remote quarters of the globe in proclaiming the Gospel to the heathen. At the time of Ignatius Loyola's death, in 1556, the Jesuits had thirteen provinces, mainly in Spain, Portugal and Italy. Their influence was very great; as they took possession of the pulpits, schools and confessionals wherever they established themselves. They were the most accomplished and popular preachers, and occupied anew the deserted churches. They supplanted other priests in the care of consciences; and, as they taught gratuitously and well, their schools were soon filled with the children of all classes.

The efforts of the Jesuits to counteract the Reformation were prosecuted zealously and effectively, contributing immensely in Spain, Italy and Germany to arrest and prevent the spread of Protestantism. Distinguished for their learning, their zeal and their disinterestedness, devoting themselves in the pulpit and in the school with singleness of purpose to the fulfillment of the mission to which they had consecrated their lives, their influence was everywhere felt as a formidable adversary to the Protestant doctrine.

Instead of wasting their time in austerities, as did the older monastic orders, the Jesuits were encouraged to cultivate all their intellectual faculties by the liberal pursuits of art, science and general literature. As they thus became the most accomplished instructors of youth, they acquired a controlling influence over the leading minds of Europe during the most impressible years of life—an influence clearly discernible in the later policy of the Austrian House of Hapsburg.

The General of the Order had the most absolute authority in assigning every member the work for which he was adapted and qualified. While the superior talents of some of the Order directed the subtle diplomacy of European courts, the pious zeal of others found active employment in the most toilsome and self-denying missions among the forests of America or in the crowded cities of China and Japan.

Jesuit missionaries converted many of the American Indians to Christianity, and were pioneers in the exploration of the Great Lakes of North America. In Paraguay Jesuit missionaries gained possession of the civil government of the country, converted and civilized the Indians, and rescued them from the system of slavery under which they had been reduced by the Spaniards and the Portuguese, at the same time teaching them agriculture, building, and the arts of social life, and inducing them to exclude all other influences.

The most illustrious of Jesuit missionaries was the celebrated St. Francis Xavier, who began his career in the East Indies in 1542, who preached in Goa, Ceylon, Malacca, Cochin-China and Japan, and who baptized hundreds of thousands in those distant lands, dying on his way to China, in 1551, after a missionary career of nine years. Another was Robert de Nobili, who went to India as a missionary in 1605, arriving at Goa, where St. Francis Xavier had landed sixty-three years before, and who made converts to Christianity by disguising himself as a Brahman, in this way practicing Ignatius Loyola's doctrine that the end justifies the means.

The Jesuits encountered great opposition and fierce abuse from other Catholic orders whom they supplanted, as well as from Protestants. They were accused of all manner of false beliefs and wicked actions. Some of these accusations were well founded, but others were merely the result of the jealousy of their rivals. The system of studies which they introduced into their schools took Europe by surprise, and involved them in a struggle with the Sorbonne of Paris and with the University of Coimbra in Portugal and that of Salamanca in Spain. They were vehemently assailed, their doctrines and practices were bitterly denounced, and their Order was often suppressed even in Catholic countries and by Catholic rulers.

Says Macaulay: "With what vehemence, with what policy, with what exact discipline, with what dauntless courage, with what self-denial, with what forgetfulness of the dearest private ties, with what intense and stubborn devotion to a single end, with what unscrupulous laxity and versatility in the choice of means, the Jesuits fought the battles of their Church, is written in every page of the annals of Europe during several generations. The history of the Order of Jesus is the history of the great Catholic reaction against Protestantism in the seventeenth century."

SECTION XI.—THE REFORMATION IN SCANDINAVIA.

SWEDEN.

COMPLETE political and religious revolution occurred in the three Scandinavian kingdoms in the sixteenth century. The tyrant Christian II. of Denmark—"the Nero of the North"—was the last king who reigned over the three Scandinavian kingdoms under the Union of Calmar. He irritated the Danish and Swedish nobility to such an extent by his severity and cruelty that insurrections broke out in Denmark and Sweden at the same time—a result which led to the dissolution of the Union of Calmar and the establishment of Lutheranism in the three Scandinavian kingdoms.

The valiant GUSTAVUS VASA, a brave youth, endowed with the wisdom and valor of his relatives, the Stures, inaugurated the political and ecclesiastical revolution in Sweden, and founded a dynasty of vigorous monarchs, who raised Sweden to the ascendency in the North. He was carried into Denmark as a hostage by Christian II.; but he soon escaped to Lübeck, where he was provided with money and encouraged with promises of the liberation of his native land.

In 1520 Christian II. caused ninety-four Swedish nobles to be perfidiously massacred at Stockholm. Among these massacred nobles was the heroic Gustavus Vasa's father. This atrocity excited universal horror in Sweden. In the same year the brave Gustavus Vasa landed on the shores of Sweden. In the midst of a thousand perils and adventures, he escaped the pursuing emissaries of Christian II., who were constantly at his heels, until he found aid and refuge among the rude inhabitants of the mining region in the North of Dalecarlia.

Gustavus Vasa aroused the Dalecarlians to an effort to recover the independence of Sweden, and with a force of hardy peasants he conquered Falun, repulsed the Danish troops and their allies, and took Upsala. His fame and his call to freedom soon resounded through all lands and brought many warriors to his side. He obtained troops, money and artillery from the Lübeckers, and forced the Danish garrison to retreat. After being elected King of Sweden by the Diet of Strengnas, he entered Stockholm in triumph, in June, 1523, thus restoring the independence of Sweden.

The restored Kingdom of Sweden remained an elective monarchy for twenty years, but in 1544 the Swedish Diet declared the Swedish crown to be hereditary in the male line of the Vasa family. As the possessions of the Swedish throne had been so dilapidated by neglect as to be inadequate to support the expenditure, the new royal dignity could only be maintained with honor by augmenting the royal revenue, and for this the Reformation afforded a welcome opportunity.

The Swedish people, instructed in the Lutheran doctrines by the brothers Olaus and Laurentius Petri, gladly embraced the Lutheran faith; and, as the clergy in Sweden had sided with the Danes during the war for Swedish independence, the Swedish Diet placed the possessions of the clergy at Gustavus Vasa's disposal, in 1527. Thus supported by the Diet's resolution, the new Swedish king gradually introduced Lutheranism into his kingdom, and confiscated most of the possessions of the Romish Church in Sweden for the benefit of the Swedish crown. As the Swedish nobility were enriched by this proceeding they supported the king in his policy. After a long resistance, the Swedish bishops yielded to the new system, remained as Estates of the kingdom and heads of the Church, but were dependent upon their king and held in check by the consistories.

Gustavus Vasa, who sought to make Sweden prosperous by good and wise laws and by encouraging trade and industry, died in 1560, after a reign of thirty-seven years; and the dynasty which he founded occupied the throne of Sweden for almost three centuries, A. D. 1523-1818. Evil times came upon Sweden during the reigns of his sons, who successively occupied the Swedish throne.

ERIK XIV., the first son and successor of Gustavus Vasa, was of so passionate a disposition that he finally became hopelessly insane; and while in that condition he murdered several of the Sture family with his own hand, and caused all the Swedish nobles to tremble in fear of a similar fate. His brothers placed him in confinement, and finally poisoned him in 1568.

JOHN III., another son of Gustavus Vasa, then became King of Sweden. This monarch was a weak-minded sovereign of vascillating disposition. Being led astray by his wife, who was a rigid Catholic and a Polish princess, and by a Jesuit who lived secretly at Stockholm as an ambassador, John III. endeavored to reëstablish the Catholic religion in Sweden, and consented that his son Sigismund, who was to be King of Sweden and Poland, should be educated as a Catholic. This scheme failed, because of the resistance of the Swedish people to the Catholic ceremonies. John III. himself afterward repented of his project, when his second wife exerted herself in favor of Lutheranism.

John III. died in 1592; and his son SIGISMUND, who was King Sigismund III. of Poland, became King of Sweden. Sigismund's attachment to the Roman Catholic Church proved very detrimental to his reign in Sweden. He stubbornly refused to comply with the resolution of the Swedish Diet that the Evangelical Lutheran Church should be the state religion of Sweden and alone tolerated in that kingdom. Thereupon the Diet appointed his uncle Charles, Duke of Sudermania, also a son of Gustavus Vasa, to administer the government of Sweden as regent, A. D. 1598.

Sigismund endeavored vainly to maintain his right to the crown of Sweden by force of arms. He was defeated by his uncle; whereupon the Swedish Diet demanded that he either renounce popery and govern Sweden in person, or send his son to Sweden so that the prince might be educated in the Lutheran religion. As Sigismund refused to comply with this demand he was deposed in 1599; whereupon his uncle, the Duke of Sudermania, was made King of Sweden with the title of CHARLES IX.; and a new law of succession secured the Swedish crown to his family.

DENMARK AND NORWAY.

In the meantime, while Lutheranism was thus triumphant in Sweden, the Lutheran Church was also established in Denmark. The tyrant CHRISTIAN II., who was at first favorable to the Reformation, was deposed by the Danish Diet in 1523, the same year in which Gustavus Vasa became King of Sweden; whereupon his uncle Frederick, Duke of Holstein, became King FREDERICK I. of Denmark. Frederick I., who was acknowledged as king by the Danish nobility and people, supported the Lutheran doctrines, in order to strengthen himself against his dethroned rival.

The deposed Christian II. then became a firm adherent of the Romish Church, in order to gain the support of the Pope and of the Emperor Charles V. in his efforts to recover possession of the crowns of Denmark and Sweden. In the meantime, while Frederick I., at the Diet of Odensee, admitted Protestants in Denmark to equal civil rights with Catholics, and made the Danish Church independent of the Pope, Christian II. made an attack upon Denmark from Norway; but he was taken prisoner, and was incarcerated in a gloomy tower for sixteen years with a Norwegian dwarf as his only companion.

Frederick I. died in 1534, after a reign of ten years, and was succeeded on the Danish throne by his son CHRISTIAN III., during whose reign the Lutheran Church was fully established in Denmark. Most of the possessions of the Romish clergy in Denmark were confiscated, and became the property of the Danish crown and nobility; and the Danish bishops, whose titles were retained, became utterly dependent upon their government. Lutheranism was quietly established in Norway by the peasantry, but the Protestant party in Iceland fell with the sword in their hands. The Danish nobility, like the Swedish, acquired great wealth, power and privileges by the Reformation.

Christian III. of Denmark and Norway died in 1559, and was succeeded by his son FREDERICK II., who reduced the free people of the Republic of Ditmarsen under the dominion of Denmark, after they had successfully resisted the Danes for several centuries. Denmark finally acknowledged Sweden's independence by the Peace of Stettin, in 1570, which closed the Northern Seven Years' War, but left the seven southern provinces of Sweden in the possession of the King of Denmark. The reign of Frederick II. was prosperous, and was celebrated for the progress of art and science, which were now cultivated in Denmark for the first time. The great astronomer, Tycho Brahe, founded an observatory at Uranienborg. Frederick II. died in 1588, and was succeeded on the throne of Denmark and Norway by his son CHRISTIAN IV., who reigned sixty years.

THE REFORMERS.

www.ingramcontent.com/pod-product-compliance
Lightning Source LLC
Chambersburg PA
CBHW051848300426
44117CB00006B/304